NATIONAL SECURITY LAWS

Law and Justice in an Age of Terror

NATIONAL SECURITY LAWS

Law and Justice in an Age of Terror

Major Suresh Goel (Retd)

MD PUBLICATIONS PVT LTD
NEW DELHI
www.mdppl.com

Published by :

MD Publications Pvt Ltd
"MD House", 11, Darya Ganj,
New Delhi - 110002
Phone : +91-11-45355555
E-mail : contact@mdppl.com
Website: www.mdppl.com

ISBN: 978-81-7533-453-3

Published and Printed by Mr. Pranav Gupta on behalf of **MD Publications Pvt Ltd** at Mohit Enterprises, Delhi.

PREFACE

National Security is the requirement to maintain the survival of the state through the use of economic power, diplomacy, power projection and political power. The concept developed mostly in the whole world. Initially focusing on military might, it now encompasses a broad range of facets, all of which impinge on the non military or economic security of the nation and the values espoused by the national society. Accordingly, in order to possess national security, a nation needs to possess economic security, energy security, environmental security, etc. Security threats involve not only conventional foes such as other nation-states but also non-state actors such as violent non-state actors, narcotic cartels, multinational corporations and non-governmental organisations; some authorities include natural disasters and events causing severe environmental damage in this category.

There is no single universally accepted definition of "National Security" since there are some differences on describing National as State and everything consist in a nation. The variety of definitions provide an overview of the many usages of this concept. The concept still remains ambiguous, having originated from simpler definitions which initially emphasised the freedom from military threat and political coercion to later increase in sophistication and include other forms of non-military security as suited the circumstances of the time.

"The distinctive meaning of national security means freedom from foreign dictation."

Arnold Wolfers, while recognising the need to segregate the subjectivity of the conceptual idea from the objectivity, talks of threats to acquired values:

> *"An ambiguous symbol meaning different things to different people. National security objectively means the absence of threats to acquired values and subjectively, the absence of fear that such values will be attacked."*

> *"National security is an appropriate and aggressive blend of political resilience and maturity, human resources, economic structure and capacity, technological competence, industrial base and availability of natural resources and finally the military might."*

> *"National security then is the ability to preserve the nation's physical integrity and territory; to maintain its economic relations with the rest of the world on reasonable terms; to preserve its nature, institution, and governance from disruption from outside, and to control its borders."*

"National security is best described as a capacity to control those domestic and foreign conditions that the public opinion of a given community believes necessary to enjoy its own self-determination or autonomy, prosperity and wellbeing."

The origin of the modern concept of "national security" as a philosophy of maintaining a stable nation state can be traced to the Peace of Westphalia, wherein the concept of a sovereign state, ruled by a sovereign, became the basis of a new international order of nation states.

National security was achieved by this voluntary accession by the leadership to a higher order than the nation-state, viz. "international security".

The notion that national security encompasses more than just military security was present, though understated, from the beginning. The Act established the National Security Council so as to "advise the President on the integration of domestic, military and foreign policies relating to national security".

The national valuables in this broad sense include current assets and national interests, as well as the sources of strength upon which our future as a nation depends. Some valuables are tangible and earthy; others are spiritual or intellectual. They range widely from political assets such as the Bill of Rights, our political institutions and international friendships, to many economic assets which radiate worldwide from a highly productive domestic economy supported by rich natural resources. It is the urgent need to protect valuables such as these which legitimizes and makes essential the role of national security.

The military aspect of security is an important, but not the sole, component of national security. To be truly secure, a nation needs other forms of security.

Although national security measures are imposed to protect society as a whole, many such measures will restrict the rights and freedoms of all individuals in society. The concern is that where the exercise of national security laws and powers is not subject to good governance, the rule of law, and strict checks and balances, there is a risk that "national security" may simply serve as a pretext for suppressing unfavorable political and social views.

In preparation of this book, I am thankful to my family, friends and colleagues for their constant support and guidance. I am grateful to Mr Pranav Gupta, Director of MD Publications Pvt Ltd, for his encouragement in preparation of this book.

Major Suresh Goel (Retd)

Contents

1

The Air Force Act, 1950

AN ACT to consolidate and amend the law relating to the government of the Air Force.

Be it enacted by Parliament as follows -

CHAPTER - I : PRELIMINARY

1. Short title and commencement.

(1) This Act may be called the Air Force Act, 1950.

(2) It shall come into force on such date[2] as the Central Government may, by notification in the Official Gazette, appoint in this behalf.

2. Persons subject to this Act. The following persons shall be subject to this Act wherever they may be, namely: -

(a) officers and warrant officers of the Air Force;

(b) persons enrolled under this Act;

3 (c) persons belonging to the Regular Air Force Reserve or the Air Defence Reserve or the Auxiliary Air Force, in the circumstances specified in Section 26 of the Reserve and Auxiliary Air Forces Act, 1952] (62 of 1952);

(d) persons not otherwise subject to air force law, who on active service, in camp, on the march, or at any frontier post specified by the Central Government by notification in this behalf, are employed by, or are in the service of, or are followers of, or accompany any portion of the Air Force

3. Termination of application of the Act. Every person subject to this Act under clauses (a) to (c) of Section 2 shall remain so subject until duly retired, discharged, released, removed, dismissed or cashiered from the service.

4. Definitions. In this Act, unless the context otherwise requires -

(i) "active service", as applied to a person subject to this Act, means the time during which such person-

(a) is attached to, or forms part of, a force which is engaged in operations against an enemy; or

(b) is engaged in air force operations in, or is on the line of march to, a country or place wholly or partly occupied by an enemy; or

(c) is attached to, or forms part of, a force which is in military occupation of any foreign country;

(ii) "aircraft" includes aeroplanes, balloons, kite balloons, airships, gliders or other machines for flying;

(iii) "aircraft material" includes any engines, fittings, guns, gear, instruments or apparatus for use in connection with aircraft, and any of its components and accessories and petrol oil, and any other substance used for providing motive power for planes;

(iv) "Air Force" means officers and airmen who by their commission, warrant, terms of enrolment or otherwise, are liable to render continuously for a term air force service to the Union in every part of the world or any specified part of the world, including persons belonging to [1][any Air Force Reserve or the Auxiliary Air Force] when called out on permanent service;

(v) "air force custody" means the arrest or confinement of a person according to the usages of the service and includes militarly or naval custody;

(vi) "air force law" means the law enacted by this Act and the rules made thereunder and includes the usages of the service;

(vii) "air force reward" includes any gratuity or annuity for long service or good conduct, badge pay or pension, and any other air force pecuniary reward;

(viii) "airman" means any person subject to this Act other than an officer;

(ix) "air officer" means any officer of the Air Force above the rank of group captain;

(x) "air signal" means any signal intended for the guidance of aircraft, whether given by flag, ground signal, light, wind indicator or in any manner whatsoever;

(xi) "Chief Legal Adviser" means a person appointed as such by [1][the Chief of the Air Staff] to give advice on matters relating to air force law and to perform such other duties of a legal character as may arise in connection therewith;

(xii) "civil offence" means an offence which is triable by a criminal court;

(xiii) "civil prison" means any jail or place used for the detention of any criminal prisoner under the Prisons Act, 1894 (9 of 1894), or under any other law for the time being in force;

[2][(xiv) "Chief of the Air Staff" means the officer commanding the Air Force;]

(xv) "commanding officer" used in relation to a person subject to this Act, means the officer for the time being in command of the unit or detachment to which such person belongs or is attached;

(xvi) "court-martial" means a court-martial held under this Act;

(xvii) "criminal court" means a court of ordinary criminal justice in any part of India [3] * * *;

(xvii) "enemy" includes all armed mutineers, armed rebels, armed rioters, pirates and any person in arms against whom it is the duty of any person subject to air force law to act;

(xix) "the force" means the regular Army, Navy and Air Force or any part of any one or more of them; 3 The words "other than the State of Jammu and Kashmir" omitted by Act 13 of 1975, s. 2 (w.e.f. 25-1-1975);

(xx) "non-commissioned officer" means a person holding a non-commissioned rank or an acting non-commissioned rank in the Air-Force, and includes any person holding a non-commissioned rank or an acting non-commissioned rank in [1][any Air Force Reserve or the Auxiliary Air Force] when subject to this Act;

(xxi) "notification" means a notification published in the Official Gazette;

(xxii) "offence" means any act or omission punishable under this Act, and includes a civil offence, as hereinbefore defined;

(xxiii) "officer" means a person commissioned, gazetted or in pay as an officer in the Air Force, and includes-

(a) an officer of [1][any Air Force Reserve or the Auxiliary Air Force] who is for the time being subject to this Act;

(b) in relation to a person subject to this Act when serving under such conditions as may be prescribed, an officer of the regular Army or the Navy, but does not include a junior commissioned officer, warrant officer, petty officer or non-commissioned officer;

(xxiv) "prescribed" means prescribed by rules made under this Act;

(xxv) "provost-marshal" means a person appointed as such under Section 108 and includes any of his deputies or assistants or any other person legally exercising authority under him or on his behalf;

(xxvi) "regulation" includes a regulation made under this Act;

(xxvii) "superior officer", when used in relation to a person subject to this Act, includes a warrant officer and a non-commissioned officer, and as regards persons serving under such conditions as may be prescribed, an officer, junior commissioned officer, warrant officer, petty officer and non-commissioned officer of the regular Army or the Navy;

(xxviii) "unit" includes -

(a) any body of officers and. airmen for which a separate authorised establishment exists 150A

(b) any separate body of persons subject to this Act employed on any service and not attached to a unit as aforesaid;

(c) any other separate body of persons composed wholly or partly of persons subject to this Act, and specified as a unit by the Central Government;

(xxix) "warrant officer" means a person appointed, gazetted or in pay as a warrant officer of the Air Force and includes an acting warrant officer, a master warrant officer, and a warrant officer of 1[any Air Force Reserve or the Auxiliary Air Force] who is for the time being subject to this Act;

(xxx) [2][all words (except the word "India")] and expressions used herein and defined in the Indian Penal Code (45 of 1860) and not hereinbefore defined, shall be deemed to have the meanings respectively assigned to them by that Code.

CHAPTER - II : SPECIAL PROVISIONS FOR THE APPLICATION OF ACT IN CERTAIN CASES

5. Application of Act to certain forces under the Central Government.

(1) The Central Government may, by notification, apply, with or without modifications, all or any of the provisions of this Act to any force raised and maintained in India and suspend the operation of any other enactment for the time being applicable to the said force.

(2) The provisions of this Act so applied shall have effect in respect of persons belonging to the said force as they have effect in respect of persons subject to this Act holding in the Air Force the same or equivalent rank as the aforesaid persons hold for the time being in the said force.

(3) The provisions of this Act so applied shall also have effect in respect of persons who are employed by, or are in the service of, or are followers of, or accompany any portion of the said force as they have effect in respect of persons subject to this Act under clause (d) of Section 2.

(4) While any of the provisions of this Act apply to the said force, the Central Government may, by notification, direct by what authority any jurisdiction, powers or duties incident to the operation of these provisions shall be exercised or performed in respect of the said force.

6. Special provisions as to rank in certain cases.

(1) The Central Government may, by notification, direct that any persons or class of persons subject to this Act under clause (d) of Section 2, shall be so subject as officers, warrant officers or non-commissioned officers, and may authorise any officer to give a like direction and to cancel such direction.

(2) All persons subject to this Act other than officers, warrant officers and non-commissioned officers shall, if they are not persons in respect of whom notification or direction under sub-section (1) is in force, be deemed to be of rank inferior to that of a non-commissioned officer.

7. Commanding officer of persons subject to air force law under clause (d) of Section 2.

(1) Every person subject to this Act, under clause (d) of Section 2, shall, for the purposes of this Act, be deemed to be under the commanding officer of the unit, or detachment, if any, to which he is attached, and if he is not so attached under the command of any officer who may for the time being be named as his commanding officer by the officer commanding the force with which such person

may for the time being be serving, or of any other prescribed officer, or, if no such officer is named or prescribed, under the command of the said officer commanding the force.

(2) An officer commanding a force shall not place a person subject to this Act under clause (d) of Section 2 under the command of an officer of official rank inferior to that of such person if there is present at the place where such person is any officer of higher rank under whose command he can be placed.

8. Officers exercising powers in certain cases.

(1) Whenever persons subject to this Act are serving under an officer commanding any air force formation not in this Section specifically named, and being, in the opinion of the Central Government, not less than a squadron, the said Government may prescribe the officer by whom the powers which, under this Act, may be exercised by air officers in charge of commands, and officers commanding groups, wings and squadrons shall, as regards such persons, be exercised.

(2) The Central Government may confer such powers either absolutely, or subject to such restrictions, reservations, exceptions and conditions as it may think fit.

9. Power to declare persons to be on active service. Notwithstanding anything contained in clause (i) of Section 4, the Central Government may, by notification, declare that any person or class of persons subject to this Act shall, with reference to any area in which they may be serving or with reference to any provision of this Act or of any other law for the time being in force, be deemed to be on active service within the meaning of this Act.

CHAPTER - III : COMMISSION, APPOINTMENT AND ENROLMENT

10. Commission and appointment. The President may grant, to such person as he thinks fit a commission as an officer or appoint any person as a warrant officer of the Air Force.

11. Ineligibility of aliens for enrolment. No person who is not a citizen of India shall, except with the consent of the Central Government signified in writing, be enrolled in the Air Force:

PROVIDED that nothing contained in this Section shall bar the enrolment of the subjects of Nepal in the Air Force.

12. Ineligibility of females for enrolment or employment. No female shall be eligible for enrolment or employment in the Air Force, except in such corps, department, branch or other body forming part of, or attached to any portion of, the Air Force as the Central Government may, by notification, specify in this behalf :

PROVIDED that nothing contained in this Section shall affect the provisions of any law for the time being in force providing for the raising and maintenance of any service auxiliary to the Air Force or any branch thereof in which females are eligible for enrolment or employment.

13. Procedure before enrolling officer. Upon the appearance before the prescribed enrolling officer of any person desirous of being enrolled, the enrolling officer shall read and explain to him, or cause to be read and explained to him in his presence, the conditions of the service for which he is to be enrolled; and shall put to him the questions set forth in the prescribed form of enrolment, and shall, after having cautioned him that if he makes a false answer to any such question he will be liable to punishment under this Act, record or cause to be recorded his answer to each such question.

14. Mode of enrolment. If, after complying with the provisions of Section 13, the enrolling officer is satisfied that the person desirous of being enrolled fully understands the questions put to him and consents to the conditions of service, and if such officer perceives no impediment, he shall sign and shall also cause such person to sign the enrolment paper, and such person shall thereupon be deemed to be enrolled.

15. Validity of enrolment. Every person who has for the space of three months been in receipt of pay as a person enrolled under this Act and been borne on the rolls of any unit shall be deemed to have been duly enrolled, and shall not be entitled to claim his discharge on the ground of any irregularity or illegality in his enrolment or on any other ground whatsoever; and if any person, in receipt of such pay and borne on the rolls as aforesaid, claims his discharge before the expiry of three months from his enrolment, no such irregularity or illegality or other ground shall, until he is discharged in pursuance of his claim, affect his position as an enrolled person under this Act or invalidate any proceedings, act or thing taken or done prior to his discharge.

16. Persons to be attested. The following persons shall be attested, namely:–

(a) all persons enrolled as combatants;

(b) all persons selected to hold a non-commissioned or acting non-commissioned rank; and

(c) all other persons subject to this Act as may be prescribed by the Central Government.

17. Mode of attestation.

(1) When a person who is to be attested is reported fit for duty, or has completed the prescribed period of probation, an oath or affirmation shall be administered to him in the prescribed form by his commanding officer in front of his unit or such portion thereof as may be present, or by any other prescribed person.

(2) The form of oath or affirmation prescribed under this Section shall contain a promise that the person to be attested will bear true allegiance to the Constitution of India as by law established, and that he will serve in the Air Force and go wherever he is ordered by land, sea of air, and that he will obey all commands of any officer set over him, even to the peril of his life.

(3) The fact of an enrolled person having taken the oath or affirmation directed by this Section to be taken shall be entered on his enrolment paper, and authenticated by the signature of the officer administering the oath or affirmation.

CHAPTER - IV : CONDITIONS OF SERVICE.

18. Tenure of service under the Act. Every person subject to this Act shall hold office during the pleasure of the President.

19. Termination of service by Central Government. Subject to the provisions of this Act and the rules and regulations made thereunder, the Central Government may dismiss, or remove from the service any person subject to this Act.

20. Dismissal, removal or reduction by Chief of the Air Staff and other officers.

(1) 1[The Chief of the Air Staff] may dismiss or remove from the service any person subject to this Act other than an officer.

(2) 1[The Chief of the Air Staff] I may reduce to a lower grade or rank or the ranks, any warrant officer or any non-commissioned officer.

(3) An officer having power not less than an air officer in charge of a command or equivalent commander or any prescribed officer may dismiss or remove from the service any person serving under his command other than an officer or a warrant officer.

(4) On active service, an officer commanding the air forces in the field may reduce to a lower rank or to the ranks any warrant officer or non-commissioned officer under his command.

(5) 1[The Chief of the Air Staff] or an officer specified in sub-section (3) may reduce to a lower class in the ranks any airman other than a warrant officer or non-commissioned officer.

(6) The commanding officer of an acting non-commissioned officer may order him to revert to his substantive rank as a non-commissioned officer, or if he has no such substantive rank, to the ranks.

(7) The exercise of any powers under this Section shall be subject to the other provisions contained in this Act and the rules and regulations made thereunder.

21. Power to modify certain fundamental rights in their application to persons subject to this Act. Subject to the provisions of any law for the time being in force relating to the Air Force or to any branch thereof, the Central Government may, by notification, make rules restricting in such manner and to such extent as may be specified the right of any person subject to this Act-

(a) to be a member of, or to be associated in any way with, any trade union or labour union, or any class of trade or labour unions or any society, institution or association, or any class of societies, institutions or associations;

(b) to attend or address any meeting or to take part in any demonstration organised by any body of persons for any political or other purposes;

(c) to communicate with the press or to publish or cause to be published any book, letter or other document.

22. Retirement, release or discharge. Any person subject to this Act may be retired, released or discharged from the service by such authority and in such manner as may be prescribed.

23. Certificate on termination of service. Every warrant officer, or enrolled person who is dismissed, removed, discharged, retired or released from the service shall be furnished by his commanding officer with a certificate, in the language which is the mother tongue of such person and also in the English language setting forth-

(a) the authority terminating his service;

(b) the cause for such termination; and

(c) the full period of his service in the Air Force.

24. Discharge or dismissal when out of India.

(1) Any person enrolled under this Act who is entitled under the conditions of his enrolment to be discharged, or whose discharge is ordered by competent authority, and who, when he is so entitled or ordered to be discharged, is serving out of India, and requests to be sent to India, shall, before being discharged, be sent to India with all convenient speed.

(2) Any person enrolled under this Act who is dismissed from the service and who, when he is so dismissed, is serving out of India, shall be sent to India with all convenient speed.

(3) Where any such person as is mentioned in sub-section (2) is sentenced to dismissal combined with any other punishment, such other punishment, or, in the case of a sentence of transportation, imprisonment or detention, a portion of such sentence, may be inflicted before he is sent to India.

(4) For the purposes of this Section, the word "discharge" shall include release, and the word "dismissal" shall include removal.

CHAPTER - V : SERVICE PRIVILEGES

25. Authorised deductions only to be made from pay. The pay of every person subject to this Act due to him as such under any regulation, for the time being in force, shall be paid without any deduction other than the deductions authorised by or under this or any other Act.

26. Remedy of aggrieved airmen.

(1) Any airman who deems himself wronged by any superior or other officer may, if not attached to a unit or detachment, complain to the officer under whose command or orders he is serving; and may, if attached to a unit or detachment, complain to the officer commanding the same.

(2) When the officer complained against is the officer to whom any complaint should, under sub-section (1), be preferred, the aggrieved airman may complain to such officers next superior officer, and if he thinks himself wronged by such superior officer, he may complain to [1][the Chief of the Air Staff].

(3) Every officer receiving any such complaint shall make as complete an investigation into it as may be possible for giving full redress to the complainant; or, when necessary, refer the complaint to superior authority.

(4) Every such complaint shall be preferred in such manner as may from time to time be specified by the proper authority.

(5) The Central Government may revise any decision by 1[the Chief of the Air Staff] under sub-section (2), but subject-thereto, the decision of 1[the Chief of the Air Staff] shall be final.

27. Remedy of aggrieved officers. Any officer who deems himself wronged by his commanding officer or any superior officer and who on due application made to his commanding officer does not receive the redress to which he considers himself entitled, may complain to the Central Government in such manner as may from time to time be specified by the proper authority.

28. Immunity from attachment. The arms, clothes, equipment, accoutrements or necessaries of any person subject to this Act shall not be seized, and the pay and allowances of any such person or any part thereof shall not be attached, by direction of any civil or revenue court or any revenue officer, in satisfaction of any decree or order enforceable against him.

29. Immunity from arrest for debt.

(1) No person subject to this Act shall, so long as he belongs to the Forces, be liable to be arrested for debt under any process issued by, or by the authority of, any civil or revenue court or revenue officer.

(2) The judge of any such court or the said officer may examine into any complaint made by such person or his superior officer of the arrest of such person contrary to the provisions of this Section, and may, by warrant under his hand, discharge the person, and award reasonable costs to the complainant, who may recover those costs in like manner as he might have recovered costs awarded to him by a decree against the person obtaining the process.

(3) For the recovery of such costs no court-fee shall be payable by the complainant.

30. Immunity of persons attending courts-martial from arrest.

(1) No presiding officer or member of a court-martial, no judge advocate, no party to any proceeding before a court-martial, or his legal practitioner or agent, and no witness acting in obedience to a summons to attend a court-martial shall, while proceeding to, attending, or returning from, a court-martial, be liable to arrest under civil or revenue process.

(2) If any such person is arrested under any such process, he may be discharged by order of the court-martial.

31. Privileges of reservists. Every person belonging to [1][any Air Force Reserve or the Auxiliary Air Force] shall, when called out for, or engaged in, or returning from, training or service, be entitled to all the privileges accorded by Sections 28 and 29 to a person subject to this Act.

32. Priority in respect of Air Force personnels litigation.

(1) On the presentation to any court by or on behalf of any person subject to this Act of a certificate, from the proper air force authority, of leave of absence having been granted to or applied for by him for the purpose of prosecuting or defending any suit or other proceeding in such court, the court shall, on the application of such person, arrange, so far as may be possible, for the hearing

and final disposal of such suit or other proceeding within the period of the leave so granted or applied for.

(2) The certificate from the proper air force authority shall state the first and last day of the leave or intended leave, and set forth a description of the case with respect to which the leave was granted or applied for.

(3) No fee shall be payable to the court in respect of the presentation of any such certificate, or of any application by or on behalf of any such person, for priority for the hearing of his case.

(4) Where the court is unable to arrange for the hearing and final disposal of the suit or other proceeding within the period of such leave or intended leave as aforesaid, it shall record its reasons for its inability to do so, and shall cause a copy thereof to be furnished to such person on his application without any payment whatever by him in respect either of the application for such copy or of the copy itself.

(5) If in any case a question arises as to the proper air force authority qualified to grant such certificate as aforesaid, such question shall be at once referred by the court to an officer having power not less than a group commander or equivalent commander whose decision shall be final.

33. Saving of rights and privileges under other laws. The rights and privileges specified in the preceding Sections of this Chapter shall be in addition to any others conferred on persons subject to this Act or on members of the regular Army, Navy and Air Force generally by any other law for the time being in force.

CHAPTER - VI : OFFENCES

34. Offence in relation to the enemy and punishable with death. Any person subject to this Act who commits any of the following offences, that is to say -

(a) shamefully abandons or delivers up any garrison, fortress, post, place or guard, committed to his charge, or which it is his duty to defend, or uses any means to compel or induce any commanding officer or other person to commit the said act; or

(b) intentionally uses any means to compel or induce any person subject to military, naval or air force law to abstain from acting against the enemy, or to discourage such person from acting against the enemy; or

(c) in the presence of the enemy, shamefully casts away his arms, ammunition, tools or equipment or misbehaves in such manner as to show cowardice; or

(d) treacherously holds correspondence with, or communicates intelligence to, the enemy or any person in arms against the Union; or

(e) directly or indirectly assists the enemy with money, arms, ammunition, stores or supplies;

(f) or treacherously or through cowardice sends a flag of truce to the enemy; or

(g) in time of war or during any air force operation, intentionally occasions a false alarm in action, camp or quarters or spreads reports calculated to create alarm or despondency; or

(h) in time of action leaves his commanding officer or his post, guard, piquet, patrol or party without being regularly relieved or without leave; or

(i) having been made a prisoner of war, voluntarily serves with or aids the enemy; or

(j) knowingly harbours or protects an enemy not being a prisoner; or

(k) being a sentry in time of war or alarm, sleeps upon his post or is intoxicated; or

(l) knowingly does any act calculated to imperil the success of the military, naval or air forces of India or any forces co-operating therewith or any part of such forces; or

(m) treacherously or shamefully causes the capture or destruction by the enemy of any aircraft belonging to the Forces; or

(n) treacherously uses any false air signal or alters or interferes with any air signal; or

(o) when ordered by his superior officer or otherwise under orders to carry out any air force operations, treacherously or shamefully fails to use his utmost exertions to carry such orders into effect;

shall, on conviction by court-martial, be liable to suffer death or such less punishment as is in this Act mentioned.

35. Offences in relation to the enemy and not punishable with death. Any person subject to this Act who commits any of the following offences, that is to say -

(a) is taken prisoner, by want of due precaution, or through disobedience of orders, or wilful neglect of duty, or having been taken prisoner, fails to rejoin his service when able to do so; or

(b) without due authority holds correspondence with or communicates intelligence to the enemy; or having come by the knowledge of any such correspondence or communication wilfully omits to discover it immediately to his commanding or other superior officer; or

(c) without due authority sends a Rag of truce to the enemy;

or

(d) negligently causes the capture or destruction by the enemy of any aircraft belonging to the Government; or

(e) when ordered by his superior officer, or otherwise under orders to carry out any warlike operations in the air, negligently or through other default fails to use his utmost exertions to carry such orders into effect;

shall, on conviction by court-martial, be liable to suffer imprisonment for a term which may extend to fourteen years or such less punishment as is in this Act mentioned.

36. Offences punishable more severely on active service than at other times. Any person subject to this Act who commits any of the following offences, that is to say -

(a) forces a safeguard, or forces or uses criminal force to a sentry; or

(b) breaks into any house or other place in search of plunder or

(c) being a sentry sleeps upon his post, or is intoxicated; or

(d) without orders from his superior officer leaves his guard, piquet, patrol or post; or

(e) intentionally or through neglect occasions a false alarm in camp or quarters; or spreads reports calculated to create unnecessary alarm or despondency; or

(f) makes known the parole, watchword or countersign to any person not entitled to receive it; or knowingly gives a parole, watchword or countersign different from what he received; or

(g) without due authority alters or interferes with any air signal; shall, on conviction by court-martial, if he commits any such offence when on active service, be liable to suffer imprisonment for a term which may extend to fourteen years or such less punishment as is in this Act mentioned; and if he commits any such offence when not on active service, be liable to suffer imprisonment for a term which may extend to seven years or such less punishment as is in this Act mentioned.

37. Mutiny. Any person subject to this Act who commits any of the following offences, that is to say -

(a) begins, incites, causes, or conspires with any other persons to cause, any mutiny in the military, naval or air forces of India or any forces co-operating therewith; or

(b) joins in any such mutiny; or

(c) being present at any such mutiny, does not use his utmost endeavours to suppress the same; or

(d) knowing or having reason to believe in the existence of any such mutiny, or of any intention to commit such mutiny or any such conspiracy, does not, without delay, give information thereof to his commanding or other superior officer; or

(e) endeavours to seduce any person in the military, naval or air forces of India from his duty or allegiance to the Union; shall, on conviction by court-martial, be liable to suffer death or such less punishment as is in this Act mentioned.

38. Desertion and aiding desertion.

(1) Any person subject to this Act who deserts or attempts to desert the service shall on conviction by court-martial, if he commits the offence on active service or when under orders for active service, be liable to suffer death or such less punishment as is in this Act mentioned; and if he commits the offence under any other circumstances, be liable to suffer imprisonment for a term which may extend to seven years or such less punishment as is in this Act mentioned.

(2) Any person subject to this Act who knowingly harbours any such deserter shall, on conviction by court-martial, be liable to suffer imprisonment for a term which may extend to seven years or such less punishment as is in this Act mentioned.

(3) Any person subject to this Act who, being cognizant of any desertion or attempt at desertion of a person subject to this Act, does not forthwith give notice to his own or some other superior officer, or take any steps in his power to cause such person to be apprehended, shall, on conviction by court-martial, be liable to suffer imprisonment for a term which may extend to two years or such less punishment as is in this Act mentioned.

39. Absence without leave. Any person subject to this Act who commits any of the following offences, that is to say,-

(a) absents himself without leave; or

(b) without sufficient cause overstays leave granted to him; or

(c) being on leave of absence and having received information from proper authority that any unit or detachment, to which he belongs, has been ordered on active service, fails, without sufficient cause, to rejoin without delay; or

(d) without sufficient cause fails to appear at the time fixed, at the parade or place appointed for exercise or duty; or

(e) when on parade, or on the line of march, without sufficient cause or without leave from his superior officer, quits the parade or line of march; or

(f) when in camp or elsewhere, is found beyond any limits fixed, or in any place prohibited, by any general, local or other order, without a pass or written leave from his superior officer; or

(g) without leave from his superior officer or without due cause, absents himself from any school when duly ordered to attend there; shall, on conviction by court-martial, be liable to suffer imprisonment for a term which may extend to three years or such less punishment as is in this Act mentioned.

40. Striking or threatening superior officer. Any person subject to this Act who commits any of the following offences, that is to say,-

(a) uses criminal force to, or assaults his superior officer; or

(b) uses threatening language to such officer; or

(c) uses insubordinate language to such officer;

shall, on conviction by court-martial, if such officer is at the time in the execution of his office or, if the offence is committed on active service, be liable to suffer imprisonment for a term which may extend to fourteen years or such less punishment as is in this Act mentioned; and in other cases, be liable to suffer imprisonment for a term which may extend to ten years or such less punishment as is in this Act mentioned:

PROVIDED that in the case of an offence specified in clause (c), the imprisonment shall not exceed five years.

41. Disobedience to superior officer.

(1) Any person subject to this Act who disobeys in such manner as to show a wilful defiance of authority any lawful command given personally by his superior officer in the execution of his office whether the same is given orally or in

writing or by signal or otherwise shall, on conviction by court martial, be liable to suffer imprisonment for a term which may extend to fourteen years or such less punishment as is in this Act mentioned.

(2) Any person subject to this Act who disobeys any lawful command given by his superior officer shall, on conviction by court martial, if he commits such offence when on active service, be liable to suffer imprisonment for a term which may extend to fourteen years or such less punishment as is in this Act mentioned; and if he commits such offence when not on active service, be liable to suffer imprisonment for a term which may extend to five years or such less punishment as is in this Act mentioned.

42. Insubordination and obstruction. Any person subject to this Act who commits any of the following offences, that is to say,-

(a) being concerned in any quarrel, affray or disorder, refuses to obey any officer, though of inferior rank, who orders him into arrest, or uses criminal force to or assaults any such officer; or

(b) uses criminal force to, or assaults any person, whether subject to this Act or not, in whose custody he is lawfully placed, and whether he is or is not his superior officer; or

(c) resists an escort whose duty it is to apprehend him or to have him in charge; or

(d) breaks out of barracks, camp or quarters; or

(e) neglects to obey any general, local or other order; or

(f) impedes the provost-marshal or any person lawfully acting on his behalf or, when called upon, refuses to assist in the execution of his duty a provost-marshal or any person lawfully acting on his behalf; or

(g) uses criminal force to or assaults any person bringing provisions or supplies to the Forces;

shall, on conviction by court-martial, be liable to suffer imprisonment for a term which may extend, in the case of the offences specified in clauses (d) and (e) to two years, and in the case of the offences specified in the other clauses to ten years, or such less punishment as is in this Act mentioned.

43. Fraudulent enrolment. Any person subject to this Act who commits any of the following offences, that is to say -

(a) without having obtained a regular discharge from the Air Force or otherwise fulfilled the conditions enabling him to enrol or enter, enrols himself in, or enters the said force or any part of the military or the naval forces of India; or

(b) is concerned in the enrolment in any part of the Forces, of any person when he knows or has reason to believe such person to be so circumstanced that by enrolling he commits an offence against this Act; shall, on conviction by court-martial, be liable to suffer imprisonment for a term which may extend to five years or such less punishment as is in this Act mentioned.

44. False answers on enrolment. Any person having become subject to this Act who is discovered to have made at the time of enrolment a wilfully false answer to any question set forth in the prescribed form of enrolment which has been put to him by the enrolling officer before whom he appears for the purpose of being enrolled, shall, on conviction by court-martial, be liable to suffer imprisonment for a term which may extend to five years or such less punishment as is in this Act mentioned.

45. Unbecoming conduct. Any officer or warrant officer who behaves in a manner unbecoming his position and the character expected of him shall, on conviction by court-martial, if he is an officer, be liable to be cashiered or to suffer such less punishment as is in this Act mentioned; and if he is a warrant officer, be liable to be dismissed or to suffer such less punishment as is in this Act mentioned.

46. Certain forms of disgraceful conduct. Any person subject to this Act who commits any of the following offences, that is to say -

(a) is guilty of any disgraceful conduct of a cruel, indecent or unnatural kind; or

(b) malingers, or feigns, or produces disease or infirmity in himself, or intentionally delays his cure or aggravates his disease or infirmity; or

(c) with intent to render himself or any other person unfit for service, voluntarily causes hurt to himself or that person; shall, on conviction by court-martial, be liable to suffer imprisonment for a term which may extend to seven years or such less punishment as is in this Act mentioned.

47. Ill-treating a subordinate. Any officer, warrant officer or non-commissioned officer, who uses criminal force to or otherwise ill-treats any person subject to this Act, being his subordinate in rank or position, shall, on conviction by court-martial, be liable to suffer imprisonment for a term which may extend to seven years or such less punishment as is in this Act mentioned.

48. Intoxication.

(1) Any person subject to this Act who is found in a state of intoxication, whether on duty or not, shall, on conviction by court-martial, if he is an officer, be liable to be cashiered or to suffer such less punishment as is in this Act mentioned; and if he is not an officer, be liable, subject to the provisions of sub-section (2), to suffer imprisonment for a term which may extend to two years or such less punishment as is in this Act mentioned.

(2) Where an offence of being intoxicated is committed by a person other than an officer when not on active service or not on duty, the period of imprisonment awarded shall not exceed six months.

49. Permitting escape of person in custody. Any person subject to this Act who commits any of the following offences, that is to say -

(a) when in command of a guard, picquet, patrol or post, releases without proper authority, whether wilfully or without reasonable excuse, any person committed to his charge or refuses to receive any prisoner or person so committed; or

(b) wilfully or without reasonable excuse allows to escape any person who is committed to his charge, or whom it is his duty to keep or guard; shall, on conviction by court-martial, be liable, if he has acted wilfully, to suffer imprisonment for a term which may extend to fourteen years or such less punishment as is in this Act mentioned; and if he has not acted wilfully, to suffer imprisonment for a term which may extend to two years or such less punishment as is in this Act mentioned.

50. Irregularity in connection with arrest or confinement. Any person subject to this Act who commits any of the following offences, that is to say -

(a) unnecessarily detains a person in arrest or confinement without bringing him to trial, or fails to bring his case before the proper authority for investigation; or

(b) having committed a person to air force custody fails without reasonable cause to deliver at the time of such committal, or as soon as practicable, and in any case within forty-eight hours thereafter, to the officer or other person into whose custody the person arrested is committed, an account in writing signed by himself of the offence with which the person so committed is charged; shall, on conviction by court-martial, be liable to suffer imprisonment for a term which may extend to two years or such less punishment as is in this Act mentioned.

51. Escape from custody. Any person subject to this Act who, being in lawful custody, escapes or attempts to escape, shall, on conviction by court-martial, be liable to suffer imprisonment for a term which may extend to five years or such less punishment as is in this Act mentioned.

52. Offences in respect of property. Any person subject to this Act who commits any of the following offences, that is to say -

(a) commits theft of any property belonging to the Government, or to any military, naval or air force mess, band or institution, or to any person subject to military, naval or air force law; or

(b) dishonestly misappropriates or converts to his own use any such property; or

(c) commits criminal breach of trust in respect of any such property; or

(d) dishonestly receives or retains any such property in respect of which any of the offences under clauses (a), (b) and (c) has been committed, knowing or having reason to believe the commission of such offence; or

(e) wilfully destroys or injures any property of the Government entrusted to him; or

(f) does any other thing with intent to defraud, or to cause wrongful gain to one person or wrongful loss to another person; shall, on conviction by court-martial, be liable to suffer imprisonment for a term which may extend to ten years or such less punishment as is in this Act mentioned.

53. Extortion and corruption. Any person subject to this Act who commits any of the following offences, that is to say -

(a) commits extortion; or

(b) without proper authority exacts from any person money, provisions or service;

shall, on conviction by court-martial, be liable to suffer imprisonment for a term which may extend to ten years or such less punishment as is in this Act mentioned.

54. Making away with equipment. Any person subject to this Act who commits any of the following offences, that is to say -

(a) makes away with, or is concerned in making away with, any arms, ammunition, equipment, instruments, tools, clothing or any other thing being the property of the Government issued to him for his use or entrusted to him; or

(b) loses by neglect anything mentioned in clause (a); or

(c) sells, pawns, destroys or defaces any medal or decoration granted to him;

shall, on conviction by court-martial, be liable to suffer imprisonment for a term which may extend, in the case of the offences specified in clause (a) to ten years, and in the case of the offences specified in the other clauses to five years, or such less punishment as is in this Act mentioned.

54A. Relief of tax on capital gains on transfer of property held under trust for charitable or religious purposes or by certain institutions.

55. Injury to property. Any person subject to this Act who commits any of the following offences, that is to say -

(a) destroys or injures any property mentioned in clause (a) of Section 54, or any property belonging to any military, naval or air force mess, band or institution, or to any person subject to military, naval or air force law, or serving with, or attached to, the Air Force; or

(b) commits any act which causes damage to, or destruction of, any property of the Government by fire; or

(c) kills, injures, makes away with, ill-treats or loses any animal entrusted to him shall, on conviction by court-martial, be liable, if he has acted wilfully, to suffer imprisonment for a term which may extend to fourteen years or such less punishment as is in this Act mentioned; and if he has acted without reasonable excuse to suffer imprisonment for a term which may extend to seven years or such less punishment as is in this Act mentioned.

56.False accussation. Any person subject to this Act who commits any of the following offences, that is to say -

(a) makes a false accusation against any person subject to this Act, knowing or having reason to believe such accusation to be false; or

(b) in making a complaint under Section 26 or Section 27 makes any statement affecting the character of any person subject to this Act, knowing or having reason to believe such statement to be false, or knowingly and wilfully suppresses any material facts; shall, on conviction by court-martial, be liable to suffer imprisonment for a term which may extend to five years or such less punishment as is in this Act mentioned.

57. Falsifying official documents and false declaration. Any person subject to this Act who commits any of the following offences, that is to say -

(a) in any report, return, list, certificate, book or other document made or signed by him, or of the contents of which, it is his duty to ascertain the accuracy, knowingly makes, or is privy to the making of, any false or fraudulent statement; or

(b) in any document of the description mentioned in clause (a) knowingly makes, or is privy to the making of, any omission, with intent to defraud; or

(c) knowingly and with intent to injure any person, or knowingly and with intent to defraud, suppresses, defaces, alters or makes away with any document which it is his duty to preserve or produce; or

(d) where it is his official duty to make a declaration respecting any matter, knowingly makes a false declaration; or

(e) obtains for himself, or for any other person, any pension, allowance or other advantage or privilege by a statement which is false, and which he either knows or believes to be false or does not believe to be true, or by making or using a false entry in any book or record, or by making any document containing a false statement, or by omitting to make a true entry or document containing a true statement; shall, on conviction by court-martial, be liable to suffer imprisonment for a term which may extend to fourteen years or such less punishment as is in this Act mentioned.

58. Signing in blank and failure to report. Any person subject to this Act who commits any of the following offences, that is to say -

(a) when signing any document relating to pay, arms, ammunition, equipment, clothing, supplies or stores, or any property of the Government fraudulently leaves in blank any material part for which his signature is a voucher; or

(b) refuses or by culpable neglect omits to make or send a report or return which it is his duty to make or send; shall, on conviction by court-martial, be liable to suffer imprisonment for a term which may extend to seven years or such less punishment as is in this Act mentioned.

59. Offences relating to courts martial. Any person subject to this Act who commits any of the following offences, that is to say -

(a) being duly summoned or ordered to attend as a witness before a court-martial, wilfully or without reasonable excuse, makes default in attending; or

(b) refuses to take an oath or make an affirmation legally required by a court-martial to be taken or made; or

(c) refuses to produce or deliver any document in his power or control legally required by a court-martial to be produced or delivered by him; or

(d) refuses when a witness to answer any question which he is by law bound to answer; or

(e) is guilty of contempt of court-martial by using insulting or threatening language, or by causing any interruption or disturbance in the proceedings of such court;

shall, on conviction by court-martial, be liable to suffer imprisonment for a term which may extend to three years or such less punishment as is in this Act mentioned.

60. False evidence. Any person subject to this Act who, having been duly sworn or affirmed before any court-martial or other court competent under this Act to administer an oath or affirmation, makes any statement which is false, and which he either knows or believes to be false or does not believe to be true, shall, on conviction by court-martial, be liable to suffer imprisonment for a term which may extend to seven years or such less punishment as is in this Act mentioned.

61. Unlawful detention of pay. Any officer, warrant officer or non-commissioned officer who, having received the pay of a person subject to this Act unlawfully detains or refuses to pay the same when due, shall, on conviction by court-martial, be liable to suffer imprisonment for a term which may extend to ten years or such less punishment as is in this Act mentioned.

62. Offences in relation to aircraft and flying. Any person subject to this Act who commits any of the following offences, that is to say -

(a) wilfully or without reasonable excuse damages, destroys or loses any aircraft or aircraft material belonging to the Government; or

(b) is guilty of any act or neglect likely to cause such damage, destruction or loss; or

(c) without lawful authority disposes of any aircraft or aircraft material belonging to the Government; or

(d) is guilty of any act or neglect in flying, or in the use of any aircraft, or in relation to any aircraft or aircraft material, which causes or is likely to cause loss of life or bodily injury to any person; or

(e) during a state of war, wilfully and without proper occasion, or negligently, causes the sequestration, by or under the authority of a neutral State, or the destruction in a neutral State, of any aircraft belonging to the Government;

shall, on conviction by court-martial, be liable, if he has acted wilfully, to suffer imprisonment for a term which may extend to fourteen years or such less punishment as is in this Act mentioned, and, in any other case, to suffer imprisonment for a term which may extend to five years or such less punishment as is in this Act mentioned.

63. Other offences relating to aircraft and flying. Any person subject to this Act who commits any of the following offences, that is to say -

(a) signs any certificate in relation to an aircraft or aircraft material belonging to the Government without ensuring the accuracy thereof; or

(b) being the pilot of an aircraft belonging to the Government, flies it at a height less than such height as may be specified by [1][the Chief of the Air Staff], except while taking off or landing, or in such other circumstances as may be specified by [1][the Chief of the Air Staff]; or

(c) being the pilot of an aircraft belonging to the Government, flies it so as to cause, or to be likely to cause, unnecessary annoyance to any person; shall, on conviction by court-martial, be liable to suffer imprisonment for a term which may extend to two years or such less punishment as is in this Act mentioned.

64. Disobedience of lawful command of captain of aircraft. Any person subject to this Act who, whatever his rank, commits any of the following offences, that is to say -

(a) while he is in an aircraft disobeys any lawful command given by the captain of the aircraft, whether such captain is subject to this Act or not, as respects all matters relating to the flying or handling of the aircraft, or affecting the safety thereof; or

(b) being the captain of a glider aircraft towed by another aircraft disobeys any lawful command given by the captain of the towing aircraft, whether the latter is subject to this Act or not, as respects all matters aforesaid; shall on conviction by court-martial, be liable to suffer imprisonment for a term which may extend to fourteen years or such less punishment as is in this Act mentioned.

65. Violation of good order and air force discipline. Any person subject to this Act who is guilty of any act or omission which though not specified in this Act, is prejudicial to good order and air force discipline shall, on conviction by court-martial, be liable to suffer imprisonment for a term which may extend to seven years or such less punishment as is in this Act mentioned.

66. Miscellaneous offences. Any person subject to this Act who commits any of the following offences, that is to say -

(a) being in command at any post or on the march, and receiving a complaint that any one under his command has beaten or otherwise maltreated or oppressed any person, or has disturbed any fair or market, or committed any riot or trespass, fails to have due reparation made to the injured person or to report the case to the proper authority; or

(b) by defiling any place of worship, or otherwise, intentionally insults the religion or wounds the religious feelings of any person; or

(c) attempts to commit suicide, and in such attempt does any act towards the commission of such offence; or

(d) being below the rank of warrant officer, when off duty, appears, without proper authority, in or about camp or cantonments, or in or about, or when going to or returning from, any town or bazar, carrying a rifle, sword or other offensive weapon; or

(e) directly or indirectly accepts or obtains, or agrees to accept or attempts to obtain, for himself or for any other person, any gratification as a motive or reward for procuring the enrolment of any person, or leave of absence, promotion or any other advantage or indulgence for any person in the service; or

(f) commits any offence against the property or person of any inhabitant of, or resident in, the country in which he is serving; shall, on conviction by court-martial, be liable to suffer imprisonment for a term which may extend to seven years or such less punishment as is in this Act mentioned.

67. Attempt. Any person subject to this Act who attempts to commit any of the offences specified in Sections 34 to 66 inclusive, and in such attempt does any act towards the commission of the offence shall, on conviction by court-martial, where no express provision is made by this Act for the punishment of such attempt, be liable, if the offence attempted to be committed is punishable with death, to suffer imprisonment for a term which may extend to fourteen years or such less punishment as is in this Act mentioned; and if the offence attempted to be committed is punishable with imprisonment, to suffer imprisonment for a term which may extend to one-half of the longest term provided for that offence or such less punishment as is in this Act mentioned.

68. Abetment of offences that have been committed. Any person subject to this Act who abets the commission of any of the offences specified in Sections 34 to 66 inclusive, shall, on conviction by court-martial, if the act abetted is committed in consequence of the abetment and no express provision is made by this Act for the punishment of such abetment, be liable to suffer the punishment provided for that offence or such less punishment as is in this Act mentioned.

69. Abetment of offences punishable with death and not committed. Any person subject to this Act who abets the commission of any of the offences punishable with death under Sections 34, 37 and sub-section (1) of Section 38 shall, on conviction by court-martial, if that offence be not committed in consequence of the abetment, and no express provision is made by this Act for the punishment of such abetment, be liable to suffer imprisonment for a term which may extend to fourteen years or such less punishment as is in this Act mentioned.

70. Abetment of offences punishable with imprisonment and not committed. Any person subject to this Act who abets the commission of any of the offences specified in Sections 34 to 66 inclusive, and punishable with imprisonment shall, on conviction by court-martial, if that offence be not committed in consequence of the abetment, and no express provision is made by this Act for the punishment of such abetment, be liable to suffer imprisonment for a term which may extend to one-half of the longest term provided for that offence or such less punishment as is in this Act mentioned.

71. Civil offences. Subject to the provisions of Section 72, any person subject to this Act who at any place in or beyond India commits any civil offence shall be deemed to be guilty of an offence against this Act and, if charged therewith under this Section shall be liable to be tried by a court-martial and, on conviction, be punishable as follows, that is to say -

(a) if the offence is one which would be punishable under any law in force in India with death, or with transportation, he shall be liable to suffer any punishment, other than whipping, assigned for the offence by the aforesaid law and such less punishment as is in this Act mentioned; and

(b) in any other case, he shall be liable to suffer any punishment other than whipping, assigned for the offence by any law in force in India, or imprisonment for a term which may extend to seven years or such less punishment as is in this Act mentioned.

72. Civil offences not triable by court-martial. A person subject to this Act who commits an offence of murder against a person not subject to military, naval or air force law, or of culpable homicide not amounting to murder against such a person or of rape in relation to such a person, shall not be deemed to be guilty of an offence against this Act and shall not be tried by a court-martial, unless he commits any of the said offences-

(a) while on active service, or

(b) at any place outside India, or

(c) at a frontier post specified by the said Government by notification in this behalf.

CHAPTER - VII : PUNISHMENTS

73. Punishments awardable by courts-martial. Punishments may be inflicted in respect of offences committed by persons subject to this Act and convicted by courts-martial according to the scale. following, that is to say -

(a) death;

(b) transportation for life or for any period not less than seven years, in respect of civil offences;

(c) imprisonment, either rigorous or simple, for any period not exceeding fourteen years;

(d) detention for a term not exceeding two years in the case of airmen;

(e) cashiering, in the case of officers;

(f) dismissal from service;

(g) reduction to the ranks or to a lower rank or classification, in the case of warrant officers and non-commissioned officers:

PROVIDED that a warrant officer reduced to the ranks shall not be required to serve in the ranks as an airman;

(h) forfeiture of seniority of rank, in the case of officers, warrant officers and non-commissioned officers; and forfeiture of all or any part of their service for the purpose of promotion, in the case of any of them whose promotion depends upon length of service;

(i) forfeiture of service for the purpose of increased pay, pension or any other prescribed purpose;

(j) severe reprimand or reprimand, in the case of officers, warrant officers and non-commissioned officers;

(k) forfeiture of pay and allowances for a period not exceeding three months for an offence committed on active service;

(l) forfeiture in the case of a person sentenced to cashiering or dismissal from the service of all arrears of pay and allowances and other public money due to him at the time of such cashiering or dismissal;

(m) stoppage of pay and allowances until any proved loss or damage occasioned by the offence of which he is convicted is made. good.

74. Alternative punishments awardable by court-martial. Subject to the provisions of this Act, a court-martial may, on convicting a person subject to this Act of any of the offences specified in Sections 34 to 70 inclusive, award either the particular punishment with which the offence is stated in the said Sections to be punishable, or, in lieu thereof, any one of the punishments lower in the scale set out in Section 73, regard being had to the nature and degree of the offence.

75. Combination of punishments. A sentence of a court-martial may award in addition to, or without any one other punishment, the punishment specified in clause (e) or clause (f) of Section 73 and any one or more of the punishments specified in clauses (g) to (m) of that Section.

76. Cashiering of officers. An officer shall be sentenced to be cashiered before he is awarded any of the punishments specified in clauses (a) to (c) of Section 73.

77. Field punishment.

(1) Where any person subject to this Act and under the rank of warrant officer commits any offence on active service, it shall be lawful for a court-martial to award for that offence any such punishment as is prescribed as a field punishment.

(2) Field punishment shall be of the character of personal restraint or of hard labour but shall not be of a nature to cause injury to life or limb and shall not include flogging.

78. Position of field punishment in scale of punishments. Field punishment shall for the purpose of commutation be deemed to stand next below dismissal in the scale of punishments specified in Section 73.

79. Result of certain punishments in the case of a warrant officer or a noncommissioned officer. A warrant officer or a non-commissioned officer sentenced by a court-martial to transportation, imprisonment, detention, field punishment or dismissal from the service shall be deemed to be reduced to the ranks.

80. Retention in the ranks of a person convicted on active service. When, on active service, any enrolled person has been sentenced by a court-martial to dismissal, or to transportation, imprisonment or detention, whether combined with dismissal or not, the prescribed officer may direct that such person may be retained to serve in the ranks and such service shall be reckoned as part of his term of transportation, imprisonment or detention, if any.

81. Punishments otherwise than by court martial. Punishments may also be inflicted in respect of offences committed by persons subject to this Act without the intervention of a court-martial and in the manner stated in Sections 82 and 86.

82.Punishment of persons other than officers and warrant officers. Subject to the provisions of Section 84, a commanding officer or such other officer as is, with the consent of the Central Government, specified by [1][the Chief of the Air Staff], may, in the prescribed manner, proceed against a person subject to this Act otherwise than as an officer or warrant officer who is charged with an offence under this Act and award such person, to the extent prescribed, one or more of the following punishments, that is to say -

(a) detention up to twenty-eight days;
(b) confinement to the camp up to fourteen days;
(c) extra guards or duties not exceeding three in number;
(d) deprivation of acting rank;
(e) forfeiture of badge pay;
(f) severe reprimand or reprimand;
(g) fine up to fourteen days pay in any one month;
(h) penal deductions under clause (g) of Section 92;
(i) admonition;
(j) any prescribed field punishment up to twenty-eight days, in the case of a person on active service.

83. Requirement of sanction in certain cases.

(1) Subject to the provisions of sub-section (2), the punishments mentioned in Section 82 shall not be inflicted in respect of an offence under any of the Sections 34, 35 and 36 when committed on active service or under any of the Sections 37, 38, 40, 42 (f) and (g), 43, 47, 52, 60, 62, 63, 64, 66(a), (b) and (c) and 71 except with the previous sanction in writing of an officer having power to convene a district court-martial.

(2) The said punishments may be awarded without such sanction in the case of any offence, other than an offence under Section 34 or Section 71, committed by persons who have not been enrolled as combatants.

84. Limit of punishments under Section 82.

(1) An award of punishment under Section 82 shall not include field punishment in addition to one or more of the punishments specified in clauses (a) and (b) of that Section.

(2) In the case of an award of two or more of the punishments specified in clauses (a), (b) and, (c) of the said Section, the punishment specified in clause (b) or clause (c) shall take effect only at the end of the punishment specified in clause (a).

(3) When two or more of the punishments specified in the said clauses (a) and (b) are awarded to a person conjointly, or when already undergoing one or more of the said punishments, the whole extent of the punishments shall not exceed in the aggregate forty-two days.

(4) The punishments specified in clauses (a), (b), (c), (e), (g) and (j) of Section 82 shall not be awarded to any person who is of the rank of non-commissioned officer or was, at the time of committing the offence for which he is punished, of such rank.

(5) The punishment specified in clause (f) of the said Section shall not be awarded to any person below the rank of a non-commissioned officer.

85. Punishments in addition to those specified in Section 82. [1][The Chief of the Air Staff] may, with the consent of the Central Government, specify such other punishments as may be awarded under Section 82 in addition to or without any of the punishments specified in the said Section, and the extent to which such other punishments may be awarded.

86. Punishment of officers and warrant officers. An officer having power to convene a general court-martial or such other officer as is, with the consent of the Central Government, specified by [1][the Chief of the Air Staff] may, in the prescribed manner, proceed against an officer below the rank of squadron leader or a warrant officer, who is charged with an offence under this Act, and award one or more of the following punishments, that is to say -

(a) forfeiture of seniority, or in the case of any of them whose promotion depends upon length of service, forfeiture of service for the purpose of promotion for a period not exceeding twelve months, but subject to the right of the accused previous to the award to elect to be tried by a court-martial;

(b) severe reprimand or reprimand;

(c) stoppage of pay and allowance until any proved loss or damage occasioned by the offence of which he is convicted is made good but subject to the right of the accused specified in clause (a);

(d) forfeiture of pay and allowances for a period not exceeding three months for an offence under clause (e) of Section 42 insofar as it consists of neglect to obey flying orders or under Section 62 or Section 63.

87. Transmission of proceedings. In every case in which punishment has been awarded under Section 86, certified true copies of the proceedings shall be forwarded, in the prescribed manner, by the officer awarding the punishment, to a superior air force authority as defined in Section 89.

88. Review of proceedings. If any punishment awarded under Section 86 appears to a superior air force authority as defined in Section 89 to be illegal, unjust or excessive, such authority may cancel, vary or remit the punishment and make such other direction as may be appropriate in the circumstances of the case.

89. Superior air force authority. For the purposes of Sections 87 and 88, a "superior, air force authority" means-

(a) in the case of punishments awarded by a commanding officer, any officer superior in command to such commanding officer;

(b) in the case of punishments awarded by any other authority, the Central Government, [1][the Chief of the Air Staff] or other officer specified by [1][the Chief of the Air Staff].

90. Collective fines.

(1) Whenever any weapon or part of a weapon forming part of the equipment of a unit or detachment is lost or stolen, the officer commanding such unit or detachment may, after obtaining the report of a court of inquiry, impose a collective fine upon the warrant officers, non-commissioned officers and men

of such unit, or upon so many of them as, in his judgment, should be held responsible-for such loss or theft.

(2) Such fine shall be assessed as a percentage on the pay of the individuals on whom it falls.

CHAPTER - VIII : PENAL DEDUCTIONS

91. Deductions from pay and allowances of officers. The following penal deductions may be made from the pay and allowances of an officer, that is to say -

(a) all pay and allowances due to an officer for every day he absents himself without leave, unless a satisfactory explanation has been given to his commanding officer and has been approved by the Central Government;

(b) all pay and allowances for every day while he is in custody or under suspension from duty on a charge for an offence of which he is afterwards convicted by a criminal court or a court-martial or by an officer exercising authority under Section 86;

(c) any sum required to make good the pay of any person subject to this Act which he has unlawfully retained or unlawfully refused to pay;

(d) any sum required to make good such compensation for any expenses, loss, damage or destruction occasioned by the commission of an offence as may be determined by the court-martial by whom he is convicted of such offence, or by an officer exercising authority under Section 86;

(e) all pay and allowances ordered by a court-martial or an officer exercising authority under Section 86 to be forfeited or stopped;

(f) any sum required to pay a fine awarded by a criminal court or a court-martial exercising jurisdiction under Section 71;

(g) any sum required to make good any loss, damage, or destruction of public or service property which, after due investigation, appears to the Central Government to have been occasioned by the wrongful act or negligence on the part of the officer;

(h) all pay and allowances forfeited by order of the Central Government if the officer is found by a court of inquiry constituted by [1][the Chief of the Air Staff] in this behalf, to have deserted to the enemy, or while in enemy hands, to have served with, or under the orders of, the enemy or in any manner to have aided the enemy, or to have allowed himself to be taken prisoner by the enemy through want of due precaution or through disobedience of orders or wilful neglect of duty, or having been taken prisoner by the enemy, to have failed to rejoin his service when it was possible to do so;

(i) any sum required by order of the Central Government to be paid for the maintenance of his wife or his legitimate or illegitimate child or towards the cost of any relief given by the said Government to the said wife or child.

92. Deductions from pay and allowances of airmen. Subject to the provisions of Section 95, the following penal deductions may be made from the pay and allowances of an airman, that is to say -

(a) all pay and allowances for every day of absence either on desertion or without leave, or as a prisoner of war, and for every day of transportation or imprisonment awarded by a criminal court, or a court-martial, or of detention, or field punishment awarded by a court-martial or an officer exercising authority under Section 82.

(b) all pay and allowances for every day while he is in custody on a charge for an offence of which he is afterwards convicted by a criminal court or a court-martial, or on a charge of absence without leave for which he is afterwards awarded detention or field punishment by an officer exercising authority under Section 82;

(c) all pay and allowances for every day on which he is in hospital on account of sickness certified by the medical officer attending on him to have been caused by an offence under this Act committed by him;

(d) for every day on which he is in hospital on account of sickness certified by the medical officer attending on him to have been caused by his own misconduct or imprudence, such sum as may be specified by order of the Central Government or by such officer as may be specified by that Government;

(e) all pay and allowances ordered by a court-martial or by an officer exercising authority under Section 82 or Section 86 to be forfeited or stopped;

(f) all pay and allowances for every day between his being recovered from the enemy and his dismissal from the service in consequence of his conduct when being taken prisoner by, or while in the hands of, the enemy;

(g) any sum required to make good such compensation for any expenses, loss, damage or destruction caused by him to the Central Government or to any building or property as may be awarded by his commanding officer;

(h) any sum required to pay a fine awarded by a criminal court, a court-martial exercising jurisdiction under Section 71, or an officer exercising authority under Section 82 or Section 90;

(i) any sum required by order of the Central Government or any prescribed officer to be paid for the maintenance of his wife or his legitimate or illegitimate child or towards the cost of any relief given by the said Government to the said wife or child.

93. Computation of time of absence or custody. For the purposes of clauses (a) and (b) of Section 92-

(a) no person shall be treated as absent or in custody for a day a unless the absence or custody has lasted, whether wholly in one day, or partly in one day and partly in another, for six consecutive hours or upwards;

(b) any absence or custody for less than a day may be reckoned as absence or custody for a day if such absence or custody prevented the absentee from fulfilling any air force duty which was thereby thrown upon some other person;

(c) absence or custody for twelve consecutive hours or upwards may be reckoned as absence or custody for the whole of each day during any portion of which the person was absent or in custody;

(d) a period of absence, or imprisonment, which commences before and ends after, midnight may be reckoned as a day.

94. Pay and allowances during trial. In the case of any person subject to this Act who is in custody or under suspension-from duty on a charge for an offence, the prescribed officer may direct that the whole or any part of the pay and allowances of such person shall be withheld, pending the result of his trial on the charge against him, in order to give effect to the provisions of clause (b) of Sections 91.and 92.

95. Limit of certain deductions. The total deductions from the pay and allowances of a person made under clauses (e) and (g) to (i) of Section 92 shall not, except where he is sentenced to dismissal, exceed in any one month one-half of his pay and allowances for that month.

96. Deduction from public money due to a person. Any sum authorised by this Act to be deducted from the pay and allowances of any person may, without prejudice to any other mode of recovering the same, be deducted from any public money due to him other than a pension.

97. Pay and allowances of prisoner of war during inquiry into his conduct. Where the conduct of any person subject to this Act when being taken prisoner by, or while in the hands of, the enemy, is to be inquired into under this Act or any other law, 1 [the Chief of the Air Staff] or any officer authorised by him may order that the whole or any part of the pay and allowances of such person shall be withheld pending the result of such inquiry.

98. Remission of deductions. Any deduction from pay and allowances authorised by this Act may be remitted in such manner, and to such extent, and by such authority, as may from time to time be prescribed.

99. Provision for dependants of prisoner of war from remitted deductions. In the case of all persons subject to this Act, being prisoners of war, whose pay and allowances have been forfeited under clause (h) of Section 91 or clause (a) of Section 92, but in respect of whom a remission has been made under Section 98, it shall be lawful for proper provision to be made by the prescribed authorities out of such pay and allowances for any dependants of such persons, and any such remission shall in that case be deemed to apply only to the balance thereafter remaining of such pay and allowances.

100. Provision for dependants of prisoner of war from his pay and allowances. It shall be lawful for proper provision to be made by the prescribed authorities for any dependants of any person subject to this Act, who is a prisoner of war or is missing, out of his pay and allowances.

101. Period during which a person is deemed to be a prisoner of war. For the purposes of Sections 99 and 100, a person shall be deemed to continue to be a prisoner of war until the conclusion of any inquiry into his conduct such as is referred to in Section 97, and if he is cashiered or dismissed from the service in consequence of such conduct, until the date of such cashiering or dismissal.

CHAPTER - IX : ARREST AND PROCEEDINGS BEFORE TRIAL

102. Custody of offenders.

(1) Any person subject to this Act who is charged with a offence may be taken into air force custody.

(2) Any such person may be ordered into air force custody by any superior officer.

(3) Any officer may order into air force custody any officer, though he may be of a higher rank, engaged in a quarrel, affray or disorder.

103. Duty of commanding officer in regard detention.

(1) It shall be the duty of every commanding officer to take care that a person under his command when charged with an offence is not detained in custody for more than forty-eight hours after the committal of such person into custody is reported to him, without the charge being investigated, unless investigation within that period seems to him to be impracticable with due regard to the public service.

(2) Every case of a person being detained in custody beyond a period of forty-eight hours, and the reason thereof shall be reported by the commanding officer to the air or other officer to whom application would be made to convene a general or district court-martial for the trial of the person charged.

(3) In reckoning the period of forty-eight hours specified in subsection (1), Sundays and public holidays shall be excluded.

(4) Subject to the provisions of this Act, the Central Government may make rules providing for the manner in which and the period for which any person subject to this Act may be taken into and detained in air force custody, pending the trial by any competent authority for any offence committed by him.

104. Interval between committal and court-martial. In every case where any such person as is mentioned in Section 102 and as is not on active service remains in such custody for a longer period than eight days, without a court-martial for his trial being ordered to assemble, a special report giving reasons for the delay shall be made by his commanding officer in the manner prescribed; and a similar report shall be forwarded every eight days until a court-martial is assembled or such person is released from custody.

105. Arrest by civil authorities. Whenever any person subject to this Act, who is accused of any offence under this Act, is within the jurisdiction of any magistrate or police officer, such magistrate or police officer shall aid in the apprehension and delivery to air force custody of such person upon receipt of a written application to that effect signed by his commanding officer.

106. Capture of deserters.

(1) Whenever any person subject to this Act deserts, the commanding officer of the unit or detachment to which he belongs, shall give written information of the desertion to such civil authorities as, in his opinion, may be able to afford assistance towards the capture of the deserter; and such authorities shall thereupon take steps for the apprehension of the said deserter in like manner

as if he were a person for whose apprehension a warrant had been issued by a magistrate, and shall deliver the deserter, when apprehended, into air force custody.

(2) Any police officer may arrest without warrant any person reasonably believed to be subject to this Act, and to be a deserter or to be travelling without authority, and shall bring him without delay before the nearest magistrate, to be dealt with according to law.

107. Inquiry into absence without leave.

(1) When any person subject to this Act has been absent from his duty without due authority for a period of thirty days, a court of inquiry shall, as soon as practicable, be assembled, and such court shall, on oath or affirmation administered in the prescribed manner, inquire respecting the absence of the person, and the deficiency, if any, in the property of the Government entrusted to his care, or in any arms, ammunition, equipment, instruments, clothing or necessaries, and if satisfied of the fact of such absence without due authority or other sufficient cause, the court shall declare such absence and the period thereof, and the said deficiency, if any; and the commanding officer of the unit to which the person belongs shall enter in the court-martial book of the unit a record of declaration.

(2) If the person declared absent does not afterwards surrender or is not apprehended, he shall, for the purposes of this Act, be deemed to be a deserter.

108. Provost marshals.

(1) Provost-marshals may be appointed by [1][the Chief of the Air Staff], or by any prescribed officer.

(2) The duties of a provost-marshal are to take charge of persons confined for any offence, to preserve good order and discipline, and to prevent breaches of the same by persons serving in, or attached to the Air Force.

(3) A provost-marshal may at any time arrest and detain for trial any person subject to this Act who commits, or is charged with an offence, and may also carry into effect any punishment to be inflicted in pursuance of the sentence awarded by a court-martial, or by an officer exercising authority under Section 82 but shall not inflict any punishment on his own authority:

PROVIDED that no officer shall be so arrested or detained otherwise than on the order of another officer.

(4) For the purposes of sub-sections (2) and (3), a provost-marshal shall be deemed to include a provost-marshal appointed under the Army Act or the Navy Act and any person legally exercising authority under him or on his behalf.

CHAPTER - X : COURTS-MARTIAL

109. Different kinds of courts martial. For the purposes of this Act there shall be three kinds of courts-martial, that is to say -

(a) general courts-martial
(b) district courts-martial and
(c) summary general courts-martial.

110. Power to convene a general court martial. A general court-martial may be convened by the Central Government or [1][the Chief of the Air Staff], or by any officer empowered in this behalf by warrant of [1][the Chief of the Air Staff].

111. Power to convene a district court martial. A district court-martial may be convened by an officer having power to convene a general court-martial, or by any officer empowered in this behalf by warrant of any such officer.

112. Contents of warrants issued under Sections 110 and 111. A warrant issued under Section 110 or Section 111 may contain such restrictions, reservations or conditions as the officer issuing it may think fit.

113. Power to convene a summary general court martial. The following authorities shall have the power to convene a summary general court-martial, namely:-

(a) an officer empowered in this behalf by an order of the Central Government or of [1][the Chief of the Air Staff];
(b) on active service, the officer commanding the forces in the field, or any officer empowered by him in this behalf;
(c) an officer commanding any detached portion of the Air Force on active service when, in his opinion, it is not practicable, with due regard to discipline and the exigencies of the service, that an offence should be tried by a general court-martial.

114. Composition of general court martial. A general court-martial shall consist of not less than five officers, each of whom has held a commission for not less than three whole years and of whom not less than four are of a rank not below that of flight-lieutenant.

115. Composition of district court-martial. A district court-martial shall consist of not less than three officers, each of whom has held a commission for not less than two whole years.

116. Composition of summary general court-martial. A summary general court-martial shall consist of not less than three officers.

117. Dissolution of court-martial.

(1) If a court-martial after the commencement of a trial is reduced below the minimum number of officers required by this Act, it shall be dissolved.
(2) If on account of the illness of the judge advocate or of the accused before the finding, it is impossible to continue the trial, a court-martial shall be dissolved.
(3) The officer who convened a court-martial may dissolve such court-martial if it appears to him that the exigencies of the service or the necessities of discipline render it impossible or inexpedient to continue the said court-martial.
(4) Where a court-martial is dissolved under this Section, the accused may be tried again.

118. Powers of general and summary general courts-martial. A general or summary general court-martial shall have power to try any person subject to this Act for any offence punishable therein and to pass any sentence authorised thereby.

119. Powers of district court-martial. A district court-martial shall have power to try any person subject to this Act other than an officer or warrant officer for any offence made punishable therein, and to pass any sentence authorised by this Act other than a sentence of death, transportation, or imprisonment for a term exceeding two years.

120. Prohibition of second trial. When any person subject to this Act has been acquitted or convicted of an offence by a court-martial or by a criminal court, or has been dealt with under Section 82 or Section 86, he shall not be liable to be tried again for the same offence by a court-martial or dealt with under the said Sections.

121. Period of limitation for trial.

(1) Except as provided by sub-section (2), no trial by court-martial of any person subject to this Act for any offence shall be commenced after the expiration of a period of three years from the date of such offence.

(2) The provisions of sub-section (1) shall not apply to a trial for an offence of desertion or fraudulent enrolment or for any of the offences mentioned in Section 37.

(3) In the computation of the period of time mentioned in sub-section (1) anytime spent by such person as a prisoner of war, or in enemy territory, or in evading arrest after the commission of the offence, shall be excluded.

(4) No trial for an offence of desertion, other than desertion on active service or of fraudulent enrolment shall be commenced if the person in question, not being an officer has, subsequently to the commission of the offence, served continuously in an exemplary manner for not less than three years with any portion of the Air Force.

122. Liability of offender who ceases to be subject to Act.

(1) Where an offence under this Act had been committed by any person while subject to this Act, and he has ceased to be so subject, he may be taken into and kept in air force custody, and tried and punished for such offence as if he continued to be so subject.

(2) Except as provided by sub-sections (3) and (4), any such person shall, not be tried for an offence, unless his trial commences within six months after he had ceased to be subject to this Act.

(3) The provisions of sub-section (2) shall not apply to the trial of any such person for an offence of desertion or fraudulent enrolment or for any of the offences, mentioned in Section 37.

(4) Nothing contained in sub-section (2) shall affect the jurisdiction of a civil court to try any offence triable by such court as well as by a court-martial.

(5) When a person subject to this Act is sentenced by a court martial to transportation or imprisonment, this Act shall apply to him during the term of his sentence, though he is cashiered or dismissed from the Air Force, or has

otherwise ceased to be subject to this Act, and he may be kept, removed, imprisoned and punished as if he continued to be subject to this Act.

(6) When a person subject to this Act is sentenced by a court-martial to death, this Act shall apply to him till the sentence is carried out.

123. Place of trial. Any person subject to this Act who commits any offence against it may be tried and punished for such offence in any place whatever.

124. Choice between criminal court and court-martial. When a criminal court and a court-martial have each jurisdiction in respect of an offence, it shall be in the discretion of [1][the Chief of the Air Staff], the officer commanding any group, wing or station in which the accused prisoner is serving or such other officer as may be prescribed to decide before which court the proceedings shall be instituted, and, if that officer decides that they should be instituted before a court-martial, to direct that the accused person shall be detained in air force custody.

125. Power of criminal court to require delivery of offender.

(1) When a criminal court having jurisdiction is of opinion that proceedings shall be instituted before itself in respect of any alleged offence, it may, by written notice, require the officer referred to in Section 124 at his option, either to deliver over the offender to the nearest magistrate to be proceeded against according to law, or to postpone proceedings pending a reference to the Central Government.

(2) In every such case the said officer shall either deliver over the offender in compliance with the requisition, or shall forthwith refer the question as to the court before which the proceedings are to be instituted for the determination of the Central Government whose order upon such reference shall be final.

126. Successive trials by a criminal court and a court-martial.

(1) A person convicted or acquitted by a court-martial may, with the previous sanction of the Central Government, be tried again by a criminal court for the same offence, or on the same facts.

(2) If a person sentenced by a court-martial under this Act or punished under Section 82 or Section 86 is afterwards tried and convicted by a criminal court for the same offence, or on the same facts, that court shall, in awarding punishment have regard to the punishment he may already have undergone for the said offence.

CHAPTER - XI : PROCEDURE OF COURTS-MARTIAL

127. Presiding officer. At every general, district or summary general court-martial the senior member shall be the presiding officer.

128. Judge advocate. Every general court-martial shall, and every district or summary general court-martial may, be attended by a judge advocate, who shall be either an officer belonging to the department of the Chief Legal Adviser or if no such officer is available, an officer approved by the Chief Legal Adviser or any of his deputies.

129. Challenges.

(1) At all trials by general, district or summary general courts-martial, as soon as the court is assembled, the names of the presiding officer and members shall be read over to the accused, who shall thereupon be asked whether he objects to being tried by any officer sitting on the court.

(2) If the accused objects to any such officer, his objection, and also the reply thereto of the officer objected to, shall be heard and recorded, and the remaining officers of the court shall, in the absence of the challenged officer, decide on the objection.

(3) If the objection is allowed by one-half or more of the votes of the officers entitled to vote, the objection shall be allowed, and the member objected to shall retire, and his vacancy may be filled in the prescribed manner by another officer, subject to the same right of the accused to object.

(4) When no challenge is made, or when challenge has been made and disallowed, or the place of every officer successfully challenged has been filled by another officer to whom no objection is made or allowed, the court shall proceed with the trial.

130. Oaths of member, judge advocate and witness.

(1) An oath or affirmation in the prescribed manner shall be administered to every member of every court-martial and to the judge advocate before the commencement of the trial.

(2) Every person giving evidence before a court-martial shall be examined after being duly sworn or affirmed in the prescribed form.

(3) The provisions of sub-section (2) shall not apply where the witness is a child under twelve years of age and the court-martial is of opinion that though the witness understands the duty of speaking the truth, he does not understand the nature of an oath or affirmation.

131. Voting by members.

(1) Subject to the provisions of sub-sections (2) and (3), every decision of a court-martial shall be passed by an absolute majority of votes; and where there is an equality of votes on either the finding or the sentence, the decision shall be in favour of the accused.

(2) No sentence of death shall be passed by a general court-martial without the concurrence of at least two-thirds of the members of the court.

(3) No sentence of death shall be passed by a summary general court-martial without the concurrence of all the members.

(4) In matters other than a challenge or the finding or sentence, the presiding officer shall have a casting vote.

132. General rule as to evidence. The Indian Evidence Act, 1872 (1 of 1872) shall, subject to the provisions of this Act, apply to all proceedings before a court-martial.

133. Judicial notice. A court-martial may take judicial notice of any matter within the general air force knowledge of the members.

134. Summoning witnesses.

(1) The convening officer, the Presiding officer of a court-martial, the judge advocate or the commanding officer of the accused person, may, by summons under his hand, require the attendance, at a time and place to be mentioned in the summons, of any person either to give evidence or to produce any document or other thing.

(2) In the case of a witness amenable to air force authority, the summons shall be sent to his commanding officer, and such officer shall serve it upon him accordingly.

(3) In the case of any other witness, the summons shall be sent to the magistrate within whose jurisdiction he may be or reside, and such magistrate shall give effect to the summons as if the witness were required in the court of such magistrate.

(4) When a witness is required to produce any particular document or other thing in his possession or power, the summons shall describe it with reasonable precision.

135. Documents exempted from production.

(1) Nothing in Section 134 shall be deemed to affect the operation of Sections 123 and 124 of the Indian Evidence Act, 1872, or to apply to any letter, postcard, telegram or other document in the custody of the postal or telegraph authorities.

(2) If any document in such custody is, in the opinion of any district magistrate, chief presidency magistrate, High Court or Court of Session, wanted for the purpose of any court-martial, such magistrate or court may require the postal or telegraph authorities, as the case may be, to deliver such document to such person as such magistrate or court may direct.

(3) If any such document is, in the opinion of any other magistrate or of any commissioner of police or district superintendent of police, wanted for any such purpose, he may require the postal or telegraph authorities, as the case may be, to cause search to be made for and to detain such document pending the orders of any such district magistrate, chief presidency magistrate or High Court or Court of Session.

136. Commissions for examination of witnesses.

(1) Whenever, in the course of a trial by court-martial, it appears to the court that the examination of a witness is necessary for the ends of justice, and that the attendance of such witness cannot be procured without an amount of delay, expense or inconvenience which, in the circumstances of the case, would be unreasonable, such court may address the Chief Legal Adviser in order that a commission to take the evidence of such witness may be issued.

(2) The Chief Legal Adviser may then, if he thinks necessary, issue a commission to any district magistrate or magistrate of the first class, within the local limits of whose jurisdiction such witness resides, to take the evidence of such witness.

(3) The magistrate or officer to whom the commission is issued, or, if he is the district magistrate, he or such magistrate of the first class as he appoints in this behalf, shall proceed to the place where the witness is or shall summon the witness before him and shall take down his evidence in the same manner, and may for this purpose exercise the same powers, as in trials of warrant cases under the Code of Criminal Procedure, 1898, (5 of 1898) or any corresponding law in force in [1][the State of Jammu and Kashmir].

(4) When the witness resides in a tribal area or in any place outside India, the commission may be issued in the manner specified in Chapter XL of the Code of Criminal Procedure, 1898, (5 of 1898) or of any corresponding law in force in [1][the State of Jammu and Kashmir].

(5) In this and the next succeeding Section, the expression Chief Legal Adviser includes a Deputy Chief Legal Adviser.

137. Examination of a witness on commission.

(1) The prosecutor and the accused person in any case in which a commission is issued under Section 136 may respectively forward any interrogatories in writing which the court may think relevant to the issue, and the magistrate or officer executing the commission shall examine the witness upon such interrogatories.

(2) The prosecutor and the accused person may appear before such magistrate or officer by counsel or except in the case of an accused person in custody, in person, and may examine, cross-examine and re-examine, as the case may be, the said witness.

(3) After a commission issued under Section 136 has been duly executed, it shall be returned, together with the deposition of the witness examined thereunder to the Chief Legal Adviser.

(4) On receipt of a commission and deposition returned under sub-section (3), the Chief Legal Adviser shall forward the same to the court at whose instance the commission was issued or, if such court has been dissolved, to any other court convened for the trial of the accused person; and the commission, the return thereto and the deposition shall be open to inspection by the prosecutor and the accused person, and may, subject to all just exceptions, be read in evidence in the case by either the prosecutor or the accused, and shall form part of the proceedings of the court.

(5) In every case in which a commission is issued under Section 136, the trial may be adjourned for a specified time reasonably sufficient for the execution and return of the commission.

138. Conviction of offence not charged.

(1) A person charged before a court-martial with desertion may be found guilty of attempting to desert or of being absent without leave.

(2) A person charged before a court-martial with attempting to desert may be found guilty of being absent without leave.

(3) A person charged before a court-martial with using criminal force may be found guilty of assault.

(4) A person charged before a court-martial with using threatening language may be found guilty of using insubordinate language.

(5) A person charged before a court-martial with any one of the offences specified in clauses (a), (b), (c) and (d) of Section 52 may be found guilty of any other of these offences with which he might have been charged.

(6) A person charged before a court-martial with an offence punishable under Section 71 may be found guilty of any other offence of which he might have been found guilty if the provisions of the Code of Criminal Procedure, 1898 (5 of 1898) were applicable.

(7) A person charged before a court-martial with any offence under this Act may, on failure of proof of an offence having been committed in circumstances involving a more severe punishment, be found guilty of the same offence as having been committed in circumstances involving a less severe punishment.

(8) A person charged before a court-martial with any offence under this Act may be found guilty of having attempted or abetted the commission of that offence, although the attempt or abetment is not separately charged.

139. Presumption as to signatures. In any proceeding under this Act, any application, certificate, warrant, reply, or other document purporting to be signed by an officer in the service of the Government shall, on production, be presumed to have been duly signed by the person by whom and in the character in which it purports to have been signed, until the contrary is shown.

140. Enrolment paper.

(1) Any enrolment paper purporting to be signed by an enrolling officer shall, in proceedings under this Act, be evidence of the person enrolled having given the answers to questions which he is therein represented as having given.

(2) The enrolment of such person may be proved by the production of the original or a copy of his enrolment paper purporting to be certified to be a true copy by the officer having the custody of the enrolment paper.

141. Presumption as to certain documents.

(1) A letter, return or other document respecting the service of any person in, or the cashiering, dismissal or discharge of any person from, any portion of the Air Force, or respecting the circumstance of any person not having served in, or belonged to, any portion of the Forces, if purporting to be signed by or on behalf of the Central Government or [1][the Chief of the Air Staff], or by any prescribed officer, shall be evidence of the facts stated in such letter, return or other document.

(2) An Army, Navy or Air Force List or Gazette purporting to be published by authority shall be evidence of the status and rank of the officers or warrant officers therein mentioned, and of any appointment held by them and of the unit or branch of the services to which they belong.

(3) Where a record is made in any service book in pursuance of this Act or of any rules made thereunder or otherwise in pursuance of air force duty, and purports to be signed by the commanding officer or by the officer whose duty it is to make such record, such record shall be evidence of the facts therein stated.

(4) A copy of any record in any service book purporting to be certified to be a true copy by the officer having custody of such book shall be evidence of such record.

(5) Where any person subject to this Act is being tried on a charge of desertion or of absence without leave, and such person has surrendered himself into the custody of any officer or other person subject to this Act, or any portion of the Air Force, or has been apprehended by such officer or person, a certificate purporting to be signed by such officer, or by the commanding officer of that portion of the Air Force, or by the commanding officer of the unit, or detachment to which such person belongs, as the case may be, and stating the fact, date and place of such surrender or apprehension, and the manner in which he was dressed, shall be evidence of the matters so stated.

(6) Where any person subject to this Act is being tried on a charge of desertion or of absence without leave, and such person has surrendered himself into the custody of, or has been apprehended by, a police officer not below the rank of an officer-in-charge of a police station, a certificate purporting to be signed by such police officer and stating the fact, date and place of such surrender or apprehension and the manner in which he was dressed shall be evidence of the matters so stated.

(7) Any document purporting to be a report under the hand of any Chemical Examiner or Assistant Chemical Examiner to Government upon any matter or thing duly submitted to him for examination or analysis and report may be used as evidence in any proceeding tinder this Act.

142. Reference by accused to Government Officer.

(1) If at any trial for desertion or absence without leave, overstaying leave or not rejoining when warned for service, the person tried states in his defence any sufficient or reasonable excuse for his unauthorised absence, and refers in support thereof to any officer in the service of the Government, or if it appears that any such officer is likely to prove or disprove the said statement in the defence, the court shall address such officer and adjourn the proceedings until his reply is received.

(2) The written reply of any officer so referred to shall, if signed by him, be received in evidence and have the same effect as if made on oath before the court.

(3) If the court is dissolved before the receipt of such reply, or if the court omits to comply with the provisions of this Section, the convening officer may, at his discretion, annul the proceedings and order a fresh trial.

143. Evidence of previous convictions and general character.

(1) When any person subject to this Act has been convicted by a court-martial of any offence, such court-martial may inquire into, and receive and record evidence

of any previous convictions of such person, either by a court-martial or by a criminal court, or any previous award of punishment under Section 82 or Section 86 and may further inquire into and record the general character of such person and such other matters as may be prescribed.

(2) Evidence received under this Section may be either oral, or in the shape of entries in, or certified extracts from, court-martial books or other official records, and it shall not be necessary to give notice before trial to the person tried that evidence as to his previous convictions or character will be received.

144. Lunacy of accused.

(1) Whenever, in the course of a trial by a court-martial, it appears to the court that the person charged is by reason of unsoundness of mind incapable of making his defence, or that he committed the act alleged but was by reason of unsoundness of mind incapable of knowing the nature of the act or knowing that it was wrong or contrary to law, the court shall record a finding accordingly.

(2) The presiding officer of the court shall forthwith report the case to the confirming officer.

(3) The confirming officer to whom the case is reported under sub-section (2) may, if he does not confirm the finding, take steps to have the accused person tried by the same or another court-martial for the offence with which he was charged.

(4) A confirming officer confirming a finding in any case so reported to him under sub-section (2) shall order the accused person to be kept in custody in the prescribed manner and shall report the case for the orders of the Central Government.

(5) On receipt of a report under sub-section (4) the Central Government may order the accused person to be detained in a lunatic asylum or other suitable place of safe custody.

145. Subsequent fitness of lunatic accused for trial. Where any accused person, having been found by reason of unsoundness of mind to be incapable of making his defence, is in custody or under detention under Section 144, the officer commanding a unit or detachment within the area of whose command the accused is in custody or is detained, or any other officer prescribed in this behalf, may -

(a) if such person is in custody under sub-section (4) of Section 144, on the report of a medical officer that he is capable of making his defence, or

(b) if such person is detained in a jail under sub-section (5) of Section 144, on a certificate of the Inspector-General of Prisons and if such person is detained in a lunatic asylum under the said sub-section on a certificate of any two or more of the visitors of such asylum that he is capable of making his defence take steps to have such person tried by the same or another court-martial for the offence with which he was originally charged, or, if the offence is a civil offence, by a criminal court.

146. Transmission to Central Government of orders under Section 145. A copy of every order made by an officer under Section 145 for the trial of the accused shall forthwith be sent to the Central Government.

147. Release of lunatic accused. Where any person is in custody under sub-section (4) of Section 144 or under detention under sub-section (5) of that Section-

(a) if such person is in custody under the said sub-section (4), on the report of a medical officer, or

(b) if such person is detained under the said sub-section (5), on a certificate from any of the authorities mentioned in clause (b) of Section 145 that, in the judgment of such officer or authority such person may be released without danger of his doing injury to himself or to any other person, the Central Government may order that such person be released, or detained in custody, or transferred to a public lunatic asylum if he has not already been sent to such an asylum.

148. Delivery of lunatic accused to relatives. Where any relative or friend of any person who is in custody under sub-section (4) of Section 144 or under detention under sub-section (5) of that Section desires that he should be delivered to his care and custody, the Central Government may upon application by such relative or friend and on his giving security to the satisfaction of that Government that the person delivered shall be properly taken care of and prevented from doing injury to himself or any other person, and be produced for the inspection of such officer, and at such times and places, as the Central Government may direct, order such person to be delivered to such relative or friend.

149. Order for custody and disposal of property pending trial. When any property regarding which any offence appears to have been committed, or which appears to have been used for the commission of any offence, is produced before a court-martial during a trial, the court may make such order as it thinks fit for the proper custody of such property pending the conclusion of the trial, and if the property is subject to speedy or natural decay may, after recording such evidence as it thinks necessary, order it to be sold or otherwise disposed of.

150. Order for disposal of property regarding which offence is committed.

(1) After the conclusion of a trial before any court-martial, the court or the officer confirming the finding or sentence of such court-martial or any authority superior to such officer, may make such order as it or he thinks fit for the disposal by destruction, confiscation, delivery to any person claiming to be entitled to possession thereof, or otherwise of any property or document produced before the court or in its custody, or regarding which any offences appears to have been committed or which has been used for the commission of any offence.

(2) Where any order has been made under sub-section (1) in respect of property regarding which an offence appears to have been committed, a copy of such order signed and certified by the authority making the same may, whether the trial was held within India or not, be sent to a magistrate within whose jurisdiction such property for the time being is situated, and such magistrate shall thereupon cause the order to be carried into effect as if it were an order passed by him under the provisions of the Code of Criminal Procedure, 1898, (5 of 1898) or any corresponding law in force in [1][the State of Jammu and Kashmir].

(3) In this Section the term "property" includes, in the case of property regarding which an offence appears to have been committed, not only such property as has been originally in the possession or under the control of any person, but also any property into or for which the same may have been converted or exchanged, and anything acquired by such conversion or exchange whether immediately or otherwise.

151. Powers of courts martial when certain offences are committed by persons not subject to this Act. Any trial by a court-martial under the provisions of this Act shall be deemed to be a judicial proceeding within the meaning of Sections 193 and 228 of the Indian Penal Code, (45 of 1860) and the court-martial shall be deemed to be a court within the meaning of Sections 480 and 482 of the Code of Criminal Procedure, 1898 (5 of 1898).

CHAPTER - XII : CONFIRMATION AND REVISION

152. Finding and sentence not valid, unless confirmed. No finding or sentence of a general, district or summary general court-martial shall be valid except so far as it may be confirmed as provided by this Act.

153. Power to confirm finding and sentence of general court-martial. The findings and sentences of general courts-martial may be confirmed by the Central Government, or by any officer empowered in this behalf by warrant of the Central Government.

154. Power to confirm finding and sentence of district court-martial. The findings and sentences of district courts-martial may be confirmed by any officer having power to convene a general court-martial or by any officer empowered in this behalf by warrant of such officer.

155. Limitation of powers of confirming authority. A warrant issued under Section 153 or Section 154 may contain such restrictions, reservations or conditions as the authority issuing it may think fit.

156. Power to confirm finding and sentence of summary general court-martial. The findings and sentences of summary general courts-martial may be confirmed by the convening officer or if he so directs, by an authority superior to him.

157. Power of confirming authority to mitigate, remit or commute sentences.

(1) Subject to such restrictions, reservations or conditions as may be contained in any warrant issued under Section 153 or Section 154 and to the provisions of sub-sections (2) and (3), a confirming authority may, when confirming the sentence of a court-martial, mitigate or remit the punishment thereby awarded, or commute that punishment for any punishment or punishments lower in the scale laid down in Section 73.

(2) A sentence of transportation shall not be commuted for a sentence of imprisonment or detention for a term exceeding the term of transportation awarded by the court.

(3) A sentence of imprisonment shall not be computed for a sentence of detention for a term exceeding the term of imprisonment awarded by the court.

158. Confirming of findings and sentences on board a ship. When any person subject to this Act is tried and sentenced by a court-martial while on board a ship, the finding and sentence so far as not confirmed and executed on board the ship, may be confirmed and executed in like manner as if such person had been tried at the port of disembarkation.

159. Revision of finding or sentence.

(1) Any finding or sentence of a court-martial may be once revised by order of the confirming authority and on such revision, the court, if so directed by the confirming authority, may take additional evidence.

(2) The court, on revision, shall consist of the same officers as were present when the original decision was passed, unless any of those officers are unavoidably absent.

(3) In case of such unavoidable absence the cause thereof shall be duly certified in the proceedings, and the court shall proceed with the revision, provided that, if a general court-martial, it still consists of five officers, or, if a summary general or district court-martial, of three officers.

160. Alteration of finding or sentence in certain cases.

(1) Where a finding of guilty by a court-martial, which has been confirmed, is found for any reason to be invalid or cannot be supported by the evidence, the authority which would have had power under Section 177 to commute the punishment awarded by the sentence, if the finding had been valid, may substitute a new finding and pass a sentence for the offence specified or involved in such finding:

PROVIDED that no such substitution shall be made unless such finding could have been validly made by the court-martial on the charge and unless it appears that the court-martial must have been satisfied of the facts establishing the offence.

(2) Where a sentence passed by a court-martial which has been confirmed not being a sentence passed in pursuance of a new finding substituted under sub-section (1), is found for any reason to be invalid, the authority referred to in sub-section (1) may pass a valid sentence.

(3) The punishment awarded by a sentence passed under subsection (1) or sub-section (2) shall not be higher in the scale of punishments than, or in excess of, the punishment awarded by, the sentence for which a new sentence is substituted under this Section.

(4) Any finding substituted, or any sentence passed, under this Section shall for the purposes of this Act and the rules made thereunder have effect as if it were a finding or sentence, as the case may be, of a court-martial.

161. Remedy against order finding or sentence of court-martial.

(1) Any person subject to this Act who considers himself aggrieved by any order passed by a court-martial may present a petition to the officer or authority empowered to confirm any finding or sentence of such court-martial, and the confirming authority may take such steps as may be considered necessary to

satisfy itself as to the correctness, legality or propriety of the order passed or as to the regularity of any proceeding to which the order relates.

(2) Any person subject to this Act who considers himself aggrieved by a finding or sentence of a court-martial which has been confirmed, may present a petition to the Central Government, [1][the Chief of the Air Staff] or any prescribed officer superior in command to the one who confirmed such finding or sentence, and the Central Government, [1][the Chief of the Air Staff] or other officer, as the case may be, may pass such order thereon as it or he thinks fit.

162. Annulment of proceedings. The Central Government, 1[the Chief of the Air Staff] or any prescribed officer may annul the proceedings of any court-martial on the ground that they are illegal or unjust.

CHAPTER -XIII : EXECUTION OF SENTENCES

163. Form of sentence of death. In awarding a sentence of death, a court-martial shall, in its discretion, direct that the offender shall suffer death by being hanged by the neck until he be dead, or shall suffer death by being shot to death.

164. Commencement of sentence of transportation or imprisonment. Whenever any person is sentenced by a court-martial under this Act to transportation, imprisonment or detention the term of his sentence shall, whether it has been revised or not, be reckoned to commence on the day on which the original proceedings were signed, by the presiding officer.

165. Execution of sentence of transportation. Whenever any sentence of transportation is passed under this Act or whenever any sentence of death be commuted to transportation, the commanding officer of the person under sentence or such other officer as may be prescribed shall forward a warrant in the prescribed form to the officer-in-charge of the civil prison in which such person is to be confined and shall arrange for his despatch to such prison with the warrant.

166. Execution of sentence of imprisonment.

(1) Whenever any sentence of imprisonment is passed under this Act or whenever any sentence of death or transportation is commuted to imprisonment, the confirming officer or such other officer as may be prescribed, shall, save as otherwise provided in sub-sections (3) and (4), direct either that the sentence shall be carried out by confinement in a military or air force prison or that it shall be carried out by confinement in a civil prison.

(2) When a direction has been made under sub-section (1) the commanding officer of the person under sentence or such other officer as may be prescribed shall forward a warrant in the prescribed form to the officer-in-charge of the prison in which such person is to be confined and shall arrange for his despatch to such prison with the warrant.

(3) In the case of a sentence of imprisonment for a period not exceeding three months, the officers referred to in sub-section (1) may direct that the sentence shall be carried out by confinement in air force custody instead of in a civil or military or air force prison.

(4) On active service, a sentence of imprisonment may be carried out by confinement in such place as the officer commanding the forces in the field may from time to time appoint.

167. Temporary custody of offender. Where a sentence of transportation or imprisonment is directed to be undergone in a civil prison, the offender may be kept in military or air force custody or in any other fit place, till such time as it, is possible to send him to a civil prison.

168. Execution of sentence of imprisonment in special cases. Whenever, in the opinion of an air or other officer commanding a group, any sentence or portion of a sentence of imprisonment cannot for special reasons conveniently be carried out in a military or air force prison or in air force custody in accordance with the provisions of Section 166 such officer may direct. that such sentence or portion of sentence shall be carried out by confinement in any civil prison or other fit place.

169. Conveyance of prisoner from place to place. A person under sentence of transportation or imprisonment may, during his conveyance from place to place, or when on board ship, aircraft, or otherwise, be subjected to such restraint as is necessary for his safe conduct and removal.

170. Execution of sentence of detention. Whenever any sentence of detention is passed under this Act, or whenever any sentence of death, transportation or imprisonment is commuted to detention, the sentence shall be carried out by detaining the offender in any military or air force detention barracks, detention cells or other military or air force custody; and when the sentence is to be carried out by detention in any military or air force detention barracks, the commanding officer of the person under sentence or such other officer as may be prescribed shall forward a warrant in the prescribed form to the officer-in-charge of the detention barracks in which the person under sentence is to be detained and shall forward the person under sentence to such detention barracks with the warrant.

171. Communication of certain orders to prison officers. Whenever an order is duly made under this Act setting aside or varying any sentence, order or warrant under which any person is confined in a civil, military or air force prison or detained in a military or air force detention barracks a warrant in accordance with such order shall be forwarded by the officer making the order, or his staff officer, or such other person as may be prescribed, to the officer-in-charge of the prison or detention barracks in which such person is confined.

172. Execution of sentence of fine. When a sentence of fine is imposed by a court-martial under Section 71 whether the trial was held within India or not, a copy of such sentence, signed and certified by the confirming officer may be sent to any magistrate in India, and such magistrate shall thereupon cause the fine to be recovered in accordance with the provisions of the Code of Criminal Procedure, 1898 (5 of 1898) or any corresponding law in force in [1][the State of Jammu and Kashmir] for the levy of fines as if it were a sentence of fine imposed by such magistrate.

173. Establishment and regulation of air force prisons. The Central Government may set apart any building or part of a building, or any place under its control, as an air force prison or detention barracks for the confinement of persons sentenced to imprisonment or detention under this Act.

174. Informality or error in the order or warrants. Whenever a person is sentenced to transportation, imprisonment or detention under this Act, and is undergoing the sentence in any place or manner in which he might be confined under a lawful order or warrant in pursuance of this Act, the confinement of such person shall not be deemed to be illegal only by reason of any informality or error in or as respects the order, warrant or other document, or the authority by which, or in pursuance whereof such person was brought into or is confined in any such place, and any such order, warrant or document may be amended accordingly.

175. Power to make rules in respect of prisons and prisoners. The Central Government may make rules providing.

(a) for the government, management and regulation of air force prisons and detention barracks;

(b) for the appointment, removal and powers of inspectors, visitors, governors and officers thereof;

(c) for the labour of prisoners undergoing confinement therein, and for enabling such prisoners or persons to earn by special industry and good conduct, a remission of a portion of their sentence;

(d) for the safe custody of such prisoners or persons and the maintenance of discipline among them and the punishment, by personal correction, restraint or otherwise, of offences committed by them;

(e) for the application to air force prisons or detention barracks of any of the provisions of the Prisons Act, 1894, (9 of 1894) relating to the duties of officers of prisons and the punishment of persons not being prisoners;

(f) for the admission into any prison, at proper times and subject to proper restrictions, of persons with whom prisoners may desire to communicate, and for the consultation by prisoners under trial with their legal advisers without the presence as far as possible of any third party within hearing distance.

176. Restriction of rule-making power in respect to corporal punishment. Rules made under Section 175 shall not authorise corporal punishment to be inflicted for any offence, nor render the imprisonment more severe than it is under any law for the time being in force relating to civil prisons in India.

CHAPTER -XIV : PARDONS, REMISSIONS AND SUSPENSIONS

177. Pardon and remission. When any person subject to this Act has been convicted by a court-martial of any offence, the Central Government, 1[the Chief of the Air Staff], an air or other officer commanding a group of, or the prescribed officer, may-

(a) either with or without conditions which the person sentenced accepts, pardon the person or remit the whole or any part of the punishment awarded; or

(b) mitigate the punishment awarded; or

(c) commute such punishment for any less punishment or punishments mentioned in this Act:

PROVIDED that a sentence of transportation shall not be commuted for a sentence of imprisonment for a term exceeding the term of transportation awarded by the court; and a sentence of imprisonment shall not be commuted for a sentence of detention for a term exceeding the term of imprisonment so awarded;

(d) either with or without conditions which the person sentenced accepts, release the person on parole.

178. Cancellation of conditional pardon, release on parole or remission.

(1) If any condition on which a person has been pardoned or released on parole or a punishment has been remitted is, in the opinion of the authority which granted the pardon, release or remission, not fulfilled, such authority may cancel the pardon, release or remission, and thereupon the sentence of the court shall be carried into effect as if such pardon, release or remission had not been granted.

(2) A person whose sentence of transportation, imprisonment or detention is carried into effect under the provisions of sub-section (1) shall undergo only the unexpired portion of his sentence.

179. Reduction of warrant officer or non-commissioned officer. When under the provisions of Section 79 a warrant officer or a non-commissioned officer is deemed to be reduced to the ranks, such reduction shall, for the purpose of Section 177 be treated as a punishment awarded by a sentence of a court-martial.

180. Suspension of sentence of transportation, imprisonment or detention.

(1) Where a person subject to this Act is sentenced by a court-martial to transportation, imprisonment or detention, the Central Government, [1][the Chief of the Air Staff], or any officer empowered to convene a general or a summary general court-martial may suspend the sentence whether or not the offender has already been committed to prison or to air force custody.

(2) The authority or officer specified in sub-section (1) may in the case of an offender so sentenced direct that, until the orders of such authority or officer have been obtained, the offender shall not be committed to prison or to air force custody.

(3) The powers conferred by sub-sections (1) and (2) may be exercised in the case of any such sentence which has been confirmed, reduced or commuted.

181. Orders pending suspension. A confirming officer may, when confirming any sentence referred to in Section 180, direct that the offender be not committed to prison or to air force custody until the orders of the authority or officer specified in Section 180 have been obtained.

182. Release in suspension. Where a sentence is suspended under Section 180, the offender shall forthwith be released from custody.

183. Computation of period of suspension. Any period during which the sentence is under suspension shall be reckoned as part of the term of such sentence.

184. Order after suspension. The authority or officer specified in Section 180 may, at any time while a sentence is suspended, order-

(a) that the offender be committed to undergo the unexpired portion of the sentence, or

(b) that the sentence be remitted.

185. Reconsideration of case after suspension.

(1) Where a sentence has been suspended, the case may at any time, and shall, at intervals of not more than four months, be reconsidered by the authority or officer specified in Section 180, or by any air or other officer not below the rank of squadron leader duly authorised by the authority or officer specified in Section 180.

(2) Where on such reconsideration by the officer so authorised it appears to him that the conduct of the offender since his conviction has been such as to justify a remission of the sentence, he shall refer the matter to the authority or officer specified in Section 180.

186. Fresh sentence after suspension. Where an offender, while a sentence on him is suspended under this Act, is sentenced for any other offence, then-

(a) if the further sentence is also suspended under this Act, the two sentences shall run concurrently;

(b) if the further sentence is for a period of three months or more and is not suspended under this Act, the offender shall also be committed to prison or air force custody for the unexpired portion of the previous sentence, but both sentences shall run concurrently; and

(c) if the further sentence is for a period of less than three months and is not suspended under this Act, the offender shall be so committed on that sentence only, and the previous sentence shall, subject to any order which may be passed under Section 184 or Section 185, continue to be suspended.

187. Scope of power of suspension. The powers conferred by Sections 180 and 184 shall be in addition to and not in derogation of, the power of mitigation, remission and commutation.

188. Effect of suspension and remission on dismissal.

(1) Where in addition to any other sentence the punishment of dismissal has been awarded by a court-martial, and such other sentence is suspended under Section 180, then, such dismissal shall not take effect until so ordered by the authority or officer specified in Section 180.

(2) If such other sentence is remitted under Section 184, the punishment of dismissal shall also be remitted.

CHAPTER -XV : RULES

189. Power to make rules.

(1) The Central Government may make rules for the purpose of carrying into effect the provisions of this Act.

(2) Without prejudice to the generality of the power conferred by sub-section (1), the rules made thereunder may provide for-

(a) the removal, retirement, release or discharge from the service of persons subject to this Act;

(b) the amount and incidence of fines to be imposed under Section 90;

(c) the specification of the punishment which may be awarded as field punishments under Sections 77 and 82;

(d) the assembly and procedure of courts of inquiry, the recording of summaries of evidence and the administration of oaths or affirmations by such courts;

(e) the convening and constituting of courts-martial and the appointment of prosecutors at trials by courts-martial;

(f) the adjournment, dissolution and sitting of courts-martial;

(g) the procedure to be observed in trials by courts-martial and the appearance of legal practitioners thereat;

(h) the confirmation, revision and annulment of, and petitions against the findings and sentences of courts-martial;

(i) the carrying into effect of sentences or courts-martial;

(j) the forms of orders to be made under the provisions of this Act relating to courts-martial, transportation, imprisonment and detention;

(k) the constitution of authorities to decide for what persons, to what amounts and in what manner, provision should be made for dependants under Section 100 and the due carrying out of such decisions;

(l) the relative rank of the officers, junior commissioned officers, warrant officers, petty officers and non-commissioned officers of the regular Army, Navy and Air Force when acting together;

(m) any other matter directed by this Act to be prescribed.

190. Power to make regulations. The Central Government may make regulations for all or any of the purposes of this Act other than those specified in Section 189.

191. Publication of rules and regulations in Gazette. All rules and regulations made under this Act shall be published in the Official Gazette and, on such publication, shall have effect as if enacted in this Act.

[1]**[191A. Laying of rules and regulations before Parliament.** Every rule and every regulation made under this Act shall be laid, as soon as may be after it is made, before each House of Parliament, while it is in session, for a total period of thirty days which may be comprised in one session or in two or more successive sessions, and if, before the expiry of the session immediately following the session or the successive sessions aforesaid, both Houses agree in making any modification in the rule or regulation or both Houses agree that the rule or regulation should not be made, the rule or regulation shall thereafter have effect only in such modified form or be of no effect, as the case may be; no, however, that any such modification or annulment shall be without prejudice to the validity of anything previously done under that rule or regulation.]

192. [Repeal.] *Rep. by the Repealing and Amending Act, 1957 (36.of 1957), S. 2 and Sch. I.*

CHAPTER -XVI : TRANSITORY PROVISIONS

193. Definition of "British officer".

(1) In this Chapter "British officer" means a person of non-Indian domicile holding a commission in His Majestys Air Forces and serving in the Air Force.

(2) The expression "superior officer" in this Act shall be deemed to include a British officer.

194. Powers of British officer. A British officer shall have all the powers conferred by this Act on an officer of corresponding rank or holding a corresponding appointment.

❑❑❑

2

The Anti - Hijacking Act, 1982

Act No. 65 OF 1982

(Received the assent of the President on 6th November, 1982)

AN ACT to give effect to the Convention for the Suppression of Unlawful Seizure of Aircraft and for matters connected therewith.

WHEREAS a Convention for the Suppression of Unlawful Seizure of Aircraft was, on the 16th day of December, 1970, signed at The Hague;

AND WHEREAS it is expedient that India should accede to the said Convention and make provisions for giving effect thereto and for matters connected there with;

Be it enacted by Parliament in the Thirty-third Year of the Republic of India as follows:-

CHAPTER - I : PRELIMINARY

1. Short title, extent application and commencement.

(1) This Act may be called the Anti-Hijacking Act, 1982.

(2) It extends to the whole of India and, save as otherwise provided in this Act, it applies also to any offence thereunder committed outside India by any person.

(3) It shall come into force on such date as the Central Government may, by notification in the Official Gazette, appoint.

2. Definitions. In this Act, unless the context otherwise requires -

(a) "aircraft" means any aircraft, whether or not registered in India, other than a military aircraft or an aircraft used in customs or police service;

(b) "aircraft registered in India" means an aircraft which is for the time being registered in India;

(c) "Convention country" means a country in which The Hague Convention is for the time being in force;

(d) "Hague Convention" means the Convention for the Suppression of Unlawful Seizure of Aircraft signed at The Hague on the 16th day of December, 1970;

(e) "military aircraft" means an aircraft of the naval, military, air force or any other armed forces of any country and includes every aircraft commanded for the time being by a person in any such force detailed for the purpose.

CHAPTER - II : HIJACKING AND CONNECTED OFFENCES

3. Hijacking.

(1) Whoever on broad an aircraft in flight, unlawfully, by force or threat of force or by any other form of intimidation, seizes or exercises control of that aircraft, commits the offence of hijacking of such aircraft.

(2) Whoever attempts to commit any of the acts referred to in sub-section (1) in relation to any aircraft, or abets the commission of any such act, shall also be deemed to have committed the offence of hijacking of such aircraft.

(3) For the purposes of this section, an aircraft shall be deemed to be in flight at any time from the moment when all its external doors are closed following embarkation until the moment when any such door is opened for disembarkation, and in the case of a forced landing, the fight shall be deemed to continue until the competent authorities of the country in which such forced lading takes place take over the responsibility for the aircraft and for persons and property on board.

4. Punishment for hijacking. Whoever commits the offence of hijacking shall be punished with imprisonment for life and shall also be liable to fine.

5. Punishment for acts to violence connected with hijacking. Whoever, being a person committing the offence of hijacking of an aircraft, commits, in connection with such offence, any act of violence against any passenger or member of the crew of such aircraft, shall be punished with the same punishment with which he would have been punishable under any law for the time being in force in India if such act had been committed in India.

6. Jurisdiction.

(1) Subject to the provision of sub-section (2), where an offence under Section 4 or Section 5 is committed outside India, the person committing such offence may be dealt with in respect thereof as if such offence had been committed at any place within India at which he may be found.

(2) No court shall take cognizance of an offence punishable under Section 4 or Section 5 which is committed outside India unless -

(a) such offence is committed on board an aircraft registered in India;

(b) such offence is committed on board an aircraft which is for the time being leased without crew to a lessee who has his principal place of business or where he had no such place of business, his permanent residence in India; or

(c) the alleged offender is a citizen of India or is on board the aircraft in relation to which such offence is committed when it lands in India or is found in India.

CHAPTER - III : MISCELLANEOUS

7. Provisions as to extradition.

1. The offences under Section 4 and Section 5 shall be deemed to have been included as extraditable offences and provided for in all the extradition treaties made by India with Convention countries and which extend to, and are binding on, India on the date of commencement of this Act.
2. For the purposes of the application of the Extradition Act, 1962 (34 of 1962) the offences under this Act, any aircraft registered in a Convention country shall, at any time while that aircraft is in flight, be deemed to be within the jurisdiction of that country, whether or not it is for the time being also within the jurisdiction of any other country.

8. Contracting parties of Convention. The Central Government may, by notification in the Official Gazette, certify as to who are the contracting parties to The Hague Convention and to what extent they have availed themselves of the provisions of the Convention, and any such notification shall be conclusive evidence of the matters certified therein.

9. Power to treat certain aircraft to be registered in Convention countries. If the Central Government is satisfied that the requirements of Article 5 of The Hague Convention have been satisfied in relation to any aircraft, it may, by notification in the Official Gazette, direct that such aircraft shall, for the purposes of this Act, be treated as registered in such Convention country as may be specified in the notification.

10. Previous sanction necessary for prosecution. No prosecution for an offence under this Act shall be instituted except with the previous sanction of the Central Government.

11. Protection of action taken in good faith.

(1) No suit, prosecution or other legal proceeding shall lie against any person for anything which is in good faith done or intended to be done in pursuance of the provisions of this Act.

(2) No suit or other legal proceedings shall lie against the Central Government for any damage caused or likely to be caused for anything which is in good faith done or intended to be done in pursuance of the provisions of this Act.

❑❑❑

3

The Armed Forces (Emergency Duties) Act, 1947

(Act No.15 of 1947) [20th March, 1947]

(The Act was extended to the new Provinces and merged States by the Merged States (Laws) Act, 1949 (59 of 1949), s. 3 and Sch.; to the States of Manipur, Tripura and Vindhya Pradesh by the Part C States (Laws) Act, 1950 (30 of 1950), s.3; in Pondicherry on 1-10-1963 vide Reg. 7 of 1963, s.3 and Sch.I; to lakshadweep (w.e.f.1-10-1987); vide Reg. 8 of 10965, s.3 and Sch., to Goa, Daman and Diu with modifications by Reg. 12 of 1962, s.3 and Sch. and in Dadra and Nagar Haveli (w.e.f. 1-7-1965) by Reg. 6 of 1963, s.2 and Sch.I)

AN ACT to enable duties in connection with vital services to be imposed in an emergency on the Armed Forces. (The words of the Crown omitted by the A.O.1950)

WHEREAS it is expedient to enable duties in connection with vital services to be imposed in an emergency on the Armed Forces. (The words "of the Crown" omitted by the A.O. 1950)

It is hereby enacted as follows :-

1. Short title and extent. (The brackets and figure "(l)" and sub-section (2) rep. by Act 4 of 1948, s.2) This Act may be called the Armed Forces (Emergency Duties) Act, 1947. (The brackets and figure "(l)" and sub-section (2) rep. by Act 4 of 1948, s.2)

2. Emergency duties of Armed Forces.

(1) The Central Government may, by notification in the Official Gazette, declare any specified service. *(The brackets and figure "(l)" and sub-section (2) rep. by Act 4 of 1948, s.2)* [in a State] to be a service of vital importance to the community:

PROVIDED that such notification shall remain in force for one month in the first instance, but may be extended, from time to time, by a like notification.

(2) Upon a declaration being made under sub-section *(1)* and until it is rescinded, it shall be the duty of every person subject to *(Subs. by s.3 and Sch., ibid., for "the Indian Army Act, 1911, or the Indian Air Force Act, 1932")* [the Army Act, 1950 (46 of 1950) or the Air Force Act, 1950 945 of 1950)], or *(Subs. by s.3 and Sch., ibid., for "the Indian Army Act, 1911, or the Indian Air Force Act, 1932").(Subs. by Act 58 of 1960, s.3 and Sch.II, for "the Indian Navy (Discipline) Act, 1934")*[the Navy Act, 1957 (62 of 1957)], to obey any command given by any superior officer in relation to employment upon or in connection with the service specified in the declaration; and every such command shall be deemed to be a lawful command within the meaning and for the purposes of the said Acts.

3. Violation of certain past commands. Every command given, after the 30th day of September, 1946, and before the commencement of this Act, to any person referred to in sub-section (2) of Section 2 by any superior officer in relation to employment upon or in connection with any such service as the Central Government may, by notification in the Official Gazette, specify in this behalf, shall be deemed to have been a lawful command within the meaning and for the purposes of the Acts referred to in that sub-section, so however that no such person shall be punished by reason only of his not having obeyed any such command.

STATEMENT OF OBJECTS AND REASONS

The Armed Forces (Emergency Duties) Act, 1947 (XV of 1947) was passed early this year to enable the Central Government to authorise the use of persons subject to the Indian Army Act, 1911, the Indian Air Force Act, 1932 or the Naval Discipline Act, as set forth in the First Schedule to the Indian Navy (Discipline) Act, 1934, to maintain essential services in an emergency. This Act applies at present only to the Provinces of India.

With the accession of the most of the States to the Dominion of India, it is desirable that the Central Government should have the power to authorise the employment of the personnel referred to above for the maintenance over the Acceding States of any essential service in an emergency, if so requested by the Government of that State. The Bill is designed to confer this power on the Central Government.

❑❑❑

4

The Arms Act, 1959

Act No. 54 of 1959 [23rd December, 1959]

AN ACT to consolidate and amend the law relating to arms and ammunition.

CHAPTER - I : PRELIMINARY

1. Short title, extent and commencement.

(1) This Act may be called the Arms Act, 1959.

(2) It extends to the whole of India.

(3) It shall come into force on such date[1] as the Central Government may, by notification in the Official Gezette, appoint.

2. Definition and interpretation.

(1) In this Act, unless the context otherwise requires —

(a) "acquisition", with its grammatical variations and cognate expressions, includes hiring, borrowing, or accepting as a gift;

(b) "ammunition" means ammunition for any firearm, and includes—

(i) rockets, bombs, grenades, shells [and other missiles] [2]

(ii) articles, designed for torpedo service and submarine mining,

(iii) other articles containing, or designed or adapted to contain, explosive, fulminating or fissionable material or noxious liquid, gas or other such thing, whether capable of use with firearms or not,

(iv) charges for firearms and accessories for such charges,

(v) fuses and friction tubes,

(vi) parts of, and machinery for manufacturing ammunition, and

(vii) such ingredients of ammunition as the Central Government may, by notification in the Official Gazette, specify in this behalf;

(c) "arms" means articles of any description designed or adapted as weapons for offence or defence, and includes firearms, sharpedged and other deadly weapons, and parts of, and machinery for manufacturing, arms, but does not include articles designed solely for domestic or agricultural uses such as a lathi or an ordinary walking stick and weapons incapable of being used otherwise than as toys or of being converted into serviceable weapons;

[1][(d) "district magistrate", in relation to any area for which a Commissioner of Police has been appointed, means the Commissioner of Police thereof and includes any such Deputy Commissioner of Police, exercising jurisdiction over the whole or any part of such area, as may be specified by the State Government in this behalf in relation to such area or part];

(e) "firearms" means arms of any description designed or adapted to discharge a projectile or projectiles of any kind by the action of any explosive or other forms of energy, and includes —

(i) artillery, hand-grenades, riot-pistols or weapons of any kind designed or adapted for the discharge of any noxious liquid, gas or other such thing,

(ii) accessories for any such firearm designed or adapted to diminish the noise or flash caused by the firing thereof,

(iii) parts of, and machinery for manufacturing, firearms, and

(iv) carriages, platforms and appliances for mounting, transporting and serving artillery.

(f) "licensing authority" means an officer or authority empowered to grant or renew licences under rules made under this Act, and includes the Government;

[1][(ff) "magistrate" means an Executive Magistrate under the Code of Criminal Procedure, 1973 (2 of 1974)];

(g) "prescribed" means prescribed by rules made under this Act,

(h) "prohibited ammunition" means any ammunition containing or designed or adapted to contain, any noxious liquid, gas or other such thing, and includes rockets, bombs, grenades, shells, [2][missiles] articles designed for torpedo service and submarine mining and such other articles as the Central Government may, by notification in the Official Gazette, specify to be prohibited ammunition;

(i) "prohibited arms" means —

(i) firearms so designed or adapted that, if pressure is applied to the trigger, missiles continue to be discharged until pressure is removed from the trigger or the magazine containing the missiles is empty, or

(ii) weapons of any description designed or adapted for the discharge of any noxious liquid, gas or other such thing, and includes artillery, anti-aircraft and anti-tank firearms and such other arms as the Central Government may, by notification in the Official Gazette, specify to be prohibited arms;

(j) "public servant" has the same meaning as in Section 21 of the Indian Penal Code (45 of 1860);

(k) "transfer", with its grammatical variations and cognate expressions, includes letting on hire, lending, giving and parting with possession.

(2) For the purposes of this Act, the length of the barrel of a firearm shall be measured from the muzzle to the point at which the charge is exploded on firing.

(3) Any reference in this Act to any law which is not in force in any area shall, in relation to that area, be construed as a reference to the corresponding law, if any, in force in that area.

(4) Any reference in this Act to any officer or authority shall, in relation to any area in which there is no officer or authority with the same designation, be construed as a reference to such officer or authority as may be specified by the Central Government by notification in the Official Gazette.

CHAPTER - II : ACQUISITION, POSSESSION, MANUFACTURE, SALE, IMPORT, EXPORT AND TRANSPORT OF ARMS AND AMMUNITION

3. Licence for acquisition and possession of fire-arms and ammunition.

[1][(1) No person shall acquire, have in his possession, or carry any firearm or ammunition unless he holds in this behalf a licence issued in accordance with the provisions of this Act and the rules made thereunder:

PROVIDED that a person may, without himself holding a licence, carry any firearm or ammunition in the presence, or under the written authority, of the holder of the licence for repair or for renewal of the licence or for use by such holder.

[2][(2) Notwithstanding anything contained in sub-section (1), no person, other than a person referred to in sub-section (3), shall acquire, have in his possession or carry, at any time, more than three firearms:

PROVIDED that a person who has in his possession more firearms than three at the commencement of the Arms (Amendment) Act, 1983, may retain with him any three of such firearms and shall deposit, within ninety days from such commencement, the remaining firearms with the officer in charge of the nearest police station or, subject to the conditions prescribed for the purposes of sub-section (1) of Section 21, with a licensed dealer or, where such person is a member of the armed forces of the Union, in a unit armoury referred to in that sub-section.

(3) Nothing contained in sub-section (2) shall apply to any dealer in firearms or to any member of a rifle club or rifle association licensed or recognised by the Central Government using a point 22 bore rifle or an air rifle for target practice.

(4) The provisions of sub-sections (2) to (6) (both inclusive) of Section 21 shall apply in relation to any deposit of firearms under the proviso to sub-section (2) as they apply in relation to the deposit of any arm or ammunition under sub-section (1) of that Section."]

4. Licence for acquisition and possession of arms of specified description in certain cases. If the Central Government is of opinion that having regard to the circumstances prevailing in any area it is necessary or expedient in the public interest that the acquisition, possession or carrying of arms other than firearms should also be regulated, it may, by notification in the Official Gazette, direct that this Section shall apply to the area specified in the notification, and thereupon no person shall acquire, have in his possession or carry in that area arms of such class or description as may be specified in that notification unless he holds in this behalf a licence issued in accordance with the provisions of this Act and the rules made thereunder.

5. Licence for manufacture, sale, etc., of arms and ammunition.

[1][(1)] No person shall—

(a) [2][use, manufacture] sell, transfer, convert, repair, test or prove, or

(b) expose or offer for sale or transfer or have in his possession for sale, transfer, conversion, repair, test or proof, any firearm or any other arms of such class or description as may be prescribed or any ammunition, unless he holds in this behalf a licence issued in accordance with the provisions of this Act and the rules made thereunder:

[3] * * *

[4][(2) Notwithstanding anything contained in sub-section (1) a person may, without holding a licence in this behalf, sell or transfer any arms or ammunition which he lawfully possesses for his own private use to another person who is entitled by virtue of this Act or any other law for the time being in force to have, or is not prohibited by this Act or such other law from having in his possession such arms or ammunition:

PROVIDED that no firearm or ammunition in respect of which a licence is required under Section 3 and no arms in respect of which a licence is required under Section 4 shall be so sold or transferred by any person unless—

(a) he has informed in writing the district magistrate having jurisdiction or the officer in charge of the nearest police station of his intention to sell or transfer such firearms, ammunition or other arms and the name and address of the person to whom he intends to sell or transfer such firearms, ammunition or the other arms, and

(b) a period of not less than forty-five days has expired after the giving of such information].

6. Licence for the shortening of guns or conversion of imitation firearms into firearms. No person shall shorten the barrel of a firearm or convert an imitation firearm into a firearm unless he holds in this behalf a licence issued in accordance with the provisions of this Act and the rules made thereunder.

EXPLANATION: In this Section, the expression "imitation firearm" means anything which has the appearance of being a firearm, whether it is capable of discharging any shot, bullet or other missile or not.

7. Prohibition of acquisition or possession, or of manufacture or sale, of prohibited arms or prohibited ammunition. No person shall —

(a) acquire, have in his possession or carry; or

(b) [2][use, manufacture] sell, transfer, convert, repair, test or prove; or

(c) expose or offer for sale or transfer or have in his possession for sale, transfer, conversion, repair, test or proof; any prohibited arms or prohibited ammunition unless he has been specially authorised by the Central Government in this behalf.

8. Prohibition of sale or transfer of firearms not bearing identification marks.

(1) No person shall obliterate, remove, alter or forge any name, number or other identification mark stamped or otherwise shown on a firearm.

(2) No person shall sell or transfer any firearm which does not bear the name of the maker, manufacturers number or other identification mark stamped or otherwise shown thereon in a manner approved by the Central Government.

(3) Whenever any person has in his possession any firearm without such name, number or other identification mark or on which such name, number or other identification mark has been obliterated, removed, altered or forged, it shall be presumed unless the contrary is proved, that he has obliterated, removed, altered or forged that name, number or other identification mark:

PROVIDED that in relation to a person who has in his possession at the commencement of this Act any firearm without such name, number or other identification mark stamped or otherwise shown thereon, the provisions of this sub-section shall not take effect until after the expiration of one year from such commencement.

9. Prohibition of acquisition or possession by, or of sale or transfer to, young persons and certain other persons of firearms, etc.

(1) Notwithstanding anything in the foregoing provisions of this Act -

(a) no person,—

(i) who has not completed the age of 2[twenty-one years], or

(ii) who has been sentenced on conviction of any offence involving violence or moral turpitude to imprisonment for [1][any term], at any time during a period of five years after the expiration of the sentence, or

(iii) who has been ordered to execute under Chapter VIII of the [1][Code of Criminal Procedure, 1973 (2 of 1974)], a bond for keeping the peace or for good behaviour, at any time during the term of the bond, shall acquire, have in his possession or carry any firearm or ammunition;

(b) no person shall sell or transfer any firearm or ammunition to, or convert, repair, test or prove any firearm or ammunition for, any other person whom he knows, or has reason to believe —

(i) to be prohibited under clause (a) from acquiring, having in his possession or carrying any firearm or ammunition, or

(ii) to be of unsound mind at the time of such sale or transfer, or such conversion, repair, test or proof.

(2) Notwithstanding anything in sub-clause (i) of clause (a) of sub-section (1), a person who has attained the prescribed age-limit may use under prescribed conditions such firearms as may be prescribed in the course of his training in the use of such firearms:

PROVIDED that different age-limits may be prescribed in relation to different types of firearms.

10. Licence for import and export of arms, etc.

(1) No person shall bring into, or take out of, India by sea, land or air any arms or ammunition unless he holds in this behalf a licence issued in accordance with the provisions of this Act and the rules made thereunder:

PROVIDED that—

(a) a person who is entitled by virtue of this Act or any other law for the time being in force to have, or is not prohibited by this Act or such other law from having, in his possession any arms or ammunition, may without a licence in this behalf bring into, or take out of, India such arms or ammunition in reasonable quantities for his own private use;

(b) a person being a bona fide tourist belonging to any such country as the Central Government may, by notification in the Official Gazette, specify, who is not prohibited by the laws of that country from having in his possession any arms or ammunition, may, without a licence under this Section but in accordance with such conditions as may be prescribed, bring with him into India arms and ammunition in reasonable quantities for use by him for purposes only of sport and for no other purpose;

EXPLANATION: For purposes of clause (b) of this proviso, the word "tourist" means a person who not being a citizen of India visits India for a period not exceeding six months with no other object than recreation, sight-seeing, or participation in a representative capacity in meetings convened by the Central Government or in international conferences, associations or other bodies.

(2) Notwithstanding anything contained in the proviso to sub-section (1), where the collector of customs or any other officer empowered by the Central Government in this behalf has any doubt as to the applicability of clause (a) or clause (b) of that proviso to any person who claims that such clause is applicable to him, or as to the reasonableness of the quantities of arms or ammunition in the possession of any person referred to in such clause, or as to the use to which such arms or ammunition may be put by such person, may detain the arms or ammunition in the possession of such person until he receives the orders of the Central Government in relation thereto.

(3) Arms and ammunition taken from one part of India to another by sea or air or across any intervening territory not forming part of India, are taken out of, and brought into, India within the meaning of this Section.

11. Power to prohibit import or export of arms, etc. The Central Government may, by notification in the Official Gazette, prohibit the bringing into, or the taking out of, India, arms or ammunition of such classes and descriptions as may be specified in the notification.

12. Power to restrict or prohibit transport of arms.

(1) The Central Government may, by notification in the Official Gazette,—

(a) direct that no person shall transport over India or any part thereof arms or ammunition of such classes and descriptions as may be specified in the notification unless he holds in this behalf a licence issued in accordance with the provisions of this Act and the rules made there-under; or

(b) prohibit such transport altogether.

(2) Arms or ammunition trans-shipped at a seaport or an airport in India are transported within the meaning of this Section.

CHAPTER - III : PROVISIONS RELATING TO LICENCES

13. Grant of licences.

(1) An application for the grant of a licence under Chapter II shall be made to the licensing authority and shall be in such form, contain such particulars and be accompanied by such fee, if any, as may be prescribed.

[1][(2) On receipt of an application, the licensing authority shall call for the report of the officer in charge of the nearest police station on that application, and such officer shall send his report within the prescribed time.

(2A) The licensing authority, after such inquiry, if any, as it may consider necessary, and after considering the report received under sub-section (2), shall, subject to the other provisions of this Chapter, by order in writing either grant the licence or refuse to grant the same:

PROVIDED that where the officer-in-charge of the nearest police station does not send his report on the application within the prescribed time, the licensing authority may, if it deems fit, make such order, after the expiry of the prescribed time, without further waiting for that report.]

(3) The licensing authority shall grant—

(a) a licence under Section 3 where the licence is required-

(i) by a citizen of India in respect of a smooth bore gun having a barrel of not less than twenty inches in length to be used for protection or sport or in respect of a muzzle loading gun to be used for *bona fide* crop protection:

PROVIDED that where having regard to the circumstances of any case, the licensing authority is satisfied that a muzzle loading gun will not be sufficient for crop protection, the licensing authority may grant a licence in respect of any other smooth bore gun as aforesaid for such protection, or

(ii) in respect of a point 22 bore rifle or an air rifle to be used for target practice by a member of a rifle club or rifle association licensed or recognised by the Central Government;

(b) a licence under Section 3 in any other case or a licence under Section 4, Section 5, Section 6, Section 10 or Section 12, if the licensing authority is satisfied that the person by whom the licence is required has a good reason for obtaining the same.

14. Refusal of licences.

(1) Notwithstanding anything in Section 13, the licensing authority shall refuse to grant —

(a) a licence under Section 3, Section 4 or Section 5 where such licence is required in respect of any prohibited arms or prohibited ammunition;

(b) a licence in any other case under Chapter II —

(i) where such licence is required by a person whom the licensing authority has reason to believe —

(1) to be prohibited by this Act or by any other law for the time being in force from acquiring, having in his possession or carrying any arms or ammunition, or

(2) to be of unsound mind, or

(3) to be for any reason unfit for a licence under this Act; or

(ii) where the licensing authority deems it necessary for the security of the public peace or for public safety to refuse to grant such licence.

(2) The licensing authority shall not refuse to grant any licence to any person merely on the ground that such person does not own or possess sufficient property.

(3) Where the licensing authority refuses to grant a licence to any person it shall record in writing the reasons for such refusal and furnish to that person on demand a brief statement of the same unless in any case the licensing authority is of the opinion that it will not be in the public interest to furnish such statement.

15. Duration and renewal of licence.

(1) A licence under Section 3 shall, unless revoked earlier, continue in force for a period of three years from the date on which it is granted:

PROVIDED that such a licence may be granted for a shorter period if the person by whom the licence is required so desires or if the licensing authority for reasons to be recorded in writing considers in any case that the licence should be granted for a shorter period.

(2) A licence under any other provision of Chapter II shall, unless revoked earlier, continue in force for such period from the date on which it is granted as the licensing authority may in each case determine.

(3) Every licence shall, unless the licensing authority for reasons to be recorded in writing otherwise decides in any case, be renewable for the same period for which the licence was originally granted and shall be so renewable from time to time, and the provisions of Sections 13 and 14 shall apply to the renewal of a licence as they apply to the grant thereof.

16. Fees, etc., for licence. The fees on payment of which, the conditions subject to which and the form in which a licence shall be granted or renewed shall be such as may be prescribed:

> *PROVIDED that different fees, different conditions and different forms may be prescribed for different types of licences:*
>
> *PROVIDED FURTHER that a licence may contain in addition to prescribed conditions such other conditions as may be considered necessary by the licensing authority in any particular case.*

17. Variation, suspension and revocation of licences.

(1) The licensing authority may vary the conditions subject to which a licence has been granted except such of them as have been prescribed and may for that purpose require the licence-holder by notice in writing to deliver-up the licence to it within such time as may specified in the notice.

(2) The licensing authority may, on the application of the holder of a licence, also vary the conditions of the licence except such of them as have been prescribed.

(3) The licensing authority may by order in writing suspend a licence for such period as it thinks fit or revoke a licence —

- (a) if the licensing authority is satisfied that the holder of the licence is prohibited by this Act or by any other law for the time being in force, from acquiring, having in his possession or carrying any arms or ammunition, or is of unsound mind, or is for any reason unfit for a licence under this Act; or
- (b) if the licensing authority deems it necessary for the security of the public peace or for public safety to suspend or revoke the licence; or
- (c) if the licence was obtained by the suppression of material information or on the basis of wrong information provided by the holder of the licence or any other person on his behalf at the time of applying for it; or
- (d) if any of the conditions of the licence has been contravened; or
- (e) if the holder of the licence has failed to comply with a notice under sub-section (1) requiring him to deliverup the licence.

(4) The licensing authority may also revoke a licence on the application of the holder thereof.

(5) Where the licensing authority makes an order varying a licence under sub-section (1) or an order suspending or revoking a licence under sub-section (3), it shall record in writing the reasons therefor and furnish to the holder of the licence on demand a brief statement of the same unless in any case the licensing authority is of the opinion that it will not be in the public interest to furnish such statement.

(6) The authority to whom the licensing authority is subordinate may by order in writing suspend or revoke a licence on any ground on which it may be suspended or revoked by the licensing authority; and the foregoing provisions of this Section shall, as far as may be, apply in relation to the suspension or revocation of a

licence by such authority.

(7) A court convicting the holder of a licence of any offence under this Act or the rules made thereunder may also suspend or revoke the licence:

PROVIDED that if the conviction is set aside on appeal or otherwise, the suspension or revocation shall become void.

(8) An order of suspension or revocation under sub-section (7) may also be made by an appellate court or by the High Court when exercising its powers of revision.

(9) The Central Government may, by order in the Official Gazette, suspend or revoke or direct any licensing authority to suspend or revoke all or any licences granted under this Act throughout India or any part thereof.

(10) On the suspension or revocation of a licence under this Section the holder thereof shall without delay surrender the licence to the authority by whom it has been suspended or revoked or to such other authority as may be specified in this behalf in the order of suspension or revocation.

18. Appeals.

(1) Any person aggrieved by an order of the licensing authority refusing to grant a licence or varying the conditions of a licence or by an order of the licensing authority or the authority to whom the licensing authority is subordinate, suspending or revoking a licence may prefer an appeal against that order to such authority (hereinafter referred to as the appellate authority) and within such period as may be prescribed:

PROVIDED that no appeal shall lie against any order made by or under the direction of the Government.

(2) No appeal shall be admitted if it is preferred after the expiry of the period prescribed therefor:

PROVIDED that an appeal may be admitted after the expiry of the period prescribed therefor if the appellant satisfies the appellate authority that he had sufficient cause for not preferring the appeal within that period.

(3) The period prescribed for an appeal shall be computed in accordance with the provisions of the Indian Limitation Act, 1908 (9 of 1908), with respect to the computation of periods of limitation thereunder.

(4) Every appeal under this Section shall be made by a petition in writing and shall be accompanied by a brief statement of the reasons for the order appealed against where such statement has been furnished to the appellant and by such fee as may be prescribed.

(5) In disposing of an appeal the appellate authority shall follow such procedure as may be prescribed:

PROVIDED that no appeal shall be disposed of unless the appellant has been given a reasonable opportunity of being heard.

(6) The order appealed against shall, unless the appellate authority conditionally or unconditionally directs otherwise, be in force pending the disposal of the appeal against such order.

(7) Every order of the appellate authority confirming, modifying or reversing the order appealed against shall be final.

CHAPTER - IV : POWERS AND PROCEDURE

19. Power to demand production of licence, etc.

(1) Any police officer or any other officer specially empowered in this behalf by the Central Government may demand the production of his licence from any person who is carrying any arms or ammunition.

(2) If the person upon whom a demand is made refuses or fails to produce the licence or to show that he is entitled by virtue of this Act or any other law for the time being in force to carry such arms or ammunition without a licence, the officer concerned may require him to give his name and address and if such officer considers it necessary, seize from that person the arms or ammunition which he is carrying.

(3) If that person refuses to give his name and address or if the officer concerned suspects that person of giving a false name or address or of intending to abscond, such officer may arrest him without warrant.

20. Arrest of persons conveying arms, etc., under suspicious circumstances. Where any person is found carrying or conveying any arms or ammunition whether covered by a licence or not, in such manner or under such circumstances as to afford just grounds of suspicion that the same are or is being carried by him with intent to use them, or that the same may be used, for any unlawful purpose, any magistrate, any police officer or any other public servant or any person employed or working upon a railway, aircraft, vessel, vehicle or any other means of conveyance, may arrest him without warrant and seize from him such arms or ammunition.

21. Deposit of arms, etc., on possession ceasing to be lawful.

(1) Any person having in his possession any arms or ammunition the possession whereof has, in consequence of the expiration of the duration of a licence or of the suspension or revocation of a licence or by the issue of a notification under Section 4 or by any reason whatever, ceased to be lawful, shall without unnecessary delay deposit the same either with the officer in charge of the nearest police station or subject to such conditions as may be prescribed, with a licensed dealer or where such person is a member of the armed forces of the Union, in a unit armoury.

EXPLANATION: In this sub-section "unit armoury" includes an armoury in a ship or establishment of the Indian Navy.

(2) Where arms or ammunition have or has been deposited under sub-section (1), the depositor or in the case of his death, his legal representative, shall, at any time before the expiry of such period as may be prescribed, be entitled—

(a) to receive back anything so deposited on his becoming entitled by virtue of this Act or any other law for the time being in force to have the same in his possession, or

(b) to dispose, or authorise the disposal, of anything so deposited by sale or otherwise to any person entitled by virtue of this Act or any other law for the time being in force to have, or not prohibited by this Act or such other law from having, the same in his possession and to receive the proceeds of any such disposal:

PROVIDED that nothing in this sub-section shall be deemed to authorise the return or disposal of anything of which confiscation has been directed under Section 32.

(3) All things deposited and not received back or disposed of under sub-section (2) within the period therein referred to shall be forfeited to Government by order of the district magistrate:

PROVIDED that in the case of suspension of a licence no such forfeiture shall be ordered in respect of a thing covered by the licence during the period of suspension.

(4) Before making an order under sub-section (3) the district magistrate shall, by notice in writing to be served upon the depositor or in the case of his death, upon his legal representative, in the prescribed manner, require him to show cause within thirty days from the service of the notice why the things specified in the notice should not be forfeited.

(5) After considering the cause, if any, shown by the depositor or, as the case may be, his legal representative, the district magistrate shall pass such order as he thinks fit.

(6) The Government may at any time return to the depositor or his legal representative things forfeited to it or the proceeds of disposal thereof wholly or in part.

22. Search and seizure by magistrate.

(1) Whenever any magistrate has reason to believe —

(a) that any person residing within the local limits of his jurisdiction has in his possession any arms or ammunition for any unlawful purpose, or

(b) that such person cannot be left in the possession of any arms or ammunition without danger to the public peace or safety.

The magistrate may, after having recorded the reasons for his belief, cause a search to be made of the house or premises occupied by such person or in which the magistrate has reason to believe that such arms or ammunition are or is to be found and may have such arms or ammunition, if any, seized and detain the same in safe custody for such period as he thinks necessary, although that person may be entitled by virtue of this Act or any other law for the time being in force to have the same in his possession.

(2) Every search under this Section shall be conducted by or in the presence of a magistrate or by or in the presence of some officer specially empowered in this behalf by the Central Government.

23. Search of vessels, vehicles for arms, etc. Any magistrate, any police officer or any other officer specially powered in this behalf by the Central Government, may for the purpose of ascertaining whether any contravention of this Act or the rules made thereunder is being or is likely to be committed, stop and search any vessel, vehicle or other means of conveyance and seize any arms or ammunition that may be found therein along with such vessel, vehicle or other means of conveyance.

24. Seizure and detention under orders of the Central Government. The Central Government may at any time order the seizure of any arms or ammunition in the possession of any person, notwithstanding that such person is entitled by virtue of this Act or any other law for the time being in force to have the same in his possession, and may detain the same for such period as it thinks necessary for the public peace and safety.

24A. Prohibition as to possession of notified arms in disturbed areas, etc.

(1) Where the Central Government is satisfied that there is extensive disturbance of public peace and tranquillity or imminent danger of such disturbance in any area and that for the prevention of offences involving the use of arms in such area, it is necessary or expedient so to do, it may by notification in the Official Gazette —

(a) specify the limits of such area;

(b) direct that before the commencement of the period specified in the notification (which period shall be a period commencing from a date not earlier tan the fourth day after the date of publication of the notification in the Official Gazette), every person having in his possession in such area any arms of such description as may be specified in the notification (the arms so specified being hereafter in this Section referred to as notified arms), shall deposit the same before such commencement in accordance with the provisions of Section 21 and for this purpose the possession by such person of any notified arms shall, notwithstanding anything contained in any other provision of this Act (except Section 41) or in any other law for the time being in force, as from the date of publication of such notification in the Official Gazette be deemed to have ceased to be lawful;

(c) declare that as from the commencement of, and until the expiry of the period specified in the notification, it shall not be lawful for any person to have in his possession in such area any notified arms;

(d) authorise any such officer subordinate to the Central Government or a State Government as may be specified in the notification —

(i) to search at any time during the period specified in the notification any person in, or passing through, or any premises in, or any animal or vessel or vehicle or other conveyance of whatever nature in or passing through, or any receptacle or other container of whatever nature in, such area if such officer has reason to believe that any notified arms are secreted by such person or in such premises or on such animal or in such vessel, vehicle or other conveyance or in such receptacle or other container;

(ii) to seize at any time during the period specified in the notification any notified arms in the possession of any person in such area or discovered through a search under sub-clause (i), and detain the same during the period specified in the notification.

(2) The period specified in a notification issued under sub-section (1) in respect of any area shall not, in the first instance, exceed ninety days, but the Central Government may amend such notification to extend such period from time to time by any period not exceeding ninety days at any one time if, in the opinion of that Government, there continues to be in such area such disturbance of public peace and tranquillity as is referred to in sub-section (1) or imminent danger thereof and that for the prevention of offences involving the use of arms in such area it is necessary or expedient so to do.

(3) The provisions of the Code of Criminal Procedure 1973 (2 of 1973), relating to searches and seizures shall, so far as may be, apply to any search or seizure made under sub-section (1).

(4) For the purposes of this Section —

(a) "arms" includes ammunition;

(b) where the period specified in a notification, as originally issued under sub-section (1), is extended under sub-section (2), then, in relation to such notification, references in sub-section (1) to "the period specified in the notification" shall be construed as references to the period as so extended.

24B. Prohibition as to carrying of notified arms or through public places in disturbed areas ect.

(1) Where the Central Government is satisfied that there is extensive disturbance of public peace and tranquillity or imminent danger of such disturbance in any area and that for the prevention of offences involving the use of arms in such area it is necessary or expedient so to do, it may, by notification in the Official Gazette —

(a) specify the limits of such area;

(b) direct that during the period specified in the notification (which period shall be a period commencing from a date not earlier than the second day after the date of publication of the notification in the Official Gazette), no person shall carry or otherwise have in his possession any arms of such description as may be specified in the notification (the arms so specified being hereafter in this Section referred to as notified arms) through or in any public place in such area;

(c) authorise any such officer subordinate to the Central Government or a State Government as may be specified in the notification —

(i) to search at any time during the period specified in the notification any person in, or passing through, or any premises in or forming part of, or any animal or vessel or vehicle or other conveyance of whatever nature in or passing through, or any receptacle or other container of whatever nature in, any public place in such area if such officer has reason to believe that any notified arms are secreted by such person or in such premises or on such animal or in such vessel, vehicle or other conveyance or in such receptacle or other container;

(ii) to seize at any time during the period specified in the notification any notified arms being carried by or otherwise in the possession of any person, through or in a public place in such area or discovered through a search under sub-clause (i), and detain the same during the period specified in the notification.

(2) The period specified in a notification issued under sub-section (1) in respect of any area shall not, in the first instance, exceed ninety days, but the Central Government may amend such notification to extend such period from time to time by any period exceeding ninety days at any one time if, in the opinion of that Government, there continues to be in such area such disturbance of public peace and tranquillity as is referred to in sub-section (1) or imminent danger thereof and that for the prevention of offences involving the use of arms in such area it is necessary or expedient so to do.

(3) The provisions of the Code of Criminal Procedure, 1973 (2 of 1974) relating to searches and seizures shall, so far as may be, apply to any search or seizure made under sub-section (1).

(4) For the purposes of this Section —

(a) "arms" includes ammunition;

(b) "public place" means any place intended for use by, or accessible to the public or any Section of the public; and

(c) where the period specified in a notification, as originally issued under sub-section (1), is extended under sub-section (2), then, in relation to such notification, references in sub-section (1) to "the period specified in the notification" shall be construed as references to the period as so extended.]

CHAPTER - V : OFFENCES AND PENALTIES

25. Punishment for certain offences.

[2][(1) Whoever—

(a) manufactures, sells, transfers, converts, repairs, tests or proves, or exposes or offers for sale or transfer, or has in his possession for sale, transfer, conversion, repair, test or proof, any arms or ammunition in contravention of Section 5; or

(b) shortens the barrel of a firearm or converts an imitation firearm into a firearm in contravention of Section 6;

or

[3] * * * *

(d) brings into, or takes out of, India, any arms or ammunition of any class or description in contravention of Section 11, shall be punishable with imprisonment for a term which shall not be less than three years but which may extend to seven years and shall also be liable to fine.

[5][(1AAA)] Whoever has in contravention of a notification issued under Section 24A in his possession or in contravention of a notification issued under Section 24B carries or otherwise has in his possession, any arms or ammunition shall be punishable with imprisonment for a term which shall not be less than [6][three years, but which may extend to seven years] and shall also be liable to fine.

(1B) Whoever—

(a) acquires, has in his possession or carries any firearm or ammunition in contravention of Section 3; or

(b) acquires, has in his possession or carries in any place specified by notification under Section 4 any arms of such class or description as has been specified in that notification in contravention of that Section; or

(c) sells or transfers any firearm which does not bear the name of the maker, manufacturers number or other identification mark stamped or otherwise shown thereon as required by sub-section (2) of Section 8 or does any act in contravention of sub-section (1) of that Section; or

(d) being a person to whom sub-clause (ii) or sub-clause (iii) of clause (a) of sub-section (1) of Section 9 applies, acquires, has in his possession or carries any firearm or ammunition in contravention of that Section; or

(e) sells or transfers, or converts, repairs, tests or proves any firearm or ammunition in contravention of clause (b) of sub-section (1) of Section 9; or

(f) brings into, or takes out of, India, any arms or ammunition in contravention of Section 10; or

(g) transports any arms or ammunition in contravention of Section 12; or

(h) fails to deposit arms or ammunition as required by sub-section (2) of Section 3, or sub-section (1) of Section 21; or

(i) being a manufacturer of, or dealer in, arms or ammunition, fails, on being required to do so by rules made under Section 44, to maintain a record or account or to make therein all such entries as are required by such rules or intentionally makes a false entry therein or prevents or obstructs the inspection of such record or account or the making of copies of entries therefrom or prevents or obstructs the entry into any premises or other place where arms or ammunition are or is manufactured or kept or intentionally fails to exhibit or conceals such arms or ammunition or refuses to point out where the same are or is manufactured or kept, shall be punishable with imprisonment for a term which shall not be less than [6][one year] but which may extend to three years and shall also be liable to fine:

PROVIDED that the Court may for any adequate and special reasons to be recorded in the judgment impose a sentence of imprisonment for a term of less than [6][one year]

[7][(1C) Notwithstanding anything contained in sub-section (1B), whoever commits an offence punishable under that sub-section in any disturbed area shall be punishable with imprisonment for a term which shall not be less than three years but which may extend to seven years and shall also be liable to fine.

EXPLANATION: For the purposes of this sub-section, "disturbed area" means any area declared to be a disturbed area under any enactment, for the time being in force, making provision for the suppression of disorder and restoration and maintenance of public order, and includes any areas specified by notification under Section 24A or Section 24B.]

(2) Whoever being a person to whom sub-clause (i) of clause (a) of sub-section (1) of Section 9 applies, acquires, has in his possession or carries any firearm or ammunition in contravention of that Section shall be punishable with imprisonment for a term which may extend to one year, or with fine, or with both.

[1][(3) Whoever sells or transfers any firearm, ammunition or other arms—

(i) without informing the district magistrate having jurisdiction or the officer in charge of the nearest police station, of the intended sale or transfer of that firearm, ammunition or other arms; or

(ii) before the expiration of the period of forty-five days from the date of giving such information to such district magistrate or the officer-in-charge of the police station, in contravention of the provisions of clause (a) or clause (b) of the proviso to sub-section (2) of Section 5, shall be punishable with imprisonment for a term which may extend to six months, or with fine of an amount which may extend to five hundred rupees, or with both.]

(4) Whoever fails to deliver-up a licence when so required by the licensing authority under sub-section (1) of Section 17 for the purpose of varying the conditions specified in the licence or fails to surrender a licence to the appropriate authority under sub-section (10) of that Section on its suspension or revocation shall be punishable with imprisonment for a term which may extend to six months, or with fine of an amount which may extend to five hundred rupees, or with both.

(5) Whoever, when required under Section 19 to give his name and address, refuses to give such name and address or gives a name or address which subsequently transpires to be false shall be punishable with imprisonment for a term which may extend to six months, or with fine of an amount which may extend to two hundred rupees, or with both.

[2][**26. Secret contraventions.**

(1) Whoever does any act in contravention of any of the provisions of Section 3, 4, 10 or 12 in such manner as to indicate an intention that such act may not be known to any public servant or to any person employed or working upon a railway, aircraft, vessel, vehicle or any other means of conveyance, shall be punishable with imprisonment for a term which shall not be less than six months but which may extend to seven years and also with fine.

(2) Whoever does any act in contravention of any of the provisions of Section 5, 6, 7 or 11 in such manner as to indicate an intention that such act may not be known to any public servant or to any person employed or working upon a railway, aircraft, vessel, vehicle or any other means of conveyance, shall be punishable with imprisonment for a term which shall be punishable with imprisonment for a term which shall not be less than five years but which may extend to ten years and also with fine.

(3) Whoever on any search being made under Section 22 conceals or attempts to conceal any arms or ammunition, shall be punishable with imprisonment for a term which may extend to ten years and also with fine.]

[1][**27. Punishment for using arms, etc.**

(1) Whoever uses any arms or ammunition in contravention of Section 5 shall be punishable with imprisonment for a term which shall not be less than three years but which may extend to seven years and shall also be liable to fine.

(2) Whoever uses any prohibited arms or prohibited ammunition in contravention of Section 7 shall be punishable with imprisonment for a term which shall not be less than seven years but which may extend to imprisonment for life and shall also be liable to fine.

(3) Whoever uses any prohibited arms or prohibited ammunition or does any act in contravention of Section 7 and such use or act results in the death of any other person, shall be punishable with death.]

28. Punishment for use and possession of firearms or imitation firearms in certain cases. Whoever makes or attempts to make any use whatsoever of a firearm or an imitation firearm with intent to resist or prevent the lawful arrest or detention of himself or any other person shall be punishable with imprisonment for a term which may extend to seven years, [4][and with fine]

EXPLANATION: In this Section the expression "imitation fire arm" has the same meaning as in Section 6.

29. Punishment for knowingly purchasing arms, etc., from unlicensed person or for delivering arms, etc., to person not entitled to possess the same. Whoever—

(a) purchases any firearm or any other arms of such class or description as may be prescribed or any ammunition from any other person knowing that such other person is not licensed or authorised under Section 5; or

(b) delivers any arms or ammunition into the possession of another person without previously ascertaining that such other person is entitled by virtue of this Act or any other law for the time being in force to have, and is not prohibited by this Act or such other law from having, in his possession the same; shall be punishable with imprisonment for a term which may extend to [2][three years, or with fine, or with both]

30. Punishment for contravention of licence or rule. Whoever contravenes any condition of a licence or any provision of this act or any rule made thereunder, for which no punishment is provided elsewhere in this Act shall be punishable with imprisonment for a term which may extend to [3][six month], or with fine which may extend to 4[two thousand] rupees, or with both.

31. Punishment for subsequent offences. Whoever having been convicted of an offence under this Act is again convicted of an offence under this Act shall be punishable with double the penalty provided for the latter offence.

32. Power to confiscate.

(1) When any person is convicted under this Act of any offence committed by him in respect of any arms or ammunition, it shall be in the discretion of the convicting court further to direct that the whole or any portion of such arms or ammunition, and any vessel, vehicle or other means of conveyance and any resceptacle or thing containing, or used to conceal, the arms or ammunition shall be confiscated:

PROVIDED that if the conviction is set aside on appeal or otherwise, the order of confiscation shall become void.

(2) An order of confiscation may also be made by the appellate court or by the High Court when exercising its powers of revision.

33. Offences by companies.

(1) Whenever an offence under this Act has been committed by a company, every person who at the time the offence was committed was in charge of, or was responsible to the company for the conduct of, the business of the company, as well as the company, shall be deemed to be guilty of the offence and shall be liable to be proceeded against and punished accordingly:

PROVIDED that nothing contained in this sub-section shall render any such person liable to any punishment under this Act if he proves that the offence was committed without his knowledge and that he exercised all due diligence to prevent the commission of such offence.

(2) Notwithstanding anything contained in sub-section (1), where an offence under this Act has been committed by a company and it is proved that the offence has been committed with the consent or connivance of, or is attributable to any neglect on the part of, any director, manager, secretary or other officer of the company, such director, manager, secretary or other officer shall also be deemed to be guilty of that offence and shall be liable to be proceeded against and punished accordingly.

EXPLANATION: For the purposes of this Section —

(a) "company" means any body corporate, and includes a firm or other association of individuals; and

(b) "director", in relation to a firm, means a partner in the firm.

CHAPTER - VI : MISCELLANEOUS

34. Sanction of Central Government for warehousing of arms. Notwithstanding anything contained in the [1][Customs Act, 1962 (52 of 1962)] no arms or ammunition shall be deposited in any warehouse licensed under [1][Section 58] of that Act without the sanction of the Central Government.

35. Criminal responsibility of persons in occupation of premises in certain cases. Where any arms or ammunition in respect of which any offence under this Act has been or is being committed are or is found in any premises, vehicle or other place in the joint occupation or under the joint control of several persons, each of such persons in respect of whom there is reason to believe that he was aware of the existence of the arms or ammunition in the premises, vehicle or other place shall, unless the contrary is proved, be liable for that offence in the same manner as if it has been or is being committed by him alone.

36. Information to be given regarding certain offences.

(1) Every person aware of the commission of any offence under this Act shall, in the absence of reasonable excuse the burden of proving which shall lie upon such person, give information of the same to the officer in charge of the nearest police station or the magistrate having jurisdiction.

(2) Every person employed or working upon any railway, aircraft, vessel, vehicle or other means of conveyance shall, in the absence of reasonable excuse the burden of proving which shall lie upon such person, give information to the officer in charge of the nearest police station regarding any box, package or bale in transit which he may have reason to suspect contains arms or ammunition in respect of which an offence under this Act has been or is being committed.

37. Arrest and searches. Save as otherwise provided in this Act -

(a) all arrests and searches made under this Act or under any rules made thereunder shall be carried out in accordance with the provisions of the [2][Code of Criminal Procedure, 1973 (2 of 1974)], relating respectively to arrests and searches made under that Code;

(b) any person arrested and any arms or ammunition seized under this Act by a person not being a magistrate or a police officer shall be delivered without delay to the officer in charge of the nearest police station and that officer shall—

   (i) either release that person on his executing a bond with or without sureties to appear before a magistrate and keep the things seized in his custody till the appearance of that person before the magistrate, or

   (ii) should that person fail to execute the bond and to furnish, if so required, sufficient sureties, produce that person and those things without delay before the magistrate.

38. Offences to be cognizable. Every offence under this Act shall be cognizable within the meaning of the [1][Code of Criminal Procedure, 1973 (2 of 1974)]

39. Previous sanction of the district magistrate necessary in certain cases. No prosecution shall be instituted against any person in respect of any offence under Section 3 without the previous sanction of the district magistrate.

40. Protection of action taken in good faith. No suit, prosecution or other legal proceeding shall lie against any person for any thing which is in good faith done or intended to be done under this Act.

41. Power to exempt. Where the Central Government is of the opinion that it is necessary or expedient in the public interest so to do, it may, by notification in the Official Gazette and subject to such conditions, if any, as it may specify in the notification —

(a) [2][exempt any person or class of persons (either generally or in relation to such description of arms and ammunition as may be specified in the notification)], or exclude any description of arms or ammunition, or withdraw any part of India, from the operation of all or any of the provisions of this Act;

and

(b) as often as may be, cancel any such notification and again subject, by a like notification, the person or class of persons or the description of arms and ammunition or the part of India to the operation of such provisions.

42. Power to take census of firearms.

(1) The Central Government may, by notification in the Official Gazette, direct a census to be taken of all firearms in any area and empower any officer of Government to take such census.

(2) On the issue of any such notification all persons having in their possession any firearm in that area shall furnish to the officer concerned such information as he may require in relation thereto and shall produce before him such firearms if he so requires.

43. Power to delegate.

(1) The Central Government may, by notification in the Official Gazette, direct that any power or function which may be exercised or performed by it under this Act other than the power under Section 41 or the power under Section 44, may, in relation to such matters and subject to such conditions, if any, as it may specify in the notification, be exercised or performed also by —

  (a) such officer or authority subordinate to the Central Government, or

  (b) such State Government or such officer or authority subordinate to the State Government, as may be specified in the notification.

(2) Any rules made by the Central Government under this Act may confer powers or impose duties or authorise the conferring of powers or imposition of duties upon any State Government or any officer or authority subordinate thereto.

44. Power to make rules.

(1) The Central Government may, by notification in the Official Gazette, make rules for carrying out the purposes of this Act.

(2) In particular, and without prejudice to the generality of the foregoing power, such rules may provide for all or any of the following matters, namely :

(a) the appointment, jurisdiction, control and functions of licensing authorities [1][“including the areas and the categories of arms and ammunition for which they may grant licences];

(b) the form and particulars of application for the grant or renewal of a licence and where the application is for the renewal of a licence, the time within which it shall be made;

(c) the form in which and the conditions subject to which any licence may be granted or refused, renewed, varied, suspended or revoked;

(d) where no period has been specified in this Act, the period for which any licence shall continue to be in force;

(e) the fees payable in respect of any application for the grant or renewal of a licence and in respect of any licence granted or renewed and the manner of paying the same;

(f) the manner in which the makers name, the manufacturers number or other identification mark of a firearm shall be stamped or otherwise shown thereon;

(g) the procedure for the test or proof of any firearms;

(h) the firearms that may be used in the course of training, the age-limits of persons who may use them and the conditions for their use by such persons;

(i) the authority to whom appeals may be preferred under Section 18, the procedure to be followed by such authority and the period within which appeals shall be preferred, the fees to be paid in respect of such appeals and the refund of such fees;

(j) the maintenance of records or accounts of anything done under a licence other than a licence under Section 3 or Section 4, the form of, and the entries to be made in, such records or accounts and the exhibition of such records or accounts to any police officer or to any officer of Government empowered in this behalf;

(k) the entry and inspection by any police officer or by any officer of Government empowered in this behalf of any premises or other place in which arms or ammunition are or is manufactured or in which arms or ammunition are or is kept by a manufacturer of or dealer in such arms or ammunition and the exhibition of the same to such officer;

(l) the conditions subject to which arms or ammunition may be deposited with a licensed dealer or in a unit armoury as required by sub-section (1) of Section 21 and the period on the expiry of which the things so deposited may be forfeited;

(m) any other matter which is to be, or may be, prescribed.

(3) Every rule made under this Section shall be laid as soon as may be after it is made before each House of Parliament while it is in session for a total period of thirty days which may be comprised in one session or in [1][two or more successive sessions, and if, before the expiry of the session immediately following the session or the successive sessions aforesaid], both Houses agree in making any modification in the rule or both Houses agree that the rule should not be made, the rule shall thereafter have effect only in such modified form or be of no effect, as the case may be, so however that any such modification or annulment shall be without prejudice to the validity of anything previously done under that rule.

45. Nothing in this Act shall apply to.

(a) arms or ammunition on board any sea-going vessel or any aircraft and forming part of the ordinary armament or equipment of such vessel or aircraft;

(b) the acquisition, possession or carrying, the manufacture, repair, conversion, test or proof, the sale or transfer or the import, export or transport of arms or ammunition —

  (i) by or under orders of the Central Government, or

  (ii) by a public servant in the course of his duty as such public servant, or

  (iii) by a member of the National Cadet Corps raised and maintained under the National Cadet Corps Act, 1948 (31 of 1948), or by any officer or enrolled person of the Territorial Army Act, 1948 (56 of 1948), or by any member of any other forces raised and maintained or that may hereafter be raised and maintained under any Central Act, or by any member of such other forces as the Central Government may, by notification in the Official Gazette, specify, in the course of his duty as such member, officer or enrolled person;

(c) any weapon of an obsolete pattern or of antiquarian value or in disrepair which is not capable of being used as a firearm either with or without repair;

(d) the acquisition, possession or carrying by a person of minor parts of arms or ammunition which are not intended to be used along with complementary parts acquired or possessed by that or any other person.

46. Repeal of Act 11 of 1878.

(1) The Indian Arms Act, 1878 (11 of 1878), is hereby repealed.

(2) Notwithstanding the repeal of the Indian Arms Act, 1878 (11 of 1878) and without prejudice to the provisions of Sections 6 and 24 of the General Clauses Act, 1897 (10 of 1897), every licence granted or renewed under the first-mentioned Act shall, unless sooner revoked, continue in force after such commencement for the unexpired portion of the period for which it has been granted or renewed.

❑❑❑

5

The Army Act, 1950[1]

ACT NO. 46 OF 1950 [20TH MAY, 1950]

AN ACT to consolidate and amend the law relating to the government of the regular Army.

Be it enacted by Parliament as follows -

CHAPTER - I : PRELIMINARY

1. Short title and commencement.

(1) This Act may be called the Army Act, 1950.

(2) It shall come into force on such date as the Central Government may, by notification in the Official Gazette, appoint in this behalf.

2. Persons subject to this Act.

(1) The following persons shall be subject to this Act wherever they may be, namely:-

(a) officers, junior commissioned officers and warrant officers of the regular Army;

(b) persons enrolled under this Act;

(c) persons belonging to the Indian Reserve Forces;

(d) persons belonging to the Indian Supplementary Reserve Forces when called out for service or when carrying out the annual test;

(e) officers of the Territorial Army, when doing duty as such officers, and enrolled persons of the said Army when called out or embodied or attached to any regular forces, subject to such adaptations and modifications as may be made in the application of this Act to such persons under sub-section (1) of Section 9 of the Territorial Army Act, 1948 (56 of 1948).

(f) persons holding commissions in the Army in India Reserve of Officers, when ordered on any duty or service for which they are liable as members of such reserve forces;

(g) officers appointed to the Indian Regular Reserve of Officers, when ordered on any duty or service for which they are liable as members of such reserve forces;

(i) persons not otherwise subject to military law who, on active service, in camp, on the march or at any frontier post specified by the Central Government by notification in this behalf, are employed by, or are in the service of, or are followers of, or accompany any portion of, the regular Army.

(2) Every person subject to this Act under clauses (a) to [2][(g) of sub-section (1) shall remain so subject until duly retired, discharged, released, removed, dismissed or cashiered from the service.

3. Definition. In this Act, unless the context otherwise requires -

(i) "active service", as applied to a person subject to this Act, means the time during which such person-

(a) is attached to, or forms part of, a force which is engaged in operations against an enemy, or

(b) is engaged in military operations in, or is on the line of march to, a country or place wholly or partly occupied by an enemy, or

(c) is attached to or forms part of a force which is in military occupation of a foreign country;

(ii) "civil offence" means an offence which is triable by a Criminal Court;

(iii) "civil prison" means any jail or place used for the detention of any criminal prisoner under the Prisons Act, 1894 (9 of 1894) or under any other law for the time being in force;

(iv) [3][Chief of the Army Staff" means the officer commanding the regular Army];

(v) "commanding officer", when used in any provision of this Act, with reference to any separate portion of the regular Army or to any department thereof, means the officer whose duty it is under the regulations of the regular Army, or in the absence of any such regulations, by the custom of the service, to discharge with respect to that portion of the regular Army or that department, as the case may be, the functions of a commanding officer in regard to matters of the description referred to in that provision;

(vi) "corps" means any separate body of persons subject to this Act, which is prescribed as a corps for the purposes of all or any of the provisions of this Act;

(vii) "court-martial" means a court-martial held under this Act;

(viii) "Criminal Court" means a Court of ordinary criminal justice in any part of India;

(ix) "department" includes any division or branch of a department;

(x) "enemy" includes all armed mutineers, armed rebels, armed rioters, pirates and any person in arms against whom it is the duty of any person subject to military law to act;

(xi) "the Forces" means the regular Army, Navy and Air Force or any part of any one or more of them;

(xii) "junior commissioned officer" means a person commissioned, gazetted or in pay as a junior commissioned officer in the regular Army or the Indian Reserve Forces, and includes a person holding a junior commission in the Indian Supplementary Reserve Forces or the Territorial Army, [2][who is for the time being subject to this Act;

(xiii) "military custody" means the arrest or confinement of a person according to the usages of the service and includes naval or air force custody;

(xiv) "military reward" includes any gratuity or annuity for long service or good conduct, good service pay or pension, and any other military pecuniary reward;

(xv) "non-commissioned officer" means a person holding a non-commissioned rank or an acting non-commissioned rank in the regular Army or the Indian Reserve Forces, and includes a non-commissioned officer or acting non-commissioned officer of the Indian Supplementary Reserve Forces or the Territorial Army, [1][who is for the time being subject to this Act;

(xvi) "notification" means a notification published in the Official Gazette;

(xvii) "offence" means any act or omission punishable under this Act and includes a civil offence as hereinbefore defined;

(xviii) "officer" means a person commissioned, gazetted are in pay as an officer in the regular Army, and includes-

(a) an officer of the Indian Reserve Forces;

(b) an officer holding a commission in the Territorial Army granted by the President with designation of rank corresponding to that of an officer of the regular Army who is for the time being subject to this Act;

(c) an officer of the Army in India Reserve of Officers who is for the time being subject to this Act;

(d) an officer of the Indian Regular Reserve of Officers who is for the time being subject to this Act;

(f) in relation to a person subject to this Act when serving under such conditions as may be prescribed, an officer of the Navy or Air Force; but does not include a junior commissioned officer, warrant officer, petty officer or non-commissioned officer;

(xix) "prescribed" means prescribed by rules made under this Act;

(xx) "provost-marshal" means a person appointed as such under Section 107 and includes any of his deputies or assistants or any other person legally exercising authority under him or on his behalf;

(xxi) "regular Army" means officers, junior commissioned officers, warrant officers, non-commissioned officers and other enrolled persons who, by their commission, warrant, terms of enrolment or otherwise, are liable to warrant, terms of enrolment or otherwise, are liable to Union in any part of the world, including persons belonging to the Reserve Forces and the Territorial Army when called out on permanent service;

(xxii) "regulation" includes a regulation made under this Act;

(xxiii) "superior officer", when used in relation to a person subject to this Act, includes a junior commissioned officer, warrant officer and a non-commissioned officer, and, as regards persons placed under his orders, an officer, warrant officer, petty officer and non-commissioned officer of the Navy or Air Force;

(xxiv) "warrant officer" means a person appointed, gazetted or in pay as a warrant officer of the regular Army or of the Indian Reserve Forces, and includes a warrant officer of the Indian Supplementary Reserve Forces or of the Territorial Army 1[who is for the time being subject to this Act;

(xxv) [2][all words (except the word "India")] and expressions used but not defined in this Act and defined in the Indian Penal Code (45 of 1860) shall be deemed to have the meanings assigned to them in that Code.

CHAPTER - II : SPECIAL PROVISIONS FOR THE APPLICATION OF ACT IN CERTAIN CASES

4. Application of Act to certain forces under Central Government.

(1) The Central Government may, by notification, apply, with or without modifications, all or any of the provisions of this Act to any force raised and maintained in India under the authority of that Government, [3][and suspend the operation of any other enactment for the time being applicable to the said force.

(2) The provisions of this Act so applied shall have effect in respect of persons belonging to the said force as they have effect in respect of persons subject to this Act holding in the regular Army the same or equivalent rank as the aforesaid persons hold for the time being in the said force.

(3) The provisions of this Act so applied shall also have effect in respect of persons who are employed by or are in the service of or are followers of or accompany any portion of the said force as they have effect in respect of persons subject to this Act under 1[clause (i) of sub-section (1) of Section (2)].

(4) While any of the provisions of this Act apply to the said force, the Central Government may, by notification, direct by what authority any jurisdiction, powers or duties incident to the operation of these provisions shall be exercised or performed in respect of the said force.

5. [Application of Act to forces of Part B States.] *Rep. by the Adaptation of Laws (No. 3) Order, 1956.*

6. Special provision as to rank in certain cases.

(1) The Central Government may, by notification, direct that any persons or class of persons subject to this Act under [1][clause (i), of sub-section (1) of Section 2]

shall be so subject as officers, junior commissioned officers, warrant officers or non-commissioned officers and may authorise any officer to give a like direction and to cancel such direction.

(2) All persons subject to this Act other than officers, junior commissioned officers, warrant officers and non-commissioned officers shall, if they are not persons in respect of whom a notification or direction under sub-section (1) is in force, be deemed to be of a rank inferior to that of a non-commissioned officer.

7. Commanding officer of persons subject to military law under clause (i) of Section 2.

(1) Every person subject to this Act under [1][clause (i) of sub-section (1) of Section 2] shall, for the purposes of this Act, be deemed to be under the commanding officer of the corps, department of detachment, if any, to which he is attached, and, if he is not so attached, under the command of any officer who may for the time being be named as his commanding officer by the officer commanding the force with which such person for the time being is serving, or any other prescribed officer, or, if no such officer is named or prescribed, under the command of the said officer commanding the force.

(2) An officer commanding a force shall not place a person subject to this Act under [2][clause (i) of sub-section (1) of Section 2] under the command of an officer of rank inferior to that of such person, if there is present at the place where such person is any officer of a higher rank under whose command he can be placed.

8. Officers exercising powers in certain cases.

(1) Whenever persons subject to this Act are serving under an officer commanding any military Organisation, not in this Section specifically named and being in the opinion of the Central Government not less than a brigade, that Government may prescribe the officer by whom the powers, which under this Act may be exercised by officers commanding armies, army corps, divisions and brigades, shall, as regards such, persons, be exercised.

(2) The Central Government may confer such powers, either absolutely or subject to such restrictions, reservations, exceptions and conditions, as it may think fit.

9. Power to declare persons to be on active service. Notwithstanding anything contained in clause (i) of Section 3, the Central Government may, by notification, declare that any person or class of persons subject to this Act shall, with reference to any area in which they may be serving or with reference to any provision of this Act or of any other law for the time being in force, be deemed to be on active service within the meaning of this Act.

CHAPTER - III : COMMISSION, APPOINTMENT AND ENROLMENT

10. Commission and appointment. The President may grant, to such person as he thinks fit, a commission as, an officer, or as a junior commissioned officer or appoint any person, as a warrant officer of the regular Army.

11. Ineligibility of aliens for enrolment. No person who is not a citizen of India shall, except with the consent of the Central Government signified in writing, be enrolled in the regular Army:

PROVIDED that nothing contained in this Section shall bar the enrolment of the subjects of Nepal in the regular Army.

12. Ineligibility of females for enrolment or employment. No female shall be eligible for enrolment or employment in the regular Army, except in such corps, department, branch or other body forming part of, or attached to any portion of, the regular Army as the Central Government may, by notification in the Official Gazette, specify in this behalf:

PROVIDED that nothing contained in this Section shall affect the provisions of any law for the time being in force providing for the raising and maintenance of any service auxiliary to the regular Army, or any branch thereof in which females are eligible for enrolment or employment.

13. Procedure before enrolling officer. Upon the appearance before the prescribed enrolling officer of any person desirous of being enrolled, the enrolling officer shall read and explain to him, or cause to be read and explained to him in his presence, the conditions of the service for which he is to be enrolled; and shall put to him the questions set forth in the prescribed form of enrolment, and shall, after having cautioned him that if he makes a false answer to any such question, he will be liable to punishment under this Act, record or cause to be recorded his answer to each such question.

14. Mode of enrolment. If, after complying with the provisions of Section 13, the enrolling officer is satisfied that the person desirous of being enrolled fully understands the questions put to him and consents to the conditions of service, and if such officer perceives no impediment, he shall sign and shall also cause such person to sign the enrolment paper, and such person shall thereupon be deemed to be enrolled.

15. Validity of enrolment. Every person who has for the space of three months been in receipt of pay as a person enrolled under this Act and been borne on the rolls of any corps or department shall be deemed to have been duly enrolled, and shall not be entitled to claim his discharge on the ground of any irregularity or illegality in his enrolment or on any other ground whatsoever; and if any person, in receipt of such pay and borne on the rolls as aforesaid, claims his discharge before the expiry of three months from his enrolment, no such irregularity or illegality or other ground shall, until he is discharged in pursuance of his claim, affect his position as an enrolled person under this Act or invalidate any proceeding, act or thing taken or done prior to his discharge.

16. Persons to be attested. The following persons shall be attested, namely :-

(a) all persons enrolled as combatants;

(b) all persons selected to hold a non-commissioned or acting non-commissioned rank; and

(c) all other persons subject to this Act as may be prescribed by the Central Government.

17. Mode of attestation.

(1) When a person who is to be attested is reported fit for duty, or has completed the prescribed period of probation, an oath or affirmation shall be administered to

him in the prescribed form by his commanding officer in front of his corps or such portion thereof or such members of his department as may be present, or by any other prescribed person.

(2) The form of oath or affirmation prescribed under this Section shall contain a promise that the person to be attested will bear true allegiance to the Constitution of India as by law established, and that he will serve in the regular Army and go wherever he is ordered by land, sea or air, and that he will obey all commands of any officer set over him, even to the peril of his life.

(3) The fact of an enrolled person having taken the oath or affirmation directed by this Section to be taken shall be entered on his enrolment paper, and authenticated by the signature of the officer administering the oath or affirmation.

CHAPTER - IV : CONDITIONS OF SERVICE

18. Tenure of service under the Act. Every person subject to this Act shall hold office during the pleasure of the President.

19. Termination of service by Central Government. Subject to the provisions of this Act and the rules and regulations made thereunder the Central Government may dismiss, or remove from the service, any person subject to this Act.

20. Dismissal, removal or reduction by the Chief of the Army Staff and by other officers.

(1) 1[The Chief of the Army Staff] may dismiss or remove from the service any person subject to this Act other than an officer.

(2) [3][The Chief of the Army Staff] may reduce to a lower grade or rank or the ranks, any warrant officer or any non-commissioned officer.

(3) An officer having power not less than a brigade or equivalent commander or any prescribed officer may dismiss or remove from the service any person serving under his command other than an officer or a junior commissioned officer.

(4) Any such officer as is mentioned in sub-section (3) may reduce to a lower grade or rank or the ranks, any warrant officer or any non-commissioned officer under his command.

(5) A warrant officer reduced to the ranks under this Section shall not, however, be required to serve in the ranks as a sepoy.

(6) The commanding officer of an acting non-commissioned officer may order him to revert to his permanent grade as a non-commissioned officer, or if he has no permanent grade above the ranks, to the ranks.

(7) The exercise of any power under this Section shall be subject to the said provisions contained in this Act and the rules and regulations made thereunder.

21. Power to modify certain fundamental rights in their application to persons subject to this Act. Subject to the provisions of any law for the time being in force relating to the regular Army or to any branch thereof, the Central Government may, by notification, make rules restricting to such extent and in such manner as may be necessary the right of any person subject to this Act-

(a) to be a member of, or to be associated in any way with, any trade union or labour union, or any class of trade or labour unions or any society, institution or association, or any class of societies, institutions or associations

(b) to attend or address any meeting or to take part in any demonstration organised by any body of persons for any political or other purposes

(c) to communicate with the press or to publish or cause to be published any book, letter or other document.

22. Retirement, release or discharge. Any person subject to this Act may be retired, released or discharged from the service by such authority and in such manner as may be prescribed.

23. Certificate on termination of service. Every junior commissioned officer, warrant officer, or enrolled person who is dismissed, removed, discharged, retired or released from the service shall be furnished by his commanding officer with a certificate, in the language which is the mother tongue of such person and also in the English language setting forth-

(a) the authority terminating his service

(b) the cause for such termination; and

(c) the full period of his service in the regular Army.

24. Discharge or dismissal when out of India.

(1) Any person enrolled under this Act who is entitled under the conditions of his enrolment to be discharged, or whose discharge is ordered by competent authority, and who, when he is so entitled or ordered to be discharged, is serving out of India, and requests to be sent to India, shall, before being discharged, be sent to India with all convenient speed.

(2) Any person enrolled under this Act who is dismissed from the service and who, when he is so dismissed, is serving out of India, shall be sent to India with all convenient speed.

(3) Where any such person as is mentioned in sub-section (2) is sentenced to dismissal combined with any other punishment, such other punishment, or, in the case of a sentence of transportation or imprisonment, a portion of such sentence may be inflicted before he is sent to India.

(4) For the purposes of this Section, the word "discharge" shall include release, and the word "dismissal" shall include removal.

CHAPTER - V : SERVICE PRIVILEGES

25. Authorised deductions only to be made from pay. The pay of every person subject to this Act due to him as such under any regulation for the time being in force shall be paid without any deduction other than the deductions authorised by or under this or any other Act.

26. Remedy of aggrieved persons other than officers.

(1) Any person subject to this Act other than an officer who deems himself wronged by any superior or other officer may, if not attached to a troop or company, complain to the officer under whose command or orders he is serving; and may, if attached to a troop or company, complain to the officer commanding the same.

(2) When the officer complained against is the officer to whom any complaint should, under sub-section (1), be preferred, the aggrieved person may complain to such officer' s next superior officer.

(3) Every officer receiving any such complaint shall make as complete an investigation into it as may be possible for giving full redress to the complainant; or, when necessary, refer the complaint to superior authority.

(4) Every such complaint shall be preferred in such manner as may from time to time be specified by the proper authority.

(5) The Central Government may revise any decision by [4][the Chief of the Army Staff] under sub-section (2), but, subject thereto, the decision of [4][the Chief of the Army Staff] shall be final.

27. Remedy of aggrieved officers. Any officer who deems himself wronged by his commanding officer or any superior officer and who on due application made to his commanding officer does not receive the redress to which he considers himself entitled, may complain to the Central Government in such manner as may from time to time be specified by the proper authority.

28. Immunity from attachment. Neither the arms, clothes, equipment, accoutrements or necessaries of any person subject to this Act, nor any animal used by him for the discharge of his duty, shall be seized, nor shall the pay and allowances of any such person or any part thereof be attached, by direction of any civil or revenue court or any revenue officer in satisfaction of any decree or order enforceable against him.

29. Immunity from arrest for debt.

(1) No person subject to this Act shall, so long as he belongs to the Forces, be liable to be arrested for debt under any process issued by, or by the authority of, any civil or revenue court or revenue officer.

(2) The judge of any such court or the said officer may examine into any complaint made by such person or his superior officer of the arrest of such person contrary to the provisions of this Section and may, by warrant under his hand, discharge the person, and award reasonable costs to the complainant, who may recover those costs in like manner as he might have recovered costs awarded to him by a decree against the person obtaining the process.

(3) For the recovery of such costs no court-fee shall be payable by the complainant.

30. Immunity of persons attending courts-martial from arrest.

(1) No presiding officer or member of a court-martial, no judge advocate, no party to any proceeding before a court-martial, or his legal practitioner or agent, and no witness acting in obedience to a summons to attend a court-martial shall, while proceeding to, attending or returning from, a court-martial, be liable to arrest under civil or revenue process.

(2) If any such person is arrested under any such process, he may be discharged by order of the court-martial.

31. Privileges of reservists. Every person belonging to the Indian Reserve Forces shall, when called out for or engaged in or returning from, training or service, be entitled to all the privileges accorded by Sections 28 and 29 to a person subject to this Act.

32. Priority in respect of army personnel's litigation.

(1) On the presentation to any court by or on behalf of any person subject to this Act of a certificate from the proper military authority of leave of absence having been granted to or applied for by him for the purpose of prosecuting or defending any suit or other proceeding in such court, the court shall, on the application of such person, arrange, so far as may be possible, for the hearing and final disposal of such suit or other proceeding within the period of the leave so granted or applied for.

(2) The certificate from the proper military authority shall state the first and last day of the leave or intended leave, and set forth a description of the case with respect to which the leave was granted or applied for.

(3) No fee shall be payable to the court in respect of the presentation of any such certificate, or of any application by or on behalf of any such person, for priority for the hearing of his case.

(4) Where the court is unable to arrange for the hearing and final disposal of the suit or other proceeding within the period of such leave or intended leave as aforesaid, it shall record its reasons for its inability to do so, and shall cause a copy thereof to be furnished to such person on his application without any payment whatever by him in respect either of the application for such copy or of the copy itself.

(5) If in any case a question arises as to the proper military authority qualified to grant such certificate as aforesaid, such question shall at once be referred by the court to an officer having power not less than a brigade or equivalent commander whose decision shall be final.

33. Saving of rights and privileges under other laws. The rights and privileges specified in the preceding Sections of this Chapter shall be in addition to, and not in derogation of, any other rights and privileges conferred on persons subject to this Act or on members of the regular Army, Navy and Air Force generally by any other law for the time being in force.

CHAPTER - VI : OFFENCES

34. Offences in relation to the enemy and punishable with death. Any person subject to this Act who commits any of the following offences, that is to say -

(a) shamefully abandons or delivers up any garrison, fortress, post, place or guard, committed to his charge, or which it is his duty to defend, or uses any means to compel or induce any commanding officer or other person to commit any of the said acts; or

(b) intentionally uses any means to compel or induce any person subject to military, naval or air force law to abstain from acting against the enemy, or to discourage such person from acting against the enemy; or

(c) in the presence of the enemy, shamefully casts away his arms, ammunition, tools or equipment or misbehaves in such manner as to show cowardice; or

(d) treacherously holds correspondence with, or communicates intelligence to, the enemy or any person in arms against the Union; or

(e) directly or indirectly assists the enemy with money, arms, ammunition, stores or supplies; or

(f) treacherously or through cowardice sends a flag of truce to the enemy; or

(g) in time of war or during any military operation, intentionally occasions a false alarm in action, camp, garrison or quarters, or spreads reports calculated to create alarm or despondency; or

(h) in time of action leaves his commanding officer or his post, guard, picquet, patrol or party without being regularly relieved or without leave; or

(i) having been made a prisoner of war, voluntarily serves with or aids the enemy; or

(j) knowingly harbours or protects an enemy not being a prisoner; or

(k) being a sentry in time of war or alarm, sleeps upon his post or is intoxicated; or

(l) knowingly does any act calculated to imperil the success of the military, naval or air forces of India or any forces co-operating therewith or any part of such forces; shall, on conviction by court-martial, be liable to suffer death or such less punishment as is in this Act mentioned.

35. Offences in relation to the enemy and not punishable with death. Any person subject to this Act who commits any of the following offences, that is to say -

(a) is taken prisoner, by want of due precaution, or through disobedience of orders, or wilful neglect of duty, or having been taken prisoner, fails to rejoin his service when able to do so; or

(b) without due authority holds correspondence with or communicates intelligence to the enemy or having come by the knowledge of any such correspondence or communication, wilfully omits to discover it immediately to his commanding or other superior officer; or

(c) without due authority sends a flag of truce to the enemy; shall, on conviction by court-martial, be liable to suffer imprisonment for a term which may extend to fourteen years or such less punishment as is in this Act mentioned.

36. Offences punishable more severely on active service than at other times. Any person subject to this Act who commits any of the following offences, that is to say -

(a) forces a safeguard, or forces or uses criminal force to a sentry; or

(b) breaks into any house or other place in search of plunder; or

(c) being a sentry sleeps upon his post, or is intoxicated; or

(d) without orders from his superior officer leaves his guard, picquet, patrol or post; or

(e) intentionally or through neglect occasions a false alarm in camp, garrison, or quarters; or spreads reports calculated to create unnecessary alarm or despondency; or

(f) makes known the parole, watchword or countersign to any person not entitled to receive it; or knowingly gives a parole, watchword or countersign different from what he received; shall, on conviction by court-martial, if he commits any such offence when on active service, be liable to suffer imprisonment for a term which may extend to fourteen years or such less punishment as is in this Act mentioned; and if he commits any such offence when not on active service, be liable to suffer imprisonment for a term which may extend to seven years or such less punishment as is in this Act mentioned.

37. Mutiny. Any person subject to this Act who commits any of the following offences, that is to say -

(a) begins, incites, causes, or conspires with any other persons to cause any mutiny in the military, naval or air forces of India or any forces co-operating therewith; or

(b) joins in any such mutiny; or

(c) being present at any such mutiny, does not use his utmost endeavours to suppress the same; or

(d) knowing or having reason to believe in the existence of any such mutiny, or of any intention to mutiny or of any such conspiracy, does not, without delay, give information thereof to his commanding or other superior officer; or

(e) endeavours to seduce any person in the military, naval. or air forces of India from his duty or allegiance to the Union; shall, on conviction by court-martial, be liable to suffer death or such less punishment as is in this Act mentioned.

38. Desertion and aiding desertion.

(1) Any person subject to this Act who deserts or attempts to desert the service shall, on conviction by court-martial, if he commits the offence on active service or when under orders for active service, be liable to suffer death or such less punishment as is in this Act mentioned; and if he commits the offence under any other circumstances, be liable to suffer imprisonment for a term which may extend to seven years or such less punishment as is in this Act mentioned.

(2) Any person subject to this Act who, knowingly harbours any such deserter shall, on conviction by court-martial, be liable to suffer imprisonment for a term which may extend to seven years or such less punishment as is in this Act mentioned.

(3) Any person subject to this Act who, being cognizant of any desertion or attempt at desertion of a person subject to this Act, does not forthwith give notice to his own or some other superior officer, or take any steps in his power to cause

such person to be apprehended, shall, on conviction by court-martial, be liable to suffer imprisonment for a term which may extend to two years or such less punishment as is in this Act mentioned.

39. Absence without leave. Any person subject to this Act who commits any of the following offences, that is to say -

(a) absents himself without leave; or

(b) without sufficient cause overstays leave granted to him; or

(c) being on leave of absence and having received information from proper authority that any corps, or portion of a corps, or any department, to which he belongs, has been ordered on active service, fails, without sufficient cause, to rejoin without delay; or

(d) without sufficient cause fails to appear at the time fixed at the parade or place appointed for exercise or duty; or

(e) when on parade, or on the line of march, without sufficient cause or without leave from his superior officer, quits the parade or line of march; or

(f) when in camp or garrison or elsewhere, is found beyond any limits fixed, or in any place prohibited, by any general, local or other order, without a pass or written leave from his superior officer; or

(g) without leave from his superior officer or without due cause, absents himself from any school when duly ordered to attend there; shall, on conviction by court-martial, be liable to suffer imprisonment for a term which may extend to three years or such less punishment as is in this Act mentioned.

40. Striking or threatening superior officers. Any person subject to this Act who commits any of the following offences, that is to say -

(a) uses criminal force to or assaults his superior officer; or

(b) uses threatening language to such officer; or

(c) uses insubordinate language to such officer; shall, on conviction by court-martial, if such officer is at the time in the execution of his office or, if the offence is committed on active service, be liable to suffer imprisonment for a term which may extend to fourteen years or such less punishment as is in this Act mentioned; and in other cases, be liable to suffer imprisonment for a term which may extend to ten years or such less punishment as is in this Act mentioned:

PROVIDED that in the case of an offence specified in clause (c), the imprisonment shall not exceed five years.

41. Disobedience to superior officer.

(1) Any person subject to this Act who disobeys in such manner as to show a wilful defiance of authority any lawful command given personally by his superior officer in the execution of his office whether the same is given orally, or in writing or by signal or otherwise shall on conviction by court-martial, be liable to suffer imprisonment for a term which may extend to fourteen years or such less punishment as is in this Act mentioned.

(2) Any person subject to this Act who disobeys any lawful command given by his superior officer shall, on conviction by court-martial, if he commits such offence when on active service, be liable to suffer imprisonment for a term which may extend to fourteen years or such less punishment as is in this Act mentioned; and if he commits such offence when not on active service, be liable to suffer imprisonment for a term which may extend to five years or such less punishment as is in this Act mentioned.

42. Insubordination and obstruction. Any person subject to this Act who commits any of the following offences, that is to say -

(a) being concerned in any quarrel, affray, or disorder, refuses to obey any officer, though of inferior rank, who orders him into arrest, or uses criminal force to or assaults any such officer; or

(b) uses criminal force to, or assaults any person, whether subject to this Act or not, in whose custody he is lawfully placed, and whether he is or is not his superior officer; or

(c) resists an escort whose duty it is to apprehend him or to have him in charge; or

(d) breaks out of barracks, camp or quarters; or

(e) neglects to obey any general, local or other order; or

(f) impedes the provost-marshal or any person lawfully acting on his behalf, or when called upon, refuses to assist in the execution of his duty a provost-marshal or any person lawfully acting on his behalf; or

(g) uses criminal force to or assaults any person bringing provisions or supplies to the forces; shall, on conviction by court-martial, be liable to suffer imprisonment for a term which may extend, in the case of the offences specified in clauses (d) and (e) to two years, and in the case of the offences specified in the other clauses to ten years or such less punishment as is in this Act mentioned.

43. Fraudulent enrolment. Any person subject to this Act who commits any of the following offences, that is to say -

(a) without having obtained a regular discharge from the corps or department to which he belongs, or otherwise fulfilled the conditions enabling him to enrol or enter, enrols himself in, or enters the same or any other corps or department or any part of the naval or air forces of India or the Territorial Army; or

(b) is concerned in the enrolment in any part of the Forces of any person when he knows or has reason to believe such person to be so circumstanced that by enrolling he commits an offence against this Act; shall, on conviction by court-martial, be liable to suffer imprisonment for a term which may extend to five years or such less punishment as is in this Act mentioned.

44. False answers on enrolment. Any person having become subject to this Act who is discovered to have made at the time of enrolment a wilfully false answer to any question set forth in the prescribed form of enrolment which has been put to him by the enrolling officer before whom he appears for the purpose of being enrolled shall, on conviction by court-martial, be liable to suffer imprisonment for a term which may extend to five years or such less punishment as is in this Act mentioned.

45. Unbecoming conduct. Any officer, junior commissioned officer or warrant officer who behaves in a manner unbecoming his position and the character expected of him shall, on conviction by court-martial, if he is an officer, be liable to be cashiered or to suffer such less punishment as is in this Act mentioned; and, if he is a junior commissioned officer or a warrant officer, be liable to be dismissed or to suffer such less punishment as is in this Act mentioned.

46. Certain forms of disgraceful conduct. Any person subject to this Act who commits any of the following offences, that is to say -

(a) is guilty of any disgraceful conduct of a cruel, indecent or unnatural kind; or

(b) malingers, or feigns, or produces disease or infirmity in himself, or intentionally delays his cure or aggravates his disease or infirmity; or

(c) with intent to render himself or any other person unfit for service, voluntarily causes hurt to himself or that person; shall, on conviction by court-martial, be liable to suffer imprisonment for a term which may extend to seven years or such less punishment as is in this Act mentioned.

47. Ill-treating a subordinate. Any officer, junior commissioned officer, warrant officer or non-commissioned officer who uses criminal force to or otherwise illtreats any person subject to this Act, being his subordinate in rank or position, shall, on conviction by court-martial, be liable to suffer imprisonment for a term which may extend to seven years or such less punishment as is in this Act mentioned.

48. Intoxication.

(1) Any person subject to this Act who is found in a state of intoxication, whether on duty or not, shall, on conviction by court-martial, if he is an officer, be liable to be cashiered or to suffer such less punishment as is in this Act mentioned; and, if he is not an officer, be liable, subject to the provisions of sub-section (2), to suffer imprisonment for a term which may extend to two years or such less punishment as is in this Act mentioned.

(2) Where an offence of being intoxicated is committed by a person other than an officer when not on active service or not on duty, the period of imprisonment awarded shall not exceed six months.

49. Permitting escape of person in custody. Any person subject to this Act who commits any of the following offences, that is to say -

(a) when in command of a guard, picquet, patrol or post, releases without proper authority, whether wilfully or without reasonable excuse, any person committed to his charge, or refuses to receive any prisoner or person so committed; or

(b) wilfully or without reasonable excuse allows to escape any person who is committed to his charge, or whom it is his duty to keep or guard; shall, on conviction by court-martial, be liable, if he has acted wilfully to suffer imprisonment for a term which may extend to fourteen years or such less punishment as is in this Act mentioned; and if he has not acted wilfully, to suffer imprisonment for a term which may extend to two years or such less punishment as is in this Act mentioned.

50. Irregularity in connection with arrest or confinement. Any person subject to this Act who commits any of the following offences, that is to say -

(a) unnecessarily detains a person in arrest or confinement without bringing him to trial, or fails to bring his case before the proper authority for investigation; or

(b) having committed a person to military custody fails without reasonable cause to deliver at the time of such committal, or as soon as practicable, and in any case within forty-eight hours. thereafter, to the officer or other person into whose custody the person arrested is committed, an account in writing signed by himself of the offence with which the person so committed is charged; shall, on conviction by court-martial, be liable to suffer imprisonment for a term which may extend to two years or such less punishment as is in this Act mentioned.

51. Escape from custody. Any person subject to this Act who, being in lawful custody, escapes or attempts to escape, shall, on conviction by court-martial, be liable to suffer imprisonment for a term which may extend to five years or such less punishment as is in this Act mentioned.

52. Offences in respect of property. Any person subject to this Act who commits any of the following offences, that is to say -

(a) commits theft of any property belonging to the Government, or to any military, naval or air force mess, band or institution, or to any person subject to military, naval or air force law; or

(b) dishonestly misappropriates or converts to his own use any such property; or

(c) commits criminal breach of trust in respect of any such property; or

(d) dishonestly receives or retains any such property in respect of which any of the offences under clauses (a), (b) and (c) has been committed, knowing or having reason to believe the commission of such offence; or

(e) wilfully destroys or injures any property of the Government entrusted to him; or

(f) does any other thing with intent to defraud, or to cause wrongful gain to one person or wrongful loss to another person; shall, on conviction by court-martial, be liable to suffer imprisonment for a term which may extend to ten years or such less punishment as is in this Act mentioned.

53. Extortion and corruption. Any person subject to this Act who commits any of the following offences, that is to say -

(a) commits extortion; or

(b) without proper authority exacts from any person money, provisions or service; shall, on conviction by court-martial, be liable to suffer imprisonment for a term which may extend to ten years or such less punishment as is in this Act mentioned.

54. Making away with equipment. Any person subject to this Act who commits any of the following offences, that is to say -

(a) makes away with, or is concerned in making away with, any arms, ammunition, equipment, instruments tools, clothing or any other thing being the property of the Government issued to him for his use or entrusted to him; or

(b) loses by neglect anything mentioned in clause (a); or

(c) sells, pawns, destroys or defaces any medal or decoration granted to him; shall, on conviction by court-martial, be liable to suffer imprisonment for a term which may extend in the case of the offences specified in clause (a) to ten years, and in the case of the offences specified in the other clauses to five years, or such less punishment as is in this Act mentioned.

55. Injury to property. Any person subject to this Act who commits any of the following offences, that is to say -

(a) destroys or injures any property mentioned in clause (a) of Section 54 or any property belonging to any military, naval or air force mess, band or institution, or to any person subject to military, naval or air force law, or serving with, or attached to, the regular Army; or

(b) commits any act which causes damage to, or destruction of, any property of the Government by fire; or

(c) kills, injures, makes away with, ill-treats or loses any, animal entrusted to him; shall, on conviction by court-martial, be liable, if he has acted wil-fully, to suffer imprisonment for a term which may extend to fourteen years or such less punishment as is in this Act mentioned; and if he has acted without reasonable excuse, to suffer imprisonment for a term which may extend to seven years or such less punishment as is in this Act mentioned.

56. False accusations. Any person subject to this Act who commits any of the following offences, that is to say -

(a) makes a false accusation against any person subject to this Act, knowing or having reason to believe such accusation to be false; or

(b) in making a complaint under Section 26 or Section 27 makes any statement affecting the character of any person subject to this Act, knowing or having reason to believe such statement to be false or knowingly and wilfully suppresses any material facts; shall, on conviction by court-martial be liable to suffer imprisonment for a term which may extend to five years or such less punishment as is in this Act mentioned.

57. Falsifying official documents and false declaration. Any person subject to this Act who commits any of the following offences, that is to say -

(a) in any report, return, list, certificate, book or other document made or signed by him, or of the contents of which it is his duty to ascertain the accuracy, knowingly makes, or is privy to the making of any false or fraudulent statement; or

(b) in any document of the description mentioned in clause (a) knowingly makes, or is privy to the making of, any omission, with intent to defraud; or

(c) knowingly and with intent to injure any person, or knowingly and with intent to defraud, suppresses, defaces, alters or makes away with any document which it is his duty to preserve or produce; or

(d) where it is his official duty to make a declaration respecting any matter, knowingly makes a false declaration; or

(e) obtains for himself, or for any other person, any pension, allowance or other advantage or privilege by a statement which is false, and which he either knows or believes to be false or does not believe to be true, or by making or using a false entry in any book or record or by making any document containing a false statement, or by omitting to make a true entry or document containing a true statement; shall, on conviction by court-martial, be liable to suffer imprisonment for a term which may extend to fourteen years or such less punishment as is in this Act mentioned.

58. Signing in blank and failure to report. Any person subject to this Act who commits any of the following offences, that is to say -

(a) when signing any document relating to pay, arms, ammunition, equipment, clothing, supplies or stores, or any,. property of the Government fraudulently leaves in blank any material part for which his signature is a voucher; or

(b) refuses or by culpable neglect omits to make or send a report or return which it is his duty to make or send; shall, on conviction by court-martial, be liable to suffer imprison-ment for a term which may extend to seven years or such less punishment as is in this Act mentioned.

59. Offences relating to courts-martial. Any person subject to this Act who commits any of the following offences, that is to say -

(a) being duly summoned or ordered to attend as a witness before a court martial, wilfully or without reasonable excuse, makes default in attending; or

(b) refuses to take an oath or make an affirmation legally required by a court-martial to be taken or made; or

(c) refuses to produce or deliver any document in his power or control legally required by a court-martial to be produced or delivered by him; or

(d) refuses when a witness to answer any question which he is by law bound to answer; or

(e) is guilty of contempt of court-martial by using insulting or threatening language, or by causing any interruption or disturbance in the proceedings of such court; shall, on conviction by court-martial, be liable to suffer imprisonment for a term which may extend to three years or such less punishment as is in this Act mentioned.

60. False evidence. Any person subject to this Act who, having been duly sworn or affirmed before any court-martial or other court competent under this Act to administer an oath or affirmation, makes any statement which is false, and which he either knows or believes to be false or does not believe to be true, shall, on conviction by court-martial, be liable to suffer imprisonment for a term which may extend to seven years or such less punishment as is in this Act mentioned.

61. Unlawful detention of pay. Any officer, junior commissioned officer, warrant officer or non-commissioned officer who, having received the pay of a person subject to this Act unlawfully detains or refuses to pay the same when due, shall, on conviction by court-martial, be liable to suffer imprisonment for a term which may extend to ten years or such less punishment as is in this Act mentioned.

62. Offences in relation to aircraft and flying. Any person subject to this Act who commits any of the following offences, that is to say -

(a) wilfully or without reasonable excuse damages, destroys or loses any aircraft or aircraft material belonging to the Government: or

(b) is guilty of any act or neglect likely to cause such damage, destruction or loss; or

(c) without lawful authority disposes of any aircraft or aircraft material belonging to the Government; or

(d) is guilty of any act or neglect in flying, or in the use of any aircraft, or in relation to any aircraft or aircraft material, which causes or is likely to cause loss of life or bodily injury to any person; or

(e) during a state of war, wilfully and without proper occasion, or negligently, causes the sequestration, by or under the authority of a neutral State, or the destruction in a neutral State of any aircraft, belonging to the Government shall, on conviction by court-martial, be liable, if he has acted wilfully, to suffer imprisonment for a term which may extend to fourteen years or such less punishment as is in this Act mentioned, and, in any other case, to suffer imprisonment for a term which may extend to five years or such less punishment as is in this Act mentioned.

63. Violation of good order and discipline. Any person subject to this Act who is guilty of any act or omission which, though not specified in this Act, is prejudicial to good order and military discipline shall, on conviction by court-martial, be liable to suffer imprisonment for a term which may extend to seven years or such less punishment as is in this Act mentioned.

64. Miscellaneous offences. Any person subject to this Act who commits any of the following offences, that is to say -

(a) being in command at any post or on the march, and receiving a complaint that any one under his command has beaten or otherwise maltreated or oppressed any person, or has disturbed any fair or market, or committed any riot or trespass, fails to have due reparation made to the injured person or to report the case to the proper authority; or

(b) by defiling any place of worship, or otherwise, intentionally insults the religion or wounds the religious feelings of any person; or

(c) attempts to commit suicide, and in such attempt does any act towards the commission of such offence; or

(d) being below the rank of warrant officer, when off duty, appears without proper authority, in or about camp or cantonments, or in or about, or when going to or returning from, any town or bazar, carrying a rifle, sword or other offensive weapon; or

(e) directly or indirectly accepts or obtains, or agrees to accept or attempts to obtain, for himself or for any other person, any gratification as a motive or reward for procuring the enrolment of any person, or leave of absence, promotion or any other advantage or indulgence for any person in the service; or

(f) commits any offence against the property or person of any inhabitant of, or resident in, the country in which he is serving; shall, on conviction by court-martial, be liable to suffer imprisonment for a term which may extend to seven years or such less punishment as is in this Act mentioned.

65. Attempt. Any person subject to this Act who attempts to commit any of the offences specified in Sections 34 to 64 inclusive and in such attempt does any act towards the commission of the offence, shall, on conviction by court-martial, where no express provision is made by this Act for the punishment of such attempt, be liable, if the offence attempted to be committed is punishable with death, to suffer imprisonment for a term which may extend to fourteen years or such less punishment as is in this Act mentioned; and if the offence attempted to be committed is punishable with imprisonment, to suffer imprisonment for a term which may extend to one-half of the longest term provided for that offence or such less punishment as is in this Act mentioned.

66. Abetment of offences that have been committed. Any person subject to this Act who abets the commission of any of the offences specified in Sections 34 to 64 inclusive shall, on conviction by court-martial, if the Act abetted is committed in consequence of the abetment and no express provision is made by this Act for the punishment of such abetment, be liable to suffer the punishment provided for that offence or such less punishment as is in this Act mentioned.

67. Abetment of offences punishable with death and not committed. Any person subject to this Act who abets the commission of any of the offences punishable with death under Sections 34, 37 and sub-section (1) of Section 38 shall, on conviction by court-martial, if that offence be not committed in consequence of the abetment, and no express provision is made by this Act for the punishment of such abetment, be liable to suffer imprisonment for a term which may extend to fourteen years or such less punishment as is in this Act mentioned.

68. Abetment of offences punishable with imprisonment and not committed. Any person subject to this Act who abets the commission of any of the offences specified in Sections 34 to 64 inclusive and punishable with imprisonment shall, on conviction by court-martial, if that offence be not committed in consequence of the abetment, and no express provision is made by this Act for the punishment of such abetment, be liable to suffer imprisonment for a term which may extend to one-half of the longest term provided for that offence or such less punishment as is in this Act mentioned.

69. Civil offences. Subject to the provisions of Section 70, any person subject to this Act who at any place in or beyond India commits any civil offence shall be deemed to be guilty of an offence against this Act and, if charged therewith under this Section, shall be liable to be tried by a court-martial and, on conviction, be punishable as follows, that is to say -

(a) if the offence is one which would be punishable under any law in force in India with death or with transportation, he shall be liable to suffer any punishment, other than whipping, assigned for the offence, by the aforesaid law and such less punishment as is in this Act mentioned; and

(b) in any other case, he shall be liable to suffer any punishment, other than whipping, assigned for the offence by the law in force in India, or imprisonment for a term which may extend to seven years, or such less punishment as is in this Act mentioned.

70. Civil offence not triable by court-martial. A person subject to this Act who commits an offence of murder against a person not subject to military, naval or air force law, or of culpable homicide not amounting to murder against such a person or of rape in relation to such a person, shall not be deemed to be guilty of an offence against this Act and shall not be tried by a court-martial, unless he commits any of the said offences-

(a) while on active service, or

(b) at any place outside India, or

(c) at a frontier post specified by the Central Government by notification in this behalf.

CHAPTER - VII : PUNISHMENTS

71. Punishments awardable by courts-martial. Punishments may be inflicted in respect of offences committed by persons subject to this Act and convicted by courts-martial, according to the scale following, that is to say -

(a) death;

(b) transportation for life or for any period not less than seven years;

(c) imprisonment, either rigorous or simple, for any period not exceeding fourteen years;

(d) cashiering, in the case of officers;

(e) dismissal from the service;

(f) reduction to the ranks or to a lower rank or grade or place in the list of their rank, in the case of warrant officers;

(g) forfeiture of seniority of rank, in the case of officers, junior commissioned officers, warrant officers and non-commissioned officers; and forfeiture of all or any part of their service for the purpose of promotion, in the case of any of them whose promotion depends upon length of service;

(h) forfeiture of service for the purpose of increased pay, pension or any other prescribed purpose;

(i) severe reprimand or reprimand, in the case of officers, junior commissioned officers, warrant officers and non-commissioned officers;

(j) forfeiture of pay and allowances for a period not exceeding three months for an offence committed on active service;

(k) forfeiture in the case of a person sentenced to cashiering or dismissal from the service of all arrears of pay and allowances and other public money due to him at the time of such cashiering or dismissal;

(l) stoppage of pay and allowances until any proved loss or damage occasioned by the offence of which he is convicted is made good.

72. Alternative punishments awardable by court-martial. Subject to the provisions of this Act, a court-martial may, on convicting a person subject to this Act of any of the offences specified in Sections 34 to 68 inclusive, award either the particular punishment with which the offence is stated in the said Sections to be punishable, or, in lieu thereof, any one of the punishments lower in the scale set out in Section 71, regard being had to the nature and degree of the offence.

73. Combination of punishments. A sentence of a court-martial may award in addition to, or without any one other punishment, the punishment specified in clause (d) or clause (e) of Section 71 and any one or more of the punishments specified in clauses (f) to (l) of that Section.

74. Cashiering of officers. An officer shall be sentenced to be cashiered before he is awarded any of the punishments specified in clauses (a) to (c) of Section 71.

77. Result of certain punishments in the case of a warrant officer or non-commissioned officer. A warrant officer or a non-commissioned officer sentenced by a court-martial to transportation, imprisonment, [5][or dismissal from the service, shall be deemed to be reduced to ranks.

78. Retention in the ranks of a person convicted on active service. When, on active service, any enrolled person has been sentenced by a court-martial to dismissal, or to transportation or imprisonment whether combined with dismissal or not, the prescribed officer may direct that such person may be retained to serve in the ranks, and such service shall be reckoned as part of his term of transportation or imprisonment, if any.

79. Punishments otherwise than by court-martial. Punishments may also be inflicted in respect of offences committed by persons subject to this Act without the intervention of a court-martial and in the manner stated in Sections 80, 83, 84 and 85.

80. Punishment of persons other than officers, junior commissioned officers and warrant officers. Subject to the provisions of Section 81, a commanding officer or such other officer as is, with the consent of the Central Government, specified by [4][the Chief of the Army Staff], may, in the prescribed manner, proceed against a person subject to this Act otherwise than as an officer, junior commissioned officer or warrant officer who is charged with an offence under this Act and award such person, to the extent prescribed, one or more of the following punishments, that is to say -

(a) imprisonment in military custody up to twenty-eight days;

(b) detention up to twenty-eight days;

(c) confinement to the lines up to twenty-eight days;
(d) extra guards or duties;
(e) deprivation of a, position of the nature of an appointment or of corps or working pay, and in the case of non-commissioned officers, also deprivation of acting rank or reduction to a lower grade of pay;
(f) forfeiture of good service and good conduct pay;
(g) severe reprimand or reprimand;
(h) fine up to fourteen days' pay in any one month;
(i) penal deductions under clause (g) of Section 91.

81. Limit of punishments under Section 80.

[6][1. * * * *

(2) In the case of an award of two or more of the punishments specified in clauses (a), (b), (c) and (d) of the said Section, the punishment specified in clause (c) or clause (d) shall take effect only at the end of the punishment specified in clause (a) or clause (b).

(3) When two or more of the punishments specified in the said clauses (a), (b) and (c) are awarded to a person conjointly, or when already undergoing one or more of the said punishments, the whole extent of the punishments shall not exceed in the aggregate forty-two days.

(4) The punishments specified in clauses [7][(a), (b) and (c)] of Section 80 shall not be awarded to any person who is of the rank of non-commissioned officer or was, at the time of committing the offence for which he is punished, of such rank.

(5) The punishment specified in clause (g) of the said Section shall not be awarded to any person below the rank of a non-commissioned officer.

82. Punishments in addition to those specified in Section 80. [4][The Chief of the Army Staff] may, with the consent of the Central Government, specify such other punishments as may be awarded under Section 80 in addition to or without any of the punishments specified in the said Section, and the extent to which such other punishments may be awarded.

83. Punishment of officers, junior commissioned officers and warrant officers by brigade commanders and others. An officer having power not less than a brigade, or an equivalent commander or such other officer as is, with the consent of the Central Government, specified by [4][the Chief of the Army Staff] may in the prescribed manner, proceed against an officer below the rank of a field officer, a junior commissioned officer or a warrant officer, who is charged with an offence under this Act, and award one or more of the following punishments, that is to say -

(a) severe reprimand or reprimand;
(b) stoppage of pay and, allowances until any proved loss or damage occasioned by the offence of which he is convicted is made good.

84. Punishment of officers, junior commissioned officers and warrant officers by area commanders and others. An officer having power not less than an area commander or an equivalent commander or an officer empowered to convene a general court-martial or such other officer as is, with the consent of the Central Government, may, in the prescribed manner, proceed against an officer below the rank of lieutenant-colonel, a junior commissioned officer or a warrant officer, who is charged with an offence under this Act, and award one or more of the following punishments, that is to say -

(a) forfeiture of seniority, or in the case of any of them whose promotion depends upon length of service, forfeiture of service for the purpose of promotion for a period not exceeding twelve months, but subject to the right of the accused previous to the award to elect to be tried by a court-martial;

(b) severe reprimand or reprimand;

(c) stoppage of pay and allowances until any proved loss or damage occasioned by the offence of which he is convicted is made good.

85. Punishment of junior commissioned officers. A commanding officer or such other officer as is, with the consent of the Central Government, specified by [4][the Chief of the Army Staff] may, in the prescribed manner, proceed against a junior commissioned officer who is charged with an offence under this Act [5][and award one or more of the following punishments, that is to say -

(i) severe reprimand or reprimand;

(ii) stoppage of pay and allowances until any proved loss or damage occasioned by the offence of which he is convicted is made good:

PROVIDED that the punishment specified in clause (i) shall not be awarded if the commanding officer or such other officer is below the rank of Colonel]

86. Transmission of proceedings. In every case in which punishment has been awarded under any of the Sections 83, 84 and 85, certified true copies of the proceedings shall be forwarded, in the prescribed manner, by the officer awarding the punishment, to a superior military authority as defined in Section 88.

87. Review of proceedings. If any punishment awarded under any of the Sections 83, 84 and 85 appears to a superior military authority as defined in Section 88 to be illegal, unjust or excessive, such authority may cancel, vary or remit the punishment and make such other direction as may be appropriate in the circumstances of the case.

88. Superior military authority. For the purpose of Sections 86 and 87, a "superior military authority" means-

(a) in the case of punishments awarded by a commanding officer, any officer superior in command to such commanding officer;

(b) in the case of punishments awarded by any other authority, the Central Government, [4][the Chief of the Army Staff] or other officer specified by [4][the Chief of the Army Staff]

89. Collective fines.

(1) Whenever any weapon or part of a weapon forming part of the equipment of a half squadron, battery, company or other similar unit is lost or stolen, the officer commanding the army, army corps, division or independent brigade to which such unit belongs may, after obtaining the report of a court of inquiry, impose a

collective fine upon the junior commissioned officers, warrant officers, non-commissioned officers and men of such unit, or upon so many of them as, in his judgment, should be held responsible for such loss or theft.

(2) Such fine shall be assessed as a percentage on the pay of the individuals on whom it falls.

CHAPTER - VIII : PENAL DEDUCTIONS

90. Deductions from pay and allowances of officers. The following penal deductions may be made from the pay and allowances of an officer, that is to say -

(a) all pay and allowances due to an officer for every day he absents himself without leave, unless a satisfactory explanation has been given to his commanding officer and has been approved by the Central Government;

(b) all pay and allowances for every day while he is in custody or under suspension from duty on a charge for an offence for which he is afterwards convicted by a criminal court or a court-martial or by an officer exercising authority under Section 83 or Section 84;

(c) any sum required to make good the pay of any person subject to this Act which he has unlawfully retained or unlawfully refused to pay;

(d) any sum required to make good such compensation for any expenses, loss, damage or destruction occasioned by the commission of an offence as may be determined by the court-martial by whom he is convicted of such offence, or by an officer exercising authority under Section 83 or Section 84

(e) all pay and allowances ordered by a court-martial [4][to be forfeited or stopped;

(f) any sum required to pay a fine awarded by a criminal court or a court-martial exercising jurisdiction under Section 69;

(g) any sum required to make good any loss, damage, or destruction of public or regimental property which, after due investigation, appears to the Central Government to have been occasioned by the wrongful act or negligence on the part of the officer;

(h) all pay and allowances forfeited by order of the Central Government if the officer is found by a court of inquiry constituted by [4][the Chief of the Army Staff] in this behalf, to have deserted to the enemy, or while in enemy hands, to have served with, or under the orders of the enemy, or in any manner to have aided the enemy, or to have allowed himself to be taken prisoner by the enemy through want of due precaution or through disobedience of orders or wilful neglect of duty, or having been taken prisoner by the enemy, to have failed to rejoin his service when it was possible to do so;

(i) any sum required by order of the Central Government [5][or any prescribed officers] to be paid for the maintenance of his wife or his legitimate or illegitimate child or towards the cost of any relief given by the said Government to the said wife or child.

91. Deductions from pay and allowances of persons other than officers. Subject to the provisions of Section 94 the following penal deductions may be made from the pay and allowances of a person subject to this, Act other than an officer, that is to say -

(a) all pay and allowances for every day of absence either on desertion or without leave, or as a prisoner of war, and for every day of transportation or imprisonment awarded by a criminal court, a court-martial or an officer exercising authority under Section 80;

(b) all pay and allowances for every day while he is in custody on a charge for an offence of which he is afterwards convicted by a criminal court or a court-martial, or on a charge of absence without leave for which he is afterwards awarded imprisonment [6][by an officer exercising authority under Section 80;

(c) all pay and allowances for every day on which he is in hospital on account of sickness certified by the medical officer attending on him to have been caused by an offence under this Act committed by him;

(d) for every day on which he is in hospital on account of sickness certified by the medical officer attending on him to have been caused by his own misconduct or imprudence, such sum as may be specified by order of the Central Government or such officer as may be specified by that Government;

(e) all pay and allowances ordered by a court-martial or by an officer exercising authority under any of the Sections 80, 83, 84 and 85, to be forfeited or stopped;

(f) all pay and allowances for every day between his being recovered from the enemy and his dismissal from the service in consequence of his conduct when being taken prisoner by, or while in the hands of, the enemy;

(g) any sum required to make good such compensation for any expenses, loss, damage or destruction caused by him to the Central Government or to any building or property as may be awarded by his commanding officer;

(h) any sum required to, pay a fine awarded by a criminal court, a court-martial exercising jurisdiction under Section 69, or an officer exercising authority under any of the Sections 80 and 89;

(i) any sum required by order of the Central Government or any prescribed officer to be paid for the maintenance of his wife or his legitimate or illegitimate child or towards the cost of any relief given by the said Government to the said wife or child.

92. Computation of time of absence or custody. For the purposes of clauses (a) and (b) of Section 91 -

(a) no person shall be treated as absent or in custody for a day unless the absence or custody has lasted, whether wholly in one day, or partly in one day and partly in another, for six consecutive hours or upwards;

(b) any absence or custody for less than a day may be reckoned as absence or custody for a day if such absence or custody prevented the absentee from fulfilling any military duty which was thereby thrown upon some other person;

(c) absence or custody for twelve consecutive hours or upwards may be reckoned as absence or custody for the whole of each day during any portion of which the person was absent or in custody;

(d) a period of absence, or imprisonment, which commences before, and ends after, midnight may be reckoned as a day.

93. Pay and allowances during trial. In the case of any person subject to this Act who is in custody or under suspension from duty on a charge for an offence, the prescribed officer may direct that the whole or any part of the pay and allowances of such person shall be withheld, pending the result of his trial on the charge against him, in order to give effect to the provisions of clause (b) of Sections 90 and 91.

94. Limit of certain deductions. The total deductions from the pay and allowances of a person made under clauses (e), (g) to (i) of Section 91 shall not, except where he is sentenced to dismissal, exceed in any one month one-half of his pay and allowances for that month.

95. Deduction from public money due to a person. Any sum authorised by this Act to be deducted from the pay and allowances of any person may, without prejudice to any other mode of recovering the same, be deducted from any public money due to him other than a pension.

96. Pay and allowances of prisoner of war during inquiry into his conduct. Where the conduct of any person subject to this Act when being taken prisoner by, or while in the hands of the enemy, is to be inquired into under this Act or any other law, [4][the Chief of the Army Staff] or any officer authorised by him may order that the whole or any part of the pay and allowances of such person shall be withheld pending the result of such inquiry.

97. Remission of deductions. Any deduction from pay and allowances authorised by this Act may be remitted in such manner and to such extent, and by such authority, as may from time to time be prescribed.

98. Provision for dependants of prisoner of war from remitted deductions. In the case of all persons subject to this Act, being prisoners of war, whose pay and allowances have been forfeited under clause (h) of Section 90 or clause (a) of Section 91, but in respect of whom a remission has been made under Section 97, it shall be lawful for proper provision to be made by the prescribed authorities out of such pay and allowances for any dependants of such persons, and any such remission shall in that case be deemed to apply only to the balance thereafter remaining of such pay and allowances.

99. Provision for dependants of prisoner war from his pay and allowances. It shall be lawful for proper provision to be made by the prescribed authorities for any dependants of any person subject to this Act who is a prisoner of war or is missing, out of his pay and allowances.

100. Period during which a person is deemed to be a prisoner of war. For the purposes of Sections 98 and 99, a person shall be deemed to continue to be a prisoner of war until the conclusion of any inquiry into his conduct such as is referred to in Section 96, and if he is cashiered or dismissed from the service in consequence of such conduct, until the date of such cashiering or dismissal.

CHAPTER - IX : ARREST AND PROCEEDINGS BEFORE TRIAL

101. Custody of offenders.

(1) Any person subject to this Act who is charged with an offence may be taken into military custody.

(2) Any such person may be ordered into military custody by any superior officer.

(3) An officer may order into military custody any officer, though he may be of a higher rank, engaged in a quarrel, affray or disorder.

102. Duty of commanding officer in regard to detention.

(1) It shall be the duty of every commanding officer to take care that a person under his command when charged with an offence is not detained in custody for more than forty-eight hours after the committal of such person into custody is reported to him, without the charge being investigated, unless investigation within that period seems to him to be impracticable having regard to the public service.

(2) The case of every person being detained in custody beyond a period of forty-eight hours, and the reason thereof, shall be reported by the commanding officer to the general or other officer to whom application would be made to convene a general or district court-martial for the trial of the person charged.

(3) In reckoning the period of forty-eight hours specified in sub-section (1), Sundays and other public holidays shall be excluded.

(4) Subject to the provisions of this Act, the Central Government may make rules providing for the manner in which and the period for which any person subject to this Act may be taken into and detained in military custody, pending the trial by any competent authority for any offence committed by him.

103. Interval between commital and court-martial. In every case where any such person as is mentioned in Section 101 and as is not on active service remains in such custody for a longer period than eight days, without a court-martial for his trial being ordered to assemble, a special report giving reasons for the delay shall be made by his commanding officer in the manner prescribed, and a similar report shall be forwarded at intervals of every eight days until a court-martial is assembled or such person is released from custody.

104. Arrest by civil authorities. Whenever any person subject to this Act, who is accused of any offence under this Act, is within the jurisdiction of any magistrate or police officer, such magistrate or police officer shall aid in the apprehension and delivery to military custody of such person upon receipt of a written application to that effect signed by his commanding officer.

105. Capture of deserters.

(1) Whenever any person subject to this Act deserts, the commanding officer of the corps, department or detachment to which he belongs, shall give written information of the desertion to such civil authorities as, in his opinion, may be able to afford assistance towards the capture of the deserter; and such authorities shall thereupon take steps for the apprehension of the said deserter in like manner as if he were a person for whose apprehension a warrant had been

issued by a magistrate, and shall deliver the deserter. when apprehended, into military custody.

(2) Any police officer may arrest without warrant any person reasonably believed to be subject to this Act, and to be a deserter or to be travelling without authority, and shall bring him without delay before the nearest magistrate, to be dealt with according to law.

106. Inquiry into absence without leave.

(1) When any person subject to this Act has been absent from his duty without due authority for a period of thirty days, a court of inquiry shall, as soon as practicable, be assembled, and such court shall, on oath or affirmation administered in the prescribed manner, inquire respecting the absence of the person, and the deficiency, if any, in the property of the Government entrusted to his care, or in any arms, ammunition, equipment, instruments, clothing or necessaries; and if satisfied of the fact of such absence without due authority or other sufficient cause, the court shall declare such absence and the period thereof, and the said deficiency, if any, and the commanding officer of the corps or department to which the person belongs shall enter in the court-martial book of the corps or department a record of the declaration.

(2) If the person declared absent does not afterwards surrender or is not apprehended, he. shall, for the purposes of this Act, be deemed to be a deserter.

107. Provost-marshals.

(1) Provost-marshals may be appointed by [4][the Chief of the Army Staff] or by any prescribed officer.

(2) The duties of a provost-marshal are to take charge of persons confined for any offence, to preserve good order and discipline, and to prevent breaches of the same by persons serving in, or attached to, the regular Army.

(3) A provost-marshal may act any time arrest and detain for trial any person subject to this Act who commits, or is charged with, an offence, and may also carry into effect any punishment to be inflicted in pursuance of the sentence awarded by a court-martial, or by an officer exercising authority under Section 80 but shall not inflict any punishment on his own authority:

PROVIDED that no officer shall be so arrested or detained otherwise than on the order of another officer.

(4) For the purposes of sub-sections (2) and (3), a provost-marshal shall be deemed to include a provost-marshal appointed under any law for the time being in force relating to the Government of the Navy or Air Force, and any person legally exercising authority under him or on his behalf.

CHAPTER - X : COURTS-MARTIAL

108. Kinds of courts-martial. For the purposes of this Act there shall be four kinds of courts-martial, that is to say -

(a) general courts-martial;

(b) district courts-martial;

(c) summary general courts-martial; and

(d) summary courts-martial.

109. Power to convene a general court-martial. A general court-martial may be convened by the Central Government or [4][the Chief of the Army Staff] or by any officer empowered in this behalf by warrant of [4][the Chief of the Army Staff].

110. Power to convene a district court-martial. A district court-martial may be convened by an officer having power to convene a general court-martial or by any officer empowered in this behalf by warrant of any such officer.

111. Contents of warrants issued under Sections 109 and 110. A warrant issued under Section 109 or Section 110 may contain such restrictions, reservations or conditions as the officer issuing, it may think fit.

112. Power to convene a summary general court-martial. The following authorities shall have power to convene a summary general court-martial, namely -

(a) an officer empowered in this behalf by an order of the Central Government or of [4][the Chief of the Army Staff];

(b) on active service, the officer commanding the forces in the field, or any officer empowered by him in this behalf;

(c) an officer commanding any detached portion of the regular Army on active service when, in his opinion, it is not practicable, with due regard to discipline and the exigencies of the service, that an offence should be tried by a general court-martial.

113. Composition of general court-martial. A general court-martial shall consist of not less than five officers, each of whom has held a commission for not less than three whole years and of whom not less than four are of a rank not below that of captain.

114. Composition of district court-martial. A district court-martial shall consist of not less than three officers, each of whom has held a commission for not less than two whole years.

115. Composition of summary general court-martial. A summary general court-martial shall consist of not less than three officers.

116. Summary court-martial.

(1) A summary court-martial may be held by the commanding officer of any corps, department or detachment of the regular Army, and he shall alone constitute the court.

(2) The proceedings shall be attended throughout by two other persons who shall be officers or junior commissioned officers or one of either, and who shall not as such, be sworn or affirmed.

117. Dissolution of courts-martial.

(1) If a court-martial after the commencement of a trial is reduced below the minimum number of officers required by this Act, it shall be dissolved.

(2) If, on account of the illness of the judge advocate or of the accused before the finding, it is impossible to continue the trial, a court-martial shall be dissolved.

(3) The officer who convened a court-martial may dissolve such court-martial if it appears to him that military exigencies or the necessities of discipline render it impossible or inexpedient to continue the said court-martial.

(4) Where a court-martial is dissolved under this Section, the accused may be tried again.

118. Powers of general and summary general courts-martial. A general or summary general court-martial shall have power to try any person subject to this Act for any offence punishable therein and to pass any sentence authorised thereby.

119. Powers of district courts-martial. A district court-martial shall have power to try any person subject to this Act other than an officer or a junior commissioned officer for any offence made punishable therein, and to pass any sentence authorised by this Act other than a sentence of death, transportation, or imprisonment for a term exceeding two years:

PROVIDED that a district court-martial shall not sentence a warrant officer to imprisonment.

120. Powers of summary courts-martial.

(1) Subject to the provisions of sub-section (2), a summary court-martial may try any offence punishable under this Act.

(2) When there is no grave reason for immediate action and reference can without detriment to discipline be made to the officer empowered to convene a district court-martial or on active service a summary general court-martial for the trial of the alleged offender, an officer holding a summary court-martial shall not try without such reference any offence punishable under any of the Sections 34, 37 and 69, or any offence against the officer holding the court.

(3) A summary court-martial may try any person subject to this Act and under the command of the officer holding the court, except an officer, junior commissioned officer or warrant officer.

(4) A summary court-martial may pass any sentence which may be passed under this Act, except a sentence of death or transportation, or of imprisonment for a term exceeding the limit specified in sub-section (5).

(5) The limit referred to in sub-section (4) shall be one year if the officer holding the summary court-martial is of the rank of lieutenant-colonel and upwards, and three months if such officer is below that rank.

121. Prohibition of second trial. When any person subject to this Act has been acquitted or convicted of an offence by a court-martial or by a criminal court, or has been dealt with under any of the Sections 80, 83, 84 and 85, he shall not be liable to be tried again for the same offence by a court-martial or dealt with under the said Sections.

122. Period of limitation for trial.

(1) Except as provided by sub-section (2), no trial by court-martial of any person subject to this Act for any offence shall be commenced after the expiration of a period of three years 1[and such period shall commence -

(a) on the date of the offence; or

(b) where the commission of the offence was not known to the person aggrieved by the offence or to the authority com-petent to initiate action, the first day on which such offence comes to the knowledge of such person or authority, whichever is earlier; or

(c) where it is not known by whom the offence was committed, the first day on which the identity of the offender is known to the person aggrieved by the offence or to the authority competent to initiate action, whichever is earlier.]

(2) The provisions of sub-section (1) shall not apply to a trial for an offence of desertion or fraudulent enrolment or for any of the offences mentioned in Section 37.

(3) In the computation of the period of time mentioned in sub-section (1), any time spent by such person as a prisoner of war, or in enemy territory, or in evading arrest after the commission of the offence, shall be excluded.

(4) No trial for an offence of desertion other than desertion on active service or of fraudulent enrolment shall be commenced if the person in question, not being an officer, has subsequently to the commission of the offence, served continuously in an exemplary manner for not less than three years with any portion of the regular Army.

123. Liability of offender who ceases to be subject to Act.

(1) Where an offence under this Act had been committed by any person while subject to this Act, and he has ceased to be so subject, he may be taken into and kept in military custody, and tried and punished for such offence as if he continued to be so subject.

(2) No such person shall be tried for an offence, unless his trial commences 1[within a period of three years after he had ceased to be subject to this Act; and in computing such period, the time during which such person has avoided arrest by absconding or concealing himself or where the institution of the proceeding in respect of the offence has been stayed by an injunction or order, the period of the continuance of the injunction or order, the day on which it was issued or made, and the day on which it was withdrawn, shall be excluded]:

PROVIDED that nothing contained in this sub-section shall apply to the trial of any such person for an offence of desertion or fraudulent enrolment or for any of the offences mentioned in Section 37 or shall affect the jurisdiction of a criminal court to try any offence triable by such court as well as by a court-martial.

(3) When a person subject to this Act is sentenced by a court-martial to transportation or imprisonment, this Act shall apply to him during the term of his sentence, though he is cashiered or dismissed from the regular Army, or has otherwise ceased to be subject to this Act, and he may be kept, removed, imprisoned and punished as if he continued to be subject to this Act.

(4) When a person subject to this Act is sentenced by a court-martial to death, this Act shall apply to him till the sentence is carried out.

124. Place of trial. Any person subject to this Act who commits any offence against it may be tried and punished for such offence in any place whatever.

125. Choice between criminal court and court-martial. When a criminal court and a court-martial have each jurisdiction in respect of an offence, it shall be in the discretion of the officer commanding the army, army corps, division or independent brigade in which the accused person is serving or such other officer as may be prescribed to decide before which court the proceedings shall be instituted, and, if that officer decides that they should be instituted before a court-martial, to direct that the accused person shall be detained in military custody.

126. Power of criminal court to require delivery of offender.

(1) When a criminal court having jurisdiction is of opinion that proceedings shall be instituted before itself in respect of any alleged offence, it may, by written notice, require the officer referred to in Section 125 at his option, either to deliver over the offender to the nearest magistrate to be proceeded against according to law, or to postpone proceedings pending a reference to the Central Government.

(2) In every such case the said officer shall either deliver over the offender in compliance with the requisition, or shall forthwith refer the question as to the court before which the proceedings are to be instituted for the determination of the Central Government, whose order upon such reference shall be final.

CHAPTER - XI : PROCEDURE OF COURTS-MARTIAL

128. Presiding officer. At every general, district or summary general court-martial the senior member shall be the presiding officer.

129. Judge advocate. Every general court-martial shall, and every district or summary general court-martial may, be attended by a judge advocate, who shall be either an officer belonging to the department of the Judge Advocate General, or if no such officer is available, an officer approved of by the Judge Advocate General or any of his deputies.

130. Challenges.

(1) At all trials by general, district or summary general court-martial, as soon as the court is assembled, the names of the presiding officer and members shall be read over to the accused, who shall thereupon be asked whether he objects to being tried by any officer sitting on the court.

(2) If the accused objects to any such officer, his objection, and also the reply thereto of the officer objected to, shall be heard and recorded, and the remaining officers of the court shall, in the absence of the challenged officer decide on the objection.

(3) If the objection is allowed by one-half or more of the votes of the officers entitled to vote, the objection shall be allowed, and the member objected to shall retire, and his vacancy may be filled in the prescribed manner by another officer subject to the same right of the accused to object.

(4) When no challenge is made, or when challenge has been made and disallowed, or the place of every officer successfully challenged has been filled by another officer to whom no objection is made or allowed, the court shall proceed with the trial.

131. Oaths of member, judge advocate and witness.

(1) An oath or affirmation in the prescribed manner shall be administered to every member of every court-martial and to the judge advocate before the commencement of the trial.

(2) Every person giving evidence before a court-martial shall be examined after being duly sworn or affirmed in the prescribed form.

(3) The provisions of sub-section (2) shall not apply where the witness is a child under twelve years of age and the court-martial is of opinion that though the witness understands the duty of speaking the truth, he does not understand the nature of an oath or affirmation.

132. Voting by members.

(1) Subject to the provisions of sub-sections (2) and (3), every decision of a court-martial shall be passed by an absolute majority of votes; and where there is an equality of votes on either the finding or the sentence, the decision shall be in favour of the accused.

(2) No sentence of death shall be passed by a general court-martial without the concurrence of at least two-thirds of the members of the court.

(3) No sentence of death shall be passed by a summary general court-martial without the concurrence of all the members.

(4) In matters, other than a challenge or the finding or sentence, the presiding officer shall have a casting vote.

133. General rule as to evidence. The Indian Evidence Act, 1872 (1 of 1872), shall, subject to the provisions of this Act, apply to all proceedings before a court-martial.

134. Judicial notice. A court-martial may take judicial notice of any matter within the general military knowledge of the members.

135. Summoning withnesses.

(1) The convening officer, the presiding officer of a court-martial, 1[or courts of inquiry] the judge advocate or the commanding officer of the accused person may, by summons under his hand, require the attendance, at a time and place to be mentioned in the summons, of any person either to give evidence or to produce any document or other thing.

(2) In the case of a witness amenable to military authority, the summons shall be sent to his commanding officer, and such officer shall serve it upon him accordingly.

(3) In the case of any other witness, the summons shall be sent to the magistrate within whose jurisdiction he may be or reside, and such magistrate shall give effect to the summons as if the witness were required in the court of such magistrate.

(4) When a witness is required to produce any particular document or other thing in his possession or power, the summons shall describe it with reasonable precision.

136. Documents exempted from production.

(1) Nothing in Section 135 shall be deemed to affect the operation of Sections 123 and 124 of the Indian Evidence Act 1872 (1 of 1872), or to apply to any letter, postcard, telegram or other document in the custody of the postal or telegraph authorities.

(2) If any document in such custody is, in the opinion of any district magistrate, chief presidency magistrate, High Court or Court of Session, wanted for the purpose of any court-martial, such magistrate or Court may require the postal or telegraph authorities, as the case may be, to deliver such document to such person as such magistrate or Court may direct.

(3) If any such document is, in the opinion of any other magistrate or of any commissioner of police or district superintendent of police, wanted for any such purpose, he may require the postal or telegraph authorities, as the case may be, to cause search to be made for and to detain such document pending the orders of any such district magistrate, chief presidency magistrate or High Court or Court of Session.

137. Commissions for examination of withness.

(1) Whenever, in the course of a trial by court-martial, it appears to the Court that the examination of a witness is necessary for the ends of justice, and that the attendance of such witness cannot be procured without an amount of delay, expense or inconvenience which, in the circumstances of the case, would be unreasonable, such Court may address the Judge Advocate General in order that a commission to take the evidence of such witness may be issued.

(2) The Judge Advocate General may then, if he thinks necessary, issue a commission to any district magistrate or magistrate of the first class, within the local limits of whose jurisdiction such witness resides, to take the evidence of such witness.

(3) The magistrate or officer to whom the commission is issued, or, if he is the district magistrate, he or such magistrate of the first class as he appoints in this behalf, shall proceed to the place where the witness is or shall summon the witness before him and shall take down his evidence in the same manner, and may for this purpose exercise the same powers, as in trials of warrant-cases under the [5][code of Criminal Procedure, 1973] (2 of 1974) on any corresponding law in force in the State of Jammu and Kashmir.

(4) When the witness resides in a tribal area or in any place outside India, the commission may be issued in the manner specified in [5][Chapter XXII of the Code of Criminal Procedure, 1973] (2 of 1974) or of any corresponding law om force in the State of Jammu and Kashmir.

(5) In this and the next succeeding Section, the expression “Judge Advocate General” includes a Deputy Judge Advocate General.

138. Examination of a withness on commission.

(1) The prosecutors and the accused person in any case in which a commission is issued under Section 137 may respectively forward any interrogatories in writing which the Court may think relevant to the issue, and the magistrate or officer executing the commission shall examine the witness upon such interrogatories.

(2) The prosecutor and the accused person may appear before such magistrate or officer by counsel or, except in the case of an accused person in custody, in person, and may examine, cross-examine and re-examine, as the case may be, the said witness.

(3) After a commission issued under Section 137 has been duly executed, it shall be returned, together with the deposition of the witness examined thereunder, to the Judge Advocate General.

(4) On receipt of a commission and deposition returned under subsection (3), the Judge Advocate General shall forward the same to the Court at whose instance the commission was issued or, if such Court has been dissolved, to any other Court convened for the trial of the accused person; and the commission, the return thereto and the deposition shall be open to inspection by the prosecutor and the accused person, and may, subject to all just exceptions, be read in evidence in the case by either the prosecutor or the accused, and shall form part of the proceedings of the Court.

(5) In every case in which a commission is issued under Section 137, the trial may be adjourned for a specified time reasonably sufficient for the execution and return of the commission.

139. Conviction of offence not charged.

(1) A person charged before a court-martial with desertion may be found guilty of attempting to desert or of being absent without leave.

(2) A person charged before a court-martial with attempting to desert may be found guilty of being absent without leave.

(3) A person charged before a court-martial with using criminal force may be found guilty of assault.

(4) A person charged before a court-martial with using threatening language may be found guilty of using insubordinate language.

(5) A person charged before a court-martial with any one of the offences specified in clauses (a), (b), (c) and (d) of Section 52 may be found guilty of any other of these offences with which he might have been charged.

(6) A person charged before a court-martial with an offence punishable under Section 69 may be found guilty of any other offence of which he might have been found guilty if the provisions of the 1[Code of Criminal Procedure, 1973] (2 of 1974) were applicable.

(7) A person charged before a court-martial with any offence under this Act, may,

on failure of proof of an offence having been committed in circumstances involving a more severe punishment, be found guilty of the same offence as having been committed in circumstances involving a less severe punishment.

(8) A person charged before a court-martial with any offence under this Act may be found guilty of having attempted or abetted the commission of that offence, although the attempt or abetment is not separately charged.

140. Presumption as to signatures. In any proceeding under this Act, any application, certificate, warrant, reply or other document purporting to be signed by an officer in the service of the Government shall, on production, be presumed to have been duly signed by the person by whom and in the character in which it purports to have been signed, until the contrary is shown.

141. Enrolment paper.

(1) Any enrolment paper purporting to be signed by an enrolling officer shall, in proceedings under this Act, be evidence of the person enrolled having given the answers to questions which he is therein represented as having given.

(2) The enrolment of such person may be proved by the production of the original or a copy of his enrolment paper purporting to be certified to be a true copy by the officer having the custody of the enrolment paper.

142. Presumption as to certain documents.

(1) A letter, return or other document respecting the service of any person in, or the cashiering, dismissal or discharge of any person from, any portion of the regular Army, or respecting the circumstance of any person not having served in, or belonged to, any portion of the Forces, if purporting to be signed by or on behalf of the Central Government or [4][the Chief of the Army Staff], or by any prescribed officer, shall be evidence of the facts stated in such letter, return or other document.

(2) An Army, Navy or Air Force List or Gazette purporting to be published by authority shall be evidence of the status and rank of the officers, junior commissioned officers or warrant officers therein mentioned, and of any appointment held by them and of the corps, battalion or arm or branch of the services to which they belong.

(3) Where a record is made in any regimental book in pursuance of this Act or of any rules made thereunder or otherwise in pursuance of military duty, and purports to be signed by the commanding officer or by the officer whose duty it is to make such record, such record shall be evidence of the facts therein stated.

(4) A copy of any record in any regimental book purporting to be certified to be a true copy by the officer having custody of such book shall be evidence of such record.

(5) Where any person subject to this Act is being tried on a charge of desertion or of absence without leave, and such person has surrendered himself into the custody of any officer or other person subject to this Act, or any portion of the regular Army, or has been apprehended by such officer or person, a certificate purporting to be signed by such officer, or by the commanding officer of that portion of the regular Army, or by the commanding officer of the corps, department

or detachment to which such person belongs, as the case may be, and stating the fact, date and place of such surrender or apprehension, and the manner in which he was dressed, shall be evidence of the matters so stated.

(6) Where any person subject to this Act is being tried on a charge of desertion or of absence without leave, and such person has surrendered himself into the custody of, or has been apprehended by, a police officer not below the rank of an officer in charge of a police station, a certificate purporting to be signed by such police officer and stating the fact, date and place of such surrender or apprehension and the manner in which he was dressed shall be evidence of the matters so stated.

(7) Any document purporting to be a report under the hand of any Chemical Examiner or Assistant Chemical Examiner to Government [4][or any of the Government scientific experts namely, the Chief Inspector of the Explosives, the Director of Finger Print Bureau, the Director, Haffkeine Institute, Bombay, the Director of a Central Forensic Science Laboratory or a State Forensic Science Laboratory and the Serologist to the Government] upon any matter or thing duly submitted to him for examination or analysis and report may be used as evidence in any proceeding under this Act.

143. Reference by accused to Government officer.

(1) If at any trial for desertion or absence without leave, overstaying leave or not rejoining when warned for service, the person tried states in his defence any sufficient or reasonable excuse for his unauthorised absence, and refers in support thereof to any officer in the service of the Government, or if it appears that any such officer is likely to prove or disprove the said statement in the defence, the court shall address such officer and adjourn the proceedings until his reply is received.

(2) The written reply of any officer so referred to shall, if signed by him be received in evidence and have the same effect as if made on oath before the court.

(3) If the court is dissolved before the receipt of such reply, or if the court omits to comply with the provisions of this Section, the convening officer may, at his discretion, annul the proceedings and order a fresh trial.

144. Evidence of previous convictions and general character.

(1) When any person subject to this Act has been convicted by a court-martial of any offence, such court-martial may inquire into, and receive and record evidence of any previous convictions of such person, either by a court-martial or by a criminal court, or any previous award of punishment under any of the Sections 80, 83, 84 and 85, and may further inquire into and record the general character of such person and such other matters as may be prescribed.

(2) Evidence received under this Section may be either oral, or in the shape of entries in, or certified extracts from, court-martial books or other official records; and it shall not be necessary to give notice before trial to the person tried that evidence as to his previous convictions or character will be received.

(3) At a summary court-martial the officer holding the trial may, if he thinks fit, record any previous convictions against the offender, his general character, and such other matters as may be prescribed, as of his own knowledge, instead of requiring them to be proved under the foregoing provisions of this Section.

145. Lunacy of accused.

(1) Whenever, in the course of a trial by a court-martial, it appears to the court that the person charged is by reason of unsoundness of mind incapable of making his defence, or that he committed the act alleged but was by reason of unsoundness of mind incapable of knowing the nature of the act or knowing that it was wrong or contrary to law, the court shall record a finding accordingly.

(2) The presiding officer of the court, or, in the case of a summary court-martial, the officer holding the trial, shall forthwith report the case to the confirming officer, or to the authority empowered to deal with its finding under Section 162, as the case may be.

(3) The confirming officer to whom the case is reported under subsection (2) may, if he does not confirm the finding, take steps to have the accused person tried by the same or another court-martial for the offence with which he was charged.

(4) The authority to whom the finding of a summary court-martial is reported under sub-section (2), and a confirming officer confirming a finding in any case so reported to him shall order the accused person to be kept in custody in the prescribed manner and shall report the case for the orders of the Central Government.

(5) On receipt of a report under sub-section (4) the Central Government may order the accused person to be detained in a lunatic asylum or other suitable place of safe custody.

146. Subsequent fitness of lunatic accused for trial. Where any accused person, having been found by reason of unsoundness of mind to be incapable of making his defence, is in custody or under detention under Section 145, the officer commanding the army, army corps, division or brigade within the area of whose command the accused is in custody or is detained, or any other officer prescribed in this behalf, may-

(a) if such person is in custody under sub-section (4) of Section 145, on the report of a medical officer that he is capable of making his defence, or

(b) if such person is detained in a jail under sub-section (5) of Section 145, on a certificate of the Inspector General of Prisons, and if such person is detained in a lunatic asylum under the said sub-section on a certificate of any two or more of the visitors of such asylum that he is capable of making his defence, take steps to have such person tried by the same or another court-martial for the offence with which he was originally charged or, if the offence is a civil offence, by a criminal court.

147. Transmission to Central Government of orders under Section 146. A copy of every order made by an officer under Section 146 for the trial of the accused shall forthwith be sent to the Central Government.

148. Release of lunatic accused. Where any person is in custody under sub-section (4) of Section 145 or under detention under sub-section (5) of that Section-

(a) if such person is in custody under the said sub-section (4), on the report of a medical officer, or

(b) if such person is detained under the said sub-section (5), on a certificate from any of the authorities mentioned in clause (b) of Section 146 that, in the judgment of such officer or authority such person may be released without danger of his doing injury to himself or to any other person, the Central Government may order that such person be released or detained in custody, or transferred to a public lunatic asylum if he has not already been sent to such an asylum.

149. Delivery of lunatic accused to relatives. Where any relative or friend of any person who is in custody under sub-section (4) of Section 145 or under detention under sub-section (5) of that Section desires that he should be delivered to his care and custody, the Central Government may upon application by such relative or friend and on his giving security to the satisfaction of that Government that the person delivered shall be properly taken care of and prevented from doing injury to himself or any other person, and be produced for the inspection of such officer, and at such times and places, as the Central Government may direct, order such person to be delivered to such relative or friend.

150. Order for custody and disposal of property pending trial. When any property regarding which any offence appears to have been committed, or which appears to have been used for the commission of any offence, is produced before a court-martial during a trial, the court may make such order as it thinks fit for the proper custody of such property pending the conclusion of the trial, and if the property is subject to speedy or natural decay may, after recording such evidence as it thinks necessary, order it to be sold or otherwise disposed of.

151. Order for disposal of property regarding which offence is committed.

(1) After the conclusion of a trial before any court-martial, the Court or the officer confirming the finding or sentence of such court-martial, or any authority superior to such officer, or, in the case of a court-martial whose finding or sentence does not require confirmation, the officer commanding the army, army corps, division or brigade within which the trial was held, may make such order as it or he thinks fit for the disposal by destruction, confiscation, delivery to any person claiming to be entitled to possession thereof, or otherwise, of any property or document produced before the Court or in its custody, or regarding which any offence appears to have been committed or which has been used for the commission of any offence.

(2) Where any order has been made under sub-section (1) in respect of property regarding which an offence appears to have been committed, a copy of such order signed and certified by the authority making the same may, whether the trial was held within India or not, be sent to a magistrate within whose jurisdiction such property for the time being is situated, and such magistrate shall thereupon cause the order to be carried into effect as if it were an order passed by him under the provisions of the [5][Code of Criminal Procedure, 1973]

(2 of 1974), or any corresponding law in force in [4][the State of Jammu and Kashmir].

(3) In this Section the term "property" includes, in the case of property regarding which an offence appears to have been committed, not only such property as has been originally in the possession or under the control of any person, but also any property into or for which the same may have been converted or exchanged, and anything acquired by such conversion or exchange whether immediately or otherwise.

152. Powers of court-martial in relation to proceedings under this Act. Any trial by a court-martial under the provisions of this Act shall be deemed to be a judicial proceeding within the meaning of Sections 193 and 228 of the Indian Penal Code (45 of 1860), and the court-martial shall be deemed to be a Court within the meaning of Sections 345 and 346 of the Code of Criminal Procedure, 1973 (2 of 1974).

CHAPTER - XII : CONFIRMATION AND REVISION

153. Finding and sentence not valid, unless confirmed. No finding or sentence of a general, district or summary general, court-martial shall be valid except so far as it may be confirmed as provided by this Act.

154. Power to confirm finding and sentence of general court-martial. The findings and sentences of general courts-martial may be confirmed by the Central Government, or by any officer empowered in this behalf by warrant of the Central Government.

155. Power to confirm finding and sentence of district court-martial. The findings and sentences of district courts-martial may be confirmed by any officer having power to convene a general court-martial or by any officer empowered in this behalf by warrant of such officer.

156. Limitation of powers of confirming authority. A warrant issued under Section 154 or Section 155 may contain such restrictions, reservations or conditions as the authority issuing it may think fit.

157. Power to confirm finding and sentence of summary general court-martial. The findings and sentences of summary general courts-martial may be confirmed by the convening officer or if he so directs, by an authority superior to him.

158. Power of confirming authority to mitigate, remit or commute sentences.

(1) Subject to such restrictions, reservations or conditions as may be contained in any warrant issued under Section 154 or Section 155 and to the provision of sub-section (2), a confirming authority may, when confirming the sentence of a court-martial, mitigate or remit the punishment thereby awarded, or commute that punishment for any punishment or punishments lower in the scale laid down in Section 71.

(2) A sentence of transportation shall not be commuted for a sentence of imprisonment for a term exceeding the term of trans-portation awarded by the Court.

159. Confirming of findings and sentences on board a ship. When any person subject to this Act is tried and sentenced by a court-martial while on board a ship, the finding and sentence so far as not confirmed and executed on board the ship, may be confirmed and executed in like manner as if such person had been tried at the port of disembarkation.

160. Revision of finding or sentence.

(1) Any finding or sentence of a court-martial which requires confirmation may be once revised by order of the confirming authority and on such revision, the Court, if so directed by the confirming authority, may take additional evidence.

(2) The Court, on revision, shall consist of the same officers as were present when the original decision was passed, unless any of those officers are unavoidably absent.

(3) In case of such unavoidable absence the cause thereof shall be duly certified in the proceedings, and the Court shall proceed with the revision, provided that, if a general court-martial, it still consists of five officers, or, if a summary general or district court-martial, of three officers.

161. Finding and sentence of a summary court-martial.

(1) Save as otherwise provided in sub-section (2), the finding and sentence of a summary court-martial shall not require to be confirmed, but may be carried out forthwith.

(2) If the officer holding the trial is of less than five years service, he shall not, except on active service, carry into effect any sentence until it has received the approval of an officer commanding not less than a brigade.

162. Transmission of proceedings of summary court-martial. The proceedings of every summary court-martial shall without delay be forwarded to the officer commanding the division or brigade within which the trial was held, or to the prescribed officer; and such officer, or [4][the Chief of the Army Staff], or any officer empowered in this behalf by [4][the Chief of the Army Staff], may, for reasons based on the merits of the case, but not any merely technical grounds, set aside the proceedings or reduce the sentence to any other sentence which the court might have passed.

163. Alteration of finding or sentence in certain cases.

(1) Where a finding of guilty by a court-martial, which has been confirmed, or which does not require confirmation, is found for any reason to be invalid or cannot be supported by the evidence, the authority which would have had power under Section 179 to commute the punishment awarded by the sentence, if the finding had been valid, may substitute a new finding and pass a sentence for the offence specified or involved in such finding:

PROVIDED that no such substitution shall be made unless such finding could have been validly made by the court-martial on the charge and unless it appears that the court-martial must have been satisfied of the facts establishing the said offence.

(2) Where a sentence passed by a court-martial which has been confirmed, or which does not require confirmation, not being a sen-tence passed in pursuance of a new finding substituted under sub-section (1), is found for any reason to be invalid, the authority referred to in sub-section (1) may pass a valid sentence.

(3) The punishment awarded by a sentence passed under sub-section (1) or sub-section (2) shall not be higher in the scale of punishments than, or in excess of, the punishment awarded by, the sentence for which a new sentence is substituted under this Section.

(4) Any finding substituted, or any sentence passed, under this Section shall, for the purposes of this Act and the rules made thereunder, have effect as if it were a finding or sentence, as the case may be, of a court-martial.

164. Remedy against order, finding or sentence of court-martial.

(1) Any person subject to this Act who considers himself aggrieved by any order passed by any court-martial may present a petition to the officer or authority empowered to confirm any finding or sentence of such court-martial, and the confirming authority may take such steps as may be considered necessary to satisfy itself as to the correctness, legality or propriety of the order passed or as to the regularity of any proceeding to which the order relates.

(2) Any person subject to this Act who considers himself aggrieved by a finding or sentence of any court-martial which has been confirmed, may present a petition to the Central Government, [4][the Chief of the Army Staff] or any prescribed officer superior in command to the one who confirmed such finding or sentence, and the Central Government, [4][the Chief of the Army Staff] or other officer, as the case may be, may pass such order thereon as it or he thinks fit.

165. Annulment of proceedings. The Central Government, [4][the Chief of the Army Staff] or any prescribed officer may annul the proceedings of any court-martial on the ground that they are illegal or unjust.

CHAPTER - XIII : EXECUTION OF SENTENCES

166. Form of sentence of death. In awarding a sentence of death a court-martial shall, in its discretion, direct that the offender shall suffer death by being hanged by the neck until he be dead, or shall suffer death by being shot to death.

167. Commencement of sentence of transportation or imprisonment. Whenever any person is sentenced by a court-martial under this Act to transportation or imprisonment, the term of his sentence shall, whether it has been revised or not, be reckoned to commence on the day on which the original proceedings were signed by the presiding officer or, in the case of a summary court-martial, by the court.

168. Execution of sentence of transportation. Whenever any sentence of transportation is passed under this Act or whenever any sentence of death is commuted to transportation, the commanding officer of the person under sentence or such other officer as may be prescribed shall forward a warrant in the prescribed form to the officer in charge of the civil prison in which such person is to be confined and shall arrange for his despatch to such prison with the warrant.

169. Execution of sentence of imprisonment.

(1) Whenever any sentence of imprisonment is passed under this Act by a court-martial or whenever any sentence of death or transportation is commuted to

imprisonment, the confirming officer or in case of a summary court-martial the officer holding the Court or such other officer as may be prescribed, shall, save as otherwise provided in sub-sections (3) and (4), direct either that the sentence shall be carried out by confinement in a military prison or that it shall be carried out by confinement in a civil prison.

(2) When a direction has been made under sub-section (1) the commanding officer of the person under sentence or such other officer as may be prescribed shall forward a warrant in the prescribed form to the officer in charge of the prison in which such person is to be confined and shall arrange for his despatch to such prison with the warrant.

(3) In the case of a sentence of imprisonment for a period not exceeding three months and passed under this Act by a court-martial, the appropriate officer under sub-section (1) may direct that the sentence shall be carried out by confinement in military custody instead of in a civil or military prison.

(4) On active service, a sentence of imprisonment may be carried out by confinement in such place as the officer commanding the forces in the field may from time to time appoint.

169A. [4][Period of custody undergone by the officer or person to be set off against the imprisonment. When a person or officer subject to this Act is sentenced by a court-martial to a term of imprisonment, not being an imprisonment in default of payment of fine, the period spent by him in civil or military custody during investigation, inquiry or trial of the same case, and before the date of order of such sentence, shall be set off against the term of imprisonment imposed upon him, and the liability of such person or officer to undergo imprisonment on such order of sentence shall be restricted to the remainder, if any, of the term of imprisonment imposed upon him.]

170. Temporary custody of offender. Where a sentence of transportation or imprisonment is directed to be undergone in a civil prison the offender may be kept in a military prison or in military custody or in any other fit place, till such time as it is possible send him to a civil prison.

171. Execution of sentence of imprisonment in special cases. Whenever, in the opinion of an officer commanding an army, army corps, division or independent brigade, any sentence or portion of a sentence of imprisonment cannot for special reasons, conveniently be carried out in a military prison or in military custody in accordance with the provision of Section 169 such officer may direct that such sentence or portion of sentence shall be carried out by confinement in any civil, prison or other fit place.

172. Conveyance of prisoner from place to place. A person under sentence of transportation or imprisonment may during his conveyance from place to place, or when on board ship, aircraft, or otherwise, be subjected to such restraint as is necessary for his safe conduct and removal.

173. Communication of certain orders to prison officers. Whenever an order is duly made under this Act setting aside or varying any sentence, order or warrant under which any person is confined in a civil or military prison, a warrant in accordance with such order shall be forwarded by the officer making the order or his staff officer or such other person as may be prescribed to the officer in charge of the prison in which such person is confined.

174. Execution of sentence of fine. When a sentence of fine is imposed by a court-martial under Section 69 whether the trial was held within India or not, a copy of such sentence, signed and certified by the confirming officer, or where no confirmation is required, by the officer holding the trial may be sent to any magistrate in India, and such magistrate shall thereupon cause the fine to be recovered in accordance with the provision of the [5][Code of Criminal Procedure, 1973] (2 of 1974), or any corresponding law in force in [4][the State of Jammu and Kashmir] for the levy of fines as if it were a sentence of fine imposed by such magistrate.

175. Establishment and regulation of military prisons. The Central Government may set apart any building or part of a building, or any place under its control, as a military prison for the confinement of persons sentenced to imprisonment under this Act.

176. Informality or error in the order or warrant. Whenever any person is sentenced to transportation or imprisonment under this Act, and is undergoing the sentence in any place or manner in which he might be confined under a lawful order or warrant in pursuance of this Act, the confinement of such person shall not be deemed to be illegal only by reason of any informality or error in or as respects the order, warrant or other document, or the authority by which, or in pursuance whereof such person was brought into or is confined in any such place, and any such order, warrant or document may be amended accordingly.

177. Power to make rules in respect of prisons and prisoners. The Central Government may make rules providing-

(a) for the government, management and regulation of military prisons;

(b) for the appointment, removal and powers of inspectors, visitors, governors and officers thereof;

(c) for the labour of prisoners undergoing confinement therein, and for enabling persons to earn, by special industry and good conduct, a remission of a portion of their sentence;

(d) for the safe custody of prisoners and the maintenance of discipline among them and the punishment, by personal correction, restraint or otherwise, of offences committed by prisoners;

(e) for the application to military prisons of any of the provisions of the Prisons Act, 1894 (9 of 1894), relating to the duties of officers of prisons and the punishment of persons not being prisoners;

(f) for the admission into any prison, at proper times and subject to proper restrictions, of persons with whom prisoners may desire to communicate, and for the consultation by prisoners under trial with their legal advisers without the presence as far as possible of any third party within hearing distance.

178. Restriction of rule-making power in regard to corporal punishment. Rules made under Section 177 shall not authorise corporal punishment to be inflicted for any offence, nor render the imprisonment more severe than it is under the law for the time being in force relating to civil prisons.

CHAPTER - XIV : PARDONS, REMISSIONS AND SUSPENSIONS

179. Pardon and remission. When any person subject to this Act has been convicted by a court-martial of any offence, the Central Government or [4][the Chief of the Army Staff] or, in the case of a sentence, which he could have confirmed or which did not, require confirmation, the officer commanding the army, army corps, division or independent brigade in which such person at the time of conviction was serving, or the prescribed officer may-

(a) either with or without conditions which the person sentenced accepts, pardon the person or remit the whole or any part of the punishment awarded; or

(b) mitigate the punishment awarded; or

(c) commute such punishment for any less punishment or punishments mentioned in this Act:

PROVIDED that a sentence of transportation shall not be commuted for a sentence of imprisonment for a term exceeding the term of transportation awarded by the court; or

(d) either with or without conditions which the person sentenced accepts, release the person on parole.

180. Cancellation of conditional pardon, release on parole or remission.

(1) If any condition on which a person has been pardoned or released on parole or a punishment has been remitted is, in the opinion of the authority which granted the pardon, release or remission, not fulfilled, such authority may cancel the pardon, release or remission, and thereupon the sentence of the court shall be carried into effect as if such pardon, release or remission had not been granted.

(2) A person whose sentence of transportation or imprisonment is carried into effect under the provisions of sub-section (1) shall undergo only the unexpired portion of his sentence.

181. Reduction of warrant officer or non-commissioned officer. When under the provisions of Section 77 a warrant officer or a non-commissioned officer is deemed to be reduced to the ranks, such reduction shall, for the purpose of Section 179, be treated as a punishment awarded by a sentence of a court-martial.

182. Suspension of sentence of transportation or imprisonment.

(1) Where a person subject to this Act is sentenced by a court-martial to transportation or imprisonment, the Central Government, [4][the Chief of the Army Staff] or any officer empowered to convene a general or a summary general court-martial may suspend the sentence whether or not the offender has already been committed to prison or to military custody.

(2) The authority or officer specified in sub-section (1) may in the case of an offender so sentenced direct that, until the orders of such authority or officer have been obtained the offender shall not be committed to prison or to military custody.

(3) The powers conferred by sub-sections (1) and (2) may be exercised in the case of any such sentence which has been confirmed, reduced or commuted.

183. Orders pending suspension.

(1) Where the sentence referred to in Section 182 is imposed by a court-martial other than a summary court-martial, the confirming officer may, when confirming the sentence, direct that the offender be not committed to prison or to military custody until the orders of the authority or officer specified in Section 182 have been obtained.

(2) Where a sentence of imprisonment is imposed by a summary court-martial, the officer holding the trial or the officer authorised to approve of the sentence under sub-section (2) of Section 161 may make the direction referred to in sub-section (1).

184. Release on suspension. Where a sentence is suspended under Section 182, the offender shall forthwith be released from custody.

185. Computation of period of suspension. Any period during which the sentence is under suspension shall be reckoned as part of the term of such sentence.

186. Order after suspension. The authority or officer specified in Section 182 may, at any time while a sentence is suspended, order-

(a) that the offender be committed to undergo the unexpired portion of the sentence, or

(b) that the sentence be remitted.

187. Reconsideration of case after suspension.

(1) Where a sentence has been suspended, the case may at any time, and shall at intervals of not more than four months, be reconsidered by the authority or officer specified in Section 182, or by any general or other officer not below the rank of field officer duly authorised by the authority or officer specified in Section 182.

(2) Where on such reconsideration by the officer so authorised it appears to him that the conduct of the offender since his conviction has been such as to justify a remission of the sentence, he shall refer the matter to the authority or officer specified in Section 182.

188. Fresh sentences after suspension. Where an offender, while a sentence on him is suspended under this Act, is sentenced for any other offence, then-

(a) if the further sentence is also suspended under this Act, the two sentences shall run concurrently;

(b) if the further sentence is for a period of three months or more and is not suspended under this Act, the offender shall also be committed to prison or military custody for the unexpired portion of the previous sentence, but both sentences shall run concurrently; and

(c) if the further sentence is for a period of less than three months and is not suspended under this Act, the offender shall be so committed on that sentence only, and the previous sentence shall, subject to any order which may be passed under Section 186 or Section 187, continue to be suspended.

189. Scope of power of suspension. The powers conferred by Sections 182 and 186 shall be in addition to and not in derogation of the power of mitigation, remission and commutation.

190. Effect of suspension and remission on dismissal.

(1) Where in addition to any other sentence the punishment of dismissal has been awarded by a court-martial, and such other' sentence is suspended under Section 182, then, such dismissal shall not take effect until so ordered by the authority or officer specified in Section 182.

(2) If such other sentence is remitted under Section 186, the punishment of dismissal shall also be remitted.

CHAPTER - XV : RULES

191. Power to make rules.

(1) The Central Government may make rules for the purpose of carrying into effect the provisions of this Act.

(2) Without prejudice to the generality of the power conferred by sub-section (1), the rules made thereunder may provide for-

- (a) the removal, retirement, release or discharge from the service of persons subject to this Act;
- (b) the amount and incidence of fines to be imposed under Section 89;
- (d) the assembly and procedure of courts of inquiry, the recording of summaries of evidence and the administration of oaths or affirmations by such courts;
- (e) the convening and constituting of courts-martial and the appointment of prosecutors at trials by courts-martial;
- (f) the adjournment, dissolution and sitting of courts-martial;
- (g) the procedure to be observed in trials by courts-martial and the appearance of legal practitioners thereat;
- (h) the confirmation, revision and annulment of, and petitions against, the findings and sentences of courts-martial;
- (i) the carrying into effect of sentences of courts-martial;
- (j) the forms of orders to be made under the provisions of this Act relating to courts-martial, transportation and imprisonment;
- (k) the constitution of authorities to decide for what persons, to what amounts and in what manner, provision should be made for dependants under Section 99, and the due carrying out of such decisions;
- (l) the relative rank of the officers, junior commissioned officers, warrant officers, petty officers and non-commissioned officers of the regular Army, Navy and Air Force when acting together;
- (m) any other matter directed by this Act to be prescribed.

192. Power to make regulations. The Central Government may make regulations for all or any of the purposes of this Act other than those specified in Section 191.

193. Publication of rules and regulations in Gazette. All rules and regulations made under this Act shall be published in the Official Gazette and on such publication, shall have effect as if enacted in this Act.

193A. [4][Rules and regulations to be laid before Parliament. Every rule and every regulation made by the Central Government under this Act shall be laid, as soon as may be after it is made, before each House of Parliament while it is in session, for a total period of thirty days which may be comprised in one session or in two or more successive sessions, and if, before the expiry of the session immediately following the session, or the successive sessions aforesaid, both Houses agree in making any modification in the rule or regulation should not be made the rule or regulation on shall thereafter have effect only in such modified form or be of no effect, as the case may be; so, however that any such modification or annulment shall be without prejudice to the validity of anything previously done under that rule or regulation.]

194. [Repeals] *Rep. by the Repealing and Amending Act, 1957 (36 of 1957), s. 2 and Sch. I.* [THE SCHEDULE.] *Rep. by the Repealing and Amending Act, 1957 (36 of 1957) s. 2 and Sch. I.*

❑❑❑

1. Subs. by Act 56 of 1974, s. 3 and Sch. II, for" clause (i) of Section".
2. Subs. by Act 58 of 1974, s. 3 and Sch. II, for" clause (i) of Section 2".
3. Subs. by Act 19 of 1955, s. 2 and Sch., for" The Commander-in-Chief".
4. Subs. by Act 19 of 1955, s. 2 and Sch., for" the Commander-in-Chief".

6

The Army and Air Force (Disposal of Private Property) Act, 1950

Act No. 40 of 1950 [28th April, 1950]

AN ACT to provide for the disposal of the private property of persons subject to the Army Act, 1950 (46 of 1950), or the Air Force Act, 1950 (45 of 1950), who die or desert or are ascertained to be of unsound mind or while on active service are officially reported to be missing.

Be it enacted by Parliament as follows:-

1. Short title, extent and commencement.

(1) This Act may be called the Army and Air Force (Disposal of Private Property) Act, 1950.

(2) It extends to the whole of India, and applies to citizens of India and persons subject to the Army Act, 1950 (46 of 1950), or the Air Force Act, 1950 (45 of 1950), wherever they may be.

(3) It shall come into force on such date[2] as the Central Government may, by notification in the Official Gazette, appoint in this behalf.

2. Definitions. In this Act, unless the context otherwise requires -

(1) "Committee" means the Committee of Adjustment constituted under Section 4;

(2) "prescribed" means prescribed by rules made under this Act;

(3) "regimental and other debts in camp or quarters" includes-

(i) in relation to any person subject to the Army Act, 1950, (46 of 1950) moneys due as military debts, namely, sums due in respect of or of any advance in respect of-

(a) quarters;

(b) mess, band and other regimental accounts;

(c) military clothing, appointments and equipments, not exceeding a sum equal to three months' pay of the deceased and having become due within eighteen months before the date of his death; and

(ii) in relation to any person subject to the Air Force Act, 1950 (45 of 1950) moneys due as air force debts, namely, sums due in respect of or of any advance in respect of-

(a) quarters;

(b) mess, band and other service accounts;

(c) air force clothing, appointments and equipments, not exceeding a sum equal to three months' pay of the deceased and having become due within eighteen months before the date of his death;

(4) "representation" includes probate, letters of administration, with or without the will annexed and a succession certificate, constituting a person executor or administrator of the estate of a deceased person or authorising him to receive or realise the assets of a deceased person;

(5) "representative" means any person who has taken out representation, but does not include in Administrator General;

(6) all words and expressions used herein and defined in the Army Act, 1950, (46 of 1950) or the Air Force Act, 1950 (45 of 1950) and not in this Act defined shall be deemed to have the meanings respectively attributed to them by those Acts.

3. Property of deceased persons and deserters other than officers.

(1) On the death or desertion of any person, not being an officer, subject to the Army Act, 1950 (46 of 1950) or the Air Force Act, 1950 (45 of 1950), as the case may be, the commanding officer of the corps, department, detachment or unit to which the deceased or deserter belonged, shall, as soon as may be and subject to any rules that may be made in this behalf-

(a) secure all the movable property belonging to the deceased or deserter that is in camp or quarters, and cause an inventory thereof to be made,

(b) draw the pay and allowances due to such person,

(c) make due provision for the payment of regimental and other debts in camp or quarters, if any, of such persons.

(2) In the case of a deceased person, the commanding officer -

(a) if in any case not otherwise provided for by rules made under this Act it appears to him to be necessary to make provision for the payment of regimental and other debts in camp or quarters, the funeral expenses of the deceased and the expenses, if any, incurred by the commanding officer in respect of the estate of the deceased, shall, and-

(b) in any other case, may,— collect all moneys left by the deceased in any banking company (including any post office savings bank, co-operative bank or society or any other institution receiving deposits in money however named) and for that purpose may require the agent, manager or other proper officer of such banking company, society or other institution to pay the moneys to the commanding officer forthwith, notwithstanding anything in the rules of the banking company, society or other institution, and such agent, manager or other officer shall be bound to comply with the requisition.

(3) Where any money has been paid by a banking company, society or other institution in compliance with a requisition made under sub-section (2), no person shall have any claim against the banking company, society or other institution in respect of such money.

(4) Where the representative of a deceased has given security to the satisfaction of the commanding officer for the payment of the regimental and other debts in camp or quarters, if any, and of the funeral expenses of the deceased in cases where no provision for the payment of such expenses has been made otherwise and of the expenses, if any, incurred by the commanding officer in respect of the estate of the deceased, the commanding officer shall deliver over the property received by him under sub-sections (1) and (2) to that representative, whereupon his responsibility for the administration of the estate of the deceased shall cease.

(5) In the case of a deceased whose estate has not been dealt with under sub-section (4), or under Section 10, and in the case of a deserter, the commanding officer -

(i) if in any case it is necessary in his opinion so to do for the purpose of securing the payment of the regimental and other debts in camp or quarters of the deceased or deserter, the funeral expenses of the deceased, if any, and the expenses, if any, incurred by the commanding officer in respect of the estate of the deceased or deserter, shall, and

(ii) in any other case, may cause the movable property of the deceased or deserter, as the case may be, to be sold or converted into money.

(6) The commanding officer shall, out of the moneys received, collected or realised under sub-sections (1), (2) and (5), pay the regimental and other debts in camp or quarters, if any, of the deceased or deserter, as the case may be, the expenses, if any, incurred by the commanding officer in respect of the estate of the deceased or deserter, and in the case of a deceased his funeral expenses in cases where no provision for the payment of such expenses has been made otherwise.

(7) The surplus, if any, after payment of the debts and expenses specified in sub-section (6), shall -

(a) in the case of a deceased, be paid to his representative, if any, or in the event of no claim to such surplus being established within twelve months after the death, to the prescribed person; and

(b) in the case of a deserter, be forthwith paid to the prescribed person, and shall, on the expiry of three years from the date of desertion, be forfeited to the Central Government, unless the deserter shall have surrendered or been apprehended in the meantime:

PROVIDED that the prescribed person may, if the deserter has not surrendered or been apprehended in the meantime, pay the whole or any part of the surplus received by him under clause (b) to the wife or children or any other dependent of the deserter at any time during the said period of three years.

EXPLANATION. In this Section and in Section 4, the word "officer" with reference to persons subject to the Air Force Act, 1950 (45 of 1950), includes a warrant officer who has died or deserted.

4. Property of officers who die or desert. The provisions of Section 3 shall also apply to the disposal of the property of any officer subject to the Army Act, 1950 (46 of 1950) or the Air Force Act, 1950 (45 of 1950), who dies or deserts, but with the following modifications, namely:-

(i) the functions of the commanding officer under Section 3 shall be performed by a Committee of Adjustment constituted in this behalf in the prescribed manner;

(ii) the surplus, if any, after payment of the debts and expenses specified in sub-section (6) of Section 3, shall in the case of a deceased officer, be paid to the prescribed person.

5. Decision of questions as to regimental and other debts in camp quarters. If in any case a doubt or difference arises as to what are the regimental and other debts in camp or quarters of a deceased or deserter or as to the amount payable in respect thereof, the decision of the prescribed person shall be final and shall be binding on all persons for all purposes.

6. Representative powers of commanding officer or Committee. For the purpose of the exercise of his or its duties under Section 3 or Section 4, the commanding officer or the Committee, as the case may be, shall, to the exclusion of all other persons and authorities whomsoever or whatsoever, have the same rights and powers as if he or it had taken out representation to the estate of the deceased, and any receipt given by the commanding officer or the Committee, as the case may be, shall have effect accordingly.

7. Power of Central Government to hand over estate of deceased person to the Administrator General.

(1) Notwithstanding anything contained in the Administrator General's Act, 1913, (3 of 1913) an Administrator General shall not interpose in any manner in relation to any property of a deceased which has been dealt with under the provisions of Section 3 or Section 4, except insofar as he is expressly required or permitted to do so by or under the provisions of this Act.

(2) The Central Government may, at any time and in such circumstances as it thinks fit, direct that the estate of a deceased shall be handed over by the commanding officer or the Committee, as the case may be, to the Administrator General of a State for administration, and thereupon the commanding officer

or the Committee, as the case may be, shall make over the estate to such Administrator General.

(3) Where under this Section any estate is handed over to the Administrator General, the Administrator General shall administer such estate in accordance with the provisions of the Administrator General's Act, 1913 (3 of 1913) or, if that Act is not in force in any State, of the corresponding law in force in that State:

PROVIDED that the regimental and other debts in camp or quarters of the deceased, if any, shall be paid by the Administrator General in priority to any other debts due by the deceased.

(4) The Administrator General shall pay the surplus, if any, remaining in his hands after discharging all debts and charges, to the heirs of the deceased, and, if no heir is traceable, shall make over the surplus in the prescribed manner to the prescribed person.

(5) The Administrator General shall not charge in respect of his duties under this Section any fee exceeding three per cent. of the gross amount coming to or remaining in his hands after payment of the regimental and other debts in camp or quarters.

8. Disposal of surplus by prescribed persons. On receipt of the surplus referred to in sub-section (7) of Section 3 or clause (ii) of Section 4 or sub-section (4) of Section 7, the prescribed person shall -

(a) if he knows of a representative of the deceased, pay the surplus to that representative;

(b) if he does not know of any such representative and the surplus has not been disposed of under Section 10, publish every year a notice in the prescribed form and manner for six consecutive years and if no claim to the surplus is made by a representative of the deceased within six months even after the publication of the last of such notices, the prescribed person shall deposit the surplus together with any income or accumulation of income accrued therefrom to the credit of the Central Government:

PROVIDED that such deposit shall not bar the claim of any person to such surplus or any part thereof, if he is otherwise entitled to it.

9. Disposal of effects, not money. Where any part of the estate of a deceased person consists of effects, securities or other property not converted into money, the provisions of sub-section (7) of Section 3, clause (ii) of Section 4 and Section 8, with respect to the payment of the surplus, shall, save as may be prescribed, extend to the delivery, transmission or transfer of such effects, securities or property, and the prescribed person shall have the same power of converting the same into money as a representative of the deceased.

10. Disposal of certain property without production of probate, etc. Property deliverable and money payable to the representative of a deceased under Section 3 or Section 4 or Section 8 may, if the total amount or value thereof does not exceed [1][ten thousand] rupees and if the prescribed person thinks fit, be delivered or paid to any person appearing to him to be entitled to receive it or to administer the estate of the deceased without requiring such person to produce any probate, letters of administration, succession certificate or other such conclusive evidence of title.

11. Discharge of Commanding Officer, Committee, prescribed person and the Central Government. Any payment or application of money or application, delivery, sale or other disposition of any property made, or purported to be made, by the commanding officer, the Committee or the prescribed person in good faith in pursuance of Section 3, Section 4, Section 8, Section 9 or Section 10 shall be valid and shall be a full discharge to the commanding officer, the Committee or the prescribed person, as the case may be, and to the Central Government from all further liability in respect of that money or property; but nothing herein contained shall affect the right of any executor or administrator or other representative, or of any creditor of the deceased against any person to whom such payment or delivery has been made.

12. Property in the hands of commanding officer, Committee or prescribed person not to be assets where commanding officer, Committee or prescribed person is stationed. Any Property coming into the hands of the commanding officer or the Committee or the prescribed person under Section 3, Section 4, or sub-section (4) of Section 7 shall not, by reason thereof, be deemed to be assets or effects at the place in which that commanding officer or the Committee or the prescribed person is stationed, and it shall not be necessary by reason thereof that representation be taken out in respect of that property for that place.

13. Saving of rights of representative. After the commanding officer, or the Committee has paid to the prescribed person the surplus of the property of any deceased under sub-section (7) of Section 3 or clause (ii) of Section 4, any representative of the deceased or any Administrator General, shall, as regards any property of the deceased not collected by the commanding officer or the Committee, as the case may be, and not forming part of the aforesaid surplus, have the same rights and duties as if Sections 3 and 4 had not been enacted.

14. Application of Sections 3 to 13 to persons of unsound mind or to persons reported missing on active service. The provisions of Sections 3 to 13 shall, so far as they can be made applicable, also apply in the case of a person subject to the Army Act, 1950 (46 of 1950), or the Air Force Act, 1950 (45 of 1950), as the case may be, who, notwithstanding anything contained in the Indian Lunacy Act, 1912, (4 of 1912), is ascertained in the prescribed manner to be of unsound mind, or who, while on active service, is officially reported missing, as if he had died on the day on which his unsoundness of mind is so ascertained or, as the case may be, on the day on which he is officially reported missing:

> *PROVIDED that in the case of a person so reported missing, no action shall be taken under sub-sections (2) to (6) of Section 3 or Section 4 or Section 7 until such time as he is officially presumed to be dead.*

15. Appointment of Standing Committee of Adjustment in certain cases. When an officer dies or deserts or is ascertained in the prescribed manner to be of unsound mind or while on active service is officially reported missing, the references in the foregoing provisions of this Act to the Committee shall be construed as references to the Standing Committee of Adjustment, if any, constituted in this behalf in the prescribed manner and such Standing Committee shall alone be entitled to perform all the functions of the Committee under this Act,

16. Power to make rules.

(1) The Central Government may, by notification in the Official Gazette, make rules 1 for the purpose of carrying into effect the purposes of this Act.

(2) In particular, and without prejudice to the generality of the foregoing power, such rules may-

(a) prescribe the manner in which any property belonging to a deceased or deserter may be secured or collected and his regimental and other debts in camp or quarters paid;

(b) provide for the payment of the funeral expenses of any deceased;

(c) provide for the constitution of the Committee of Adjustment or any Standing Committee of Adjustment under this Act;

(d) specify the person who shall be regarded as the prescribed person for the purposes of this Act;

(e) prescribe the circumstances in which the estate of any deceased shall be handed over to the Administrator General;

(f) prescribe the form and manner in which a notice under Section 8 shall be published;

(g) prescribe the procedure by which any person may be ascertained to be of unsound mind.

(3) 2[Every rule made by the Central Government under this Act shall be laid, as soon as may be after it is made, before each House of Parliament while it is in session, for a total period of thirty days which may be comprised in one session or in two or more successive sessions, and if, before the expiry of the session immediately following the session or the successive sessions aforesaid, both Houses agree in making any modification in the rule or both Houses agree that the rule should not be made, the rule shall thereafter have effect only in such modified form or be of no effect, as the case may be; so, however, that any such modification or annulment shall be without prejudice to the validity of anything previously done under that rule.]

17. [Repeals]. *Rep. by the Repealing and Amending Act, 1957 (36 of 1957), s. 2 and Sch. I.*

❑❑❑

7

The Assam Rifles Act, 2006

ACT NO. 47 OF 2006 [3RD NOVEMBER, 2006]

AN ACT to consolidate and amend the law relating to the governance of the Assam Rifles, an Armed Force of the Union for ensuring the security of the borders of India, to carry out Counter Insurgency Operations in the specified areas and to act in aid of civil authorities for the maintenance of the law and order and for matters connected therewith.

Be it enacted by Parliament in the Fifty-seventh Year of the Republic of India as follows:-

CHAPTER - I : PRELIMINARY

1. Short title and commencement.

(1) This Act may be called the Assam Rifles Act, 2006.

(2) It shall come into force on such date as the Central Government may, by notification in the Official Gazette, appoint.

2. Definitions.

(1) In this Act, unless the context otherwise requires -

(a) "active duty", in relation to a person subject to this Act, means any duty as a member of the Force during the period in which such person is attached to, or forms part of, a unit of the Force-

(i) which is engaged in operations against an enemy or an insurgent or a terrorist or any person in arms against the Union, or

(ii) which is operating at a picket or engaged on patrol or other guard duty along the borders of India, and includes duty by such person during any period declared by the Central Government, by notification in the Official Gazette, as a period of active duty with reference to any area in which or under any provision of this Act or for the purposes of any other law for the time being in force, any person or class of persons subject to this Act may be serving;

(b) "Assam Rifles Court" means a Court referred to in Section 86;

(c) "battalion" means a unit of the Force constituted as battalion by the Central Government;

(d) "Chief Law Officer" and" Law Officer" mean, respectively, the Chief Law Officer and a Law Officer of the Force appointed by the Central Government;

(e) "civil offence" means an offence which is triable by a criminal court;

(f) "civil prison" means any jail or place used for the detention of any criminal prisoner under the Prisons Act, 1894 , or under any other law for the time being in force;

(g) "Commandant", when used in any provision of this Act with reference to any unit of the Force, means the officer whose duty it is under the rules or regulations or in the absence of such rules or regulations, by custom of the service, to discharge with respect to that unit, the functions of a Commandant in regard to matters of the description referred to in that provision;

(h) "criminal court" means a court of ordinary criminal justice in any part of India;

(i) "deputation" means a period for which the services of a person belonging to any department of the Central Government are placed at the disposal of the Director-General;

(j) "Director-General" and "Additional Director-General" mean, the Director-General and Additional Director-General of the Force appointed under sub-sections (1) and (2) of Section 5, respectively;

(k) "enemy" includes all armed mutineers, armed rebels, armed rioters, pirates, terrorists and any person in arms against whom it is the duty of any person subject to this Act to take action;

(l) "enrolled person" means an under-officer or other person enrolled under this Act;

(m) "Force" means the Assam Rifles;

(n) "Force custody" means the arrest or confinement of a member of the Force according to rules and includes any military custody of such member under the Army Act, 1950;

(o) "Inspector-General" and "'Deputy Inspector-General" mean, respectively, the Inspector-General and the Deputy Inspector-General of the Force appointed under sub-section (2) of Section 5;

(p) "member of the Force" means an officer, a subordinate officer, an under-officer or other enrolled person and includes the persons on deputation;

(q) "notification" means a notification published in the Official Gazette;

(r) "offence" means any act or omission punishable under this Act and includes a civil offence;

(s) "officer" means a person appointed or in pay as an officer of the Force; but does not include a subordinate officer or an under-officer;

(t) "prescribed" means prescribed by rules made under this Act;

(u) "regulations" means the regulations made by the Central Government under this Act;

(v) "rule" means a rule made under this Act;

(w) "subordinate officer" means a person appointed or in pay as a Subedar Major, a Subedar or a Naib Subedar of the Force;

(x) "superior officer", when used in relation to a person subject to this Act, means-

  (i) any member of the Force or a person on deputation to whose command such person is for the time being subject in accordance with the rules;

  (ii) any officer of higher rank or class or of a higher grade in the same class, and includes when such person is not an officer, a subordinate officer or an under-officer of higher rank, class or grade;

(y) "terrorist" means any person who, with intent to overawe the Government as by law established or to strike terror in the people or any Section of the people or to alienate any Section of the people or to adversely affect the harmony amongst different Sections of the people, does any act or thing by using bombs, dynamite or other explosive substances or inflammable substances or fire-arms or other lethal weapons or poisons or noxious gases or other chemicals or any other substances (whether biological or otherwise) of a hazardous nature in such a manner, as to cause or is likely to cause death of, or injury to, any person or persons, or damage to, or destruction of, property or disruption of any supplies or services essential to the life of the community;.

(z) "under-officer" means a Warrant Officer, Havildar, Naik and Lance Naik of the Force;

(za) "unit" means any-

  (i) battalion; or

  (ii) regiment; or

  (iii) training institution; or

  (iv) Head Quarters of Deputy Inspector-General; or

  (v) Head Quarters of Inspector-General; or

  (vi) Head Quarters of Director-General, of the Force and includes any other formation of the Force specified, by notification, by the Central Government.

(2) Words and expressions used and not defined in this Act but defined in the Indian Penal Code shall have the meanings assigned to them in that Code.

(3) In this Act, reference to any law not in force in the State of Jammu and Kashmir shall be construed as references to the corresponding law in force in that State.

3. Persons subject to this Act.

(1) The following persons (whether on deputation or otherwise employed) shall be subject to this Act, wherever they may be, namely:-

(a) officers and subordinate officers; and

(b) under-officers and other persons enrolled under this Act.

(2) Members of the Force in existence at the commencement of this Act shall be deemed to have been appointed or, as the case may be, enrolled as such under this Act.

(3) Notwithstanding anything contained in sub-section (1), any person who is employed in the Force on deputation from the regular Army as defined under clause (xxi) of Section 3 of the Army Act, 1950 shall not be subject to this Act and shall, during the period of such deputation, be deemed to be subject to the Army Act, 1950 :

PROVIDED that such person in regard to his duties and discipline shall be deemed to be under the command of the member of the Force under whose command such person for the time being is placed:

PROVIDED FURTHER that, in case of such person, for the purposes of his duties and discipline, the expression "active duty" defined in clause (a) of sub-section (1) of Section 2 shall be deemed to be the "active service" as defined in clause (i) of Section 3 of the Army Act, 1950 for taking any action against him under the provisions of the said Army Act.

(4) Any person who is not subject to this Act is posted for any service with the members of the Force or engaged to accompany with or to provide any service in any manner to the members of the Force in such-

(i) camp;

(ii) line of march;

(iii) frontier post;

(iv) active duty; or

(v) counter insurgency operations, as may be specified, by notification, by the Central Government in this behalf shall be deemed to be a member of the Force, till he is so posted or engaged in such corresponding rank as may be determined, by notification, by the Central Government for the purposes of this Act.

(5) Every person subject to this Act shall remain so subject until retired, discharged, released, removed or dismissed from the Force in accordance with the provisions of this Act and the rules.

CHAPTER -II : CONSTITUTION OF THE FORCE AND CONDITIONS OF SERVICE OF THE MEMBERS OF THE FORCE

4. Constitution of Force.

(1) There shall be an armed force of the Union called the Assam Rifles for ensuring the security of the borders of India, to carry out counter insurgency operations in the specified areas and to act in aid of civil authorities for the maintenance of law and order and the matters connected therewith.

(2) Subject to the provisions of this Act, the Force shall be reconstituted in such manner as may be prescribed and the conditions of service of the members of the Force shall be such as may be prescribed.

5. Control, direction, etc.

(1) The general superintendence, direction and control of the Force shall vest in, and be exercised by the Central Government and subject thereto and to the provisions of this Act and the rules and regulations, the command and supervision of the Force shall vest in an officer to be appointed by the Central Government as the Director-General of the Force.

(2) The Director-General shall, in the discharge of his duties under this Act, be assisted by such number of Additional Director-General, Inspectors-General, Deputy Inspectors-General, Commandants and other officers as may be appointed by the Central Government.

6. Enrolment.

(1) The persons to be enrolled to the Force, the mode of enrolment and the procedure for enrolment shall be such as may be prescribed by the Central Government.

(2) Notwithstanding anything contained in this Act and the rules and regulations, every person who has, for a continuous period of three months, been in receipt of pay as a person enrolled under this Act and borne on the rolls of the Force shall be deemed to have been duly enrolled.

(3) No person who is not a citizen of India shall, except by the consent of the Central Government signified in writing, be enrolled in the Force.

7. Liability for service outside India. Every member of the Force shall be liable to serve in any part of India as well as outside India.

8. Resignation and withdrawal from the post. No member of the Force shall be at liberty-

(a) to resign his appointment during the term of his engagement; or

(b) to withdraw himself from all or any of the duties of his appointment, except with the previous permission in writing of the prescribed authority.

9. Tenure of service under the Act. Every person subject to this Act shall hold office during the pleasure of the President.

10. Termination of service by Central Government. Subject to the provisions of this Act and the rules and regulations, the Central Government may dismiss or remove from the service any person subject to this Act.

11. Dismissal, removal or reduction by Director-General and by other officers.

(1) The Director-General, Additional Director-General or any Inspector-General may dismiss or remove from service or reduce to a lower grade or rank or the ranks any person subject to this Act other than an officer.

(2) An officer not below the rank of Deputy Inspector-General may dismiss or remove from the service any person under his command other than an officer or a subordinate officer of such rank or the ranks as may be prescribed.

(3) Any such officer as is mentioned in sub-section (2) may reduce to a lower grade or rank or the ranks any person under his command except an officer or a subordinate officer.

(4) The exercise of any power under this Section shall be subject to the provisions of this Act and the rules and regulations.

12. Certificate of termination of service. A subordinate officer or an under-officer or other enrolled person who is retired, discharged, released, removed or dismissed from service shall be furnished by the officer, to whose command he is subject, with a certificate in the language which is the mother-tongue of such person and also in Hindi and English language setting forth-

(a) the authority terminating his service;

(b) the cause for such termination; and

(c) the full period of his service in the Force.

13. Restrictions on right to form association, freedom of speech, etc.

(1) No person subject to this Act shall, without the previous sanction in writing of the Central Government or of the prescribed authority -

(a) be a member of, or be associated in any way with, any trade union, labour union, political association or with any class of trade unions, labour unions or political associations; or

(b) be a member of, or be associated in any way with, any society, institution, association or organisation that is not recognised as part of the Force or is not of a purely social, recreational or religious nature; or

(c) communicate with the press or publish or cause to be published any book, letter or other document except where such communication or publication is in the bonafide discharge of his duties or is of a purely literary, artistic or scientific character or is of a prescribed nature.

EXPLANATION. If any question arises as to whether any society, institution, association or organisation is of a purely social, recreational or religious nature under clause (b) of this sub-section, the decision of the Central Government thereon shall be final.

(2) No person subject to this Act shall participate in, or address, any meeting or take part in any demonstration organised by any body or persons for any political purposes or for such other purposes as may be prescribed.

CHAPTER -III : SERVICE PRIVILEGES

14. Authorised deduction only to be made from pay. The pay of every person subject to this Act due to him as such under any rules or regulations for the time being in force shall be paid without any deduction other than the deductions authorised by or under this Act or any other Act.

15. Remedy of aggrieved persons other than officers.

(1) Any person subject to this Act other than an officer who deems himself wronged by any officer or subordinate officer may complain to the officer under whose command or orders he is serving.

(2) When the officer complained against is the officer to whom any complaint should, under sub-section (1), be preferred, the aggrieved person may complain to such officer' s next superior officer.

(3) Every officer receiving any such complaint shall make as complete an investigation into it as may be possible for giving full redress to the complainant; or when necessary, refer the complaint to superior authority.

(4) Every such complaint shall be preferred in such manner as may, from time to time, be specified by the Director-General.

(5) The Central Government may revise any decision by the Director-General under sub-section (2), but, subject thereto, the decision of the Director-General shall be final.

16. Remedy of aggrieved officers. Any officer who deems himself wronged by his Commandant or any superior officer and who on due application made to his Commandant or such superior officer does not receive the redress to which he considers himself entitled, may complain to the Central Government in such manner as may, from time to time, be specified by the Director-General.

17. Immunity from attachment. Neither the arms, clothes, equipment, accoutrements or necessaries of any person subject to this Act, nor any animal used by him for the discharge of his duty shall be seized, nor shall, the pay and allowances of any such person or any part thereof, be attached, by direction of any civil or revenue court or any revenue officer in satisfaction of any decree or order enforceable against him.

18. Immunity from arrest for debt.

(1) No person subject to this Act shall, so long as he belongs to the Force, be liable to be arrested for debt under any process issued by, or by the authority of, any civil or revenue court or revenue officer, except with the prior consent of the Central Government.

(2) The Judge of any such court or the said officer may examine into any complaint made by such person or his superior officer of the arrest of such person contrary to the provisions of this Section and may, by warrant under his hand, discharge the person, and award reasonable costs to the complainant, who may recover

those costs in like manner as he might have recovered costs awarded to him by a decree against the person obtaining the process.

(3) For the recovery of such costs no court-fee shall be payable by the complainant.

19. Immunity of persons attending Assam Rifles Court from arrest.

(1) No Presiding Officer or member of an Assam Rifles Court, no Law Officer, no party to any proceeding before an Assam Rifles Court, or his legal practitioner or agent and no witness acting in obedience to a summons to attend an Assam Rifles Court shall, while proceeding to, attending or returning from, an Assam Rifles Court, be liable to arrest under civil or revenue process.

(2) If any such person is arrested under any such process, he may be discharged by order of the Assam Rifles Court.

20. Savings of rights and privileges under other laws. The rights and privileges specified in the preceding Section of this Chapter shall be in addition to, and not in derogation of, any other rights and privileges conferred on persons subject to this Act generally by any other law for the time being in force.

CHAPTER -IV : OFFENCES CHAPTER IV OFFENCES

21. Offences in relation to the enemy and punishable with death. Any person subject to this Act who commits any of the following offences, that is to say -

(a) shamefully abandons or delivers up any post, place or guard, committed to his charge or which it is his duty to defend; or

(b) intentionally uses any means to compel or induce any person subject to this Act or to army, naval, air force law or any member of other armed forces to abstain from acting against the enemy or to discourage such person from acting against the enemy; or

(c) in the presence of enemy, shamefully casts away his arms, ammunition, tools or equipment or misbehaves in such manner as to show cowardice; or

(d) treacherously holds correspondence with, or communicates intelligence to, the enemy or any person in arms against the Union; or

(e) directly or indirectly assists the enemy with money, arms, ammunition, stores or supplies or in any other manner whatsoever; or

(f) in time of active operation against the enemy intentionally occasions a false alarm in action, camp, quarters or spreads or causes to be spread reports calculated to create alarm or despondency; or

(g) in time of action leaves his Commandant or other superior officer or his post, guard, picket, patrol or party without being regularly relieved or without leave; or

(h) having been captured by the enemy or made a prisoner of war, voluntarily serves with or aids the enemy; or

(i) knowingly harbours or protects an enemy not being a prisoner; or

(j) being a sentry in time of active operation against the enemy or alarm, sleeps upon his post or is intoxicated; or

(k) knowingly does any act calculated to imperil the success of the Force or the army, naval, air forces of India or any other armed forces of the Central Government co-operating therewith or any part of such forces, shall, on conviction by an Assam Rifles Court, be liable to suffer death or such less punishment as is in this Act mentioned.

22. Offences in relation to the enemy and not punishable with death. Any person subject to this Act who commits any of the following offences, that is to say -

(a) is taken prisoner or captured by the enemy, by want of due precaution or through disobedience of orders, or wilful neglect of duty, or having been taken prisoner or so captured fails to rejoin his service when able to do so; or

(b) without due authority holds correspondence with, or communicates intelligence to, the enemy or any person in league with the enemy or having come by the knowledge of any such correspondence or communication, wilfully omits to discover it immediately to his Commandant or other superior officer, shall, on conviction by an Assam Rifles Court, be liable to suffer imprisonment for a term which may extend to fourteen years or such less punishment as is in this Act mentioned.

23. Offences punishable more severely on active duty than at other times. Any person subject to this Act who commits any of the following offences, that is to say -

(a) forces a safeguard or forces or uses criminal force to a sentry; or

(b) breaks into any house or other place in search of plunder; or

(c) being a sentry, sleeps upon his post or is intoxicated; or

(d) without orders from his superior officer, leaves his guard, picket, patrol or posts; or

(e) intentionally or through neglect occasions a false alarm in camp or quarters, or spreads or causes to be spread reports calculated to create unnecessary alarm or despondency; or

(f) makes known the parole, watchword or countersign to any person not entitled to receive it; or

(g) knowingly gives a parole, watchword or countersign different from what he received, shall, on conviction by an Assam Rifles Court -

(i) if he commits any such offence when on active duty, be liable to suffer imprisonment for a term which may extend to fourteen years or such less punishment as is in this Act mentioned; and

(ii) if he commits any such offence when not on active duty, be liable to suffer imprisonment for a term which may extend to seven years or such less punishment as is in this Act mentioned.

24. Mutiny. Any person subject to this Act who commits any of the following offences, that is to say -

(a) begins, incites, causes or conspires with any other person to cause any mutiny in the Force or in the army, naval or air forces of India or any forces co-operating therewith; or

(b) joins in any such mutiny; or

(c) being present at any such mutiny, does not use his utmost endeavours to suppress the same; or

(d) knowing or having reason to believe in the existence of any such mutiny, or of any intention to mutiny or of any such conspiracy, does not, without delay, give information thereof to his Commandant or other superior officer; or

(e) endeavours to seduce any person in the Force or in the army, naval or air forces of India or any forces cooperating therewith from his duty or allegiance to the Union, shall, on conviction by an Assam Rifles Court, be liable to suffer death or such less punishment as is in this Act mentioned.

25. Desertion and aiding desertion.

(1) Any person subject to this Act who deserts or attempts to desert the service shall, on conviction by an Assam Rifles Court -

(a) if he commits the offence when on active duty or when under orders for active duty, be liable to suffer death or such less punishment as is in this Act mentioned; and

(b) if he commits the offence under any other circumstances, be liable to suffer imprisonment for a term which may extend to seven years or such less punishment as is in this Act mentioned.

(2) Any person subject to this Act who knowingly harbours any such deserter shall, on conviction by an Assam Rifles Court, be liable to suffer imprisonment for a term which may extend to seven years or such less punishment as is in this Act mentioned.

(3) Any person subject to this Act who, being cognisant of any desertion or attempt at desertion of a person subject to this Act, does not forthwith give notice to his own or some other superior officer, or take any steps in his power to cause such person to be apprehended, shall, on conviction by an Assam Rifles Court, be liable to suffer imprisonment for a term which may extend to two years or such less punishment as is in this Act mentioned.

26. Absence without leave. Any person subject to this Act who commits any of the following offences, that is to say -

(a) absents himself without leave; or

(b) without sufficient cause, overstays leave granted to him; or

(c) being on leave of absence and having received information from the appropriate authority that any battalion or part thereof or any other unit of the Force, to which he belongs, has been ordered on active duty, fails, without sufficient cause, to rejoin without delay; or

(d) without sufficient cause, fails to appear at the time fixed at the parade or place appointed for exercise or duty; or

(e) when on parade, or on the line of march, without sufficient cause or without leave from his superior officer, quits the parade or line of march; or

(f) when in camp or elsewhere, is found beyond any limits fixed, or in any place prohibited, by any general, local or other order, without a pass or written leave from his superior officer; or

(g) without leave from his superior officer or without due cause, absents himself from any school when duly ordered to attend there, shall, on conviction by an Assam Rifles Court, be liable to suffer imprisonment for a term which may extend to three years or such less punishment as is in this Act mentioned.

27. Striking or threatening superior officers. Any person subject to this Act who commits any of the following offences, that is to say -

(a) uses criminal force to or assaults his superior officer; or

(b) uses threatening language to such officer; or

(c) uses insubordinate language to such officer, shall, on conviction by an Assam Rifles Court -

(i) if such officer is at the time in the execution of his office or, if the offence is committed on active duty, be liable to suffer imprisonment for a term which may extend to fourteen years or such less punishment as is in this Act mentioned; and

(ii) in other cases, be liable to suffer imprisonment for a term which may extend to ten years or such less punishment as is in this Act mentioned:

PROVIDED that in the case of an offence specified in clause (c), the imprisonment shall not exceed five years.

28. Disobedience to superior officer.

(1) Any person subject to this Act who disobeys, in such manner as to show a wilful defiance of authority, any lawful command given personally by his superior officer in the execution of his office whether the same is given orally, or in writing or by signal or otherwise, shall, on conviction by an Assam Rifles Court, be liable to suffer imprisonment for a term which may extend to fourteen years or such less punishment as is in this Act mentioned.

(2) Any person subject to this Act who disobeys any lawful command given by his superior officer shall, on conviction by an Assam Rifles Court -

(a) if he commits such offence when on active duty, be liable to suffer imprisonment for a term which may extend to fourteen years or such less punishment as is in this Act mentioned; and

(b) if he commits such offence when not on active duty, be liable to suffer imprisonment for a term which may extend to five years or such less punishment as is in this Act mentioned.

29. Insubordination and obstruction. Any person subject to this Act who commits any of the following offences, that is to say -

(a) being concerned in any quarrel, affray or disorder, refuses to obey any officer, though of inferior rank, who orders him into arrest, or uses criminal force to or assaults any such officer; or

(b) uses criminal force to, or assaults any person, whether subject to this Act or not, in whose custody he is lawfully placed, and whether he is or is not his superior officer; or

(c) resists an escort whose duty it is to apprehend him or to have him in charge; or

(d) breaks out of barracks, camp or quarters; or

(e) neglects to obey any general, local or other order; or

(f) impedes the Force Police referred to in Section 85 or any person lawfully acting on its behalf, or when called upon, refuses to assist in the execution of his duty a Force Police or any person lawfully acting on his behalf, shall, on conviction by an Assam Rifles Court, be liable to suffer imprisonment for a term which may extend, in the case of the offences specified in clauses (d) and (e), to two years, and in the case of the offences specified in the other clauses, to ten years, or in either case such less punishment as is in this Act mentioned.

30. Fraudulent enrolment. Any person subject to this Act who knowingly attempts to get enrolled or enrolls any other person who does not fulfil the conditions enabling him to be enrolled, shall, on conviction by the Assam Rifles Court, be liable to suffer imprisonment for a term which may extend to five years or such less punishment as is in this Act mentioned.

31. False answers on enrolment. Any person having become subject to this Act who is discovered to have made at the time of enrolment a wilfully false answer to any question set-forth in the prescribed form of enrolment which has been put to him by the enrolling officer before whom he appears for the purpose of being enrolled, shall, on conviction by an Assam Rifles Court, be liable to suffer imprisonment for a term which may extend to five years or such less punishment as is in this Act mentioned.

32. Unbecoming conduct. Any officer, subordinate officer or an under-officer who behaves in a manner unbecoming his position and the character expected of him shall, on conviction by an Assam Rifles Court, be liable to be dismissed or to suffer such less punishment as is in this Act mentioned.

33. Certain forms of disgraceful conduct. Any person subject to this Act who commits any of the following offences, that is to say -

(a) is guilty of any disgraceful conduct of a cruel, indecent or unnatural kind; or

(b) malingers, or feigns or produces disease or infirmity in himself or intentionally delays his cure or aggravates his disease or infirmity; or

(c) with intent to render himself or any other person unfit for service, voluntarily causes hurt to himself or that person, shall, on conviction by an Assam Rifles Court, be liable to suffer imprisonment for a term which may extend to seven years or such less punishment as is in this Act mentioned.

34. Ill-treating a subordinate. Any officer, subordinate officer or an under-officer who uses criminal force to or otherwise ill-treats any person subject to this Act, being his subordinate in rank or position, shall, on conviction by an Assam Rifles Court, be liable to suffer imprisonment for a term which may extend to seven years or such less punishment as is in this Act mentioned.

35. Intoxication. Any person subject to this Act who is found in a state of intoxication whether on duty or not, shall, on conviction by an Assam Rifles Court, be liable to suffer imprisonment for a term which may extend to six months or such less punishment as is in this Act mentioned.

36. Permitting escape of person in custody. Any person subject to this Act who commits any of the following offences, that is to say -

(a) when in command of guard, picket, patrol or post, releases without proper authority, whether illfully or without reasonable excuse, any person committed to his charge, or refuses to receive any prisoner or person so committed; or

(b) illfully or without reasonable excuse allows to escape any person who is committed to his charge, or whom it is his duty to keep or guard, shall, on conviction by an Assam Rifles Court, be liable, if he has acted illfully, to suffer imprisonment for a term which may extend to ten years or such less punishment as is in this Act mentioned; and if he has not acted illfully, to suffer imprisonment for a term which may extend to two years or such less punishment as is in this Act mentioned.

37. Irregularity in connection with arrest or confinement. Any person subject to this Act who commits any of the following offences, that is to say -

(a) unnecessarily detains a person in arrest or confinement without bringing him to trial, or fails to bring his case before the proper authority for investigation; or

(b) having committed a person to Force custody fails without reasonable cause to deliver at the time of such committal, or as soon as practicable, and in any case within forty-eight hours, thereafter, to the officer or other person into whose custody the person arrested is committed, an account in writing signed by himself of the offence with which the person so committed is charged, shall, on conviction by an Assam Rifles Court, be liable to suffer imprisonment for a term which may extend to one year or such less punishment as is in this Act mentioned.

38. Escape from custody. Any person subject to this Act who, being in lawful custody, escapes or attempts to escape, shall, on conviction by an Assam Rifles Court, be liable to suffer imprisonment for a term which may extend to three years or such less punishment as is in this Act mentioned.

39. Offences in respect of property. Any person subject to this Act who commits any of the following offences, that is to say -

(a) commits theft of any property belonging to the Government, or to any Force mess, band or institution, or to any person subject to this Act; or

(b) dishonestly misappropriates or converts to his own use any such property; or

(c) commits criminal breach of trust in respect of any such property; or

(d) dishonestly receives or retains any such property in respect of which any of the offences under clauses (a), (b) and (c) has been committed, knowing or having reason to believe the commission of such offence; or

(e) wilfully destroys or injures any property of the Government entrusted to him; or

(f) does any other thing with intent to defraud, or to cause wrongful gain to one person or wrongful loss to another person, shall, on conviction by an Assam Rifles Court, be liable to suffer imprisonment for a term which may extend to ten years or such less punishment as is in this Act mentioned.

40. Extortion and corruption. Any person subject to this Act who commits any of the following offences, that is to say -

(a) commits extortion; or

(b) without proper authority extracts from any person money, provisions or service, shall, on conviction by an Assam Rifles Court, be liable to suffer imprisonment for a term which may extend to ten years or such less punishment as is in this Act mentioned.

41. Making away with equipment. Any person subject to this Act who commits any of the following offences, that is to say -

(a) makes away with, or is concerned in making away with any arms, ammunition, equipment, instruments, tools, clothing or any other thing being the property of the Government issued to him for his use or entrusted to him; or

(b) loses by neglect anything mentioned in clause (a); or

(c) sells, pawns, destroys or defaces any medal or decoration granted to him, shall, on conviction by an Assam Rifles Court, be liable to suffer imprisonment for a term which may extend, in the case of the offences specified in clause (a), to ten years, and in the case of the offences specified in the other clauses, to five years, or in either case such less punishment as is in this Act mentioned.

42. Injury to property. Any person subject to this Act who commits any of the following offences, that is to say -

(a) destroys or injures any property mentioned in clause (a) of Section 41 or any property belonging to any Force mess, band or institution, or to any person subject to this Act; or

(b) commits any act which causes damage to, or destruction of, any property of the Government by fire; or

(c) kills, injures, makes away with, ill-treats or loses any animal entrusted to him, shall, on conviction by an Assam Rifles Court, be liable, if he has acted wilfully, to suffer imprisonment for a term which may extend to ten years or such less punishment as is in this Act mentioned; and if he has acted without reasonable excuse, to suffer imprisonment for a term which may extend to five years or such less punishment as is in this Act mentioned.

43. False accusations. Any person subject to this Act who commits any of the following offences, that is to say -

(a) makes a false accusation against any person subject to this Act, knowing or having reason to believe such accusation to be false; or

(b) in making complaint against any person subject to this Act, makes any statement affecting the character of such person, knowing or having reason to believe such statement to be false, or knowingly and wilfully suppresses any material facts, shall, on conviction by an Assam Rifles Court, be liable to suffer imprisonment for a term which may extend to three years or such less punishment as is in this Act mentioned.

44. Falsifying official document and false declarations. Any person subject to this Act who commits any of the following offences, that is to say -

(a) in any report, return, list, certificate, book or other document made or signed by him, or of the contents of which it is his duty to ascertain the accuracy, knowingly makes, or is privy to the making of, any false or fraudulent statement; or

(b) in any document of the description mentioned in clause (a), knowingly makes, or is privy to the making of, any omission, with intent to defraud; or

(c) knowingly and with intent to injure any person or knowingly and with intent to defraud, suppresses, defaces, alters or makes away with any document which it is his duty to preserve or produce; or

(d) where it is his official duty to make a declaration respecting any matter, knowingly makes a false declaration; or

(e) obtains for himself, or for any other person, any pension, allowance or other advantage or privilege by a statement which is false, and which he either knows or believes to be false or does not believe to be true, or by making or using false entry in any book or record, or by making any document containing a false statement, or by omitting to make a true entry or document containing a true statement, shall, on conviction by an Assam Rifles Court, be liable to suffer imprisonment for a term which may extend to ten years or such less punishment as is in this Act mentioned.

45. Signing in blank and failure to report. Any person subject to this Act who commits any of the following offences, that is to say -

(a) when signing any document relating to pay, arms, ammunition, equipment, clothing, supplies or stores, or any property of the Government fraudulently leaves in blank any material part for which his signature is a voucher; or

(b) refuses or by culpable neglect omits to make or send a report or return which it is his duty to make or send, shall, on conviction by an Assam Rifles Court, be liable to suffer imprisonment for a term which may extend to three years or such less punishment as is in this Act mentioned.

46. Offences relating to Assam Rifles Court. Any person subject to this Act who commits any of the following offences, that is to say -

(a) being duly summoned or ordered to attend as a witness before an Assam Rifles Court, wilfully or without reasonable excuse, makes default in attending; or

(b) refuses to take an oath or make an affirmation legally required by an Assam Rifles Court to be taken or made; or

(c) refuses to produce or deliver any document in his power or control legally required by an Assam Rifles Court to be produced or delivered by him; or

(d) refuses, when a witness, to answer any question which he is by law bound to answer; or

(e) is guilty of contempt of the Assam Rifles Court by using insulting or threatening language, or by causing any interruption or disturbance in the proceedings of such Court, shall, on conviction by an Assam Rifles Court, be liable to suffer imprisonment for a term which may extend to three years or such less punishment as is in this Act mentioned.

47. False evidence. Any person subject to this Act who, having been duly sworn or affirmed before any Assam Rifles Court or other court competent under this Act to administer an oath or affirmation, makes any statement which is false, and which he either knows or believes to be false or does not believe to be true, shall, on conviction by an Assam Rifles Court, be liable to suffer imprisonment for a term which may extend to seven years or such less punishment as is in this Act mentioned.

48. Unlawful detention of pay. Any officer, subordinate officer or an under-officer who, having received the pay of a person subject to this Act, unlawfully detains or refuses to pay the same when due, shall, on conviction by an Assam Rifles Court, be liable to suffer imprisonment for a term which may extend to five years or such less punishment as is in this Act mentioned.

49. Violation of good order and discipline. Any person subject to this Act who is guilty of any act or omission which, though not specified in this Act, is prejudicial to good order and discipline of the Force shall, on conviction by an Assam Rifles Court, be liable to suffer imprisonment for a term which may extend to seven years or such less punishment as is in this Act mentioned.

50. Miscellaneous offences. Any person subject to this Act who commits any of the following offences, that is to say -

(a) being in command at any post or on the march, and receiving a complaint that anyone under his command has beaten or otherwise mal-treated or oppressed any person, or has disturbed any fair or market, or committed any riot or trespass, fails to have due reparation made to the injured person or to report the case to the proper authority; or

(b) by defiling any place of worship, or otherwise, intentionally insults the religion, or wounds the religious feelings of any person; or

(c) attempts to commit suicide, and in such attempt does any act towards the commission of such offence; or

(d) being below the rank of subordinate officer, when off duty, appears without proper authority, in or about camp, or when going to, or returning from, any town or bazaar, carrying a rifle, sword or other offensive weapons; or

(e) directly or indirectly accepts or obtains, or agrees to accept, or attempts to obtain, for himself or for any other person, any gratification as a motive or reward for procuring the enrolment of any person or leave of absence, promotion or any other advantage or indulgence for any person in the service; or

(f) commits any offence against the property or person of any inhabitant of, or resident in, the country in which he is serving, shall, on conviction by an Assam Rifles Court, be liable to suffer imprisonment for a term which may extend to seven years or such less punishment as is in this Act mentioned.

51. Attempt. Any person subject to this Act who attempts to commit any of the offences specified in Sections 21 to 50 (both inclusive) and in such attempt does any act towards the commission of the offence shall, on conviction by an Assam Rifles Court, where no express provision is made by this Act for the punishment of such attempt, be liable -

(a) if the offence attempted to be committed is punishable with death, to suffer imprisonment for a term which may extend to fourteen years or such less punishment as is in this Act mentioned; and

(b) if the offence attempted to be committed is punishable with imprisonment to suffer imprisonment for a term which may extend to one-half of the longest term provided for that offence or such less punishment as is in this Act mentioned.

52. Abetment of offences that have been committed. Any person subject to this Act who abets the commission of any of the offences specified in Sections 21 to 50 (both inclusive) shall, on conviction by an Assam Rifles Court, if the Act abetted is committed in consequence of the abetment and no express provision is made by this Act for the punishment of such abetment, be liable to suffer the punishment provided for that offence or such less punishment as is in this Act mentioned.

53. Abetment of offences punishable with death and not committed. Any person subject to this Act who abets the commission of any of the offences punishable with death under Sections 21, 24 and clause (a) of sub-section (1) of Section 25 shall, on conviction by an Assam Rifles Court, if that offence, be not committed in consequence of the abetment, and no express provision is made by this Act for the punishment of such abetment, be liable to suffer imprisonment for a term which may extend to fourteen years of such less punishment as is in this Act mentioned.

54. Abetment of offences punishable with imprisonment and not committed. Any person subject to this Act who abets the commission of any of the offences specified in Sections 21 to 50 (both inclusive) and punishable with imprisonment shall, on conviction by an Assam Rifles Court, if that offence, be not committed in consequence of the abetment, and no express provision is made by this Act for the punishment of such abetment, be liable to suffer imprisonment for a term which may extend to one-half of the longest term provided for that offence or such less punishment as is in this Act mentioned.

55. Civil offences. Subject to the provisions of Section 56, any person subject to this Act who at any place in, or beyond, India commits any civil offence shall be deemed to be guilty of an offence against this Act and, if charged therewith under this Section, shall be liable to be tried by an Assam Rifles Court and, on conviction, be punishable as follows, that is to say -

(a) if the offence is one which would be punishable under any law in force in India with death, he shall be liable to suffer any punishment assigned for the offence, by the aforesaid law and such less punishment as is in this Act mentioned; and

(b) in any other case, he shall be liable to suffer any punishment assigned for the offence by the law in force in India, or imprisonment for a term which may extend to seven years, or such less punishment as in this Act mentioned.

56. Civil offences not triable by an Assam Rifles Court. A person subject to this Act who commits an offence of murder or of culpable homicide not amounting to murder against, or of rape in relation to, a person not subject to this Act shall not be deemed to be guilty of an offence against this Act and shall not be tried by an Assam Rifles Court, unless he commits any of the said offences -

(a) while on active duty; or

(b) at any place outside India; or

(c) at any place specified by the Central Government, by notification in this behalf.

CHAPTER -V : PUNISHMENTS

57. Punishment awardable by Assam Rifles Courts.

(1) Punishments may be inflicted in respect of offences committed by persons subject to this Act and convicted by the Assam Rifles Courts, according to the scale following, that is to say -

(a) death;

(b) imprisonment which may be for the term of life or any other lesser term but excluding imprisonment for a term not exceeding three months in Force custody;

(c) dismissal from the service;

(d) compulsory retirement from service;

(e) imprisonment for a term not exceeding three months in Force custody except in case of officers and subordinate officers;

(f) reduction to the ranks or to a lower rank or grade or place in the list of their rank in the case of an under-officer;

(g) forfeiture of seniority of rank and forfeiture of all or any part of the service for the purpose of promotion;

(h) forfeiture of service for the purpose of increased pay, pension or any other prescribed purpose;

(i) fine;

(j) severe reprimand or reprimand except in the case of persons below the rank of an under-officer;

(k) forfeiture of pay and allowances for a period not exceeding three months for an offence committed on active duty;

(l) forfeiture in the case of person sentenced to dismissal from the service of all arrears of pay and allowances and other public money due to him at the time of such dismissal;

(m) stoppage of pay and allowances until any proved loss or damage occasioned by the offence for which he is convicted is made good.

(2) Each of the punishments specified in sub-section (1) shall be deemed to be inferior in degree to every punishment preceding it in the above scale.

58. Alternative punishments awardable by Assam Rifles Courts. Subject to the provisions of this Act, an Assam Rifles Court may, on convicting a person subject to this Act of any of the offences specified in Sections 21 to 54 (both inclusive) award either the particular punishment with which the offence is stated in the said Sections to be punishable or, in lieu thereof, any of the punishments lower in the scale set out in Section 57 regard being had to the nature and degree of the offence.

59. Combination of punishments. A sentence of an Assam Rifles Court may award in addition to, or without any one other punishment, the punishment specified in clause (c) of sub-section (1) of Section 57, and any one more of the punishments specified in clauses (f) to (m) (both inclusive) of that sub-section.

60. Retention in the Force of a person convicted on active duty. When on active duty, any enrolled person has been sentenced by an Assam Rifles Court to dismissal or to imprisonment whether combined with dismissal or not, the prescribed officer may direct that such person may be retained to serve in the ranks, and such service shall be reckoned as part of his term of imprisonment, if any.

61. Punishments otherwise than by Assam Rifles Courts. Punishments may also be inflicted in respect of offences committed by persons subject to this Act without the intervention of an Assam Rifles Court in the manner stated in Sections 62, 64, 65 and 66.

62. Minor punishments. Subject to the provisions of Section 63, a Commandant or such other officer as is, with the consent of the Central Government, specified by the Director-General may, in the prescribed manner, proceed against a person subject to this Act, otherwise than as an officer or a subordinate officer or a Warrant Officer who is charged with an offence under this Act and award such person to the extent prescribed, one or more of the following punishments, that is to say -

(a) imprisonment in Force custody up to twenty-eight days;

(b) detention up to twenty-eight days;

(c) confinement to the lines up to twenty-eight days;

(d) extra guards or duties;

(e) deprivation of any special position or special emoluments or any acting rank or reduction to a lower grade of pay;

(f) forfeiture of good service and good conduct pay;

(g) severe reprimand or reprimand;

(h) fine up to fourteen days' pay in any one month;

(i) deduction from his pay and allowances of any sum required to make good such compensation for any expense, loss, damage or destruction caused by him to the Central Government, or any building or property as may be awarded by his Commandant.

63. Limit of punishments under Section 62.

(1) In the case of an award of two or more of the punishments specified in clauses (a), (b), (c) and (d) of Section 62, the punishments specified in clause (c) or clause (d) shall take effect only at the end of the punishment specified in clause (a) or clause (b).

(2) When two or more of the punishments specified in the said clauses (a), (b) and (c) are awarded to a person conjointly, or when already undergoing one or more of the said punishments, the whole extent of the punishments shall not exceed in the aggregate forty-two days.

(3) The punishments specified in the said clauses (a), (b) and (c) shall not be awarded to any person who is of the rank of an under-officer or was at the time of committing the offence for which he is punished of such rank.

(4) The punishments specified in clause (g) of Section 62 shall not be awarded to any person below the rank of an under-officer.

64. Punishment of officers below the rank of Deputy Commandant, subordinate officers and Warrant Officer by Deputy Inspectors-General and others.

(1) An officer not below the rank of the Deputy Inspector-General or such other officer as is, with the consent of the Central Government, specified by the Director-General may, in the prescribed manner, proceed against an officer below the rank of a Deputy Commandant and of any rank of subordinate officer and of the rank of Warrant Officer who is charged with an offence under this Act and award one or more of the following punishments, that is to say -

  (a) forfeiture of seniority, or in the case of any of them whose promotion depends upon the length of service, forfeiture of service for the purpose of promotion for a period not exceeding twelve months, but subject to the right of the accused previous to the award to elect to be tried by an Assam Rifles Court;

  (b) severe reprimand or reprimand;

  (c) stoppage of pay and allowances until any proved loss or damage occasioned by the offence of which he is convicted is made good.

(2) In every case in which punishment has been awarded under sub-section (1), certified true copies of the proceedings shall be forwarded, in the prescribed manner, by the officer awarding the punishment to the prescribed superior authority who may, if the punishment awarded, appears to him to be illegal, unjust or excessive, cancel, vary or remit the punishment and make such other direction as may be appropriate in the circumstances of the case.

65. Punishment of officers below the rank of a Commandant, subordinate officers and Warrant Officer by the Inspectors-General and others.

(1) An officer not below the rank of the Inspector-General or such other officer as is, with the consent of the Central Government, specified by the Director-General may, in the prescribed manner, proceed against an officer below the rank of a Commandant and any subordinate officer and a Warrant Officer who

is charged with an offence under this Act and award one or more of the following punishments, that is to say -

(a) forfeiture of seniority, or in the case of any of them whose promotion depends upon the length of service, forfeiture of service for the purpose of promotion for a period not exceeding twelve months, but subject to the right of the accused previous to the award to elect to be tried by an Assam Rifles Court;

(b) severe reprimand or reprimand;

(c) stoppage of pay and allowances until any proved loss or damage occasioned by the offence of which he is convicted is made good.

(2) In every case in which punishment has been awarded under sub-section (1), certified true copies of the proceedings shall be forwarded, in the prescribed manner, by the officer awarding the punishment to the prescribed superior authority who may, if the punishment awarded appears to him to be illegal, unjust or excessive, cancel, vary or remit the punishment and make such other direction as may be appropriate in the circumstances of the case.

66. Punishment of subordinate officers and Warrant Officer by Commandant, etc. A Commandant or such other officer as is, with the consent of the Central Government, specified by the Director-General may, in the prescribed manner, proceed against any subordinate officer or a Warrant Officer who is charged with an offence under this Act and award one or more of the following punishments, that is to say -

(a) severe reprimand or reprimand;

(b) stoppage of pay and allowances until any proved loss or damage occasioned by the offence of which he is convicted is made good:

PROVIDED that the punishment mentioned under clause (a) shall only be awarded by an officer not below the rank of Commandant authorised by the Director-General to award such punishment.

67. Collective fines.

(1) Whenever any weapon or part of a weapon, or ammunition, forming part of the equipment of a unit of the Force, is lost or stolen, an officer not below rank of the Commandant of a battalion may, after making such inquiry as he thinks fit and subject to the rules and regulations, impose a collective fine upon the subordinate officer, under-officer and men of such unit, or upon so many of them as, in his judgment, should be held responsible for such loss or theft.

(2) Such fine shall be assessed as a percentage on the pay of the individuals on whom it falls.

CHAPTER -VI : PENAL DEDUCTIONS

68. Deductions from pay and allowances of officers. The following penal deductions may be made from the pay and allowances of an officer, that is to say -

(a) all pay and allowances due to an officer for every day he absents himself without leave, unless a satisfactory explanation has been given to his commanding officer and has been approved by the Central Government;

(b) all pay and allowances for every day while he is in custody or under suspension from duty on a charge for an offence for which he is afterwards convicted by a criminal court or an Assam Rifles Court or by an officer exercising authority under Section 64 or Section 65;

(c) any sum required to make good the pay of any person subject to this Act which he has unlawfully retained or unlawfully refused to pay;

(d) any sum required to make good such compensation for any expenses, loss, damage or destruction occasioned by the commission of an offence as may be determined by an Assam Rifles Court by whom he is convicted of such offence or by an officer exercising authority under Section 64 or Section 65;

(e) all pay and allowances ordered by an Assam Rifles Court to be forfeited or stopped;

(f) any sum required to pay a fine awarded by a criminal court or an Assam Rifles Court;

(g) any sum required to make good any loss, damage or destruction of public or regimental property which, after due investigation, appears to the Central Government to have been occasioned by the wrongful act or negligence on the part of the officer;

(h) all pay and allowances forfeited by order of the Central Government if the officer is found by a Court of inquiry constituted by the Director-General in this behalf, to have deserted to the enemy, or while in enemy hands, to have served with, or under the orders of, the enemy, or in any manner to have aided the enemy, or to have allowed himself to be taken prisoner by the enemy through want of due precaution or through disobedience of orders or wilful neglect of duty, or having been taken prisoner by the enemy, to have failed to rejoin his service when it was possible to do so;

(i) any sum required by order of the Central Government to be paid for the maintenance of his wife or his legitimate or illegitimate child or towards the cost of any relief given by the said Government to the said wife or child.

69. Deductions from pay and allowances of persons other than officers. Subject to the provisions of Section 72, the following penal deductions may be made from the pay and allowances of a person subject to this Act other than an officer, that is to say -

(a) all pay and allowances for every day of absence either on desertion or without leave, or as a prisoner of war unless a satisfactory explanation has been given and accepted by his Commandant, and for every day of imprisonment awarded by a criminal court, an Assam Rifles Court or an officer exercising authority under Section 62;

(b) all pay and allowances for every day while he is in custody on a charge for an offence of which he is afterwards convicted by a criminal court or an Assam Rifles Court or on a charge of absence without leave for which he is afterwards awarded imprisonment by an officer exercising authority under Section 62;

(c) all pay and allowances for every day on which he is in hospital on account of sickness certified by the medical officer attending on him to have been caused by an offence under this Act committed by him;

(d) for every day on which he is in hospital on account of sickness certified by the medical officer attending on him to have been caused by his own misconduct or imprudence, such sum as may be specified by the order of the Central Government or such officer as may be specified by that Government;

(e) all pay and allowances ordered by an Assam Rifles Court or by an officer exercising authority under any of the Sections 62, 64, 65 and 66 to be forfeited or stopped;

(f) all pay and allowances for every day between his being recovered from the enemy and his dismissal from the service in consequence of his conduct when being taken prisoner by, or while in the hands of the enemy;

(g) any sum required to make good such compensation for any expenses, loss, damage or destruction caused by him to the Central Government or to any building or property as may be awarded by his Commandant;

(h) any sum required to pay a fine awarded by a criminal court, an Assam Rifles Court or an officer exercising authority under any of the Sections 62 and 67;

(i) any sum required by order of the Central Government or any prescribed officer to be paid for the maintenance of his wife or his legitimate or illegitimate child or towards the cost of any relief given by the said Government to the said wife or child.

70. Computation of time of absence of custody. For the purpose of clauses (a) and (b) of Section 69 -

(a) no person shall be treated as absent or in custody for a day unless the absence or custody has lasted, whether wholly in one day, or partly in one day and partly in another, for six consecutive hours or upwards;

(b) any absence or custody for less than a day may be reckoned as absence or custody for a day if such absence or custody prevented the absentee from fulfilling any duty which was thereby thrown upon some other person;

(c) absence or custody for twelve consecutive hours or upward may be reckoned as absence or custody for the whole of each day during any portion of which the person was absent or in custody;

(d) a period of absence or imprisonment, which commences before, and ends after, midnight may be reckoned as a day.

71. Pay and allowances during trial. In case of any person subject to this Act who is in custody or under suspension from duty on a charge for an offence, the prescribed officer may direct that the whole or any part of the pay and allowances of such person shall be withheld, pending the result of his trial on the charge against him, in order to give effect to the provisions of clause (b) of Section 68 and Section 69.

72. Limit of certain deductions. The total deductions from the pay and allowances of a person made under clauses (e), (g) to (i) of Section 69 shall not, except where he is sentenced to dismissal or removal, exceed in any one month one-half of his pay and allowances of that month.

73. Deduction from public money due to a person. Any sum authorised by this Act to be deducted from the pay and allowances of any person may, without prejudice to any other mode of recovering the same, be deducted from any public money due to him other than a pension.

74. Pay and allowances of prisoner of war during inquiry into his conduct. Where the conduct of any person subject to this Act when being taken prisoner by, or while in the hands of the enemy, is to be inquired into under this Act or any other law, the Director-General or any officer authorised by him may order that the whole or any part of the pay and allowances of such person shall be withheld pending the result of such inquiry.

75. Remission of deductions. Any deduction from pay and allowances authorised by this Act may be remitted in such manner and to such extent and by such authority, as may, from time to time be prescribed.

76. Provision for dependents of prisoner of war from remitted deductions. In the case of all persons subject to this Act, being prisoners of war, whose pay and allowances have been forfeited under clause (a) of Section 69, but in respect of whom a remission has been made under Section 75, it shall be lawful for proper provision to be made by the prescribed authorities out of such pay and allowances for any dependants of such persons, and any such remission shall in that case be deemed to apply only to the balance thereafter remaining of such pay and allowances.

77. Provision for dependents of prisoner of war from his pay and allowances. It shall be lawful for proper provision to be made by the prescribed authorities for any dependants of any person subject to this Act who is prisoner of war or is missing, out of his pay and allowances.

78. Period during which a person is deemed to be a prisoner of war. For the purposes of Sections 76 and 77, a person shall be deemed to continue to be prisoner of war until the conclusion of any inquiry into his conduct such as is referred to in Section 74 and if he is dismissed or removed from the service in consequence of such conduct, until the date of such dismissal or removal.

CHAPTER -VII : ARREST AND PROCEEDINGS BEFORE TRIAL

79. Custody of offenders.

(1) Any person subject to this Act who is charged with an offence may be taken into Force custody, under the order of any superior officer.

(2) Notwithstanding anything contained in sub-section (1), an officer may order into Force custody any other officer, though such other officer may be of a higher rank, engaged in a quarrel, affray or disorder.

80. Duty of Commandant in regard to detention.

(1) It shall be the duty of every Commandant to take care that a person under his command when charged with an offence is not detained in custody for more than forty-eight hours after the committal of such person into custody is reported

to him without the charge being investigated, unless investigation within that period seems to him to be impracticable having regard to the public service.

(2) The case of every person, being detained in custody beyond a period of forty-eight hours, and reason thereof, shall be reported by the Commandant to the Deputy Inspector-General under whom he is serving or such other officer to whom an application may be made to convene an Assam Rifles Court for the trial of the person charged.

(3) In reckoning the period of forty-eight hours specified in sub-section (1), Sundays and other public holidays shall be excluded.

(4) Subject to the provisions of this Act, the Central Government may make rules providing for the manner in which and the period for which any person subject to this Act may be taken into and detained in Force custody, pending the trial by any competent authority for any offence committed by him.

81. Interval between committal and trial. In every case where any such person as is mentioned in Section 79 and as not on active duty, remains in such custody for a longer period than eight days, without his trial by an Assam Rifles Court being ordered to be convened, a special report giving reasons for the delay shall be made by his Commandant in the manner prescribed, and a similar report shall be forwarded at intervals of every eight days until an Assam Rifles Court is convened or such person is released from custody.

82. Arrest by civil authorities. Whenever any person subject to this Act who is accused of an offence under this Act, is within the jurisdiction of any magistrate or police officer, such magistrate or police officer shall aid in the apprehension and delivery to Force custody of such person upon receipt of a written application to that effect signed by his Commandant or an officer authorised by the Commandant in that behalf.

83. Capture of deserters.

(1) Whenever any person subject to this Act deserts, the Commandant of the unit to which he belongs, shall give information of the desertion to such civil authorities as, in his opinion, may be able to afford assistance towards the capture of the deserter; and such authorities shall thereupon take steps for the apprehension of the said deserter in like manner as if he were a person for whose apprehension a warrant had been issued by a magistrate and shall deliver the deserter, when apprehended, into Force custody.

(2) Any police officer may arrest without warrant any person reasonably believed to be subject to this Act, and to be a deserter or to be travelling without authority, and shall bring him without delay before the nearest magistrate, to be dealt with according to law.

84. Inquiry into absence without leave.

(1) When any person subject to this Act has been absent from his duty without due authority for a period of thirty days, a court of inquiry shall, as soon as practicable, be assembled and such court shall, on oath or affirmation administered in the prescribed manner, inquire respecting the absence of the person, and the deficiency, if any, in the property of the Government entrusted to his care, or

in any arms, ammunition, equipment, instruments, clothing or necessaries; and if satisfied of the fact of such absence without due authority or other sufficient cause, the court shall declare such absence and the period thereof and the said deficiency, if any, and the Commandant of the unit to which the person belongs shall make a record thereof in the prescribed manner.

(2) If the person declared absent does not afterwards surrender or is not apprehended, he shall, for the purpose of this Act, be deemed to be deserter.

85. Force Police Officers.

(1) The Director-General or any prescribed officer may appoint persons (in this Act referred to as Force Police) for discharging the functions specified in sub-sections (2) and (3).

(2) The duties of a person appointed under sub-section (1), are to take charge of persons confined for any offence, to preserve good order and discipline and to prevent breaches of the same by persons serving in, or attached to, the Force.

(3) Notwithstanding anything contained in Section 79, a person appointed under sub-section (1) may, at any time, arrest and detain for trial, any person subject to this Act who commits, or is charged with, an offence, and may also carry into effect any punishment to be inflicted in pursuance of a sentence awarded by an Assam Rifles Court or by an officer exercising authority under Section 62 but shall not inflict any punishment on his own authority:

PROVIDED that no officer shall be arrested or detained otherwise than on the order of another officer.

CHAPTER -VIII : ASSAM RIFLES COURTS

86. Kinds of Assam Rifles Courts. For the purposes of this Act there shall be three kinds of Assam Rifles Courts, that is to say -

(a) General Assam Rifles Courts;

(b) Petty Assam Rifles Courts; and

(c) Summary Assam Rifles Courts.

87. Power to convene a General Assam Rifles Court. A General Assam Rifles Court may be convened by the Central Government or the Director-General or by any officer empowered in this behalf by warrant of the Director-General.

88. Power to convene a Petty Assam Rifles Court. A Petty Assam Rifles Court may be convened by an officer having power to convene a General Assam Rifles Court or by an officer empowered in this behalf by warrant of any such officer.

89. Contents of warrants issued under Sections 87 and 88. A warrant issued under Section 87 or Section 88 may contain such restrictions, reservations or conditions as the officer issuing it may think fit.

90. Composition of General Assam Rifles Court. A General Assam Rifles Court shall consist of not less than five officers, each of whom has held the post of Assistant Commandant for not less than three whole years and of whom not less than four are of a rank not below that of a confirmed Assistant Commandant.

EXPLANATION. For the purpose of this Section and Section 91, "Assistant Commandant" includes any post of a higher rank and any post declared by the Central Government, by notification, to be an equivalent post as also any post higher in rank than the post so declared.

91. Composition of a Petty Assam Rifles Court. A Petty Assam Rifles Court shall consist of not less than three officers, each of whom has held the post of Assistant Commandant for not less than two whole years.

92. Summary Assam Rifles Court.

(1) A Summary Assam Rifles Court may be held by the Commandant of any unit of the Force and he alone shall constitute the Court.

(2) The proceedings shall be attended throughout by two other persons who shall be officers or subordinate officers or one of either, and who shall not as such, be sworn or affirmed.

93. Dissolution of an Assam Rifles Court.

(1) If an Assam Rifles Court after the commencement of a trial is reduced below the minimum number of officers required by this Act, it shall be dissolved.

(2) If, on account of the illness of the Law Officer or of the accused before the finding, it is impossible to continue the trial, an Assam Rifles Court shall be dissolved.

(3) The officer who convened an Assam Rifles Court may dissolve the same if it appears to him that the exigencies of the service or necessities of discipline render it impossible or inexpedient to continue the said Assam Rifles Court.

(4) Where an Assam Rifles Court is dissolved under this Section, the accused may be tried again.

94. Power of General Assam Rifles Court. A General Assam Rifles Court shall have the power to try any person subject to this Act for any offence punishable thereunder and to pass any sentence authorised thereby.

95. Power of a Petty Assam Rifles Court. A Petty Assam Rifles Court shall have power to try any person subject to this Act other than an officer or a subordinate officer for any offence made punishable thereunder and to pass any sentence authorised by this Act other than a sentence of death or imprisonment for a term exceeding two years.

96. Power of a Summary Assam Rifles Court.

(1) Subject to the provisions of sub-section (2), a Summary Assam Rifles Court may try any offence punishable under this Act.

(2) When there is no grave reason for immediate action and reference can, without detriment to discipline, be made to the officer empowered to convene a Petty Assam Rifles Court for the trial of the alleged offender, an officer holding a Summary Assam Rifles Court shall not try without such reference any offence punishable under any of the Sections 21, 24 and 55, or any offence against the officer holding the Court.

(3) A Summary Assam Rifles Court may try any person subject to this Act and under the command of the officer holding the Court, except an officer or a subordinate officer.

(4) A Summary Assam Rifles Court may pass any sentence which may be passed under this Act except the sentence of death or of imprisonment for a term exceeding the limit specified in sub-section (5).

(5) The limit referred to in sub-section (4) shall be-

(a) one year, if the officer holding the Assam Rifles Court has held either the post of Commandant or a post declared by the Central Government, by notification, to be equivalent thereto for a period of not less than three years or holds a post of higher rank than either of the said posts; and

(b) three months, in any other case.

97. Prohibition of second trial.

(1) When any person subject to this Act has been acquitted or convicted of an offence by an Assam Rifles Court or by a criminal court or has been dealt with under Section 62 or Section 64 or Section 65 or Section 66, he shall not be liable to be tried again for the same offence by an Assam Rifles Court or dealt with under the said Sections.

(2) When any person, subject to this Act has been acquitted or convicted of an offence by an Assam Rifles Court or has been dealt with under Section 62 or Section 64 or Section 65 or Section 66, he shall not be liable to be tried again by a criminal court for the same offence or on the same facts.

98. Period of limitation for trial.

(1) Except as provided by sub-section (2), no trial by an Assam Rifles Court of any person subject to this Act for any offence shall be commenced after the expiration of a period of three years and such period shall commence-

(a) on the date of the offence; or

(b) where the commission of the offence was not known to the person aggrieved by the offence or to the authority competent to initiate action, from the first day on which such offence comes to the knowledge of such person or authority, whichever is earlier; or

(c) where it is not known by whom the offence was committed, from the first day on which the identity of the offender is known to the person aggrieved by the offence or to the authority competent to initiate action, whichever is earlier:

PROVIDED that in computing any period under this Section, the period during which the proceedings of investigation has been stayed by any court in such offence by injunction or order, the period of the continuance of the injunction or order, the day on which it was issued or made; and the day on which it was withdrawn, shall be excluded.

(2) The provisions of sub-section (1) shall not apply to a trial for an offence of desertion or for any of the offences mentioned in Section 24 or an offence under Section 30.

(3) In computation of the period of three years under sub-section (1), any time spent by such person in evading arrest after the commission of the offence, shall be excluded.

99. Trial, etc., of offender who ceases to be subject to this Act.

(1) Where an offence under this Act had been committed by any person while subject to this Act and he had ceased to be so subject, he may be taken into and kept in Force custody and tried and punished for such offence as if he continued to be so subject.

(2) No such person shall be tried for an offence, unless his trial commences within a period of three years after he had ceased to be subject to this Act; and in computing such period, the time during which such person has avoided arrest by absconding or concealing himself or where the institution of the proceeding in respect of the offence has been stayed by an injunction or order, the period of the continuance of the injunction or order, the day on which it was issued or made, and the day on which it was withdrawn, shall be excluded:

PROVIDED that nothing contained in this sub-section shall apply to the trial of any such person for an offence of desertion or for any of the offences mentioned in Section 24 or shall affect the jurisdiction of a criminal court to try an offence triable by such court as well as by an Assam Rifles Court.

100. Application of this Act during term of sentence.

(1) When a person subject to this Act is sentenced by an Assam Rifles Court to imprisonment, this Act shall apply to him during the term of his sentence, though he is dismissed from the Force or has otherwise ceased to be subject to this Act, and he may be kept, removed, imprisoned and punished as if he continued to be subject to this Act.

(2) When a person subject to this Act is sentenced by an Assam Rifles Court to death, this Act shall apply to him till the sentence is carried out.

101. Place of trial. Any person subject to this Act who commits any offence against it may be tried and punished for such offence in any place whatever.

102. Choice between criminal court and Assam Rifles Court. When a criminal court and an Assam Rifles Court each have jurisdiction in respect of an offence, it shall be in the discretion of the Director-General, or the Inspector-General or the Deputy Inspector-General within whose command the accused person is serving or such other officer as may be prescribed, to decide before which court proceedings shall be instituted, and, if that officer, decides that they shall be instituted before an Assam Rifles Court, to direct that the accused person shall be detained in Force custody.

103. Power of criminal court to require delivery of offender.

(1) When a criminal court having jurisdiction is of opinion that proceedings shall be instituted before itself in respect of any alleged offence, it may, by written notice, require the officer referred to in Section 102 at his option, either to deliver over the offender to the nearest Magistrate to be proceeded against according to law, or to postpone proceedings, pending a reference to the Central Government.

(2) In every such case the said officer shall either deliver over the offender in compliance with the requisition, or shall forthwith refer the question as to the

court before which the proceedings are to be instituted, for the determination of the Central Government whose order upon such reference shall be final.

CHAPTER -IX : PROCEDURE OF ASSAM RIFLES COURTS

104. Presiding officer. At every General Assam Rifles Court or Petty Assam Rifles Court, the senior member shall be the presiding officer.

105. Law Officer. Every General Assam Rifles Court shall, and every Petty Assam Rifles Court may, be attended by a Law Officer, or if no such officer is available, an officer approved by the Chief Law Officer or a Law Officer.

106. Challenges.

(1) At all trials by a General Assam Rifles Court or by a Petty Assam Rifles Court, as soon as the Court is assembled, the names of the presiding officer and members shall be read over to the accused, who shall thereupon be asked whether he objects to being tried by any officer sitting on the court.

(2) If the accused objects to such officer, his objection and also the reply thereto of the officer objected to, shall be heard and recorded, and the remaining officers of the court shall, in the absence of the challenged officer, decide on the objection.

(3) If the objection is allowed by one-half or more of the votes of the officers entitled to vote, the objection shall be allowed, and the member objected to shall retire, and his vacancy may be filled in the prescribed manner, by another officer subject to the same right of the accused to object.

(4) When no challenge is made, or when a challenge has been made and disallowed, or the place of every officer successfully challenged has been filled by another officer to whom no objection is made or allowed, the court shall proceed with the trial.

107. Oath of member, Law Officer and witness.

(1) An oath or affirmation in the prescribed manner shall be administered to every member of an Assam Rifles Court and to the Law Officer or, as the case may be, the officer approved under Section 105 before the commencement of the trial.

(2) Every person giving evidence before an Assam Rifles Court shall be examined after being duly sworn or affirmed in the prescribed form.

(3) The provisions of sub-section (2) shall not apply where the witness is a child under twelve years of age and the Assam Rifles Court is of opinion that though the witness understands the duty of speaking the truth, he does not understand the nature of an oath or affirmation.

108. Voting by members.

(1) Subject to the provisions of sub-sections (2) and (3), every decision of an Assam Rifles Court shall be passed by a majority of votes; and where there is an equality of votes on either the finding or the sentence, the decision shall be in favour of the accused.

(2) No sentence of death shall be passed by a General Assam Rifles Court without the concurrence of at least two-thirds of the members of the Court.

(3) In matters, other than a challenge or the finding or sentence, the presiding officer shall have a casting vote.

109. General rule as to evidence. The Indian Evidence Act, 1872 shall, subject to the provisions of this Act, apply to all proceedings before an Assam Rifles Court.

110. Judicial notice. An Assam Rifles Court may take judicial notice of any matter within the general knowledge of the members as officers of the Force.

111. Summoning of witness.

(1) The convening officer, the presiding officer of an Assam Rifles Court or court of inquiry or the Law Officer or, as the case may be, the officer approved under Section 105 or the Commandant of the accused person may, by summons under his hand, require the attendance, at a time and place to be mentioned in the summons, of any person either to give evidence or to produce any document or other thing.

(2) In the case of a witness, who is subject to this Act, the summons shall be sent to his Commandant and such officer shall serve it upon him accordingly.

(3) In the case of any other witness, the summons shall be sent to the Magistrate within whose jurisdiction he may be, or resides, and such Magistrate shall give effect to the summons as if the witness were required in the court of such Magistrate.

112. Documents exempted from production.

(1) Nothing in Section 111 shall be deemed to affect the operation of Sections 123 and 124 of the Indian Evidence Act, 1872 or to apply to any letter, postcard, telegram or other document in the custody of the postal or telegraph authorities.

(2) If any document in such custody is, in the opinion of any Chief Judicial Magistrate, Chief Metropolitan Magistrate, Court of Session or High Court, wanted for the purpose of any Assam Rifles Court, such Magistrate or Court may require the postal or telegraph authorities, as the case may be, to deliver such document to such person as such Magistrate, or Court may direct.

(3) If any such document is, in the opinion of any other Magistrate or of any Commissioner of Police or District Superintendent of Police, wanted for any such purpose, he may require the postal or telegraph authorities, as the case may be, to cause such search to be made for, and to detain such document pending the orders of any such Chief Judicial Magistrate, Chief Metropolitan Magistrate or Court of Session or High Court.

113. Commission for examination of witness.

(1) Whenever, in the course of a trial by an Assam Rifles Court, it appears to the Court that the examination of a witness is necessary for the ends of justice, and that the attendance of such witness cannot be procured without an amount of delay, expense or inconvenience which, in the circumstances of the case, would be unreasonable, such court may address the Chief Law Officer in order that a commission to take the evidence of such witness may be issued.

(2) The Chief Law Officer may then, if he thinks necessary, issue a commission to any Chief Judicial Magistrate or Judicial Magistrate of the first class, within the local limits of whose jurisdiction such witness resides, to take the evidence of such witness.

(3) The Chief Judicial Magistrate or Judicial Magistrate of the first class to whom the commission is issued, or, if he is the Chief Judicial Magistrate, he or such Judicial Magistrate of the first class as he appoints in this behalf, shall summon the witness before him and shall take down his evidence in the same manner, and may for this purpose exercise the same powers, as in the trials of warrant-cases under the Code of Criminal Procedure, 1973.

(4) When the witness resides in a tribal area or in any place outside India, the commission may be issued in the manner specified in sub-heading" B.- Commissions for the examination of witnesses" of Chapter XXIII of the Code of Criminal Procedure, 1973.

114. Examination of witness on commission.

(1) The prosecutor and the accused person in any case in which a commission is issued under Section 113 may respectively forward any interrogatories in writing which the court may think relevant to the issue, and the Chief Judicial Magistrate or the Judicial Magistrate of the first class executing the commission shall examine the witness upon such interrogatories.

(2) The prosecutor and the accused person may appear before such Chief Judicial Magistrate or the Judicial Magistrate of the first class by counsel or, except in the case of an accused person in custody, in person, and may examine, cross-examine and re-examine, as the case may be, the said witness.

(3) After a commission issued under Section 113 has been duly executed, it shall be returned, together with the deposition of the witness examined thereunder to the Chief Law Officer.

(4) On receipt of a commission, and deposition returned under sub-section (3), the Chief Law Officer shall forward the same to the court at whose instance the commission was issued or, if such court has been dissolved, to any other court convened for the trial of the accused person and the commission, the return thereto and the deposition shall be open to inspection by the prosecutor and the accused person, and may, subject to all just exceptions, be read in evidence in the case by either the prosecutor or the accused, and shall form part of the proceedings of the court.

(5) In every case in which a commission is issued under Section 113, the trial may be adjourned for specified time reasonably sufficient for the execution and return of the commission.

115. Conviction of offences not charged. A person charged before an Assam Rifles Court-

(a) with desertion may be found guilty of attempting to desert or of being absent without leave;

(b) with attempting to desert may be found guilty of being absent without leave;

(c) with using criminal force may be found guilty of assault;

(d) with using threatening language may be found guilty of using insubordinate language;

(e) with any one of the offences specified in clauses (a), (b), (c) and (d) of Section 39 may be found guilty of any other of these offences with which he might have been charged;

(f) with an offence punishable under Section 55 may be found guilty of any other offence of which he might have been found guilty, if the provisions of the Code of Criminal Procedure, 1973, were applicable;

(g) with any offence under this Act may, on failure of proof of an offence having been committed in circumstances involving a more severe punishment, be found guilty of the same offence as having been committed in circumstances involving a less severe punishment;

(h) with any offence under this Act may be found guilty of having attempted or abetted the commission of that offence, although the attempt or abetment is not separately charged.

116. Presumption as to signatures. In any proceeding under this Act, any application, certificate, warrant, reply or other document purporting to be signed by an officer in the service of the Government shall, on production, be presumed to have been duly signed by the person by whom and in the character in which it purports to have been signed, until the contrary is shown.

117. Enrolment paper.

(1) Any enrolment paper purporting to be signed by an enrolling officer shall, in proceedings under this Act, be evidence of the person enrolled having given the answers to questions which he is therein represented as having given.

(2) The enrolment of such person may be proved by the production of the original or a copy of this enrolment paper purporting to be certified to be a true copy by the officer having custody of enrolment paper.

118. Presumption as to certain documents.

(1) A letter, return or other document respecting the service of any person in, or the dismissal, removal or discharge of any person from, any unit of the Force, or respecting the circumstances of any person not having served in, or belonged to any unit of the Force, if purporting to be signed by or on behalf of the Central Government or the Director-General, or by any prescribed officer, shall be the evidence of facts stated in such letter, return or other document.

(2) An Assam Rifles list or Gazette purporting to be published by authority shall be evidence of the status and rank of the officers, subordinate officers therein mentioned, and of any appointment held by them and of the battalion, unit or branch of the Force to which they belong.

(3) Where a record is made in any battalion book in pursuance of this Act or of any rules or otherwise in the discharge of official duties, and purporting to be signed

by the Commandant or by the officer whose duty it is to make such record, such record shall be evidence of the facts therein stated.

(4) A copy of any record in any battalion book purporting to be certified to be a true copy by the officer having custody of such book shall be evidence of such record.

(5) Where any person subject to this Act is being tried on a charge of desertion or of absence without leave, and such person has surrendered himself into the custody of any officer or other person subject to this Act, or any unit of the Force, or has been apprehended by such officer or person, a certificate purporting to be signed by such officer or by the Commandant of the unit to which such person belongs, as the case may be, and stating the fact, date and place of such surrender or apprehension, and the manner in which he was dressed, shall be the evidence of the matters so stated.

(6) Where any person subject to this Act is being tried on a charge of desertion or of absence without leave and such person has surrendered himself into the custody of, or has been apprehended by, a police officer not below the rank of an officer in charge of a police station, a certificate purporting to be signed by such police officer and stating facts, the date and place of such surrender or apprehension, and the manner in which he was dressed shall be evidence of the matters so stated.

(7) Any document purporting to be the report under the hand of a Government scientific expert, upon any matter or thing duly submitted to him for examination or analysis and report in the course of any proceeding under this Act, may be used as evidence in any inquiry, trial or other proceeding under this Act.

(8) The Assam Rifles Court may, if it thinks fit, summon and examine the expert referred to in sub-section (7) as to the subject matter of his report.

(9) Where any such expert is summoned by an Assam Rifles Court and he is unable to attend personally, he may, unless the Court has expressly directed him to appear personally, depute any responsible officer working with him to attend the Court, if such deputed officer is conversant with the facts of the case and satisfactorily depose in the Court on his behalf.

(10) The provisions of sub-sections (7), (8) and (9) shall apply to such Government scientific experts as specified in sub-section (4) of Section 293 of the Code of Criminal Procedure, 1973.

119. Reference by accused to Government officer.

(1) If at any trial for desertion or absence without leave, overstaying leave or not rejoining when warned for service, the accused person states in his defence any sufficient or reasonable excuse for his unauthorised absence, and refers in support thereof to any officer in the service of the Government, or if it appears that any such officer is likely to prove or disprove the said statement in the defence, the Court shall address such officer and adjourn the proceedings until his reply is received.

(2) The written reply of any officer so referred to shall, if signed by him, be received in evidence and have the same effect as if made on oath before the Court.

(3) If the Court is dissolved before the receipt of such reply or if the Court omits to comply with the provisions of this Section, the convening officer may, at his discretion, annul the proceedings and order a fresh trial.

120. Evidence of previous convictions and general character.

(1) When any person subject to this Act has been convicted by an Assam Rifles Court of any offence, such Assam Rifles Court may inquire into, and receive, and record evidence of any previous convictions of such person, either by an Assam Rifles Court or by a criminal court, or any previous award of punishment under Section 62 or Section 64 or Section 65 or Section 66, and may further inquire into and record the general character of such person and such other matters as may be prescribed.

(2) Evidence received under this Section may be either oral, or in the shape of entries in, or certified extracts from, books of an Assam Rifles Court, or other official records; and it shall not be necessary to give notice before trial to the person tried that evidence as to his previous convictions or character will be received.

(3) At a Summary Assam Rifles Court, the officer holding the trial may, if he thinks fit, record any previous convictions against the offender, his general character, and such other matters as may be prescribed, as of his own knowledge, instead of requiring them to be proved under the foregoing provisions of this Section.

121. Lunacy of accused.

(1) Whenever, in the course of a trial by an Assam Rifles Court, it appears to the Court that the person charged is by reason of unsoundness of mind incapable of making his defence, or that he committed the act alleged but was by reason of unsoundness of mind incapable of knowing the nature of the act or knowing that it was wrong or contrary to law, the Court shall record a finding accordingly.

(2) The presiding officer of the Court, or in the case of a Summary Assam Rifles Court, the officer holding the trial, shall forthwith report the case to the confirming officer, or to the authority empowered to deal with its findings under Section 137, as the case may be.

(3) The confirming officer to whom the case is reported under sub-section (2) may, if he does not confirm the finding, take steps to have the accused person tried by the same or another Assam Rifles Court for the offence with which he was charged.

(4) The authority to whom the finding of a Summary Assam Rifles Court is reported under sub-section (2), and a confirming officer confirming the finding in any case so reported to him shall order the accused person to be kept in custody in the prescribed manner and shall report the case for the orders of the Central Government.

(5) On receipt of a report under sub-section (4), the Central Government may order the accused person to be detained in a lunatic asylum or other suitable place of safe custody.

122. Subsequent fitness of lunatic accused for trial. Where any accused person, having been found by reason of unsoundness of mind to be incapable of making his defence, is in custody or under detention under Section 121, any officer prescribed in this behalf, may -

(a) if such person is in custody under sub-section (4) of Section 121, on the report of a medical officer that he is capable of making his defence, or

(b) if such person is detained in a jail under sub-section (5) of Section 121 on a certificate of the Inspector-General of Prisons, and if such person is detained in a lunatic asylum under the said sub-section, on a certificate of any two or more of the visitors of such asylum and if he is detained in any other place under that sub-section, on a certificate of the prescribed authority, that he is capable of making his defence, take steps to have such person tried by the same or another Assam Rifles Court for the offence with which he was originally charged or, if the offence is a civil offence, by a criminal court.

123. Transmission to Central Government of orders under Section 122. A copy of every order made by an officer under Section 122 for the trial of the accused shall forthwith be sent to the Central Government.

124. Release of lunatic accused. Where any person is in custody under sub-section (4) of Section 121 or under detention under sub-section (5) of that Section -

(a) if such person is in custody under the said sub-section (4), on the report of a medical officer, or

(b) if such person is detained under the said sub-section (5), on a certificate from any of the authorities mentioned in clause (b) of Section 122 that in the judgment of such officer or authority such person may be released without danger of his doing injury to himself or to any other person, the Central Government may order that such person be released or detained in custody, or transferred to a public lunatic asylum if he has not already been to such an asylum.

125. Delivery of lunatic accused to relatives. Where any relative or friend of any person who is in custody under sub-section (4) of Section 121 or under detention under sub-section (5) of that Section desires that he should be delivered to his care and custody, the Central Government may, upon application by such relative or friend and, on his giving security to the satisfaction of that Government that the person delivered shall be properly taken care of, and, prevented from doing injury to himself or to any other person, and be produced for the inspection of such officer, and at such times and places, as the Central Government may direct, order such person to be delivered to such relative or friend.

126. Order for custody and disposal of property pending trial. When any property regarding which any offence appears to have been committed, or which appears to have been used for the commission of any offence, is produced before an Assam Rifles Court during a trial, the Court may make such order as it thinks fit for the proper custody of such property pending the conclusion of the trial, and if the property is subject to speedy or natural decay may, after recording such evidence as it thinks necessary, order it to be sold otherwise disposed of.

127. Order of disposal of property regarding which offence is committed.

(1) After the conclusion of a trial before any Assam Rifles Court, the Court or the officer confirming the finding or sentence of such Assam Rifles Court, or any authority superior to such officer, or, in the case of Summary Assam Rifles Court whose finding or sentence does not require confirmation, an officer not below the rank of Deputy Inspector-General within whose command the trial was held, may make such order as it or he thinks fit for the disposal by destruction, confiscation, delivery to any person claiming to be entitled to possession thereof, or otherwise, of any property or document produced before the Court or in its custody, or regarding which any offence appears to have been committed or which has been committed or which has been used for the commission of any offence.

(2) Where any order has been made under sub-section (1) in respect of property regarding which an offence appears to have been committed, a copy of such order signed and certified by the authority making the same may, whether the trial was held within India or not, be sent to a Magistrate within whose jurisdiction such property for the time being is situated, and such Magistrate shall thereupon cause the order to be carried into effect as if it were an order passed by him under the provisions of the Code of Criminal Procedure, 1973.

(3) In this Section, the term" property" includes, in the case of property regarding which an offence appears to have been committed, not only such property as has been originally in the possession or under the control of any person, but also any property into or for which the same may have been converted or exchanged, and anything acquired by such conversion or exchange whether immediately or otherwise.

128. Powers of Assam Rifles Court in relation to proceedings under this Act. Any trial by an Assam Rifles Court under the provisions of the Act shall be deemed to be a judicial proceeding within the meaning of Section 193 and 228 of the Indian Penal Code and the Assam Rifles Court shall be deemed to be the Court within the meaning of Sections 345 and 346 of the Code of Criminal Procedure, 1973.

CHAPTER -X : CONFIRMATION AND REVISION

129. Finding and sentence not valid unless confirmed. No finding or sentence of a General Assam Rifles Court or a Petty Assam Rifles Court shall be valid except so far as it may be confirmed as provided by this Act.

130. Power to confirm finding and sentence of General Assam Rifles Court. The findings and sentences of General Assam Rifles Courts may be confirmed by the Central Government or by any officer empowered in this behalf by warrant of the Central Government.

131. Power to confirm finding and sentence of Petty Assam Rifles Court. The findings and sentences of Petty Assam Rifles Courts may be confirmed by an officer having power to convene a General Assam Rifles Court or by any officer empowered in this behalf by warrant of such officer.

132. Limitation of powers of confirming authority. A warrant issued under Section 130 or Section 131 may contain such restrictions, reservations or conditions as the authority issuing it may think fit.

133. Power of confirming authority to mitigate, remit or commute sentences. Subject to such restrictions, reservations or conditions, as may be contained in any warrant issued under Section 130 or Section 131, a confirming authority may, when confirming the sentence of an Assam Rifles Court, mitigate or remit the punishment thereby awarded, or commute that punishment for any punishment or punishment lower in the scale laid down in Section 57.

134. Confirming of findings and sentences on board a ship. When any person subject to this Act is tried and sentenced by an Assam Rifles Court while on board a ship, the finding and sentence so far as not confirmed and executed on board the ship, may be confirmed and executed in like manner as if such person had been tried at the port of disembarkation.

135. Revision of finding or sentence.

(1) Any finding or sentence of an Assam Rifles Court which requires confirmation may be once revised by order of the confirming authority and on such revision, the Court, if so directed by the confirming authority, may take additional evidence.

(2) The Court, on revision, shall consist of the same officers as were present when the original decision was passed unless any of those officers are unavoidably absent.

(3) In case of such unavoidable absence the cause thereof shall be duly certified in the proceedings, and the Court shall proceed with the revision:

PROVIDED that, if a General Assam Rifles Court, still consists of five officers, or, if a Petty Assam Rifles Court, of three officers.

136. Finding and sentence of a Summary Assam Rifles Court.

(1) Save as otherwise provided in sub-section (2), the finding and sentence of a Summary Assam Rifles Court shall not require to be confirmed, but may be carried out forthwith.

(2) If the officer holding the trial is of the rank of Deputy Commandant or of a rank declared under clause (a) of sub-section (5) of Section 96 as equivalent thereto or of a lower rank and has held such rank for less than five years, he shall not, except on active duty, carry into effect any sentence, until it has received the approval of an officer not below the rank of a Deputy Inspector-General.

137. Transmission of proceedings of Summary Assam Rifles Court. The proceedings of every Summary Assam Rifles Court shall, without delay, be forwarded to the officer not below the rank of Deputy Inspector-General within whose command the trial was held, or to the prescribed officer, and such officer or the Director-General or any officer empowered by him in this behalf may, for reasons based on the merits of the case, but not on merely technical grounds, set aside the proceedings, or reduce the sentence to any other sentence which the court might have passed.

138. Alteration of finding or sentence in certain cases.

(1) Where a finding of guilty by an Assam Rifles Court, which has been confirmed or which does not require confirmation, is found for any reason to be invalid or cannot be supported by the evidence, the authority which would have had power under Section 150 to commute the punishment awarded by the sentence, if the finding had been valid may substitute a new finding and pass a sentence for the offence specified or involved in such finding:

PROVIDED that no such substitution shall be made unless such finding could have been validly made by the Assam Rifles Court on the charge and unless it appears that the Assam Rifles Court must have been satisfied of the facts establishing the said offence.

(2) Where a sentence passed by an Assam Rifles Court which has been confirmed, or which does not require confirmation, not being a sentence passed in pursuance of a new finding substituted under sub-section (1) is found for any reason to be invalid, the authority referred to in sub-section (1) may pass a valid sentence.

(3) The punishment awarded by a sentence passed under sub-section (1) or sub-section (2) shall not be higher in the scale of punishment than, or in excess of, the punishment awarded by, the sentence for which a new sentence is substituted under this Section.

(4) Any finding substituted, or any sentence passed, under this Section shall, for the purpose of this Act and the rules, have effect as if it were a finding or sentence, as the case may be, of an Assam Rifles Court.

139. Remedy against order, finding or sentence of Assam Rifles Court.

(1) Any person subject to this Act who considers himself aggrieved by any order passed by any Assam Rifles Court may present a petition to the officer or authority empowered to confirm any finding or sentence of the Assam Rifles Court and the confirming authority may take such steps as may be considered necessary to satisfy itself as to the correctness, legality or propriety of the order passed or as to the regularity of any proceeding to which the order relates.

(2) Any person subject to this Act who considers himself aggrieved by a finding or sentence of any Assam Rifles Court which has been confirmed may present a petition to the Central Government, the Director-General or any prescribed officer superior in command to the one who confirmed such finding or sentence, and the Central Government, the Director-General or the prescribed officer, as the case may be, may pass such order thereon as it or he thinks fit.

140. Annulment of proceedings. The Central Government, the Director-General or any prescribed officer may annul the proceeding of any Assam Rifles Court on the ground that they are illegal or unjust.

CHAPTER -XI : EXECUTION OF SENTENCE, PARDON, REMISSION, ETC.

141. Form of sentence of death. In awarding a sentence of death, an Assam Rifles Court shall in its discretion direct that the offender shall suffer death by being hanged by the neck until he be dead, or shall suffer death by being shot to death.

142. Commencement of sentence of imprisonment. Whenever any person is sentenced by an Assam Rifles Court under this Act to imprisonment, the term of his sentence shall, whether it has been revised or not, be reckoned to commence on the day in which the original proceedings were signed by the presiding officer, or in the case of a Summary Assam Rifles Court, by the Court:

PROVIDED that when a person subject to this Act is sentenced by an Assam Rifles Court to a term of imprisonment, not being an imprisonment in default of payment of fine, the period spent by him in civil or Force custody during investigation, inquiry or trial of the same case, and before the date of order, such sentence shall be set off against the term of imprisonment imposed upon him and the liability of such person or officer to undergo imprisonment on such order of sentence shall be restricted to the remainder, if any, of the term of imprisonment imposed upon him.

143. Execution of sentence of imprisonment.

(1) Whenever any sentence of imprisonment is passed under this Act by an Assam Rifles Court or whenever any sentence of death is commuted to imprisonment, the confirming officer or in case of a Summary Assam Rifles Court, the officer holding the Court or such other officer as may be prescribed, shall, save as otherwise provided in sub-sections (3) and (4), direct that the sentence shall be carried out by confinement in a civil prison.

(2) When a direction has been made under sub-section (1), the Commandant of the person under sentence or such other officer as may be prescribed shall forward a warrant in the prescribed form to the officer in charge of the prison in which such person is to be confined and shall arrange for his despatch to such prison with the warrant.

(3) In the case of a sentence of imprisonment for a period not exceeding three months and passed under this Act by an Assam Rifles Court the appropriate officer under sub-section (1) may direct that the sentence shall be carried out by confinement in force custody instead of in a civil prison.

(4) On active duty, a sentence of imprisonment may be carried out by confinement in such place as the Deputy Inspector-General within whose command the person sentenced is serving or any prescribed officer may from time to time appoint.

144. Temporary custody of offender. Where a sentence of imprisonment is directed to be undergone in a civil prison, the offender may be kept in Force custody or in any other fit place till such time as it is possible to send him to a civil prison.

145. Execution of sentence of imprisonment in special cases. Whenever, in the opinion of an officer not below the rank of Deputy Inspector-General within whose command the trial is held, any sentence or portion of a sentence of imprisonment cannot for special reasons, conveniently be carried out in Force custody in accordance with the provisions of Section 143, such officer may direct that such sentence or portion of sentence shall be carried out by confinement in any civil prison or other fit place.

146. Conveyance of prisoner from place to place. A person under sentence of imprisonment may, during his conveyance from place to place, or when on board ship, aircraft or otherwise, be subjected to such restraint as is necessary for his safe conduct and removal.

147. Communication of certain orders to prison officers. When an order is duly made under this Act setting aside or varying any sentence, order or warrant under which any person is confined in a civil prison, a warrant in accordance with such order shall be forwarded by the officer making the order or his staff officer or such other person as may be prescribed, to the officer in charge of the prison in which such person is confined.

148. Execution of sentence of fine. When a sentence of fine is imposed by an Assam Rifles Court under Section 55, a copy of such sentence signed and certified by the confirming officer, or where no confirmation is required by the officer holding the trial may be sent to any Magistrate in India and such Magistrate shall thereupon cause the fine to be recovered in accordance with the provisions of the Code of Criminal Procedure, 1973 , as if it were a sentence of fine imposed by such Magistrate.

149. Informality or error in order or warrant. Whenever any person is sentenced to imprisonment under this Act and is undergoing the sentence in any place or manner in which he might be confined under a lawful order or warrant in pursuance of this Act, the confinement of such person shall not be deemed to be illegal only by reason of informality or error in, or as respects the order, warrant or other document, or the authority by which, or in pursuance whereof such person was brought into, or is confined in any such place, and any such order, warrant or document may be amended accordingly.

150. Pardon and remission. When any person subject to this Act has been convicted by an Assam Rifles Court of any offence, the Central Government or the Director-General, or in the case of a sentence which he could have confirmed or which did not require confirmation, an officer not below the rank of Deputy Inspector-General within whose command such person at the time of conviction was serving or the prescribed officer may -

(a) either with or without conditions which the person sentenced accepts, pardon the person or remit the whole or any part of the punishment awarded; or

(b) mitigate the punishment awarded; or

(c) commute such punishment for any less punishment or punishments mentioned in this Act; or

(d) either with or without conditions which the person sentenced accepts, release the person on parole.

151. Cancellation of conditional pardon, release on parole or remission.

(1) If any condition on which a person has been pardoned or released on parole or a punishment has been remitted is, in the opinion of the authority which granted the pardon, release or remission, not fulfilled, such authority may cancel the pardon, release or remission, and thereupon the sentence of the Court shall be carried into effect as if such pardon, release or remission had not been granted.

(2) A person whose sentence of imprisonment is carried into effect under the provisions of sub-section (1) shall undergo only the unexpired portion of his sentence.

152. Suspension of sentence of imprisonment.

(1) Where a person subject to this Act is sentenced by an Assam Rifles Court to imprisonment, the Central Government, the Director-General or any officer empowered to convene a General Assam Rifles Court may suspend the sentence whether or not the offender has already been committed to prison or to Force custody.

(2) The authority or officer specified in sub-section (1) may, in the case of an offender so sentenced direct that until the order of such authority or officer have been obtained, the offender shall not be committed to prison or to Force custody.

(3) The powers conferred by sub-sections (1) and (2) may be exercised in the case of any such sentence which has been confirmed, reduced or commuted.

153. Orders pending suspension.

(1) Where sentence referred to in Section 152 is imposed by an Assam Rifles Court other than Summary Assam Rifles Court, the confirming officer may, when confirming the sentence, direct that the offender be not committed to prison or to Force custody until the orders of the authority or officer specified in Section 152 have been obtained.

(2) Where a sentence of imprisonment is imposed by a Summary Assam Rifles Court, the officer holding the trial or the officer authorised to approve the sentence under sub-section (2) of Section 136 may make the direction referred to in sub-section (1).

154. Release on suspension. Where a sentence is suspended under Section 152 the offender shall forthwith be released from custody.

155. Computation of period of suspension. Any period during which the sentence is under suspension shall be reckoned as part of the term of such sentence.

156. Order after suspension. The authority or officer specified in Section 152 may, at any time while a sentence is suspended, order-

(a) that the offender be committed to undergo the unexpired portion of the sentence; or

(b) that the sentence be remitted.

157. Reconsideration of case after suspension.

(1) Where a sentence has been suspended, the case may at any time, and shall at intervals of not more than four months, be reconsidered by the authority or officer specified in Section 152 or by any officer not below the rank of a Deputy Inspector-General duly authorised by the authority or officer specified in Section 152.

(2) Where on such reconsideration by the officer so authorised it appears to him that the conduct of offender since his conviction has been such as to justify a remission of the sentence, he shall refer the matter to the authority or officer specified in Section 150.

158. Fresh sentence after suspension. Where an offender, while a sentence on him is suspended under this Act, is sentenced for any other offence, then -

(a) if the further sentence is also suspended under this Act, the two sentences shall run concurrently;

(b) if the further sentence is for a period of three months or more and is not suspended under this Act, the offender shall be so committed to prison or to Force custody for the unexpired portion of the previous sentence, but both sentences shall run concurrently; and

(c) if the further sentence is for a period of less than three months and is not suspended under this Act, the offender shall be so committed on that sentence only, and the previous sentence shall, subject to any order which may be passed under Section 156 or Section 157, continue to be suspended.

159. Scope of power of suspension. The powers conferred by Sections 152 and 156 shall be in addition to, and not in derogation of, the power of mitigation, remission and commutation.

160. Effect of suspension and remission on dismissal.

(1) Where in addition to any other sentence the punishment of dismissal or removal has been awarded by an Assam Rifles Court, and such sentence is suspended under Section 152, then, such dismissal or removal shall not take effect until so ordered by the authority or officer specified in Section 152.

(2) If such other sentence is remitted under Section 156, the punishment of dismissal or removal shall also be remitted.

CHAPTER -XII : MISCELLANEOUS

161. Disposal of property of the members of the Force. The Central Government or any other authority empowered in this behalf by that Government may, by a general or special order, make provisions for the disposal of the private or regimental property of any person subject to this Act or any other dues including provident fund of that person, who dies or deserts, or is ascertained to be of unsound mind or while on active duty is officially reported as missing.

162. Powers and duties conferrable and imposable on members of the Force.

(1) The Central Government may, by general or special order published in the Official Gazette, direct that, subject to such conditions and limitations, and within the local limits of such area adjoining the border of India, as may be specified in the order, any member of the Force may -

(a) for the purpose of prevention of any offence punishable under the Passport (Entry into India) Act, 1920, the Registration of Foreigners Act, 1939, the Central Excise Act, 1944, the Foreigners Act, 1946 , the Customs Act, 1962, the Passports Act, 1967 or the Foreign Exchange Management Act, 1999 or of any cognizable offence punishable under any other Central Act; or

(b) for the purpose of apprehending any person who has committed any offence referred to in clause (a), exercise or discharge such of the powers or duties under that Act or any other Central Act as may be specified in the said order, being the powers and duties which, in the opinion of the Central Government, an officer of the corresponding or lower rank is by that or such other Act empowered to exercise or discharge for the said purposes.

(2) The Central Government may, by general or special order published in the Official Gazette, confer or impose, with the concurrence of the State Government concerned, any of the powers or duties which may be exercised or discharged under a State Act by a police officer upon a member of the Force who, in the opinion of the Central Government, holds a corresponding or higher rank.

(3) Every order made under this Section shall be laid, as soon as may be after it is made, before each House of Parliament while it is in session for a total period of thirty days which may be comprised in one session or in two or more successive sessions, and if, before the expiry of the session immediately following the session or the successive sessions aforesaid, both Houses agree in making any modification in the order or both Houses agree that the order should not be made, the order shall thereafter have effect only in such modified form or be of no effect, as the case may be; so, however, that any such modification or annulment shall be without prejudice to the validity of anything previously done under that order.

163. Protection for acts of members of the Force.

(1) The provision of Section 125 of the Indian Evidence Act, 1872 shall apply to such members of the Force who exercise or discharge any power or duty under sub-section (1) of Section 162 or on whom any power is conferred or duty is imposed under sub-section (2) of that Section in the same manner as it apply to a police officer.

(2) In any suit or proceeding against any member of the Force for any act done by him in pursuance of a warrant or order of a competent authority, it shall be lawful for him to plead, that such act was done by him under the authority of such warrant or order.

(3) Any such plea may be proved by the production of the warrant or order directing the act, and if it is so proved the member of the Force shall thereupon be discharged from liability in respect of the act so done by him, notwithstanding any defect in the jurisdiction of the authority which issued such warrant or order.

(4) Notwithstanding anything contained in any other law for the time being in force, any legal proceeding (whether civil or criminal) which may lawfully be brought against any member of the Force for anything done or intended to be done under the powers conferred by, or in pursuance of, any provision of this Act or the rules, shall be commenced within three months after the act complained of was committed and not otherwise, and notice in writing of such proceedings and of the cause thereof shall be given to the defendant or his superior officer at least one month before the commencement of such proceedings.

164. Power of Central Government to remove difficulties.

(1) If any difficulty arises in giving effect to the provisions of this Act, the Central Government may, by order published in the Official Gazette, make such provisions not inconsistent with the provisions of this Act as may appear to be necessary for removing the difficulty:

PROVIDED that no order shall be made under this Section after the expiry of two years from the commencement of this Act.

(2) Every order made under this Section shall, as soon as may be after it is made, be laid before each House of Parliament.

165. Power to make rules.

(1) The Central Government may, by notification, make rules for the purposes of carrying out the provisions of this Act.

(2) In particular and without prejudice to the generality of the foregoing power, such rules may provide for-

(a) the manner of re-constitution of the Force and the conditions of service of the members of the Force under sub-section (2) of Section 4;

(b) the mode of enrolment and the procedure for enrolment under sub-section (1) of Section 6;

(c) the authority whose previous permission in writing is required for resigning from appointment or withdrawing from all or any of the duties under Section 8;

(d) rank or ranks of an officer or a subordinate officer referred to under sub-section (2) of Section 11;

(e) the authority who shall give previous sanction in writing under sub-section (1) of Section 13;

(f) nature of communication or publication under clause (c) of sub-section (1) of Section 13;

(g) other purposes of meeting or demonstration under sub-section (2) of Section 13;

(h) form of enrolment under Section 31;

(i) any other purpose under clause (h) of sub-section (1) of Section 57;

(j) the officer who may direct that an enrolled person who has been sentenced to dismissal or imprisonment whether combined with dismissal or not may be retained to serve in the ranks under Section 60;

(k) the manner of proceedings against a person and the extent of awarding punishment under Section 62;

(l) the manner of proceeding against an officer below the rank of a Deputy Commandant and of the rank of subordinate officer and of the rank of Warrant Officer under sub-section (1) of Section 64;

(m) the manner of forwarding certified true copies of the proceedings and the superior authority to whom such copies shall be forwarded under sub-section (2) of Section 64;

(n) the manner of proceeding against an officer below the rank of Commandant and of any rank of subordinate officer and of the rank of Warrant Officer under sub-section (1) of Section 65;

(o) the manner of proceeding against any subordinate officer or a Warrant Officer under Section 66;

(p) the officer by whose order any sum is required to be paid, for the maintenance of wife or legitimate or illegitimate child of a person subject to this Act other than an officer, under clause (i) of Section 69;

(q) the officer who may direct that the whole or any part of the pay and allowances of person subject to this Act shall be withheld under Section 71;

(r) the manner and the extent of remission of deductions from pay and allowances authorised by this Act and the authority by which such remission shall be made under Section 75;

(s) the authorities by whom proper provision to be made out of the pay and allowances of all persons subject to this Act, being prisoners of war, for the dependents of such persons under Section 76;

(t) the authorities who shall make proper provision out of the pay and allowances of any person subject to this Act, who is prisoner of war or is missing under Section 77;

(u) the manner in which and the period for which any person subject to this Act may be taken into and detained in Force custody under sub-section (4) of Section 80;

(v) the manner of making special report giving reasons for delay under Section 81;

(w) the authority to appoint, and the manner of appointment of, a court of inquiry; the manner of administering oath or affirmation by such court of inquiry and the manner of making record under sub-section (1) of Section 84;

(x) the officer who may appoint Force Police under sub-section (1) of Section 85;

(y) the other officer having the discretion to decide before which court the proceeding shall be instituted under Section 102;

(z) the manner of filling up the vacancy of member by another officer under sub-section (3) of Section 106;

(za) the manner for administering oath or affirmation to every member of an Assam Rifles Court and to the Law Officer, or, as the case may be, the officer approved under Section 105 before the commencement of the trial, under sub-section (1) of Section 107;

(zb) the form for being duly sworn or affirmed under sub-section (2) of Section 107;

(zc) the officer by whom the letter, return or other documents purported to be signed shall be the evidence of the facts stated in such letter, return or other document under sub-section (1) of Section 118;

(zd) the other matters to be further inquired and recorded under sub-section (1) of Section 120;

(ze) the other matters to be recorded under sub-section (3) of Section 120;

(zf) the manner of keeping in custody of the accused person under sub-section (4) of Section 121;

(zg) the officer who may take steps to have certain persons tried under Section 122;

(zh) the authority for issuing certificate in case of detention in any other place under clause (b) of Section 122;

(zi) the officer to whom the proceedings of every Summary Assam Rifles Courts shall be forwarded under Section 137;

(zj) the officer superior in command, to the one who confirmed the findings or sentence referred to in sub-section (2) of Section 139, to whom petition may be presented under that sub-section;

(zk) the officer who may annul the proceeding of any Assam Rifles Court under Section 140;

(zl) the other officer who shall direct that sentence shall be carried out by the confinement in a civil prison under sub-section (1) of Section 143;

(zm) the officer who shall forward a warrant and the form of such warrant under sub-section (2) Section 143;

(zn) the officer who may from time to time appoint the place of confinement under sub-section (4) of Section 143;

(zo) the other person by whom the warrant shall be forwarded to the officer in charge of the prison under Section 147;

(zp) the officer who may pardon or exercise other powers as specified under clauses (a) to (c) of Section 150;

(zq) any other matter which is to be, or may be, prescribed, or in respect of which provision is to be, or may be, made by rules.

166. Power to make regulations. The Director-General may make regulations for all or any of the purposes of this Act other than those specified in Section 165, subject to approval of the Central Government.

167. Rules and regulations to be laid before Parliament. Every rule or regulation made under this Act shall be laid, as soon as may be after it is made, before each House of Parliament, while it is in session for a total period of thirty days which may be comprised in one session or in two or more successive sessions, and if, before the expiry of the session immediately following the session, or the successive sessions aforesaid, both Houses agree in making any modification in the rule or regulation or both Houses agree that the rule or regulation should not be made, the rule or regulation shall thereafter have effect only in such modified form or be of no effect, as the case may be, so, however, that any such modification or annulment shall be without prejudice to the validity of anything previously done under that rule or regulation.

168. Repeal and savings.

(1) The Assam Rifles Act, 1941 is hereby repealed.

(2) Notwithstanding such repeal -

(a) the Assam Rifles in existence at the commencement of this Act and constituted under the Act so repealed shall be deemed to be reconstituted under this Act;

(b) members of the Assam Rifles in existence at the commencement of this Act and appointed under the Act so repealed shall be deemed to have been appointed or, as the case may be, enrolled as such under this Act;

(c) any appeal, application, trial, inquiry or investigation pending immediately before the commencement of this Act shall be disposed of, continued, held or made, as the case may be, in accordance with the provisions of the Assam Rifles Act, 1941 , as if this Act had not come into force;

(d) any thing done or any action taken before the commencement of this Act, in relation to any person appointed or enrolled, shall be valid and as effective in law as if such thing or action was done or taken under the corresponding provisions of this Act.

❏❏❏

8

The Assam Rifles Act, 1941

(Act V of 1941) (17 March, 1941)

AN ACT to provide for the regulation of and the maintenance of discipline in the Assam Rifles.

WHEREAS it is expedient to provide for the regulations of and the maintenance of discipline in the Assam Rifles.

1. Short title, extent and application.

(1) This Act may be called THE ASSAM RIFLES ACT, 1941.

(2) It extends to [1](the whole of India) and applies to all members of the Assam Rifles wherever they may be serving.

2. Definitions. In this Act unless there is anything repugnant in the subject or context.

(1) "active service" means service at outposts or against hostile tribes or other persons in the field.

(2) "Commandant" or "Assistant Commandant" means a person appointed by the Central government to be Commandant or an Assistant Commandant of the Assam Rifles.

(3) [2]("District Magistrate" includes a Deputy Commissioner).

(4) "Rifleman" means a person appointed as such under Section 4 after he has signed the statement in the Schedule in accordance with the provision of sub Section (2) of Section 4, and includes a rifleman appointed under the Assam Rifles Act 1920[3] and a Military Police Officer appointed under the Eastern Bengal and Assam Military Police Act, 1912 [4], [5](and non-combatant appointed as such, whether before or after the commencement[6] of the Assam Rifles (Amendment) Act 1951).

(5) "Superior Officer" means, in relation to any rifleman :-

(a) An officer of higher class than, or of a higher grade in the same class as, himself and

(b) Any Assistant Commandant or Commandant.

(6) The expressions "reason to believe", "criminal force", "assault", "fraudulently" and "voluntarily causing hurt" have the meaning assigned to them respectively in the Indian Penal Code.

3. General Superintendence and Control of the Force. General superintendence and control of the Assam Rifles shall be exercised by such person or authority as the Central Government may appoint in this behalf, and, in the exercise of such superintendence and control, the person or authority so appointed shall be governed by such rules and orders as the Central Government may make in this behalf.

4. Appointment and Discharge.

(1) The appointment of all riflemen shall rest with the Commandant.

(2) Before any person is appointed to be a rifleman, the statement in the Schedule shall be read if necessary explained to him in the presence of a Magistrate, Commandant or Assistant Commandant, and shall be signed by him in acknowledgment of its having been so read to him.

(3) A rifleman shall not be entitled to be discharged except in accordance with the terms of statement which he has signed under this Act or under the Assam Rifles Act, 1920. [7]

[8]5. Class and Rank.

(1) There may be all or any of the classes of riflemen specified in the table hereunder namely :-

TABLE

1. Combatants

(i) Subedars Major

(ii) Subedars

(iii) Jemadars and Transport Jemadars

(iv) Havildars-Major

(v) Havildars and Dafadars

(vi) Nalbands

(vii) Naiks

(viii) Lance Naiks

(ix) Buglers riflemen and mule drivers

2. Non-Combatants

(i) Hospital attendants

(ii) Cooks

(iii) Water Carriers

(iv) Cart man

(v) Range warders
(vi) Barbars
(vii) Washer men
(viii) Sweepers

And such grades in each class as the Central Government may from time to time.

(2) The person specified in column 1 of the table in sub-section (1) shall take rank in order mentioned in that column.

6. Heinous offences. A rifleman who.

(a) Begine, exces, causes or joins in any mutiny or being present at any mutiny does not use his ulmost endeavours to suppress it, or knowing or having reason to believe in the existence of any mutiny does not without delay give information thereof to his commencing or other superior officer, or

(b) Uses, or attempts to use, criminal force to, or commits an assault on his superior officer, knowing or having reason to believe him to be such, whether on or off duty, or

(c) Shamefully abandons or delivers up any garrison, fortress, post or guard which is committed to his charge or which it is his duty to defend, or

(d) In the presence of an enemy or of any person in arms against whom it is his duty to act, shamefully casts away his arms or his ammunition, or intentionally uses words or any other means to induce any other rifleman to abstain from acting against the enemy, or to discourage any other rifleman from acting against the enemy, or

(e) Directly or indirectly holds correspondence with, or communicates intelligence to, or assists or relieves any person in arms against the State, or omits to discover immediately to his Commanding or other superior officer any such correspondence or communications coming to his knowledge, or

(f) Directly or indirectly assists or relieve with money, victuals or ammunition, or knowing harbours or protects, any enemy or person in arms against the State, or who while on active service,

(g) Disobeys the lawful command of his superior, or

(h) Deserts or attempts to desert the service, or

(i) Being a sentry, sleeps upon his post, or quits it without being regularly relieved or without leave, or

(j) Leaves his Commanding Officer, or his post or party, to go in search of plunder, or

(k) Quits his guard, piquet, party or patrol without being regularly relieved or without leave, or

(l) Uses criminal force to, or commits an assault on, any person bringing provisions or other necessaries to camp or quarters, or forces a safeguard, or breaks into any hours or other place for plunder, or plunders, destroys or damages any property of any kind, or

(m) Intentionally causes or spreads a false alarm in action or in camp, garrison or quarters, shall be punished with transportation for life[9] or with imprisonment which may extend to fourteen years, or with fine which may extend to five hundred rupees, or with both such imprisonment and fine.

7. Other offences including acts prejudicial to good order and discipline. A rifleman who:-

(a) Is in a state of intoxication when on or detailed for any duty, or on parade, or on the line of march, or

(b) strikes, or forces or attempts to force, an sentry, or

(c) being in command of a guard, piquet or patrol, refuses to receive any prisoner duty committed to his charge, or whether in such command or not, releases any prisoner without proper authority or negligently suffers any prisoner to escape, or

(d) being deputed to any guard, piquet or patrol, quite it without being regularly relieved or without leave, or

(e) being in command of a guard, piquet or patrol, permits gambling or other behavior prejudicial to good order and discipline, or

(f) being under arrest or in confinement, leaves his arrest or confinement before he is set at liberty be proper authority, or

(g) is grossly insubordinate or insolent to his superior officer in the execution of his office, or

(h) refuses to superintend or assist in the making of any field work or other military work or any description ordered to be made either in quarters or in the field, or

(i) strikes or otherwise ill uses any rifleman subordinate to him in rank or position, or

(j) being in command at any post or on the march and receiving a complaint that the one under his command has beaten or otherwise maltreated or oppressed any person, or has committed any riot or trespass, fails, on proof of the truth of the complaint, to have due reparation made as far as possible to the injured person and to report the case to the proper authority, or

(k) designecty or through neglect injures or losses or fraudulently or without due authority disposes of his arms, clothes, tools, equipment, ammunition, accoutrements or other necessaries, or any such articles entrusted to him or belonging to any other person, or

(l) malingers, resigns or produces disease or infirmity in himself, intentionally delays his care, or aggravates his disease or infirmity, or

(m) with intent to render himself or any other person unfit for service, voluntarily causes hurt to himself or any other person, or

(n) commits extortion, or without proper authority exacts from any person carriage, porterage or provisions, or

(o) designecty or through neglect kills, injures, makes away with ill-treats or loses his horse, or any animal used in the public service, or who, while not on active service;

(p) disobeys the lawful command of his superior officer, or

(q) Plunders, destroys or damaged any property of any kind, or

(r) being a sentry, sleeps upon his post, or quite it without being regularly relieved or without leave, or

(s) deserts or attempts to desert the service, or

(t) neglects to obey any battalion or other orders, or commits any act or omission prejudicial to good order and discipline such act of omission not constituting an offence under the Indian Penal Code or other Act in force in Assam.

Shall be punished with imprisonment for a term which may extend to one year, or with the fine which may extend to two hundred rupees, or with both.

Note: The next Section makes provision for punishment for minor offences against discipline which are not otherwise provided for or which are not of a sufficiently serious nature to call for prosecution before a Criminal Court.

8. Minor Offences and Punishment.

(1) District Magistrate or a Commandant, or subject to the control of the Commandant, an Assistant Commandant, or subject to the control of the Commandant an officer not below the rant of a Jemadar commanding a separate detachment or an outpost or in temporary command at the headquarters of a District during the absence of the District Magistrate, Commandant and Assistant Commandant, may, without a formal trial, award to any rifleman below the rank of Naik, who is subject to his authority, any of the following punishments for the commission of any petty offence against the discipline, which is not otherwise provide for in this Act, or which is not of a sufficiently serious nature to call for prosecution before a criminal court, that is to say :-

(a) Imprisonment in the Quarter Guard, or such other place as maybe considered suitable, for a term which may extend to twenty eight days when the order is passed by a District Magistrate or a Commandant [10](or an Assistant Commandant) or to seven days when it is passed by any other officer.

(b) punishment drill, extra guard, fatigue or other duty, not exceeding twenty-eight days in duration, with or without confinement to lines,

(c) forfeiture of pay and allowances for a period not exceeding twenty eight days.

(2) Any of the punishments specified in sub Section (1) may be awarded separately or in combination with any one or more of the others, but no award or awards including imprisonment and confinement to lines shall exceed twenty eight consecutive days.

[11]*EXPLANATION:* For the purposes of this Section, every non-combatant shall be deemed to be below the rank of a Naik).

9. Manner of imprisonment. Any rifleman sentenced under this Act to imprisonment for a period not exceeding three months shall, when he is also dismissed from the Assam Rifles, be imprisoned in a civil jail, but when his not also dismissed from the Assam Rifles he, may, if the convicting court of the District Magistrate so directs, be confined in the Quarter Guard or such other place as the Court of Magistrate may consider suitable.

10. Privileges of and protection for acts done by Commandant, Assistant Commandant etc.

(1) A Commandant, Assistant Commandant or rifleman shall be entitled to all the privileges which a police officer has under Section 125 of the Indian Evidence Act, 1872, and any other enactment for the time being in force.

(2) In any suit or proceeding against Commandant, Assistant Commandant or Rifleman for any act done by him in pursuance of a warrant or order of a competent authority, it shall be lawful for him to plead that such act was done by him under the authority of such warrant or order.

(3) Any such plea may be proved by the production of the warrant or order directing the act, and if it is so proved, the Commandant, Assistant Commandant or Rifleman, as the case may be, act so done by him, notwithstanding any defect in the jurisdiction of the authority which issued such warrant or order.

(4) Notwithstanding anything contained in any other law for the time being in force, any legal proceedings (whether civil or criminal) which may lawfully be brought against a Commandant, Assistant Commandant or a rifleman for anything done or intended to be done under the powers conferred by, or in pursuance of, any provision of this Act or the orders or rules made thereunder, shall be commenced within three months after the act complained of was committed and not otherwise, and notice in writing of such proceeding and of the cause thereof shall be given, where the defendant is a rifleman, to his superior officer, and in other cases, to the defendant, at least one month before the commencement of such proceedings).

[12]**10-A. Powers and duties that may be conferred or imposed by the Central Government on Commandant, Assistant Commandant, etc.**

(1) The Central Government may, be general or special order, confer or impose upon any Commandant, Assistant Commandant or Rifleman, any of the powers or duties conferred or imposed on police officer of any class or grade by any lay for the being in force.

(2) Notwithstanding anything contained in the Code of Criminal Procedure 1898, the Central Government may invest any Commandant or Assistant Commandant with the powers of a Magistrate of any class for the purpose of inquiring into or trying any offence committed by a rifleman and punishable under the Act or any offence committed by a rifleman against the person or property of another rifleman or of any person acting with or assisting the Assam Rifles.

11. Members of the Assam Rifles to be deemed part of the Indian Army for certain purposes. For the purposes of Ss 128, 130 and 131 of the Code of Criminal Procedure, 1898, a Commandant, Assistant Commandant, Subedar Major, Subedar or Jemadar of the Assam Rifles shall be deemed to be a officer, a Havildar Major, Havildar or Naik shall be deemed to be non-commissioned officer and a bugler or rifleman shall be deemed to be a soldier of the Indian Army.

12. Power of Central Government to make rules. The Central Government may, as regards the Assam Rifles, make such orders and rules consistent with this Act, as it thinks expedient, relative to the several matters respecting which the Inspector General of Police, with the approval of the State Government, may, as regards the Police Force, frame orders and rules under Section 12 of the Police Act 1861.

13. Cesser of Assam Rifles Act 1 of 1920 and of appointment of rifleman as Police Officers. The Assam Rifles Act, 1920 shall cease to apply to the Assam Rifles and to riflemen, and all riflemen shall, on the commencement of this Act cease to be police officers under the Police Act, 1861.

THE SCHEDULE
STATEMENT
[*See* Section 2(4) and 4 (2)]

1. After you have served for four years in the first instance in the Assam Rifles you have the option of extending the term of your service in the Assam Rifles indefinitely, so long as the Commandant is satisfied with your service, or of claiming your discharge at any time, making your application through the officer to whom you may be subordinate, to a Commandant of the Assam Rifles or to the Magistrate of the District in which you may be serving, and you will be granted your discharge after two months from the date of your application, unless your are on active service or unless your discharge would cause the vacancies in the Assam Rifles to exceed one tenth of the sanctioned strength. In either of the above cases you must continue to serve in the Assam Rifles until the objection is waived by competent authority or removed.

2. On your enlistment, appointment or training as a musician (piper, drummer, or bandsman), bugler, signaler, writer, soldier, clerk, havildar-componder or as an artificer (armourer, mochi carpenter, stone-mason, or motor driver) [13][or as a hospital attendant, cook, water carrier, cart man, range warder, barber, washer-man or sweeper] you must inspite of the provisions of paragraph 1 above, serve in the Assam Rifles for eight years from the date of your enlistment or the completion of your training, as the case may be.

3. On you deputation for a specialist course at any Army Training Centre you must sign an undertaking, before leaving the battalion to proceed on the course, that you will not, inspite of the provisions of paragraph 1 above, apply for discharge during the eight years following your attendance at the Course.

4. On you deputation to the Educational or Veterinary course you must sign as undertaking, before leaving the battalion to proceed on the course, that you will not,

inspite of the provisions of paragraph 1 above, apply for discharge during the eight years following your attendance at the Course.

5. In the event of your re-enlistment after you have been discharged, you will have no claim to reckon for pension or any other purpose your service previous to your discharge.

Signature of Rifleman in acknowledgement of the above having been rea ______ to him the A.B

Signature in my presence after I had ascertained that A.B understood _____ purport of what he signed
C.D Magistrate, Commandant or Assistant Commandant

❑❑❑

Endnotes

1. Substituted for the words "the whole of Assam" by the Assam Rifles (Amendment) Act, 1962 S.1 (11-9-1962).
2. Substituted by N.E.A. (Reorganisation) A.L.O 1974 (21-1-1972).
3. Assam Act of 1920.
4. Eastern Bangal and Assam Act III of 1912.
5. Added by the Assam Rifles (Amendment) Act, 1951 (XXXIV of 1951), Sec 2 (17-5-1951).
6. That is, 17th May 1951.
7. Assam Rifles Act (1 of 1920).
8. Substituted for the former Section by the Assam Rifles (Amendment Act, 1951 (XXXIV of 1951), S. 3 (17-5-1951).
9. For the construction of the expression, see the Penal Code, 1860, S. 53-A
10. Inserted by the Assam Rifles (Amendment) Act, 1958 (XLVII of 1958), S.2 (26-12-1958).
11. Inserted, ibid, 1951 (XXXIV of 1951),S.4(17-5-1951).
12. Sections 10 and 10A were substituted for the original Section 10, by the Assam Rifles (Amendment) Act, 1962 (30 of 1962), S.2(11.9.1962).
13. Inserted by the Assam Rifles (Amendment) Act 1951(XXXIV of 1951), S.3 (17.5.1951).

9

The Border Security Force (Amendment) Act, 2000

ACT NO. 35 OF 2000 [1ST SEPTEMBER, 2000]

AN ACT further to amend the Border Security Force Act, 1968.

Be it enacted by Parliament in the Fifty-first Year of the Republic of India as follows:-

1. Short title. This Act may be called the Border Security Force (Amendment) Act, 2000.

2. Insertion of new Section 121A. In the Border Security Force Act, 1968 (47 of 1968), after Section 121, the following section shall be inserted, namely:-

"**121A. Period of custody undergone by a person to be set-off against the imprisonment.** When any person subject to this Act is sentenced by a Security Force Court to a term of imprisonment, not being an imprisonment in default of payment of fine, the period spent by him in civil or Force custody during investigation, inquiry or trial of the same case, and before the date of order of such sentence, shall be set off against the term of imprisonment imposed upon him, and the liability of such person to under o imprisonment on such order of sentence shall be restricted to the remainder, if any, of the term of imprisonment imposed upon him."

❒❒❒

10

The Border Security Force Act, 1968

ACT NO. 47 OF 1968 [2ND SEPTEMBER, 1968]

AN ACT to provide for the constitution and regulation of an Armed Force of the Union for ensuring the security of the borders of India and for matters connected therewith.

CHAPTER -I : PRELIMINARY

1. Short title and commencement.

(1) This Act may be called the Border Security Force Act, 1968.

(2) It shall come into force on such date as the Central Government may, by notification in the Official Gazette, appoint.

2. Definitions.

(1) In this Act, unless the context otherwise requires -

(a) "active duty", in relation to a person subject to this Act, means any duty as a member of the Force during the period in which such person is attached to or forms part of, a unit of the Force-

(i) Which is engaged in operations against an enemy, or

(ii) which is operating at a picket or engaged on patrol or other guard duty along the borders of India, and includes duty by such person during any period declared by the Central Government by notification in the Official Gazette as a period of active duty with reference to any area in which any person or class of persons subject to this Act may be serving:

(b) "battalion" means a unit of the Force constituted as a battalion by the Central Government;

(c) "Chief Law Officer" and "Law Officer" mean, respectively, the Chief Law officer and a Law Officer of the Force appointed by the Central Government;

(d) "Civil offence" means an offence which is triable by a criminal court;

(e) "Civil prison" means any jail or place used for the detention of any criminal prisoner under the Prisons Act, 1894 (9 of 1894), or under any other law for the time being in force;

(f) "Commandant", when used in any provision of this Act with reference to any unit of the Force, means the officer whose duty it is under the rules to discharge with respect to that unit, the functions of a Commandant in regard to matters of the description referred to in that provision;

(g) "criminal court" means a court of ordinary criminal justice in any part of India;

(h) "Deputy Inspector-General" means a Deputy Inspector-General of the Force appointed under Section 5;

(i) "Director-General" means the Director-General of the Force appointed under Section 5;

(j) "enemy" includes all armed mutineers, armed rebels, armed rioters, pirates and any person in arms against whom it is the duty of any person subject to this Act to take action;

(k) "enrolled person" means an under-officer or other person enrolled under this Act;

(l) "Force" means the Border Security Force;

(m) "Force custody" means the arrest or confinement or a member of the Force according to rules;

(n) "Inspector-General" means the Inspector.-General of the Force appointed under Section 5;

(o) "member of the Force" means an officer, a subordinate officer, an under-officer or other enrolled person;

(p) "notification" means a notification published in the Official Gazette;

(q) offence" means any act or omission punishable under this Act and includes a civil offence,

(r) "officer" means a person appointed or in pay as an officer of the Force, but does not include a subordinate officer or an under-officer;

(s) "prescribed" means prescribed by rules made under this Act;

(t) "rule" means a rule made under this Act;

(u) "Security Force Court" means a Court referred to in Section 64;

(v) "Subordinate officer" means a person appointed or in pay is a Subedar Major, a Subedar or a Sub-Inspector of the Force;

(w) "superior officer", when used in relation to a person subject to this Act, means —

(i) any member of the Force to whose command such person is for the time being subject in accordance with the rules;

(ii) any officer of higher rank or class of a higher grade in the same class; and includes when such person is not an officer, a subordinate officer or an under-officer of higher rank, class or grade;

(x) "under-officer" means a Head Constable, Naik and Lance Naik of the Force;

(y) all words and expressions used and not defined in this Act but defined in the Indian Penal Code (45 of 1860), shall have the meanings assigned to them in that Code.

(2) In this Act, references to any law not in force in the State of Jammu and Kashmir shall be construed as references to the corresponding law in force in that State.

3. Persons subject to this Act.

(1) The following persons shall be subject to this Act, wherever they may be, namely:-

(a) officers and subordinate officers; and

(b) under-officers and other persons enrolled under this Act.

(2) Every person subject to this Act shall remain so subject until, retired, discharged, released, removed or dismissed from the Force in accordance with the provisions of this Act and the rules.

CHAPTER -II : CONSTITUTION OF THE FORCE AND CONDITIONS OF SERVICE OF THE MEMBERS OF THE FORCE

4. Constitution of the Force.

(1) There shall be an armed force of the Union called the Border Security Force for ensuring the security of the Borders of India.

(2) Subject to the provisions of this Act, the Force shall be constituted in such manner as may be prescribed and the conditions of service of the members of the Force shall be such as may be prescribed.

5. Control, direction, etc.

(1) The general superintendence, direction and control of the Force shall vest in, and be exercised by, the Central Government and subject thereto, and to the provisions of this Act and the rules, the command and supervision of the Force shall vest in an officer to be appointed by the Central Government as the Director-General of the Force.

(2) The Director-General shall, in the discharge of his duties under this Act, be assisted by such number of Inspectors-General, Deputy Inspectors-General, Commandants and other officers as may be appointed by the Central Government.

6. Enrolment.

(1) The persons to be enrolled to the Force, the mode of enrolment, and the procedure for enrolment shall be such as may be prescribed by the Central Government.

(2) Notwithstanding anything contained in this Act and the rules, every person who has, for a continuous period of three months, been in receipt of pay as a person enrolled under this Act and borne on the rolls of the Force shall be deemed tc have been duly enrolled.

7. Liability for service outside India. Every member of the Force shall be liable to serve in any part of India as well as outside India.

8. Resignation and withdrawal from the post. No member of the Force shall be at liberty -

(a) to resign his appointment (during the term of his engagement); or

(b) to withdraw himself from all or any of the duties of his appointment, except with the previous permission in writing of the prescribed authority.

9. Tenure of service under the Act. Every person subject to this Act shall hold office during the pleasure of the President.

10. Termination of service by Central Government. Subject to the provisions of this Act and the rules, the Central Government may dismiss or remove from the service any person subject to this Act.

11. Dismissal, removal of reduction by the Director General and by other officers.

(1) The Director-General or any Inspector-General may dismiss or remove from the service or reduce to a lower grade or rank or the ranks any person subject to this Act other than an officer.

(2) An officer not below the rank of Deputy Inspector-General or any prescribed officer may dismiss or remove from the service any person under his command other than an officer or a subordinate officer of such rank or ranks is may be prescribed.

(3) Any such officer as is mentioned in sub-section (2) may reduce to a lower grade or rank or the ranks any person under his command except an officer or a subordinate officer.

(4) The exercise of any power under this Section shall be subject to the provisions of this Act and the rules.

12. Certificate of termination of service. A subordinate officer, or an under-officer or other enrolled person who is retired, discharged, released, removed or dismissed from the service shall be furnished by the officer, to whose command he is subject, with a certificate in the language which is the mother tongue of such person and also in Hindi or English language setting forth—

(a) the authority terminating his service;

(b) the cause for such termination; and

(c) the full period of his service in the Force.

13. Restrictions respecting right to form association, freedom of speech, etc.

(1) No person subject to this Act shall, without the previous sanction in writing of the Central Government or of the prescribed authority —

(a) be a member of, or be associated in any way with, any trade union, labour union, political association or with any class trade unions, labour unions or political associations; or

(b) be a member of, or be associated in any way with, any society, institution, association or organisation that is not recognised as part of the Force or is not of a purely social, recreational or religious nature; or

(c) communicate with the press or publish or cause to be published any book, letter or other document except where such communication or publication is in the *bona fide* discharge of his duties or is of a purely literary artistic or scientific character or is of a prescribed nature.

EXPLANATION. If any question arises as to whether any society, institution, association or organisation is of a purely social, recreational or religious nature under clause (b) of this sub-section, the decision or the Central Government thereon shall be final.

(2) No person subject to this Act shall participate in, or address, any meeting or take part in any demonstration organised by any body of persons for any political purposes or for such other purposes as may be prescribed.

CHAPTER -III : OFFENCES

14. Offences in relation to the enemy and punishable with death. Any person subject to this Act who commits any of the following offences, that is to say -

(a) shamefully abandons or delivers up any post, place or guard, committed to his charge or which it is his duty to defend; or

(b) intentionally uses any means to compel or induce any person subject to this Act or to military, naval or air force law to abstain from acting against the enemy or to discourage such person from acting against the enemy; or

(c) in the presence of the enemy shamefully casts away his arms, ammunition, tools or equipment or misbehaves in such mantier as to show cowardice; or

(d) treacherously holds correspondence with, or communicates intelligence to the enemy or any person in arms against the union; or

(e) directly or indirectly assists the enemy with money, arms, ammunition, stores or supplies or in any other-manner whatsoever; or

(f) in time of active operation against the enemy, intentionally occasions a false alarm in action, camp, quarters, or spreads or causes, to be spread reports calculated to create alarm or despondency; or

(g) in time of action, leaves his Commandant or other superior officer or his post, guard, picket, patrol or party without being regularly relieved or without leave; or

(h) having been captured by the enemy or made a prisoner of war, voluntarily serves with or, aids the enemy; or

(i) knowingly harbours or protects an enemy not being a prisoner; or

(j) being a sentry in time of active operation against the enemy or alarm, sleeps upon his post or is intoxicated; or

(k) knowingly does any act calculated to imperil the success of the Force or the military, naval or air forces of India or any forces co-operating therewith or any part of such forces, shall, on conviction by a Security Force Court be liable to suffer death or such less punishment as is in this Act mentioned.

15. Offences in relation to the enemy and not punishable with death. Any person subject to this Act who commits any of the following offences, that is to say -

(a) is taken prisoner or captured by the enemy, by want of due precaution or through disobedience of orders, or wilful neglect of duty, or having been taken prisoner or so captured fails to rejoin his service when able to do so; or

(b) without due authority holds corresponding with, or communicates intelligence to, the enemy or any person in league with the enemy or having come by the knowledge of any such correspondance or communication, wilfully omits to discover it immediately to his commandant or other superior officer, shall, on conviction by a Security force Court, be liable to suffer imprisonment for a term which may extend to fourteen years or such less punishment as is in this Act mentioned.

16. Offences punishable more severly on active duty than at other times. Any person subject to this Act who commits any of the following offences, that is to say -

(a) forces a safeguard, or forces or uses criminal force to a sentry; or

(b) breaks into any house or other place in search of plunder; or

(c) being a sentry sleeps upon his post, or is intoxicated; or

(d) without orders from his superior officer leaves his guard, picket, patrol or post; or

(e) intentionally or through neglect occasions a false alarm in camp or quarters, or spreads or causes to be spread reports calculated to create unnecessary alarm or dispondency; or

(f) makes known the parole, watchword or countersign to any person not entitled to receive it; or knowingly gives a parole, watchword or countersign different from what he received, shall, on conviction by a Security Force Court -

   (i) if he commits any such offence when on active duty, be liable to suffer imprisonment for a term which may extend to fourteen years or such less punishment as is in this Act mentioned; and

   (ii) if he commits any such offence when not on active duty, be liable to suffer imprisonment for a term which may extend to seven years or such less punishment as is in this Act mentioned.

17. Mutiny. Any person subject to this Act who commits any of the following offences, that, is. to say -

(a) begins, incites, causes or conspires with any other person to cause any mutiny in the Force or in the military, naval or air forces of India or any forces co-operating therewith; or

(b) joins in any such mutiny; or

(c) being present at any such mutiny, does not use his utmost endeavours to suppress the same; or

(d) Knowing or having reason to believe in the existence of any such mutiny, or of any intention to mutiny or of any such conspiracy, does not, without delay, give information thereof to his Commandant or other superior officer; or

(e) endeavours to seduce any person in the Force or in the military, naval or air forces of India or any forces co-operating therewith from his duty or allegiance to the Union, shall, on conviction by a Security Force Court, be liable to suffer death or such less punishment as is in this Act mentioned.

18. Desertion and aiding desertion.

(1) Any person subject to this Act who deserts or attempts to desert the service shall, on conviction by a Security Force Court -

(a) if he commits the offence when on active duty or when under orders for active duty, be liable to suffer death or such less punishment as is in this Act mentioned; and

(b) if he commits the offence under any other circumstances, be liable to suffer imprisonment for a term which may extend to seven years, or such less punishment as is in this Act mentioned.

(2) Any person subject to this Act who knowingly harbours any such deserter shall, on conviction by a Security Force Court, be liable to suffer imprisonment for a term which may extend to seven years or such less punishment as is in this Act mentioned.

(3) Any person subject to this Act who, being cognizant of any desertion or attempt at desertion of a person subject to this Act, does not forthwith give notice to his own or some other superior officer, or take any steps in his power to cause such person to be apprehended, shall, on conviction by a Security Force Court, be liable to suffer imprisonment for a term which may extend to two years or such less punishment as is in this Act mentioned.

19. Absence without leave. Any person subject to this Act who commits any of the following offences, that is to say -

(a) absents himself without leave; or

(b) without sufficient cause overstays leave granted to him; or

(c) being on leave of absence and having received information from the appropriate authority that any battalion or part thereof or any other unit of the Force, to which he belongs, has been ordered on active duty, fails, without sufficient cause, to rejoin without delay; or

(d) without sufficient cause fails to appear at the time fixed at the parade or place appointed for exercise or duty; or

(e) when on parade, or on the line of march, without sufficient cause without leave from his superior officer, quits the parade or line of march; or

(f) when in camp or elsewhere, is found beyond any limits fixed, or in any place prohibited, by any general, local or other order, without a pass or written leave from his superior officer; or

(g) without leave from his superior officer or without, due cause, absents himself from any school when duly ordered to attend there, shall, on conviction by a Security Force Court, be liable to suffer imprisonment for a term which may extend to three years or such less punishment as is in this Act mentioned.

20. Striking or threatening superior officers. Any person subject to this Act who commits any of the following offences, that is to say,—

(a) uses criminal force to or assaults his superior officer; or

(b) uses threatening language to such officer; or

(c) uses insubordinate language to such officer; shall, on conviction by a Security Force Court -

(i) if such officer is at the time in the execution of his office or, if the offence is committed on active duty, be liable to suffer imprisonment for a term which may extend to fourteen years or such loss punishment as is in this Act mentioned; and

(ii) in other cases, be liable to suffer imprisonment for a term which may extend to ten years or such less punishment as is in this Act mentioned:

PROVIDED that in the case of any offence specified in clause (c), the imprisonment shall not exceed five years.

21. Disobedience to superior officer.

(1) Any person subject to this Act who disobeys in such manner as to show a wilful defiance of authority any lawful command given personally by his superior officer in the execution of his office whether the same is given orally, or in writing or by signal or otherwise, shall, on conviction by a Security Force Court, be liable to suffer imprisonment for a term which may extend to fourteen years or such less punishment as in this Act mentioned.

(2) Any person subject to this Act who disobeys any lawful command given by his superior officer shall, on conviction by a Security Force Court,—

(a) if he commits such offence when on active duty, be liable to suffer imprisonment for a term which may extend to fourteen years or such less punishment as is in this Act mentioned; and

(b) if he commits such offence when not on active duty, be liable to suffer imprisonment for a term which may extend to five years or such less punishment as is in this Act mentioned.

22. Insubordination and obstruction. Any person subject to this Act who commits any of the following offences, that is to say -

(a) being concerned in any quarrel, affray or disorder, refuses to obey any officer, though of inferior rank, who orders him into arrest, or uses criminal force to or assaults any such officer; or

(b) uses criminal force to, or assaults any person, whether subject to this Act or not, in whose custody he is lawfully placed, and whether be is or is not his superior officer; or

(c) resists an escort whose duty it is to apprehend him or to have him in charge; or

(d) breaks out of barracks, camp or quarters; or

(e) neglects to obey any general, local or other order; or

(f) impedes the Force Police referred to in Section 63 or any person lawfully acting on his behalf, or when called upon, refuses to assist in the execution of his duty a Force Police or any person lawfully acting on his behalf, shall on conviction by a Security Force Court, be liable to suffer imprisonment for a term which may extend, in the case of the offences specified in clauses (d) and (e), to two years, and in the case of the offences specified in the other clauses, to ten years, or in either case such less punishment as is in this Act mentioned.

23. False answers on enrolment. Any person having become subject to this Act who is discovered to have made at the time of enrolment a wilfully false answer to any question set forth in the prescribed form of enrolment which has been put to him by the enrolling officer before whom he appears for the purpose of being enrolled, shall, on conviction by a Security Force Court, be liable to suffer imprisonment for a term which may extend to five years or such less punishment as is in this Act mentioned.

24. Certain forms of disgraceful conduct. Any person subject to this Act who commits any of the following offences, that is to say -

(a) is guilty of any disgraceful conduct of a cruel, indecent or unnatural kind; or

(b) malingers, or feigns, or produces disease or infirmity in himself or intentionally delays his cure or aggravates his disease or infirmity; or

(c) with intent to render himself or any other person unfit for service, voluntarily causes hurt to himself or that person, shall, on conviction by a Security Force Court, be liable to suffer imprisonment for a term which may extend to seven years or such less punishment as is in this Act mentioned.

25. Ill-treating a subordinate. Any officer, subordinate officer or under-officer, who uses criminal force to or otherwise ill-treats any person subject to this Act, being his subordinate in rank or position, shall, on conviction by a Security Force Court, be liable to suffer imprisonment for a term which may extend to seven years or such less punishment as is in this Act mentioned.

26. Intoxication. Any person subject to this Act who is found in a state of intoxication, whether on duty or not, shall, on conviction by a Security Force Court, be liable to suffer imprisonment for a term which may extend to six months or such less punishment as is in this Act mentioned.

27. Permitting escape of person in custody. Any person subject to this Act who commits any of the following offences, that is to say -

(a) when in command of a guard, picket, patrol or post, releases without proper authority, whether wilfully or without reasonable excuse, any person committed to his charge, or refuses to receive any prisoner or person so committed; or

(b) wilfully or without reasonable excuse allows to escape any person who is committed to his charge, or whom it is his duty to keep or guard, shall, on conviction by a Security Force Court, be liable, if he has acted wilfully, to suffer imprisonment for a term which may extend to ten years or such less punishment as is in this Act mentioned; and if he has not acted wilfully, to suffer imprisonment for a term which may extend to two years or such less punishment as is in this Act mentioned.

28. Irregularity in connection with arrest or confinement. Any person subject to this Act who commits any of the following offences, that is to say -

(a) unnecessarily detains a person in arrest or confinement without bringing him to trial, or fails to bring his case before the proper authority for investigation; or

(b) having committed a person to Force custody fails without reasonable cause to deliver at the time of such committal, or as soon as practicable, and in any case within forty-eight hours thereafter, to the officer or other person into whose custody the person arrested is committed, an account in writing signed by himself of the offence with which the person so committed is charged, shall, on conviction by a Security Force Court, be liable to suffer imprisonment for a term which may extend to one year or such less punishment as is, in this Act mentioned.

29. Escape from custody. Any person subject to this Act who, being in lawful custody, escapes or attempts to escape, shall, on conviction by a Security Force Court, be liable to suffer imprisonment for a term which may extend to three years or such less punishment as is in this Act mentioned.

30. Offences in respect of property. Any person subject to this Act who commits any of the following offences, that is to say -

(a) commits theft of any property belonging to the Government, or to any Force mess, band or institution, or to any person subject to this Act; or

(b) dishonestly misappropriates or converts to his own use any such property; or

(c) commits criminal breach of trust in respect of any such property; or

(d) dishonestly receives or retains any such property in respect of which any of the offence under clauses (a), (b) and (c) has been committed, knowing or having reason to believe the commission of such offence; or

(e) wilfully destroys or injures any property of the Government entrusted to him; or

(f) does any other thing with intent to defraud, or to cause wrongful gain to one person or wrongful loss to another person, shall, on conviction by a Security

Force Court, be liable to suffer imprisonment for a term which may extend to ten years or such less punishment as is in this Act mentioned.

31. Extortion and corruption. Any person subject to this, Act who commits any of the following offences, that is to say -

(a) commits extortion; or

(b) without proper authority exacts from any person money, provisions or service, shall, on conviction by a Security Force Court, be liable to suffer imprisonment for a term which may extend to ten years or such less punishment as is in this Act mentioned.

32. Making away with equipment. Any person subject to this Act who commits any of the following offences, that is to say -

(a) makes away with, or is concerned in making away with, any arms, ammunition, equipment, instruments, tools, clothing or any other thing being the property of the Government issued to him for his use or entrusted to him; or

(b) loses by neglect anything mentioned in clause (a); or

(c) sells, pawns, destroys or defaces any medal or decoration granted to him, shall, on conviction by a Security Force Court be liable to suffer imprisonment for a term which may extend in the case of the offences specified in clause (a), to ten years, and in the case of the offences specified in the other clauses, to five years, or in either case such less punishment as is in this Act mentioned.

33. Injury to property. Any person subject to this Act who commits any of the following offencess, that is to say,—

(a) destroys or injures any property mentioned in clause (a) of Section 32, or any property belonging to any Force mess, band or institution or to any person subject to this Act; or

(b) commits any act which causes damage to, or destruction of, any property of the Government by fire; or

(c) kills, injures, makes away with, ill-treats or loses any, animal entrusted to him, shall, on conviction by a Security Force Court, be liable, if he has acted wilfully, to suffer imprisonment for a term which may extend to ten years or such less punishment as is in this Act mentioned; and if he has acted without reasonable excuse, to suffer imprisonment for a term which may extend to five years or such less punishment as is in this Act mentioned.

34. False accusations. Any person subject to this Act who commits any of the following offences, that is to say -

(a) makes a false accusation against any person subject to this Act, knowing or having reason to believe such accusation to be false; or

(b) in making a complaint against any person subject to this Act makes any statement affecting the character of such person, knowing or having reason to believe such statement to be false, or knowingly and wilfully suppresses any material facts, shall, on conviction by a Security Force Court, be liable to suffer imprisonment for a term which may extend to three years or such less punishment as is in this Act mentioned.

35. Falsifyng official documents and false declarations. Any person subject to this Act who commits any of the following offences, that is to say -

(a) in any report, return, list, certificate, book or other document made or signed by him, or of the contents of which it is his duty to ascertain the accuracy, knowingly makes, or is privy to the making of, any false or fraudulent statement; or

(b) in any document of the description mentioned in clause (a) knowingly makes, or is privy to the making of, any omission, with intent to defraud; or

(c) knowingly and with intent to injure any person, or knowingly and with intent to defraud, suppresses, defaces, alters or makes away with any document which it is his duty to preserve or produce; or

(d) where it is his official duty to make a declaration respecting any matter knowingly makes a false declaration; or

(e) obtains for himself, or for any other person, any pension, allowance or other advantage or privilege by a statement which is false, and which he either knows or believes to be false or does not believe to be true, or by making or using a false entry in any book or record, or by making any document containing a false statement, or by omitting to make a true entry or document containing a true statement, shall, on conviction by a Security Force Court, be liable to suffer imprisonment for a term which may extend to ten years or such less punishment as is in this Act mentioned.

36. Signing in blank and failure to report. Any person subject to this Act who commits any of the following offences, that is to say -

(a) when signing any document relating to pay, arms, ammunition, equipment, clothing, supplies or stores, or any property of the Government fraudulently leaves in blank any material part for which his signature is a voucher; or

(b) refuses or by culpable neglect omits to make or send a report or return which it is his duty to make or send, shall, on conviction by a Security Force Court, be liable to suffer imprisonment for a term which may extend to three years or such less punishment as is in this Act mentioned.

37. Offences relating to Security Force Court. Any person subject to this Act who commits any of the following offences, that is to say -

(a) being duly summoned or ordered to attend as a witness before a Security Force Court, wilfully or without reasonable excuse, makes default in attending; or

(b) refuses to take an oath or make an affirmation legally required by a Security Force Court to be taken or made; or

(c) refuses to produce or deliver any document in his power or control legally required by a Security Force Court to be produced or delivered by him; or

(d) refuses, when a witness, to answer any question which he is by law bound to answer; or

(e) is guilty of contempt of the Security Force Court by using insulting or threatening language, or by causing any interruption or disturbance in the proceedings of such court, shall, on conviction by a Security Force Court, be liable to suffer imprisonment for a term which may extend to three years or such less punishment as is in this Act mentioned.

38. False evidence. Any person subject to this Act who, having been duly sworn or affirmed before any Security Force Court or other court competent under this Act to administer an oath or affirmation, makes any statement which is false, and which he either knows or believes to be false or does not believe to be true, shall, on conviction by a Security Force Court, be liable to suffer imprisonment for a term which may extend to seven years or such less punishment as is in this Act mentioned.

39. Unlawful detention of pay. Any officer, subordinate officer or an under-officer who, having received the pay of a person subject to this Act unlawfully detains or refuses to pay the same when due, shall, on conviction by a Security Force Court, be liable to suffer imprisonment for a term which may extend to five years or such less punishment as is in this Act mentioned.

40. Violation of good order and discipline. Any person subject to this Act who is guilty of any act or omission which, though not specified in this Act, is prejudicial to good order and discipline of the Force shall, on conviction by a Security Force Court, be liable to suffer imprisonment for a term which may extend to seven years or such less punishment as is in this Act mentioned.

41. Miscellaneous offences. Any person subject to this Act who commits any of the following offences, that is to say -

(a) being in command at any post or on the march, and receiving a complaint that any one under his command has beaten or otherwise maltreated or oppressed any person, or has disturbed any fair or market, or committed any riot or trespass, fails to have due preparation made to the injured person or to report the case to the proper authority; or

(b) by defiling any place of worship, or otherwise, intentionally insults the religion, or wounds the religious feelings of any person; or

(c) attempts to commit suicide, and in such attempt does any act towards the commission of such offence; or

(d) being below the rank of subordinate officer, when off duty, appears without proper authority, in or about camp, or in or about, or when going to, or returning from, any town or bazaar, carrying a rifle, sword or other offensive weapon; or

(e) directly or indirectly accepts or obtains, or agrees to accept, or attempts to obtain, for himself or for any other person, any gratification as a motive or reward for procuring the enrolment of any person, or leave of absence, promotion or any other advantage or indulgence for any person in the service; or

(f) commits any offence against the property or person of any inhabitant of, or resident in, the country in which he is serving, shall, on conviction by a Security Force Court, be liable to suffer imprisonment for a term which may extend to seven years or such less punishment as is in this Act mentioned.

42. Attempt. Any person subject to this Act who attempts to commit any of the offences specified in Sections 14 to 41 (both inclusive) and in such attempt does any act towards the commission of the offence shall, on conviction by a Security Force Court, where no express provision is made by this Act for the punishment of such attempt, be liable -

(a) if the offence attempted to be committed is punishable with death, to suffer imprisonment for a term which may extend to fourteen years or such less punishment as is in this Act mentioned; and

(b) if the offence attempted to be committed is punishable with imprisonment, to suffer imprisonment for a term which may extend to one-half of the longest term provided for that offence or such less punishment as is in this Act mentioned.

43. Abetment of offences that have been committed. Any person subject to this Act who abets the commission of any of the offences specified in Sections 14 to 41 (both inclusive) shall, on conviction by a Security Force Court, if the Act abetted is committed in consequence of the abetment and no express provision is made by this Act for the punishment of such abetment, be liable to suffer the punishment provided for that offence or such less punishment as is in this Act mentioned.

44. Abetment of offences punishable with death and not committed. Any person subject to this Act who abets the commission of any of the offences punishable with death under Sections 14, 17 and sub-section (1) of Section 18 shall, on conviction by a Security Force Court, if that offence be not committed in consequence of the abetment, and no express provision is made by this Act for the punishment of such abetment, be liable to suffer imprisonment for a term which may extend to fourteen years or such less punishment as is in this Act mentioned.

45. Abetment of offences punishable with imprisonment and not committed. Any person subject to this Act who abets the commission of any of the offences specified in Sections 14 to 41 (both inclusive) and punishable with imprisonment shall, on conviction by a Security Force Court, if that offence be not committed in consequence of the abetment, and no express provision is made by this Act for the punishment of such abetment, be liable to suffer imprisonment for a term which may extend to one-half of the longest term provided for that offence or such less punishment as is in this Act mentioned.

46. Civil offences. Subject to the provisions of Section 47, any person subject to this Act who at any place in, or beyond, India commits any civil offence shall be deemed to be guilty of an offence against this Act and, if charged therewith under this Section shall be liable to be tried by a Security Force Court and, on conviction, be punishable as follows, that is to say -

(a) if the offence is one which would be punishable under any law in force in India with death, he shall be liable to suffer any punishment, assigned for the offence, by the aforesaid law and such less punishment as is in this Act mentioned; and

(b) in any other case, he shall be liable to suffer any punishment, assigned for the offence by the law in force in India, or imprisonment for a term which may extend to seven years, or such less punishment as is in this Act mentioned.

47. Civil offences not triable by a Security Force Court. A person subject to this Act who commits an offence of murder or of culpable homicide not amounting to murder against, or of rape in relation to, a person not subject to this Act shall not be deemed to be guilty of an offence against this Act and shall not be tried by a Security Force Court, unless he commits any of the said offences -

(a) while on active duty; or

(b) at any place outside India; or

(c) at any place specified by the Central Government by notification in this behalf.

CHAPTER -IV : PUNISHMENTS

48. Punishments awardable by Security Force Courts.

(1) Punishments may be inflicted in respect of offences committed by persons subject to this Act and convicted by Security Force Courts according to the scale following, that is to say -

(a) death;

(b) imprisonment which may be for the term of life or any other lesser term but excluding imprisonment for a term not exceeding three months in Force custody;

(c) dismissal from the service;

(d) imprisonment for a term not exceeding three months in Force custody;

(e) reduction to the ranks or to a lower rank or grade or place in the list of their rank in the case of an under-officer;

(f) forfeiture of seniority of rank and forfeiture of all or any part of the service for the purpose of promotion;

(g) forfeiture of service for the purpose of increased pay, pension or any other prescribed purpose;

(h) fine, in respect of civil offences;

(i) severe reprimand or reprimand except in the case of persons below the rank of an under-officer;

(j) forfeiture of pay and allowances for a period not exceeding three months for an offence committed on active duty;

(k) forfeiture in the case of person sentenced to dismissal from the service of all arrears of pay and allowances and other public money due to him at the time of such dismissal;

(l) stoppage of pay and allowances until any proved loss or damage occasioned by the offence for which he is convicted is made good.

(2) Each of the punishments specified in sub-section (1) shall be deemed to be inferior in degree to every punishment preceding it in the above scale.

49. Alternative punishments awardable by Security Force Courts. Subject to the provisions of this Act, a Security Force Court may, on convicting a person subject to this Act of any of the offences specified in Sections 14 to 45 (both inclusive) award either the particular punishment with which the offence is stated in the said Sections to be punishable or, in lieu thereof, any one of the punishments lower in the scale set out in Section 48 regard being had to the nature and degree of the offence.

50. Combination of punishments. A sentence of a Security Force Court may award in addition to, or without any one other punishment, the punishment specified in clause (c) of sub-section (1) of Section 48, and any one or more of the punishments specified in clauses (e) to (l) (both inclusive) of that sub-section.

51. Retention in the Force of a person convicted on active duty. When on active duty any enrolled person has been sentenced by a Security Force Court to dismissal or to imprisonment whether combined with dismissal or not, the prescribed officer may direct that such person may be retained to, serve in the ranks, and such service shall be reckoned as part of his term of imprisonment if any.

52. Punishments otherwise than by Security Force Courts. Punishments may also be inflicted in respect of offences committed by persons subject to this Act without the intervention of a Security Force Court in the manner stated in Sections 53 and 55.

53. Minor punishments. Subject to the provisions of Section 54, a Commandant or such other officer as is, with the consent of Central Government, specified by the Director-General may, in the prescribed manner, proceed against a person subject to this Act, otherwise than as an officer or a subordinate officer, who is charged with an offence under this Act and award such person, to the extent prescribed, one or more of the following punishments, that is to say -

(a) imprisonment in Force custody up to twenty-eight days;

(b) detention up-to twenty-eight days;

(c) confinement to the lines up to twenty-eight days;

(d) extra guards or duties;

(e) deprivation of any special position or special emoluments or any acting rank or reduction to a lower grade of pay;

(f) forfeiture of good service and good conduct pay;

(g) severe reprimand or reprimand;

(h) fine up to fourteen days' pay in any one month;

(i) deductions from his pay of any sum required to make good such compensation for any expense, loss, damage or destruction caused by him to the Central Government, or to any building or property as may be awarded by his Commandant.

54. Limit of punishments under Section 53.

(1) In the case of an award of two or more of the punishments specified in clauses (a), (b), (c) and (d) of Section 53, the punishments specified in clause (c) or clause (d) shall take effect only at the end of the punishment specified in clause (a) or clause (b).

(2) When two or more of the punishments specified in the said clauses (a), (b) and (c) are awarded to a person conjointly, or when already undergoing one or more

of the said punishments, the whole extent of the punishments shall not exceed in the aggregate forty-two days.

(3) The punishments specified in the said clauses (a), (b) and (c) shall not be awarded to any person who is of the rank of an under-officer or was, at the time of committing the offence for which he is punished, of such rank.

(4) The punishment specified in clause (g) of Section 53 shall not be awarded to any person below the rank of an under-officer.

55. Punishment of persons of and below the rank of subordinate officers by Deputy Inspectors-General and others.

(1) An officer not below the rank of the Deputy Inspector-General or such other officer as is, with the consent of the Central Government, specified by the Director-General may, in the prescribed manner, proceed against a person of or below the rank of a subordinate officer who is charged with an offence under this Act and award one or more of the following punishments, that is to say -

   (a) forfeiture of seniority, or in the case of any of them whose promotion depends upon the length of service forfeiture of service for the purpose of promotion for a period not exceeding twelve months, but subject to the right of the accused previous to the award to elect to be tried by a Security Force Court;

   (b) severe reprimand or reprimand;

   (c) stoppage of pay and allowances until any proved loss or damage occasioned by the offence of which he is convicted is made good.

(2) In every case in which punishment has been awarded under sub-section (1), certified true copies of the proceedings shall be forwarded, in the prescribed manner, by the officer awarding the punishment to the prescribed superior authority who may, if the punishment awarded appears to him to be illegal, unjust or excessive, cancel, vary or remit the punishment and make such other direction as may be appropriate in the circumstances of the case.

56. Collective fines.

(1) Whenever any weapon or part of a weapon, or ammunition, forming part of the equipment of a unit of the Force, is lost or stolen, an officer not below the rank of the Commandant of a battalion may, after making such enquiry as he thinks fit and subject to the rules, impose a collective fine upon the subordinate officers, under-officers and men of such unit, or upon so many of them as, in his judgment, should be held responsible for such loss or theft.

(2) Such fine shall be assessed as a percentage on the pay of the individuals on whom it falls.

CHAPTER -V : ARREST AND PROCEEDINGS BEFORE TRIAL

57. Custody of offenders.

(1) Any person subject to this Act who is charged with an offence may be taken into Force custody, under the order of any superior officer.

(2) Notwithstanding anything contained in sub-section (1), an officer may order into Force custody any other officer, though such other officer may be of a higher rank, engaged in a quarrel, affray or disorder.

58. Duty of Commandant in regard to detention.

(1) It shall be the duty of every Commandant to take care that a person under his command when charged with an offence is not detained in custody for more than forty-eight hours after the committal of such person into custody is reported to him, without the charge being investigated, unless investigation within that period seems to him to be impracticable having regard to the public service.

(2) The case of every person being detained in custody beyond a period of forty-eight hours, and the reasons therefore, shall be reported by the Commandant to the Deputy Inspector-General under whom he is serving or such other officer to whom an application may be made to convene a Security Force Court for the trial of the person charged.

(3) In reckoning the period of forty-eight hours specified in sub-section (1). Sundays and other public holidays shall be excluded.

(4) Subject to the provisions of the Act, Central Government may make rules providing for the manner in which and the period for which any person subject to this Act may be taken into and detained in Force custody, pending the trial any competent authority for any offence committed by him.

59. Interval between committal and trial. In every case where any such person as is mentioned in Section 57 and as is not on active duty, remains in such custody for a longer period then eight days without a Security force Court for his trial being convened, a special report giving reasons for the delay shall be made by his commandant in the manner prescribed, and a similar report shall be forwarded at intervals of every eight days until a Security Force Court is convened or such person is released from custody.

60. Arrest by civil authorities. Whenever any person subject to this Act, who is accused of an offence under this Act, is within the jurisdiction of any magistrate or police officer, such magistrate or police officer shall aid in the apprehension and delivery to Force custody of such person upon receipt of a written application to that effect signed by his Commandant or an officer by the Commandant in that behalf.

61. Capture of deserters.

(1) Whenever any person subject to this Act deserts, the Commandant of the unit to which he belongs, shall give information of the desertion to such civil authorities as, in his opinion, may be able to afford assistance towards the capture of the deserter; and such authorities shall thereupon take steps for the apprehension of the said deserter in like manner as if he were a person for whose apprehension a warrant had been issued by a magistrate, and shall deliver the deserter, when apprehended, into Force custody.

(2) Any police officer may arrest without warrant any person reasonably believed to be subject to this Act, and to be a deserter or to be travelling without authority, and shall bring him without delay before the nearest magistrate, to be dealt with according to law.

62. Inquiry into absence without leave.

(1) When any person subject to this Act has been absent from duty without due authority for a period of thirty days, a court of inquiry shall, as soon as practicable, be appointed by such authority and in such manner as may be prescribed; and such court shall, on oath or affirmation administered in the prescribed manner, inquire respecting the absence of the person, and the deficiency, if any, in the property of the Government entrusted to his care, or in any arms, ammunition, equipment, instruments, clothing or necessaries; and if satisfied of the fact of such absence without due authority or other sufficient cause, the court shall declare such absence and the period thereof and the said deficiency, if any, and the Commandant of the unit to which the person belongs shall make a record thereof in the prescribed manner.

(2) If the person declared absent does not afterwards surrender or is not apprehended, he shall for the purposes of this Act, be deemed to be a deserter.

63. Force police officers.

(1) The Director-General or any prescribed officer may appoint persons (in this Act referred to as Force police) for discharging the functions specified in sub-sections (2) and (3).

(2) The duties of a person appointed under sub-section (1), are to take charge of persons confined for any offence, to preserve good order and discipline and to prevent breaches of the same by persons serving in, or attached to, the Force.

(3) Notwithstanding anything contained in Section 57, a person appointed under sub-section (1) may, at any time, arrest and detain for trial any person subject to this Act who commits, or is charged with, an offence, and may also carry into effect any punishment to be inflicted in pursuance of a sentence awarded by a Security Force Court or by an officer exercising authority under Section 53 but shall not inflict any punishment on his own authority:

PROVIDED that no officer shall be so arrested or detained otherwise than on the order of another officer.

CHAPTER - VI : SECURITY FORCE COURTS

64. Kinds of Security Force Courts. For the purposes of this Act there shall be three kinds of Security Force Courts, that is to say -

(a) General Security Force Courts;

(b) Petty Security Force Courts; and

(c) Summary Security Force Courts.

65. Power to convence a General Security Force Court. A General Security Force Court may be convened by the Central Government or the Director-General or by any officer empowered in this behalf by warrant of the Director-General.

66. Power to convence a Petty Security Force Court. A Petty Security Force Court may be convened by an officer having power to convene a General Security Force Court or by an officer empowered in this behalf by warrant or any such officer.

67. Contents of warrants issued under Sections 65 and 66. A warrant, issued under Section 65 or Section 66 may contain such restrictions, reservations or conditions as the officer issuing it may think fit.

68. Composition of General Security Force Court. A General Security Force Court shall consist of not less than five officers, each of whom has held the post of Deputy Superintendent of Police for not less than three whole years and of whom not less than four are of a rank not below that of a confirmed Deputy Superintendent of Police.

EXPLANATION. For the purposes of this Section and Section 69, "Deputy Superintendent of Police" includes any post of a higher rank and any post declared by Central Government by notification to be an equivalent post as also any post higher in rank than the post so declared.

69. Composition of a Petty Security Force Court. A Petty Security Force Court shall consist of not less than three officers each of whom has held the post of Deputy Superintendent of Police for not less than two whole years.

70. Summary Security Force Court.

(1) A Summary Security Force Court may be held by the Cornandant of any unit of the Force and he alone shall constitute the Court.

(2) The proceedings shall be attended throughout by two other persons who shall be officers or subordinate officers or one of either, and who shall not as such, be sworn or affirmed.

71. Dissolution of a Security Force Court.

(1) If a Security Force Court after the commencement of a trial is reduced below the minimum number of officers required by this Act, it shall be dissolved.

(2) If, on account of the illness of the Law Officer or of the accused before the finding, it is impossible to continue the trial, a Security Force Court shall be dissolved.

(3) The officer who convened a Security Force Court may dissolve the same if it appears to, him that the exigencies of the service or necessities of discipline render it impossible or inexpedient to continue the said Security Force Court.

(4) Where a Security Force Court is dissolved under this Section, the accused may be tried again.

72. Power of a General Security Force Court. A General Security Force Court shall have the power to try any person subject to this Act for any offence punishable thereunder and to pass any sentence authorised thereby.

73. Powers of a Petty Security Force Court. A Petty Security Force Court shall have power to try any person subject to this Act other than an officer or subordinate officer for any offence made punishable thereunder and to pass any sentence authorised by this Act other than a sentence of death, or imprisonment for a term exceeding two years.

74. Power of a Summary Security Force Court.

(1) Subject to the provisions of sub-section (2), a Summary Security Force Court may try any offence punishable under this Act.

(2) When there is no grave reason for immediate action and reference can without detriment to discipline be made to the officer empowered to convene a Petty Security Force Court for the trial of the alleged offender, an officer holding a Summary Security Force Court shall not try without such reference any offence punishable under any of the Sections 14, 17 and 46 of this Act or any offence against the officer holding the court.

(3) A Summary Security Force Court may try any person subject to this Act and under the command of the officer holding the court, except an officer, or a subordinate officer.

(4) A Summary Security Force Court may pass any sentence which may be passed under this Act. except the sentence of death or of imprisonment for a term exceeding the limit specified in sub-section (5).

(5) The limit referred to in sub-section (4) shall be,—

- (a) one year, if the officer holding the Security Force Court has held either the post of Superintendent of Police or a post declared by the Central Government by notification to be equivalent thereto, for a period of not less than three years or holds a post of higher rank than either of the said posts; and
- (b) three months, in any other case.

75. Prohibition of second trial.

(1) When any person subject to this Act has been acquitted or convicted of an offence by a Security Force Court or by a criminal court or has been dealt with under Section 53 or under Section 55, he shall not be liable to be tried again for the same offence by a Security Force Court or dealt with under the said Sections.

(2) When any person, subject to this Act, has been acquitted or convicted of an offence by a Security Force Court or has been dealt with under Section 53 or Section 55, he shall not be liable to be tried again by a criminal court for the same offence or on the same facts.

76. Period of limitation for trial for an offence of desertion in certain cases. No trial for an offence of desertion, other than desertion on active duty, shall be commenced if the person in question, not being an officer, has subsequently to the commission of the offence, served continuously in an exemplary manner for not less than years with any unit of the Force.

77. Trial, etc., of offender who ceases to be subject to this Act.

(1) Where an offence under this Act had been committed by any person while subject to this Act, and he has ceased to be so subject, he may be taken into and kept in Force custody and tried and punished for such offence as if he continued to be so subject.

(2) No such person shall be tried for an offence, unless his trial commences within six months after he had ceased to be this Act:

PROVIDED that nothing contained in this sub-section shall apply to the trial of any such person for an offence of description or for any of the offences mentioned in Section 17 or shall affect the jurisdiction of a criminal court to try any offence triable by such court as well as by a Security Force Court.

78. Application of Act during term of sentence.

(1) When a person subject to this Act is sentenced by a Security Force Court to imprisonment, this Act shall apply to him during the term of his sentence, though he is dismissed from the Force, or has otherwise ceased to be subject to this Act, and he may be kept, removed, imprisoned and punished as if he continued to be subject to this Act.

(2) When a person subject to his Act is sentenced by a Security Force Court to death, this Act shall apply to him till the sentence is carried out.

79. Place of trial. Any person subject to this Act who commits any offence against it may be tried and punished for such offence in any place whatever.

80. Choice between criminal court and Security Force Court. When a criminal court and a Security Force Court have each jurisdiction in respect of an offence, it shall be in the discretion of the Director-General, or the Inspector-General or the Deputy Inspector-General within whose command the accused person is serving or such other officer as may be prescribed, to decide before which court the proceedings shall be instituted, and, if that officer decides that they shall be instituted before a Security Force Court, to direct that the accused person shall be detained in Force custody.

81. Power of criminal court to require delivery of offender.

(1) When a criminal court having jurisdiction is of opinion that proceedings shall be instituted before itself in respect of any alleged offence. It may, by written notice, require the officer referred to in Section 80 at his option, either to deliver over the offender to the nearest Magistrate to be proceeded against according to law, or to postpone proceedings, pending a reference to the Central Government.

(2) In every such case the said officer shall either deliver over the offender in compliance with the requisition, or shall forthwith refer the question as to the court before which the proceedings are to be instituted, for the determination of the Central Government whose order upon such reference shall be final.

CHAPTER -VII : PROCEDURE OF SECURITY FORCE COURTS

82. Presiding officer. At every General Security Force Court or Petty Security Force Court, the senior member shall be the presiding officer.

83. Law officers. Every General Security Force Court shall, and every Petty Security Force Court may, be attended by a Law Officer, or if no such officer is available, an officer approved by the Chief Law Officer, or a Law Officer.

84. Challenges.

(1) At all trials by a General Security Force Court or by a Petty Security Force Court, as soon as the court is assembled, the names of the presiding officer and members shall be read over to the accused, who shall thereupon be asked whether he objects to being tried by any officer sitting on the Court.

(2) If the accused objects to such officer, his objection and also the reply thereto- of the officer objected to shall be heard and recorded, and the remaining officers of the court shall, in the absence of the challenged officer decide on the objection.

(3) If the objection is allowed by one-half or more of the votes of the officers entitled to vote, the objection shall be allowed, and the member objected to shall retire, and his vacancy may be filled in the prescribed manner, by another officer subject to the same right of the accused to object.

(4) When no challenge is made, or when a challenge has been made and disallowed, or the place of every officer successfully challenged has been filled by another officer to whom no objection is made or allowed, the court shall proceed with the trial.

85. Oaths of member, Law Officer and witness.

(1) An oath or affirmation in the prescribed manner shall be administered to every member of every Security Force Court and to the Law Officer or as the case may be the officer approved under Section 83, before the commencement of the trial.

(2) Every person giving evidence before a Security Force Court shall be examined after being duly sworn or affirmed in the prescribed form.

(3) The provisions of slab-section (2) shall not apply where the witness is a child under twelve years of age and the Security Force Court is of opinion that though the witness understands the duty of speaking the truth, he does not understand the nature of an oath or affirmation.

86. Voting by members.

(1) Subject to the provisions of sub-sections (2) and (3), every decision of a Security Force Court shall be passed by an absolute majority of votes; and where there is an equality of votes on either the finding or the sentence, the decision shall be in favour of the accused.

(2) No sentence of death shall be passed by a General Security Force Court without the concurrence of at least two-thirds of the members of the court.

(3) In matters, other than a challenge or the finding or sentence, the presiding officer shall have a casting vote.

87. General rule as to evidence. The Indian Evidence Act, 1872 (1 of 1872), shall, subject to the provisions of this Act, apply to all proceedings before a Security Force Court.

88. Judicial notice. A Security Force Court may take judicial notice of any matter within the general knowledge of the members as officers of the Force.

89. Summoning witnesses.

(1) The convening officer, the presiding officer of a Security Force Court, the Law Officer or, as the case may be, the officer approved under Section 83 or the Commandant of the accused person may, by summons under his hand, require the attendance, at a time and place to be mentioned in the summons, of any person either to give evidence or to produce any document or other thing.

(2) In the case of a witness who is subject to this Act, the summons shall be sent to his Commandant and such officer shall serve it upon him accordingly.

(3) In the case of any other witness; the summons shall be sent to the magistrate within whose jurisdiction he may be, or resides, and such magistrate shall give effect to the summons as if the witness were required in the court of such a magistrate.

(4) When a witness is required to produce any particular document of other thing in his possession or power, the summons shall describe it with reasonable precision.

90. Documents exempted from production.

(1) Nothing in Section 89 shall be deemed to affect the operation of Sections 123 and 124 of the Indian Evidence Act, 1872 (1 of 1872), or to apply to any letter, postcard, telegram or other document in the custody of the postal or telegraph authorities.

(2) If any document in such custody is, in the opinion of any district Magistrate, Chief Presidency MAgistrate, High Court or Court of Sessions, wanted for the purpose of any Security Force Court, such magistrate, or Court may require the postal or telegraph authorities, as the case may be, to deliver such document to such person as such magistrate, or Court may direct.

(3) If any such document is, in the opinion of any other magistrate or of any Commissioner of Police or District Superintendent of Police wanted for any such purpose, he may require the postal or telegraph authorities, as the case may be, to cause such search to be made for, and to detain such document pending the orders of any such district Magistrate, Chief Presidency Magistrate or High Court or Court of Sessions.

91. Commissions for examination of witnesses.

(1) Whenever, in the course of a trial by a Security Force Court, it appears to the court that the examination of a witness is necessary for the ends of justice, and that the attendance of such witness cannot be procured without an amount of delay, expense or inconvenience which, in the circumstances of the case, would be unreasonable, such court may address the Chief Law Officer in order that a commission to take the evidence of such witness may be issued.

(2) The Chief Law Officer may then, if he thinks necessary, issue a Commission to any district magistrate or magistrate of the first class, within the local limits of whose jurisdiction such witness resides, to take the evidence of such witness.

(3) The magistrate or officer to whom the commission is issued, or, if he is the District Magistrate, he or such Magistrate of the first class as he appoints in this behalf, shall proceed to the place where the witness is, or shall summon the witness before him and shall take down his evidence in the same manner, and may for this purpose exercise the same powers, as in the trials of warrant-cases under the Code of Criminal Procedure, 1898 (5 of 1898).

(4) When the witness resides in a tribal area or in any place outside India, the commission may be issued in the manner specified in Chapter XL of the Code of Criminal Procedure, 1898 (5 of 1898).

92. Examination of a witness on commission.

(1) The prosecutor and the accused person in any case in which a commission is issued under Section 91 may respectively forward any interrogatories in writing which the court may think relevant to the issue, and the Magistrate or officer executing the commission shall examine the witness upon such interrogatories.

(2) The prosecutor and the accused person may appear before such Magistrate or officer by counsel or, except in the case of an accused person in custody, in person, and may examine, cross-examine and re-examine, as the case may be, the said witness.

(3) After a commission issued under Section 91 has been duly executed, it shall be returned, together with the deposition of the witness examined thereunder to the Chief Law officer.

(4) On receipt of a Commission, and deposition returned under sub-section (3), the Chief Law Officer shall forward the same to the court at whose instance the commission was issued or, if such court has been dissolved, to any other court convened for the trial of the accused person; and the commission, the return thereto and the deposition shall be open to inspection by the prosecutor and the accused person, and may, subject to all just exceptions, be read in evidence in the case by either the prosecutor or the accused, and shall form part of the proceedings of the court.

(5) In every case in which a commission is issued under Section 91, the trial may be adjourned for specified time reasonably sufficient for the execution and return of the commission.

93. Conviction of offence not charged.

(1) A person charged before a Security Force Court with desertion may be found guilty of attempting to desert or of being absent without leave.

(2) A person charged before a Security Force Court with attempting to desert may be found guilty of being absent without leave.

(3) A person charged before a Security Force Court with using criminal force may be found guilty of assault.

(4) A person charged before a Security Force Court with using threatening language may be found guilty of using insubordinate language.

(5) A person charged before a Security Force Court with any one of the offences specified in clauses (a), (b), (c) and (d) of Section 30 may be found guilty of any other of these offences with which he might have been charged.

(6) A person charged before a Security Force Court with an offence punishable under Section 46 may be found guilty of any other offence of which he might have been found guilty, if the provisions of the Code of Criminal Procedure, 1898 (5 of 1898), were applicable.

(7) A person charged before a Security Force Court with any offence under this Act may, on failure of proof of an offence having been committed in circumstances involving a more severe punishment, be found guilty of the same offence as having been committed in circumstances involving a less severe punishment.

(8) A person charged before Security Force Court with any offence under this Act may be found guilty of having attempted or abetted the commission of that offence, although the attempt or abetment is not separately charged.

94. Presumption as to signatures. In any proceeding under this Act, any application, certificate warrant, reply or other document purporting to be signed by an officer in the service of the Government shall, on production, be presumed to have been duly signed by the person by whom and in the character in which it purports to have been signed, until the contrary is shown.

95. Enrolment paper.

(1) Any enrolment paper purporting to be signed by an enrolling officer shall, in proceedings under this Act, be evidence of the person enrolled having given the answers to questions which he is therein represented as having given.

(2) The enrolment of such person may be proved by the production of the original or a copy of his enrolment paper purporting to be certified to be a true copy by the officer having the custody of the enrolment paper.

96. Presumption as to certain documents.

(1) A letter, return or other document respecting the service of any person in, or the dismissal or discharge of any person from, any unit of the Force, or respecting the circumstances of any person not having served in, or belonged to, any unit of the Force, if purporting to be signed by or on behalf of the Central Government or the Director-General, or by any prescribed officer, shall be evidence of the facts stated in such letter, return or other document.

(2) A Border Security Force List or Gazette purporting to be published by authority shall be evidence of the status and rank of the officers, subordinate officers therein mentioned, and of any appointment held by them and of the battalion, unit, or branch of the Force to which they belong.

(3) Where a record is made in any battalion book in pursuance of this Act or of any rules made thereunder or otherwise in the discharge of official duties, and purports to be signed by the Commandant or by the officer whose duty it is to make such record, such record shall be evidence of the facts therein stated.

(4) A copy of any record in any battalion book purporting to be certified to be a true copy by the officer having custody of such book shall be evidence of such record.

(5) Where any person subject to this Act is being tried on a charge of desertion or of absence without leave, and such person has surrendered himself into the custody of any officer or other person subject to this Act, or any unit of the Force, or has been apprehended by such officer or person, a certificate purporting to be signed by such officer, or by the Commandant of the unit to which such per on belongs, as the case may be, and stating the fact, date and place of such

surrender or apprehension, and the manner in which he was dressed, shag be evidence of the matters so stated.

(6) Where any person subject to this Act is being tried on a charge of desertion or of absence without leave and such person has surrendered himself into the custody of, or has been apprehended by, a police officer not below the rank of an officer in charge of a police station a certificate purporting to be signed by such police officer and stating the fact, date and place of such surrender or apprehension and the manner in which he was dressed shall be evidence of the matters so stated.

(7) Any document purporting to be a report under the hand of any Chemical Examiner or Assistant Chemical Examiner to Government upon any matter or thing duly submitted to him for examination or analysis and report, may be used as evidence in any proceeding under this Act.

97. Reference by accused to Government Officer.

(1) If at any trial for desertion or absence without leave, overstaying leave or not rejoining when warned for service, the accused person states in his defence any sufficient or reasonable excuse for his unauthorised absence, and refers in support thereof to any officer in the service of the Government, or if it appears that any such officer is likely to prove or disprove the said statement in the defence, the court shall address such officer and adjourn the proceedings until his reply is received.

(2) The written reply of any officer so referred to shall, if signed by him, be received in evidence and have the same effect as if made on oath before the court.

(3) If the court is dissolved before the receipt of such reply, or if the court omits to comply with the provisions of this Section, the convening officer may, at his discretion, annul the proceedings and order a fresh trial.

98. Evidence of previous convictions and general character.

(1) When any person subject to this Act has been convicted by a Security Force Court of any offence, such Security Force Court may inquire into, and receive, and record evidence of any previous convictions of such person, either by a Security Force Court or by a criminal court, or any previous award of punishment under Section 53 or 55, and may further inquire into and record the general character of such person and such other matters as may be prescribed.

(2) Evidence received under this Section may be either oral, or in the shape of entries in, or certified extracts from, books of Security Force Courts or other official records; and it shall not be necessary to give notice before trial to the person tried that evidence as to his previous convictions or character will be received.

(3) At a Summary Security Force Court, the officer holding the trial may, if he thinks fit, record any previous convictions against the offender, his general character, and such other matters as may be prescribed, as of his own knowledge, instead of requiring them to be proved under the foregoing provisions of this Section.

99. Lunacy of accused.

(1) Whenever, in the course of a trial by a Security Force Court, it appears to the court that the person charged is by reason of unsoundness of mind incapable of making his defence, or that he committed the act alleged but was by reason of unsoundness of mind incapable of knowing the nature of the act or knowing that it was wrong or contrary to law, the court shall record a finding accordingly.

(2) The presiding officer of the court, or, in the case of a Summary Security Force Court, the officer holding the trial, shall forthwith report the case to the confirming officer, or to the authority empowered to deal with its finding under Section 115, as the case may be.

(3) The confirming officer to whom the case is reported under sub-section (2) may, if he does not confirm the finding, take steps to have the accused person tried by the same or another Security Force Court for the offence with which he was charged.

(4) The authority to whom the finding of a Summary Security Force Court is reported under sub-section (2), and a confirming officer confirming the finding in any case so reported to him shall order the accused person to be kept in custody in the prescribed manner and shall report the case for the orders of the Central Government.

(5) On receipt of a report under sub-section (4), the Central Government may order the accused person to be detained in a lunatic asylum or other suitable place of safe custody.

100. Subsequent fitness of lunatic accused for trial. Where any accused person, having been found by reason of unsoundness of mind to be incapable of making his defence, is in custody or under detention under Section 99, any officer prescribed in this behalf, may -

(a) if such person is in custody under sub-section (4) of Section 99, on the report of a medical officer that he is capable of making his defence, or

(b) if such person is detained in a jail under sub-section (5) of Section 99, on a certificate of the Inspector General of Prisons, and if such person is detained in a lunatic asylum under the said sub-section, on a certificate of any two or more of the visitors of such asylum and if he is detained in any other place under that sub-section, on a certificate of the prescribed authority, that he is capable of making his defence, take steps to have such person tried by the same or another Security Force Court for the offence with which he was originally charged or, if the offence is a civil offence, by a criminal court.

101. Transmission to Central Government of orders under Section 100. A copy of every order-made by an officer under Section 100 for the trial of the accused shall forthwith be sent to the Central Government.

102. Release of lunatic accused. Where any person is in custody under sub-section (4) of Section 99 or under detention under subsection (5) of that Section -

(a) if such person is in custody under the said sub-section (4), on the report of a medical officer, or

(b) if such person is detained under the said sub-section (5), on a certificate from any of the authorities mentioned in clause (b) of Section 100 that in the judgment of such officer or authority such person may be released without danger of his doing injury to himself or to any other person, the Central Government may order that such person be released or detained in custody, or transferred to a public lunatic asylum if he has not already been sent to such an asylum.

103. Delivery of lunatic accused to relatives. Where any relative or friend of any person who is in custody under sub-section (4) of Section 99 or under detention under sub-section (5) of that Section desires that he should be delivered to his care and custody, the Central Government may, upon application by such relative or friend and, on his giving security to the satisfaction of that Government that the person delivered shall be properly taken care of, and, prevented from doing injury to himself or to any other person, and be produced for the inspection of such officer, and at such times and places, as the Central Government may direct, order such person to be delivered to such relative or friend.

104. Order for custody and disposal of property pending trial. When any property regarding which any offence appears to have been committed, or which appears to have been used for the commission of any offence, is produced before a Security Force Court during a trial, the court may make such order as it thinks fit for the proper custody of such property pending the conclusion of the trial, and if the property is subject to speedy or, natural decay may after recording such evidence as it thinks necessary, order it to be' sold or otherwise disposed of.

105. Order for disposal of property regarding which offence is committed.

(1) After the conclusion of a trial before any Security Force Court, the court or the officer confirming the finding or sentence of such Security Force Court, or any authority superior to such officer, or, in the case of a Summary Security Force Court whose finding or sentence does not require confirmation, an officer not below the rank of Deputy Inspector-General within whose command the trial was held, may make such order as it or he thinks fit for the disposal by destruction, confiscation, delivery to any person claiming to be entitled to possession thereof, or otherwise, of any property or document produced before the court or in its custody, or regarding which any offence appears to have been committed or which has been used for the commission of any offence.

(2) Where any order has been made under sub-section (1) in respect of property regarding which an offence appears to have been committed, a copy of such order signed and certified by the authority making the same may, whether the trial was held within India or not, be sent to a magistrate within whose jurisdiction such property for the time being is situated, and such magistrate shall thereupon cause the order to be carried into effect as if it were an order passed by him under the provisions of the Code of Criminal Procedure, 1898 (5 of 1898).

(3) In this Section, the term "property" includes, in the case of property regarding which an offence appears to have been committed, not only such property as has been originally in the possession or under the control of any person, but also any property into or for which the same may have been converted or exchanged, and anything acquired by such conversion or exchange whether immediately or otherwise.

106. Powers of Security Force Court in relation to proceedings under this Act. Any trial by a Security Force Court under the provisions of this Act shall be deemed to be a judicial proceeding within the meaning of Sections 193 and 228 of the Indian Penal Code (45 of 1860), and the Security Force Court shall be deemed to be a court within the meaning of Sections 480 and 482 of the Code of Criminal Procedure, 1898 (5 of 1898).

CHAPTER -VIII : CONFIRMATION AND REVISION

107. Finding and sentence not valid, unless confirmed. No finding or sentence of a General Security Force Court or a Petty Security Force Court shall be valid except, so far as it may be confirmed as provided by this Act.

108. Power to confirm finding and sentence of General Security Force Court. The findings and sentences of General Security Force Courts made confirmed by the Central Government or by any officer empowered in this behalf by warrant of the Central Government.

109. Power to confirm finding and sentence of Petty Security Force Court. The findings and sentences of Petty Security Force Courts may be confirmed by an officer having power to convene a General Security Force Court or by any officer empowered in this behalf by warrant of such officer.

110. Limitation of powers of confirming authority. A warrant issued under Section 108 or Section 109 may contain such restrictions, reservations or conditions as the authority issuing it may think fit.

111. Power of confirming authority to mitigate, remit or commute sentences. Subject to such restrictions, reservations or conditions, as may be contained in any warrant issued under Section 108 or Section 109, a confirming authority may, when confirming the sentence of a Security Force Court, mitigate or remit the punishment thereby awarded, or commute that punishment for any punishment or punishments lower in the scale laid down in Section 48.

112. Confirming of findings and sentences on board a ship. When any person subject to this Act is tried and sentenced by a Security Force Court while on board a ship, the finding and sentence so far as not confirmed and executed on board the ship, may be confirmed and executed in like manner as if such person had been tried at the port of disembarkation.

113. Revision of finding of sentence.

(1) Any finding or sentence of a Security Force Court which requires confirmation may be once revised by order of the confirming authority and on such revision, the court, if so directed by the confirming authority, may take additional evidence.

(2) The court, on revision, shall consist of the same officers as were present when the original decision was passed, unless any of those officers are unavoidably absent.

(3) In case of such unavoidable absence the cause thereof shall be duly certified in the proceedings, and the court shall proceed with the revision, provided that, if a General Security Force Court, it still consists of five officers, or, if a Petty Security Force Court of three officers.

114. Finding and sentence of a Summary Security Force Court.

(1) Save as otherwise provided in sub-section (2), the finding and sentence of a Summary Security Force Court shall not require to be confirmed, but may be carried out forthwith.

(2) If the officer holding the trial is of the rank of Superintendent of Police or of a rank declared under clause (a) of sub-section (5) of Section 74 as equivalent thereto or of a lower rank and has held such rank for less than five years, he shall not, except on active duty, carry into effect any sentence, until it has received the approval of an officer not below the rank of Deputy Inspector-General.

115. Transmission of proceedings of Summary Security Force Courts. The proceedings of every Summary Security Force Court shall, without delay, be forwarded to the officer not below the rank of Deputy Inspector-General within whose command the trial was held, or to the prescribed officer, and such officer, or the Director-General or any officer empowered by him in this behalf may, for reasons based on the merits of the case, but not on merely technical grounds, set aside the proceedings, or reduce the sentence to any other sentence which the court might have passed.

116. Alteration of finding or sentence in certain cases.

(1) Where a finding of guilty by a Security Force Court, which has been confirmed or which does not require confirmation, is found for any reason to be invalid or cannot be supported by the evidence, the authority which would have had power under Section 128 to commute the punishment awarded by the sentence, if the finding had been valid may substitute a new finding and pass a sentence for the offence specified or involved in such finding:

PROVIDED that no such substitution shall be made unless such finding could have been validly made by the Security Force Court on the charge and unless it appears that the Security Force Court must have been satisfied of the facts establishing the said offence.

(2) Where a sentence passed by a Security Force Court which has been confirmed, or which does not require confirmation, not being a sentence passed in pursuance of a new finding substituted under sub-section (1), is found for any reason to be invalid, the authority referred to in sub-section (1) may pass a valid sentence.

(3) The punishment awarded by a sentence passed under sub-section (1) or sub-section (2) shall not be higher in the scale of punishments than, or in excess of, the punishment awarded by, the sentence for which a new sentence is substituted under this Section.

(4) Any finding substituted, or any sentence passed, under this Section shall, for the purposes of this Act and the rules, have effect as if it were a finding or sentence, as the case may be, of a Security Force Court.

117. Remedy against order, finding or sentence of Security Force Court.

(1) Any person subject to this Act who considers himself aggrieved by any order passed by any Security Force Court may present a petition to the officer or authority empowered to confirm any finding or sentence of such Security Force Court, and the confirming authority may take such steps as may be considered necessary to satisfy itself as to the correctness, legality or propriety of the order passed or as to the regularity of any proceeding to which the order relates.

(2) Any person subject to this Act who considers himself aggrieved by a finding or sentence of any Security Force Court which has been confirmed, may present a petition to the Central Government, the Director-General, or any prescribed officer superior in command to the one who confirmed such finding or sentence, and the Central Government, the Director-General, or the prescribed officer, as the case may be, may. pass such order thereon as it or he thinks fit.

118. Annulment of proceedings. The Central Government, the Director-General, or any prescribed officer may annul the proceedings of any Security Force Court on the ground that they are illegal or unjust.

CHAPTER - IX : EXECUTION OF SENTENCE, PARDONS, REMISSIONS, ETC.

119. Form of sentence of death. In awarding a sentence of death, a Security Force Court shall, in its discretion direct that the offender shall suffer death by being hanged by the neck until he be dead, or shall suffer death by being shot to death.

120. Commencement of sentence of imprisonment. Whenever any person is sentenced by a Security Force Court under this Act to imprisonment, the term of his sentence shall, whether it has been revised or not, be reckoned to commence on the day on which the original proceedings were signed by the presiding officer, or in the case of a Summary Security Force Court, by the court.

121. Execution of sentence of imprisonment.

(1) Whenever any sentence of imprisonment is passed under this Act by a Security Force Court or whenever any sentence of death is commuted to imprisonment, the confirming officer or in case of a Summary Security Force Court the officer holding the court or such other officer as may be prescribed shall, save as otherwise provided in sub-sections (3) and (4) direct that the sentence shall be carried out by confinement in a civil prison.

(2) When a direction has been made under sub-section (1) the Commandant of the person under sentence or such other officer as may be prescribed shall forward a warrant in the prescribed form to the officer in charge of the prison in which such person is to be confined and shall arrange for his despatch to such prison with the warrant.

(3) In the case of a sentence of imprisonment for a period not exceeding three months and passed under this Act by a Security Force Court, the appropriate officer under sub-section (1) may direct that the sentence shall be carried out by confinement in Force custody instead of in a civil prison.

(4) On active duty, a sentence of imprisonment may be carried out by confinement in such place as the Deputy Inspector-General within whose command the person sentenced is serving or any prescribed officer, may from time to time appoint.

122. Temporary custody of offender. Where a sentence of imprisonment is directed to be undergone in a civil prison the offender may be kept in Force custody or in any other fit place, till such time as it is possible to send him to a civil prison.

123. Execution of sentence of imprisonment in special cases. Whenever, in the opinion of an officer not below the rank of Deputy Inspector-General within whose command the trial is held, any sentence or portion of a sentence of imprisonment cannot for special reasons, conveniently be carried out in Force custody in accordance with the provisions of Section 121, such officer may direct that such sentence or portion of sentence shall be carried out by confinement in any civil prison or other fit place.

124. Conveyance of prisoner from place to place. A person under sentence of imprisonment may during his conveyance from place to place, or when on board ship, aircraft, or otherwise, be subjected to such restraint as, is necessary, for his safe conduct and removal.

125. Communication of certain orders to prison officers. Whenever an order is duly made under this Act setting aside or varying any sentence, order or warrant under which any person is confined in a civil prison, a warrant in accordance with such order shall be forwarded by the officer making the order or his staff officer or such other person as may be prescribed, to the officer in charge of the prison in which such person is confined.

126. Execution of sentence of fine. When a sentence of fine is imposed by a Security Force Court under Section 46, a copy of such sentence signed and certified by the confirming officer, or where no confirmation is required, by the officer holding the trial may be sent to any magistrate in India, and such magistrate shall thereupon cause the fine to be recovered in accordance with the provisions of the Code of Criminal Procedure, 1898 (5 of 1898), as if it were a sentence of fine imposed by such magistrate.

127. Informality or error in the order or warrant. Whenever any person is sentenced to imprisonment under this Act, and is undergoing the sentence in any place or manner in which he might be confined under a lawful order or warrant in pursuance of this Act, the confinement of such person shall not be deemed to be illegal only by reason of informality or error in, or as respects, the order, warrant or other document, or the authority by which, or in pursuance whereof such person was brought into, or, is confined in any such place, and any such order, warrant or document may be amended accordingly.

128. Pardon and remission. When any person subject to this Act has been convicted by a Security Force Court of any offence, the Central Government or the Director-General or, in the case of a sentence, which he could have confirmed or which did not require confirmation, an officer not below the rank of Deputy Inspector-General within whose command such person at the time of conviction was, serving, or the prescribed officer may -

(a) either with or without conditions which the person sentenced accepts, pardon the person or remit the whole or any part of the punishment awarded; or

(b) mitigate the punishment awarded; or

(c) commute such punishment for any less punishment or punishments mentioned in this Act;

(d) either with or without conditions which the person sentenced accepts, release the person on parole.

129. Cancellation of conditional pardon, release on parole or remission.

(1) If any condition on which a person has been pardoned or released on parole or a punishment has been remitted is, in the opinion of the authority which granted the pardon, release or remission, not fulfilled, such authority may cancel the pardon, release or remission, and thereupon the sentence of the court shall be carried into effect as if such pardon, release or remission had not been granted.

(2) A person whose sentence of imprisonment is carried into effect under the provisions of sub-section (1) shall undergo only the unexpired portion of his sentence.

130. Suspension of sentence of imprisonment.

(1) Where a person subject to this Act is sentenced by a Security Force Court to imprisonment, the Central Government, the Director-General or any officer empowered to convene a General Security Force Court may suspend the sentence whether or not the offender has already been committed to prison or to Force custody.

(2) The authority or officer specified in sub-section (1) may, in the case of an offender so sentenced direct that until the orders of such authority or officer have been obtained, the offender shall not be committed to prison or to Force custody.

(3) The powers conferred by sub-sections (1) and (2) may be exercised in the case of any such sentence which has been confirmed, reduced or commuted.

131. Orders pending suspension.

(1) Where the sentence referred to in Section 130 is imposed by a Security Force Court other than a Summary Security Force Court, the confirming officer may, when confirming the sentence, direct that the offender be not committed to prison or to Force custody until the orders of the authority or officer specified in Section 130, have been obtained.

(2) Where a sentence of imprisonment is imposed by a Summary Security Force Court, the officer holding the trial or the officer authorised to approve of the sentence under sub-section (2) of Section 114 may make the direction referred to in sub-section (1).

132. Release on suspension. Where a sentence is suspended under Section 130, the offender shall forthwith be released from custody.

133. Computation of period of suspension. Any period during which the sentence is under suspension shall be reckoned as part of the term of such sentence.

134. Order after suspension. The authority or officer specified in Section 130 may, at any time while a sentence is suspended, order-

(a) that the offender be committed to undergo the unexpired portion of the sentence; or

(b) that the sentence be remitted.

135. Reconsideration of case after suspension.

(1) Where a sentence has been suspended, the case may at any time, and shall at intervals of not more than four months, be reconsidered by the authority or officer specified in Section 130, or by any officer not below the rank of a Deputy Inspector-General duly authorised by the authority or officer specified in Section 130.

(2) Where on such reconsideration by the officer so authorised it appears to him that the conduct of offender since his conviction has been such as to justify a remission of the sentence, he shall refer the matter to the authority or officer specified in Section 130.

136. Fresh sentence after suspension. Where an offender, while a sentence on him is suspended under this Act, is. sentenced for any other offence, then-

(a) if the further sentence is also suspended under this Act, the two sentences shall run concurrently;

(b) if the further sentence is for a period of three months or more and is not suspended under this Act, the offender shall also be committed to prison or Force custody for the unexpired portion of the previous sentence, but both sentences shall run concurrently; and

(c) if the further sentence is for a period of less than three months and is not suspended under this Act, the offender shall be so committed on that sentence only, and the previous sentence shall, subject to any order which may be passed under Section 134 or Section 135 continue to be suspended.

137. Scope of power of suspension. The powers conferred by Sections 130 and 134 shall be in-addition to, and not in derogation of, the power of mitigation, remission and commutation.

138. Effect of suspension and remission on dismissal.

(1) Where in addition to any other sentence the punishment of dismissal has been awarded by a Security Force Court, and such other sentence is suspended under Section 130, then, such dismissal shall not take effect until so ordered by the authority or officer specified in Section 130.

(2) If such other sentence is remitted under Section 134, the punishment of dismissal shall also be remitted.

CHAPTER -X : MISCELLANEOUS

139. Powers and duties conferrable and imposable on members of the Force.

(1) The Central Government may, by general or special order published in the Official Gazette direct that, subject to such conditions and limitations, and within the local limits of such area adjoining the borders of India, as may be specified in the order, any member of the Force may -

(i) for the purpose of prevention of any offence punishable under the Passport (Entry into India) Act, 1920 (34 of 1920), the Registration of Foreigners Act, 1939 (16 of 1939), the Central Excises and Salt Act, 1944 (1 of 1944), the Foreigners Act, 1946 (31 of 1946), the Foreign Exchange Regulation Act, 1947 (7 of 1947), the Customs Act, 1962 (52 of 1962), or the Passports Act, 1967 (15 of 1967), or of any cognizable offence punishable under any other Central Act; or

(ii) for the purpose of apprehending any person who has committed any offence referred to in clause (i), exercise or discharge such of the powers or duties under that Act or any other Central Act as may be specified in the said order, being the powers and duties which, in the opinion of the Central Government, an officer of the corresponding or lower rank is by that or such other Act empowered to exercise or discharge for the said purposes.

(2) The Central Government may, by general or special order published in the Official Gazette, confer or impose, with the concurrence of the State Government concerned, any of the powers or duties which may be exercised or discharged under a State Act by a police officer upon a member of the Force who, in the opinion of the Central Government, holds a corresponding or higher rank.

(3) Every order made under this Section shall be laid, as soon as may be after it is made, before each House of Parliament while it is in session for a total period of thirty days which may be comprised in one session or [1][in two or more successive sessions, and if, before the expiry of the session immediately following the session or the successive sessions aforesaid] both Houses agree in making any modification in the order or both Houses agree that the order should not be made, the order shall thereafter have effect only in such modified form or be of no effect, as the case may be; so, however, that any such modification or annulment shall be without prejudice to the validity of anything previously done under that order.

140. Protection for acts of members of the Force.

(1) In any suit or proceeding against any member of the Force for any act done by him in pursuance of a warrant or order of a competent authority, it shall be lawful for him to plead that such act was done by him under the authority of such warrant or order.

(2) Any such plea may be proved by the production of the warrant or order directing the act, and if it is so proved the member of the Force shall thereupon be

discharged from liability in respect of the act so done by him, notwithstanding any defect in the jurisdiction of the authority which issued such warrant or order.

(3) Notwithstanding anything contained in any other law for the time being in force, any legal proceeding (whether civil or criminal) which may lawfully be brought against any member of the Force for anything done or intended to be done under the powers conferred by, or in pursuance of, any provision of this Act or the rules, shall be commenced within three months after the act complained of was committed and not otherwise, and notice in writing of such proceeding and of the cause thereof shall be given to the defendant or his superior officer at least one month before the commencement of such proceeding.

141. Power to make rules.

(1) The Central Government may, by notification, make rules for the purpose of carrying into effect the provisions of this Act.

(2) In particular and without prejudice to the generality of the foregoing power, such rules may provide for -

(a) the constitution, governance, command and discipline of the Force;

(b) the enrolment of persons to the Force and the recruitment of other members of the Force;

(c) the conditions of service (including deductions from pay and allowances) of members of the Force;

(d) the rank, precedence, powers of command and authority of the officers, subordinate officers, under-officers and other persons subject to this Act;

(e) the removal, retirement release or discharge from the service of persons subject to this Act;

(f) the purposes and other matters required to be prescribed under Section 13;

(g) the convening, constitution, adjournment, dissolution and sittings of Security Force Courts, the procedure to be observed in trials by such courts, the persons by whom an accused may be defended in such trials and the appearance of such persons thereat;

(h) the confirmation, revision and annulment of, and petitions against, the findings and sentences of Security Force Courts;

(i) the [2][forms of orders] to be made under the provisions of this Act relating to Security Force Courts and the awards and infliction of death, imprisonment and detention;

(j) the carrying into effect of sentences of Security Force Courts;

(k) any matter necessary for the purpose of carrying this Act into execution, as far as it relates to the investigation, arrest, custody, trial and punishment of offences triable or punishable under this Act;

(l) the ceremonials to be observed and marks of respect to be paid in the Force;

(m) the convening of, the constitution, procedure and practice of, courts of inquiry, the summoning of witnesses before them and the administration of oaths by such Courts;

(n) the recruitment and conditions of service of the Chief Law Officer and the Law Officers;

(o) any other matter which is to be, or may be prescribed or in respect of which this Act makes no provision or makes insufficient provision and provision is, in the opinion of the Central Government, necessary for the proper implementation of this Act.

(3) Every rule made under this Act shall be laid, as soon as may be after it is made, before each House of Parliament while it is in session for a total period of thirty days which may be comprised in one session or [1][in two more successive sessions, and if, before the expiry of the session immediately following the session or the successive sessions aforesaid] both Houses agree in making any modification in the rule or both Houses agree that the rule should not be made the rule shall thereafter have effect only in such modified form or be of no effect, as the case may be; so, however, that any such modification or annulment shall be without prejudice to the validity of anything previously done under that rule.

142. Provisions as to existing Border Security Force.

(1) The Border Security Force in existence at the commencement of this Act shall be deemed to be the Force constituted under this Act.

(2) Members of the Border Security Force in existence at the commencement of this Act shall be deemed to have been appointed or as the case may be, enrolled as such under this Act.

(3) Anything done or any action taken before the commencement of this Act in relation to the constitution of the Border Security Force referred to in sub-section (1), in relation to any person appointed or enrolled, as the case may be, thereto, shall be as valid and as effective in law as if such thing or action was done or taken under this Act:

PROVIDED that nothing in this sub-section shall render any person guilty of any offence in respect of anything done or omitted to be done by him before the commencement of this Act.

❏❏❏

Endnotes

1. 1-3-1969, vide Notification No. S.O. 732, dated the 20th February, 1969, Gazette of India, Extraordinary, Pt. II, Sec. 3 (ii), p. 235.

11

The Cantonments (Extension of Rent Control Laws) Act, 1957

[ACT NO.46 OF 1957] [18TH DECEMBER, 1957]

AN ACT to provide for the extension to cantonments of laws relating to the control of rent and regulation of house accommodation.

Be it enacted by Parliament in the Eighth Year of the Republic of India as follows.

2. Definitions. In this Act, "cantonment" means any place declared to be a cantonment under Section 3 of the Cantonments Act, 1924 (2 of 1924).

3. Power to extend to cantonments laws relating to control of rents and regulation of house accommodation. The Central Government may, by notification in the Official Gazette, extend to any cantonment with such restrictions and modifications as it thinks fit, any enactment relating to the control of rent and regulation of house accommodation which is in force on the date of the notification in the State in which the cantonment is situated:

PROVIDED that nothing contained in any enactment so extended shall apply to-

(a) *Any premises within the cantonment belonging to the Government;*

(b) *Any tenancy or other like relationship created by a grant from the Government in respect of premises within the cantonment taken on lease or requisitioned by the Government; or*

(c) *Any house within the cantonment which is, or may be, appropriated by the Central Government on lease under the Cantonments (House Accommodation) Act, 1923 (6 of 1923).*

4. Extension of the Madhya Bharat Accommodation Control Act, 1955 to the cantonment of Mhow. The Madhya Bharat Accommodation Control Act, 1955 (M.B. Act 23 of 1955), as in force in that part of the State of Madhya Pradesh which immediately before the 1st day of November, 1956, formed the State of Madhya Bharat is hereby extended to, and brought into force in, the cantonment of Mhow with the following modifications, namely.

In the said Act -

(a) For the words "commencement of this Act" wherever they occur, the words "extension of this Act to the cantonment" shall be substituted;

(b) In Section 1, for sub-sections (2), (3) and (4), the following sub-sections shall be substituted, namely :

"(2) It extends to the Cantonment of Mhow.

(3) It shall remain in force upto the 31st day of December, 1957; but the Central Government may, by notification in the Official Gazette, direct from time to time that it shall remain in force for such further period as may be specified in the notification so, however, that the total period for which it may remain in force shall not exceed two years from the 31st day of December, 1957";

(c) In Section 2, in the clause (b) of sub-section (1), for the words "a Municipality", the words "the Cantonment Board" shall be substituted;

(d) In Section 3, in clause (e), for the word "Municipal", the words "Cantonment Board" shall be substituted;

(e) In Section 4 -

(i) In clause (g), for the words "city or town concerned", the word "cantonment" shall be substituted;

(ii) In clause (h), for the words "city or town for that purpose and if he was in occupation, has for sufficient reasons vacated it after the Act has been extended to that city or town", the words "cantonment for that purpose or if he was in occupation, has for sufficient reasons vacated it after the extension of this Act thereto" shall be substituted;

(f) In Section 6 -

(i) In sub-section (1), the words and brackets "situated in the city of Lashkar (including Gwalior and Morar), Indore, Ujjain or Ratlam" shall be omitted;

(ii) Sub-section (2) shall be omitted;

(g) In Section 14, the words "the provisions of this Act cease to be applicable to any town, or" shall be omitted;

(h) In Section 15, after the word "instituted", the words "or if instituted, continued", shall be inserted;

(i) In Section 18, sub-section (4) shall be omitted;

(j) In Section 21, the words "or deemed to have been passed" shall be omitted;

(k) In Section 22, the words "or deemed to have been made" shall be omitted;

(l) Section 23, Section 27 and the Schedule shall be omitted;

(m) In Sections 24 and 25, the words "or deemed to have been made" shall be omitted.

❑❑❑

12

The Cantonments (Extension of Rent Control Laws) Amendment Act, 1972

[ACT, NO. 22 OF 1972] [2ND JUNE, 1972]

PREAMBLE

AN ACT to amend the Cantonments (Extension of Rent Control Laws) Act, 1957.

Be it enacted by Parliament in the Twenty-third Year of the Republic of India as follows:—

1. Short title. This Act may be called the Cantonments (Extension of Rent Control Laws) Amendment Act, 1972.

2. Amendment of Section 1. In the Cantonments (Extension of Rent Control Laws) Act, 1957 (46 of 1957) (hereinafter referred to as the principal Act), Section 1 shall be renumbered as sub-section (1) thereof, and after sub-section (1), as so re-numbered, the following sub-section shall be inserted, namely:—

"(2) It shall be deemed to have come into force on the 26th day of January, 1950."

3. Amendment of Section 3. Section 3 of the principal Act shall be re-numbered as sub-section (1) thereof, and—

(i) in sub-section (1) as so renumbered, the words "on the date of the notification" shall be, and shall be deemed always to have been, omitted;

(ii) after sub-section (1), as so re-numbered, the following sub-section shall be, and shall be deemed always to have been, inserted, namely:-

'(2) The extension of any enactment under sub-section (1) may be made from such earlier or future date as the Central Government may think fit:

PROVIDED that no such extension shall be made form a date earlier than—

(a) the commencement of such enactment, or

(b) the establishment of the cantonment, or

(c) the commencement of this Act, whichever is later.

(3) Where any enactment in force in any State relating to the control of rent and regulation of house accommodation is extended to a cantonment form a date earlier than the date on which such extension is made (hereafter referred to as the "earlier date"), such enactment, as in force on such earlier date, shall apply to such cantonment, and, where any such enactment has been amended at any time after the earlier date but before the commencement of the Cantonments (Extension of Rent Control Laws) Amendment Act, 1972, (21 of 1972) such enactment, as amended, shall apply to the cantonment on and form the date on which the enactment by which such amendment was amendment was made came into force.

(4) Where, before the extension to a cantonment of any enactment relating to the control of rent and regulation of house accommodation therein (hereafter referred to as the "Rent Control Act") -

(i) any decree or order for the regulation of, or for eviction from, any house accommodation in that cantonment; or

(ii) any order in the proceedings for the execution of such decree or order, or

(iii) any order relating to the control of rent or other incident of such house accommodation, was made by any court, tribunal or other authority in accordance with any law for the control of rent and regulation of house accommodation for the time being in force in the State in which such cantonment is situated, such decree or order shall, on and form the date on which the Rent Control Act is extended to that cantonment, be deemed to have been made under the corresponding provisions of the Rent Control Act, as extended to that cantonment, as if the said Rent Control Act, as so extended, were in force in that cantonment, on the date on which such decree or order was made'.

4. Amendment of Section 4. Section 4 of the principal Act shall be re-numbered as sub-section (1) thereof, and after sub-section (1), as so re-numbered, the following sub-sections shall be inserted, namely :

"**(2) Madhya Bharat Act 23 of 1955.** Any law relating to the control of rent and regulation of house accommodation in force in the cantonment of Mhow immediately before the commencement therein of the Madhya Bharat Accommodation Control Act, 1955, shall be, and shall be deemed always to have been, extended to that cantonment under Section 3 of this Act with effect form the commencement of such law in that cantonment or form the commencement of this Act, whichever is later:

PROVIDED that no such law shall continue, and shall be deemed to have continued, in force in the cantonment of Mhow on and form the commencement therein of the Madhya Bharat Accommodation Control Act, 1955 (Madhya Bharat Act 23 of 1955).

(3) Where, before the extension under sub-section (2) of any law to the cantonment of Mhow,—

(i) any decree or order for the regulation of or for eviction form, any house accommodation in that cantonment, or

(ii) any order in the proceedings for the execution of such decree or order, or

(iii) any order relating to the control of rent or other incident of such house accommodation, was made by any court, tribunal or other authority in accordance with any law for the control of rent and regulation of house accommodation or the time being in force in that cantonment, such decree or order shall, on and form the commencement of such law in that cantonment, be deemed to have been made under the corresponding provisions of the first-mentioned Act as if the said Act were in force in that cantonment on the date on which such decree or order was made."

❑❑❑

13

The Central Industrial Security Force (Amendment and Validation) Act, 1999

Act No. 40 of 1999 [29th December, 1999]

AN ACT further to amend the Central Industrial Security Force Act, 1968, and to validate certain revision petitions disposed of under the rules made under the said Act.

Be it enacted by Parliament in the Fiftieth Year of the Republic of India as follows:-

1. Short title. This Act may be called the Central Industrial Security Force (Amendment and Validation) Act, 1999.

2. Amendment of Long title. In the Central Industrial Security Force Act, 1968 (50 of 1968)) (hereinafter referred to as the principal Act), for the long title, the following long title shall be substituted, namely :-

"AN ACT to provide for the constitution and regulation of an armed force of the Union for the better protection and security of industrial undertakings owned by the Central Government, certain other industrial undertakings, employees of all such undertakings and to provide technical consultancy services to industrial establishments in the private sector and for matters connected therewith."

3. Amendment of Section 2. In Section 2 of the principal Act, in sub-section (1), after clause (c), the following clause shall be inserted, namely:-

(ca) "industrial establishment" means an industrial undertaking or a company as defined under Section 3 of the Companies Act, 1956 (1 of 1956) or a firm registered under Section 59 of the Indian Partnership Act, 1932 (9 of 1932) which is engaged in any ndustry, or in any trade, business or service.

4. Amendment of Section 3. In Section 3 of the principal Act, in sub-section (1), the words "and to perform such other duties as may be entrusted to it by the Central Government" shall be inserted at the end.

5. Amendment of Section 8. In Section 8 of the principal Act -

(i) in clause (i), after the word "remove", the words, "order for compulsory retirement of" shall be inserted;

(ii) in clause (ii), after sub-clause (c), the following sub-clauses shall be inserted, namely:-

"(d) withholding of increment of pay with or without cumulative effect;

(e) withholding of promotion;

(f) censure."

6. In Section 9 of the principal Act -

(i) in sub-section (1), for the words, brackets and figure "subject to the provisions of sub-section (3)", the words, brackets, figures and letters "subject to the provisions of sub-section (2A), sub-section (2B) and sub-section (3)" shall be substitute;

(ii) after sub-section (2), the following sub-sections shall be inserted, namely:-

"(2A) Any enrolled member of the Force aggrieved by an order passed in appeal under sub-section (1) may, within a period of six months from the date on which the order is communicated to him, prefer a revision petition against the order to such authority as may be prescribed and in disposing of the revision petition, the said authority shall follow such procedure as may be prescribed.

(2B) The authority, as may be prescribed for the purpose of this sub-section, on a revision petition preferred by an aggrieved enrolled member of the Force or *suo moto*, may call for, within a prescribed period, the records of any proceeding under section 8 or sub-section (2) or sub-section (2A) and such authority may, after making inquiry in the prescribed manner, and subject to the provisions of this Act, pass such order thereon as it thinks fit";

(iii) in sub-section (3), for the words, figures and brackets "under Section 8 or under sub-section (2)", the words, figures, brackets and letters "under Section 8, sub-section (2), sub-section (2A) or sub-section 10 of the principal Act, after clause (e), the following clauses shall be inserted, namely:-

(2B)" shall be substituted.

7. Amendment of Section 10. In Section "(f) to provide technical consultancy services relating to security of any private sector industrial establishments under Section 14A;

(g) to protect and safeguard the organisations owned or funded by the Government and the employees of such organisations as may be entrusted to him by the Central Government;

(h) any other duty which may be entrusted to him by the Central Government from time to time."

8. Insertion of new Section 14A. After Section 14 of the principal Act, the following Section shall be inserted, namely:-

"14A. Technical Consultancy Service to industrial establishments.

(1) Subject to any general directions which may be issued by the Central Government, it shall be lawful for the Director-General, on a request received from the Managing Director of an in ustrial establishment in the private sector or any other person authorised by him in this behalf, to direct the members of the Force to provide technical consultancy services relating to security, to such industrial establishments in such manner and on payment of such fee as may be prescribed.

(2) The fee received under sub-section (1) shall be credited to the Consolidated Fund of India.

EXPLANATION. For the purposes of this Section, the expression "Managing Director", in relation to an industrial establishment, means the person (whether called general manager, manager, chief executive officer or a partner of a firm or by any other name who exercises control over the affairs of the establishment.".

9. Amendment of Section 22. In Section 22 of the principal Act, in sub-section (2) - (i) after clause (ggg), the following clauses shall be inserted, namely:- "(gggg) prescribing authority under sub-section (2A) of Section 9 and the procedure to be followed by such authority in disposing of the revision petition; (ggggg) prescribing authority under sub-section (2B) of Section 9, the period within which such authority may call for the records and the manner in which such authority may make inquiry;";

(ii) in clause (h), the word "and" occurring at the end shall be omitted; (iii) after clause (h), the following clause shall be inserted, namely:-

"(hh) the manner in which and the fee on payment of which the technical consultancy services shall be provided under sub-section (1) of Section 14A; and".

10.Validation of the disposal of certain revision pertitions. Notwithstanding any judgment, decree or order of any court to the contrary, Rule 49 of the Central Industrial Security Force Rules, 1969 published with the notification of the Government of India in the Ministry of Home Affairs number S.O. 4632, dated the 12th November, 1969 shall be deemed to be, and to have always been, made under the principal Act as amended by this Act as if the principal Act as so amended had been in force at all materia times before the commencement of this Act and accordingly the disposal of any revision petition under the said rule 49 before the commencement of this Act or any order made or purporting to have been made or any action or thing taken or done in or under such petition shall not be deemed to be invalid or ever to have become invalid merely on the ground that the Central Government had no power under the principal Act to make the said rule 49.

□□□

14

The Central Industrial Security Force Act, 1968

ACT NO. 50 OF 1968

(As modified vide Act No.14 of 1983, 20 of 1989, 40 of 1999 and 22 of 2009)

AN ACT to Provide for the constitution and regulation of an armed force of the Union for the better protection and security of Industrial Undertakings owned by the Central Government and certain other Industrial Undertaking, employees of all such Industrial Undertakings and to provide technical consultancy services to industrial establishments in the private sector and for matters connected therewith)

Be it enacted by Parliament in the Nineteenth Year of the Republic of India as follows:-

1. Short title, extent and commencement.

(1) This Act may be called the Central Industrial Security Force Act,1968.

(2) It extends to the whole of India.

(3) It shall come into force on such date as the Central Government may, by notification in the Official Gazette, appoint.

2. Definitions.

(1) In this Act, unless the context otherwise requires -

(a) "Director-General" means the Director-General of the Force appointed under Section 4;

(aa) "enrolled member of the Force" means any subordinate officer, under officer or any other member of the Force of a rank lower than that of an under officer;

(ab) "Force" means the Central Industrial Security Force constituted under Section 3;

(ac) "Force custody" means the arrest or confinement of a member of the Force in accordance with rules made under this Act.

(b) "industrial undertaking" means any undertaking pertaining to a scheduled industry and includes an undertaking engaged in any other industry, or in any trade, business or service which may be regulated by Parliament by law;

(c) "industrial undertaking in public sector" means an Industrial Undertaking owned, controlled or managed by -

(i) a Government company as defined in Section 617 of the Companies Act, 1956 (1 of 1956);

(ii) a corporation established by or under a Central Provincial or State Act, which is controlled or managed by the Government;

(ca) "industrial establishment" means an industrial undertaking or a company as defined under Section 3 of the Companies Act, 1956 or a firm registered under Section 59 of the India Partnership Act,1932 which is engaged in any industry, or in any trade, business or service;

(cb) "joint venture" means a venture jointly undertaking by the Central Government or State Government with private industrial undertaking.

(d) **Omitted...**

(e) 'Managing Director' in relation to an Industrial undertaking, means the person (whether called a managing agent, general manager, manager, chief executive officer or by any other name) who exercises control over the affairs of that undertaking;

(f) "members of the Force" means a person appointed to the Force under this Act..

(g) "prescribed" means prescribed by rules made under this Act;

(ga). "private industrial undertaking" means an industry owned, controlled or managed by a person other than the Central or State Government or any industrial undertaking in public sector.

(h) "schedule industry" means any industry engaged in the manufacture or production of the articles mentioned in the First Schedule to the Industries (Development and Regulations Act. 1951); (65 of 1951)

(ha) "subordinate officer" means a person appointed to the Force as an Inspector, a Sub-Inspector or an Asstt. Sub. Inspector.

(i) "supervisory officer" means any of the officers appointed under Section 4 and includes any other officer appointed by the Central Government as a Supervisory Officer of the Force.

(j) "under officer" means a person appointed to the Force as a Head constable, Naik or Lance Naik.

(2) Any reference in this Act to a law which is not in Force in any area shall, in relation to that area, be construed as a reference to the corresponding law, if any, in force in that area."

3. Constitution of the Force.

(1) There shall be constituted and maintained by the Central Government an armed Force of the Union to be called Central Industrial Security Force for the better protection and security of Industrial undertakings owned by that Government, joint venture or private industrial undertaking and to perform such other duties as may be entrusted to it by the Central Government.

(2) The Force shall be constituted in such manner, shall consist of such number of supervisory officers, subordinate officers, under Officers and other enrolled members of the Force who shall receive such pay and other remuneration as may be prescribed.

4. Appointment and powers of supervisory officers.

(1) The Central Government may appoint a person to be the Director General of the Force and such other supervisory officers as considered necessary.

(2) The Director-General and every other supervisory officers so appointed shall have, and may exercise, such powers and authority as provided by or under this Act.

5. Appointment of enrolled members of the Force. The appointment of the enrolled members of the Force shall rest with the Director General who shall exercise the powers in accordance with rules made under this Act.

PROVIDED that the powers of appointment under this section may also be exercised by such other supervisory officer as the Central Government may by order specify in this behalf.

6. Certificates of Members of the Force.

(1) Every enrolled members of the Force shall receive on his appointment a certificate in the form specified in the Schedule, under the seal of the Director-General or such other supervisory officer as the Director-General may specify in this behalf, by virtue of which the person holding such certificate shall be vested with the powers of an enrolled member of the Force.

(2) Such certificate shall cease to have effect whenever the person named in it ceases for any reason to be an enrolled member of the Force.

7. Superintendence and administration of the Force.

(1) The superintendence of the Force shall vest in the Central Government, and subject thereto and to the provision of this Act and of any rules made thereunder, the command, supervision and administration of the Force shall vest in the Director General.

(2) Subject to the provisions of sub-section (1), the administration of the Force within such local limits as may be prescribed shall be carried on by such other supervisory officers as considered necessary in accordance with the provisions of this Act and of any rules made thereunder and every supervisory officer

placed in charge of the protection and security of an industrial undertaking, joint venture or private industrial undertaking shall, subject to any direction that may be given by the Central Government or the Director-General in this behalf, discharge his functions under the general supervision, direction and control of the Managing Director of that Undertaking.

8. Dismissal, removal etc. of enrolled members of the Force. Subject to the provisions of article 311 of the Constitution and to such rules as the Central Government may make under this Act supervisory officer may -

(i) dismiss, remove, order of compulsory retirement or reduce in rank any enrolled member of the Force whom he thinks remiss or negligent in the discharge of his duty, or unfit for the same; or

(ii) award any one or more of the following punishments to any enrolled member of the Force who discharges his duty in a careless or negligent manner, or who by any act of his own renders himself unfit for the discharge thereof, namely :-

(a) fine to any amount not exceeding seven days pay or reduction in pay scale;

(b) drill, extra guard, fatigue or other duty.

(c) removal from any office of distinction or deprivation of any special emolument.

(d) withholding of increment of pay with or without cumulative effect.

(e) withholding of promotion.

(f) Censure.

9. Appeal and revision.

(1) Any "enrolled" member of the Force aggrieved by an order made under Section 8 may within thirty days from the date on which the order is communicated to him prefer an appeal against the order to such authority as may be prescribed, and subject to the provisions of sub-section (2A), sub-section (2B) and sub-section (3), the decision of the said authority thereon shall be final:

PROVIDED that the prescribed authority may entertain the appeal after the expiry of the said period of thirty days, if he is satisfied that the appellant was prevented by sufficient cause from filling the appeal in time.

(2) In disposing of an appeal the prescribed authority shall follow such procedure as may be prescribed.

(2A) Any enrolled members of the Force aggrieved by an order passed in appeal under sub-section (1) may, within a period of six months from the date on which the order is communicated to him, prefer a revision petition against the order to such authority as may be prescribed and in disposing of the revision petition, the said authority shall follow such procedure as may be prescribed.

(2B) The authority, as may be prescribed for the purpose of this sub-section, on a revision petition preferred by an aggrieved enrolled member of the

Force or suo-moto, may call for, within a prescribed period, the records of any proceeding under Section 8 of sub-section (2) or sub-section (2A) and such authority may, after making inquiry in the prescribed manner, and subject to the provisions of this Act, pass such order thereon as it thinks fit."

(3) The Central Government may call for an examine the record of any proceeding under Section 8 or under sub-section (2), sub-section (2A) or sub-section (2B) of this section and may make such inquiry or cause such inquiry to be made and subject to the provisions of this Act, may pass such order thereon as it thinks fit:

PROVIDED that no order imposing an enhanced penalty under sub-section (2) or sub-section (3) shall be made unless a reasonable opportunity of being heard has been given to the person affected by such order.

10. Duties of member of the Force. It shall be the duty of every member of the Force

(a) Promptly to obey and execute all orders lawfully issued to him by his superior authority;

(b) to protect and safeguard the Industrial Undertaking owned by the Central Government together with such other installations as are specified by that Government to be vital for the carrying on of work in those Undertakings, situate within the local limits of his jurisdiction:

PROVIDED that before any installation not owned or controlled by the Central Government is so specified, the Central Government shall obtain the consent of the Government of the State in which such installation is situate;

(c) to protect and safeguard any joint venture, private industrial undertaking and such other Industrial Undertakings and installation for the protection and security of which he is deputed under Section 14;

(d) to protect and safeguard the employees of the Industrial Undertakings and installations referred to in clauses (b) and (c)

(e) to do any other act conducive to the better protection and security of the industrial undertakings and installations referred to in clauses (b) and (c) and the employees referred in clause (d);

(f) to provide technical consultancy services relating to security of any private sector industrial establishment under Section 14A.

(g) to protect and safeguard the organizations owned or funded by the Government and the employees of such organizations as may be entrusted to him by the Central Government.

(h) any other duty within and outside India which may be entrusted to him by the Central Govt. from time to time.

11. Power to arrest without warrant.

(1) Any member of the Force may, without any order from a magistrate and without a warrant, arrest -

(i) any person who voluntarily cause hurt to, or attempts voluntarily to cause hurt to, or wrongfully restrains or attempts wrongfully to restrain or assaults, or uses, or threatens or attempts to use criminal force to any employee, referred to in clause (d) of Section 10, or to him or any other member of the Force, in discharge of his duty as such employee or in execution of his duty as such member, as the case may be, or with intention to prevent or to deter him from discharging his duty as such member, or in consequence of anything done or attempted to be done by him in the lawful discharge of his duty as such member.

(ii) any person who has concerned in, or against whom a reasonable suspicion exists of his having been concerned in or who is found taking precautions to conceal his presence under circumstances which afford reason to believe that he is taking such precautions with a view to committing, a cognizable offence which relates to property longing, to or in the premises of any Industrial Undertaking referred to in clause (b) and (c) of Section 10,or relates to the other installations, or to property in the premises of the other installations, referred to in those clauses;

(iii) any persons who commits or attempts to commit a cognizable offence which involves or which is likely to involve danger to the life of any person engaged in carrying on any work relating to any Undertaking or installations referred to in clauses (b) and (c) of Section 10.

(2) If any person is found trespassing on the premises of any Industrial Undertaking referred to in clauses (b) and (c) Section 10, he may without prejudice to any other proceedings which may be taken against him be removed from such premises by any member of the Force.

12. Power to search without warrant.

(1) Whenever any member of the Force not below the prescribed rank has reason to believe that any such offence as is referred to in Section 11 has been or is being committed and that a search warrant cannot be obtained without affording the offender an opportunity of escaping or of concealing evidence of the offence, he may detain the offender and search his person and belongings forthwith and, if he thinks proper, arrest any person whom he has reason to believe to have committed the offence.

(2) The provisions of the Code of Criminal Procedure, 1973 (2 of 1974) relating to searches under that Code shall, so far as may be, apply to searches under this Section.

13. Procedure to be followed after arrest. Any member of the Force making an arrest under this Act, shall, without unnecessary delay, make over the person so arrested to a police officer, or in the absence of a police officer, take such person or cause him to be taken to the nearest police station together with a report of the circumstances occasioning the arrest.

14. Deputation of the Force to industrial undertaking in public sector, joint venture or private sector.

(1) Subject to any general directions which may be issued, by the Central Government, it shall be lawful for the Director General on a request received

in this behalf from the Managing Director concerned, of an industrial Undertaking in public sector, joint venture or private sector, showing the necessity there of to depute such number of members of the Force as the Director-General may consider necessary for the protection and security of that industrial undertaking and any installations attached thereto and the members of the Force so deputed shall be at the charge the Managing Director.

PROVIDED that in the case of an Undertaking owned, controlled or managed:

(i) *by a Government company of which the Central government is not a member.*

(ii) *by a corporation established by or under a Provincial or State Act. No such request shall be entertained unless it is made with the consent of the Government of the State in which the Undertaking is situate.*

(2) If the Director General is of the opinion that circumstance necessitating the deputation of the member of the Force in relation to an Industrial Undertaking under sub-section (1) have ceased to exist or for any other reason it is necessary so to do, he may, after informing the Managing Director of that Industrial Undertaking, withdraw the member of the Force so deputed.

PROVIDED that the Managing Director may, on giving three month's notice in writing to the Director General that the members of the Force so deputed shall be withdrawn, and the Managing Director shall be relieved from the charge from the date of expiration of such notice or from any earlier date on which the Force is so withdrawn.

(3) Every member of the Force, which discharging his functions during the period of deputation, shall continue to exercise the same powers and be subject to the same responsibilities, discipline and penalties as would have been applicable to him under this Act, if he had been discharging those functions in relation to an industrial undertaking owned by the Central Government.

14A (1) Subject to any general directions which may be issued by the Central Government, it shall be lawful for the Director General, on a request received from the Managing Director of an industrial establishment in the private sector or any other person authorized by him in his behalf, to direct the members of the Force to provide technical consultancy services relating to security, to such industrial establishments in such manner and on payment of such fee as may be prescribed.

(2) The fee received under sub-section (1) shall be credited to the Consolidated Fund of India.

EXPLANATION: For the purpose of this Section, the expression "Managing Director" in relation to an industrial establishment, means the person (whether called general manager, manager, chief executive officer, or a partner of a firm or by any other name) who exercises control over the affairs of the establishment."

15. Officers and Members of the Force to be considered always on duty and liable to be employed anywhere in India.

(1) Every member of the Force shall, for the purpose of this Act, be considered to be always on duty, and shall, at any time be liable to be employed at any place within or outside India.

(2) Save as provided in Section 14, no member of the Force shall engage himself in any employment of office other than his duties under this Act.

15A. Restrictions respecting right to form association etc.

(1) No member of the Force shall, without the previous sanction in written of the Central Government or the prescribed authority -

(a) be a member of, or be associated in any way with, any trade union, labour union, political associations or with any class or trade unions, labour unions or political associations; or

(b) be a member of, or be associated in any way with, any other society, institution, association or organization that is not recognized as part of the Force or is not of a purely social, recreational or religious nature, or

(c) communicate with the press or publish or cause to be published any book letter or other document except where such communication or publication is in the bona fide discharge of his duties or is of a purely literary, artistic or scientific character or is of a prescribed nature :

EXPLANATION: In any question arises as to whether any society institution association or organization is of a purely social, recreational or religious nature under clause (b) of this sub-section the decision of the Central Government thereon shall be final.

(2) No member of the Force shall participate in, or address, any meeting or take part in any demonstration organized by any body of person for any political purposes or for such other purposes as may be prescribed.

16. Responsibilities of member of the Force during suspension. A member of the Force shall not by reason of his suspension from office cease to be a member of the Force; and he shall, during that period, be subject to the same responsibilities, discipline and penalties to which he would have been subject if he were on duty.

17. Surrender of certificate arms etc., by persons ceasing to be members of the Force.

(1) Every person who for any reason ceases to be 'an enrolled' member of the Force, shall forthwith surrender to any supervisory officer empowered to receive the same, his certificate of appointment, the arms, accoutrements, clothing and other articles which have been furnished to him for the performance of duties as an enrolled member of the Force.

(2) Any person who wilfully neglects or refuse to surrender his certificate of appointment or the arms, accoutrements, clothing and other articles furnished to him, as required by sub-section (1) shall on conviction, be punished with imprisonment for a terms which may extend to one month or with fine which may extend to two hundred rupees, or with both.

(3) Nothing in this section shall be deemed to apply to any article which, under the orders of the Director General, has become the property of the person to whom the same was furnished.

18. Penalties for neglect of duty, etc.

(1) Without prejudice to the provisions contained in Section 8, every member of the Force who shall be guilty of any violation of duty or wilful breach or neglect of any Rule or regulations or lawful orders made by a Supervisory Officer, or who shall withdraw from the duties of his office without permission, or who, being absent on leave, fails without reasonable cause, to report himself for duty on the expiration of the leave, or who engages himself without authority in any employment other than his duty as a member of the Force or who shall be guilty of cowardice, may be taken into Force custody and shall, on conviction, be punished with imprisonment for a term which may extend to one year.

(2) Notwithstanding anything contained, in the Code of Criminal Procedure, 1973 (2 at 1974) an offence punished under this Section shall be cognizable and non-bailable.

(2A) Notwithstanding anything contained in the Code of Criminal Procedure, 1973, the Central Government may invest the Commandant with the powers of a Magistrate of any class for the purpose of inquiry into or trying any offence committed by an enrolled member of the Force and punishable under this Act, or any offence committed by an enrolled member of the Force against person or property of another member of the Force.

PROVIDED that -

(i) When the offender is on leave or absent from duty; or

(ii) when the offence is not connected with the offender's duties as an enrolled member of the Force; or

(iii) when it is petty offence even if connected with the offender's duties as an enrolled member of the Force; or

(iv) when, for reason to be recorded in writing, it is not practicable for the Commandant invested with the powers of a Magistrate to inquire into or try an offence, the offence may, if the prescribed authority within the limits of whose jurisdiction the offence has been committed so requires, be inquired into or tried by an ordinary Criminal Court having jurisdiction in the matter.

(3) Nothing contained in this section shall be construed to prevent any member of the Force from being prosecuted under any other law for any offence made punishable by that law, or for being liable under any such law to any other or higher penalty or punishment than is provided for such offence by this section.

PROVIDED that no person shall be punished twice for the same offence.

19. Application of Act 22 of 1922 to member of the Force. The Police (Incitement to Disaffection) Act,1922, shall apply to members of the Force as it applies to member of a Police Force.

20. Certain Acts not to apply to Members of the Force. Nothing contained in the payment of wages Act, 1936, or the Industrial Disputes Act 1947, on the Factories Act 1948, or any corresponding law relating to investigation and settlement of industrial disputes in force in a State shall apply to member of the Force.

21. Protection of acts of members of the Force.

(1) In any suit or proceeding against any member of the Force for any act done by him in the discharge of his duties, it shall be lawful for him to plead that such act was done by him under the order of a competent authority.

(2) Any such plea may be proved by the production of the order directing and it is so proved, the member of the Force shall thereupon be discharged from any liability in respect of the act so done by him, notwithstanding any defect in the jurisdiction of the authority which issued such order.

(3) Notwithstanding anything contained in any other law for the time being in force, any legal proceeding, whichever civil or criminal, which may lawfully be brought against any member of the Force for anything done or intended to be done under the powers conferred by, or in pursuance of, any provisions of this Act or the Rules thereunder shall be commenced within three months after the act complained or shall have been committed and not otherwise; and notice in writing of such proceeding and of the cause thereof shall be given to the person concerned and his supervisory officer at least one month before the commencement of such proceeding.

22. Power to make rules.

(1) The Central Government may, by notification in the Official Gazette, make Rules for carrying out the purposes of this Act.

(2) In particular, and without prejudice to the generality of the foregoing power such rules may provide for

(a) regulating the classes, ranks grades, pay and remuneration of members of the Force and their conditions of service in the Force;

(b) regulating the powers and duties of members of the Force authorised to exercise any functions by or under this Act;

(c) fixing the period of service for Members of the Force.

(d) prescribing the description and quantity of arms, accoutrements, clothing and necessary articles to be furnished to the Members of the Force;

(e) prescribing the place of residence of members of the Force;

(f) institution, management and regulations by any fund for any purpose connected with the administration of the Force;

(g) regulating the punishments and prescribing authorities to whom appeals shall be preferred from orders of punishment or remission of fines or other punishments, and the procedure to be followed for the disposal of such appeals;

(gg) regulating matters with respect to Force custody under this Act including the procedure to be followed for taking person into such custody;

(ggg) regulating matters with respect to disposal of cases relating to offences under this Act and specifying the places in which person convicted under this Act may be confined;

(gggg) prescribing authority under sub-section (2A) of Section 9 and the procedure to be followed by such authority in disposing of the revision petition;

(ggggg) prescribing authority under sub-section (2B) of Section 9,the period within which such authority may call for the records and the manner in which such authority may make inquiry.

(h) the terms and conditions subject to which member of the Force may be deputed under Section 14 and the charges therefor;

(hh) the manner in which and the fee on payment of which the technical consultancy services shall be provided under sub-section (1) of Section 14A; and (i) any other matter which has to be or may be prescribed or in respect of which rules are required to be made under this Act.

(3) Every rules made under this section shall be laid as soon as possible may be after it is made before each House of Parliament while it is in session for a total period of thirty days, which may be comprised in one session or in two or more successive sessions and before its expiry of the session immediately following the session or the successive aforesaid both House agree in making any modification in the rule, or both Houses agree in making any modification in the rule, or both Houses agree that the rule should not be made, the rule shall thereafter have effect only in such modified form or be of no effect as the case may be, so however, that any such modification or annulment shall be without prejudice to the validity of anything previously done under that rule.

THE SCHEDULE

[*See* Section 6]

A. B. has been appointed an enrolled member of the Central Industrial Security Force under the Central Industrial Security Force Act, 1968, and is vested with the powers, functions and privileges of an enrolled member of the Force.

APPENDIX

THE CENTRAL INDUSTRIAL SECURITY FORCE (AMENDMENT) ACT, 1983

(14 of 1983)

14. (1) The force constituted under the Principal Act as functioning immediately before the commencement of this Act (hereafter in this section referred to as the existing Force) shall, on such commencement, be deemed to be the force constituted under the principal Act amended by this Act, and every member of the existing force holding immediately before such commencement an office mentioned in column (1) of the Table below shall, on such commencement, be deemed to have been appointed to the office mentioned in the corresponding entry in column (2) of the said Table.

TABLE

	(1)	(2)
1.	Chief Security Officer	Commandant
2.	Deputy Chief Security Officer	Deputy Commandant
3.	Security Officer	Assistant Commandant
4.	Head Security Guard	Head Constable
5.	Senior Security Guard	Naik
6.	Security Guard	Constable

(2) Notwithstanding anything contained in sub-section (1), any member of the existing Force may, within thirty days from the commencement of this Act, exercise his option by notice in writing to the Director General.

(a) if such a member had been on deputation to the existing Force from any other service, to revert to such other service, and

(b) in any other case, to retire from service, and an option so exercised shall be final, and member exercising such option shall be permitted, within thirty days from the date on which he exercises such option to revert to the service from which he had been on deputation or, as the case may be, to retire from service.

EXPLANATION: For the purposes of this section the expression "member" includes an officer, and the expression "Director General" shall have the same meaning as in the principal Act as amended by this Act.

❑❑❑

15

The Central Reserve Police Force Act, 1949

Act No. 66 of 1949 [28th December, 1949]

AN ACT to provide for the constitution and regulation of an armed Central Reserve Police Force.

WHEREAS it is expedient to provide for the constitution and regulation of an armed Central Reserve Police Force;

It is hereby enacted as follows:-

1. Short title and extent.

(1) This Act may be called the Central Reserve Police Force Act, 1949.

(2) It extends to the whole of India [1]* * * and applies to members of the Force, wherever they may be.

2. Definitions. In this Act, unless there is anything repugnant in the subject or context,-

(a) "active duty" means the duty to restore and preserve order in any local area in the event of any disturbance therein;

(b) "close arrest" means confinement within the Force or a detachment of the Force or a post quarter-guard building or tent under charge of a guard;

(c) "the Force" means the Central Reserve Police Force;

(d) "member of the Force" means a person who has been appointed to the Force by the Commandant, whether before or after the commencement of this Act, and in Sections 1, 3, 6, 7, 16, 17, 18 and 19, includes also a person appointed to the Force by the Central Government, whether before or after such commencement;

(e) "open arrest" means confinement within the precincts of any barracks, lines or camp for the time being occupied by any part of the Force;

(f) "prescribed" means prescribed by rules made under this Act;

(g) "subordinate officer" means a member of the Force of the rank of subedar-major, subedar, jemadar or sub-inspector;

(h) the expressions" assault", "criminal force", "fraudulently", reason to believe and "voluntarily causing hurt" have the meanings assigned to them respectively in the Indian Penal Code (45 of 1860).

3. Constitution of the Force.

(1) There shall continue to be an armed force maintained by the Central Government and called the Central Reserve Police Force.

(2) The Force shall be constituted in such manner, and the members of the Force shall receive such pay, pension and other remuneration, as may be prescribed.

4. Appointment and powers of superior officers.

(1) The Central Government may appoint to the Force a Commandant and such other persons as it thinks fit to be assistant commandants and company officers.

(2) The Commandant and every other officer so appointed shall have, and may exercise, such powers and authority as may be provided by or under this Act.

5. Enrolment. Before a person is appointed to be a member of the Force, the statement contained in the recruiting roll set out in the Schedule shall be read out and, if necessary, explained to him in the presence of an officer appointed under sub-section (1) of Section 4, and shall be signed by such person in acknowledgment of its having been so read out to him:

PROVIDED that any person who has for a period of six months served with the Force, shall, on appointment to the Force thereafter, be deemed to be a member of the Force notwithstanding that the provisions of this Section have not been complied with in his case.

6. Resignation and withdrawal from the Force. No member of the Force shall be at liberty to-

(a) resign his appointment during the term of his engagement, except before the expiration of the first three months of his service; or

(b) withdraw himself from all or any of the duties of his appointment, without the previous permission in writing of the Commandant or assistant commandant or any other officer authorised by the Commandant to grant such permission.

7. General duties of members of the Force.

(1) It shall be the duty of every member of the Force promptly to obey and to execute all orders and warrants lawfully issued to him by any competent authority, to detect and bring offenders to justice and to apprehend all persons whom he is legally authorised to apprehend and for whose apprehension sufficient grounds exist.

(2) Every member of the Force shall be liable to serve without" and beyond, as well as within, the territory of India.

8. Superintendence, control and administration of the Force.

(1) The superintendence of, and control over, the Force shall vest in the Central Government; and the Force shall be administered by the Central Government

in accordance with the provisions of this Act and of any rules made thereunder, through such officers as the Central Government may from time to time appoint in this behalf.

(2) The Headquarters of the Force shall be at Neemuch or at such other place as may from time to time be specified by the Central Government.

(3) While on active duty outside its headquarters, the Force shall be subject to the general control and direction of such authority or officer as may be prescribed or as may be specially appointed by the Central Government in this behalf.

OFFENCES AND PUNISHMENTS

9. More heinous offences. Every member of the Force who-

(a) begins, excites, causes or conspires to cause or joins in any mutiny, or, being present at any mutiny, does not use his utmost endeavour to suppress it, or knowing, or having reason to believe in, the existence of any mutiny, or of any intention or conspiracy to mutiny or of any conspiracy against the State does not, without delay, give information thereof to his superior officer; or

(b) uses, or attempts to use, criminal force to, or commits an assault on, his superior officer, whether on or off duty, knowing or having reason to believe him to be such; or

(c) shamefully abandons or delivers up any post or guard which is committed to his charge, or which it is his duty to defend; or

(d) directly or indirectly holds correspondence with, or assists or relieves any person in arms against the State or omits to discover immediately to his superior officer any such correspondence coming to his knowledge, or who, while on active duty;

(e) disobeys the lawful command of his superior officer; or

(f) deserts the Force; or

(g) being a sentry, sleeps upon his post or quits it without being regularly relieved or without leave; or

(h) leaves his commanding officer, or his post or party, to go in search of plunder; or

(i) quits his guard, picquet, party or patrol without being regularly relieved or without leave; or

(j) uses criminal force to, or commits an assault on, any person bringing provisions or other necessaries to camp or quarters, or forces a safeguard or breaks into any house or other place for plunder, or plunders, destroys or damages property of any kind; or

(k) intentionally causes or spreads a false alarm in action or in camp, garrison or quarters; or

(l) displays cowardice in the execution of his duty, shall be punishable with transportation for life for a term of not less than seven years or with imprisonment for a term which may extend to fourteen years or with fine which may extend to three months pay or with fine to that extent in addition to such sentence of transportation or imprisonment.

10. Less heinous offences. Every member of the Force who-

(a) is in a state of intoxication when on, or after having been warned for, any duty or on parade or on the line of march; or

(b) strikes or attempts to force any sentry; or

(c) being in command of a guard, picquet or patrol, refuses to receive any prisoner or person duly committed to his charge, or without proper authority releases any person or prisoner placed under his charge, or negligently suffers any such prisoner or person to escape; or

(d) being under arrest or in confinement, leaves his arrest or confinement, before he is set at liberty by lawful authority; or

(e) is grossly insubordinate or insolent to his superior officer in the execution of his office; or

(f) refuses to superintend or assist in the making of any fieldwork or other work of any description ordered to be made either in quarters or in the field; or

(g) strikes or otherwise ill-uses any member of the Force sub-ordinate to him in rank or position; or

(h) designedly or through neglect injures or loses or fraudulently disposes of his arms, clothes, tools, equipments, ammunition or accoutrements, or any such articles entrusted to him or belonging to any other person; or

(i) malingers or feigns or produces disease or infirmity in himself, or intentionally delays his cure, or aggravates his disease or infirmity; or

(j) with intent to render himself or any other person unfit for service, voluntarily causes hurt to himself or any other person; or

(k) does not, when called upon by his superior officer so to do or upon ceasing to be a member of the Force forthwith deliver up, or duly account for, all or any arms, ammunition, stores, accoutrements or other property issued or supplied to him or in his custody or possession as such member; or

(l) knowingly furnishes a false return or report of the number or state of any men under his command or charge or of any money, arms, ammunition, clothing, equipments, stores or other property in his charge, whether belonging to such men or to the Government or to any member of, or any person attached to the Force, or who, through design or culpable neglect, omits or refuses to make or send any return or report of the matters aforesaid; or

(m) absents himself without leave, or without sufficient cause over-stays leave granted to him; or

(n) is guilty of any act or omission which, though not specified in this Act, is prejudicial to good order and discipline; or

(o) contravenes any provision of this Act for which no punishment is expressly provided, or who, while not on active duty;

(p) commits any of the offences specified in clauses (e) to (1) (both inclusive) of Section 9, shall be punishable with imprisonment for a term which may extend to one year, or with fine which may extend to three months pay, or with both.

11. Minor punishments.

(1) The Commandant or any other authority or officer as may be prescribed, may, subject to any rules made under this Act, award in lieu of, or in addition to, suspension or dismissal any one or more of the following punishments to any member of the Force whom he considers to be guilty of disobedience, neglect of duty, or remissness in the discharge of any duty or of other misconduct in his capacity as a member of the Force, that is to say -

(a) reduction in rank;

(b) fine of any amount not exceeding one months pay and allowances;

(c) confinement to quarters, lines or camp for a term not exceeding one month;

(d) confinement in the quarter-guard for not more than twenty-eight days, with or without punishment drill or extra guard, fatigue or other duty; and

(e) removal from any office of distinction or special emolument in the Force.

(2) Any punishment specified in clause (c) or clause (d) of sub-section (1) may be awarded by any Gazetted Officer when in command of any detachment of the Force away from headquarters, provided he is specially authorised in this behalf by the Commandant.

(3) The assistant commandant, a company officer or a subordinate officer, not being below the rank of subedar or inspector, commanding a separate detachment or an outpost, or in temporary command at the headquarters of the Force, may, without a formal trial, award to any member of the Force who is for the time being subject to his authority any one or more of the following punishments for the commission of any petty offence against discipline which is not otherwise provided for in this Act, or which is not of a sufficiently serious nature to require prosecution before a criminal Court, that is to say -

(a) confinement for not more than seven days in the quarterguard or such other place as may be considered suitable, with forfeiture of all pay and allowances during its continuance;

(b) punishment drill, or extra guard, fatigue or other duty, for not more than thirty days, with or without confinement to quarters, lines or camp;

(c) censure or severe censure :

PROVIDED that this punishment may be awarded to a subordinate officer only by the Commandant.

(4) A jemadar or sub-inspector who is temporarily in command of a detachment or an outpost may, in like manner and for the commission of any like offence, award to any member of the Force for the time being subject to his authority

any of the punishments specified in clause (b) of sub-section (3) for not more than fifteen days.

12. Place of imprisonment and liability to dismissal on imprisonment.

(1) Every person sentenced under this Act to imprisonment may be dismissed from the Force, and shall further be liable to forfeiture of pay, allowance and any other moneys due to him, as well as of any medals and decorations received by him.

(2) Every such person shall, if he is so dismissed, be imprisoned in the prescribed prison, but if he is not also dismissed from the Force, he may, if the Court or the Commandant so directs, be confined in the quarter-guard or such other place as the Court or the Commandant may consider suitable.

13. Deductions from pay and allowances. The following penal deductions may be made from the pay and allowances of a member of the Force by his company officer, that is to say -

(a) all pay and allowances for every day of absence either on desertion or without leave and for every day of imprisonment awarded by a criminal Court or of confinement awarded under Section 11;

(b) all pay and allowances for every day whilst he is in custody on a charge for an offence of which he is afterwards convicted;

(c) all pay and allowances for every day on which he is in hospital on account of sickness certified by the medical officer attending on him at the hospital to have been caused by an offence committed by him under this Act;

(d) all pay and allowances ordered to be forfeited under Section 11; and

(e) such sum as may be ordered by the Commandant or assistant commandant in order to make good any expenses caused by the member of the Force, or any loss of, or damage or destruction done by him to, any arms, ammunition, equipment, clothing, instruments or decorations belonging to the Force or to any buildings or property.

14. Collective fines. Whenever any weapon, part of a weapon or ammunition, forming part of the equipment of a company or other similar unit of the Force, is lost or stolen the Commandant may, after making such inquiry as he thinks fit and subject to such rules as may be prescribed, impose a collective fine upon the subordinate officers and men of such unit, or upon so many of them as, in his judgment, should be held responsible for such loss or theft.

15. Arrest.

(1) Any member of the Force who commits any offence specified in Section 9 or Section 10 may be placed on open or close arrest by any officer of the Force.

(2) Where any subordinate officer orders an arrest under sub-section (1), he shall forthwith or at the earliest opportunity report the arrest to his company or detachment commander who shall after investigating the case order the release or the continued arrest of the member of the Force arrested.

MISCELLANEOUS

16. Powers and duties conferrable and imposable on members of the Force.

(1) The Central Government may, by general or special order, confer or impose upon any member of the force any of the powers or duties conferred or imposed on a police officer of any class or grade by any law for the time being in force.

(2) Notwithstanding anything contained in the Code of Criminal Procedure, 1898, (5 of 1898) the Central Government may invest the Commandant or an assistant commandant with the powers of a Magistrate of any class for the purpose of inquiring into or trying any offence committed by a member of the Force and punishable under this Act, or any offence committed by a member of the Force against the person or property of another member:

PROVIDED that-

(i) when the offender is on leave or absent from duty, or

(ii) when the offence is not connected with the offenders duties as a member of the Force, or

(iii) when it is a petty offence, even if connected with the offenders duties as a member of the Force the offence may, if the prescribed authority within the limits of whose jurisdiction the offence has been committed, so directs, be inquired into or tried by an ordinary criminal Court having jurisdiction in the matter.

17. Protection for acts of members of the Force.

(1) In any suit or proceeding against any member of the Force for any act done by him in pursuance of a warrant or order of a competent authority, it shall be lawful for him to plead that such act was done by him under the authority of such warrant or order.

(2) Any such plea may be proved by the production of the warrant or order directing the act, and if it is so proved the member of the Force shall thereupon be discharged from liability in respect of the act so done by him, notwithstanding any defect in the jurisdiction of the authority which issued such warrant or order.

(3) Notwithstanding anything contained in any other law for the time being in force, any legal proceeding (whether civil or criminal) which may lawfully be brought against any member of the Force for anything done or intended to be done under the powers conferred by, or in pursuance of, any provision of this Act or the rules thereunder, shall be commenced within three months after the act complained of was committed and not otherwise, and notice in, writing of such proceeding and of the cause thereof shall be given to the defendant or his superior officer at least one month before the commencement of such proceeding.

18. Power to make rules.

(1) The Central Government may, by notification in the Official Gazette, make rules for carrying out the purposes of this Act.

(2) In particular and without prejudice to the generality of the foregoing power, such rules may provide for all or any of the following matters, namely :-

(a) regulating the classes and grades of, and the pay, pension and other remuneration of, members of the Force, and their conditions of service in the Force;

(b) regulating the powers and duties of officers authorised to exercise any functions by or under this Act;

(c) fixing the period of service for members of the Force;

(d) regulating the award of minor punishments under Section 11, and providing for appeals from, or the revision of, orders under that Section, or the remission of fines imposed under that Section, and the remission of deductions made under Section 13;

(e) regulating the several or collective liability of members of the Force in the case of the loss or theft of weapons and ammunition;

(f) for the disposal of criminal cases arising under this Act and for specifying the prison in which a person convicted in any such case may be confined.

[2][(3) Every rule made under this Act shall be laid, as soon as may be after it is made, before each House of Parliament, while it is in session, for a total period of thirty days which may be comprised in one session or in two or more successive sessions, and if, befores the expiry of the session immediately following the session or the successive sessions aforesaid, both Houses agree in making any modification in the rule, or both Houses agree that the rule should not be made, the rule shall thereafter have effect only in such modified form or be of no effect, as the case may be; so, however, that any such modification or annulment shall be without prejudice to the validity of anything previously done under that rule.]

19. Validation of acts done before commencement of Act. Any order made, thing done, or action taken by or in relation to a member of the Force, on or after the 15th day of August, 1947, but before the commencement of this Act, shall for all purposes be deemed to have been made, done or taken under this Act as if this Act were in force on the day on which such order was made, thing was done or action was taken.

THE SCHEDULE

RECRUITING ROLL

[*See* Section 5]

After you have served in the Force for such period as the Central Government may prescribe, you may, at any time when not on active duty, apply for discharge, through the officer to whom you may be subordinate to the Commandant, and you will be granted your discharge after two months from the date of your application, unless your discharge would cause the vacancies in the Force to exceed one-tenth of the sanctioned strength in which case you shall be bound to remain until this objection is waived or removed. But when on active duty, you shall have no claim to a discharge, and you shall be bound to remain to do your duty until the necessity for retaining you in the Force ceases when you may make your application in the abovementioned manner:

PROVIDED that, if you wish to withdraw from the Force, you may submit your resignation at any time before the expiration of the first three months of your service, but not afterwards until the completion of the period prescribed as aforesaid the Commandant may either accept your resignation forthwith or at the end of three months from the date of its receipt:

PROVIDED ALSO that the Commandant may, if he thinks fit, allow you to resign at any time on your giving three months notice of your wish to do so. Signature of the member of the Force in acknowledgement of the above having been read out to him. Space for impression of the members left thumb to be taken in the presence of the enrolling officer. Signed in my presence after I had ascertained that the candidate understood the purport of what he signed.

❑❑❑

16

The Coast Guard Act, 1978

ACT NO. 30 OF 1978 [18TH AUGUST, 1978]

AN ACT to provide for the constitution and regulation of an Armed Force of the Union for ensuring the security of the maritime zones of India with a view to the protection of maritime and other national interests in such zones and for matters connected therewith.

Be it enacted by Parliament in the Twenty-ninth Year of the Republic of India as follows:-

CHAPTER - I : PRELIMINARY

1. Short title and commencement.

(1) This Act may be called the Coast Guard Act, 1978.

(2) It shall come into force on such date[1] as the Central Government may, by notification in the Official Gazette, appoint.

2. Definitions. In this Act, unless the context otherwise requires -

(a) "Chief Law Officer" and "Law Officer" mean, respectively, the Chief Law Officer and a Law Officer of the Coast Guard appointed under Section 115;

(b) "civil offence" means an offence which is triable by a criminal court;

(c) "civil prison" means any jail or place used for the detention of any criminal prisoner under the Prisons Act, 1894 (9 of 1894), or under any other law for the time being in force;

(d) "Coast Guard" means the Coast Guard constituted under this Act;

(e) "Coast Guard Court" means a court convened under Section 64;

(f) "Coast Guard custody" means the arrest or confinement of member of the Coast Guard according to rules;

(g) "Commanding Officer", when used in any provision of this Act with reference to any unit or ship of the Coast Guard, means the officer whose duty it is under the rules to discharge with respect to that unit or ship, the functions of a Commanding Officer in regard to matters of the description referred to in that provision;

(h) "Criminal Court" means a court of ordinary criminal justice in any part of India;

(i) "Deputy Inspector-General" means a Deputy Inspector-General of the Coast Guard appointed under Section 5;

(j) "Director-General" means the Director-General of the Coast Guard appointed under Section 5;

(k) "enrolled person" means a subordinate officer, sailor or other person enrolled under this Act;

(l) "Inspector-General" means an Inspector-General of the Coast Guard appointed under Section 5;

(m) "maritime zones of India" means the territorial waters, the contiguous zone, the continental shelf, the exclusive economic zone or any other maritime zone of India;

(n) "member of the Coast Guard" means an officer, a subordinate officer, a sailor or other enrolled person;

(o) "notification" means a notification published in the Official Gazette;

(P) "offence" means any act or omission punishable under this Act and includes a civil offence;

(q) "officer" means a person appointed or in pay as an officer of the Coast Guard, but does not include a subordinate officer, sailor or other enrolled person;

(r) "prescribed" means prescribed by rules made under this Act;

(s) "rule" means a rule made under this Act;

(t) "sailor" means a member of the Coast Guard other than an officer, a subordinate officer or other enrolled person;

(u) "ship", except in the expression "on board a ship", means a Coast Guard vessel, and includes any establishmcnt or station belonging to, or under the control of, the Coast Guard whether within or without India;

(v) "skipper" means a subordinate officer in command of a ship;

(w) "subordinate officer" means a person appointed or in pay as a Pradhan Adhikari, a Pradhan Sahayak Engineer, an Uttam Adhikari, an Uttam Sahayak Engineer, an Adhikari or a Sahayak Engineer of the Coast Guard;

(x) "superior officer", when used in relation to a person subject to this Act, means any officer or subordinate officer-

   (i) who is senior to that person under the rules; or

   (ii) who is entitled under this Act or the rules to give a command to that person;

(y) "territorial waters", "contiguous zone", "continental shelf" and "exclusive economic zone", shall have the meanings respectively assigned to them in the Territorial Waters, Continental Shelf, Exclusive Economic Zone and other Maritime Zones Act, 1976 (80 of 1976);

(z) all words and expressions used and not defined in this Act but defined in the Indian Penal Code (45 of 1860), shall have the meanings assigned to them in that Code.

3. Persons subject to this Act.

(1) The following persons shall be subject to this Act, wherever they may be, namely:-

- (a) officers;
- (b) subordinate officers and. other persons enrolled under this Act;
- (c) persons who have, by a general or special order of the Central Government, been required to serve in a ship, to such extent and subject to such conditions as may be prescribed; and
- (d) persons ordered to be received, or being passengers, on board any ship or aircraft of the Coast Guard, to such extent and subject to such conditions as may be prescribed.

(2) Every person referred to in clauses (a) and (b) of sub-section (1) shall remain so subject until he retires, or he is discharged, released, removed or dismissed from the Coast Guard in accordance with the provisions of this Act, and the rules.

CHAPTER - II : CONSTITUTION OF THE COAST GUARD AND CONDITIONS OF SERVICE OF THE MEMBERS OF THE COAST GUARD

4. Constitution of the Coast Guard.

(1) There shall be an armed force of the Union called the Coast Guard for ensuring the security of the maritime zones of India with a view to the protection of maritime and other national interests in such zones.

(2) Subject to the provisions of this Act, the Coast Guard shall be constituted in such manner as may be prescribed and the conditions of service of the members of the Coast Guard shall be such as may be prescribed.

5. Control direction, etc.

(1) The general superintendence, direction and control of the Coast Guard shall vest in, and be exercised by, the Central Government and subject thereto, and to the provisions of this Act and the rules, the command and supervision of the Coast Guard shall vest in an officer to be appointed by the Central Government as the Director- General of the Coast Guard.

(2) The Director-General shall, in the discharge of his duties under this Act, be assisted by such number of Inspectors-General, Deputy Inspectors-General, Commandant and such other officers as may be appointed by the Central Government.

6. Enrolment.

(1) The persons to be enrolled to the Coast Guard, the mode of enrolment and the procedure for enrolment shall be such as may be prescribed.

(2) Notwithstanding anything contained in this Act and the rules, every person who has, for a continuous period of three months, been in receipt of pay as a person enrolled under this Act and borne on the rolls of the Coast Guard shall be deemed to have been duly enrolled.

7. Liability for service outside India. Every member of the Coast Guard shall be liable to serve in any part of India as well as outside India.

8. Oath of allegiance. Every member of the Coast Guard shall, as soon as may be, after appointment or enrolment to the Coast Guard, make and subscribe before his Commanding Officer or other prescribed officer, an oath or affirmation in the prescribed form.

9. Resignation and withdrawal from the post. No member of the Coast Guard shall be at liberty-

(a) to resign his appointment during the term of his engagement; or

(b) to withdraw himself from all or any of the duties of his appointment, except with the previous permission in writing of the prescribed authority.

10. Tenure of service under the Act. Every member of the Coast Guard shall hold office during the pleasure of the President.

11. Dismissal or removal by Central Government and by other officers. Subject to the provisions of this Act and the rules-

(a) the Central Government may dismiss or remove from service any member of the Coast Guard;

(b) the Director-General or any Inspector-General may dismiss or remove from the Coast Guard any person other than an officer;

(c) any prescribed officer not below the rank of a Deputy Inspector-General may dismiss or remove from the Coast Guard any person under his command other than an officer or a subordinate officer.

12. Certificate of termination of service. An enrolled person who retires, or is discharged, released, removed or dismissed from the Coast Guard or permitted to resign therefrom, shall be furnished by the officer, to whose command he is subject, with a certificate in the language which is the mother tongue of such person and also in Hindi or English language setting forth-

(a) the authority terminating his service;

(b) the reasons for such termination; and

(c) the full period of his service in the Coast Guard.

13. Restrictions respecting right to form association, freedom of speech, etc.

(1) No member of the Coast Guard shall, without the previous sanction in writing of the Central Government or of the prescribed authority -

(a) be a member of, or be associated in any way with, any trade union, labour union, or political association; or

(b) be a member of, or be associated in any way with, any society, institution, association or Organisation that is not recognised as part of the Coast Guard or is not of a purely social, recreational or religious nature; or

(c) communicate with the press or publish or cause to be published any book, letter or other document except where such communication or publication is in the bona fide discharge of his duties or is of a purely literary, artistic or scientific character or is of a prescribed nature. *EXPLANATION:* If any question arises whether any society, institution, association or Organisation is of a purely social, recreational or religious nature under clause (b) of this sub-section, the decision of the Central Government thereon shall be final.

(2) No member of the Coast Guard shall participate in, or address, any meeting or take part in any demonstration organised by any body of persons for any political purposes or for such other purposes as may be specified in this behalf by the Central Government.

CHAPTER - III : DUTIES AND FUNCTIONS OF THE COAST GUARD

14. Duties and functions of Coast Guard.

(1) It shall be the duty of the Coast Guard to protect by such measures, as it thinks fit, the maritime and other national interests of India in the maritime zones of India.

(2) Without prejudice to the generality of the provisions of sub-section (1), the measures referred to therein may provide for-

(a) ensuring the safety and protection of artificial islands, offshore terminals, installations and other structures and devices in any maritime zone;

(b) providing protection to fishermen including assistance to them at sea while in distress;

(c) taking such measures as are necessary to preserve and protect the maritime environment and to prevent and control marine pollution;

(d) assisting the customs and other authorities in anti-smuggling operations;

(e) enforcing the provisions of such enactments as are for the time being in force in the maritime zones; and

(f) such other matters, including measures for the safety of life and property at sea and collection of scientific data, as may be prescribed.

(3) The Coast Guard shall perform its functions under this Section in accordance with, and subject to such rules, as may be prescribed and such rules may, in particular, make provisions for ensuring that the Coast Guard functions in close liaison with Union agencies, Institutions and authorities so as to avoid duplication of effort.

CHAPTER - IV : OFFENCES

15. Correspondence, etc., with offenders. Any person subject to this Act, who,—

(a) treacherously holds correspondence with, or communicates intelligence to, an offender; or

(b) wilfully fails to make known to the proper authorities any information he may have received from an offender; or

(c) assists the offender in any manner; or

(d) having been captured by an offender, voluntarily serves with or aids him, shall, on conviction by a Coast Guard Court, be liable to suffer imprisonment for a term which may extend to seven years or such less punishment as is in this Act mentioned.

EXPLANATION: For the purposes of this Section, offender includes-

(a) all armed mutineers, armed rebels, armed rioters, pirates and any person in arms against whom it is the duty of any person subject to this Act to take action; and

(b) any person or persons engaged in smuggling, unlawful exploration or exploitation or any other unlawful activity in the maritime zones of India.

16. Deserting post and neglect of duty. Any person subject to this Act, who -

(a) deserts his post; or

(b) sleeps upon his watch; or

(c) fails to perform, or negligently performs, the duty imposed on him; or

(d) wilfully conceals any words, practice or design tending to the hindrance of the Coast Guard, shall, on conviction by a Coast Guard Court, be liable to suffer imprisonment for a term which may extend to two years or such less punishment as is in this Act mentioned.

17. Mutiny. Any person subject to this Act who commits any of the following offences, that is to say -

(a) begins, incites, causes or conspires with any other person to cause any mutiny in the Coast Guard or in the military, naval or air forces of India or any forces co-operating therewith; or

(b) joins in any such mutiny; or

(c) being present at any such mutiny, does not use his utmost endeavours to suppress the same; or

(d) knowing or having reason to believe in the existence of any such mutiny, or of any intention to mutiny or of any such conspiracy, does not, without delay, give information thereof to his Commanding Officer or other superior officer; or

(e) endeavours to seduce any person in the Coast Guard or in the military, naval or air forces of India or any forces co-operating therewith from his duty or allegiance to the Union, shall, on conviction by a Coast Guard Court, be liable to suffer death or such less punishment as is in this Act mentioned:

PROVIDED that a sentence of death awarded under this Section shall not be carried out unless it is confirmed by the Central Government.

18. Persons on board ship or aircraft seducing Coast Guard personnel from allegiance. Any person not otherwise subject to this Act who, being on board any ship or aircraft belonging to or in the service of the Coast Guard endeavours to seduce any person subject to this Act from his allegiance to the Constitution or loyalty to the State or duty to his superior officers shall, on conviction by a Coast Guard Court, be liable to suffer imprisonment for a term which may extend to seven years or such less punishment as is in this Act mentioned.

19. Striking or threatening superior Officers. Any person subject to this Act who commits any of the following offences, that is to say -

(a) uses criminal forceto or assaults his superior officer; or

(b) uses threatening language to such officer; or

(c) uses insubordinate language to such officer; or

(d) behaves with contempt to such officer, shall, on conviction by a Coast Guard Court, be liable to suffer imprisonment for a term which may extend to ten years or such less punishment as is in this Act mentioned:

PROVIDED that in the case of offences specified in clauses (c) and (d), the imprisonment shall not exceed five years.

20. Disobedience to superior officer.

(1) Any person subject to this Act who disobeys in such manner as to show a wilful defiance of authority any lawful command given personally by his superior officer in the execution of his office whether the same is given orally, or in writing or by signal or otherwise, shall, on conviction by a Coast Guard Court, be liable to suffer imprisonment for a term which may extend to fourteen years or such less punishment as is in this Act mentioned.

(2) Any person subject to this Act who disobeys any lawful command given by his superior officer, shall, on conviction by a Coast Guard Court, be liable to suffer imprisonment for a term which may extend to seven years or such less punishment as is in this Act mentioned.

21. Ill-treating subordinate. Any person subject to this Act who uses criminal force to or otherwise ill-treats any other person subject to this Act, being his subordinate in rank or position, shall, on conviction by a Coast Guard Court, be liable to suffer imprisonment for a term which may extend to seven years or such less punishment as is in this Act mentioned.

22. Quarrelling fighting and disorderly behaviour. Any person subject to this Act, who -

(a) quarrels, fights with or strikes any other person, whether such person is or is not subject to this Act; or

(b) uses reproachful or provoking speeches or gestures tending to make a quarrel or disturbance; or

(c) behaves in a disorderly manner, shall, on conviction by a Coast Guard Court, be liable to suffer imprisonment for a term which may extend to two years or such less punishment as is in this Act mentioned.

23. Certain forms of disgraceful conduct. Any person subject to this Act who commits any of the following offences, that is to say -

(a) is guilty of any disgraceful conduct of a cruel, indecent or unnatural kind; or

(b) malingers, or feigns, or produces disease or infirmity in himself or intentionally delays his cure or aggravates his disease or infirmity; or

(c) with intent to render himself or any other person unfit for service, voluntarily causes hurt to himself or that person, shall, on conviction by a Coast Guard Court, be liable to suffer imprisonment for a term which may extend to seven years or such less punishment as is in this Act mentioned.

24. Drunkenness.

(1) Any person subject to this Act, who is guilty of drunkenness shall, on conviction by a Coast Guard Court, be liable to suffer imprisonment for a term which may extend to six months or such less punishment as is in this Act mentioned.

(2) For the purposes of sub-section (1), a person shall be deemed to be guilty of drunkenness if, owing to the influence of alcohol or any drug whether alone or in combination with any other circumstances, he is unfit to be entrusted with his duty or with any duty which he may be called upon to perform or behaves in a disorderly manner or in a manner likely to bring discredit to the Coast Guard.

25. Desertion and aiding desertion.

(1) Any person subject to this Act, who absents himself from his ship or from the place where his duty requires him to be, with an intention of not returning to such ship or place, or who, at any time and under any circumstances when absent from his ship or place of duty does any act which shows that he has an intention of not returning to such ship or place is said to desert.

(2) Every person who deserts or attempts to desert the Coast Guard shall, on conviction by a Coast Guard Court, be liable to suffer imprisonment for a term which may extend to seven years or such less punishment as is in this Act mentioned.

(3) Any person subject to this Act, who knowingly harbours any such deserter, shall, on conviction by a Coast Guard Court, be liable to suffer imprisonment for a term which may extend to three years or such less punishment as is in this Act mentioned.

26. Breaking out of ship and absence without leave. Any person subject to' this Act, who without being guilty of desertion improperly leaves his ship or place of duty or is absent without leave shall, on conviction by a Coast Guard Court, be liable to suffer imprisonment for a term which may extend to two years or such less punishment as is in this Act mentioned, and shall also be punished by such mulcts of pay and allowances as may be prescribed.

27. Losing ship or aircraft.

(1) Any person subject to this Act who wilfully loses, strands or hazards or suffers to be lost, stranded or hazarded any ship belonging to or in the service of the Coast Guard, or loses or suffers to be lost any aircraft belonging to or in the service of the Coast Guard shall, on conviction by a Coast Guard Court, be liable to suffer imprisonment for a term which may extend to seven years or such less punishment as is in this Act mentioned.

(2) Any person subject to this Act, who negligently or by any default loses, strands or hazards or suffers to be lost, stranded or hazarded any ship belonging to or in the service of the Coast Guard, or loses or suffers to be lost any aircraft belonging to or in the service of the Coast Guard shall, on conviction by a Coast Guard Court, be liable to suffer imprisonment for a term which may extend to two years or such less punishment as is in this Act mentioned.

28. Dangerous unauthorised flying. Any person subject to this Act who is guilty of any act or neglect in flying or in the use of any aircraft belonging to or in the service of the Coast Guard, or in relation to any such aircraft or aircraft material, which causes or is likely to cause loss of life or bodily injury to any person shall, on conviction by a Coast Guard Court -

(a) if he acts wilfully or with wilful neglect, be liable to suffer imprisonment for a term which may extend to seven years or such less punishment as is in this Act mentioned; and

(b) in any other case, be liable to suffer imprisonment for a term which may extend to two years or such less punishment as is in this Act mentioned.

29. Inaccurate certificate. Any person subject to this Act who signs any certificate in relation to an aircraft belonging to or in the service of the Coast Guard or to any, material thereof without ensuring its accuracy shall, on conviction by a Coast Guard Court, be liable to suffer imprisonment for a term which may extend to two years or such less punishment as is in this Act mentioned.

30. Low flying and annoyance by flying. Any person subject to this Act, being the pilot of an aircraft belonging to or in the service of the Coast Guard, who-

(a) flies it at a height lower than the minimum height authorised by his Commanding Officer except while taking off or landing; or

(b) flies it so as to cause or likely to cause unnecessary annoyance to any person, shall, on conviction by a Coast Guard Court, be liable to suffer imprisonment for a term which may extend to two years or such less punishment as is in this Act mentioned.

31. Disobediance of lawful command of captain of an aircraft. Any person subject to this Act, who while he is in an aircraft belonging to or in the service of the Coast Guard, disobeys any lawful command given by the captain of the aircraft whether such captain is subject to this Act or not, in relation to all matters relating to flying or handling of the aircraft or affecting the safety thereof, shall, on conviction by a Coast Guard Court, be liable to suffer imprisonment for a term which may extend to seven years or such less punishment as is in this Act mentioned.

32. False accusations. Any person subject to this Act, who commits any of the following offences, that is to say -

(a) makes a false accusation against any person subject to this Act, knowing or having reason to believe such accusation to be false; or

(b) in making a complaint against any person subject to this Act makes any statement affecting the character of such person, knowing or having reason to believe such statement to be false or knowingly or wilfully suppresses any material facts, shall, on conviction by a Coast Guard Court, be liable to suffer imprisonment for a term which may extend to three years or such less punishment as is in this Act mentioned.

33. Falsifying official documents and false declarations. Any person subject to this Act who commits any of the following offences, that is to say -

(a) in any report, return, list, certificate, book or other document made or signed by him, or of the contents of which it is his duty to ascertain the accuracy, knowingly make, or is privy to the making of, any false or fraudulents statement; or

(b) in any document of the description mentioned in clause (a) knowingly makes, or is privy to the making of, any omission, with intent to defraud; or

(c) knowingly and with intent to injure any person, or knowingly and with intent to defraud, suppresses, defaces, alters or makes away with any document which it is his duty to preserve or produce; or

(d) where it is his official duty to make a declaration respecting any matter, knowingly makes a false declaration; or

(e) obtains for himself, or for any other person, any pension, allowance or other advantage or privilege by a statement which is false, and which he either knows or believes to be false, or does not believe to be true, or by making or using a false entry in any book or record, or by making any document containing a false statement, or by omitting to make a true entry or document containing a true statement, shall, on conviction by a Coast Guard Court, be liable to suffer imprisonment for a term which may extend to ten years or such less punishment as is in this Act mentioned.

34. Offences in respect of property. Any person subject to this Act who commits any of the following offences, that is to say,—

(a) commits theft of any property belonging to the Government or to any Coast Guard mess, or institution, or to any person subject to this Act; or

(b) dishonestly misappropriates or converts to his own use any such property; or

(c) commits criminal breach of trust in respect of any such property; or

(d) dishonestly receives or retains any such property in respect of which any of the offences under clauses (a), (b) and (c) has been committed, knowing or having reason to believe the commission of such offence; or

(e) wilfully destroys or damages any property of the Government entrusted to him; or

(f) does any other thing with intent to defraud or to cause wrongful gain to one person or wrongful loss to another person, shall, on conviction by a Coast Guard Court, be liable to suffer imprisonment for a term which may extend to ten years or such less punishment as is in this Act mentioned.

35. Damage to property. Any person subject to this Act, who commits any act which causes damage to, or destruction of, any property of the Government shall, on conviction by a Coast Guard Court, be liable to suffer imprisonment for a term which may extend to seven years or such less punishment as is in this Act mentioned.

36. Taking unauthorised goods on board. Every officer or subordinate officer in command of any ship belonging to or in the service of the Coast Guard who receives on board or permits to be received on board such ship, any goods or merchandise whatsoever other than for the sole use of the ship or persons belonging to the ship, except goods and merchandise on board any ship which may be ship-wrecked or in imminent danger either on the high seas or in some port, creek or harbour for the purpose of preserving them for their proper owners, or except such goods or merchandise as he may, at any time be ordered to take or receive on board by order of the Central Government or his superior officer, shall, on conviction by a Coast Guard Court, be liable to suffer dismissal from the Coast Guard or such less punishment an is in this Act mentioned.

37. Offences in respect of papers relating to vessel, craft or aircraft taken into custody.

(1) All the papers, charter parties, bills of lading, passports and other documents that shall be taken, seized or found on board any vessel, craft or aircraft taken into custody by the Coast Guard shall be duly preserved and the Commanding Officer or skipper shall send the same to his immediate superior.

(2) Every Commanding Officer or skipper who fails to send the documents as required under sub-section (1) shall, on conviction by a Coast Guard Court, be liable to suffer dismissal from the Coast Guard or such less punishment as is in this Act mentioned.

38. Offences in respect of vessel, craft or aircraft taken into custody. Any person subject to this Act who commits any of the following offences, that is to say,—

(a) takes out without proper authority from any vessel, craft or aircraft taken into custody, any money or goods; or

(b) pillages, beats or ill-treats persons on board the said vessel, craft or aircraft; or

(c) breaks bulk on board any such vessel, craft or aircraft with intent dishonestly to misappropriate anything therein or belonging thereto shall, on conviction by a Coast Guard Court, be liable to suffer imprisonment for a term which may extend to two years or such less punishment as is in this Act mentioned.

39. Unlawful taking of ransom. Every Commanding Officer or skipper of a ship who -

(a) unlawfully agrees with any person for the ransoming of any vessel, craft, aircraft, goods or things taken into custody by the Coast Guard; or

(b) in pursuance of any unlawful agreement for ransoming or otherwise by collusion actually quits or restores any vessel, craft, aircraft, goods or things taken into custody by the Coast Guard, shall, on conviction by a Coast Guard Court, be liable to suffer imprisonment for a term which may extend to two years or such less punishment as is in this Act mentioned.

40. Offences relating to Coast Guard Courts. Any person subject to this Act who commits any of the following offences, that is to say -

(a) being duly summoned or ordered to attend as a witness before a Coast Guard Court, wilfully or without reasonable excuse, makes default in attending; or

(b) refuses to take an oath or make an affirmation legally required by a Coast Guard Court to be taken or made; or

(c) refuses to produce or deliver any document in his power or control legally required by a Coast Guard Court to be produced or delivered by him; or

(d) refuses, when a witness, to answer any question which he is by law bound to answer; or

(e) is guilty of contempt of a Coast Guard Court by using insulting or threatening language, or by causing any interruption or disturbance in the proceedings of such Court, shall, on conviction by a Coast Guard Court, be liable to suffer imprisonment for a term which may extend to three years or such less punishment as is in this Act mentioned.

41. Escape from custody. Any person subject to this Act who, being in lawful custody, escapes or attempts to escape, shall, on conviction by a Coast Guard Court, be liable to suffer imprisonment for a term which may extend to three years or such less punishment as is in this Act mentioned.

42. Violation of the Act, rules and orders. Any person subject to this Act who neglects to obey, or contravenes any provision of this Act or any rule or any order issued by any lawful authority under this Act, shall, if no other punishment is provided in this Act for such neglect or contravention, on conviction by a Coast Guard Court, be liable to suffer imprisonment for a term which may extend to two years or such less punishment as is in this Act mentioned.

43. False answers on enrolment. Any person having become subject to this Act who is discovered to have made at the time of enrolment, a wilfully false answer to any question set forth in the prescribed form of enrolment which has been put to him by the enrolling officer before whom he appears for the purpose of being enrolled, shall, on conviction by a Coast Guard Court, be liable to suffer imprisonment for a term which may extend to five years or such less punishment as is in this Act mentioned.

44. Offences against good order and discipline. Any person subject to this Act who is guilty of any act or omission or disorder or neglect, which, though not specified in this Act, is prejudicial to good order and discipline of the Coast Guard shall, on conviction by a Coast Guard Court, where no express proprisonment for a term which may extend to three years or such less punishment as is in this Act mentioned.

45. Attempt. Any person subject to this Act who attempts to commit any of the offences specified in Sections 15 to 44 (both inclusive) and in such attempt does any act towards the commission of the offence shall, on conviction by a Coast Guard Court, where no express provision is made by this Act for the punishment of such attempt, be liable -

(a) if the offence attempted to be committed is punishable with death, to suffer imprisonment for a term which may extend to fourteen years or such less punishment as is in this Act mentioned; and

(b) if the offence attempted to be committed is punishable with imprisonment, to suffer imprisonment for a term which may extend to one-half of the longest term provided for that offence or such less punishment as is in this Act mentioned.

46. Abetment of offences that have been committed. Any person subject to this Act who abets the commission of any of the offences specified in Sections 15 to 44 (both inclusive), shall, on conviction by a Coast Guard Court, if the act abetted is committed in consequence of the abetment and no express provision is made by this Act for the punishment of such abetment, be liable to suffer imprisonment provided for that offence or such less punishment as is in this Act mentioned.

47. Abetment of offence punishable with death and not committed. Any person subject to this Act, who abets the commission of an offence punishable with death under Section 17 shall, on conviction by a Coast Guard Court, if that offence be not committed in consequence of that abetment, be liable to suffer imprisonment for a term which may extend to fourteen years or such less punishment as is in this Act mentioned.

48. Abetment of offences punishable with imprisonment and not committed. Any person subject to this Act who abets the commission of any of the offences specified in Sections 15 to 44 (both inclusive) and punishable with imprisonment shall, on conviction by a Coast Guard Court, if that offence be not committed in consequence of the abetment, and no express provision is made by this Act for the punishment of such abetment, be liable to suffer imprisonment for a term which may extend to one-half of the longest term provided for that offence or such less punishment as is in this Act mentioned.

49. Civil offences. Subject to the provisions of Section 50, any person subject to this Act who at any place in, or beyond, India commits any civil offence shall be deemed to be guilty of an offence against this Act and, if charged therewith under this Section shall be liable to be tried, by a Coast Guard Court, and, on conviction, be punishable as follows, that is to say -

(a) if the offence is one which would be punishable under any law in force in India with death, he shall be liable to suffer any punishment, assigned for the offence, by the aforesaid law or such less punishment as is in this Act mentioned; and

(b) in any other case, he shall be liable to suffer any punishment, assigned for the offence by the law in force in India, or imprisonment for a term which may extend to seven years, or such less punishment as is in this Act mentioned.

50. Civil offences not triable by a Coast Guard Court. A person subject to this Act who commits an offence of murder or of culpable homicide not amounting to murder against, or of rape in relation to, a person not subject to this Act shall not be deemed to be guilty of an offence against this Act and shall not be tried by a Coast Guard Court, unless he commits any of the said offences -

(a) at any place outside India; or

(b) at any place specified by the Central Government by notification in this behalf.

51. Period of limitation for trial of offences under the Act.

(1) No person unless he is an offender who has avoided apprehension or escaped arrest or committed the offence of desertion or of giving false entry on enrolment or the offence of mutiny shall be tried or punished in pursuance of this Act for any offence committed by him unless such trial commences within three years from the commission of such offence.

(2) No trial for an offence of desertion or of giving false entry on enrolment shall be commenced if the person in question, not being an officer, has subsequent to the commission of the offence served continuously in an exemplary manner for not less than three years in the Coast Guard.

52. Trial, etc., of a person who ceases to be subject to the Act.

(1) Where an offence under this Act had been committed by any person while subject to this Act, and such person has since the commission of the offence ceased to be subject to this Act, he may be taken into and kept in the Coast Guard custody, and tried and punished for such offence as if he had continued to be so subject.

(2) No such person shall be tried for an offence, unless his trial commences within six months after he has ceased to be subject to this Act:

PROVIDED that nothing contained in this sub-section shall apply to the trial of any such person for an offence of mutiny or desertion.

CHAPTER - V : PUNISHMENTS

53. Punishments awardable by Coast Guard Courts.

(1) Punishments may' be inflicted in respect of offences committed by persons subject to this Act and convicted by Coast Guard Courts according to the scale following, that is to say -

(a) death;

(b) imprisonment which may be for the term of life or any other lesser term;

(c) dismissal from the Coast Guard;

(d) detention in Coast Guard custody for a period not exceeding two years;

(e) reduction to the ranks or to a lower rank in the case of sailors;

(f) forfeiture of seniority of rank, forfeiture of all or any part of the service for the purpose of promotion;

(g) forfeiture of service for the purpose of increased pay, pension or any other prescribed purpose;

(h) fine, in respect of civil offences;

(i) mulcts of pay and allowances;

(j) severe reprimand or reprimand except in the case of persons below the rank of an Uttam Navik or Uttam Yantrik.

(2) Each of the punishments specified in sub-section (1) shall be deemed to be inferior in degree to every punishment preceding it in the above scale.

54. Alternative punishments awardable by Coast Guard Courts. Subject to the provisions of this Act, a Coast Guard Court may, on convicting a person subject to this Act of any of the offences specified in Sections 15 to 48 (both inclusive) award either the particular punishment with which the offence is stated in the said Sections to be punishable, or in lieu thereof, any one of the punishments lower in the scale set out in Section 53 regard being had to the nature and degree of the offence.

55. Combination of punishments. Subject to the provisions of Section 58, a sentence of a Coast Guard Court may award in addition to, or without any one other punishment, the punishment specified in clause (c) of sub-section (1) of Section 53 and any one or more of the punishments specified in clauses (e) to (j) (both inclusive) of that sub-section.

56. Punishments otherwise than by Coast Guard Courts. Punishments may also be inflicted in respect of offences committed by persons subject to this Act without the intervention of a Coast Guard Court in the manner stated in Section 57.

57. Minor punishments. Subject to the provisions of Section 58, a Commanding Officer or such other officer as is, with the consent of the Central Government, specified by the Director-General may, in the prescribed manner, proceed against a person subject to this Act, otherwise than as an officer, who is charged with an offence under this Act and award such person, to the extent prescribed, one or more of the following punishments, that is to say -

(a) imprisonment for a period not exceeding three months;

(b) dismissal from the Coast Guard;

(c) detention in Coast Guard custody for a period not exceeding three months;

(d) reduction to the ranks or to a lower rank in the case of sailors;

(e) fine, in respect of civil offences;

(f) mulcts of pay and allowances;

(g) deprivation of good conduct badges;

(h) reprimand;

(i) extra work and drill for a period not exceeding fourteen days in the case of persons below the rank of an Uttam Navik or Uttam Yantrik;

(j) stoppage of leave for a period not exceeding sixty days;

(k) admonition:

PROVIDED that no punishments specified in clauses (a) to (d) (both inclusive) shall be inflicted -

(a) in the case of a subordinate officer, unless it is approved by an officer not below the rank of an Inspector-General; and

(b) in the case of others, unless it is approved by an officer not below the rank of a Deputy Inspector-General.

58. Provisions as to award of punishments.

(1) The punishments that may be inflicted under this Act shall be awarded in accordance with the provisions of this Section.

(2) A sentence of imprisonment under this Act shall in all cases be accompanied by a sentence of dismissal.

(3) A sentence of imprisonment may be rigorous or simple or partly rigorous and partly simple.

(4) No officer shall be subject to detention for any offence under this Act.

(5) No subordinate officer shall be sentenced to detention except for desertion.

(6) A sentence of detention shall not be accompanied by a sentence of dismissal from the Coast Guard.

(7) A sentence of detention for a period exceeding fourteen days shall in all cases be accompanied by stoppage of pay and allowances during the period of detention.

CHAPTER - VI : ARREST AND PROCEEDINGS BEFORE TRIAL

59. Custody of offenders.

(1) Any person subject to this Act who is charged with an offence may be taken into Coast Guard custody, under the order of any superior officer.

(2) Notwithstanding anything contained in sub-section (1), an officer may order into Coast Guard custody any other officer engaged in a quarrel, affray or disorder, though such other officer may be of a higher rank.

60. Duty of Commanding Officer in regard to detention.

(1) It shall be the duty of every Commanding Officer to take care that a person under his command when charged with an offence is not detained in custody for more than forty-eight hours after the committal of such person into custody is reported to him, without the charge being investigated, unless investigation within that period seems to him to be impracticable having regard to the public service.

(2) The case of every person being detained in custody beyond a period of forty-eight hours, and the reasons therefore, shall be reported by the Commanding Officer to the Deputy Inspector-General under whom he is serving or such other officer to whom an application may be made to convene a Coast Guard Court for the trial of the person charged.

(3) In reckoning the period of forty-eight hours specified in sub-section (1), Sundays and other public holidays shall be excluded.

(4) Subject to the provisions of this Act, the Central Government may make rules providing for the manner in which and the period for which any person subject to this Act may be taken into and detained in Coast Guard custody, pending the trial by any competent authority for any offence committed by him.

61. Arrest by civil authorities. Whenever any person subject to this Act, who is accused of an offence under this Act, is within the jurisdiction of any Magistrate or police officer, such Magistrate or police officer shall aid in the apprehension and delivery to Coast Guard custody of such person upon receipt of a written application to that effect signed by his Commanding Officer or an officer authorised by the Commanding Officer in that behalf.

62. Capture of deserters.

(1) Whenever any person subject to this Act deserts, the Commanding Officeer of the unit or ship to which be belongs, shall give information of the desertion to such civil authorities as, in his opinion, may be able to afford assistance towards the capture of the deserter; and such authorities shall thereupon take steps for the apprehension of the said deserter in like manner as if he was a person for whose apprehension a warrant had been issued by a Magistrate, and shall deliver the deserter, when apprehended, into Coast Guard custody.

(2) Any police officer may arrest without warrant any person reasonably believed to be subject to this Act, and to be a deserter or to be travelling without authority, and shall bring him without delay before the nearest Magistrate, to be dealt with according to law.

63. Coast Guard police officers.

(1) The Director-General or any prescribed officer may appoint persons for discharging the functions specified in sub-sections (2) and (3).

(2) The duties of a person appointed under subsection (1), are to take charge of persons confined for any offence, to preserve good order and discipline and to prevent breaches of the same by persons serving in, or attached to, the Coast Guard.

(3) Notwithstanding anything contained in Section 59, a person appointed under sub-section (1) may, at any time, arrest and detain for trial any person subject to this Act who commits, or is charged with, an offence, and may also carry into effect any punishment to be inflicted in pursuance of a sentence awarded by a Coast Guard Court or by an officer exercising authority under Section 57 but shall not inflict any punishment on his own authority:

PROVIDED that no officer shall be so arrested or detained otherwise than on the order of another officer.

CHAPTER - VII : COAST GUARD COURTS

64. Power to convene a Coast Guard Court.

(1) A Coast Guard Court may be convened by the Central Government or the Director-General or by any officer empowered in this behalf by warrant of the Director-General (hereafter in this Act referred to as the Convening authority).

(2) A warrant issued under sub-section (1) may contain such restrictions, reservations or conditions as the Director-General may think fit.

65. Composition of Coast Guard Courts.

(1) A Coast Guard Court shall consist of not less than five officers each of whom has held the post of Assistant Commandant for not less than three years.

EXPLANATION: For the purposes of this sub-section "Assistant Commandant" includes any post of higher rank and any post declared by the Central Government by notification to be an equivalent post as also any post higher in rank than the post so declared.

(2) At every Coast Guard Court, the senior member shall be the presiding officer.

(3) A Coast Guard Court shall not be duly constituted unless the members thereof are drawn from at least two ships.

(4) No Coast Guard Court for the trial of an officer shall be duly constituted unless the presiding officer and at least two members of the court are of the same rank as the accused or of a higher rank.

66. Dissolution of a Coast Guard Court.

(1) If a Coast Guard Court after the commencement of a trial is reduced below the minimum number of officers required by this Act, it shall be dissolved.

(2) If, on account of the illness of the Law Officer or of the accused before the finding, it is impossible to continue the trial, a Coast Guard Court shall be dissolved.

(3) The convening authority of a Coast Guard Court may dissolve the same if it considers that the exigencies of the service or necessities of discipline render it impossible or inexpedient to continue the said Coast Guard Court.

(4) Where a Coast Guard Court is dissolved under this Section, the accused may be tried again.

67. Powers of a Coast Guard Court. Every Coast Guard Court shall have the power to try any person subject to this Act for any offence punishable thereunder and to pass any sentence authorised thereby.

68. Prohibition of second trial.

(1) When any person subject to this Act has been acquitted or convicted of an offence by a Coast Guard Court or by a Criminal Court or has been dealt with under Section 57, he shall not be liable to be tried again for the same offence by a Coast Guard Court or dealt with under the said Section.

(2) When any person, subject to this Act, has been acquitted or convicted of an offence by a Coast Guard Court or has been dealt with under Section 57, he shall not be liable to be tried again by a criminal court for the same offence or on the same facts.

69. Application of Act during term of sentence.

(1) When a person subject to this Act is sentenced by a Coast Guard Court to imprisonment, this Act shall apply to him during the term of his sentence, though he is dismissed from the Coast Guard, or has otherwise ceased to be subject to this Act, and he may be kept, removed, imprisoned and punished as if he continued to be subject to this Act.

(2) When a person subject to this Act is sentenced by a Coast Guard Court to death, this Act shall apply to him till the sentence is carried out.

70. Place of trial. A Coast Guard Court may be held on shore or afloat.

71. Choice between criminal court and Coast Guard Court. When a criminal court and a Coast Guard Court have each jurisdiction in respect of an offence, it shall be in the discretion of the Director-General or the Inspector-General or the Deputy Inspector-General within whose command the accused person is serving or such other officer as may be prescribed, to decide before which court the proceedings shall be instituted, and, if that officer decides that they shall be instituted before a Coast Guard Court, to direct that the accused person shall be detained in Coast Guard custody.

72. Power of criminal court to require delivery of an offender.

(1) When a criminal court having jurisdiction is of opinion that proceedings shall be instituted before itself in respect of any alleged offence, it may, by written notice, require the officer referred to in Section 71 at his option either to deliver over the offender to the nearest Magistrate to be proceeded against according to law, or to postpone proceedings, pending a reference to the Central Government.

(2) In every such case, the said officer shall either deliver over the offender in compliance with the requisition, or shall forthwith refer the question as to the court before which the proceedings are to be instituted, for the determination of the Central Government whose order upon such reference shall be final.

CHAPTER - VIII : PROCEDURE OF COAST GUARD COURTS

73. Law Officer. Every Coast Guard Court shall be attended by a Law Officer, or if no such officer is available, an officer approved by the Chief Law Officer or a Law Officer.

74. Challenges.

(1) At all trials by a Coast Guard Court, as soon as the court is assembled, the names of the presiding officer and members shall be read over to the accused, who shall thereupon be asked whether he objects to being tried by any officer sitting on the court.

(2) If the accused objects to such officer, his objection and also the reply thereto of the officer objected to shall be heard and recorded, and the remaining officers of the court shall, in the absence of the challenged officer, decide on the objection.

(3) If the objection is allowed by one-half or more of the votes of the members entitled to vote, the objection shall be allowed, and the member objected to shall retire, and his vacancy may be filled in the prescribed manner, by another officer subject to the same right of the accused to object.

(4) Where no challenge is made. or when a challenge has been made and disallowed, or the place of every officer successfully challenged has been filled by another officer to whom no objection is made or allowed, the court shall proceed with the trial.

75. Oaths of member, Law Officer and witness.

(1) An oath or affirmation in the prescribed manner shall be administered to every member of a Coast Guard Court and to the Law Officer or as the case may be, the officer approved under and Section 73, before the commencement of the trial.

(2) [1][Every person] giving evidence before a Coast Guard Court shall be examined after being duly sworn or affirmed in the prescribed form.

(3) The provisions of sub-section (2) shall not apply where the witness is a child under twelve years of age and the Coast Guard Court is of opinion that though the witness understands the duty of speaking the truth, he does not understand the nature of an oath or affirmation.

76. Voting by members.

(1) Subject to the provisions of sub-sections (2) and (3), every decision of a Coast Guard Court shall be passed by an absolute majority of votes; and where there is an equality of votes on either the finding or the sentence, the decision shall be in favour of the accused.

(2) No sentence of death shall be passed by a Coast Guard Court without the concurrence of at least two-thirds of the members of the court.

(3) In matters, other than a challenge or the finding or sentence, the presiding officer shall have a casting vote.

77. General rule as to evidence. The Indian Evidence Act, 1872 (1 of 1872), shall, subject to the provisions of this Act, apply to all proceedings before a Coast Guard Court.

78. Judicial notice. A Coast Guard Court may take judicial notice of any matter within the general knowledge of the members as officers of the Coast Guard.

79. Summoning of witnesses.

(1) The convening authority, the presiding officer of a Coast Guard Court, the Law Officer or, as the case may be, the officer approved under Section 73 or the Commanding Officer of the accused person may, by summons under his hand, require the attendance, at a time and place to be mentioned in the summons, of any person either to give evidence or to produce any document or other thing.

(2) In the case of a witness who is subject to this Act, the summons shall be sent to his Commanding Officer and such officer shall serve it upon him accordingly.

(3) In the case of any other witness, the summons shall be sent to the Magistrate within whose jurisdiction he may be, or resides, and such Magistrate shall give effect to the summons as if the witness were required in the court of such a Magistrate.

(4) When a witness is required to produce any particular document or other thing in his possession or power, the summons shall describe it with reasonable precision.

80. Documents exempted from production.

(1) Nothing in Section 79 shall be deemed to affect the operation of Sections 123 and 124 of the Indian Evidence Act, 1872 (1 of 1872), or to apply to any letter,

postcard, telegram or other document in the custody of the postal or telegraph authorities.

(2) If any document in such custody is, in the opinion of any Chief Judicial Magistrate, Chief Metropolitan Magistrate, Court of Session or High Court, wanted for the purpose of any Coast Guard Court, such Magistrate or Court may require the postal or telegraph authorities, as the case may be, to deliver such document to such person as such Magistrate or Court may direct.

(3) If any such document is, in the opinion of any other Magistrate or of any Commissioner of Police or District Superintendent of Police wanted for any such purpose, he may require the postal or telegraph authorities, as the case may be, to cause such search to be made for, and to detain such document pending the orders of any such Chief Judicial Magistrate, Chief Metropolitan Magistrate, Court of Session or High Court.

81. Commissions for examination of witnesses.

(1) Whenever, in the course of a trial by a Coast Guard Court, it appears to the court that the examination of a witness is necessary for the ends of justice, and that the attendance of such witness cannot be procured without an amount of delay, expense or inconvenience which, in the circumstances of the case, would be unreasonable, such court may address the Chief Law Officer in order that a commission to take the evidence of such witness may be issued.

(2) The Chief Law Officer may then, if he thinks necessary, issue a commission to any Metropolitan Magistrate or Judicial Magistrate of the first class, within the local limits of whose jurisdiction such witness resides, to take the evidence of such witness.

(3) The Magistrate to whom the commission is issued, or, if he is the Chief Metropolitan Magistrate or Chief Judicial Magistrate, he or such Metropolitan Magistrate or Judicial Magistrate of the first class as he appoints in this behalf shall proceed to the place where the witness is, or shall summon the witness before him and shall take down his evidence in the same manner, and may, for this purpose, exercise the same powers, as in the trials of warrant-cases under the Code of Criminal Procedure, 1973 (2 of 1974).

(4) When the witness resides in any place outside India, the commission may be issued in the form and manner specified in sub-section (3) of Section 285 of the Code of Criminal Procedure, 1973 (2 of 1974).

82. Examination of a witness on commission.

(1) The prosecutor and the accused person in any case in which a commission is issued under Section 81 may respectively forward any interrogatories in writing which the court may think relevant to the issue, and the Magistrate executing the commission shall examine the witness upon such interrogatories.

(2) The prosecutor and the accused person may appear before such Magistrate by counsel, or except in the case of an accused person in custody, in person, and may examine, cross-examine and re-examine, as the case may be, the said witness.

(3) After a commission issued under Section 81 has been duly executed, it shall be returned together with the deposition of the witness examined thereunder to the Chief Law Officer.

(4) On receipt of a commission, and deposition returned under sub-section (3), the Chief Law Officer shall forward the same to the Coast Guard Court at whose instance the commission was issued or, if such court has been dissolved, to any other court convened for the trial of the accused person; and the commission, the return thereto and the deposition shall be open to inspection by the prosecutor and the accused person, and may subject to all just exceptions, be read in evidence in the case by either the prosecutor or the accused, and shall form part of the proceedings of the court.

(5) In every case in which a commission is issued under Section 81, the trial may be adjourned for a specified time reasonably sufficient for the execution and return of the commission.

83. Alternative findings. If an accused is charged before a Coast Guard Court with one offence and it appears in evidence that he committed a different offence, he may be convicted of the offence which he is shown to have committed although he was not charged with it.

84. Presumption as to signatures. In any proceeding under this Act, any application, certificate, warrant, reply or other document purporting to be signed by an officer in the service of the Government shall, on production, be presumed to have been duly signed by the person by whom and in the character in which it purports to have been signed, until the contrary is shown.

85. Enrolment paper.

(1) Any enrolment paper purporting to be signed by an enrolling officer shall, in proceedings under this Act, be evidence of the person enrolled having given the answers to questions which he is therein represented as having given.

(2) The enrolment of such person may be proved by the production of the original or a copy of his enrolment paper purporting to be certified to be a true copy by the officer having the custody of the enrolment paper.

86. Presumption as to certain documents.

(1) A letter, return or other document respecting the service of any person in, or the dismissal or discharge of any person from, any unit or ship of the Coast Guard, or respecting the circumstances of any person not having served in, or belonged to, any unit or ship, if purporting to be signed by or on behalf of the Central Government or the Director-General, or by any prescribed officer, shall be evidence of the facts stated in such letter, return or other document.

(2) A Coast Guard List or Gazette purporting to be published by authority shall be evidence of the status and rank of the officers therein mentioned, and of any appointment held by them and of the unit or ship of the Coast Guard to which they belong.

(3) Where a record is made in the books of a ship in pursuance of this Act or any rule or otherwise in the discharge of official duties, and purports to be signed by the Commanding Officer or by the officer whose duty it is to make such record, such record shall be evidence of the facts therein stated.

(4) A copy of any record in the books of a ship purporting to be certified to be a true copy by the officer having custody of such books shall be evidence of such record.

(5) Where any person subject to this Act is being tried on a charge of desertion or of absence without leave, and such person has surrendered himself into the custody of any officer or other person subject to this Act or any unit or ship of the Coast Guard, or has been apprehended by such officer or person, a certificate purporting to be signed by such officer, or by the Commanding Officer of the unit or ship to which such person belongs, as the case may be, and stating the fact, date and place of such surrender or apprehension, and the manner in which he was dressed shall be evidence of the matters so stated.

(6) Where any person subject to this Act is being tried on a charge of desertion or of improperly leaving a ship or of absence without leave and such person has surrendered himself into the custody of, or has been apprehended by, a police officer not below the rank of an officer in charge of a police station, a certificate purporting to be signed by such police officer and stating the fact, date and place of such surrender or apprehension and the manner in which he was dressed shall be evidence of the matters so stated.

(7) Any document purporting to be a report under the hand of a Chemical Examiner or Assistant Chemical Examiner to Government upon any matter or thing duly submitted to him for examination or analysis and report, may be used as evidence in any proceeding under this Act.

EXPLANATION: In this Section, the term"books of a ship" shall include any official book, document or list purporting to contain the name or names of persons appointed to the ship.

87. Evidence of previous convictions and general character.

(1) When any person subject to this Act has been convicted by a Coast Guard Court of any offence, such court may inquire into, and receive, and record evidence of any previous convictions of such person, either by a Coast Guard Court or by a criminal court, or any previous award of punishment under Section 57, and may further inquire into and record the general character of such person and such other matters as may be prescribed.

(2) Evidence received under this Section may be either oral, or in the shape of entries in, or certified extracts from, books of Coast Guard Courts or other official records; and it shall not be necessary to give notice before trial to the person tried, that evidence as to his previous convictions or character will be received.

88. Lunacy of accused.

(1) Whenever, in the course of a trial by a Coast Guard Court, it appears to the court that the person charged is by reason of unsoundness of mind incapable of making his defence, or that he committed the act alleged but was by reason

of unsoundness of mind incapable of knowing the nature of the act or knowing that it was wrong or contrary to law, the court shall record a finding accordingly.

(2) The presiding officer of the Coast Guard Court shall forthwith report the case to the convening authority.

(3) The convening authority to whom the finding of a Coast Guard Court is reported under sub-section (2) shall order the accused person to be kept in custody in the prescribed manner and shall report the case for the orders of the Central Government.

(4) On receipt of a report under sub-section (3), the Central Government may order the accused person to be detained in a lunatic asylum or other suitable place of safe custody.

89. Subsequent fitness of lunatic accused for trial. Where any accused person, having been found by reason of unsoundness of mind to be incapable of making his defence, is in custody or under detention under Section 88, any officer prescribed in this behalf, may -

(a) if such person is in custody under sub-section (3) of Section 88, on the report of a medical officer that he is capable of making his defence, or

(b) if such person is detained in jail under sub-section (4) of Section 88, on a certificate of the Inspector-General of Prisons, and if such person is detained in a lunatic asylum under the said sub-section, on a certificate of any two or more of the visitors of such asylum and if he is detained in any other place under that sub-section, on a certificate of the prescribed authority, that he is capable of making his defence, take steps to have such person tried by the same or another Coast Guard Court for the offence with which he was originally charged, or, if the offence is a civil offence, by a criminal court.

90. Transmission to Central Government of orders under Section 89. A copy of every order made by an officer under Section 89 for the trial of the accused shall forthwith be sent to the Central Government.

91. Release of lunatic accused. Where any person is in custody under sub-section (3) of Section 88 or under detention under sub-section (4) of that Section -

(a) if such person is in custody under the said sub-section (3), on the report of the medical officer, or

(b) if such person is detained under the said sub-section (4), on a certificate from any of the authorities mentioned in clause (b) of Section 89 that in the judgment of such officer or authority such person may be released without danger of his doing injury to himself or to any other person, the Central Government may order that such person be released or detained in custody, or transferred to a public lunatic asylum if he has not already been sent to such asylum.

92. Delivery of lunatic accused to relatives. Where any relative or friend of any person who is in custody under sub-section (3) of Section 88 or under detention under sub-section (4) of that Section desires that he should be delivered to his care and custody, the Central Government may, upon application by such relative or friend and, on his giving security to the satisfaction of that Government that the person delivered shall be properly taken care of, and, prevented from doing injury to himself or to any other person, and be produced for the inspection of such officer, and at such times and places, as the Central Government may direct, order such person to be delivered to such relative or friend.

93. Order for custody and disposal of property pending trial. When any property regarding which any offence appears to have been committed, or which appears to have been used for the commission of any offence, is produced before a Coast Guard Court during a trial, the court may make such order as it thinks fit for the proper custody of such property pending the conclusion of the trial, and if the property is subject to speedy or natural decay may, after recording such evidence as it thinks necessary, order it to be sold or otherwise disposed of.

94. Order for disposal of property regarding which offences committed.

(1) After the conclusion of a trial before a Coast Guard Court, an officer not below the rank of a Deputy Inspector-General within whose command the trial was held, may make such order as he thinks fit for the disposal by destruction, confiscation, delivery to any person claiming to be entitled to possession thereof, or otherwise, of any property or document produced before the court or in its custody, or regarding which any offence appears to have been committed or which has been used for the commission of any offence.

(2) Where any order has been made under sub-section (1) in respect of property regarding which an offence appears to have been committed, a copy of such order signed, and certified by the authority making the same may, whether the trial was held within India or not, be sent to a Magistrate within whose jurisdiction such property for the time being is situated, and such Magistrate shall thereupon cause the order to be carried out into effect as if it were an order passed by him under the provisions of the Code of Criminal Procedure, 1973 (2 of 1974).

(3) In this Section, the term “property” includes, in the case of property regarding which an offence appears to have been committed, not only such property as has been originally in the possession.

95. Powers of Coast Guard Court in relation to proceedings under this Act. Any trial by a Coast Guard Court under the provisions of this Act shall be deemed to be a judicial proceeding within the meaning of Sections 193 and 228 of the Indian Penal Code (45 of 1860) and the Coast Guard Court shall be deemed to be a court within the meaning of Sections 345 and 346 of the Code of Criminal Procedure, 1973 (2 of 1974).

CHAPTER - IX : EXECUTION AND SUSPENSION OF SENTENCES

96. Form of sentence of death. In awarding a sentence of death, a Coast Guard Court shall, in its discretion, direct that the offender shall suffer death by being hanged by the neck until he be dead or shall suffer death by being shot to death.

97. Interim custody until execution of sentence of death. A person sentenced to death may be detained in Coast Guard custody or may be removed to a civil prison to be kept in custody until further orders are received from the Central Government, the Director-General or the convening authority of the Coast Guard Court by which he was sentenced to death or other prescribed officer, and the order of the Central Government, the Director-General or the convening authority or such officer shall be sufficient warrant for detaining the person in custody.

98. Execution of sentence of death.

(1) When a sentence of death is to be executed, the Director-General or the convening authority or the prescribed officer shall give directions as to the time, place and manner in which such sentence is to be carried out and the order of such officer or authority in the prescribed form shall be sufficient warrant for the execution of such sentence.

(2) There shall be attached to the prescribed form, an order of the Central Government certifying the confirmation of the sentence by the Central Government.

99. Commencement of sentence of imprisonment or detention. Whenever any person is sentenced under this Act to imprisonment or detention, the term of the sentence shall be reckoned to commence on the date on which the sentence was awarded.

100. Execution of sentence of imprisonment.

(1) Whenever any sentence of imprisonment is passed under this Act or whenever any sentence of death is commuted to imprisonment, the presiding officer of the Coast Guard Court which passed the sentence or such other officer as may be prescribed shall direct that the sentence shall be carried out by confinement in a civil prison.

(2) When a direction has been made under sub-section (1), the Commanding Officer of the person under sentence or such other officer as may be prescribed shall forward a warrant in the prescribed form to the officer in charge of the prison in which such person is to be confined and shall arrange for his despatch to such prison with the warrant.

101. Temporary custody of offender. Where a sentence of imprisonment is directed to be undergone in a civil prison, the offender may be kept in Coast Guard custody or in any other fit place, till such time as it is possible to send him to a civil prison.

102. Conveyance of prisoner from place to place. A person under sentence of imprisonment may during his conveyance from place to place, or when on board a ship, aircraft or otherwise, be subject to such restraint as is necessary for his safe conduct and removal.

103. Communication of certain orders to prison officers. Whenever an order is duly made under this Act setting aside or varying any sentence, order or warrant under which any person is confined in a civil prison, a warrant in accordance with such order shall be forwarded by the officer making the order or his staff officer or such person as may be prescribed, to the officer in charge of the prison in which such person is confined.

104. Execution of sentence of fine. When a sentence of fine is imposed by a Coast Guard Court under Section 53, a copy of such sentence signed and certified by the presiding officer of the court may be sent to any Magistrate in India and such Magistrate shall thereupon cause the fine to be recovered in accordance with the provisions of the Code of Criminal Procedure, 1973 (2 of 1974), as if it were a sentence of fine imposed by such Magistrate.

105. Informality or error in the order or warrant. Whenever any person is sentenced to imprisonment under this Act, and is undergoing the sentence in any place or manner in which he might be confined under a lawful order or warrant in pursuance of this Act, the confinement of such person shall not be deemed to be illegal only by reason of any informality or error in, or as respects the order, warrant or other document, or the authority by which, or in pursuance whereof such person was brought into, or is confined in any such place, and any such order, warrant or document may be amended accordingly.

106. Imprisonment or detention of offender already under sentence. Whenever a sentence is passed by a Coast Guard Court on a person already under sentence either of imprisonment or detention passed on him under this Act for a former offence, the court may award a sentence of imprisonment or detention for the offence for which he is under trial to commence at the expiration of the sentence of imprisonment or detention to which he has been previously sentenced:

> *PROVIDED that so much of any term of detention imposed on a person by a sentence in pursuance of this Section as will prolong the total term of detention beyond two years shall be deemed to be remitted.*

107. Suspension of sentence of imprisoument or detention.

(1) Where a person subject to this Act is sentenced to imprisonment or detention, the Central Government, the Director-General, the Commanding Officer imposing the sentence or any prescribed officer may suspend the sentence whether or not the offender has already been committed to prison or to Coast Guard custody.

(2) The authority or officer specified in sub-section (1) may, in the case of an offender so sentenced, direct that until the orders, of such authority or officer have been obtained, the offender shall not be committed to prison or to Coast Guard custody.

(3) The powers conferred by sub-sections (1) and (2) may be exercised in the case of any such sentence which has been reduced or commuted.

108. Release on suspension. Where a sentence is suspended under Section 107, the offender shall forthwith be released from custody.

109. Computation of period of suspension. Any period during which the sentence is under suspension shall be reckoned as part of the term of such sentence.

110. Order after suspension. The authority or officer specified in Section 107 may, at any time while a sentence is suspended, order-

(a) that the offender be committed to undergo the unexpired portion of the sentence; or

(b) that the sentence be remitted.

111. Reconsideration of case after suspension.

(1) Where a sentence has been suspended, the case may at any time, and shall at intervals of not more than four months, be reconsidered by the authority or officer specified in Section 107, or by any officer not below the rank of a Deputy Inspector-General duly authorised by the authority or officer specified in Section 107.

(2) Where on such reconsideration by the officer so authorised it appears to him that the conduct of offender since his conviction has been such as to justify a remission of the sentence, he shall refer the matter to the authority or officer specified in Section 107.

112. Fresh sentence after suspension. Where an offender, while a sentence on him is suspended under this Act, is sentenced for any other offence, then-

(a) if the further sentence is also suspended under this Act the sentence shall run concurrently;

(b) if the further sentence is for a period of three months or more and is not suspended under this Act, the offender shall also be committed to prison or Coast Guard custody for the unexpired portion of the previous sentence, but both sentences shall run concurrently; and

(c) if the further sentence is for a period of less than three months and is not suspended under this Act, the offender shall be so committed on that sentence only, and the previous sentence shall, subject to any order which may be passed under Section 110 or Section 111 continue to be suspended.

113. Scope of power of suspension. The powers conferred by Sections 107 and 110 shall be in addition to, and not in derogation of, the power of mitigation, remission and commutation.

114. Effect of suspension and remission on dismissal.

(1) Where in addition to any other sentence, the punishment of dismissal has been awarded under this Act and such other sentence is suspended under Section 107, then, such dismissal shall not take effect until so ordered by the authority or officer specified in Section 107.

(2) If such other sentence is remitted under Section 110, the punishment of dismissal shall also be remitted.

CHAPTER - X : CHIEF LAW OFFICER AND LAW OFFICERS

115. Appointment of Chief Law Officer and Law Officers.

(1) There shall be appointed by the Central Government, a chief Law Officer and as many Law Officers as the Central Government may deem necessary.

(2) A person shall not be qualified for appointment as Chief Law Officer unless he-

- (a) is a citizen of India; and
- (b) has for at least ten years held a judicial office in the territory of India; or
- (c) has for at least ten years been an advocate of a High Court or two or more such Courts in succession:

PROVIDED that the Central Government may, if it is of opinion that it is necessary or expedient so to do in the exigencies of service, relax, for reasons to be recorded in writing, the qualification specified in clause (b) or clause (c) in respect of any person.

(3) A person shall not be qualified for appointment as Law Officer unless he-

(a) is a citizen of India, and

(b) is qualified for enrolment as an advocate of a High Court.

EXPLANATION. For the purposes of this Section -

(a) in computing the period during which a person has been an advocate of a High Court, there shall be included any period during which the person has held a judicial office after he became an advocate;

(b) the expression "judicial office" shall be deemed to include the post of Law Officer.

116. Functions of Chief Law Officer.

(1) It shall be the duty of the Chief Law Officer to perform such duties of a legal and judicial character pertaining to the Coast Guard as may, from time to time, be referred or assigned to him by the Central Government or the Director-General, and to discharge the functions conferred on him by or under this Act.

(2) The functions of the Chief Law Officer shall, in his absence or otherwise, be performed by such Law Officer as may be designated in this behalf by the Director-General.

CHAPTER - XI : JUDICIAL REVIEW OF PROCEEDINGS OF COAST GUARD COURTS

117. Judicial review by the Chief Law Officer.

(1) All proceedings of trials by Coast Guard Courts shall be reviewed by the Chief Law Officer either on his own motion or on application made to him within the prescribed time by any person aggrieved by any sentence or finding, and the Chief Law Officer shall transmit the report of such review together with such recommendations as may appear to him just and proper to the Director-General for his consideration and for such action as the Director-General may think fit.

(2) Where any person aggrieved has made an application under sub-section (1), the Chief Law Officer may, if the circumstances of the case so require, give him an opportunity of being heard either in person or through a legal practitioner or an officer of the Coast Guard.

118. Consideration by the Director General.

(1) On receipt of the report and recommendations, if any, under Section 117, the Director-General shall in all cases of sentences of death, and in all cases where the Coast Guard Court is convened by the Central Government, and

may, in other cases, transmit the proceedings and the report to the Central Government together with such recommendations as he may deem fit to make.

(2) Nothing in Section 117 or this Section shall authorise the Chief Law Officer or the Director-General to make any recommendation for setting aside, or the Central Government to set aside, an order of acquittal passed under this Act.

CHAPTER - XII : MODIFICATION OF FINDINGS AND SENTENCES, PARDONS, COMMUTATION AND REMISSION OF SENTENCES

119. Petitions to Central Government or Director-General against findings and sentences. Any person subject to this Act who considers himself aggrieved by a finding or sentence of any Coast Guard Court may present a petition to the Central Government or to the Director-General, and the Central Government or the Director-General, as the case may be, may pass such orders thereon as it or he may think fit.

120. Powers of Central Government and Director-General in respect of findings and sentences.

(1) Where any person is tried under the provisions of this Act, the Central Government or the Director-General may, in the case of a conviction -

(a) set aside the finding and sentence and acquit or discharge the accused or order him to be retried; or

(b) alter the finding without modifying the sentence if such sentence may be legally passed on the altered finding; or

(c) with or without altering the finding, reduce the sentence or commute the punishment awarded for any punishment inferior in scale; or

(d) either with or without conditions, pardon the person or remit the whole or any part of the punishment awarded; or

(e) with or without conditions release the person on parole: PROVIDED that a sentence of imprisonment shall not be commuted for a sentence of detention for a term exceeding the term of imprisonment awarded:

PROVIDED further that nothing in this sub-section shall authorise the Central Government or the Director-General to enhance the sentence.

(2) Any sentence modified under the provisions of sub-section (1) shall be carried into execution as if it had been originally passed.

(3) If any condition on which a person has been pardoned or has been released on parole or a punishment has been remitted is in the opinion of the authority which granted the pardon, release or remission not fulfilled, such authority may cancel the pardon or release or remission and thereupon the sentence awarded shall be carried into effect as if such pardon, release or remission had not been granted:

PROVIDED that in the case of a person sentenced to imprisonment or detention, such person shall undergo only the unexpired portion of the sentence.

CHAPTER - XIII : MISCELLANEOUS

121. Powers and duties conferrable and imposable on members of the Coast Guard.

(1) The Central Government may, by general or special order published in the Official Gazette, direct that, subject to such conditions and limitations, and within the local limits of such inland area adjoining the coast of India, as may be specified in the order, any member of the Coast Guard may -

(i) for the purpose of prevention of any offence punishable under the Passport (Entry into India) Act, 1920 (34 of 1920), the Emigration Act, 1922 (7 of 1922), the Registration of Foreigners Act, 1939 (16 of 1939), the Foreigners Act, 1946 (31 of 1946), the Merchant Shipping Act, 1958 (44 of 1958), the Customs Act, 1962 (52 of 1962), the Passports Act, 1967 (15 of 1967), the Foreign Exchange Regulation Act, 1973 (46 of 1973), or the Territorial Waters, Continental Shelf, Exclusive Economic Zone and other Maritime Zones Act, 1976 (80 of 1976), or of any cognizable offence punishable under any other Central Act; or

(ii) for the purpose of apprehending any person who has committed any offence referred to in clause (i), exercise or discharge such of the powers or duties under that Act or any other Central Act as may be specified in the said order, being the powers and duties which, in the opinion of the Central Government, an officer of the corresponding or lower rank is by that or such other Act empowered to exercise or discharge for the said purposes.

(2) The Central Government may, by general or special order published in the Official Gazette, direct, with the concurrence of the State Government concerned, that any of the powers or duties which may be exercised or discharged under a State Act by a police officer may, subject to such conditions and limitations, and within the local limits of such inland area adjoining the coast of India, as may be specified in the order, be exercised or discharged by a member of the Coast Guard who, in the opinion of the Central Government, holds a corresponding or higher rank.

(3) The Central Government may, by general or special order published in the Official Gazette, direct that, subject to such conditions and limitations, and within the local limits of such area in any maritime zone of India, as may be specified in the order, any member of the Coast Guard may -

(i) for the purpose of prevention of any offence punishable under any enactment which extends for the time being to such area; or

(ii) for the purpose of apprehending any person who has committed any offence referred to in clause (i), exercise or discharge such of the powers or duties under that enactment, as may be specified in the said order, being the powers and duties which, in the opinion of the Central Government, an officer of the corresponding or lower rank is by that enactment empowered to exercise or discharge for the said purposes.

(4) Every order made under this Section shall be laid, as soon as may be after it is

made, before each House of Parliament, while it is in session, for a total period of thirty days which may be comprised in one session or in two or more successive sessions, and if, before the expiry of the session immediately following the session or the successive sessions aforesaid, both Houses agree in making any modification in the order or both Houses agree that the order should not be made, the order shall thereafter have effect only in such modified form or be of no effect, as the case may be; so, however, that any such modification or annulment shall be without prejudice to the validity of anything previously done under that order.

122. Protection for acts of members of the Coast Guard.

(1) In any suit or proceeding against any member of the Coast Guard for any act done by him in pursuance of a warrant or order of a competent authority. it shall be lawful for him to plead that such act was done by him under the authority of such warrant or order.

(2) Any such plea may be proved by the production of the warrant or order directing the act, and if it is so proved, the member of the Coast Guard shall thereupon be discharged from liability in respect of the act so done by him, notwithstanding any defect in the jurisdiction of the authority which issued such warrant or order.

(3) Notwithstanding anything contained in any other law for the time being in force, any legal proceeding (whether civil or criminal) which may lawfully be brought against any member of the Coast Guard for anything done or intended to be done under the powers conferred by, or in pursuance of any provision of this Act or the rules, shall be commenced within three months after the act complained of was committed and not otherwise, and notice in writing of such proceeding and of the cause thereof shall be given to the defendant or his superior officer at least one month before the commencement of such proceeding.

123. Power to make rules.

(1) The Central Government may, by notification, make rules for the purpose of carrying into effect the provisions of this Act.

(2) In particular, and without prejudice to the generality of the foregoing power, such rules may provide for -

- (a) the constitution, governance, command and discipline of the Coast Guard;
- (b) the enrolment of persons to the Coast Guard and the recruitment of other members of the Coast Guard;
- (c) the conditions of service (including service privileges and deductions from pay and allowances) of members of the Coast Guard;
- (d) the rank, precedence, powers of command and authority of the officers, subordinate officers and other enrolled persons;
- (e) the removal, retirement, release or discharge from the service of officers, subordinate officers and other enrolled persons;
- (f) the purposes and other matters required to be prescribed under Section

13;

(g) the additional matters in respect of which the Coast Guard may undertake measures in the performance of its functions;

(h) the convening, constitution, adjournment, dissolution and sittings of Coast Guard Courts, the procedure to be observed in trials by such courts, the persons by whom an accused may be defended in such trials and the appearance of such persons thereat;

(i) the forms of orders to be made under the provisions of this Act relating to Coast Guard Courts and the awards and infliction of death, imprisonment and detention;

(j) the carrying into effect of sentences of Coast Guard Courts;

(k) any matter necessary for the purpose of carrying this Act into execution, as far as it relates to the investigation, arrest, custody, trial and punishment of offences triable or punishable under this Act;

(l) the procedure relating to the exercise of powers under Section 120;

(m) the ceremonials to be observed and marks of respect to be paid in the Coast Guard;

(n) any other matter which is to be, or may be prescribed or in respect of which this Act makes no provision or makes insufficient provision and provision is, in the opinion of the Central Government, necessary for the proper implementation of this Act.

(3) Every rule made under this Act shall be laid, as soon as may be after it is made, before each House of Parliament, while it is in session, for a total period of thirty days which may be comprised in one session or in two or more successive sessions, and if, before the expiry of the session immediately following the session or the successive sessions aforesaid, both Houses agree in making any modification in the rule or both Houses agree that the rule should not be made, the rule shall thereafter have effect only in such modified form or be of no effect, as the case may be; so, however, that any such modification or annulment shall be without prejudice to the validity of anything previously done under that rule.

❑❑❑

Endnotes

1. Subs. by Act 19 of 1988, S. 3 and Sch. II.

17

The Commanders-in-Chief (Change in Designation) Act, 1955

[3RD MAY, 1955]

AN ACT to amend certain enactments for the purpose of changing the design.

1. Short title and commencement.

(1) This Act may be called the Commanders-in-Chief (Change in Designation) Act, 1955.

(2) It shall come into force on such date[1] as the Central Government may, by notification in the Official Gazette, appoint.

2. [Amendment of certain enactments.] *Rep. by the Repealing and Amending Act, 1960 (58 of 1960), s. 2 and Sch. I.*

3. Construction of references to Commanders-in-Chief in enactments or instruments. Any reference, by whatever form of words, to the Commander-in-Chief of the regular Army, the Commander-in-Chief of the Indian Navy, and the Commander-in-Chief of the Air Force, in any law for the time being in force, or in any instrument or other document, shall be construed as a reference to the Chief of the Army Staff, the Chief of the Naval Staff, and the Chief of the Air Staff respectively.

[THE SCHEDULE]. *Rep. by the Repealing and Amending Act, 1960 (58.of 1960), s. 2 and Sch. I.*

Year 1	No. 2	Short title 3	Amendments 4
1881	13	The Fort William Act, 1881.	In section 3, for the words 'The Commander-in-Chief, Indian Army', the words 'The Chief of the Army Staff' shall be substituted.
1934	34	The Indian Navy (Discipline) Act, 1934.	Throughout the Act, for the words 'the Commander-in-Chief, Indian Navy' wherever they occur, the words 'the Chief of the Naval Staff' shall be substituted.
1948	31	The National Cadet Corps Act, 1948.	In sub-section (I) of Section 12, for clauses (e), (f) and (g), the following clauses shall be substituted, namely :- "(e) the Chief of the Army Staff, *ex officio*; (f) the Chief of the Naval Staff, *ex officio*; (g) the Chief of the Air Staff, *ex officio*;
1950	45	The Air Force Act, 1950.	(1) In Section 4, for clause (xiv), the following clause shall be substituted, namely:- (xiv) 'chief of the Air Staff' means the officer commanding the Air Force;". (2) Throughout the Act, unless otherwise expressly provided, for the words 'the Commander-in-Chief', wherever they occur, the words 'the Chief of the Air Staff' shall be substituted.
1950	46	The Army Act, 1950	(1) In Section 3, for clause (iv), the following clause shall be substituted, namely;- "(iv) 'Chief of the Army Staff' means the officer commanding the regular Army ;" (2) Throughout the Act, unless otherwise expressly provided, for the words 'the Commander-in-Chief', wherever they occur, the words 'the Chief of the Army Staff' shall be substituted.
1943	30	The Indian Military Nursing Service Ordinance, 1943.	In Sections 7 and 11, for the words 'Commander-in-Chief, Indian Army' the words 'Chief of the Army Staff', shall be substituted.

❑❑❑

Endnotes

1. 7th May, 1955, vide Notification No. S.R.O. 2/E, dated the 7th May, 1955, Gazette of India, 1955, Extraordinary, Pt. II, Sec. 4, p.3

18

The Explosive Act, 1884

AN ACT to regulate the manufacture, possession, use, sale, transport, import and export of explosives.

WHEREAS it is expedient to regulate the manufacture, possession, use, sale, transport and importation of explosives. It is hereby enacted as follows :

1. Short title.

(1) This Act may be called the Explosives Act, 1884; and

(2) It extends to the whole of India.

2. Commencement. This Act shall come into force on such day as the Central Government, by notification, in the Official Gazette appoints.

3. Repeal of portions of Act 12 of 1875. [*Rep. by Act X of 1889*].

4. Definitions. In Act, unless the context otherwise requires,

(a) *aircraft* means any machine which can derive support in the atmosphere from the reaction of the air, other than the reactions of the air against the earth's surface, and includes balloons, whether fixed or free, airships, kites, gliders and flying machines;

(b) *carriage* includes any carriage, wagon cart, truck, vehicle or other means of conveying goods or passengers by land, in whatever manner the same may be propelled;

(c) *District Magistrate* in relation to any area for which a Commissioner of Police has been appointed, means the Commissioner of Police thereof and includes

(i) any such Deputy Commissioner of Police, exercising jurisdiction over the whole or any part of such area, as may be specified by the State Government in this behalf in relation to such area or part; and

(ii) an additional District Magistrate;

(d) explosive means gunpowder, nitroglycerine, nitroglycol, gun cotton di-nitro-toluene, tri-nitro-toluene picric acid, di-nitro-phenol, tri-nitro-resorcinol (styphnic acid), cyclotrimethylene trinitramine, pentaerythritol-tetranitrate, totryl, nitro gannidine, lead azide, lead styphynate, fulminate of mercury or any other metal diazo-di-nitrophenol, coloured fires or any other substance whether a single chemical compoud or a mixture of substances, whether solid or liquid or gaseous used or manufactured with a view to produce a practical effect by explosion or pyrotechnic effect; and includes fog signals, fireworks, fuses, rockets, percussion-caps, detonators, cartridges, ammunition of all description and every adaptation of preparation of an explosive as defined in this clause;

(e) *export* means taking out of India to a place outside India by land, sea or air;

(f) *import* means to bring into India from a place outside India by land, sea or air;

(g) *master*,

(i) in relation to any vessel or aircraft means any person, other than a pilot, harbour master, assistant harbour master or berthing master, having for the time being the charge or control of such vessel or aircraft, as the case may be; and

(ii) in relation to any boat belonging to a ship, means the master of that ship;

(h) *manufacture* in relation to an explosive includes the process of

(1) dividing the explosive into its component parts or otherwise breaking up or unmaking the explosive, or making fit for use any damaged explosive, and

(2) re-making, altering or repairing the explosive;

(i) *prescribed* means prescribed by rules made under the Act;

(j) *vessel* includes any ship, boat, sailing vessel, or other description of vessel used in navigation whether propelled by cars or otherwise and anything made for the conveyance, mainly by water, of human beings or of goods and a caisson.

5. Power to make rules as to licensing of the manufacture, possession, use, sale, transport, import and export of explosives.

(1) The Central Government may for any part of India make rules consistent with this Act to regulate or prohibit, except under and in accordance with the conditions of a licence granted as provided by those rules, the manufacture, possession, sale, transport, import and export of explosives, or any specified class of explosives.

(2) Rules under this section may provide for all or any of the following among other matters, that is to say,

(a) the authority by which licences may be granted;

(b) the fees to be charged for licences, and the other sums (if any) to be paid for expenses by applicants for licences;

(c) the manner in which applications for licences must be made, and the matters to be specified in such applications;

(d) the form in which, and the conditions on and subject to which, licences must be granted;

(e) the period for which licences are to remain in force;

(ee) the authority to which appeals may be preferred under Section 6-F, the procedure to be followed by such authority and the period within which appeals shall be preferred, the fees to be paid in respect of such appeals and the circumstances under which such fees may be refunded;

(ee-a) the total quantity of explosives that a licensee can purchase in a given period of time;

(ee-b) the fees to be charged by the Chief Controller of Explosives or any officer authorised by him in this behalf, for services rendered in connection with the manufacture, transport, import or export of explosives;

(f) the exemption absolutely or subject to conditions of any explosives or any person or class of persons from the operation of the rules.

5-A. Persons, already in business in respect of certain explosives to carry on such business without licence fcr a certain period. Notwithstanding anything in Section 5 or in the rules made thereunder where, immediately before the commencement of the Indian Explosives (Amendment) Act, 1978, any person was carrying on the business or manufacture, sale, transport, import or export of any explosive for which no licence was required under this Act before its amendment by the Indian Explosives (Amendment) Act, 1978, then, such person shall be entitled to continue to carry on such business without licence in respect of such explosive :

(a) for a period of three months from the date of such commencement; or

(b) if before the expiry of the said period of three months, such person has made an application for grant of licence under this Act for such licences in such explosive, until the final disposal of his application, whichever is later.

6. Power for Central Government to prohibit the manufacture, possession or importation of specially dangerous explosives.

(1) Notwithstanding anything in the rules under the last foregoing section, the Central Government may from time to time, by notification in the Official Gazette, prohibit, either absolutely or subject to conditions, the manufacture, possession or importation of any explosive which is of so dangerous a character that, in the opinion of the Central Government, it is expedient for the public safety to issue the notification.

(2) The officers of sea customs at every port shall have the same power in respect of any explosive with regard to the importation of which a notification has been issued under this section and the vessel containing the explosive, as they have for the time being in respect of any article, the importation of which is prohibited

or regulated by the law relating to sea customs and the vessel containing the same, and the enactments for the time being in force relating to sea customs or any such article or vessel shall apply accordingly.

(3) Any person manufacturing, possessing or importing an explosive in contravention of a notification issued under this section shall be punishable with imprisonment for a term which may extend to three years or with fine which may extend to five thousand rupees or with both and in the case of importation by water, the owner and master of the vessel in which the explosive is imported shall, in the absence of reasonable excuse, each be punishable with fine which may extend to five thousand rupees.

6-A. Prohibition of manufacture, possession, sale, or transport of explosive by young persons and certain other persons. Notwithstanding anything in the foregoing provisions of this Act,

(a) no person,
   (i) who has not completed the age of eighteen years, or
   (ii) who has been sentenced on conviction of any offence involving violence or moral turpitude for a term of not less than six months, at any time during a period of five years after the expiration of the sentence, or
   (iii) who has been ordered to execute under Chapter VIII of the Code of Criminal Procedure, 1973 (2 of 1974), a bond for keeping the peace or for good behaviour, at any time during the term of the bond, or
   (iv) whose licence under this Act has been cancelled, whether before or after the commencement of the Indian Explosives (Amendment) Act, 1978, for contravention of the provisions of this Act or of the rules made thereunder, at any time during a period of five years from the date of cancellation of such licence, shall
      (1) manufacture, sell, transport, import or export any explosive, or
      (2) possess any such explosive as the Central Government may, having regard to the nature thereof, by notification in the Official Gazette, specify;

(b) no person shall sell, deliver or despatch any explosive to a person whom he knows or has reason to believe at the time of such sale, delivery or despatch,
   (i) to be prohibited under clause (a) to manufacture, sell, transport, import, export or possess such explosive, or
   (ii) to be of unsound mind.

6-B. Grant of licences.

(1) Where a person makes an application for licence under Section 5, the authority prescribed in the rules made under that section for grant of licences (hereinafter referred to in this Act as the licensing authority), after making such inquiry, if any, as it may consider necessary, shall, subject to the other provisions of this Act, by order in writing either grant the licence or refuse to grant the same.

(2) The licensing authority shall grant a licence

(a) where it is required for the purpose of manufacture of explosive if the licensing authority is satisfied that the person by whom licence is required

(i) possesses technical know-how and experience in the manufacture of explosives; or

(ii) has in his employment or undertaken to employ a person or persons possessing such technical know-how and experience; or

(b) where it is required for any other purpose, if the licensing authority is satisfied that the person by whom licence is required has a good reason for obtaining the same.

6-C. Refusal of licences.

(1) Notwithstanding anything contained in Section 6-B, the licensing authority shall refuse to grant a licence

(a) where such licence is required in respect of any prohibited explosive; or

(b) where such licence is required by a person whom the licensing authority has reason to believe

(i) to be prohibited by this Act or by any other law for the time being in force to manufacture, possess, sell, transport, import or export any explosive, or

(ii) to be of unsound mind, or

(iii) to be for any reason unfit for a licence under this Act; or

(c) where the licensing authority deems it necessary for the security of the public peace or for public safety to refuse to grant such licence.

(2) Where the licensing authority refuses to grant a licence to any person, it shall record in writing the reasons for such refusal and furnish to that person on demand a brief statement of the same unless in any case the licensing authority is of opinion that it will not be in the public interest to furnish such statement.

6-D. Licensing authority competent to impose conditions in addition to prescribed conditions. A licence granted under Section 6-B may contain in addition to prescribed conditions such other conditions as may be considered necessary by the licensing authority in any particular case.

6-E. Variation, suspension and revocation of licences.

(1) The licensing authority may vary the conditions subject to which a licence has been granted except such of them as have been prescribed and may for that purpose require the holder of licence by notice in writing to deliver-up the licence to it within such time as may be specified in the notice.

(2) The licensing authority may, on the application of the holder of a licence, also vary the conditions of the licence except such of them as have been prescribed.

(3) The licensing authority may, by order in writing, suspend a licence for such period as it thinks fit or revoke a licence,

(a) if the licensing authority is satisfied that the holder of the licence is prohibited by this Act or by other law for the time being in force to manufacture, possess, sell, transport, import or export any explosive, or is of unsound mind, or is for any reason unfit for a licence under this Act; or

(b) if the licensing authority deems it necessary for the security of the public peace or for public safety to suspend or revoke the licence; or

(c) if the licence was obtained by the suppression of material information or on the basis of wrong information provided by the holder of the licence or any other person on his behalf at the time of applying for the licence; or

(d) if any of the conditions of the licence has been contravened; or

(e) if the holder of the licence has failed to comply with a notice under sub-section (1) requiring him to deliver-up the licence.

(4) The licensing authority may also revoke a licence on the application of the holder thereof.

(5) Where the licensing authority makes an order varying the conditions of a licence under sub-section (1) or an order suspending or revoking a licence under sub-section (3), it shall record in writing the reasons therefor and furnish to the holder of the licence on demand a brief statement of the same unless in any case the licensing authority is of the opinion that it will not be in the public interest to furnish such statement.

(6) A court convicting the holder of a licence of any offence under this Act or the rules made thereunder may also suspend or revoke a licence :

PROVIDED that if the conviction is set aside on appeal or otherwise, the suspension or revocation shall become void.

(7) An order of suspension or revocation under sub-section (6) may also be made by an appellate court or by the High Court when exercising its powers of revision.

(8) The Central Government may, by order in the Official Gazette suspend or revoke, or direct any licensing authority to suspend or revoke, all or any licences granted under this Act throughout India or any part thereof.

(9) On the suspension or revocation of a licence under this section, the holder thereof shall without delay surrender the licence to the authority by whom it has been suspended or revoked or to such other authority as may be specified in this behalf in the order of suspension or revocation.

6-F. Appeals.

(1) Any person aggrieved by an order of the licensing authority refusing to grant a licence or varying the conditions of a licence or by an order of the licensing authority suspending or evoking a licence may prefer an appeal against that order to such authority (hereinafter referred to as the appellate authority) and within such period as may be prescribed:

PROVIDED that no appeal shall lie against an order made by, or under the direction of the Central Government.

(2) No appeal shall be admitted if it is preferred after the expiry of the period prescribed therefor :

PROVIDED that an appeal may be admitted after the expiry of the period prescribed therefor if the appellant satisfies the appellate authority that he had sufficient cause for not preferring the appeal within that period.

(3) The period prescribed for an appeal shall be computed in accordance with the provisions of the Limitation Act, 1963 (36 of 1963), with respect to the computation of periods of limitation thereunder.

(4) Every appeal under this section shall be made by a petition in writing and shall be accompanied by a brief statement of the reasons for the order appealed where such statement has been furnished to the appellant and by such fee as may be prescribed.

(5) In disposing of an appeal the appellate authority shall follow such procedure as may be prescribed :

PROVIDED that no appeal shall be disposed of unless the appellant has been given a reasonable opportunity of being heard.

(6) The order appealed against shall, unless the appellate authority conditionally or unconditionally directs otherwise, be in force pending the disposal of the appeal against such order.

(7) Every order of the appellate authority confirming, modifying or reversing the order appealed against shall be final.

7. Power to make rules conferring powers of inspection, search, seizure, detention, and removal.

(1) The Central Government may make rules consistent with this Act authorising any officer either by name or in virtue of his office

(a) to enter, inspect and examine any place, aircraft, carriage or vessel in which an explosive is being manufactured, possessed, used, sold, transported or imported under a licence granted under this Act, or in which he has reason to believe that an explosive has been or is manufactured, possessed, used, sold, transported, imported or exported, in contravention of this Act or of the rules made under this Act;

(b) to search for explosive therein;

(c) to take samples of any explosive found therein on payment of the value thereof; and

(d) to seize, detain and remove any explosive or ingredient thereof found therein and, if necessary, also destroy such explosive or ingredient.

(2) The provisions of the Code of Criminal Procedure, 1973 (2 of 1974) relating to searches under that Code shall, so far as the same are applicable, apply to searches by officers authorized by rules this section.

8. Notice of accidents.

(1) Whenever there occurs in or about, or in connection with, any place in which an explosive is manufactured, possessed or used, or any aircraft, carriage or

vessel either conveying an explosive or on or from which an explosive is being loaded or unloaded, any accident by explosion or by fire attended with loss of human life or serious injury to person or property, or of a description usually attended with such loss or injury, the occupier of the place, or the master of the aircraft or vessel or the person in charge of the carriage, as the case may be, shall within such time and in such manner as may be by rule prescribed, give notice thereof and of the attendant loss of human life or personal injury, if any, to the Chief Controller of Explosives in India and to the officer-in-charge of the nearest police station.

(2) [1][1] [* * *]

9. Inquiry into accidents.

(1) Where any accident such as is referred to in Section 8 occurs in or about or in connection with any place, aircraft, carriage or vessel under the control of any of Armed forces of the Union an inquiry into the causes of the accident shall be held by the naval, military or air force authority concerned, and where any such accident occurs in any other circumstances, the District Magistrate shall, in cases attended by loss of human life, or may, in any other case, hold or direct a Magistrate subordinate to him to hold, such an inquiry.

(2) Any person holding an inquiry under this section shall have all the powers of Magistrate in holding an inquiry into an offence under the Code of Criminal Procedure, 1973 (2 of 1974) and may exercise each of the powers conferred on any officer by rules under Section 7 as he may think it necessary or expedient to exercise for the purpose of the inquiry.

(3) The person holding an inquiry under this section shall make a report to the Central Government stating the causes of the accident and its circumstances.

(4) The Central Government may make rules -

  (a) to regulate the procedure at inquires under this section;

  (b) to enable the Chief Controller of Explosive in India to be present or represented at any such inquiry;

  (c) to permit the Chief Controller of Explosives in India or his representative to examine any witnesses at the inquiry;

  (d) to provide that where the Chief Controller of Explosives in India is not present or represented at any such inquiry, a report of the proceedings thereof shall be sent to him;

  (e) to prescribe the manner in which and the time within which notices referred to in Section 8 shall be given.

9-A. Inquiry into more serious accidents.

(1) The Central Government may, where it is of opinion, whether or not it has received the report of an inquiry under Section 9, that an inquiry of more formal character should be held into the causes of an accident such as is referred to in Section 8, appoint the Chief Controller of Explosives or any other

competent person to hold such inquiry, and may also appoint one or more persons possessing legal or special knowledge to act as assessors in such inquiry.

(2) Where the Central Government orders in an inquiry under this Section, it may also direct that any inquiry under Section 9 pending at the time shall be discontinued.

(3) The person appointed to hold an inquiry under this section, shall have all the powers of Civil Court under the Code of Civil Procedure, 1908 (V of 1980), for the purpose of enforcing the attendance of witnesses and compelling the production of documents and material objects; and every person required by such person as aforesaid to furnish any information shall be deemed to be legally bound so to do within the meaning of Section 176 of the Indian Penal Code (XLV of 1860).

(4) Any person holding an inquiry under this section may exercise such of the powers conferred on any officer by rules under Section 7 as he may think it necessary or expedient to exercise for the purposes of the inquiry.

(5) The person holding an inquiry under this section shall make a report to the Central Government stating the causes of the accident and its circumstances, and adding any observations which he or any of the assessors may think fit to make; and the Central Government shall cause every report so made to be published at such time and in such manner as it may think fit.

(6) The Central Government may make rules for regulating the procedure at inquiries under this section.

9-B. Punishment of certain offences.

(1) Whoever, in contravention of rules made under Section 5 or of the conditions of a licence granted under the said rules-

(a) manufactures, imports or exports any explosive shall be punishable with imprisonment for a term which may extend to three years, or with fine which may extend to five thousand rupees, or with both;

(b) possesses, uses, sells or transports any explosive shall be punishable with imprisonment for a term which may extend to two years or with fine which may extend to three thousand rupees or with both; and

(c) in any other case, with fine which may extend to one thousand rupees.

(2) Whoever in contravention of a notification issued under Section 6, manufactures, possesses or imports any explosive shall be punishable with imprisonment for a term which may extend to three years or with fine which may extend to five thousand rupees or with both; and in the case of importation by water, the owner and master of the vessel or in the case of importation by air, the owner and the master of the aircraft, in which the explosive is imported shall, in the absence of reasonable excuse, each to be punishable with fine which may extend to five thousand rupees.

(3) Whoever -

(a) manufactures, sells, transports, imports, exports or possesses any explosive in contravention of the provisions of clause (a) of Section 6; or

(b) sells, delivers or despatches any explosive in contravention of the provisions of Clause (b) of that section, shall be punishable with imprisonment for a term which may extend to three years or with fine or with both; or

(c) in contravention of the provisions of Section 8 fails to give notice of any accident shall be punishable -

(i) with fine which may extend to five hundred rupees, or

(ii) if the accident is attended by loss of human life, with imprisonment for a term which may which may extend to three months or fine or with both.

9-C. Offences by companies.

(1) Whenever an offence under this Act has been committed by a company, every person who at the time the offence was committed was in charge of, or was responsible to the company for the conduct of the business of the company, as well as the company, shall be deemed to be guilty of the offence and shall be liable to be proceeded against and punished accordingly :

PROVIDED that nothing contained in this sub-section shall render any such person liable to any punishment under this Act if he proves that the offence was committed without his knowledge and that he exercised all due diligence to prevent the commission of such offence.

(2) Notwithstanding anything contained in sub-section (1), where an offence under this Act has been committed by a company and it is proved that the offence has been committed with the consent or connivance of, or is attributable to any neglect on the part of, any director, manager, secretary or other officer of the company, such director, manager, secretary or other officer shall also be deemed to be guilty of that offence and shall be liable to be proceeded against and punished accordingly.

EXPLANATION: For the purposes of this section,

(a) *company* means any body corporate, and includes a firm or other association of individuals; and

(b) *director*, in relation to a firm, means a partner in the firm.

10. Forfeiture of explosives. When a person is convicted of an offence punishable under this Act, or the rules made under this Act, the court before which he is convicted may direct that the explosive, or ingredient of the explosive or the substance (if any) in respect of which the offence has been committed, or any part of that explosive, ingredient or substance, shall with the receptacles containing the same, be forfeited.

11. Distress of aircraft or vessel. Where the owner or master of any aircraft or vessel is adjudged under this Act to pay a fine for any offence committed with, or in relation to, that aircraft or vessel, the court may, in addition to any power it may have for the purpose of compelling payment of the fine, direct it to be levied by distress and sale of,

(a) the aircraft and its furniture or so much of the furniture, or

(b) the vessel and the tackle, apparel and furniture of such vessel or so much of the tackle, apparel and furniture thereof, as is necessary for the payment of the fine.

12. Abetment and attempts. Whoever abets, within the meaning of the Indian Penal Code (XLV of 1860), the commission of an offence punishable under this Act, or the rules made under this Act, or attempts to commit any such offence and in such attempt does any act towards the commission of the same, shall be punished as if he had committed the offence.

13. Power to arrest without warrant persons committing dangerous offences. Whoever is found committing any act for which he is punishable under this Act, or the rules under this Act, and which tends to cause explosion or fire in or about any place where an explosive is manufactured or stored, or any railway or port, or any carriage, aircraft or vessel may be apprehended without a warrant by a police officer or by the occupier of, or the agent or servant of, or other person authorised by the occupier of, that place or by any agent or servant of, or other person authorised by the Railway Administration or conservator of the port or officer in charge of the airport and be removed from the place where he is arrested and conveyed as soon as conveniently may be before a Magistrate.

14. Saving and power to exempt.

(1) Nothing in this Act, except Sections 8, 9 and 9-A, shall apply to the manufacture, possession, use transport or importation of any explosive -

(a) by any of Armed Forces of the Union and Ordnance Factories or other establishment or such Forces in accordance with rules or regulations made by the Central Government;

(b) by any person employed under the Central Government or under a State Government in execution of this Act.

(2) The Central Government may, by notification in the Official Gazette exempt, absolutely or subject to any such condition as it may think fit to impose, any explosive and any person or class of persons from all or any of the provisions of this Act or the rules made thereunder.

15. Saving of Indian Arms Act, 1878. Nothing under this Act shall affect the provisions of the Arms Act, 1959 (54 of 1959):

PROVIDED that an authority granting a licence under this Act for the manufacture, possession, sale, transport or importation of an explosive may, if empowered in this behalf by the rules under which the licence is granted, direct by an order in writing on the licence that it shall have the effect of a like licence granted under the said Indian Arms Act.

16. Saving as to liability under other law. Nothing in this Act or the rules under this Act shall prevent any person from being prosecuted under any other law for any act or omission which constitutes an offence against this Act or those rules, or from being liable under that other law to any other or higher punishment or penalty than that provided by this Act or those rules :

PROVIDED that a person shall not be punished twice for the same offence.

17. Extension of definition of explosive to other explosive substances. The Central Government may, from time to time, by notification in the Official Gazette, declare that any substance which appears to the Central Government to be specially dangerous to life or property, by reason either of its explosive properties or of any process in the manufacture thereof being liable to explosion, shall be deemed to be an explosive within the meaning of this Act, and the provisions of this Act (subject to such exceptions, limitations and restrictions as may be specified in the notification) shall accordingly extend to that substance in like manner as if it were included in the definition of the term explosive in this Act.

17-A. Power to delegate. The Central Government may, by notification in the Official Gazette, direct that any power to function which may be exercised or performed by it under this Act other than the power under Sections 5, 6, 6-A, 14 and 17 may, in relation to such matters and subject to such conditions, if any, as it may specify in the notification, be exercised or performed also by

(a) such officer or authority subordinate to the Central Government; or

(b) such State Government or such officer or authority subordinate to the State Government.

18. Procedure for making publication and confirmation of rules.

(1) An authority making rules under this Act shall, before making the rule, publish a draft of the proposed rules for the information of persons likely to be affected thereby.

(2) The publication shall be made in such manner as the Central Government, from time to time, by notification in the Official Gazette, prescribes.

(3) There shall be published with the draft a notice specifying date at or after which the draft will be taken into consideration.

(4) The authority making the rule, shall receive and consider any objection or suggestion which may be made by any person with respect to the draft before the date so specified.

(5) A rule made under this Act shall not take effect until it has been published in the Official Gazette.

(6) The publication in the Official Gazette of a rule purporting to be made under this Act shall be conclusive evidence that it has been duly made, and, if it requires sanction, that, it has been duly sanctioned.

(7) All powers to make rules conferred by this Act may be exercised from time to time as occasion requires.

(8) Every rule made under this Act shall be laid, as soon as may be after it is made, before each House of Parliament, while it is in session for a total period of thirty days which may be comprised in one session or in two or more successive sessions, and if, before the expiry of the session immediately following the session or the successive sessions aforesaid, both Houses agree in making

any modification in the rule or both Houses agree that the rule should not be made, the rule shall thereafter have effect only in such modified form or be of no effect, as the case may be; so, however, that any such modification or annulment shall be without prejudice to the validity of anything previously done under the rule.

❑❑❑

19

The Explosive Substances (Amendment) Act, 2001

Act No. 54 of 2001 [11th December, 2001]

AN ACT further to amend the Explosive Substances Act, 2001.

Be it enacted by Parliament in the Fifty-second Year of the Republic of India as follows:-

1. Short title and commencement.

(1) This Act may be called the Explosive Substances (Amendment) Act, 2001.

(2) It shall come into force on such date as the Central Government may, by notification in the Official Gazette, appoint.

2. Substitution of new sections for Sections 2 to 5. In the Explosive Substances Act, 1908 (6 of 1908) (hereinafter referred to as the principal Act), for Sections 2 to 5, the following sections shall be substituted, namely -

2A. Definitions. In this Act -

(a) the expression "explosive substance" shall be deemed to include any materials for making any explosive substance; also any apparatus, machine, implement or material used, or intended to be used, or adapted for causing, or aiding in causing, any explosion in or with any explosive substance; also any part of any such apparatus, machine or implement;

(b) the expression "special category explosive substance" shall be deemed to include research development explosive (RDX), penta erythritol tetra nitrate (PETN), high melting explosive (HMX), tri nitro toluene (TNT), low temperature plastic explosive (LPE), composition exploding (CE) 2, 4, 6 phenyl methyl nitramine or tetryl, OCTOL (mixture of high melting explosive and tri nitro toluene), plastic explosive kirkee-1 (PEK-1) and RDX TNT compounds and other similar type of explosive and a combination thereof and remote control devices causing explosion and any other substance and a combination thereof which the Central Government may, by notification in the Official Gazette, specify for the purposes of this Act.

3. Punishment for causing explosion likely to endanger life or property. Any person who unlawfully and maliciously causes by—

(a) any explosive substance an explosion of a nature likely to endanger life or to cause serious injury to property shall, whether any injury to person or property has been actually caused or not, be punished with imprisonment for life, or with rigorous mprisonment of either description which shall not be less than ten years, and shall also be liable to fine;

(b) any special category explosive substance an explosion of a nature likely to endanger life or to cause serious injury to property shall, whether any injury to person or property has been actually caused or not, be punished with death, or rigorous imprisonment for life, and shall also be liable to fine.

4. Punishment for attempt to cause explosion, or for making or keeping explosive with intent to endanger life or property. Any person who unlawfully and maliciously -

(a) does any act with intent to cause by an explosive substance or special category explosive substance, or conspires to cause by an explosive substance or special category explosive substance, an explosion of a nature likely to endanger life or to cause serious injury to property; or

(b) makes or has in his possession or under his control any explosive substance or special category explosive substance with intent by means thereof to endanger life, or cause serious injury to property, or to enable any other person by means thereof to ndanger life or cause serious injury to property in India, shall, whether any explosion does or does not take place and whether any injury to person or property has been actually caused or not, be punished -

  (i) in the case of any explosive substance, with imprisonment for life, or with imprisonment of either description for a term which may extend to ten years, and shall also be liable to fine;

  (ii) in the case of any special category explosive substance, with rigorous imprisonment for life, or with rigorous imprisonment for a term which may extend to ten years, and shall also be liable to fine.

5. Punishment for making or possessing explosives under suspicious circumstances. Any person who makes or knowingly has in his possession or under his control any explosive substance or special category explosive substance, under such circumstances as to give rise to a reasonable suspicion that he is not making it or does not have it in his possession or under his control for a lawful object, shall, unless he can show that he made it or had it in his possession or under his control for a lawful object, he punished,-

(a) in the case of any explosive substance, with imprisonment for a term which may extend to ten years, and shall also be liable to fine;

(b) in the case of any special category explosive substance, with rigorous imprisonment for life, or with rigorous imprisonment for a term which may extend to ten years, and shall also be liable to fine.'.

3. Amendment of Section 7.-In Section 7 of the principal Act, for the words "Central Government", the words "District Magistrate" shall be substituted.

❑❑❑

20

The Explosive Substances Act, 1908

[Act No. 6 of 1908] [8th June 1908]

AN ACT further to amend the law relating to explosive substances.

WHEREAS it is necessary further to amend the law relating to explosive substances;

It is hereby enacted as follows: -

2. Definition of "explosive substance. In this Act the expression "explosive substance" shall be deemed to include any materials for making any explosive substance; also any apparatus, machine, implement or material used or intended to be used, or adapted for causing, or aiding in causing, any explosion in or with any explosive substance; also any part of any such apparatus, machine or implement.

3. Punishment for causing explosion likely to endanger life or property. Any person who unlawfully and maliciously causes by any explosive substance an explosion of a nature likely to endanger life or to cause serious injury to property shall, whether any injury to person or property has been actually caused or not, be punished with transportation for life or any shorter terms, to which fine may be added.

4. Punishment for attempt to cause explosion, or for making or keeping explosives with intend to endanger life or property. Any person who unlawfully and maliciously -

(a) Does any act with intent to cause by an explosive substance or conspires to cause by an explosive substance, an explosion in India of a nature likely to endanger life or to cause serious injury to property; or

(b) Makes or has in his possession or under his control any explosive substance with intent by means thereof to endanger life, or cause serious injury to property in India, or to enable any other person by means thereof to endanger life or cause serious injury to property in India, shall, whether any explosion does or does not take place and whether any injury to person or property has been actually caused or not, be punished with transportation for at term which may extend to twenty years, to which fine may be added, or with imprisonment for a term which may extend to seven years to which fine may be added.

5. Punishment for making or possessing explosives under suspicious circumstances. Any person who makes or knowingly has in his possession or under his control any explosive substance, under such circumstances as to give rise to a reasonable suspicion that he is not making it or does not have it in his possession or under his control for a lawful object, shall, unless he can show that he made it or had it in his possession or under his control for a lawful object, be punishable with transportation for a term which may extend to fourteen years, to which fine may be added, or with imprisonment for a term which may extend to five years to which fine may be added.

6. Punishment of abettors. Any person who by the supply of or solicitation for money, the providing of premises, the supply of materials, or in any manner whatsoever, procures, counsels, aids, abets, or is accessory to, the commission of any offence under this Act shall be punished with the punishment provided for the offence.

7. Restriction on trial of offences. No Court shall proceed to the trial of any person for an offence against this Act except with the consent of the Central Government.

❑❑❑

21

The Indian Reserve Forces Act, 1888

ACT NO. 4 OF 1888 [AS ON 1955]

AN ACT to regulate *(Subs. by the A.O.1950, for Her Majesty's)* [the] Indian Reserve Forces.

WHEREAS it is expedient to provide for the government, discipline and regulation of *(Subs.by the A.O.1950, for "Her Majesty's")* the Indian Reserve Forces; It is hereby enacted as follows:—

1. Title and commencement.

(1) This Act may be called the Indian Reserve Forces Act, 1888; and

(2) It shall come into force on such day as the Central Government may, by notification in the Official Gazette, *(The Act came into force on the 26th May, 1888, see Gazette of India of same date, Pt. I, p. 239)* appoint in this behalf. *(Subs. by Act 12 of 1931, s.2, for the original section).*

2. Division of Reserve Forces into Regular and Supplementary Reserves. The Indian Reserve Forces shall consist of the Regular Reserve and the Supplementary Reserve]

3. Locality of Service of Reserves. *(The figure and brackets " (1)" were rep. by s.3, ibid)* A person belonging to the *(Subs. by s.3, ibid., for "Active Reserve")* [Indian Reserve Forces] shall bet liable to serve beyond the limits of *(Subs.by the A.O.1950, for "the Provinces")* [the territories comprised within Part A States and Part C States] as well as within those limits.

(Sub-section (2) rep. by s.3 of Act 12 of 1931)

4. Power to make rules for regulation of Reserve Forces. The Central Government may make rules and orders for the government, discipline and regulation of the Indian Reserve Forces.

5. Liability of Reserve Forces to military law. Subject to *(The words "the provision of s.3 with respect to persons belonging to the Garrison Reserve, and to" were rep. by s.4, ibid)* such rules and orders as may be made under Section 4, a person belonging to the Indian Reserve Forces shall, as an officer, or soldier, as the case may be, be subject to military law in the same manner and to the same extent as a person belonging to *(Subs.by the A.O 1950, for "Her Majesty's Indian Forces")* [the Regular Army].

6. Punishment of certain offences by persons belonging to Reserve Forces.

(1) If a person belonging to the Indian Reserve Forces—

(a) when required by or in pursuance of any rule or order under this Act to attend at any place, fails without reasonable excuse to attend in accordance with such requirement, or

(b) fails without reasonable excuse to comply with any such rules or order, or

(c) fraudulently obtains any pay or other sum contrary to any such rule or order, or he shall be liable—

(i) on conviction by a court-martial, to such punishment other than death, transportation or imprisonment for a term exceeding one year as such court is by the *(Subs.by Act 42 of 1953, s.4 and Sch. III, for "Indian Army Act, 1911")* [Army Act, 44 1950] empowered to award, or

(ii) on conviction by *(Ins. by Act 12 of 1931, s.5)* [a Presidency Magistrate or] a Magistrate of the first class, to imprisonment for a term which may extend, in the case of a first offence under this section, to six months, and, in the case of any subsequent offence thereunder, to one year.

(2) Where a person belonging to the Indian Reserve Forces is required by or in pursuance of any rule or order under this Act to attend at any place, a certificate purporting to be signed by an officer appointed by such a rule or order in this behalf, and stating that the person so required to attend failed to do so in accordance with Such requirement, shall, without proof of the signature or appointment of such officer, be evidence of the matters stated therein.

(3) Any person charged with an offence under this section may he taken into and kept in either military or civil custody, or partly into and in one description of custody and partly into and in the other, or be transferred from one description of custody to the other.

7. [Effect of Act on persons already in the Reserve] *Rep.by the Indian Reserve Forces (Amendment) Act, 1931 (12 of 1931), s.6.*

□□□

22

The Indian Rifles Act, 1920

ACT NO. 23 OF 1920 [31ST AUGUST, 1920]

AN ACT to provide for the better discipline of police officers enrolled in Military Police or Rifle Battalions.

WHEREAS it is expedient to provide for the better discipline of police officers enrolled under local Acts in Military Police or Rifle Battalions it is hereby enacted as follows:-

1. Short title. This Act may be called the Indian Rifles Act, 1920.

2. Police officers subject to discipline and penalities prescribed in local Acts wherever serving. All police officers enrolled under the provisions of any local Military Police or Rifles Act shall be subject to the discipline and penalties prescribed by such Act, wherever serving in India.

□□□

23

The Indo-Tibetan Border Police Force Act, 1992

ACT NO. 35 OF 1992 [1ST SEPTEMBER, 1992)

AN ACT to provide for the constitution and regulation of an armed force of the Union for ensuring the security of the borders of India and for matters connected therewith.

Be it enacted by Parliament in the Forty-third Year of the Republic of India as follows:

CHAPTER -I : PRELIMINARY

1. Short title and commencement.

(1) This Act may be called the Indo-Tibetan Border Police Force Act, 1992.

(2) It shall come into force on such date as the Central Government may, by notification, appoint.

2. Definitions.

(1) In this Act, unless the context otherwise requires,—

(a) **"active duty",** in relation to a person subject to this Act, means any duty as a member of the Force during the period in which such person is attached to or forms part of a unit of the Force:—

(i) which is engaged in operations against an enemy, or

(ii) which is operating, at a picket or engaged on patrol or other guard duty along the borders of India, and includes duty by such person during any period declared by the Central Government by order as a period of active duty with reference to any area in which any person or class of persons subject to this Act may be serving;

(b) **"battalion"** means a unit of the Force constituted as a battalion by the Central Government;

(c) **"civil offence"** means an offence which is triable by a criminal court;

(d) **"civil prison"** means any jail or place used for the detention of any criminal prisoner under the Prisons Act, 1894 (9 of 1894), or under any other law for the time being in force;

(e) **"commanding officer"**, used in relation to a person subject to this Act, means an officer for the time being in command of the unit or any separate portion of the Force to which such person belongs or is attached;

(f) **"criminal court"** means a court of ordinary criminal justice in any part of India and includes a Court of a special Judge appointed under the Criminal Law Amendment Act, 1952 (46 of 1952);

(g) **"Deputy Inspector-General" and "Additional Deputy Inspector-General"** mean respectively a Deputy Inspector-General and an Additional Deputy Inspector-General of the Force appointed under Section 5;

(h) **"Director-General" and "Additional Director-General"** mean respectively the Director-General and an Additional Director-General of the Force appointed under Section 5;

(i) **"enemy"** includes all armed mutineers, armed rebels, armed rioters, pirates and any person in arms against whom it is the duty of any person subject to this Act to take action;

(j) **"enrolled person"** means an under-officer or other person enrolled under this Act;

(k) **"Force"** means the Indo-Tibetan Border Police Force;

(l) **"Force Court"** means a Court referred to in Section 76;

(m) **"Force custody"** means the arrest or confinement of a member of the Force according to rules;

(n) **"Inspector-General"** means the Inspector-General of the Force appointed under Section 5;

(o) **"Judge Attorney General", "Additional Judge Attorney-General", "Deputy Judge Attorney-General" and "Judge Attorney"** mean respectively' the Judge Attorney-General, an Additional Judge Attorney-General, a Deputy Judge Attorney-General and a Judge Attorney of the Force appointed in the appropriate rank by the Central Government;

(p) **"member of the Force"** means an officer, a subordinate officer, an under-officer or other enrolled person;

(q) **"notification"** means a notification published in the Official Gazette;

(r) **"offence"** means any act or omission punishable under this Act and includes a civil offence;

(s) **"officer"** means a person appointed or in pay as an officer of the Force, but does not include a subordinate officer or an under-officer;

(t) **"prescribed"** means prescribed by rules made under this Act;

(u) **"rule"** means a rule made under this Act;

(v) **"subordinate officer"** means a person appointed or in pay as a Subedar Major, a Subedar or a Sub-Inspector of the Force

(w) **"superior officer",** when used in relation to a person subject to this Act; means -

(i) any member of the Force to whose command such person is for the time being subject in accordance with the rules;

(ii) any officer of a higher rank or class or of a higher grade in the same class, and includes, when such person is not an officer, a subordinate officer or an under-officer of a, higher rank, class or grade;

(x) **"under-officer"** means a Head Constable, a Naik or a Lance Naik of the Force;

(y) **"unit"** includes -

(i) any body of officers and other members of the Force for which a separate authorised establishment exists;

(ii) any separate body of persons subject to this Act employed on any service and not attached to a unit as aforesaid;

(iii) any other separate body of persons composed wholly or partly of persons subject to this Act and specified as a unit by the Central Government.

(z) all words and expressions used and not defined in this Act but defined in the Indian Penal Code (45 of 1860), the Army Act, 1950 (46 of 1950) or the National Security Guard Act, 1986 (47 of 1986), shall have the same meanings respectively assigned to them in that Code or those Acts.

(2) In this Act, references to any law not in force in the State of Jammu and shall be construed as references to the corresponding law in force in that State.

3. Persons subject to this Act.

(1) The following persons appointed (whether on deputation or in any other manner) in the Force shall be subject to this Act, wherever they may be, namely:

(a) officers and subordinate officers; and

(b) under-officers and other persons enrolled under this Act.

(2) Every person subject to this Act shall remain so subject until repatriated, retired, released, discharged, removed or dismissed from the Force in, accordance with the provisions' of this Act and the rules.

CHAPTER -II : CONSTITUTION OF THE FORCE AND CONDITIONS OF SERVICE OF THE MEMBER OF THE FORCE

4. Constitution of the Force.

(1) There shall be an armed force of the Union called the Indo-Tibetan Border Police Force for ensuring the security of the borders of India and performing such other duties as may be entrusted to it by the Central Government.

(2) Subject to the provisions of this Act, the Force, shall be constituted in such manner as may be prescribed and the conditions of service of the members of the Force shall be such as may be prescribed.

5. Control, direction, etc.

(1) The general superintendence, direction and control of the Force shall vest in, and be exercised by, the Central Government and subject thereto and to the provisions of this Act and the rules, the command and supervision of the Force shall vest in an officer to be appointed by the Central Government as the Director-General of the Force.

(2) The Director-General shall, in the discharge of his duties under this Act, be assisted by such number of Additional Directors-General, Inspectors-General, Deputy Inspectors-General, Additional Deputy Inspectors-General, Commandants and other officers as may be appointed by the Central Government.

6. Enrolment. The persons to be enrolled to the Force, the mode of enrolment, and the procedure for enrolment shall be such as may be prescribed.

7. Liability for service outside India. Every member of the Force shall be liable to serve in any part of India as well as outside India.

8. Resignation and withdrawal from the post. No member of the Force shall be at liberty,

(a) to resign his appointment during the term of his engagement; or

(b) to withdraw himself from all or any of the duties of his appointment, except with the previous permission in writing of the prescribed authority.

9. Tenure of service under the Act. Every person subject to this Act shall hold office during the pleasure of the President.

10. Termination of service by Central Government. Subject to the provisions of this Act and the rules, the Central Government may dismiss or remove from the service any person subject to this Act.

11. Dismissal, removal or reduction by the Director-General and by other officers.

(1) The Director-General any Additional Director-General or Inspector-General may dismiss or remove from the service or reduce to a lower grade or rank or ranks any person subject to this Act other than an officer.

(2) An officer not below the rank of Additional Deputy Inspector-General or any prescribed officer may dismiss or remove from the service any person under his command other than an officer or a subordinate officer of such rank or ranks as may be prescribed.

(3) Any such officer as is mentioned in sub-section (2) may reduce to a lower grade or rank or ranks any person under his command except an officer or a subordinate officer.

(4) The exercise of any power under this Section shall be subject to the provisions of this Act and the rules.

12. Certificate of termination of service. A subordinate officer, or an under-officer or other enrolled person who is retired, discharged, released, removed or dismissed from the service shall be furnished by the officer, to whose command he is subject, with a certificate in Hindi or English language setting forth -

(a) the authority terminating his service;

(b) the cause for such termination; and

(c) the full period of his service in the Force.

13. Restrictions respecting right to form association, freedom of speech, etc.

(1) No person subject to this Act shall, without the previous sanction in writing of the Central Government or of the prescribed authority,—

(a) be a member of, or be associated in any way with, any trade union, labour union, political-association; or with any class of trade unions, labour unions or political associations; or

(b) be a member of, or be associated in any way with, any society, institution, association or organisation that is not recognised as part of the Force or is not of a purely social, recreational or religious nature; or

(c) communicate with the press or publish or cause to be published any book, letter or other document except where such communication or publication is in the *bona fide* discharge of his duties or is of a purely literary, artistic or scientific character or is of a prescribed nature.

EXPLANATION: If any question arises as to whether any society, institution, association or organisation is of a purely social, recreational or religious nature under clause (b) of this sub-section, the decision of the Central Government thereon shall be final.

(2) No person subject to this Act shall participate in, or address, any meeting or take part in any demonstration organised by any body of persons for any political purposes or for such other purposes as may be prescribed.

14. Remedy of aggrieved persons other than officers.

(1) Any person subject to this Act other than an officer who deems himself wronged by any superior or other officer may complain to the officer under whose command he is serving.

(2) When the officer complained against is the officer to whom any complaint should, under sub-section (1), be preferred, the aggrieved person may complain to such officer's next superior officer.

(3) Every officer receiving any such complaint shall make as complete an investigation into it as may be possible for giving full redress to the complainant, or when necessary, refer the complaint to a superior authority.

(4) The Director-General may revise any decision made under any of the foregoing sub-sections, but, subject thereto, such decision shall be final.

15. Remedy of aggrieved officers. Any officer who deems himself wronged by his commanding officer or any other superior officer and who, on due application made to his commanding officer or such other superior officer, does not receive the redress to which he considers himself entitled, may complain to the Director-General or the Central Government through proper channel.

CHAPTER -III : OFFENCES

16. Offences in relation to the enemy or terrorist and punishable with death. Any person subject to this Act who commits any of the following offences, that is to say,—

(a) shamefully abandons or delivers up any post, place or guard, committed to his charge or which it is his duty to defend; or

(b) intentionally uses any means to compel or induce any person subject to this Act or to any other law relating to military, naval, air force or any other armed force of the Union to abstain from acting against the enemy or to discourage such person from acting against the enemy; or

(c) in the presence of the enemy or terrorist, shamefully casts away his arms, ammunition, tools or equipment or misbehaves in such manner as to show cowardice; or

(d) treacherously holds correspondence with, or communicates intelligence to the enemy, terrorist or any person in arms against the Union; or

(e) directly or indirectly assists the enemy or terrorist with money, arms, ammunition, stores or supplies or in any other manner whatsoever; or

(f) in time of-active operation against the enemy or terrorist, intentionally occasions a false alarm in action, camp, quarters or spreads or causes to be spread reports calculated to create alarm or despondency; or

(g) in time of action leaves his commanding officer or other superior officer or his post, guard, picket, patrol or party without being regularly relieved or without leave; or

(h) having been captured by the enemy or made a prisoner of war, voluntarily serves with or aids the enemy; or

(i) knowingly harbours or protects an enemy, not being a prisoner; or

(j) being a sentry in time of active operation against the enemy or alarm, sleeps upon his post or is intoxicated; or

(k) knowingly does any act calculated to imperil the success of the Force or the military naval or air force of India or any forces, co-operating therewith or any part of such forces, shall, on conviction by a Force Court, be liable to suffer death of such less punishment as is in this Act mentioned.

17. Offences in relation to the enemy and not punishable with death. Any person subject to this Act who commits any of the following offences, that is to say,—

(a) is taken prisoner or captured by the enemy, by want of due precaution or through disobedience of orders, or wilful neglect of duty, or having been taken prisoner or so captured fails 'to rejoin his service when able to do so; or

(b) without due authority holds correspondence with, or communicates intelligence to, the enemy or any person in league with the enemy or having come by the knowledge of any such correspondence or communication, wilfully omits to discover it immediately to his commanding officer or other superior officer, shall, on conviction by a Force Court, be liable to suffer imprisonment for a term which may extend to fourteen years or such less punishment as is in this Act mentioned.

18. Offences punishable more severely on active duty than at other times. Any person subject to this Act who commits any of the following offences, that is to say,—

(a) forces a safeguard, or forces' or uses criminal force to a sentry; or

(b) breaks into any house or other place in search of plunder; or

(c) being a sentry sleeps upon his post, or is intoxicated; or

(d) without orders from his superior officer leaves his guard, picket, patrol or post; or

(e) intentionally or through neglect occasions a false alarm in camp or quarters, or spreads or causes to be spread reports calculated to create unnecessary alarm or despondency; or

(f) makes known the parole, watchward or countersign to any person not entitled to receive it; or knowingly gives a parole, watch ward or a countersign different from what he received, shall, on conviction by a Force Court,—

(i) if he commits any such offence when on active duty, be liable to suffer imprisonment for a term which may extend to fourteen years or such less punishment as is in this Act mentioned; and

(ii) if he commits any such offence when not on active duty, be liable to suffer imprisonment for a term which may extend to seven years or such less punishment as is in this Act mentioned.

19. Mutiny. Any person subject to this Act who commits any of the following offences, that is to say,_

(a) begins, incites, causes or conspires with any other person to cause any mutiny in the Force or in the military, naval or air force of India or any forces co-operating therewith; or

(b) joins in any such mutiny; or

(c) being present at any such mutiny, does not use his utmost endeavours to suppress the same; or

(d) knowing or having reason to believe in the existence of any such mutiny, or of any intention to mutiny or of any such conspiracy, does not, without delay, give information thereof to his commanding officer or other superior officer; or

(e) endeavours to seduce any person in the Force or in the military, naval or air force of India of any forces co-operating therewith from his duty or allegiance to the Union, shall, on conviction by a Force Court, be liable to-suffer death or such less punishment as is in this Act mentioned.

20. Desertion and aiding desertion.

(1) Any person subject to this Act who deserts or attempts to desert the service shall, on conviction by a Force Court —

(a) if he commits the offence when on active duty or when under orders for active duty, be liable to suffer death or such less punishment as is in this Act mentioned; and

(b) if he commits the offence under any other circumstances, be liable to suffer imprisonment for a term which may extend to seven years or such less punishment as is in this Act mentioned.

(2) Any person subject to this Act who knowingly harbours any such deserter shall, on conviction by a Force Court, be liable to suffer imprisonment for a term which may extend to seven years or such less punishment as is in this Act mentioned.

(3) Any person subject to this Act who, being cognizant of any desertion or attempt at desertion of a person subject to this Act, does not forthwith give notice to his own or some other superior officer or take any steps in his power to cause such person to be apprehended,. shall, on conviction by a Force Court, be liable to suffer imprisonment for a term which may extend to two years or such less punishment as is in this Act mentioned.

(4) For the purposes of this Act, a person deserts,—

(a) if he absents from his unit or, the place of duty at any time with the intention of not reporting back to such unit or place, or who, at any time and under any circumstances when absent from his unit or place of duty, does any act which shows that he has an intention of not reporting to such unit or place of duty;

(b) if he absents himself without leave with intent to avoid any active duty.

21. Absence without leave. Any person subject to this Act who commits any of the following offences, that is to say,—

(a) absents himself without leave; or

(b) without sufficient cause overstays leave granted to him; or

(c) being on leave of absence and having received information from the appropriate authority that any battalion or part thereof or any other unit of the Force, to which he belongs, has been, ordered. on active duty, fails,,without sufficient cause, to rejoin without delay; or

(d) without sufficient cause fails to appear at the time fixed at the parade or place appointed for exercise or duty; or

(e) when on parade, or on the line of march, without sufficient cause or without leave from his superior officer, quits the parade or line of march; or

(f) when in camp or elsewhere, is found beyond any limits fixed, or in any place prohibited, by any general, local or other order, without a pass or written leave from his superior officer; or

(g) without leave from his superior officer or without due cause, absents himself from any school or training institution when duly ordered to attend there, shall; on conviction by a Force Court, be liable to suffer imprisonment for a term which may extend to three years of such less punishment as is in this Act mentioned.

22. Striking or threatening superior officer. Any person subject to this Act who commits any of the following offences, that is to say,—

(a) uses criminal force to or assaults his superior officer; or

(b) uses threatening language to such officer; or

(c) uses insubordinate language to such officer, shall, on conviction by a Force Court,

(i) if such officer is at the time in the execution of his office or, if the offence is committed on active duty, be liable to suffer imprisonment for a term which may extend to fourteen years or such less punishment as is in this Act mentioned; and

(ii) in other cases be liable to suffer imprisonment for a term which may extend to years or such less punishment as is in this Act mentioned:

PROVIDED that in the case of an offence specified in clause (c), the imprisonment shall not exceed five years.

23. Disobedience to superior officer.

(1) Any person subject to this Act who disobeys in such manner as to show a wilful defiance of authority any lawful command given personally by his superior officer in the execution of his office whether the same is given orally, or in writing or by signal or otherwise, shall, on conviction by a Force Court, be liable to suffer imprisonment for a term which may extend to fourteen years or such less punishment as is in this Act mentioned.

(2) Any person subject to this Act who disobeys any lawful command given by his superior officer shall, on conviction by a Force Court,

(a) if he commits such offence when on active duty, be liable to suffer imprisonment for a term which may extend to fourteen years or such less punishment as is in this Act mentioned; and

(b) if he commits such offence when not on active duty, be liable to suffer imprisonment for a term which may extend to five years or such less punishment as is in this Act mentioned.

24. Insubordination and obstruction. Any person subject to this Act who commits any of the following offences, that is to say,—

(a) being concerned in any quarrel, affray or disorder, refuses to obey any officer, though of inferior rank, who orders him into arrest, or uses criminal force to, or assaults, any such officer; or

(b) uses criminal force to, or assaults, any person, whether subject to this Act or not, in whose custody he is lawfully placed, and whether he is or is not his superior officer; or

(c) resists an escort whose duty it is to apprehend him or to have him in charge; or

(d) breaks out of barracks, camp or quarters; or

(e) neglects to obey any general, local or other order; or

(f) impedes the Force Police referred to in Section 75 or any person lawfully acting on his behalf, or when called upon, refuses to assist in the execution of his duty a Force Police or any person lawfully acting on his behalf, shall, on conviction by a Force Court, be liable to suffer imprisonment for a term which may extend, in the case of the offences specified in clauses (d) and (e), to two years, and in the case of the offences specified in the other clauses, to ten years, or in either case such less punishment as is in this Act mentioned.

25. False answers on enrolment. Any person having become subject to this Act who is discovered to have made at the time of enrolment a wilfully false answer to any question set forth in the prescribed form of enrolment which has been put to him by the enrolling officer before whom he appears for the purpose of being enrolled, shall, on conviction by a Force Court, be liable to suffer imprisonment for a term which may extend to five years or such less punishment as is in this Act mentioned.

26. Unbecoming conduct. Any officer or subordinate officer who behaves in a manner un-becoming of his position and the character expected of him shall, on conviction by a Force Court, be liable to be dismissed or to suffer such less punishment as is in this Act mentioned.

27. Certain forms of disgraceful conduct. Any person subject to this Act who commits any of the following offences, that is to say,—

(a) is guilty of any disgraceful conduct of a cruel, indecent or unnatural kind; or

(b) malingers or feigns or produces disease or infirmity in himself or intentionally delays his cure or aggravates his disease at infirmity; or

(c) with intent to render himself or any other person unfit for service, voluntarily causes hurt to himself or that person, shall, on conviction by a Force Court, be liable to suffer imprisonment for a term which may extend to seven years or such less punishment as is in this Act mentioned.

28. Ill-treating a subordinate. Any officer, subordinate officer or under-officer, who uses criminal force to, or otherwise ill-treats, any person subject to this Act, being his subordinate in rank or position, shall, on conviction by a Force Court, be liable to suffer imprisonment for a term which may extend to seven years or such less punishment as is in this Act mentioned.

29. Intoxication.

(1) Any person subject to this Act who is found in a state of intoxication, whether on duty or not, shall, on conviction by a Force Court, be liable to suffer imprisonment for a term which may extend to six months or such less punishment as is in this Act mentioned.

(2) For the purposes of sub-section (1), a person shall be deemed to be in a state of Intoxication if, owing to the influence of alcohol or any drug whether alone, or any, combination with any other substance, he is unfit to be entrusted with

his duty or with any duty which he may be called upon to perform or, behaves in a disorderly manner or a manner likely to bring discredit to the Force.

30. Permitting escape of person in custody. Any person subject to this Act who commits any of the following offences, that is to say,—

(a) when in command of a guard, picket, patrol, detachment or post, releases without proper authority, whether wilfully or without reasonable excuse, any person committed to his charge, or refuse to receive any prisoner or person so committed; or

(b) wilfully or without reasonable excuse allows to escape any person who is committed to his charge, or whom it is his duty to keep or guard, shall, on conviction by a Force Court, be liable, if he has acted wilfully, to suffer imprisonment for a term which may extend to ten years or such less punishment as is in this Act mentioned; and if he has not acted wilfully, to suffer imprisonment for a term which may extend to two years or such less punishment as is in this Act mentioned.

31. Irregularity in connection with arrest or confinement. Any person subject to this Act who commits any of the following offences, that is to say,—

(a) unnecessarily detains a person in arrest or confinement without bringing him to trial, or fails to bring his case before the proper authority for investigation; or

(b) having committed a person to Force custody fails without reasonable cause to deliver at the time of such committal, or as soon as practicable, and in any case within forty-eight hours thereafter, to the officer or other person into whose custody the person arrested is committed, an account in writing signed by himself of the offence with which the person so committed is charged, shall, on conviction by a Force Court, be liable to suffer imprisonment for a term which may extend to one year or such less punishment as is in this Act mentioned.

32. Escape from custody. Any person subject to this Act who, being in lawful custody, escapes or attempts to escape, shall, on conviction by a Force Court, be liable to suffer imprisonment for a term which may extend to three years or such less punishment as is in this Act mentioned.

33. Offences in respect of property. Any person subject to this Act who commits any of the following offences, that is to say,—

(a) commits theft of any property belonging to the Government, or to any Force, mess, band or institution, or to any person subject to this Act; or

(b) dishonestly misappropriates or converts to his own use any such property; or

(c) commits criminal breach of trust in respect of any such property; or

(d) dishonestly receives or retains any such property in respect of which any of the offences under clauses (a), (b) and (c) has been committed, knowing or having reason to believe the commission of such offence; or

(e) wilfully destroys or injures any property of the Government entrusted to him; or

(f) does any other thing with intent to defraud, or to cause wrongful gain to one person or wrongful loss to another person, shall, on conviction by a Force Court, be liable to suffer imprisonment for a term which may extend to ten years or such less punishment as is in this Act mentioned.

34. Extortion and exaction. Any person subject to this Act who commits any of the following offences, that is to say -

(a) commits extortion; or

(b) without proper authority exacts from any person money, provisions or service, shall, on conviction by a Force Court, be liable to suffer imprisonment for a term which may extend to ten years or such less punishment as is in this Act mentioned.

35. Making away with equipment. Any person subject to this Act who commits any of the following offences, that is to say —

(a) makes away with, or is concerned in making away with, any arms, ammunition, equipment, instruments, tools, clothing or any other thing being the property of the Government issued to him for his use or entrusted to him; or

(b) loses by neglect anything mentioned in clause (a); or

(c) sells, pawns, destroys or defaces any medal or decoration granted to him,

shall, on conviction by a Force Court, be liable to suffer imprisonment for a term which may extend, in the case of the offences specified in clause (a), to ten years, and in the case of the offences specified in the other clauses, to five years, or in either case such less punishment as is in this Act mentioned.

36. Injury to property. Any person subject to this Act who commits, any of the following offences, that is to say —

(a) destroys or injures any property mentioned in clause (a) of Section 35, or any property belonging to any Force mess, band or institution, or to any person subject to this Act; or

(b) commits any act which causes damage to, or destruction of, any property of the Government by fire; or

(c) kills, injures, makes away with, ill-treats or loses any, animal entrusted to him, shall, on conviction by a Force Court, be liable, if he has acted wilfully, to suffer imprisonment for a term which may extend to ten years, or such less punishment as is in this Act mentioned; and if he has acted without reasonable excuse, to suffer imprisonment for a term which may extend to five years or such less punishment as is in this Act mentioned.

37. False accusations. Any person subject to this Act who commits any of the following offences, that is to say —

(a) makes a false accusation against any person subject to this Act, knowing or having reason to believe such accusation to be false; or

(b) in making a complaint against any person subject to this Act makes any statement affecting the character of such person, knowing or having reason to believe such statement to be false, or knowingly and wilfully suppresses any material facts, shall, on conviction by a Force Court, be liable to suffer imprisonment for a term which may extend to three years or such less punishment as is in this Act mentioned.

38. Falsifying official documents and false declarations. Any person subject to this Act who commits any of the following offences, that is to say —

(a) in any report, return, list, certificate, book or other document made or signed by him, or of the contents of which it is his duty to ascertain the accuracy, knowingly makes, or is privy to the making of, any false or fraudulent statement; or

(b) in any document of the description mentioned in clause (a) knowingly makes, or is privy to the making of, any omission, with intent to defraud; or

(c) knowingly and 'with intent to injure any person, or knowingly and with intent to de-fraud, suppresses, defaces, alters or makes away with any document which it is his duty to preserve or produce; or

(d) where it is his official duty to make a declaration respecting any matter, knowingly makes a false declaration; or

(e) obtains for himself, or for any other person, any pension, allowance or other advantage or privilege by a statement which is false, and which he either knows or believes to be false or does not believe to be true, or by making or using a false entry in any book or record, or by making any document containing a false statement, or by omitting to make a true entry or document containing a true statement, shall, on conviction by a Force Court, be liable to suffer imprisonment for a term which may extend to ten years or such less punishment as is in this Act mentioned.

39. Signing in blank and failure to report. Any person subject to this Act who commits any of the following offences, that is to say —

(a) when signing any document relating to pay, arms, ammunition, equipment, clothing, supplies or stores, or any property of the Government fraudulently leaves in blank any material part for which his signature is a voucher; or

(b) refuses or by culpable neglect omits to make or send a report or return which it is his duty to make or send, shall, on conviction by a Force Court, be liable to suffer imprisonment for a term which may extend to three years or such less punishment as is in this Act mentioned.

40. Offences relating to Force Court. Any person subject to this Act who commits any of the following offences, that is to say —

(a) being duly summoned or ordered to attend as a witness before a Force Court wilfully or without reasonable excuse, makes default in attending; or

(b) refuses to take an oath or make an affirmation legally required by a Force Court to be taken or made; or

(c) refuses to produce or deliver any document in his power or control legally required by a Force Court to be produced or delivered by him; or

(d) refuses, when a witness, to answer any question which he is by law bound to answer; or

(e) is guilty of contempt of the Force Court by using insulting or threatening language, or by causing any interruption or disturbance in the proceedings of such Court, shall, on conviction by a Force Court, be liable to suffer imprisonment for a term which may extend to three years or such less punishment as is in this Act mentioned.

41. False evidence. Any person subject to this Act who having been duly sworn or affirmed before any Force Court or other court competent under this Act to administer an oath or affirmation, makes any statement which is false, and which he either knows or believes to be false or does not believe to be true, shall, on conviction by a Force Court, be liable to suffer imprisonment for a term which may extend to seven years or such less punishment as is in this Act mentioned.

42. Unlawful detention of pay. Any officer, subordinate officer or under-officer who, having received the pay of a person subject to this Act unlawfully detains or refuses to pay the same when due, shall, on conviction by a Force Court, be liable to suffer imprisonment for a term which may extend to five years or such less punishment as is in this Act mentioned.

43. Violation of good order and discipline. Any person subject to this Act who is guilty of any act or omission which, though not specified ill this Act, is prejudicial to good order and discipline ('the Force shall, on conviction by a Force Court, be liable to suffer imprisonment for a term which may extend to seven years or such less punishment as is in this Act mentioned.

44. Miscellaneous offences. Any person subject to this Act who commits any of the following offences, that is to say,—

(a) being in command at any post or on the march, and receiving a complaint that any one under his command has beaten or otherwise maltreated or oppressed any person, or has disturbed any fair or market, or committed any riot or trespass, fails to have due reparation made to the injured person or to report tae case to the proper authority; or

(b) by defiling any place of worship, or otherwise, intentionally insults the religion, or wounds the religious feelings of any person; or

(c) attempts to commit suicide, and in such attempt does any act towards the commission of such offence; or

(d) being below the rank of subordinate officer, when off duty, appears without proper authority, in or about camp, or in or about, or when going to, or returning from any town or bazzar, carrying a rifle, sword or other offensive weapon; or

(e) directly or indirectly accepts or obtains, or agrees to accept, or attempts to obtain, for himself or for any other person, any gratification as a motive or reward for procuring the enrolment of any person, or leave of absence, promotion or any other advantage or indulgence for any person in the service; or

(f) commits any offence against the property or person of any inhabitant of, or resident in, the country in which he is serving, shall, on conviction by a Force Court, be liable to suffer imprisonment for a term which may extend to seven years or such less punishment as is in this Act mentioned.

45. Attempt. Any person subject to this Act who attempts to commit any of the offences specified in Sections 16 to 44 (both inclusive) and in such attempt does any act towards the commission of the offence shall, on conviction by a Force Court, where no express provision is made by this Act for the punishment of such attempt, be liable,

(a) if the offence attempted to be committed is punishable with death, to suffer imprisonment for a term which may extend to fourteen years or such less punishment as is in this Act mentioned; and

(b) if the offence attempted to be committed is punishable with imprisonment, to suffer imprisonment for a term which may extend to one-half of the longest term provided for that offence or such less punishment as is in this Act mentioned.

46. Abetment of offences that have been committed. Any person subject to this Act who abets the commission of any of the offences specified in Sections 16 to 44 (both inclusive) shall, on conviction by a Force Court, if the act abetted is committed in consequence of the abetment and no express provision is made by this Act for the punishment of such abetment, be liable to suffer the punishment provided or that offence or such less punishment as is in this Act mentioned.

47. Abetment of offences punishable with death and not committed. Any person subject to this Act who abets the commission of any of the offences punishable with death under Sections 16, 19 and sub-section (1) of Section 20 shall, on conviction by a Force Court, if that offence be not committed in consequence of the abetment, and no express provision is made by this Act for the punishment of such abetment, be liable to suffer imprisonment for a term which may extend to fourteen years or such less punishment as is in this Act mentioned.

48. Abetment of offences punishable with imprisonment and not committed. Any person subject to this Act who abets the commission of any of the offences specified in Sections 16 to 44 (both inclusive) and punishable with imprisonment shall, on conviction by a Force Court, if that offence be not committed in consequence of the abetment, and no express provision is made by this Act for the punishment of such abetment, be liable to suffer imprisonment for a term which may extent to one-half of the longest term provided for that offence or such less punishment as is in this Act mentioned.

49. Civil offences. Subject to the provisions of Section 50, any person subject to this Act who at any place in, or beyond, India commits any civil offence shall be deemed to be guilty of an offence against this Act and, if charged therewith under this Section shall be liable to be tried by a Force Court and, on conviction, be punishable as follows, that is to say —

(a) if the offence is one which would be punishable under any law in force in India with death, he shall be liable to suffer any punishment, assigned for the offence, by the aforesaid law and such less punishment as is in this Act mentioned; and

(b) in any other case, he shall be liable to suffer any punishment, assigned for the offence by the Jaw in force in India, or imprisonment far a term which may extend to seven years, or such less punishment as is in this Act mentioned.

50. Civil offences not triable by a Force Court. A person subject to this Act who commits an offence of murder or culpable homicide not amounting to murder against, or of rape in relation to, a person not subject to this Act shall not be deemed to be guilty of an offence against this Act and shall not be tried by a Force Court, unless he commits any of the said offences,—

(a) while on active duty; or

(b) at any place outside India; or

(c) at any place specified by the Central Government by notification, in this behalf.

CHAPTER -IV : PUNISHMENTS

51. Punishment awardable by Force Courts.

(1) Punishments may be inflicted in respect of offences committed by persons subject to this Act and convicted by Force Courts according to the scale following, that is to say,—

(a) death;

(b) imprisonment which may be for the term of life or any other lesser term but excluding imprisonment for a term not exceeding three months in Force custody;

(c) dismissal or removal from the service;

(d) compulsory retirement from the service;

(e) imprisonment for a term not exceeding three months in Force custody;

(f) reduction to the ranks or to a lower rank or grade or a place in the list of their rank in the case of an under-officer;

(g) reduction to next lower rank in case of an officer or subordinate officer:

PROVIDED that no officer shall be reduced to a rank lower than the one to which he was initially appointed;

(h) forfeiture of seniority of rank and forfeiture of all or any part of the service for the purpose of promotion;

(i) forfeiture of service for the purpose of increased pay or pension;

(j) fine, in respect of civil offences;

(k) severe reprimand or reprimand except in the case of persons below the rank of an under-officer;

(l) forfeiture of pay and allowances for a period not exceeding three months for an offence committed on active duty;

(m) forfeiture in the case of person sentenced to dismissal from the service of all arrears of pay and allowances and other public money due to him at the time of such dismissal;

(n) stoppage of pay and allowances until any proved loss or damage occasioned by the offence for which he is convicted is made good.

(2) Each of the punishments specified in sub-section (1) shall be deemed to be inferior in degree to every punishment preceding it in the above scale.

52. Alternative punishments awardable by Force Courts. Subject to the provisions of this Act, a Force Court may, on convicting a person subject to this Act of any of the offences specified in Sections 16 to 48 (both inclusive) award either the particular punishment with which the offence is stated in the said Sections to be punishable or, in lieu thereof, anyone of the punishments lower in the scale set out in Section 51 regard being had to the nature and degree of the offence.

53. Combination of punishments. A Force Court may award in addition to, or without, any other punishment, the punishment specified in clause (c) of sub-section (1) of Section 51, or anyone or more of the punishments specified in clause (f) to (n) (both inclusive) of that sub-section.

54. Retention in the Force of a person convicted on active duty. When on active duty an enrolled person has been sentenced by a Force Court to imprisonment whether combined with dismissal or not, the prescribed officer may direct that such person may be retained to serve in the ranks, and such service shall be reckoned as part of his term of imprisonment.

55. Punishments otherwise than by Force Courts. Punishments may also be inflicted in respect of offences committed by persons subject to this Act without the intervention of a Force Court in the manner stated in Sections 56, 58 and 59.

56. Minor punishments.

(1) Subject to the provisions of Section 57, a commanding officer of and above the rank of Commandant may, in the prescribed manner, proceed against a person subject to this Act, other than an officer or a subordinate officer, who is charged with an offence under this Act and award such person, to the extent prescribed, one or more of the following punishments, that is to say,—

(a) imprisonment in Force custody up to twenty-eight days;

(b) detention up to twenty-eight days;

(c) confinement to the lines up to twenty-eight days;

(d) extra guards or duties;

(e) deprivation of any special position or special emoluments or any acting rank;

(f) severe reprimand or reprimand;

(g) fine up to fourteen days pay in anyone month;

(h) deductions from his pay and allowances of any sum required to make good any loss or damage occasioned by the offence for which he is punished.

(2) If any unit, training centre or other establishment of the Force is being temporarily Commanded by an officer of the rank of second-in-Command or Deputy Commandant, such officer shall have full powers of a commanding officer specified in sub-section (1).

(3) subject to the provisions of Section 57, a Deputy Commandant or an Assistant Commandant, commanding a company or a detachment or an outpost, shall have the power to proceed against a person subject to this Act, other than an officer or a subordinate officer, who is charged with an offence under this Act and award such person to the extent prescribed, one or more of the punishments specified in clauses (a) to (d) and (h) of sub-section (1) provided that the maximum limit of punishment awarded under each of the clauses (a), (b) and (c) shall not exceed fourteen days.

(4) A subordinate officer not below the rank of Sub-Inspector who is commanding detachment or an outpost shall have the powers to proceed against a person subject to this Act, other than a subordinate officer or an under-officer, who is charged with an offence under this Act and award such person to the extent prescribed, one or more of the punishments specified under clauses (c) and (d) of sub-section (1) provided that the maximum limit of punishment awarded under clause (c) shall not exceed fourteen days.

57. Limit of punishments under Section 56.

(1) In the case of an award of two or more of the punishments specified in clauses (a), (b), (c) and (d) of sub-section (1) of Section 56, the punishments specified in clause (c) or clause (d) shall take effect only at the end of the punishment specified in clause (a) or clause (b).

(2) When two or more of the punishments specified in clauses (a), (b) and (c) of sub-section (1) of Section 56 are awarded to a person conjointly, or when already undergoing one or more of the said punishments, the whole extent of the punishments shall not exceed in the aggregate fourty-two days.

(3) The punishments specified in clauses (a), (b) and (c) of sub-section (1) of Section 56 shall not be awarded to any person who is of the rank of an under-officer or was, at the time of committing the offence for which he is punished, of such rank.

(4) The punishment specified in clause (f) of sub-section (1) of Section 56 shall not be awarded to any person below the rank of an under-officer.

58. Punishment of persons of or below the rank of Commandant by Inspectors-General and others.

(l) An officer not below the rank of Inspector-General may, in the prescribed manner, proceed against an officer of or below the rank of Commandant who is charged with an offence under this Act and award one or more of the following punishments, that is to say,—

(a) forfeiture of seniority, or in the case of any of them whose promotion depends upon length of service, forfeiture of service for the purpose of promotion for a period not exceeding one year, but subject to the right of the accused previous to the award to elect to be tried by a Force Court;

(b) severe reprimand or reprimand;

(c) deduction from pay and allowances of any sum required to make good any proved loss or damage occasioned by the offence of which he is convicted.

(2) An officer not below the rank of Additional Deputy Inspector-General may, in the prescribed manner, proceed against a person of or below the rank of Subedar-Major who is charged with an offence under this Act and award one or more of the following punishments, that is to say,—

(a) forfeiture of seniority, or in the case of any of them whose promotion depends upon the length of service, forfeiture of service for the purpose of promotion for a period not exceeding one year, but subject to the right of the accused previous to the award to elect to be tried by a Force Court;

(b) severe reprimand or reprimand;

(c) deduction from pay and allowances of any sum-required to make good any proved loss or damage occasioned by the offence of which he is convicted.

(3) An officer not below the rank of Commandant may, in the prescribed manner, proceed against a person of or below the rank of Subedar-Major who is charged with an offence under this Act and award anyone or both of the following punishments, that is to say,—

(a) severe reprimand or reprimand;

(b) deduction from pay and allowances of any sum required to make good any proved loss or damage occasioned by the offence of which he is convicted.

59. Review of proceedings.

(1) In every case in which punishment has been awarded under Section 58, certified true copies of the proceedings shall be forwarded, in the prescribed manner, by the officer awarding the punishment to the prescribed superior authority who may, if the punishment awarded appears to him to be illegal, unjust or excessive, cancel, vary or remit the punishment and make such other direction as may be appropriate in the circumstances of the case.

(2) For the purpose of sub-section (1), a "superior authority" means,

(a) any officer superior in command to such officer who has awarded the punishment;

(b) in the case of punishment awarded by Director-General, the Central Government.

60. Collective fines.

(l) Whenever any weapon or part of weapon or ammunition, forming part of the equipment of a unit, is lost or stolen, a commanding officer not below the rank of the Commandant of that unit may, after making such enquiry as he thinks fit and subject to the rules, impose a collective fine upon the subordinate offices, under-officers and men of such unit, or upon so many of them as, in his judgment, should be held responsible for such loss or theft.

(2) Such fine shall be assessed as a percentage of the pay of the individuals on whom it.

CHAPTER -V : DEDUCTIONS FROM PAY AND ALLOWANCES

61. Deductions from pay and allowances of persons subject to this Act.

(1) The following deductions may be made from the pay and allowances of an officer, that is to say,—

(a) all pay and allowances due to an officer for every day he absents himself without leave, unless a satisfactory explanation has been given to, and accepted by, the Inspector-General under whom he is for the time being serving;

(b) all pay and allowances for every day while he is in custody on a charge for an offence for which he is afterwards convicted by a criminal court or Force Court or by an officer exercising authority under Section 58;

(c) any sum required to make good the pay of any person subject to this Act which be has unlawfully retained or unlawfully refused to pay;

(d) any sum required to make good such compensation for any expenses, loss, damage or destruction occasioned by the commission of an offence as may be determined by the Force Court by whom he is convicted of such offence or by an officer exercising authority under Section 58;

(e) an pay and allowances ordered by Force Court;

(f) any sum required to be paid as fine awarded by a criminal court or a Force Court;

(g) any sum required to make good any loss, damage or destruction of public or Force property which, after due investigation, appears to the Inspector-General under whom the officer is for the time being serving, to have been occasioned by the wrongful act or negligence on the part of the officer;

(h) all pay and allowances forfeited by order of the Central Government if the officer is found by a court of inquiry constituted by the Director-General in this behalf, to have deserted to the enemy, or while in enemy hands, to have served with, or under the orders of the enemy, or in any manner to have aided the enemy, or to have allowed himself to be taken prisoner by the enemy through want of due precaution, or through disobedience of orders or wilful neglect of duty, or having been taken prisoner by the enemy, to have failed to rejoin his service when it was possible to do so;

(i) any sum required by order of the Central Government to be paid for the maintenance of his wife or his legitimate or illegitimate child or step child or towards the cost of any relief given by the said Government to" the said wife or child.

(2) Subject to the provisions of Section 63, the following deductions may be made from the pay and allowances of a person subject to this Act other than an officer. that is to say.—

(a) all pay and allowances for every day of absence either on desertion or without leave or as a prisoner of war unless a satisfactory explanation has been given and accepted by his commanding officer and for every day of imprisonment awarded by a Criminal Court, Force Court or an officer exercising authority under Section 56;

(b) all pay and allowances for every day while he is in custody on a charge for an offence of which he is afterwards convicted by a Criminal Court or Force Court or on a charge of absence without leave for which he is afterwards awarded imprisonment by an officer exercising authority under Section 56;

(c) all pay and allowances for every day on which he is in hospital on account of sickness certified by the medical officer attending on him to have been caused by an offence-under this Act committed by him;

(d) for every day on which he is in hospital on account of sickness certified by the medical officer attending on him to have been caused by his own misconduct or imprudence, such sum as may be specified by the order of the Director-General;

(e) all pay and allowances ordered by Force Court or by an officer exercising authority under any of the Sections 56 and 58 to be forfeited or stopped;

(f) all pay and allowances for every day between his being recovered from the enemy and his dismissal from the service in consequence of his conduct when being taken prisoner by, or while in the hands of the enemy;

(g) any sum required to make good such compensation for any expenses, loss. damage or destruction caused by him to the Central Government or to any building or property or any private fund of the Force as may be awarded by his commanding officer;

(h) any Sum required to pay a fine awarded by a criminal court, Force Court exercising jurisdiction under Section 49 or an officer exercising authority under any of the Sections 56 and 60;

(i) any sum required by order of the Central Government or any prescribed officer to be: paid for the maintenance of his wife, or his legitimate child. or illegitimate child or step child or towards the cost of any relief given by the said Government to the said wife or child.

(3) For computation of time, of absence or custody under this Section,—

(a) no person shall be treated as absent or in custody for a day unless the absence or custody has lasted, whether wholly in one day, or partly in one day and partly in another for six consecutive hours or upwards;

(b) any absence or custody for less than a day may be reckoned as absence or custody for a day, if such absence or custody prevented the absentee from fulfilling any duty as member of the Force which was thereby thrown upon some other person;

(c) absence or custody for twelve consecutive hours or upwards may be reckoned as absence or custody for the whole of each day during any portion of which the person was absent or in custody;

(d) a period of absence, or imprisonment, which commences before, and ends after, midnight may be reckoned as a day.

62. Pay and allowances during trial. In the case of any person subject to this Act who is in custody or under suspension from duty on a charge for an offence, the prescribed officer may direct that the whole or any part of the pay and allowances of such person shall be withheld, pending the result of his trial on the charge against him, in order to give effect to the provisions of clause (b) of sub-sections (1) and (2) of Section 61.

63. Limit of certain deductions. The total deductions from the pay and allowances of a person made under clauses (e) and (g) to (i) of sub-section (2) of Section 61 shall not, except where he is sentenced to dismissal or removal, exceed in anyone month one-half of his pay and allowances for that month.

64. Deduction from public money due to a person. Any sum authorised by this Act to be deducted from the pay and allowances of any person may, without prejudice to any other mode of recovering the same, be deducted from any public money due to him other than a pension.

65. Pay and allowances of prisoner of war during inquiry into his conduct. Where the conduct of any person subject to this' Act when being taken prisoner by, or while in the hands of, the enemy, is to be inquired into under this Act or any other law, the Director-General or any officer authorised by him may order that the whole or any part of the pay and allowances of such person shall be withheld pending the result of such inquiry.

66. Remission of deductions. Any deduction from pay and allowances authorised by this Act may be remitted in such manner and to such extent, and by such authority, as may from time to time be prescribed.

67. Provision for dependants of prisoner of war from his remitted deductions and pay and allowances.

(1) In the case of all persons subject to this Act, being prisoners of war, whose pay and allowances have been forfeited under clause (h) of sub-section (1) or clause (a) of sub-section (2) of Section 61 but in respect of whom a remission has been made under Section 66, it shall be lawful for proper provisions to be made by the Central Government or by the Director-General when so authorised by the Central Government out of such pay and allowances for any dependants of such persons and any such remission shall in that case be deemed to apply only to the balance thereafter remaining of such pay and allowances.

(2) It shall be lawful for proper provision to be made by the Central Government or by the Director-General when so authorised by the Central Government for

any dependants of any person subject to this Act who is a prisoner of war, or is missing, out of his pay and allowances.

68. Period during which a person is deemed to be a prisoner of war. For the purposes of Section 67, a person shall be deemed to continue to be a prisoner of war until the conclusion of any inquiry into his conduct such as is referred to in Section 65 and if he is dismissed from the service in consequence of such conduct, until the date of such dismissal.

CHAPTER -VI : ARREST AND PROCEEDINGS BEFORE TRIAL

69. Custody of offenders.

(1) Any person subject to this Act who is charged with an offence may be taken into Force custody under the order of any superior officer.

(2) Notwithstanding anything contained in sub-section (1), an officer may order into Force custody any other officer, though such other officer may be of a higher rank, engaged in a quarrel, affray or disorder.

70. Duty of commanding officer in regard to detention.

(1) It shall be the duty of every commanding officer to take care that a person under his command when charged with an offence is not detained in custody for more than forty-eight hours after the committal of such person into custody is reported to him, without the charge being investigated, unless investigation within that period seems to him to be impracticable having regard to the public service.

(2) The case of every person being detained in custody beyond a period of forty-eight hours, and the reasons therefore, shall be reported by the commanding officer to the next higher officer or such other officer to whom an application may be made to convene a Force Court for the trial of the person charged.

(3) In reckoning the period of forty-eight hours specified in sub-section (1), Sundays and other public holidays shall be excluded.

(4) Subject to the provisions of this Act, the Central Government may make rules providing for the manner in which and the period for which any person subject to this Act may be taken into and detained in Force custody, pending the trial by any competent authority for any offence committed by him.

71. Interval between committal and trial. In every case where any such person as is mentioned in Section 69 and as is not on active duty, remains in such custody for a longer period than eight days without a Force Court for his trial being convened, a special report giving reasons for the delay shall be made by his commanding officer in the manner prescribed, and a similar report shall be forwarded at intervals of every eight days until a Force Court is convened or such person is released from custody.

72. Arrest by civil authorities. Whenever any person subject to this Act, who is accused of an offence under this Act, is within the jurisdiction of any magistrate or police officer, such magistrate or police officer shall aid in the apprehension and delivery to Force custody of such person upon receipt of a written application to that effect signed by his commanding officer or an officer authorised by the commanding officer in that behalf.

73. Capture of deserters.

(1) Whenever any person subject to this Act deserts, the commanding officer of the unit to which he belongs or is attached, shall give information of the desertion to such civil authorities as, in his opinion, may be able to afford assistance towards the capture of the deserter; and such authorities shall thereupon take steps for the apprehension of the said deserter in like manner as if he were a person for whose apprehension a warrant had been issued by a magistrate, and shall deliver the deserter, when apprehended, into Force custody.

(2) Any police officer may arrest without warrant any person reasonably believed to be subject to this Act, and to be a deserter or to be travelling without authority, and shall bring him without delay before the nearest magistrate, to be dealt with according to law.

74. Inquiry into absence without leave.

(1) When any person subject to this Act has been absent from duty without due authority for a period of thirty days, a court of inquiry shall, as soon as practicable, be appointed by such authority and in such manner as may be prescribed; and such court shall, on oath or affirmation administered in the prescribed manner, inquire respecting the absence of the person, and the deficiency, if any, in the property of the Government entrusted to his care, or in any arms, ammunition, equipment, instruments, clothing or necessaries; and if satisfied of the fact of such absence without due authority or other sufficient cause, the court shall declare such absence and the period thereof and the said deficiency, if any, and the commanding officer of the unit to which the person belongs or is attached, shall make a record thereof in the prescribed manner.

(2) If the person declared absent does not afterwards surrender or is not apprehended, he shall, for the purposes of this Act, be deemed to be a deserter.

75. Force Police Officers.

(1) The Director-General or any prescribed officer may appoint persons (in this Act referred to as Force Police) for discharging the functions specified in sub-sections (2) and (3).

(2) The duties of a person appointed under sub-section (1) are to take charge of persons confined for any offence, to preserve good order and discipline and to prevent breaches of the same by persons serving in, or attached to the Force.

(3) Notwithstanding anything contained in Section 69, a person appointed under sub-section (1) may, at any time, arrest and detain for trial any person subject to this Act who commits, or is charged with it offence, and may also carry into effect any punishment to be inflicted in pursuance of a sentence awarded by a Force Court or by an officer exercising authority under Section 56 but shall not inflict any punishment or his own authority:

PROVIDED that no officer shall be so arrested or detained otherwise than on the order of another officer.

CHAPTER -VII : FORCE COURTS

76. Kinds of Force Courts. For the purposes of this Act there shall be three kinds of Force Courts, that is to say,—

(a) General Force Courts;

(b) Petty Force Court; and

(c) Summary Force Courts.

77. Power to convene a General Force Court. A General Force Court may be convened by the Central Government or the Director-General or by any officer empowered in this behalf by warrant of the Director-General.

78. Power to convene a Petty Force Court. A Petty Force Court may be convened by an officer having power to convene a General Force Court or by an officer empowered in this behalf by warrant of' any such officer.

79. Contents of warrants issue under Sections 77 and 78. A warrant issued under Section 77 or Section 78 may contain such restrictions, reservations or conditions as the officer issuing it may think fit.

80. Composition of a General Force Court. A General Force Court shall consist of not less than five officers.

81. Composition of a Petty Force Court. A Petty Force Court shall consist of not less than three officers.

82. Summary Force Court.

(1) A Summary Force Court may be held by the commanding officer of any unit and be alone shall constitute the Court.

(2) The proceedings shall be attended throughout by two other persons who shall be officers or subordinate officers or are of either, and who shall not as such, be sworn or affirmed.

83. Dissolution of a Force Court.

(1) If a Force Court after the commencement of a trial is reduced below the minimum number of officers required by this Act, it shall be dissolved.

(2) If, on account of the illness of the concerned Judge Attorney or as the case maybe, Deputy Judge Attorney-General or Additional Judge Attorney-General or of the accused before the finding, it is impossible to continue the trial, the Force Court shall be dissolved.

(3) The authority or officer who convened a Force Court may dissolve the same if it appears to him that the exigencies of the service or necessities of discipline render it impossible or inexpedient to continue the said Force Court.

(4) Where a Force Court is dissolved under this Section, the accused may be tried

84. Power of It General Force Court. A General Force Court shall have the power to try any person subject to this Act for any offence punishable thereunder and to pass any sentence authorized thereby.

85. Power of a Petty Force Court. A Petty Force Court shall have the power to try any person subject to this Act other than an officer or a subordinate officer for any offence made punishable thereunder and to pass any sentence authorised by this Act other than a sentence of death or imprisonment for a term exceeding two years.

86. Power of a Summary Force Court.

(1) Subject to the provisions of sub-section (2), a Summary Force Court may try any offence punishable under this Act.

(2) When there is no grave reason for, immediate action and reference can without detriment to discipline be made to the officer empowered to convene a Petty Force Court for the trial of the alleged offender, an officer holding a Summary Force Court shall not try without such reference any offence punishable under any of the Sections 16,19 and 49, or any offence against the officer holding the Court.

(3) A Summary Force Court may try any person subject to this Act and under the command of the officer 'holding the Court, except an officer or a subordinate officer.

(4) A Summary Force Court may pass any sentence which may be passed under this Act, except the sentence of death or of imprisonment for a term exceeding the limit specified in sub-section (5).

(5) The limit referred to in sub-section (4) shall be,

(a) one year, if the officer holding the Force Court holds the rank. not below that of a Commandant;

(b) three months, in any other case.

87. Prohibition of second trial.

(1) When any person, subject to this Act has been acquired or convicted of an offence by a Force Court or by a criminal court or has been dealt with under Section 56 or Section 58, he shall not be liable to be tried again for the same offence by a Force Court or dealt with under the said Sections.

(2) When any person, subject to this Act, has been acquired or convicted of an offence by a Force Court or has been dealt with under Section 56 or Section 58, he shall not be liable to be tried again by a criminal court for the same offence or on the same facts.

88. Period of limitation for trial.

(1) Except as provided by sub-section (2), no trial by a Force Court', of any person subject to this Act for any offence shall be commenced after the expiration of a period of three, years from the date-of such offence.

(2) The provisions of sub-section (1) shall not apply to a trial for an offence of desertion or for any of the offences mentioned in Section 19.

(3) In the computation of the period of time mentioned in sub-section (1), any time spent by such 'person in evading arrest after the commission of the offence, shall be excluded.

89. Trial, etc., of offender who ceases to be subject to this Act.

(1) Where an offence under this Act had been committed by any person while subject to this Act, and he has ceased-to be so subject, he may be taken into and kept in Force custody and tried and punished for such offence as if he continued to be so subject.

(2) No such person shall be tried for an offence, unless his trial commences within six months after he had ceased to be subject to this Act:

PROVIDED that nothing contained in this sub-section shall apply to the trial of any such person for an offence of desertion or for any o[the offences mentioned in Section 19 or shall affect the jurisdiction of a criminal court to try any offence triable by such court, as well as by a Force Court.

90. Application of Act during term of sentence.

(1) When a person subject to this Act is sentenced by a Force Court to imprisonment, this Act shall apply to him during the term of his sentence, though he is dismissed from the Force, or has otherwise ceased to be subject to this Act, and he may be kept, removed, imprisoned and punished as if he continued to be subject to this Act.

(2) When a person subject to this Act is sentenced by a Force Court to death, this Act shall apply to him till the sentence is carried out.

91. Place of trial. Any person subject to this Act who commits any offence against it may be tried and punished for such offence in any place whatever.

92. Choice between Criminal Court and Force Court. When a Criminal Court and a Force Court have each jurisdiction in respect of an offence. It shall be in the discretion of the Director-General, Additional Director-General or the Inspector-General or the Deputy Inspector-General or the Additional Deputy Inspector-General within whose command the accused person is serving or such other officer as may be prescribed, to decide before which court the proceedings shall be instituted, and if that officer decides that they shall he instituted before a Force Court to direct that the accused person shall be detained in Force custody.

93. Power of criminal court to require delivery of offender.

(1) When a criminal court having jurisdiction is of opinion that proceedings shall be instituted before itself in respect of any alleged offence, it may, by written notice, require the officer referred to in Section 92 at his option, either to deliver over the offender to the nearest magistrate to be proceeded against according to law, or to postpone proceedings, pending a reference to the Central Government.

(2) In every such case the said officer shall either deliver over the offender incompliance with the requisition, or shall forthwith refer the question as to the court before which the proceedings are to be instituted, for the determination of the Central Government whose order upon such reference shall be final.

CHAPTER -VIII : PROCEDURE OF FORCE COURTS

94. Presiding Officer. At every General Force Court or Petty Force Court, the senior member shall be the presiding officer.

95. Judge Attorneys. Every General Force Court shall, and every Petty Force Court may be attended by a Judge Attorney or a Deputy Judge Attorney-General or an Additional Judge Attorney-General, or, if no such officer is, available, an officer approved by the Judge Attorney-General or by any officer authorised in this behalf by the Judge Attorney-General.

96. Challenges.

(1) At all trials by a General Force Court or by a Petty Force Court, as soon as the Court is assembled, the names of the presiding officer and members shall be read over to the accused, who shall thereupon be asked whether he objects to being tried by any officer sitting on the Court.

(2) If the accused objects to such officer, his objection and also the reply thereto of the officer objected to shall be heard and recorded, and the remaining officers of the Court shall, in the absence of the challenged officer decide on the objection.

(3) If the objection is allowed by one-half or more of the votes of the officers entitled to vote, the objection shall be allowed, and the member objected to shall retire, and his vacancy may be filled in the prescribed manner, by another officer subject to the same right of the accused to object.

(4) When no challenge is made, or when a challenge has been made and disallowed, or the place of every officer successfully challenged has been filled by another officer to whom no objection is made or allowed, the Court shall proceed with the trial.

97. Oaths of member, Judge Attorney and witness.

(1) An oath or affirmation in the prescribed manner shall be administered to every member of the Force Court and to the Judge Attorney, or as the case may be, the Deputy Judge Attorney-General or the Additional Judge Attorney-General or the officer approved under Section 95, before the commencement of the trial.

(2) Every person giving evidence before a Force Court shall be examined after being duly sworn or affirmed if the prescribed form.

(3) The provisions of sub-section (2) shall not apply where the witness is a child under twelve years of age and the Force Court is of opinion that though the witness understands the duty of speaking the truth, he does not understand the nature of an oath or affirmation.

98. Voting by members.

(1) Subject to the provisions of sub-sections (2) and (3), every decision of a Force Court shall be passed by an absolute majority of votes; and where there is an equality of votes on either the finding or the sentence, the decision shall be in favour of the accused.

(2) No sentence of death shall be passed by a General Force Court without the concurrence of at least two-thirds of the members of the Court.

(3) In matters other than a challenge or the finding or sentence, the presiding officer shall have a casting vote.

99. General rule as to evidence. The Indian Evidence Act, 1872 (1 of 1872) shall, subject to the provisions of this Act, apply to all proceedings before a Force Court.

100. Judicial notice. A Force Court may take judicial notice of any matter within the general knowledge of the members as officers of the Force.

101. Summoning Witnesses.

(1) The convening officer, the presiding officer of a Force Court, the Judge Attorney or, as the case may be, the Deputy Judge Attorney-General or the Additional Judge Attorney-General or the officer approved under Section 9 or the Commanding Officer of the accused person may, by summons under his hand, require the attendance, at a time and place to be mentioned in the summons; of any person either to give evidence or to produce any document or other thing.

(2) In the case of a witness who is subject to this Act or any other Act relating to the armed forces of the Union, the summons shall be sent to his Commanding Officer and such officer shall serve it upon him accordingly.

(3) In the case of any other witness, the summons shall be sent to the magistrate within whose jurisdiction he may be, or resides, and such magistrate shall give effect to the summons as if the witness were required in the court of such a magistrate.

(4) When a witness is required to produce any particular document or other thing in his 'possession or power', the summons shall describe it with reasonable precision.

102. Documents exempted from production.

(1) Nothing in Section 101 shall be deemed to affect the operation of Sections 123 and 124 of the Indian Evidence Act, 1872 (1 of 1872), or to apply to any letter, postcard, telegram or other document in the custody of the postal or telegraph authorities.

(2) If any document in such custody is, in the opinion of any District Magistrate, Chief Metropolitan Magistrate, Chief Judicial Magistrate, Court of Sessions or High Court wanted for the purpose of any Force Court, such Magistrate, or Court may require the postal or telegraph authorities, as the case may be, to deliver such document to such person as such Magistrate or Court may direct.

(3) If any such document is, in the opinion of any other magistrate or of any Commissioner of Police or District Superintendent of Police, wanted for any such purpose, he may require the postal or telegraph authorities, as the case may be, to cause such search to be made for, and to detain such document pending the orders of any such District Magistrate, Chief Metropolitan Magistrate, Chief Judicial Magistrate, Court of Sessions or High Court.

103. Commissions for examination of witnesses.

(1) Whenever, in the course of a trial by a Force Court, it appears to the Court that the examination of a witness is necessary for the ends of justice, and that the attendance of such witness cannot be procured without an amount of delay, expense or inconvenience which, in the circumstances of the case, would be unreasonable, such Court may address the Judge Attorney-General in order that a commission to take the evidence of such witness may be issued.

(2) The Judge Attorney-General may then, if he thinks necessary, issue a commission to any Metropolitan Magistrate or Judicial Magistrate of the first class, within the local limits of whose jurisdiction such witness resides, to take the evidence of such witness.

(3) The Magistrate to whom the commission is issued, or, if he is the Chief Metropolitan Magistrate, or Chief Judicial Magistrate, or such Metropolitan Magistrate, or Judicial Magistrate, as he appoints in this behalf, shall summon the witness before him or proceed to the place where the witness is, and shall take down his evidence in the same manner, and may for this purpose exercise the same powers, as in the trials of warrant-cases under the Code of Criminal Procedure, 1973 (2 of 1974).

(4) When the witness sides in a tribal area or in any place outside India, the commission may be issued in the manner specified in Chapter XXIII of the Code of Criminal Procedure, 1973 (2 of 1974).

104. Examination of a witness on Commission.

(1) The prosecutor and the accused person in any case in which a commission is issued under Section 103 may respectively forward any interrogatories in writing which the court may think relevant to the issue, and the Magistrate executing the commission shall examine the witness upon such interrogatories.

(2) The prosecutor and the accused person may appear before such Magistrate by counsel, or, except in the case of an accused person in custody, in person, and may examine, cross-examine and re-examine, as the case may be, the said witness.

(4) On receipt of a commission, and deposition returned under sub-section (3), the Judge Attorney-General shall forward the same to the Court at whose instance the commission was issued or, if such Court has been dissolved, to any other Court convened for the trial of the accused person; and the commission, the return thereto and the deposition shall be open to inspection by the prosecutor and the accused person, and may, subject to all just exceptions, be read in evidence in the case by either the prosecutor or the accused, and shall form part of the proceedings of the Court.

(3) After a commission issued under Section 103 has been duly executed, it shall be returned, together with the deposition of the witness examined thereunder to the Judge Attorney-General.

(5) In every case in which a commission is issued under Section 103, the trial may be adjourned for specified time reasonably sufficient for the execution and return of the commission.

105. Conviction for offences not charged. A person charged before a Force Court,—

(a) with desertion may be found guilty of attempting to desert or of being absent without leave;

(b) with attempting to desert may be found guilty of being absent without leave;

(c) with using criminal force may be found guilty of assault;

(d) with using threatening language may be found guilty of using insubordinate language;

(e) with anyone of the offences specified in clauses (a), (b), (c) and (d) of Section 33 may be found guilty of any other of these offences with which he might have been charged;

(f) with an offence punishable under Section 49 may be found guilty of any other offence of which he might have been found guilty, if the provisions of the Code of Criminal Procedure, 1973 (2 of 1974), were applicable;

(g) with any offence under this Act may, on failure of proof of an offence having been committed in circumstances involving a more severe punishment, be found guilty of the same offence as having been committed in circumstances involving a less severe punishment;

(h) with any offence under this Act may be found guilty of having attempted or abetted the commission of that offence, although the attempt or abetment is not separately charged.

106. Presumption as to signatures. In any proceeding under this Act, any application, certificate, warrant, reply or other document purporting to be signed by an officer in the service of the Government shall, on production, be presumed to have been duly signed by the person by whom and in the character in which it purports to have been signed, until the contrary is shown.

107. Enrolment paper.

(1) Any enrolment paper purporting to be signed by an enrolling officer shall, in proceedings under this Act, be evidence of the person enrolled having given the answers to questions which he is therein represented as having given.

(2) The enrolment of such person may be proved by the production of the original or a copy of his enrolment paper purporting to be certified to be a true copy by the officer having the custody of the enrolment paper or service record.

108. Presumption as to certain documents.

(1) A letter, return or other document respecting the service of any person in, or the dismissal, removal or discharge of any person from, any unit of the Force, or respecting the circumstances of any person not having served in, or belonged to, any unit of the Force, if purporting to be signed by or on behalf of the Central Government or the Director-General, or by any prescribed officer, shall be evidence of the facts stated in such letter, return or other document.

(2) A Force List or Gazette purporting to be published by authority shall be evidence of the status and rank of the officers, subordinate officers therein mentioned. and of any appointment held by them and of the battalion, unit, or branch of the Force to which they belong.

(3) Where a record is made in any battalion book in pursuance of this Act or of any rules made thereunder or otherwise in the discharge of official duties, and purports to be signed by the Commanding Officer or by the officer whose duty it is to make such record, such record shall be evidence of the facts therein stated.

(4) A copy of any record in any office of the Force purporting to be certified to be a true copy by the officer having custody of such book shall be evidence of such record.

(5) Where any person subject to this Act is being tried on a charge of desertion or of absence without leave, and such person has surrendered himself into the custody of any officer or other person subject to this Act, or any unit of the Force, or has been apprehended by such officer or person, a certificate purporting to be signed by such officer, or by the Commanding Officer of the unit to which such person belongs or is attached, as the case may be, and stating the fact, date and place of such surrender or apprehension, and the manner in which he was dressed, shall be evidence of the matters so stated.

(6) Where any person subject to this Act is being tried on a charge of desertion or of absence without leave and such person has surrendered himself into the custody of, or has been apprehended by, a police officer not below the rank of an officer-in-charge of a police station, a certificate purporting to be signed by such police officer and stating the fact, date and place of such surrender or apprehension and the manner in which he was dressed shall be evidence of the, matters so stated.

(7) (a) Any document purporting to be a report under the hand of a Government scientific expert to whom this sub-section applies, upon any matter or thing duly submitted to him for examination or analysis and report in the course of any proceeding under this Act, may be used as evidence in any inquiry, trial or other proceeding under this Act.

(b) The Force Court may, if it thinks fit, summon and examine any such expert as to the subject matter of' his report.

(c) Where any such expert is summoned by a Force Court and he is unable to attend personally, he may, unless the Court has expressly directed him to appear personally, depute an officer who is conversant with the facts of the case to depose in the Court on his behalf.

(d) This sub-section applies to the Government scientific experts, for the time being specified in sub-section (4) of Section 293 of the Code of Criminal Procedure, 1973 (2 of 1974).

109. Reference by accused to Government Officer.

(1) If at any trial for desertion or absence without leave, over-staying leave or not rejoining when warned for service, the accused person states in his defence any sufficient or reasonable excuse for his unauthorized absence, and refers in support thereof any officer in the service of the Government, or if it appears that any such officer is likely to prove or disprove the said statement in the defence, the Court shall address such officer and adjourn the proceedings until his reply is received.

(2) The written reply of any officer so referred to shall, if signed by him, be received in evidence and have the same effect as if made on oath before the Court.

(3) If the Court is dissolved before the receipt of such reply or if the Court omits to comply with the provisions of this Section, the convening officer may, at his discretion, annual the proceedings and order a fresh trial.

110. Evidence of previous convictions and general character.

(1) When any person subject to this Act has been convicted by a Force Court of any offence, such Force Court may inquire into, and receive, and record evidence of any previous convictions of such person, either by a Force Court or by a criminal court, or any previous award of punishment under Section 56 or Section 58, and may further inquire into and record the general character of such person and such other matters as may be prescribed.

(2) Evidence received under this Section may be either oral, or in the shape of entries in, or certified extracts from, books of Force Courts or other official records; and it shall not be necessary to give notice before trial to the person tried that evidence as to his previous convictions or character will be received.

(3) At a Summary Force Court, the officer holding the trial may, if he thinks fit, record any previous convictions against the offender, his general character, and such other matters as may be prescribed, as of his own knowledge, instead of requiring them to be proved under the foregoing provisions of this Section.

111. Lunacy of accused.

(1) Whenever, in the course of a trial by a Force Court, it appears to the Court that the person charged is by reason of unsoundness of mind incapable of making his defence, or that he committed the act alleged but was by reason of unsoundness of mind incapable of knowing the nature of the act or knowing that it was wrong or contrary to law, the Court shall record a finding accordingly.

(2) The presiding officer of the Court, or, in the case of a Summary Force Court, the officer holding the trial, shall forthwith report the case to the confirming officer, or to the authority empowered to deal with its finding under Section 129, as the case may be.

(3) The confirming officer to whom the case is reported under sub-section (2) may, if he does not confirm the finding, take steps to have the accused person tried by the same or another Force Court for the offence with which he was charged.

(4) The authority to whom the finding of a Summary Force Court is reported under sub-section (2) and a confirming officer confirming the finding in any case so

reported to him shall order the accused person to be kept in custody in the prescribed manner and shall report the case for the orders of the Central Government.

(5) On receipt of a report under sub-section (4), the Central Government may order the accused person to be detained in a lunatic asylum or other suitable place of safe custody.

112. Subsequent fitness of lunatic accused for trial. Where any accused person, having been found by reason of unsoundness of mind to be incapable of making his defence, is in custody or under detention under Section 111, any officer prescribed in this behalf, may —

(a) if such person is in custody under sub-section (4) of Section 111, on the report of a medical officer that he is capable of making his defence, or

(b) if such person is detained in a jail under sub-section (5) of Section 111, on a certificate of the Inspector-General of Prisons, and if such person is detained in a lunatic asylum under the said sub-section, on a certificate of any two or more of the visitors of such asylum and if he is detained in any other place under that sub-section, on a certificate of the prescribed authority, that he is capable of making his defence, take steps to have such person tried by the same or another Force Court for the offence with which he was originally charged or, if the offence is a civil offence, by a criminal court.

113. Transmission to Central Government of orders under Section 112. A copy of every order made by an officer under Section 112 for the trial of the accused shall forthwith be sent to the Central Government.

114. Release of lunatic accused. Where any person is in custody under sub-section (4) of Section 111 or under detention under sub-section (5) of that Section,—

(a) if such person is in custody under the said sub-section (4), on the report of a medical officer, or

(b) if such person is detained under the said sub-section (5), on a certificate from any of the authorities mentioned in clause (d) of Section 112 that in the judgment of such officer or authority such person may be released without danger of his doing injury to himself or to any other person, the Central Government may order that such person be released or detained in custody or transferred to a public lunatic asylum if he has not already been sent to such an asylum.

115. Delivery of lunatic accused to relatives. Where any relative or friend of any person who is in custody under sub-section (4) of Section 111 or under detention under sub-section (5) of that Section desires that he should be delivered to his care and custody, the Central Government may, upon application by such relative or friend and, on his giving security to the satisfaction of that Government that the person delivered shall be properly taken care of, and, prevented from doing injury to himself or to any other person, and be produced for the inspection of such officer, and at such times and places, as the Central Government may direct, order such person to be delivered to such relative or friend.

116. Order for custody and disposal of property pending trial. When any property regarding which any offence appears to have been committed, or which appears to have been used for the commission of any offence, is produced before a Force Court during a trial, the Court may make such order as it thinks fit for the proper custody of such property pending the conclusion of the trial, and if the property is subject to speedy or natural decay may, after recording such evidence as it thinks necessary, order it to be sold or otherwise disposed of.

117. Order for disposal of property regarding which offence is committed.

(1) After the conclusion of a trial before any Force Court, the Court or the officer confirming the finding or sentence of such Force Court, or any authority superior to such officer, or, in the case of a Summary Force Court whose finding or sentence does not require confirmation, an officer not below the rank of Additional Deputy Inspector-General within whose command the trial was held, may make such order as it or he thinks fit for the disposal by destruction, confiscation, delivery to any person claiming to be entitled to possession thereof, or otherwise, of any property or document produced before the Court or in its custody, or regarding which any offence appears to have been committed or which has been used for the commission of any offence.

(2) Where any order has been made under sub-section (1) in respect of property regarding which an offence appears to have been committed, a copy of such order signed and certified by the authority making the same may, whether the trial was held within India or not, be sent to a magistrate within whose jurisdiction such property for the time being is situated, and such magistrate shall thereupon cause the order to be carried into effect as if it were an order passed by him under the provisions of the Code of Criminal Procedure, 1973 (2 of 1974).

(3) In this Section, the term "property" includes, in the case of property regarding which an offence appears to have been committed, not only such property as has been originally in the possession or under the control of any person, but also any property into or for which the same may have been converted or exchanged, and anything acquired by such conversion or exchange whether immediately or otherwise.

118. Powers of Force Court in relation to proceedings under this Act. Any trial by a Force Court under the provisions of this Act shall be deemed to be a judicial proceeding within the meaning of Sections 193 and 228 of the Indian Penal Code (45 of 1860) and the Force Court shall be deemed to be a Court within the meaning of Sections 345 and 346 of the Code of Criminal Procedure, 1973 (2 of 1974).

119. Tender of pardon to accomplice.

(1) With a view to obtaining the evidence of any person supposed to have been directly or indirectly concerned in or privy to an offence triable by a Force Court other than a Summary Force Court under this Act, the commanding officer, the convening officer or the Force Court, at any stage of the investigation or inquiry into or the trial of, the offence, may tender a pardon to such person

on condition of his making a full and true disclosure of the whole of the circumstances within his knowledge relating to the offence and to every other person concerned, whether as principal or abettor, in the commission thereof.

(2) The commanding officer or the convening officer who tenders a pardon under sub-section (1) shall record—

(a) his reasons for so doing;

(b) whether the tender was or was not accepted by the person to whom it was made, and shall, on application made by the accused, furnish him with a copy of such record free of cost.

(3) Every person accepting a tender of pardon made under sub-section (1) —

(a) shall be examined as a witness by the commanding officer of the accused and in the subsequent trial, if any;

(b) may be detained in Force custody until the termination of the trial.

120. Trial of person not complying with conditions of pardon.

(1) Where, in regard to a person who has accepted a tender of pardon made under Section 119, the Judge Attorney, or as the case may be, the Deputy Judge Attorney-General, or the Additional Judge Attorney-General, or the officer approved under Section 95, certifies that in his opinion such person has, either by wilfully concealing anything essential or by giving false evidence, not complied with the conditions on which the tender was made, such person may be tried for the offence in respect of which the pardon was so tendered or for any other offence of which he appears to have been guilty in connection with the same matter and also for the offence of giving false evidence:

PROVIDED that such person shall not be tried jointly with any of the other accused.

(2) Any statement made by such person accepting the tender of pardon and recorded by his commanding officer or Force Court may be given in evidence against him at such trial.

(3) At such trial, the accused shall be entitled to plead that he has complied with the condition upon which such tender was made; in which case it shall be for the prosecution to prove that the condition has not been complied with.

(4) At such trial, the Force Court shall, before arraignment, ask the accused whether he pleads that he has complied with the condition on which the tender of pardon was made.

(5) If the accused does so plead, the Court shall record the plea and proceed with the trial and it shall, before giving its finding on the charge, find whether or not the accused has complied with the conditions of the pardon, and, if it finds that he has so complied, it shall give a verdict of not guilty.

CHAPTER -IX : CONFIRMATION AND REVISION

121. Finding and sentence not valid unless confirmed. No finding or sentence of a General Force Court or a Petty Force Court shall be valid except so far as it may be confirmed as provided by this Act.

122. Power to confirm finding and sentence of General Force Court. The findings and sentences of General Force Courts may be confirmed by the Central Government or by any officer empowered in this behalf by warrant of the Central Government.

123. Power to confirm finding and sentence of Petty Force Court. The findings and sentences of a Petty Force Court may be confirmed by an officer having power to convene a General Force Court or by any officer empowered in this behalf by warrant of such officer.

124. Limitation of powers of confirming authority. A warrant issued under Section 122 or Section 123 may contain such restrictions, reservations or conditions as the authority issuing it may think fit.

125. Power of confirming authority to mitigate, remit or commute sentences. Subject to such restrictions, reservations conditions, as may be contained in any warrant issued under Section 122 or Section 123 a confirming authority may, when confirming the sentence of a Force Court, mitigate or remit the punishment thereby awarded or commute that punishment for any punishment or punishments lower in the scale laid down in Section 51.

126. Confirming of findings and sentences on board a ship. When any person subject to this Act is tried and sentenced by a Force Court while on board a ship, the finding and sentence so far as not confirmed and executed on board the ship, may be confirmed and executed in like manner as if such person had been tried at the port of disembarkation.

127. Revision of finding or sentence.

(1) Any finding or sentence of a Force Court which requires confirmation may be once revised by order of the confirming authority and on such revision, the Court, if so directed by the confirming authority, may take additional evidence.

(2) The Court on revision, shall consist of the same officers as were present when the original decision was passed unless any of those officers are unavoidably absent.

(3) In case of such unavoidable absence the cause thereof shall be duly certified in the proceedings, and the Court shall proceed with the revision, provided that, if a General Force Court, it still consists of five officers, or, if a Petty Force Court, of three officers.

128. Finding and sentence of a Summary Force Court. The finding and sentence of a Summary Force Court shall not require to be confirmed, but may be carried out forthwith.

129. Transmission of proceedings of Summary Force Court. The proceedings of every Summary Force Court shall, without delay be: forwarded to the officer not below the rank of Additional Deputy Inspector-General within whose command the trial was held, or to the prescribed officer, and such officer, or the Director-General or any officer empowered by him in this behalf may, for reasons based on the merits of the case, but not on merely technical grounds, set aside the proceedings, or reduce the sentence to any other sentence which the Court might have passed.

130. Alteration of finding or sentence in certain cases.

(1) Where a finding of guilty by a Force Court, which has been confirmed or which does not require confirmation, is found for any reason to be invalid or cannot be supported by the evidence, the authority which would have had power under Section 142 to commute the punishment awarded by the sentence, if the finding had been valid may substitute a new finding and pass a sentence for the offence specified or involved in such finding:

PROVIDED that no such substitution shall be made unless such finding could have been validly made by the Force Court on the charge and unless it appears that the Force Court must have been satisfied of the facts establishing the said offence.

(2) Where a sentence passed by a Force Court which has been confirmed, or which does not require confirmation, not being a sentence passed in pursuance of a new finding substituted under sub-section (1), is found for any reason to be invalid, the authority referred to in sub-section (1) may pass a valid sentence.

(3) The punishment awarded by a sentence passed under sub-section (1) or sub-section (2) shall not be higher in the scale of punishments than, or in excess of, the punishment awarded by, the sentence for which a new sentence is substituted under this Section.

(4) Any finding substituted, or any sentence passed, under this Section shall, for the purposes of this Act and the rules, have effect as if it were a finding or sentence, as the case may be, of a Force Court.

131. Remedy against order, finding or sentence of Force Court.

(1) Any person subject to this Act who considers himself aggrieved by any order passed by any Force Court may present a petition to the officer or authority empowered to confirm any finding or sentence of such Force Court, and the confirming authority may take such steps as may be considered necessary to satisfy itself as to the correctness, legality or propriety of the order passed or as to the regularity of any proceeding to which the order relates.

(2) Any person subject to this Act who considers himself aggrieved by a finding or sentence of any Force Court which has been confirmed, may present a petition to the Central Government, the Director-General or any prescribed officer superior in command to the one who confirmed such finding or sentence, and the Central Government, the Director-General, or the prescribed officer, as the case may 'be, may pass such order thereon as it or he thinks fit.

132. Annulment of proceedings. The Central Government, the Director-General or any prescribed officer may annul the proceedings of any Force Court on the ground that they are illegal or unjust unjust.

CHAPTER -X : EXECUTION OF SENTENCES, PARDONS, REMISSIONS, ETC.

133. Form of sentence of death. In awarding a sentence of death, a Force Court shall, in its discretion direct that the offender shall suffer death by being hanged by the neck until he be dead, or shall suffer death by being shot to death.

134. Commencement of sentence of imprisonment. Whenever any person is sentenced by a Force Court under this Act to imprisonment, the term of his sentence shall, whether it has been revised or not, be reckoned to commence on the day on which the original proceedings were signed by the presiding officer, or in the case or a Summary Force Court, by the Court:

PROVIDED that —

(i) if for any reason, beyond the control of the commanding officer or superior officer, the sentence of imprisonment cannot be executed in full or in part, the convict shall be liable to undergo the whole or un-expired portion of sentence, as the case may be, when it becomes possible to carry out the same;

(ii) the period of detention or confinement, if any, undergone by an accused person, during the investigation, inquiry or trial of the case in which he is sentenced and before the date on which the original proceedings were signed shall be set off against the term of his sentence and the liability of such person to undergo imprisonment shall be restricted to the remainder, if any of the term of his sentence.

135. Execution of sentence of imprisonment.

(1) Whenever any sentence of imprisonment is passed under this Act by a Force Court or whenever any sentence of death is commuted to imprisonment, the confirming officer or in case of a Summary Force Court the officer holding the Court, or such other officer as may be prescribed shall, save as otherwise provided in sub-sections (3) and (4), direct that the sentence shall be carried out by confinement in a civil prison.

(2) When a direction has been made under sub-section (1), the commanding officer of the person under sentence or such other officer as may be prescribed shall forward a warrant in the prescribed form to the officer-in-charge of the prison in which such person is to be confined and shall arrange for his despatch to such prison with the warrant.

(3) In the case of a sentence of imprisonment for a period not exceeding three months and passed under this Act by a Force Court, the appropriate officer under sub-section (1) may direct that the sentence shall be carried out by confinement in Force custody instead of in a civil prison.

(4) On active duty, a sentence of imprisonment may be carried out by confinement in such place as the officer hot below the rank of Additional Deputy Inspector-General within whose command, the person sentenced is serving or any prescribed officer may from time to time appoint.

136. Temporary custody of offender. Where a sentence of imprisonment is directed to be undergone in a civil prison, the offender may be kept in Force custody or in any other fit place till such time as it is possible to send him to a civil prison.

137. Execution of sentence of imprisonment in special cases. Whenever, in the opinion of an officer not below the rank of Additional Deputy Inspector-General within whose command the trial is held, any sentence or portion of a sentence of imprisonment cannot for special reasons conveniently be carried out in Force custody in accordance with the provisions of Section 135, such officer may direct that such sentence or portion of sentence shall be carried out by confinement in any civil prison or other fit place.

138. Conveyance of prisoner from place to place. A person under sentence of imprisonment may during his conveyance from place to place or when on board a ship, aircraft, or otherwise, be subjected to such restraint as is necessary for his safe conduct and removal.

139. Communication of certain orders to prison officers. Whenever an order is duly made under this Act setting aside or varying any sentence, order or warrant under which any person is confined in a civil prison, a warrant in accordance with such order shall be forwarded by the officer making the order or his staff officer or such other person as may be prescribed, to the officer-in-charge of the prison in which such person is confined.

140. Execution of sentence of fine. When a sentence of fine is imposed by a Force Court under Section 49, a copy of such sentence signed and certified by the confirming officer, or where no confirmation is required, by the officer holding the trial may be sent to any magistrate in India, and such magistrate shall thereupon cause the fine to be recovered in accordance with the provisions of the Code of Criminal Procedure, 1973 (2 of 1974) as if it were a sentence of fine imposed by such magistrate.

141. Informality or error in the order or warrant. Whenever any person is sentenced to imprisonment under this Act, and is undergoing the sentence in any place or manner in which he might be confined under a lawful order or warrant in pursuance of this Act, the confinement of such person shall not be deemed to be illegal only by reason of informality or error in, or as respects, the order, warrant or other document, or the authority by which, or in pursuance whereof such person was brought into, or, is confined in any such place, and any such order, warrant or document may be amended accordingly.

142. Pardon and remission. When any person subject to this Act has been convicted by a Force Court of any offence, the Central Government or the Director-General or, in the case of a sentence, which he could have confirmed or which did not require confirmation, an officer not below the rank of Additional Deputy Inspector-General within whose command such person at the time of conviction was serving, or the prescribed officer may,

(a) either with or without conditions which the person sentenced accepts, pardon the person or remit the whole or any part of the punishments awarded; or

(b) mitigate the punishment awarded; or

(c) commute such punishment for any less punishment or punishments mentioned in this Act; or

(d) either with or without conditions which the person sentenced accepts release the person on parole.

143. Cancellation of conditional pardons, release on parole or remission.

(1) If any condition on which a person has been pardoned or released on parole or a punishment has been remitted is, in the opinion of the authority which granted the pardon, release or remission, not fulfilled, such authority may cancel the pardon, release or remission, and thereupon the sentence of the

Court shall be carried into effect as if such pardon, release or remission had riot been granted.

(2) A person whose sentence of imprisonment is carried into effect under the provisions of sub-section (1) shall undergo only the un-expired portion of his sentence.

144. Suspension of sentence of imprisonment.

(1) Where a person subject to this Act is sentenced by a Force Court to imprisonment, the Central Government, the Director-General or any officer empowered to convene a General Force Court may suspend the sentence whether or not the offender has already been committed to prison or to Force custody.

(2) The authority or officer specified in sub-section (1) may, in the case of an offender so sentenced direct that until the orders of such authority or officer have been obtained, the offender shall not be committed to prison or to Force custody.

(3) The powers conferred by sub-sections (1) and (2) may be exercised in the case of any such sentence which has been confirmed, reduced or commuted.

145. Orders pending suspension.

(1) Where the sentence referred to in Section 144 is imposed by a Force Court other than a Summary Force Court, the confirming officer may, when confirming the sentence, direct that the offender be not committed to prison or to Force custody until the orders of the authority or officer specified in Section 144 have been obtained.

(2) Where a sentence of imprisonment is imposed by a Summary Force Court, the officer holding the trial may make the direction referred to in sub-section (1).

146. Release on suspension. Where a sentence is suspended under Section 144, the offender shall forthwith be released from custody.

147. Computation of period of suspension. Any period during which the sentence is under suspension shall be reckoned as part of the term of such sentence.

148. Order after suspension. The authority or officer specified in Section 144 may, at any time while a sentence is suspended, order—

(a) that the offender be committed to undergo the un-expired portion of the sentence; or

(b) that the sentence be remitted.

149. Reconsideration of case after suspension.

(1) Where a sentence has been suspended, the case may at any time, and shall at intervals of not more than four months, be reconsidered by the authority or officer not below the rank of an Additional Deputy Inspector-General duly authorised by the authority or officer specified in Section 144.

(2) Where on such reconsideration by the officer so authorised it appears to him that the conduct of offender since his conviction has been such as to justify a remission of the sentence, he shall refer the matter to the authority or officer specified in Section 144.

150. Fresh sentence after suspension. Where an offender, while a sentence on him is suspended under this Act, is sentenced for any other offence, then—

(a) if the further sentence is also suspended under this Act, the two sentences shall run concurrently;

(b) if the further sentence is for a period of three months or more and is not suspended under this Act, the offender shall also be committed to prison or Force custody for the un-expired portion of the previous sentence, but both 'sentences' shall run concurrently; and

(c) if the further sentence is for a period of less than three months and is not suspended under this Act, the offender shall be so committed on that sentence only, and the previous sentence shall, subject to any order which may be passed under Section 148 or Section 149, continue to be suspended.

151. Scope of power of suspension. The powers conferred by Sections 144 and 148 shall be in addition to, and not in derogation of, the power of mitigation, remission and commutation.

152. Effect of suspension and remission on dismissal.

(1) Where in addition to any other sentence. the punishment of dismissal has been awarded by a Force Court, and such other sentence is suspended under Section 144, then, such dismissal shall not take effect until so ordered by the authority or officer specified in Section 144.

(2) If such other sentence is remitted under Section 148, the punishment of dismissal shall also be remitted.

CHAPTER -XI : MISCELLANEOUS

153. Rank structure.

(l) The officers and other members of the Force shall be classified in accordance with their ranks in the following categories, namely:-

(a) officers

(i) Director-General.

(ii) Additional Director-General.

(iii) Inspector-General.

(iv) Deputy Inspector-General.

(v) Additional Deputy Inspector-General

(vi) Commandant.

(vii) Second-in-Command.

(viii) Deputy Commandant.

(ix) Assistant Commandant.

(b) subordinate officers

(i) Subedar-Major.

(ii) Subedar/Inspector.

(iii) Sub-Inspector.

(c) under-officers

(i) Head Constable

(ii) Naik

(iii) Lance Naik.

(d) enrolled persons other than under-officers-constable.

(2) The matters relating to *inter se* seniority of person belonging to the same rank shall be determined in accordance with such rules as may be prescribed.

(3) Notwithstanding anything contained in this Act, the Director-General may, subject to confirmation of the Central Government as provided hereinafter, grant to an officer or a Subedar Major of the Force a rank, mentioned in clause (a) of sub-section (1) as a local rank, whenever considered necessary by him in the interest of better functioning of the Force.

(4) An officer of the Force holding a local rank,—

(a) shall exercise the command and be vested with the powers of an officer holding that rank;

(b) shall cease to hold that rank if the grant of such rank is not confirmed within one month by the Central Government or when so ordered by the Director-General or when he ceases to hold the appointment for which the rank was granted;

(c) shall not be entitled to claim any seniority over other officers of the Force by virtue of having held such rank; and

(d) shall not be entitled to any extra pay and allowances for holding such rank.

EXPLANATION I: Assistant Commandant shall also include a Joint Assistant Commandant in case of personnel belonging to cadres of Motor Mechanic, Combatant Ministerial and Combatant Stenographer of the Force.

EXPLANATION II: Sub-Inspector shall include an Assistant Sub-Inspector in case of personnel belonging to Combatant Ministerial cadre of the Force.

154. Powers and duties conferrable and imposable on members of the Force.

(1) The Central Government may, by general or special order published in the Official Gazette, direct that, subject to such conditions and limitations as may be specified in the order, any member of the Force may exercise or discharge such of the powers or duties under any Central Act as may be specified in the laid order, being the powers and duties which, in the opinion of the Central Government, an officer of the corresponding or lower rank is by such Central Act empowered to exercise or discharge for the said purposes.

(2) The Central Government may, by general or special order published in the Official Gazette, confer or impose, with the concurrence of the State Government concerned, any of the powers or duties which may be exercised or discharged

under a State Act by a police officer upon a member of the Force who, in the opinion of the Central Government, holds a corresponding or higher rank.

(3) Every order made under this Section shall be laid, as soon as may be after it is made, before each House of Parliament, while it is in session, for a total period of thirty days which may be comprised in one session or in two or more successive sessions and if, before the expiry of the session immediately following the session or the successive sessions aforesaid, both Houses agree in making any modification in the order or both Houses agree that the order should not be made, the order shall thereafter have effect only in such modified form or be of no effect, as the case may be; so, however, that any such modification or annulment shall be without prejudice to the validity of anything previously done under that order.

155. Protection for acts of members of the Force.

(1) In any suit or proceeding against any member of the Force for any act done by him in pursuance of a warrant or order of a competent authority, it shall be lawful for him to plead that such act was done by him under the authority of such warrant or order.

(2) Any such plea may be proved by the production of the warrant or order directing the act, and if it is so proved the member of the Force shall thereupon be discharged from liability in respect of the act so done by him, notwithstanding any defect in the jurisdiction of the authority which issued such warrant or order.

(3) Notwithstanding anything contained in any other law for the time being in force, any legal proceeding (whether civil or criminal) which may lawfully be brought against any member of the Force for anything done or intended to be done under the powers conferred by, or in pursuance of any provision of this Act or the rules, shall be commenced within three months after the act complained of was committed and not otherwise, and notice in writing of such proceedings and of the cause thereof shall be given to the defendant or his superior officer at least one month before the commencement of such proceedings.

156. Power to make rules.

(1) The Central Government may, by notification, make rules for the purpose of carrying into effect the provisions of this Act.

(2) In particular, and without prejudice to the generally of the foregoing power, such rules may provide for—

(a) the constitution, governance, command and discipline of the Force;

(b) the enrolment of persons to the Force and the recruitment of other members of the Force;

(c) the conditions of service (including deductions from pay and allowances) of members of the Force;

(d) the precedence, powers of command and authority of the officers, subordinate officers, under-officers and other persons subject to this Act;

(e) the dismissal, removal, retirement, release or discharge from the service of persons subject to this Act;

(f) the purposes and other matters required to be prescribed under Section 13;

(g) the amount and incidence of fine to be imposed under Section 60;

(h) the convening, constitution, adjournment, dissolution and sittings of Force Courts, the procedure to be observed in trials by such Courts, the persons by whom an accused may be defended is such trials and the appearance of such persons thereat;

(i) the confirmation, revision and annulment of, and petitions against, the findings and, sentences of Force Courts;

(j) the forms of orders to be made under the provisions of this Act relating to Force Courts and the awards and infliction of death, imprisonment and detention;

(k) the constitution of authorities to decide for what persons, to what amounts and in what manner, provisions should be made for dependants under Section 67 and the due carrying out of such decisions;

(l) the carrying into effect of sentences of Force Courts;

(m) any matter necessary for the purpose of carrying this Act into execution, as far as it relates to the investigation, arrest, custody, trial and punishment of offences triable or punishable under this Act;

(n) the ceremonials to be observed and marks of respect to be paid in the Force;

(o) the convening of, the constitution, procedure and practice of, courts of inquiry, the summoning of witnesses before them and the administration of oaths by such courts;

(p) the recruitment and conditions of service of Judge Attorney-General, Additional Judge Attorney-General, Deputy Judge Attorney-General and Judge Attorney;

(q) the disposal of the private or regimental property, or any other dues including provident fund of persons subject to this Act who die or desert or are ascertained to be of unsound mind or while on active duty are officially reported as missing;

(r) any other matter which is to be, or may be, prescribed, or in respect of which provision is to be, or may be, made by rules.

(3) Notwithstanding anything contained in any other law for the time being in force, any legal proceeding (whether civil or criminal) which may lawfully be brought against any member of the Force for anything done or intended to be done under the powers conferred by, or in pursuance of any provision of this

Act or the rules, shall be commenced within three months after the act complained of was committed and not otherwise, and notice in writing of such proceedings and of the cause thereof shall be given to the defendant or his superior officer at least one month before the commencement of such proceedings.

157. Provisions as to existing Indo-Tibetan Border Police Force.

(1) The Indo-Tibetan Border Police Force in existence at the commencement of this Act shall be deemed to be the Force constituted under this Act.

(2) The members of the Indo-Tibetan Border Police Force in existence at the commencement of this Act shall be deemed to have been appointed or, as the case may be, enrolled as such under this Act.

(3) Anything done or any action taken before the commencement of this Act in relation to the constitution of the Indo-Tibetan Border Police Force referred to in sub-section (1), in relation to any person appointed or enrolled, as the case may be, thereto, shall be as valid and as effective in law as if such thing or action was done or taken under this Act:

PROVIDED that nothing in this sub-section shall render any person guilty of any offence in respect of anything done or omitted to be done by him before the commencement of this Act.

❒❒❒

24

The Maintenance of Internal Security Act, 1971

ACT NO. 26 OR 1971

This Act has been repealed by the Maintenance of Internal Security (Repeal) Act, 1978 (27 of 1978), s. 2 (w.e.f. 3-8-1978).

□□□

25

The Manoeuvres, Field Firing and Artillery Practice Act, 1938

[Act No.5 of 1938] [12th March, 1938]

AN ACT to provide facilities for military manoeuvres and for field firing and artillery practice.

WHEREAS it is expedient to provide facilities for military manoeuvres and for field firing and artillery practice; It is hereby enacted as follows:—

It has been applied to the District of Angul and the Districts of Koraput the Khondmals and the Ganjam Agency tracts see Orissa Gaz., 1948, Pt. III, page 83 and 419 respectively: Angul District is now a sub-division of Dhenkanal district.

This act has been extended to the new provinces and merged States by the Merged States (Laws) Act 1949 (59 of 1959) Section 3 (1-1-1950) and to the States of Manipur Tripura and Vindhya Pradesh by the Union Territories (Law) act 1950 (30 of 1950). Manipur and Tripura are States now and Vindhya Pradesh has merged with the State of Madhya Pradesh - See Act 37 of 1956 sec. 9 (1) (e), see also Act 81 of 1971 Sections 3 and 4 (30-12-1971).

2. Power of State Government to authorise manoeuvres.

(1) The State Government may, by notification in the local Official Gazette, authorise the execution of military manoeuvres over any area specified in the notification during a specified period not exceeding three months:

PROVIDED that the same area or any part thereof shall not ordinarily be so specified more than once in any period of three years.

(2) The State Government shall publish notice of its intention to issue a notification under sub-section (1) as early as possible in advance of the issue of the notification, and no such notification shall be issued until the expiry of three months from the date of the first publication of such notice in the local Official Gazette.

(3) The notice required by sub-section (2) shall be given by publication in the local Official Gazette and shall also be given throughout the area which it is proposed to specify in the notification by publication in the manner prescribed by rules made under Section 13, and shall be repeated by like publication one month and one week as nearly as may be before the commencement of the manoeuvres.

3. Powers exercisable for purposes of manoeuvres.

(1) Where a notification under sub-section (1) of Section 2 has been issued, such persons as are included in the military forces engaged in the manoeuvres may, within the specified limits and during the specified periods,

(a) Pass over, or encamp, construct military works of a temporary character, or execute military manoeuvres on, the area specified in the notification, and

(b) Supply themselves with water from any source of water in such area :

PROVIDED that nothing herein contained shall authorise the taking of water from any source of supply, whether belonging to a private owner or a public authority, of an amount in excess of the reasonable requirements of the military forces or of such amount as to curtail the supply ordinarily required by those entitled to the use of such water supply.

(2) The provisions of sub-section (1) shall not authorise entry on or interference with any well or tank held sacred by any religious community or any place of worship or ground attached thereto except for the legitimate purpose of offering prayers or any place or building reserved or used for the disposal of the dead, or any dwelling house or premises attached thereto or any educational institution, factory, workshop or store or any premises used for the carrying on of any trade, business or manufacture or any garden or pleasure ground, or any ancient monument as defined in Section 2 of the Ancient Monuments Preservation Act, 1904.

4. Duty of Officer Commanding to repair damage. The Officcr in Command of the military forces engaged in the manoeuvres shall cause all lands used under the powers conferred by this Chapter to be restored, as soon and as far as practicable, to their previous condition.

5. Right to compensation for damage caused by manoeuvres. Where a notification issued under Section 2 authorises the execution of military manoeuvres compensation shall be payable from the Defence Estimates for any damage to person or property or interference with rights or privileges arising from such manoeuvres including expenses reasonably incurred in protecting person, property, rights and privileges.

6. Method of assessing compensation.

(1) The Collector of the district in which any area utilised for the purpose of manoeuvres is situated shall depute one or more Revenue Officers to accompany the forces engaged in the manoeuvres for the purpose of determining the amount of any compensation payable under Section 5.

(2) The Revenue Officer shall consider all claims for compensation under Section 5 and determine, on local investigation and where possible after hearing the claimant, the amount of compensation, if any, which shall be awarded in each case; and shall disburse on the spot to the claimant the compensation so determined as payable.

(3) Any claimant, dissatisfied with a refusal of the Revenue Officer to award him compensation or with the amount of compensation awarded to him by the Revenue Officer, may, at any time within fifteen days from the communication to him of the decision of the Revenue Officer, give notice to the Revenue Officer of his intention to appeal against the decision.

(4) Where any such notice has been given, the Collector of the district shall constitute a commission consisting of himself as chairman, a person nominated by the Officer Commanding the forces engaged in the manoeuvres and two persons nominated by the District Board, and the commission shall decide all appeals of which notice has been given.

(5) The commission may exercise its powers notwithstanding the absence of any member of the commission, and the chairman of the commission shall have a casting vote in the case of an equal division of opinion.

(6) The decision of the commission shall be final and no suit shall lie in any Civil Court in respect of any matter decided by the commission.

(7) No fee shall be charged in connection with any claim, notice, appeal, application or document filed before the Revenue Officer, Collector or the commission under this Section.

7. Offences. If, within the area and during the period specified in a notification under sub-section (1) of Section 2, any person

(a) Wilfully obstructs or interferes with the execution of the manoeuvres, or

(b) Without due authority enters or remains in any camp, or

(c) Without due authority interferes with any flag or mark or any apparatus used or the purposes of the manoeuvres. He shall be punishable with fine which may extend to ten rupees.

8. Definitions. In this Chapter-

(a) "Field firing" includes air armament practice;

(b) "Notified area" means an area defined in a notification issued under sub-section (1) of Section 9.

9. Power of State Government to authorise field firing and artillery Practice.

(1) The State Government may, by notification in the local Official Gazette, define any area as an area within which for a specified term of years the carrying out periodically of field firing and artillery practice may be authorised.

(2) The State Government may, by notification in the local Official Gazette, authorise the carrying out of field firing and artillery practice throughout a notified area or any specified part thereof during any period or periods specified in the notification.

(3) Before any notification under sub-section (2) is issued, the State Government shall publish notice of its intention to issue such notification as early as possible in advance of the issue of the notification, and no such notification shall be issued until the expiry of two months from the date of the first publication of the notice in the local Official Gazette.

(4) The notice required by sub-section (3) shall be given by publication in the local Official Gazette and shall also be given throughout the notified area by publication in some newspaper circulating in and in the language commonly understood in that area and by beat of drum and by affixation in all prominent places of copies of the said notice in the language of the locality and in such other manner as may be prescribed by rules made under Section 13 and shall be repeated by like publication one week as nearly as may be before the commencement of the period or of each period specified in the notification :

PROVIDED that the fact of the said beat of drum and affixation shall be verified in writing by one headman and two other literate inhabitants of the locality and provided further that such notice by the beat of drum shall be given seven and two days as nearly as may be before the commencement of such field firing and artillery practice.

10. Powers exercisable for purposes of field firing and artillery practice.

(1) Where a notification under sub-section (2) of Section 9 has been issued, such persons as are included in the forces engaged in field firing or artillery practice may, within the notified area or specified part thereof during the specified period or periods,—

(a) Carry out field firing and artillery practice with lethal missiles, and

(b) Exercise, subject to the provisions of Sections 3 and 4, any of the rights conferred by Section 3 on forces engaged in military manoeuvres :

PROVIDED that the provisions of sub-section (2) of Section 3 shall not debar entry into, or interference with, any place specified in that sub-section, if it is situated in an area declared to be a danger zone under sub-section (2) of this Section, to the extent that may be necessary to ensure the exclusion from it of persons and domestic animals :

PROVIDED FURTHER that in the case of a dwelling house occupied by women adequate warning shall be given through a local inhabitant and entry shall be effected after such warning in the presence of two respectable inhabitants of the locality.

(2) The Officer Commanding the forces engaged in any such practice may, within the notified area or specified part thereof, declare any area to be a danger zone, and thereupon the Collector shall, on application made to him by the Officer

Commanding the forces engaged in the practice, prohibit the entry into and secure the removal from such danger zone of all persons and domestic animals during the times when the discharge of lethal missiles is taking place or there is danger to life or health.

11. Compensation. The provisions of Sections 5 and 6 shall apply in the case of field firing and artillery practice as they apply in the case of military manoeuvres :

PROVIDED that the compensation payable under this Section shall include compensation for exclusion or removal from any place declared to be a danger zone of persons or domestic animals, such compensation to be disbursed at not less than the minimum rates prescribed by rules made under Section 13 before the exclusion or removal is enforced, and shall also include compensation for any loss of employment or deterioration of crops resulting from any such exclusion or removal.

12. Offences. If, during any period specified in a notification issued under sub-section (2) of Section 9, any person within a notified area-

(a) wilfully obstructs or interferes with the carrying out of field firing or artillery practice; or

(b) without due authority enters or remains in any camp; or

(c) without due authority enters or remains in any area declared to be a danger zone at a time when entry thereto is prohibited; or

(d) without due authority interferes with any flag or mark or target or any apparatus used for the purposes of the practice. He shall be punishable with fine which may extend to ten rupees.

13. Power to make rules. The State Government may, by notification in the local Official Gazette, make rules-

(a) Prescribing the manner in which the notices required by sub-section (2) of Section 2 and sub-section (3) of Section 9 shall be published in the areas concerned;

(b) Regulating the use under this Act of land for manoeuvres or field firing and artillery practice in such manner as to secure the public against danger and to enable the manoeuvre, or practice, to be carried out without interference and with the minimum inconvenience to the inhabitants of the areas affected;

(c) Regulating the procedure of the Revenue Officers and commissions referred to in Section 6 in such manner as to secure due publicity regarding the method of making claims for compensation and preferring appeals from original awards of compensation, the expeditious settlement of claims and of appeals and the payment of compensation so far as possible direct to the claimants; and

(d) Defining the principles to be followed by the Revenue Officers and commissions referred to in Section 6 in assessing the amount of compensation to be awarded.

❑❑❑

26

The National Cadet Corps Act, 1948

[ACT No. 31 OF 1948] [16TH APRIL, 1948]

AN ACT to provide for the constitution of a National Cadet Corps.

WHEREAS it is expedient to provide for the constitution of a National Cadet Corps. It is hereby enacted as follows:—

2. Definitions. In this Act, unless there is anything repugnant in the subject or context -

"Corps" means the National Cadet Corps constituted under this Act;

"Enrolled" means enrolled in the Corps under this Act;

"Prescribed" means prescribed by rules made under this Act;

"School" includes any institution recognised in this behalf by the Central Government or the State Government;

"University" means any university established by law in India and includes colleges affiliated to universities, intermediate colleges and such technical institutions of collegiate status, as are recognised in this behalf by the Central Government or the State Government.

3. Constitution of the National Cadet Corps. There shall be raised and maintained in the manner hereinafter provided a Corps to be designated the National Cadet Corps:

PROVIDED that the Central Government may establish all or any of the units of the Corps as and when necessary.

4. Constitution and disbandment of units. The Central Government may constitute in any State[1] one or more units of the Corps, members of which shall be recruited from amongst the students of any university or school, and may disband or reconstitute any unit so constituted.

5. Division of the Corps into Divisions. There shall be three Divisions of the Corps, namely :-

(i) The Senior Division, recruitment to which shall be from amongst the students of the male sex of any university;

(ii) The Junior Division, recruitment to which shall be from amongst the students of the male sex of any school; and

(iii) The Girls Division, recruitment to which shall be from amongst the students of the female sex of any university or school.

6. Enrolment.

(1) Any student of the male sex of any university may offer himself for enrolment as a cadet in the Senior Division, and any student of the male sex of any school may offer himself for enrolment as a cadet in the Junior Division if he is of the prescribed age or over.

(2) Any student of the female sex of any university or school may offer herself for enrolment as a cadet in the Girls Division:

PROVIDED that in the latter case she is of the prescribed age or over.

7. Central Government may raise other units. Notwithstanding anything contained in this Act, the Central Government may, by notification, provide for the constitution of any other units of the Corps in any place and prescribe the persons or class of persons who may be eligible for enrolment therein.

8. Discharge. Every person enrolled under this Act shall be entitled to receive his or her discharge from the Corps on the expiration of the period for which he or she was enrolled or on his or her ceasing to be borne on the roll of the university or school to which he or she may belong :

PROVIDED that any person enrolled may be discharged at any time by such authority and subject to such conditions as may be prescribed.

9. Appointment of officers. The Central Government may provide for the appointment of officers in or for any unit of the Corps either from amongst members of the staff of any university or school or otherwise and may prescribe the duties, powers and functions of such officers.

10. Duties of persons subject to this Act. No person subject to this Act shall by virtue of being a member of the Corps be liable for active military service, but subject thereto any such person shall be liable to perform such duties and discharge such obligations as may be prescribed.

11. Punishment for offences under this Act. Any person enrolled under this Act may be punished for the contravention of any rule made under this Act with fine which may extend to fifty rupees to be recovered in such manner and by such authority as may be prescribed.

12. Power to appoint Advisory Committees.

(1) The Central Government may for the purpose of advising it on all matters of policy connected with the constitution and administration of the Corps appoint a Central Advisory Committee consisting of the following persons, namely:-

(a) The Minister for Defence, who shall be the Chairman of the Committee;

(b) The Secretary to the Government of India, Ministry of Defence, *ex-officio*;

(c) The Secretary to the Government of India, Ministry of Education, *ex-officio*;

(d) The Financial Adviser, Defence, *ex-officio*;

[2][(e) the Chief of the Army Staff, *ex-officio*;

(f) The Chief of the Naval Staff, *ex-officio*;

(g) The Chief of the Air Staff, *ex-officio*;

(h) Five non-official members to be nominated by the Central Government; and

[3][(i) two-members to be elected by the House of the People and one member to be elected by the Council of States annually.]

(2) The Central Government may also appoint, for the same purpose as is specified in sub-section (1), such [The words "Provincial or" were omitted by the A.O. 1950.] State Advisory Committees as it may consider desirable from time to time and may prescribe their duties and functions.

13. Power to make rules.

(1) The Central Government may make rules [For National Cadet Corps Rules, 1948, see Notification No. 289, Gazette of India, 1949, Pt. I, Sec. 3, p. 239] to carry out the objects of this Act.

(2) In particular and without prejudice to the generality of the foregoing power such rules may -

(a) prescribe the conditions subject to which universities or schools shall be allowed to raise units under this Act;

(b) prescribe the persons or class of persons who may be eligible for enrolment under section 7;

(c) prescribe the manner in which, the period for which and the conditions subject to which any person or class of persons may be enrolled under this Act;

(d) provide for the medical examination of persons offering themselves for enrolment under this Act;

(e) prescribe preliminary and periodical military training for any person or class of persons subject to this Act;

(f) prescribe the military or other obligations to which members of the Corps shall be liable when undergoing military training and provide generally for the maintenance of discipline amongst members of the Corps;

(g) prescribe the duties, powers and functions of officers appointed under this Act;

(h) prescribe the allowances or other remuneration payable to persons subject to this Act;

(i) provide for the removal or discharge of any person subject to this Act;

(j) prescribe the offences for which any person subject to this Act may be tried and provide for the trial thereof;

(k) prescribe the manner in which fines levied under this Act may be recovered;

(l) prescribe the duties, powers and functions of Central or State Advisory Committees; and

(m) provide for any other matter which under this Act is to be or may be prescribed.

❑❑❑

Endnotes

1. The words " or Acceding State " omitted by the A.O 1950.
2. Subs. by Act 19 of 1955, s.2 and Sch. for the former clauses (e), (f) and (g).
3. Subs. by Act 57 of 1952, s.2.

27

The National Commission For Minority Educational Institutions Act, 2004

Act No. 2 of 2005 [6th January, 2005]

AN ACT to constitute a National Commission for Minority Educational Institutions and to provide for matters connected therewith or incidental thereto.

Be it enacted by Parliament in the Fifty-fifth Year of the Republic of India as follows:-

CHAPTER - I : PRELIMINARY

1. Short title, extent and commencement.

(1) This Act may be called the National Commission for Minority Educational Institutions Act, 2004.

(2) It extends to the whole of India except the State of Jammu and Kashmir.

(3) It shall be deemed to have come into force on the 11th day of November, 2004.

2. Definitions. In this Act, unless the context otherwise requires -

(a) "affiliation" together with its grammatical variations, includes, in relation to a college, recognition of such college by, association of such college with, and admission of such college to the privileges of, a Scheduled University;

(b) "college" means a college or teaching institution (other than a University) established or maintained by a person or group of persons from amongst a minority community;

(c) "Commission" means the National Commission for Minority Educational Institutions constituted under Section 3;

(d) "degree" means any such degree as may, with previous approval of the Central Government, be specified in this behalf by the University Grants Commission, by notification in the Official Gazette;

(e) "Member" means a member of the Commission and includes the Chairperson;

(f) "minority", for the purpose of this Act, means a community notified as such by the Central Government;

(g) "Minority Educational Institution" means a college or institution (other than a University) established or maintained by a person or group of persons from amongst the minorities;

(h) "prescribed" means prescribed by rules made unuer this Act;

(i) "qualification" means a degree or any other qualification awarded by a University;

(j) "Scheduled University" means a University specified in the Schedule;

(k) "technical education" has the meaning assigned to it in clause (g) of Section 2 of the All India Council for Technical Education Act, 1987 (52 of 1987);

(l) "University" means a university defined under clause (f) of Section 2 of the University Grants Commission Act, 1956 (1 of 1956), and includes an institution deemed to be a University under Section 3 of that Act, or an institution specifically empowered by an Act of Parliament to confer or grant degrees.

CHAPTER - II : THE NATIONAL COMMISSION FOR MINORITY EDUCATIONAL INSTITUTIONS

3. Constitution of National Commission for Minority Educational Institutions.

(1) The Central Government shall, by notification in the Official Gazette, constitute a body to be known as the National Commission for Minority Educational Institutions to exercise the powers conferred on, and to perform the functions assigned to, it under this Act.

(2) The Commission shall consist of a Chairperson and two members to be nominated by the Central Government.

4. Qualifications for appointment as Chairperson or other Member.

(1) A person shall not be qualified for appointment as the Chairperson unless he -

(a) is a member of a minority community; and

(b) has been a Judge of a High Court.

(2) A person shall not be qualified for appointment as a Member unless he -

(a) is a member of a minority community; and

(b) is a person of eminence, ability and integrity.

5. Term of office and conditions of service of Chairperson and Members.

(1) Every Member shall hold office for a term of five years from the date on which he assumes office.

(2) A Member may, by writing under his hand addressed to the Central Government, resign from the office of Chairperson or, as the case may be, of Member at any time.

(3) The Central Government shall remove a person from the office of Member if that person-

(a) becomes an undischarged insolvent;

(b) is convicted and sentenced to imprisonment for an offence which, in the opinion of the Central Government, involves moral turpitude;

(c) becomes of unsound mind and stands so declared by a competent court;

(d) refuses to act or becomes incapable of acting;

(e) is, without obtaining leave of absence from the Commission, absent from three consecutive meetings of the Commission; or

(f) in the opinion of the Central Government, has so abused the position of Chairperson or Member as to render that person's continuance in office detrimental to the public interest:

PROVIDED that no person shall be removed under this clause until that person has been given an opportunity of being heard in the matter.

(4) A vacancy caused under sub-section (2) or otherwise shall be filled by fresh nomination and a person so nominated shall hold office for the unexpired period of the term for which his predecessor in office would have held office if such vacancy had not arisen.

(5) The salaries and allowances payable to, and the other terms and conditions of service of, the Chairperson and Members shall be such as may be prescribed.

6. Officers and other employees of Commission.

(1) The Central Government shall provide the Commission with a Secretary and such other officers and employees as may be necessary for the efficient performance of the functions of the Commission under this Act.

(2) The salaries and allowances payable to, and the other terms and conditions of service of, the Secretary, officers and other employees appointed for the purpose of the Commission shall be such as may be prescribed.

7. Salaries and allowances to be paid out of grants. The salaries and allowances payable to the Chairperson and Members and the administrative expenses, including salaries, allowances and pensions payable to the Secretary, officers and other employees referred to in Section 6, shall be paid out of the grants referred to in sub-section (1) of Section 14.

8. Vacancies, etc., not to invalidate proceedings of Commission. No act or proceeding of the commission shall be questioned or shall be invalid on the ground merely of the existence of any vacancy or defect in the constitution of the Commission.

9. Procedure to be regulated by Commission.

(1) The Commission shall meet as and when necessary at such time and place as the Chairperson may think fit.

(2) The Commission shall regulate its own procedure.

(3) All orders and decisions of the Commission shall be authenticated by the Secretary or any other officer of the Commission duly authorised by the Secretary in this behalf.

CHAPTER - III : RIGHT OF A MINORITY EDUCATIONAL INSTITUTION

10. Right of a Minority Educational Institution to seek affiliation to a Scheduled University.

(1) Notwithstanding anything contained in any other law for the time being in force, a Minority Educational Institution may seek recognition as an affiliated college of a Scheduled University of its choice.

(2) The Scheduled University shall consult the Government of the State in which the minority educational institution seeking affiliation under sub-section (1) is situate and views of such Government shall be taken into consideration before granting affiliation.

CHAPTER - IV : FUNCTIONS AND POWERS OF COMMISSION

11. Functions of Commission. Notwithstanding anything contained in any other law for the time being in force, the Commission shall-

(a) advise the Central Government or any State Government on any question relating to the education of minorities that may be referred to it;

(b) look into specific complaints regarding deprivation or violation of rights of minorities to establish and administer educational institutions of their choice and any dispute relating affiliation to a Scheduled University and report its findings to the Central Government for its implementation; and

(c) to do such other acts and things as may be necessary, incidental or conducive to the attainment of all or any of the objects of the Commission.

12. Powers of Commission.

(1) If any dispute arises between a minority educational institution and a Scheduled University relating to its affiliation to such University, the decision of the Commission thereon shall be final.

(2) The Commission shall, for the purposes of discharging its functions under this Act, have all the powers of a civil court trying a suit and in particular, in respect of the following matters, namely:-

  (a) summoning and enforcing the attendance of any person from any part of India and examining him on oath;

  (b) requiring the discovery and production of any document;

  (c) receiving evidence on affidavits;

  (d) subject to the provisions of Sections 123 and 124 of the Indian Evidence Act, 1872 (1 of 1872), requisitioning any public record or document or copy of such record or document from any office;

  (e) issuing commissions for the examination of witnesses or documents; and

  (f) any other matter which may be prescribed.

13. Financial and administrative powers of Chairperson. The Chairperson shall exercise such financial and administrative powers as may be vested in him by the rules made under this Section:

PROVIDED that the Chairperson shall have authority to delegate such of the financial and administrative powers as he may think fit to any Member or Secretary or any other officer of the Commission subject to the condition that such Member or Secretary or officer shall, while exercising such delegated powers, continue to act under the direction, control and supervision of the Chairperson.

CHAPTER - V : FINANCE, ACCOUNTS AND AUDIT

14. Grants by Central Government.

(1) The Central Government shall, after due appropriation made by Parliament by law in this behalf, pay to the Commission by way of grants such sums of money as the Central Government may think fit for being utilised for the purposes of this Act.

(2) The Commission may spend such sums of money as it thinks fit for performing the functions under this Act, and such sums shall be treated as expenditure payable out of the grants referred to in sub-section (1).

15. Accounts and audit.

(1) The Commission shall maintain proper accounts and other relevant records and prepare an annual statement of accounts in such form as may be prescribed by the Central Government in consultation with the Comptroller and Auditor-General of India.

(2) The accounts of the Commission shall be audited by the Comptroller and Auditor-General at such intervals as may be specified by him and any expenditure incurred in connection with such audit shall be payable by the Commission to the Comptroller and Auditor-General.

(3) The Comptroller and Auditor-General and any person appointed by him in connection with the audit of the accounts of the Commission under this Act shall have the same rights and privileges and the authority in connection with such audit as the Comptroller and Auditor-General generally has in connection with the audit of Government accounts and, in particular, shall have the right to demand the production of books, accounts, connected vouchers and other documents and papers and to inspect any of the offices of the Commission.

16. Annual report. The Commission shall prepare, in such form and at such time, for each financial year, as may be prescribed, its annual report, giving a full account of its activities during the previous financial year and forward a copy thereof to the Central Government.

17. Annual report and audit report to be laid before Parliament. The Central Government shall cause the annual report, together with a memorandum of action taken on the advice tendered by the Commission under Section 11 and the reasons for the non-acceptance, if any, of any such advice, and the audit report to be laid as soon as may be after they are received before each House of Parliament.

CHAPTER - VI : MISCELLANEOUS

18. Power to amend Schedule.

(1) The Central Government if deems it fit may, by notification in the Official Gazette, amend the Schedule by including therein any other University or omitting therefrom any University already specified therein and on the publication of such notification, such University shall be deemed to be included in or, as the case may be, omitted from the Schedule.

(2) Every notification issued under sub-section (1), shall be laid before each House of Parliament.

19. Chairperson, Members, Secretary, employees, etc., of Commission to be public servants. The Chairperson, Members, Secretary, officers and other employees of the Commission shall be deemed to be public servants within the meaning of Section 21 of the Indian Penal Code (45 of 1860).

20. Directions by Central Government.

(1) In the discharge of its functions under this Act, the Commission shall be guided by such direction on questions of policy relating to national purposes, as may be given to it by the Central Government.

(2) If any dispute arises between the Central Government and the Commission as to whether a question is or is not a question of policy relating to national purposes, the decision of the Central Government shall be final.

21. Protection of action taken in good faith. No suit, prosecution or other legal proceeding shall lie against the Central Government, Commission, Chairperson, Members, Secretary or any officer or other employee of the Commission for anything which is in good faith done or intended to be done under this Act.

22. Act to have overriding effect. The provisions of this Act shall have effect notwithstanding anything inconsistent therewith contained in any other law for the time being in force or in any instrument having effect by virtue of any law other than this Act.

23. Returns or information.-The Commission shall furnish to the Central Government such returns or other information with respect to its activities as the Central Government may, from time to time, require.

24. Power to make rules.

(1) The Central Government may, by notification in the Official Gazette, make rules for carrying out the provisions of this Act.

(2) In particular, and without prejudice to the generality of the foregoing powers, such rules may provide for all or any of the following matters, namely:-

(a) the salaries and allowances payable to, and the other terms and conditions of the service of, the Chairperson and Members under sub-section (5) of Section 5 and of the Secretary, officers and other employees under sub-section (2) of Section 6;

(b) the financial and administrative powers to be exercised by the Chairperson under Section 13;

(c) the form in which the annual statement of accounts shall be prepared under sub-section (1) of Section 15;

(d) the form in, and the time at, which the annual report shall be prepared under Section 16;

(e) any other matter which is required to be, or may be, prescribed.

(3) Every rule made under this Act shall be laid, as soon as may be after it is made, before each House of Parliament, while it is in session, for a total period of thirty days which may be comprised in one session or in two or more successive sessions, and if, before the expiry of the session immediately following the session or the successive sessions aforesaid, both Houses agree in making any modification in the rule or both Houses agree that the rule should not be made, the rule shall thereafter have effect only in such modified form or be of no effect, as the case may be; so, however, that any such modification or annulment shall be without prejudice to the validity of anything previously done under that rule.

25. Power to remove difficulties.

(1) If any difficulty arises in giving effect to the provisions of this Act, the Central Government may, by order published in the Official Gazette, make such provisions not inconsistent with the provisions of this Act, as appear to it to be necessary or expedient, for removing the difficulty:

PROVIDED that no such order shall be made after the expiry of a period of two years from the date of commencement of this Act.

(2) Every order made under this Section shall, as soon as may be after it is made, be laid before each House of Parliament.

26. Repeal and saving.

(1) The National Commission for Minority Educational Institutions Ordinance, 2004 (Ord. 6 of 2004) is hereby repealed.

(2) Notwithstanding the repeal of the said Ordinance, anything done or any action taken under the said Ordinance shall be deemed to have been done or taken under the corresponding provisions of this Act.

THE SCHEDULE

[*See* Section 2 (j)]

Sl. No.	Name of the University
1.	University of Delhi.
2.	North-Eastern Hill University.
3.	Pondicherry University.
4.	Assam University.
5.	Nagaland University.
6.	Mizoram University.

❏❏❏

28

The National Security Act, 1980

27TH DECEMBER, 1980

AN ACT to provide for preventive detention in certain cases and for matters connected therewith.

Be it enacted by Parliament in the Thirty-first Year of the Republic of India as follows: —

2. Definitions. In this Act, unless the context otherwise requires, —

(a) "appropriate Government" means, as respects a detention order made by the Central Government or a person detained under such order, the Central Government, and as respects a detention order made by a State Government or by an officer subordinate to a State Government or as respects a person detained under such order, the State Government;

(b) "detention order" means an order made under Section 3;

(c) "foreigner" has the same meaning as in the Foreigners Act, 1946 (31 of 1946);

(d) "person" includes a foreigner;

(e) "State Government", in relation to a Union territory, means the administrator thereof.

3. Power to make orders detaining certain persons.

(1) The Central Government or the State Government may, —

(a) if satisfied with respect to any person that with a view to preventing him from acting in any manner prejudicial to the defence of India, the relations of India with foreign powers, or the security of India, or

(b) if satisfied with respect to any foreigner that with a view to regulating his continued presence in India or with a view to making arrangements for his expulsion from India, it is necessary so to do, make an order directing that such person be detained.

(2) The Central Government or the State Government may, if satisfied with respect to any person that with a view to preventing him from acting in any manner prejudicial to the security of the State or from acting in any manner prejudicial to the maintenance of Public order or from acting in any manner prejudicial to the maintenance of supplies and services essential to the community it is necessary so to do, make an order directing that such person be detained.

EXPLANATION: For the purposes of this sub-section, "acting in any manner prejudicial to the maintenance of supplies and services essential to the community" does not include "acting in any manner prejudicial to the maintenance of supplies of commodities essential to the community" as defined in the Explanation to sub-section (1) of Section 3 of the Prevention of Black-marketing and Maintenance of Supplies of Essential Commodities Act, 1980 (7 of 1980), and accordingly, no order of detention shall be made under this Act on any ground on which an order of detention may be made under that Act.

(3) If, having regard to the circumstances prevailing or likely to prevail in any area within the local limits of the jurisdiction of a District Magistrate or a Commissioner of Police, the State Government is satisfied that it is necessary so to do, it may, by order in writing, direct, that during such period as may be specified in the order, such District Magistrate or Commissioner of Police may also, if satisfied as provided in sub-section (2), exercise the powers conferred by the said sub-section:

***PROVIDED** that the period specified in an order made by the State Government under this sub-section shall not, in the first instance, exceed three months, but the State Government may, if satisfied as aforesaid that it is necessary so to do, amend such order to extend such period from time to time by any period not exceeding three months at any one time.*

(4) When any order is made under this Section by an officer mentioned in sub-section (3), he shall forthwith report the fact to the State Government to which he is subordinate together with the grounds on which the order has been made and such other particulars as, in his opinion, have a bearing on the matter, and no such order shall remain in force for more than twelve days after the making thereof unless, in the meantime, it has been approved by the State Government:

***PROVIDED** that where under Section 8 the grounds of detention are communicated by the officer making the order after five days but not later than ten days from the date of detention, this sub-section shall apply subject to the modification that, for the words "twelve days", the words "fifteen days" shall be substituted.*

(5) When any order is made or approved by the State Government under this Section, the State Government shall, within seven days, report the fact to the Central Government together with the grounds on which the order has been made and such other particulars as, in the opinion of the State Government, have a bearing on the necessity for the order.

4. Execution of detention orders. A detention order may be executed at any place in India in the manner provided for the execution of warrants of arrest under the Code of Criminal Procedure, 1973 (2 of 1974).

5. Power to regulate place and conditions of detention. Every person in respect of whom a detention order has been made shall be liable—

(a) to be detained in such place and under such conditions,

(b) including conditions as to maintenance, discipline and punishment for breaches of discipline, as the appropriate Government may, by general or special order, specify; and

(c) to be removed from one place of detention to another place of detention, whether within the same State or in another State, by order of the appropriate Government:

PROVIDED that no order shall be made by a State Government under clause

(d) for the removal of a person from one State to another State except with the consent of the Government of that other State.

6. Detention orders not to be invalid or inoperative on certain grounds. No detention order shall be invalid or inoperative merely by reason—

(a) that the person to be detained thereunder is outside the limits of the territorial jurisdiction of the Government or officer making the order, or

(b) that the place of detention of such person is outside the said limits.

7. Powers in relation to absconding persons.

(1) If the Central Government or the State Government or an officer mentioned in sub-section (3) of Section 3, as the case may be, has reason to believe that a person in respect of whom a detention order has been made has absconded or is concealing himself so that the order cannot be executed, that Government or officer may—

  (a) make a report in writing of the fact to a Metropolitan Magistrate or a Judicial Magistrate of the first class having jurisdiction in the place where the said person ordinarily resides;

  (b) by order notified in the Official Gazette direct the said person to appear before such officer, at such place and within such period as may be specified in the order.

(2) Upon the making of a report against any person under clause (a) of sub-section (1), the provisions of Sections 82, 83, 84 and 85 of the Code of Criminal Procedure, 1973 (2 of 1974), shall apply in respect of such person and his property as if the detention order made against him were a warrant issued by the Magistrate.

(3) If any person fails to comply with an order issued under clause (b) of sub-section (1), he shall, unless he proves that it was not possible for him to comply therewith and that he had, within the period specified in the order, informed the officer mentioned in the order of the reason which rendered compliance

therewith impossible and of his whereabouts, be punishable with imprisonment for a term which may extend to one year, or with fine, or with both.

(4) Notwithstanding anything contained in the Code of Criminal Procedure, 1973 (2 of 1974), every offence under sub-section (3) shall be cognizable.

8. Grounds of order of detention to be disclosed to persons affected by the order.

(1) When a person is detained in pursuance of a detention order, the authority making the order shall, as soon as may be, but ordinarily not later than five days and in exceptional circumstances and for reasons to be recorded in writing, not later than ten days from the date of detention, communicate to him the grounds on which the order has been made and shall afford him the earliest opportunity of making a representation against the order to the appropriate Government.

(2) Nothing in sub-section (1) shall require the authority to disclose facts which it considers to be against the public interest to disclose.

9. Constitution of Advisory Boards.

(1) The Central Government and each State Government shall, whenever necessary, constitute one or more Advisory Boards for the purposes of this Act.

(2) Every such Board shall consist of three persons who are, or have been, or are qualified to be appointed as, Judges of a High Court, and such persons shall be appointed by the appropriate Government.

(3) The appropriate Government shall appoint one of the members of the Advisory Board who is, or has been, a Judge of a High Court to be its Chairman, and in the case of a Union territory, the appointment to the Advisory Board of any person who is a Judge of the High Court of a State shall be with the previous approval of the State Government concerned.

10. Reference to Advisory Boards. Save as otherwise expressly provided in this Act, in every case where a detention order has been made under this Act, the appropriate Government shall, within three weeks from the date of detention of a person under the order, place before the Advisory Board constituted by it under Section 9, the grounds on which the order has been made and the representation, if any, made by the person affected by the order, and in case where the order has been made by an officer mentioned in sub-section (3) of Section 3, also the report by such officer under sub-section (4) of that Section.

11. Procedure of Advisory Boards.

(1) The Advisory Board shall, after considering the materials placed before it and, after calling for such further information as it may deem necessary from the appropriate Government or from any person called for the purpose through the appropriate Government or from the person concerned, and if, in any particular case, it considers it essential so to do or if the person concerned desires to be heard, after hearing him in person, submit its report to the appropriate Government within seven weeks from the date of detention of the person concerned.

(2) The report of the Advisory Board shall specify in a separate part thereof the opinion of the Advisory Board as to whether or not there is sufficient cause for the detention of the person concerned.

(3) When there is a difference of opinion among the members forming the Advisory Board, the opinion of the majority of such members shall be deemed to be the opinion of the Board.

(4) Nothing in this Section shall entitle any person against whom a detention order has been made to appear by any legal practitioner in any matter connected with the reference to the Advisory Board; and the proceedings of the Advisory Board and its report, excepting that part of the report in which the opinion of the Advisory Board is specified, shall be confidential.

12. Action upon the report of the Advisory Board.

(1) In any case where the Advisory Board has reported that there is, in its opinion, sufficient cause for the detention of a person, the appropriate Government may confirm the detention order and continue the detention of the person concerned for such period as it thinks fit.

(2) In any case where the Advisory Board has reported that there is, in its opinion, no sufficient cause for the detention of a person, the appropriate Government shall revoke the detention order and cause the person concerned to be released forthwith.

13. Maximum period of detention. The maximum period for which any person may be detained in pursuance of any detention order which has been confirmed under Section 12 shall be twelve months from the date of detention:

PROVIDED that nothing contained in this Section shall affect the power of the appropriate Government to revoke or modify the detention order at any earlier time.

14. Revocation of detention orders.

(1) Without prejudice to the provisions of Section 21 of the General Clauses Act, 1897 (10 of1897), a detention order may, at any time, be revoked or modified,—

(a) notwithstanding that the order has been made by an officer mentioned in sub-section (3) of Section 3, by the State Government to which that officer is subordinate or by the Central Government;

(b) notwithstanding that the order has been made by a State Government, by the Central Government.

15. Temporary release of persons detained.

(1) The appropriate Government may, at any time, direct that any person detained in pursuance of a detention order may be released for any specified period either without conditions or upon such conditions specified in the direction as that person accepts, and may, at any time, cancel his release.

(2) In directing the release of any person under sub-section (1), the appropriate Government may require him to enter into a bond with or without sureties for the due observance of the conditions specified in the direction.

(3) Any person released under sub-section (1) shall surrender himself at the time and place, and to the authority, specified in the order directing his release or cancelling his release, as the case may be.

(4) If any person fails without sufficient cause to surrender himself in the manner specified in sub-section (3), he shall be punishable with imprisonment for a term which may extend to two years, or with fine, or with both.

(5) If any person released under sub-section (1) fails to fulfil any of the conditions imposed upon him under the said sub-section or in the bond entered into by him, the bond shall be declared to be forfeited and any person bound thereby shall be liable to pay thepenalty thereof.

16. Protection of action taken in good faith. No suit or other legal proceeding shall lie against the Central Government or a State Government, and no suit, prosecution or other legal proceeding shall lie against any person, for anything in good faith done or intended to be done in pursuance of this Act.

17. Act not to have effect with respect to detentions under State laws.

(1) Nothing in this Act shall apply or have any effect with respect to orders of detention, made under any State law, which are in force immediately before the commencement of the National Security Ordinance, 1980 (11 of 1980), and accordingly every person in respect of whom an order of detention made under any State law is in force immediately before such commencement, shall be governed with respect to such detention by the provisions of such State law or where the State law under which such order of detention is made is an Ordinance (hereinafter referred to as the State Ordinance) promulgated by the Governor of that State and the State Ordinance has been replaced—

(i) before such commencement, by an enactment passed by the Legislature of that State, by such enactment; or

(ii) after such commencement, by an enactment which is passed by the Legislature of that State and the application of which is confined to orders of detention made before such commencement under the State Ordinance, by such enactment, as if this Act had not been enacted.

(2) Nothing in this Section shall be deemed to bar the making under Section 3, of a detention order against any person referred to in sub-section (1) after the detention order in force in respect of him as aforesaid immediately before the commencement of the National Security Ordinance, 1980 (11 of 1980), ceases to have effect for any reason whatsoever.

EXPLANATION: For the purposes of this Section, "State law" means any law providing for preventive detention on all or any of the grounds on which an order of detention may be made under sub-section (2) of Section 3 and in force in any State immediately before the commencement of the said Ordinance.

18. Repeal and saving.

(1) The National Security Ordinance, 1980 (11 of 1980), is hereby repealed.

(2) Notwithstanding such repeal, anything done or any action taken under the

said Ordinance shall be deemed to have been done or taken under the corresponding provisions of this Act, as if this Act had come into force on the 23rd day of September, 1980, and, in particular, any reference made under Section 10 of the said Ordinance and pending before any Advisory Board immediately before the date on which this Act receives the assent of the President may continue to be dealt with by that Board after that date as if such Board had been constituted under Section 9 of this Act.

❑❑❑

29

The Naval Forces (Miscellaneous Provisions) Act, 1950

The Naval Forces (Miscellaneous Provisions) Act, 1950. *Rep. by the Navy Act, 1957 (62 of 1957), s.186 (w.e.f. 1.1.1958).*

❑❑❑

30

The Police (Incitement to Disaffection) Act, 1922

ACT NO. 22 OF 1922 [5TH OCTOBER, 1922]

AN ACT to provide a penalty for spreading disaffection among the police and for kindred offences.

WHEREAS it is expedient to penalize the spreading of disaffection among the police and other kindred offences. It is hereby enacted as follows: -

1. Short title, extent and commencement.

(1) This Act may be called the Police (Incitement to Disaffection) Act, 1922.

[1][(2) It extends to the whole of India except [2][the territories which, immediately before the 1st November, 1956, were comprised in Part B States].]

(3) It shall come into force in any State or part of a State on such date as the State Government may, by notification in the Official Gazette, direct.

2. Definition. In this Act, the expression "member of a policeforce" means any person appointed or enrolled for the performance of police duties under any enactment specified in the Schedule.

3. Penalty for causing disaffection etc. Whoever intentionally causes or attempts to cause, or does any act which he knows is likely to cause, disaffection towards [3]***.

The Government established by law in [4][India] amongst the members of a police-force, or induces or attempts to induce, or does any act which he knows is likely to induce, any member of a police-force to withhold his services or to commit a breach of discipline shall be punished with imprisonment which may extend to six months. or with fine which may extend to two hundred rupees, or with both.

EXPLANATION: Expressions of disapprobation of the measures of the Government with a view to obtain their alteration by lawful means, or of disapprobation of the administrative or other action of the Government, do not constitute an offence under this section unless they cause or are made for the purpose of causing or are likely to cause disaffection.

4. Saving of acts done by police associations and other persons for certain purposes. Nothing shall be deemed to be an offence under this Act which is done in good faith-

(a) for the purpose of promoting the welfare or interests of any member of a police-force by inducing him to withhold his services in any manner authorised by law; or

(b) by or on behalf of any association formed for the purpose of furthering the interests of members of a policeforce as such, where the association has been authorised or recognised by the Government and the act done is done under any rules or articles of the association which have been approved by the Government.

5. Sanction to trial of offences by Subordinate Courts. No Court shall proceed to the trial of any offence under this Act except with the previous sanction, or on the complaint, of the District Magistrate or in the case of a Presidency-town [5]*** of the Commissioner of Police.

6. Trial of cases.

(1) No Court inferior to that of a Presidency Magistrate or Magistrate of the first class shall try any offence under this Act.

(2) Notwithstanding anything contained in Chapter XXII of the Code of Criminal Procedure, 1898 (5 of 1988), no offence under this Act shall be triable summarily.

THE SCHEDULE
[See Section 2]

ACTS OF THE GOVERNOR-GENERAL IN COUNCIL

Year.	**No.**	**Short title**
1859	XXIV	The Madras District Police Act, 1859, 1861 V The Police Act, 1961. [6]* * * *
1888	III	The Police Act, 1888, 1892 V The Bengal Military Police Act, 1892, Madras Act.
1888	III	The Madras City Police Act, 1888, Bombay Acts.
1890	IV	The Bombay District Police Act, 1890.
1902	IV	The City of Bombay Police Act, 1902. Bengal Acts.
1866	II	The Calcutta Suburban Police Act, 1866. IV The Calcutta Police Act, 1866, 1890 III The Calcutta Port, l et, 1890.
1920	II	The Eastern Frontier Rifles (Bengal Battalion) Act, 1920.

❑❑❑

31

The Police Act, 1849

WHEREAS it is expedient to provide for the constitution of a general police district embracing two or more Union territories and for the establishment of police force therefor.

It is hereby enacted as follows:

1. Short title, extent and commencement.

(1) This Act may be called the Police Act, 1949.

(2) It extends to all the Union territories.

(3) It shall come into force in Union territories on such date as the Central Government may, by notification in the Official Gazette, appoint in this behalf for such Union territories.

2. Definition. In this Act "general police district" means the general police district constituted under Section 3.

3. Constitution of general police district embracing two or more Union territories. Notwithstanding anything contained in the Police Act, 1861, the Central Government may, be notification in the Official Gazette, constitute general police district embracing two or more Union territories.

4. Constitution of one police force for general police district. The entire police establishment in a general police district shall be one police force and shall consist of such number of officers and men and shall be constituted in such manner as the Central Government may, by order, direct.

5. Superintendence and administration of police.

(1) The superintendence of the police throughout a general police district shall vest in and be exercised by, the Central Government.

(2) The administration of the said police force shall vest in an officer appointed in this behalf by the Central Government, who shall exercise in respect of that

police force such of the powers exercisable by an Inspector-General of Police under the Police Act, 1861, as the Central Government may, by notification in the Official Gazette, specify in this behalf.

6. Application of the Police Act, 1861. Save as otherwise expressly provided in this Act, the provisions of the Police Act, 1861, shall apply to the police force constituted for the general police district as if it were one police force constituted for a territory and members of the said police force shall have, in every part of any territory which is included in the general police district, the same powers, duties and privileges, and shall be subject to the same liabilities, as they would have had, or would have been subject to, as police officer if they had formed a police establishment under one State Government.

7. Saving. Nothing in this Act shall be deemed to affect the provisions contained in the Delhi Special Police Establishment Act, 1946 (XXV of 1946).

❑❑❑

32

The Police Act, 1861

Act No. 5 of 1861 [22nd March, 1861]

AN ACT for the Regulation of Police.

WHEREAS it is expedient to reorganize the police and to make it a more efficient instrument for the prevention and detection of crime. It is enacted as follows:-

1. Interpretation clause. The following words and expressions in this Act shall have the meaning assigned to them, unless there be something in the subject or context repugnant to such construction, that is to say, —

The words "Magistrate of the district" shall mean the chief-officer charged with the executive administration of a district and exercising the powers of a Magistrate, by whatever designation the chief officer charged with such executive administration as styled;

The word "Magistrate" shall include all persons within the general police-district, exercising all or any of the powers of a Magistrate;

The word "police" shall include all persons who shall be enrolled under his Act;

The words "general police district" shall embrace any Presidency, State or place, or any part of any Presidency, State or place, in which this Act shall be ordered to take effect;

The words "District Superintendent" and "District Superintendent of Police" shall include any Assistant District Superintendent or other person appointed by general or special order of the State Government to perform all or any of the duties of a District Superintendent of Police under this Act in any District;

The word "property" shall include any movable property, money, or valuable security;

The word "person" shall include a company or corporation; The word "month" shall mean a calendar month;

The word "cattle" shall, besides horned cattle, include elephants, camels, horses, asses, mules, sheep, goats and swine.

References, to the subordinate ranks of a police force, shall be construed a reference to members of that force below the rank of Deputy Superintendent.

2. Constitution of the force. The entire police-establishment under a State Government shall; for the purposes of this Act, be deemed to be one [1][police force, and shall be formally enrolled and shall consist of such number of officers and men, and shall be constituted in such manner, [2][as shall from time to time be ordered by the State Government [3][[4][Subject to the provisions of this Act the pay and all other conditions of service of members of the subordinate ranks of any police force shall be such as may be determined by the State Government.]

3. Superintendence in the State Government. The superintendence of the police throughout a general police-district shall vest in and [4][shall be exercised by the State Government to which such district is subordinate; and except as authorized under the provisions of this Act, no person, officer, or Court shall be empowered by the State Government to [5][supersede, or control any police functionary.

4. Inspector-General of Police, etc. [6][The administration of the police throughout a general police district shall be vested in an officer to be styled the Inspector-General of Police, and in such Deputy Inspectors-General and Assistant Inspectors-General as to the State Government shall seem fit.

The administration of the police throughout the local jurisdiction of the Magistrate of the district shall, under the general control and direction of such Magistrate, be vested in a District Superintendent and such Assistant District Superintendents as the State Government shall consider necessary.

5. Powers of Inspector-General [Exercise of powers]. The Inspector-General of Police shall have the full powers of a Magistrate throughout the general police-district; but shall exercise those powers subject to such limitation as may from time to time be imposed by the State Government.

6. [Magisterial powers of police-officers.] *Rep. by the Code of Criminal Procedure, 1882 (Act 10 of 1882), s. 2 and Sch. I (b).*

7. Appointment, dismissal, etc., of inferior officers. [6][[7][Subject to the provisions of article 311 of the Constitution, and to such rules] as the State Government may from time to time make under this Act, the Inspector-General, Deputy Inspectors-General, Assistant Inspector-General and District Superintendents of Police may at any time dismiss, suspend or reduce any police-officer of the subordinate ranks] whom they shall think remiss or negligent in the discharge of his duty, or unfit for the same; [8][or may award any one or more of the following punishments to any police-officer [9][of the subordinate ranks] who shall discharge his duty in a careless or negligent manner, or who by any act of his own shall render himself unfit for the discharge thereof, namely:-

- (a) fine to any amount not exceeding one month's pay;
- (b) confinement to quarters for a term not exceeding fifteen days, with or without punishment-drill, extra guard, fatigue or other duty;

(c) deprivation of good-conduct pay;

(d) removal from any office of distinction or special emolument.] [10]

8. Certificates to police-officers. [11][Every police-officer [12][appointed to the police force other than an officer mentioned in Section 4] shall receive on his appointment a certificate in the form annexed to this Act under the seal of the Inspector-General or such other officer as the Inspector-General shall appoint, by virtue of which the person holding such certificate shall be vested with the powers, functions, and privileges of a police-officer.

9. Police-officers not to resign without leave or two months' notice. No police-officer shall be at liberty to withdraw himself from the duties of his office unless expressly allowed to do so by the District Superintendent or by some other officer authorized to grant such permission or, without the leave of the District Superintendent, to resign his office unless he shall have given to his superior officer notice in writing, for a period of not less than two months, of his intention to resign.

10. Police-officers not to engage in other employment. No police-officer shall engage in any employment or office whatever other than his duties under this Act, unless expressly permitted to do so in writing by the Inspector-General.

11. [Police superannuation fund.] *Rep. by the Repealing Act, 1874 (16 of 1874) s. 1 and Sch., Pt. I.*

12. Power of Inspector-General to make rules. The Inspector-General of Police may, from time to time, subject to the approval of the State Government, frame such orders and rules as he shall deem expedient relative to the organization, classification and distribution of the police-force, the places at which the members of the force shall reside, and the particular services to be performed by them; their inspection, the description of arms, accoutrements and other necessaries to be furnished to them; the collecting and communicating by them of intelligence and information; and all such other orders and rules relative to the police-force as the Inspector-General shall, from time to time, deem expedient for preventing abuse or neglect of duty, and for rendering such force efficient in the discharge of its duties.

13. Additional police-officers employed at cost of individuals. It shall be lawful for the Inspector-General of Police, or any Deputy Inspector-General, or Assistant Inspector-General, or for the District Superintendent, subject to the general direction of the Magistrate of the district, on the application of any person showing the necessity thereof, to depute any additional number of police-officers to keep the peace at any place within the general police-district, and for such time as shall be deemed proper. Such force shall be exclusively under the orders of the District Superintendent, and shall be at the charge of the person making the application:

> *PROVIDED that it shall be lawful for the person on whose application such deputation shall have been made, on giving one month's notice in writing to the Inspector-General, Depute Inspector-General, or Assistant Inspector-General, or to the District Superintendent, to require that the police-officers so deputed shall be withdrawn; and such person shall be relieved from the charge of such additional force from the expiration of such notice.*

14. Appointment of additional force in the neighbourhood of railway and other works. Whenever any railway, canal or other public work, or any manufactory or commercial concern shall be carried on, or be in operation in any part of the country, and it shall appear to the Inspector-General that the employment of an additional police-force in such place is rendered necessary by the behaviour or reasonable apprehension of the behaviour of the persons employed upon such work, manufactory or concern, it shall be lawful for the Inspector-General, with the consent of the State Government, to depute such additional force to such place, and to employ the same so long as such necessity shall continue, and to make orders, from time to time, upon the person having the control or custody of the funds used in carrying on such work, manufactory or concern, for the payment of the extra force so rendered necessary, and such person shall thereupon cause payment to be made accordingly.

15. 1[Quartering of additional police in disturbed or dangerous districts.

(1) It shall be lawful for the State Government, by proclamation to be notified in the Official Gazette, and in such other manner as the State Government shall direct, to declare that any area subject to its authority has been found to be in a disturbed or dangerous state, or that, from the conduct of the inhabitants of such area or of any class or section of them, it is expedient to increase the number of police.

(2) It shall thereupon be lawful for the Inspector-General of Police, or other officer authorized by the State Government in this behalf, with the sanction of the State Government, to employ any police-force in addition to the ordinary fixed complement to be quartered in the area specified in such proclamation as aforesaid.

(3) Subject to the provisions of sub-section (5) of this section, the cost of such additional police-force shall be borne by the inhabitants of such area described in the proclamation.

(4) The Magistrate of the district, after such enquiry as he may deem necessary, shall apportion such cost among the inhabitants who are, as aforesaid, liable to bear the same and who shall not have been exempted under the next succeeding sub-section. Such apportionment shall be made according to the Magistrate' s judgement of the respective means within such area of such inhabitants.

(5) It shall be lawful for the State Government by order to exempt any persons or class or section of such inhabitants from liability to bear any portion of such cost.

(6) Every proclamation issued under sub-section (1) of this section shall state the period for which it is to remain in force, but it may be withdrawn at any time or continued from time to time for a further period or periods as the State Government may in each case think fit to direct.

EXPLANATION. For the purposes of this section, "inhabitants" shall include persons who themselves or by their agents or servants occupy or hold land or other immovable property within such area, and landlords who themselves or by their agents or servants collect rents direct from raiyats or occupiers in such area, notwithstanding that they do not actually reside therein.]

15A. [14][Awarding compensation to sufferers from misconduct of inhabitants or persons interested in land.

(1) If, in any area in regard to which any proclamation notified under the last preceding section is in force, death or grievous hurt or loss of, or damage to, property has been caused by or has ensued from the misconduct of the inhabitants of such area or any class or section of them it shall be lawful for any person, being an inhabitant of such area, who claims to have suffered injury from such misconduct to make, within one month from the date of the injury or such shorter period as may be prescribed, an application for compensation to the Magistrate of the district or of the sub-division of a district within which such area is situated.

(2) It shall thereupon be lawful for the Magistrate of the district, with the sanction of the State Government after such enquiry as he may deem necessary, and whether any additional police force has or has not been quartered in such area under the last preceding section, to-

(a) declare the persons to whom injury has been caused by or has ensued from such misconduct;

(b) fix the amount of compensation to be paid to such persons and the manner in which it is to be distributed among them; and

(c) access the proportion in which the same shall be paid by the inhabitants of such area other than the applicant who shall not have been exempted from liability to pay under the next succeeding sub-section:

PROVIDED that the Magistrate shall not make any declaration or assessment under this sub-section, unless he is of opinion that such injury as aforesaid has arisen from a riot or unlawful assembly within such area, and that the person who suffered the injury was himself free from blame in respect of the occurrences which led to such injury.

(3) It shall be lawful for the State Government, by order, to exempt any persons or class or section of such inhabitants from liability to pay any portion of such compensation.

(4) Every declaration or assessment made or order passed by the Magistrate of the district under sub-section (2) shall be subject to revision by the Commissioner of the Division of the State Government, but save as aforesaid shall be final.

(5) No civil suit shall be maintainable in respect of any injury for which compensation has been awarded under this section.

EXPLANATION: In this section the word "inhabitants" shall have the same meaning as in the last preceding section.]

16. [15][Recovery of moneys payable under Sections 13, 14, 15 and 15A, and disposal of same when recovered.

(1) All moneys payable under Sections 13, 14, 15 and 15A shall be recoverable by the Magistrate of the district in the manner provided by Sections 386 and 387 of the Code of Criminal Procedure, 1882 [16][(10 of 1882), for the recovery of fines, or by suit in any competent Court.

(2) All moneys paid or recovered under Section 15A shall be paid by the Magistrate of the district to the persons to whom and in the proportions in which the same are payable under that section.]

17. Special police-officers. When it shall appear that any unlawful assembly, or riot or disturbance of the peace has taken place, or may be reasonably apprehended, and that the police-force ordinarily employed for preserving the peace is not sufficient for its preservation and for the protection of the inhabitants and the security of property in the place where such unlawful assembly or riot or disturbance of the peace has occurred, or is apprehended, it shall be lawful for any police-officer not below the rank of Inspector to apply to the nearest Magistrate to appoint so many of the residents of the neighbourhood as such police-officers may require to act as special police-officers for such time and within such limits as he shall deem necessary; and the Magistrate to whom such application is made shall, unless he see cause to the contrary, comply with the application.

18. Powers of special police-officers. Every special police-officer so appointed shall have the same powers, privileges and protection, and shall be liable to perform the same duties and shall be amenable to the same penalties, and be subordinate to the same authorities, as the ordinary officers of police.

19. Refusal to serve as special police-officers. If any person being appointed a special police-officer as aforesaid shall without sufficient excuse, neglect or refuse to serve as such, or to obey such lawful order or direction as may be given to him for the performance of his duties, he shall be liable, upon conviction before a Magistrate, to a fine not exceeding fifty rupees for every such neglect, refusal or disobedience.

20. [17][Authority to be exercised by Police Officers. Police-officers enrolled under this Act shall not exercise any authority, except the authority provided for a police-officer under this Act and any Act which shall hereafter be passed for regulating criminal procedure.

21. Village police-officers. Nothing in this Act shall affect any hereditary or other village police-officer, unless such officer shall be enrolled as a police-officer under this Act. When so enrolled, such officer shall be bound by the provisions of the last preceding section. No hereditary or other village police-officer shall be enrolled without his consent and the consent of those who have the right of nomination.

Police-chaukidars in the Presidency of Fort William. If any police-officer appointed under [18][Act XX of 1856 (to make better provision for the appointment and maintenance of Police-chaukidars in Cities, Towns, Stations, Suburbs and Bazars in the Presidency of Fort William in Bengal) is employed out of the district for which he shall have been appointed under that Act, he shall not be paid out of the rates levied under the said Act for that district.

22. Police-officers always on duty and may be employed in any part of district. Every police-officer shall, for all purposes in this Act contained, be considered to be always on duty, and may at any time be employed as a police-officer in any part of the general police-district.

23. Duties of police-officers. It shall be the duty of every police-officer promptly to obey and execute all orders and warrants lawfully issued to him by any competent authority; to collect and communicate intelligence affecting the public peace; to prevent the commission of offences and public nuisances; to detect and bring offenders to justice and to apprehend all persons whom he is legally authorized to apprehend, and for whose apprehension sufficient ground exists; and it shall be lawful for every police-officer, for any of the purposes mentioned in this section, without a warrant, to enter and inspect any drinking-shop, gaming-house or other place of resort of loose and disorderly characters.

24. Police-officer may lay information, etc. It shall be lawful for any police-officer to lay any information before a Magistrate, and to apply for a summons, warrant, search warrant or such other legal process as may by law issue against any person committing an offence 3.

25. Police-officer to take charge of unclaimed property, and be subject to Magistrate's orders as to disposal. It shall be the duty of every police-officer to take charge of all unclaimed property, and to furnish an inventory thereof to the Magistrate of the district.

26. Magistrate may detain property and issue proclamation.

(1) The Magistrate of the district may detain the property and issue a proclamation, specifying the articles of which it consists, and requiring any person who has any claim thereto to appear and establish his right to the same within six months from the date of such proclamation.

(2) [19][The provisions of Section 525 of the [20][Code of Criminal Procedure, 1882 (10 of 1882), shall be applicable to property referred to in this section.]

27. [21][Conflscation of property if no claimant appears.

(1) If no person shall within the period allowed claim such property, or the proceeds thereof, if sold, it may, if not already sold under sub-section (2) of the last preceding section, be sold under the orders of the Magistrate of the district.

(2) The sale-proceeds of property sold under the preceding sub-section and the proceeds of property sold under Section 26 to which no claim has been established shall be [22][at the disposal of the State Government].]

28. Persons refusing to deliver up certificate, etc., on ceasing to be police-officers. Every person, having ceased to be an enrolled police-officer under this Act, who shall not forthwith deliver up his certificate, and the clothing, accoutrements, appointments and other necessaries which shall have been supplied to him for the execution of his duty, shall be liable, on conviction before a Magistrate, to a penalty not exceeding two hundred rupees, or to imprisonment with or without hard labour, for a period not exceeding six months, or to both.

29. Penalties for neglect of duty, etc. Every police-officer who shall be guilty of any violation of duty or wilful breach or neglect of any rule or regulation or lawful order made by competent authority, or who shall withdraw from the duties of his office without permission, or without having given previous notice for the period of two months, [23][or who, being absent on leave, shall fail, without reasonable cause, to report himself for duty on the expiration of such leave,] or who shall engage without authority in any employment other than his police-duty, or who shall be guilty of cowardice, or who shall offer any unwarrantable personal violence to any person in his custody, shall be liable, on conviction before a Magistrate, to a penalty not exceeding three months' pay, or to imprisonment with or without hard labour, for a period not exceeding three months, or to both.

30. [24][Regulation of public assemblies and processions and licensing of the same.

(1) The District Superintendent or Assistant District Superintendent of Police may, as occasion requires, direct the conduct of all assemblies and processions on the public roads, or in the public streets or thoroughfares, and prescribe the routes by which, and the times at which, such processions may pass.

(2) He may also, on being satisfied that it is intended by any persons or class of person to convene or collect an assembly in any such road, street or thoroughfare, or to form a procession which would, in the judgment of the Magistrate of the district, or of the sub-division of a district, if uncontrolled, be likely to cause a breach of the peace, require by general or special notice that the persons convening or collecting such assembly or directing or promoting such procession shall apply for a licence.

(3) On such application being made, he may issue a license specifying the names of the licensees and defining the conditions on which alone such assembly or such procession is to be permitted to take place and otherwise giving effect to this section:

PROVIDED that no fee shall be charged on the application for, or grant of, any such licence.

(4) Music in the streets. He may also regulate the extent to which music may be used in the streets on the occasion of festivals and ceremonies.]

30A. [25][Powers with regard to assemblies and processions violating conditions of icense.

(1) Any Magistrate or District Superintendent of Police or Assistant District Superintendent of Police or Inspector of Police or any police-officer-in-charge of a station may stop any procession which violates the conditions of a licence granted under the last foregoing section, and may order it or any assembly which violates any such conditions as aforesaid to disperse.

(2) Any procession or assembly which neglects or refuses to obey any order given under the last preceding sub-section shall be deemed to be an unlawful assembly.]

31. Police to keep order in public roads, etc. It shall be the duty of the police to keep order on the public roads, and in the public streets, thoroughfares, ghats and landing-places, and at all other places of public resort, and to prevent obstructions on the occasions of assemblies and processions on the public roads and in the public streets, or in the neighbourhood of places of worship, during the time of public worship, and in any case when any road, street, thoroughfare, ghat or landing-place may be thronged or may be liable to be obstructed.

32. Penalty for disobeying orders issued under last three sections, etc. Every person opposing or not obeying the orders issued under the last [26][three] preceding sections, or violating the conditions of any license granted by the District Superintendent or Assistant District Superintendent of Police for the use of music, or for the conduct of assemblies and processions, shall be liable, on conviction before a Magistrate, to a fine not exceeding two hundred rupees.

33. Saving of control of Magistrate of district. Nothing in the last [27][four] preceding sections shall be deemed to interfere with the general control of the Magistrate of the district over the matters referred to therein.

34. Punishment for certain offences on roads, etc. Any person who, on any road or in any [28][open place or] street or thoroughfare within the limits of any town to which this section shall be specially extended by the State Government, commits any of the following offences, to the obstructions inconvenience, annoyance, risk, danger or damage of the [29][residents or passengers] shall, on conviction before a Magistrate, be liable to fine not exceeding fifty rupees, or to imprisonment [30][with or without hard labour] not exceeding eight days; and it shall be lawful for any police-officer to take into custody, without a warrant, any person who within his view commits any of such offences, namely:-

First - Slaughtering cattle, furious riding, etc. Any person who slaughters any cattle or cleans any carcass; any person who rides or drives any cattle recklessly or furiously, or trains or breaks any horse or other cattle;

Second - Cruelty to animals. Any person who wantonly or cruelly beats, abuses or tortures any animal;

Third - Obstructing passengers. Any person who keeps any cattle or conveyance of any kind standing longer than is required for loading or unloading or for taking up or setting down passengers, or who leaves any conveyance in such a manner as to cause inconvenience or danger to the public;

Fourth - Exposing goods for sale. Any person who exposes any goods for sale;

Fifth.-Throwing dirt into street. Any person who throws or lays down any dirt, filth, rubbish or any stones or building materials, or who constructs any cowshed, stable or the like, or who causes any offensive matter to run from any house, factory, dungheap, or the like;

Sixth - Being found drunk or riotous. Any person who is found drunk or riotous or who is incapable of taking care of himself;

Seventh - Indecent exposure of person. Any person who wilfully and indecently exposes his person, or any offensive deformity or disease, or commits nuisance by easing himself, or by bathing or washing in any tank or reservoir not being a place set apart for that purpose;

Eighth - Neglect to protect dangerous places. Any person who neglects to fence in or duly to protect any well, tank or other dangerous place or structure.

35. Jurisdiction. [31][Any charge against a police-officer above the rank of a constable under this Act shall be enquired into and determined only by on officer exercising the powers of a Magistrate.

36. Power to prosecute under other law not affected. Nothing contained in this Act shall be construed to prevent any person from being prosecuted under any other Regulation or Act for any offence made punishable by this Act, or from being liable under any other Regulation or Act or any other or higher penalty or punishment than is provided for such offence by this Act:

PROVIDED that on person shall be punished twice for the same offence.

37. [32]**[Recovery of penalties and fines imposed by Magistrate.** The provisions of Sections 64 to 70, both inclusive, of the Indian Penal Code (45 of 1860), and of Sections 386 to 389, both inclusive, of the [33][Code of Criminal Procedure, 1882 (10 of 1882), with respect to fines, shall apply to penalties and fines imposed under this Act on conviction before Magistrate:

PROVIDED that, notwithstanding anything contained in Section 65 of the first-mentioned Code, any person sentenced to fine under Section 34 of this Act may be imprisoned in default of payment of such fine for any period not exceeding eight days.]

38. [Procedure until return is made to warrant of distress]. *Rep. by the Police Act (1861) Amendment Act, 1895 (8 of 1895), s. 14.*

39. [Imprisonment if distress not sufficient.] *Rep. by the Police Act (1861) Amendment Act, 1895 (8 of 1895), s. 14.*

40. [Levy of fines from European British Subjects.] *Rep., ibid.*

41. [Rewards to police and informer payable to General Police Fund.] Rep. by the A. O. 1937 [34][Proviso.

[35]**[42. Limitation of actions.** All actions and prosecutions against any person, which may be lawfully brought for anything done or intended to be done under the provisions of this Act, or under the general police-powers hereby given shall be commenced within three months after the act complained of shall have been committed, and not otherwise; and notice in writing of such action and of the cause thereof shall be given to the defendant, or to the District Superintendent or an Assistant District Superintendent of the District in which the act was committed, one month at least before the commencement of the action. **Tender of amends.** No plaintiff shall rocover in any such action if tender of sufficient amend shall have been made before such action brought, or if a sufficient sum of money shall have been paid into Court after such action brought, by or on behalf of the defendant, and, though a decree shall be given for the plaintiff in any such action, such plaintiff shall not have costs against the defendant, unless the Judge before whom the trial is held shall certify his approbation of the action.

Proviso — *PROVIDED always that no action shall in any case lie where such officers shall have been prosecuted criminally for the same act.*

43. Plea that act was done under warrant. When any action or prosecution shall be brought or any proceedings held against any police-officer for any act done by him in such capacity, it shall be lawful him to plead that such act was done by him under the authority of a warrant issued by a Magistrate. Such plea shall be proved by the production of the warrant directing, the act, and purporting to be signed by such Magistrate and the defendant shall thereupon be entitled to a decree in his favour, not withstanding any defect of jurisdiction in such Magistrate. No proof of the signature of such Magistrate shall be necessary, unless the Court shall see reason to doubt its being genuine:

> ***Proviso.*** *— PROVIDED always that any remedy which the party may have against the authority issuing such warrant shall not be affected by anything contained in this section.*

44. Police-officers to keep diary. It shall be the duty of every officer in charge of a police-station to keep a general diary in such form shall, from time to time, be prescribed by the State Government and to record therein all complaints and charges preferred, the names of all persons arrested, the names of the complainants, the offences charged against them, the weapons or property that shall have been taken from their possession or otherwise, and the names of the witnesses who shall have been examined. The Magistrate of the district shall be at liberty to call for and inspect such diary.

45. State Government may prescribe form of returns. The State Government may direct the submission of such returns by the Inspector-General and other police-officers as to such State Government shall seem proper, and may prescribe the form in which such returns shall made:

46. [36][Scope of Act.

(1) This Act shall not by its own operation take effect in any presidency, State or place. But the [37][State Government] by an order to be published in the Official Gazette may extend the whole or any part of this Act to any presidency, State or place, and the whole or such portion of this Act as shall be specified in such order shall thereupon take effect in such presidency, State or place.

(2) When the whole or any part of this Act shall have been so extended, the State Government may, from time to time, by notification in the Official Gazette, make rules consistent with this Act—

- (a) to regulate the procedure to be followed by Magistrates and police-officers in the discharge of any duty imposed upon them by or under this Act;
- (b) to prescribe the time, manner and conditions within and under which claims for compensation under Section 15A are to be made, the particulars to be stated in such claims, the manner in which the same are to be verified, and the proceedings (including local enquiries if necessary) which are to be taken consequent thereon; and
- (c) generally, for giving effect to the provisions of this Act.

(3) All rules made under this Act may from time to time be amended, added to or cancelled by the State Government.]

47. Authority of District Superintendent of Police over village police. It shall be lawful for the State Government in carrying this Act into effect in any part of the territories subject to such State Government, to declare that any authority which now is or may be exercised by the Magistrate of the district over any village-watchman or other village police-officer for the purposes of police, shall be exercised, subject to the general control of the Magistrate of the district, by the District Superintendent of Police.

❑❑❑

33

The Police Act, 1888

Act No. 3 of 1888 [17th February, 1888]

AN ACT to amend the law relating to the Regulation of Police.

WHEREAS it is expedient to relax those provisions of Acts for the regulation of police which restrict the employment of police-officers to the presidency, province or place of the police-establishment of which they are members. It is hereby enacted as follows :

1. Title and extent.

(1) This Act may be called the Police Act, 1888 .

(2) [1][It extends to the whole of India.] [2][[3][.

2. [4][Constitution of police forces for special purposes.

(1) Notwithstanding anything in the Madras District Police Act, 1859 , the Indian Police Act, 1861, the Bombay District Police Act, 1890 , or any Act relating to the police in any Presidency-town, [5][the Central Government may, by notification [6][in the Official Gazette, create a special police district embracing parts of two or more States, and extend to every part of the said district the powers and jurisdiction of members of a police force belonging to [7][a State] specified in the notification.

(2) Subject to any orders which the Central Government may make in this behalf, members of the said police force shall have, within every part of any State of which any part is included in the said district, the powers, duties, privileges and liabilities which, as police officers, they have in their own State.

(3) Any member of the said police force whom the Central Government shall generally or specially empower to act under this sub section may, subject to any orders which the Central Government may make in this behalf, exercise

within any State any part of which is included in the said district any of the powers of the officer in charge of a police-station in that State, and when so exercising any such powers, shall, subject to any such Order as aforesaid, be deemed to be an officer in charge of a police-station discharging the functions of such an officer within the limits of his station.

(4) A part of a State included in the said district shall not by reason of that inclusion cease, for the purposes of any enactment relating to police to be part of that State.]

3. Employment of police-officers beyond the State to which they belong. Notwithstanding anything in any of the Acts mentioned or referred to in the last foregoing section, but subject to any orders which the Central Government may make in this behalf, a member of the [8][police force] of any [9][State] may discharge the functions of a police-officer in any part of [10][any other State] and shall, while so discharging such functions, be deemed to be a member of the [police force] of that part and be vested with the powers, functions and privileges, and be subject to the liabilities, of a police- officer belonging to [11][that police force].

4. [12][Consent of State Government to exercise of powers and jurisdiction. Nothing in this Act shall be deemed to enable the police of one State to exercise powers and jurisdiction in any area within another State, not being a railway area, without the consent of the Government of that other State.]

❐❐❐

34

The Police Act, 1949

Act No. 64 of 1949 [27th December, 1949]

AN ACT to provide for the constitution of a general police-district embracing two or more [1][Union territories] and for the establishment of a police force therefor.

WHEREAS it is expedient to provide for the constitution of a general police-district embracing two or more [1][Union territories] and for the establishment of a police force therefor.

1. Short title, extent and commencement.

(1) This Act may be called the Police Act, 1949.

(2) It extends to all the [2][Union territories].

(3) It shall come into force in a [3][Union territory] on such date as the Central Government may, by notification in the Official Gazette, appoint in this behalf for [4]such territory].

2. Definition. In this Act "general police-district" means the general police district constituted under section 3.

3. Constitution of general police-district embracing two or more Union territories. Notwithstanding anything contained in the Police Act, 1861 (5 of 1861), the Central Government may, by notification in the Official Gazette, constitute a general police-district embracing two or more [2][Union territories].

4. Constitution of one police force for general police-district. The entire police establishment in a general police-district shall be one police force and shall consist of such number of officers and men and shall be constituted in such manner as the Central Government may, by order, direct.

5. Superintendence and administration of police.

(1) The superintendence of the police throughout a general police-district shall vest in, and be exercised by, the Central Government.

(2) The administration of the said police force shall vest in an officer, appointed in this behalf by the Central Government, who shall exercise in respect of that police force such of the powers exercisable by an Inspector-General of Police under the Police Act, 1861 (5 of 1961), as the Central Government may, by notification in the Official Gazette, specify in this behalf.

6. Application of the Police Act, 1861. Save as otherwise expressly provided in this Act, the provisions of the Police Act, 1861 (5 of 1861), shall apply to the police force constituted for the general police-district as if it were one police force constituted for a State, and members of the said police force shall have, in every part of [1][any territory] which is included in the general police-district, the same powers, duties and privileges, and shall be subject to the same liabilities, as they would have had, or would have been subject, to, as police officers if they had formed a police establishment under one State Government.

7. Saving. Nothing in this Act shall be deemed to affect the provisions contained in the Delhi Special Police Establishment Act, 1946 (25 of 1946).

❑❑❑

35

The Police-Forces (Restriction of Rights) Act, 1966

ACT No. 33 OF 1966 [2ND DECEMBER, 1966]

AN ACT to provide for the restriction of certain rights conferred by Part III of the Constitution in their application to the members of the Forces charged with the maintenance of public order so as to ensure the proper discharge of their duties and the maintenance of discipline among them.

Be it enacted by Parliament in the Seventeenth Year of the Republic of India as follows:

1. Short title, extent and commencement.

(1) This Act may be called the Police-Forces (Restriction of Rights) Act, 1966.

(2) It extends to the whole of India.

(3) It shall come into force on such date as may be appointed in this behalf by notification in the Official Gazette -

(a) in a Union territory, [1][by the Central Government; and

(b) in a State by the Government of that State:

PROVIDED that different dates may be appointed by the Central Government for different Union territories.

2. Definition. In this Act, unless the context otherwise requires,-

(a) "member of a police-force" means any person appointed or enrolled under any enactment specified in the Schedule;

(b) "police-force" includes any force charged with the maintenance of public order;

(c) "prescribed" means prescribed by rules made under this Act.

3. Restrictions respecting right to form association, freedom of speech, etc.

(1) No member of, a police-force shall, without the express sanction of the Central Government or of the prescribed authority -

(a) be a member of, or be associated in any way with, any trade union, labour union, political association or with any class of trade unions, labour unions or political associations; or

(b) be a member of, or be associated in any way with, any other society, institution, association or organisation that

(c) communicate with the press or publish or cause to be published any book, letter or other document except where such communication or publication is in the *bona fide* discharge of his duties or is of a purely literary, artistic or scientific character or is of a prescribed nature.

EXPLANATION. If any question arises as to whether any society, institution, association or Organisation is of a purely social, recreational or religious nature under clause (b) of this sub-section, the decision of the Central Government thereon shall be final.

(2) No member of a police-force shall participate in, or address, any meeting or take part in any demonstration organised by any body of persons for any political purposes or for such other purposes as may be prescribed.

4. Penalty. Any person who contravenes the provisions of Section 3 shall, without prejudice to any other action that may be taken against him be punishable with imprisonment for a term which may extend to two years, or with fine which may extend to two thousand rupees, or with both.

5. Power to amend Schedule.

(1) The Central Government may, by notification in the Official Gazette, amend the Schedule by including therein any other enactment relating to a force charged with the maintenance of public order or by omitting therefrom any enactment already specified therein and on the publication of the notification such enactment shall be deemed to be specified in, or as the case may be, omitted from, the Schedule.

(2) A copy of every notification issued under sub-section (1) shall be laid before each House of Parliament, as soon as may be, after it is issued.

6. Power to make rules.

(1) The Central Government may, by notification in the Official Gazette, make rules to carry out the purposes of this Act.

(2) Every rule made under this section shall be laid, as soon as may be after it is made, before each House of Parliament while it is in session for a total period of thirty days, which may be comprised in one session or ["in two or more successive sessession immediately following the session or the successive sessions aforesaid" both Houses agree in making any modification in the rule or both], Houses agree that the rule should not be made.

❑❑❑

36

The Prevention of Terrorism (Amendment) Act 2003

Act No. 4 of 2004 [2nd January, 2004]

AN ACT to amend the Prevention of Terrorism Act, 2002.

Be it enacted by Parliament in the Fifty-fourth Year of the Republic of India as follows:

1. Short title and commencement.

(1) This Act may be called the Prevention of Terrorism (Amendment) Act, 2003.

(2) It shall be deemed to have come into force on the 27th day of October, 2003.

2. Amendment of Section 60. In Section 60 of the Prevention of Terrorism Act, 2003 (15 of 2002), after sub-section (3), the following sub-sections shall be inserted, namely:

"(4) Without prejudice to the other provisions of this Act, any Review Committee constituted under sub-section (1) shall, on an application by any aggrieved person, review whether there is a *prima facie* for proceeding against the accused under this Act and issue directions accordingly.

(5) Any direction issued under sub-section (4) -

(i) by the Review Committee constituted by the Central Government, shall be binding on the Central Government, the State Government and the police officer investigating the offence; and

(ii) by the Review Committee constituted by the State Government, shall be binding on the State Government and the police officer investigating the offence.

(6) Where the reviews under sub-section (4) relating to the same offence under this Act, have been made by a Review Committee constituted by the Central Government and a Review Committee constituted by the State Government, under sub-section (1), any

direction issued by the Review Committee constituted by the Central Government shall prevail.

(7) Where any Review Committee constituted under sub-section (1) is of opinion that there is no *prima facie* case for proceeding against the accused and issues directions under sub-section (4), then, the proceedings pending against the accused shall be deemed to have been withdrawn from the date of such direction.".

3. Repeal and saving.

(1) The Prevention of Terrorism (Amendment) Ordinance, 2003 (Ord. 4 of 2003), is hereby repealed.

(2) Notwithstanding such repeal, anything done or any action taken under the Prevention of Terrorism Act, 2002 (15 of 2002), as amended by the said Ordinance, shall be deemed to have been done or taken under the said Act, as amended by this Act.

❏❏❏

37

The Prevention of Terrorism Act, 2002

Act No. 15 of 2002

AN ACT to make provisions for the prevention of, and for dealing with, terrorist activities and for matters connected therewith.

Be it enacted by Parliament in the Fifty-third Year of the Republic of India as follows:—

CHAPTER - I : PRELIMINARY

1. Short title, application, commencement, duration and savings.

(1) This Act may be called the Prevention of Terrorism Act, 2002.

(2) It extends to the whole of India.

(3) Every person shall be liable to punishment under this Act for every act or omission contrary to the provisions thereof, of which he is held guilty in India.

(4) Any person who commits an offence beyond India which is punishable under this Act shall be dealt with according to the provisions of this Act in the same manner as if such act had been committed in India.

(5) The provisions of this Act apply also to—

(a) citizens of India outside India;

(b) persons in the service of the Government, wherever they may be; and

(c) persons on ships and aircrafts, registered in India, wherever they may be.

(6) Save as otherwise provided in respect of entries at serial numbers 24 and 25 of the Schedule to this Act, it shall be deemed to have come into force on the 24th day of October, 2001 and shall remain in force for a period of three years from

the date of its commencement, but its expiry under the operation of this sub-section shall not affect—

(a) the previous operation of, or anything duly done or suffered under this Act, or

(b) any right, privilege, obligation or liability acquired, accrued or incurred under this Act, or

(c) any penalty, forfeiture or punishment incurred in respect of any offence under this Act, or

(d) any investigation, legal proceeding or remedy in respect of any such right, privilege, obligation, liability, penalty, forfeiture or punishment as aforesaid, and, any such investigation, legal proceeding or remedy may be instituted, continued or enforced and any such penalty, forfeiture or punishment may be imposed as if this Act had not expired.

2. Definitions.

(1) In this Act, unless the context otherwise requires,—

(a) "Code" means the Code of Criminal Procedure, 1973 (2 of 1974);

(b) "Designated Authority" shall mean such officer of the Central Government not below the rank of Joint Secretary to the Government, or such officer of the State Government not below the rank of Secretary to the Government, as the case may be, as may be specified by the Central Government or, as the case may be, the State Government, by a notification published in the Official Gazette;

(c) "proceeds of terrorism" shall mean all kinds of properties which have been derived or obtained from commission of any terrorist act or have been acquired through funds traceable to a terrorist act, and shall include cash irrespective of person in whose name such proceeds are standing or in whose possession they are found;

(d) "property" means property and assets of every description, whether corporeal or incorporeal, movable or immovable, tangible or intangible and deeds and instruments evidencing title to, or interest in, such property or assets and includes bank account;

(e) "Public Prosecutor" means a Public Prosecutor or an Additional Public Prosecutor or a Special Public Prosecutor appointed under Section 28 and includes any person acting under the directions of the Public Prosecutor;

(f) "Special Court" means a Special Court constituted under Section 23;

(g) "terrorist act" has the meaning assigned to it in sub-section (1) of Section 3, and the expression "terrorist" shall be construed accordingly;

(h) "State Government", in relation to a Union territory, means the Administrator thereof;

(i) words and expressions used but not defined in this Act and defined in the Code shall have the meanings respectively assigned to them in the Code.

(2) Any reference in this Act to any enactment or any provision thereof shall, in relation to an area in which such enactment or such provision is not in force, be construed as a reference to the corresponding law or the relevant provision of the corresponding law, if any, in force in that area.

CHAPTER - II : PUNISHMENT FOR, AND MEASURES FOR DEALING WITH, TERRORIST ACTIVITIES

3. Punishment for terrorist acts.

(1) Whoever,—

(a) with intent to threaten the unity, integrity, security or sovereignty of India or to strike terror in the people or any Section of the people does any act or thing by using bombs, dynamite or other explosive substances or inflammable substances or firearms or other lethal weapons or poisons or noxious gases or other chemicals or by any other substances (whether biological or otherwise) of a hazardous nature or by any other means whatsoever, in such a manner as to cause, or likely to cause, death of, or injuries to any person or persons or loss of, or damage to, or destruction of, property or disruption of any supplies or services essential to the life of the community or causes damage or destruction of any property or equipment used or intended to be used for the defense of India or in connection with any other purposes of the Government of India, any State Government or any of their agencies, or detains any person and threatens to kill or injure such person in order to compel the Government or any other person to do or abstain from doing any act;

(b) is or continues to be a member of an association declared unlawful under the Unlawful Activities (Prevention) Act, 1967 (37 of 1967), or voluntarily does an act aiding or promoting in any manner the objects of such association and in either case is in possession of any unlicensed firearms, ammunition, explosive or other instrument or substance capable of causing mass destruction and commits any act resulting in loss of human life or grievous injury to any person or causes significant damage to any property,

commits a terrorist act.

EXPLANATION. For the purposes of this sub-section, "a terrorist act" shall include the act of raising funds intended for the purpose of terrorism.

(2) Whoever commits a terrorist act, shall,—

(a) if such act has resulted in the death of any person, be punishable with death or imprisonment for life and shall also be liable to fine;

(b) in any other case, be punishable with imprisonment for a term which shall not be less than five years but which may extend to imprisonment for life and shall also be liable to fine.

(3) Whoever conspires or attempts to commit, or advocates, abets, advises or incites or knowingly facilitates the commission of, a terrorist act or any act preparatory

to a terrorist act, shall be punishable with imprisonment for a term which shall not be less than five years but which may extend to imprisonment for life and shall also be liable to fine.

(4) Whoever voluntarily harbors or conceals, or attempts to harbour or conceal any person knowing that such person is a terrorist shall be punishable with imprisonment for a term which shall not be less than three years but which may extend to imprisonment for life and shall also be liable to fine:

PROVIDED that this sub-section shall not apply to any case in which the harbour or concealment is by the husband or wife of the offender.

(5) Any person who is a member of a terrorist gang or a terrorist organisation, which is involved in terrorist acts, shall be punishable with imprisonment for a term which may extend to imprisonment for life or with fine which may extend to rupees ten lakh or with both.

EXPLANATION. For the purposes of this sub-section, "terrorist organisation" means an organisation which is concerned with or involved in terrorism.

(6) Whoever knowingly holds any property derived or obtained from commission of any terrorist act or has been acquired through the terrorist funds shall be punishable with imprisonment for a term which may extend to imprisonment for life or with fine which may extend to rupees ten lakh or with both.

(7) Whoever threatens any person who is a witness or any other person in whom such witness may be interested, with violence, or wrongfully restrains or confines the witness, or any other person in whom the witness may be interested, or does any other unlawful act with the said intent, shall be punishable with imprisonment which may extend to three years and fine.

4. Possession of certain unauthorized arms, etc. Where any person is in unauthorised possession of any—

(a) arms or ammunition specified in columns (2) and (3) of Category I or Category III (a) of Schedule I to the Arms Rules, 1962, in a notified area,

(b) bombs, dynamite or hazardous explosive substances or other lethal weapons capable of mass destruction or biological or chemical substances of warfare in any area, whether notified or not, he shall be guilty of terrorist act notwithstanding anything contained in any other law for the time being in force, and be punishable with imprisonment for a term which may extend to imprisonment for life or with fine which may extend to rupees ten lakh or with both.

EXPLANATION. In this Section, "notified area" means such area as the State Government may, by notification in the Official Gazette, specify.

5. Enhanced penalties.

(1) If any person with intent to aid any terrorist contravenes any provision of, or any rule made under the Explosives Act, 1884 (4 of 1884), the Explosive Substances Act, 1908 (6 of 1908), the Inflammable Substances Act, 1952 (20 of 1952) or the Arms Act, 1959 (54 of 1959), he shall, notwithstanding anything

contained in any of the aforesaid Acts or the rules made thereunder, be punishable with imprisonment for a term which may extend to imprisonment for life and shall also be liable to fine.

(2) For the purposes of this Section, any person who attempts to contravene or abets, or does any act preparatory to the contravention of any provision of any law, rule or order, shall be deemed to have contravened that provision, and the provisions of sub-section (1) shall, in relation to such person, have effect subject to the modification that the reference to "imprisonment for life" shall be construed as a reference to "imprisonment for ten years".

6. Holding of proceeds of terrorism illegal.

(1) No person shall hold or be in possession of any proceeds of terrorism.

(2) Proceeds of terrorism, whether held by a terrorist or by any other person and whether or not such person is prosecuted or convicted under this Act, shall be liable to be forfeited to the Central Government or the State Government, as the case may be, in the manner provided under this Chapter.

7. Powers of investigating officers and appeal against order of Designated Authority.

(1) If an officer (not below the rank of Superintendent of Police) investigating an offence committed under this Act, has reason to believe that any property in relation to which an investigation is being conducted, represents proceeds of terrorism, he shall, with the prior approval in writing of the Director General of the Police of the State in which such property is situated, make an order seizing such property and where it is not practicable to seize such property, make an order of attachment directing that such property shall not be transferred or otherwise dealt with except with the prior permission of the officer making such order, or of the Designated Authority before whom the properties seized or attached are produced and a copy of such order shall be served on the person concerned.

(2) For the removal of doubts, it is hereby provided that where an organisation is declared as a terrorist organisation under this Act and the investigating officer has reason to believe that any person has custody of any property which is being used or is intended to be used for the purpose of such terrorist organisation, he may, by an order in writing, seize or attach such property.

(3) The investigating officer shall duly inform the Designated Authority within forty-eight hours of the seizure or attachment of such property.

(4) It shall be open to the Designated Authority before whom the seized or attached properties are produced either to confirm or revoke the order of attachment so issued:

PROVIDED that an opportunity of making a representation by the person whose property is being attached shall be given.

(5) In the case of immovable property attached by the investigating officer, it shall be deemed to have been produced before the Designated Authority, when the

investigating officer notifies his report and places it at the disposal of the Designated Authority.

(6) The investigating officer may seize and detain any cash to which this Chapter applies if he has reasonable grounds for suspecting that—

(a) it is intended to be used for the purposes of terrorism;

(b) it forms the whole or part of the resources of an organisation declared as terrorist organisation under this Act:

PROVIDED that the cash seized under this sub-section by the investigating officer shall be released not later than the period of forty-eight hours beginning with the time when it is seized unless the matter involving the cash is before the Designated Authority and such Authority passes an order allowing its retention beyond forty-eight hours.

EXPLANATION: For the purposes of this sub-section, "cash" means —

(a) coins and notes in any currency;

(b) postal orders;

(c) traveller's cheques;

(d) banker's drafts; and

(e) such other monetary instruments as the Central Government or, as the case may be, the State Government may specify by an order made in writing.

(7) Any person aggrieved by an order made by the Designated Authority may prefer an appeal to the Special Court and the Special Court may either confirm the order of attachment of property or seizure so made or revoke such order and release the property.

8. Forfeiture of proceeds of terrorism. Where any property is seized or attached on the ground that it constitutes proceeds of terrorism and the Special Court is satisfied in this regard under sub-section (7) of Section 7, it may order forfeiture of such property, whether or not the person from whose possession it is seized or attached, is prosecuted in a Special Court for an offence under this Act.

9. Issue of show cause notice before forfeiture of proceeds of terrorism.

(1) No order forfeiting any proceeds of terrorism shall be made under Section 8 unless the person holding or in possession of such proceeds is given a notice in writing informing him of the grounds on which it is proposed to forfeit the proceeds of terrorism and such person is given an opportunity of making a representation in writing within such reasonable time as may be specified in the notice against the grounds of forfeiture and is also given a reasonable opportunity of being heard in the matter.

(2) No order of forfeiture shall be made under sub-section (1), if such person establishes that he is a *bona fide* transferee of such proceeds for value without knowing that they represent proceeds of terrorism.

(3) It shall be competent for the Special Court to make an order in respect of property seized or attached,—

(a) directing it to be sold if it is a perishable property and the provisions of Section 459 of the Code shall, as nearly as may be practicable, apply to the net proceeds of such sale;

(b) nominating any officer of the Central or State Government, in the case of any other property, to perform the function of the Administrator of such property subject to such conditions as may be specified by the Special Court.

10. Appeal.

(1) Any person aggrieved by an order of forfeiture under Section 8 may, within one month from the date of the receipt of such order, appeal to the High Court within whose jurisdiction, the Special Court, who passed the order appealed against, is situated.

(2) Where an order under Section 8 is modified or annulled by the High Court or where in a prosecution instituted for the contravention of the provisions of this Act, the person against whom an order of forfeiture has been made under Section 8 is acquitted, such property shall be returned to him and in either case if it is not possible for any reason to return the forfeited property, such person shall be paid the price therefor as if the property had been sold to the Central Government with reasonable interest calculated from the day of seizure of the property and such price shall be determined in the manner prescribed.

11. Order of forfeiture not to interfere with other punishments. The order of forfeiture made under this Act by the Special Court, shall not prevent the infliction of any other punishment to which the person affected thereby is liable under this Act.

12. Claims by third party.

(1) Where any claim is preferred, or any objection is made to the seizure of any property under Section 7 on the ground that such property is not liable to seizure, the Designated Authority before whom such property is produced, shall proceed to investigate the claim or objection:

PROVIDED that no such investigation shall be made where the Designated Authority considers that the claim or objection is designed to cause unnecessary delay.

(2) In case claimant or objector establishes that the property specified in the notice issued under Section 9 is not liable to be forfeited under the Act, the said notice shall be withdrawn or modified accordingly.

13. Powers of Designated Authority. The Designated Authority, acting under the provisions of this Act, shall have all the powers of a civil court required for making a full and fair enquiry into the matter before it.

14. Obligation to furnish information.

(1) Notwithstanding anything contained in any other law, the officer investigating any offence under this Act, with prior approval in writing of an officer not below the rank of a Superintendent of Police, may require any officer or authority of

the Central Government or a State Government or a local authority or a bank, or a company, or a firm or any other institution, establishment, organisation or any individual to furnish information in their possession in relation to such offence, on points or matters, where the investigating officer has reason to believe that such information will be useful for, or relevant to, the purposes of this Act.

(2) Failure to furnish the information called for under sub-section (1), or deliberately furnishing false information shall be punishable with imprisonment for a term which may extend to three years or with fine or with both.

(3) Notwithstanding anything contained in the Code, the offence under sub-section (1) shall be tried as a summary case and the procedure prescribed in Chapter XXI of the said Code [except sub-section (2) of Section 262] shall be applicable thereto.

15. Certain transfers to be null and void. Where, after the issue of an order under Section 7 or issue of a notice under Section 9, any property referred to in the said order or notice is transferred by any mode whatsoever, such transfer shall, for the purpose of the proceedings under this Act, be ignored and if such property is subsequently forfeited, the transfer of such property shall be deemed to be null and void.

16. Forfeiture of property of certain persons.

(1) Where any person is accused of any offence under this Act, it shall be open to the Special Court trying him to pass an order that all or any of the properties, movable or immovable or both belonging to him, shall, during the period of such trial, be attached, if not already attached under this Act.

(2) Where a person has been convicted of any offence punishable under this Act, the Special Court may, in addition to awarding any punishment, by order in writing, declare that any property, movable or immovable or both, belonging to the accused and specified in the order, shall stand forfeited to the Central Government or the State Government, as the case may be, free from all encumbrances.

17. Company to transfer shares to Government. Where any shares in a company stand forfeited to the Central Government or the State Government, as the case may be, under this Act, then, the company shall, on receipt of the order of the Special Court, notwithstanding anything contained in the Companies Act, 1956 (1 of 1956), or the articles of association of the company, forthwith register the Central Government or the State Government, as the case may be, as the transferee of such shares.

CHAPTER - III : TERRORIST ORGANISATIONS

18. Declaration of an organization as a terrorist organization.

(1) For the purposes of this Act, an organisation is a terrorist organisation if—

(a) it is listed in the Schedule, or

(b) it operates under the same name as an organisation listed in that Schedule.

(2) The Central Government may by order, in the Official Gazette —

(a) add an organisation to the Schedule;

(b) remove an organisation from that Schedule;

(c) amend that Schedule in some other way.

(3) The Central Government may exercise its power under clause (a) of sub-section (2) in respect of an organisation only if it believes that it is involved in terrorism.

(4) For the purposes of sub-section (3), an organisation shall be deemed to be involved in terrorism if it—

(a) commits or participates in acts of terrorism,

(b) prepares for terrorism,

(c) promotes or encourages terrorism, or

(d) is otherwise involved in terrorism.

19. Denotification of a terrorist organization.

(1) An application may be made to the Central Government for the exercise of its power under clause (b) of sub-section (2) of Section 18 to remove an organisation from the Schedule.

(2) An application may be made by—

(a) the organisation, or

(b) any person affected by inclusion of the organisation in the Schedule as a terrorist organisation.

(3) The Central Government may make rules to prescribe the procedure for admission and disposal of an application made under this Section.

(4) Where an application under sub-section (1) has been refused, the applicant may apply for a review to the Review Committee constituted by the Central Government under sub-section (1) of Section 60 within one month from the date of receipt of the order by the applicant.

(5) The Review Committee may allow an application for review against refusal to remove an organisation from the Schedule, if it considers that the decision to refuse was flawed when considered in the light of the principles applicable on an application for judicial review.

(6) Where the Review Committee allows review under sub-section (5) by or in respect of an organisation, it may make an order under this sub-section.

(7) Where an order is made under sub-section (6), the Central Government shall, as soon as the certified copy of the order is received by it, make an order removing the organisation from the list in the Schedule.

20. Offence relating to membership of a terrorist organization.

(1) A person commits an offence if he belongs or professes to belong to a terrorist organisation:

PROVIDED that this sub-section shall not apply where the person charged is able to prove :

(a) that the organisation was not declared as a terrorist organisation at the time when he became a member or began to profess to be a member; and

(b) that he has not taken part in the activities of the organisation at any time during its inclusion in the Schedule as a terrorist organisation.

(2) A person guilty of an offence under this Section shall be liable, on conviction, to imprisonment for a term not exceeding ten years or with fine or with both.

21. Offence relating to support given to a terrorist organization.

(1) A person commits an offence if—

(a) he invites support for a terrorist organisation, and

(b) the support is not, or is not restricted to, the provision of money or other property within the meaning of Section 22.

(2) A person commits an offence if he arranges, manages or assists in arranging or managing a meeting which he knows is—

(a) to support a terrorist organisation, or

(b) to further the activities of a terrorist organisation, or

(c) to be addressed by a person who belongs or professes to belong to a terrorist organisation.

(3) A person commits an offence if he addresses a meeting for the purpose of encouraging support for a terrorist organisation or to further its activities.

(4) A person guilty of an offence under this Section shall be liable on conviction, to imprisonment for a term not exceeding ten years or with fine or with both.

EXPLANATION: For the purposes of this Section, the expression "meeting" means a meeting of three or more persons whether or not the public are admitted.

22. Fund raising for a terrorist organization to be an offence.

(1) A person commits an offence if he—

(a) invites another to provide money or other property, and

(b) intends that it should be used, or has reasonable cause to suspect that it may be used, for the purposes of terrorism.

(2) A person commits an offence if he—

(a) receives money or other property, and

(b) intends that it should be used, or has reasonable cause to suspect that it may be used, for the purposes of terrorism.

(3) A person commits an offence if he—

(a) provides money or other property, and

(b) knows or has reasonable cause to suspect that it will or may be used for the purposes of terrorism.

(4) In this Section, a reference to the provision of money or other property is a reference to its being given, lent or otherwise made available, whether or not for consideration.

(5) A person guilty of an offence under this Section shall be liable on conviction, to imprisonment for a term not exceeding fourteen years or with fine or with both.

CHAPTER - IV : SPECIAL COURTS

23. Special Courts.

(1) The Central Government or a State Government may, by notification in the Official Gazette, constitute one or more Special Courts for such area or areas, or for such case or class or group of cases, as may be specified in the notification.

(2) Where a notification constituting a Special Court for any area or areas or for any case or class or group of cases is issued by the Central Government under sub-section (1), and a notification constituting a Special Court for the same area or areas or for the same case or class or group of cases has also been issued by the State Government under that sub-section, the Special Court constituted by the Central Government, whether the notification constituting such Court is issued before or after the issue of the notification constituting the Special Court by the State Government, shall have, and the Special Court constituted by the State Government shall not have, jurisdiction to try any offence committed in that area or areas or, as the case may be, the case or class or group of cases and all cases pending before any Special Court constituted by the State Government shall stand transferred to the Special Court constituted by the Central Government.

(3) Where any question arises as to the jurisdiction of any Special Court, it shall be referred to the Central Government whose decision in the matter shall be final.

(4) A Special Court shall be presided over by a judge to be appointed by the Central Government or, as the case may be, the State Government, with the concurrence of the Chief Justice of the High Court.

(5) The Central Government or, as the case may be, the State Government may also appoint, with the concurrence of the Chief Justice of the High Court, additional judges to exercise jurisdiction of a Special Court.

(6) A person shall not be qualified for appointment as a judge or an additional judge of a Special Court unless he is, immediately before such appointment, a sessions judge or an additional sessions judge in any State.

(7) For the removal of doubts, it is hereby provided that the attainment, by a person appointed as a judge or an additional judge of a Special Court, of the age of superannuation under the rules applicable to him in the service to which he belongs, shall not affect his continuance as such judge or additional judge.

(8) Where any additional judge or additional judges is or are appointed in a Special Court, the judge of the Special Court may, from time to time, by general or special order, in writing, provide for the distribution of business of the Special Court among all judges including himself and the additional judge or additional judges and also for the disposal of urgent business in the event of his absence or the absence of any additional judge.

24. Place of sitting. A Special Court may, on its own motion, or on an application made by the Public Prosecutor and if it considers it expedient or desirable so to do, sit for any of its proceedings at any place other than its ordinary place of sitting:

PROVIDED that nothing in this Section shall be construed to change the place of sitting of a Special Court constituted by a State Government to any place outside that State.

25. Jurisdiction of Special Courts.

(1) Notwithstanding anything contained in the Code, every offence punishable under any provision of this Act shall be triable only by the Special Court within whose local jurisdiction it was committed or, as the case may be, by the Special Court constituted for trying such offence under Section 23.

(2) If, having regard to the exigencies of the situation prevailing in a State,—

(a) it is not possible to have a fair, impartial or speedy trial; or

(b) it is not feasible to have the trial without occasioning the breach of peace or grave risk to the safety of the accused, the witnesses, the Public Prosecutor and a judge of the Special Court or any of them; or

(c) it is not otherwise in the interests of justice, the Supreme Court may transfer any case pending before a Special Court to any other Special Court within that State or in any other State and the High Court may transfer any case pending before a Special Court situated in that State to any other Special Court within the State.

(3) The Supreme Court or the High Court, as the case may be, may act under this Section either on the application of the Central Government or a party interested and any such application shall be made by motion, which shall, except when the applicant is the Attorney-General of India, be supported by an affidavit or affirmation.

26. Power of Special Courts with respect to other offences.

(1) When trying any offence, a Special Court may also try any other offence with which the accused may, under the Code, be charged at the same trial if the offence is connected with such other offence.

(2) If, in the course of any trial under this Act of any offence, it is found that the accused person has committed any other offence under this Act or under any other law, the Special Court may convict such person of such other offence and pass any sentence or award punishment authorised by this Act or such rule or, as the case may be, under such other law.

27. Power to direct for samples, etc.

(1) When a police officer investigating a case requests the Court of a Chief Judicial Magistrate or the Court of a Chief Metropolitan Magistrate in writing for obtaining samples of handwriting, finger-prints, foot-prints, photographs, blood, saliva, semen, hair, voice of any accused person, reasonably suspected to be involved in the commission of an offence under this Act, it shall be lawful for the Court of a Chief Judicial Magistrate or the Court of a Chief Metropolitan Magistrate to

direct that such samples be given by the accused person to the police officer either through a medical practitioner or otherwise, as the case may be.

(2) If any accused person refuses to give samples as provided in sub-section (1), the Court shall draw adverse inference against the accused.

28. Public Prosecutors.

(1) For every Special Court, the Central Government or, as the case may be, the State Government, shall appoint a person to be the Public Prosecutor and may appoint one or more persons to be the Additional Public Prosecutor or Additional Public Prosecutors:

PROVIDED that the Central Government or, as the case may be, the State Government, may also appoint for any case or class or group of cases, a Special Public Prosecutor.

(2) A person shall not be qualified to be appointed as a Public Prosecutor or an Additional Public Prosecutor or a Special Public Prosecutor under this Section unless he has been in practice as an Advocate for not less than seven years or has held any post, for a period of not less than seven years, under the Union or a State, requiring special knowledge of law.

(3) Every person appointed as a Public Prosecutor or an Additional Public Prosecutor or a Special Public Prosecutor under this Section shall be deemed to be a Public Prosecutor within the meaning of clause (u) of Section 2 of the Code, and the provisions of the Code shall have effect accordingly.

29. Procedure and powers of Special Courts.

(1) Subject to the provisions of Section 50, a Special Court may take cognizance of any offence, without the accused being committed to it for trial, upon receiving a complaint of facts that constitute such offence or upon a police report of such facts.

(2) Where an offence triable by a Special Court is punishable with imprisonment for a term not exceeding three years or with fine or with both, the Special Court may, notwithstanding anything contained in sub-section (1) of Section 260 or Section 262 of the Code, try the offence in a summary way in accordance with the procedure prescribed in the Code and the provisions of Sections 263 to 265 of the Code, shall so far as may be, apply to such trial:

PROVIDED that when, in the course of a summary trial under this sub-section, it appears to the Special Court that the nature of the case is such that it is undesirable to try it in a summary way, the Special Court shall recall any witnesses who may have been examined and proceed to re-hear the case in the manner provided by the provisions of the Code for the trial of such offence and the said provisions shall apply to and in relation to a Special Court as they apply to and in relation to a Magistrate:

PROVIDED further that in the case of any conviction in a summary trial under this Section, it shall be lawful for a Special Court to pass a sentence of imprisonment for a term not exceeding one year and with fine which may extend to rupees five lakh.

(3) Subject to the other provisions of this Act, a Special Court shall, for the purpose of trial of any offence, have all the powers of a Court of Session and shall try

such offence as if it were a Court of Session so far as may be in accordance with the procedure prescribed in the Code for the trial before a Court of Session.

(4) Subject to the other provisions of this Act, every case transferred to a Special Court under Section 25 shall be dealt with as if such case had been transferred under Section 406 of the Code to such Special Court.

(5) Notwithstanding anything contained in the Code, but subject to the provisions of Section 299 of the Code, a Special Court may, if it thinks fit and for reasons to be recorded by it, proceed with the trial in the absence of the accused or his pleader and record the evidence of any witness, subject to the right of the accused to recall the witness for cross-examination.

30. Protection of witnesses.

(1) Notwithstanding anything contained in the Code, the proceedings under this Act may, for reasons to be recorded in writing, be held in camera if the Special Court so desires.

(2) A Special Court, if on an application made by a witness in any proceeding before it or by the Public Prosecutor in relation to such witness or on its own motion, is satisfied that the life of such witness is in danger, it may, for reasons to be recorded in writing, take such measures as it deems fit for keeping the identity and address of such witness secret.

(3) In particular, and without prejudice to the generality of the provisions of sub-section (2), the measures which a Special Court may take under that sub-section may include—

(a) the holding of the proceedings at a place to be decided by the Special Court;

(b) the avoiding of the mention of the names and addresses of the witnesses in its orders or judgments or in any records of the case accessible to public;

(c) the issuing of any directions for securing that the identity and address of the witnesses are not disclosed;

(d) a decision that it is in the public interest to order that all or any of the proceedings pending before such a Court shall not be published in any manner.

(4) Any person who contravenes any decision or direction issued under sub-section (3) shall be punishable with imprisonment for a term which may extend to one year and with fine which may extend to one thousand rupees.

31. Trial by Special Courts to have precedence. The trial under this Act of any offence by a Special Court shall have precedence over the trial of any other case against the accused in any other court (not being a Special Court) and shall be concluded in preference to the trial of such other case and accordingly the trial of such other case shall remain in abeyance.

32. Certain confessions made to police officers to be taken into consideration.

(1) Notwithstanding anything in the Code or in the Indian Evidence Act, 1872 (1 of 1872), but subject to the provisions of this Section, a confession made by a person before a police officer not lower in rank than a Superintendent of Police

and recorded by such police officer either in writing or on any mechanical or electronic device like cassettes, tapes or sound tracks from out of which sound or images can be reproduced, shall be admissible in the trial of such person for an offence under this Act or the rules made thereunder.

(2) A police officer shall, before recording any confession made by a person under sub-section (1), explain to such person in writing that he is not bound to make a confession and that if he does so, it may be used against him:

PROVIDED that where such person prefers to remain silent, the police officer shall not compel or induce him to make any confession.

(3) The confession shall be recorded in an atmosphere free from threat or inducement and shall be in the same language in which the person makes it.

(4) The person from whom a confession has been recorded under sub-section (1), shall be produced before the Court of a Chief Metropolitan Magistrate or the Court of a Chief Judicial Magistrate along with the original statement of confession, written or recorded on mechanical or electronic device within forty-eight hours.

(5) The Chief Metropolitan Magistrate or the Chief Judicial Magistrate, shall, record the statement, if any, made by the person so produced and get his signature or thumb impression and if there is any complaint of torture, such person shall be directed to be produced for medical examination before a Medical Officer not lower in rank than an Assistant Civil Surgeon and thereafter, he shall be sent to judicial custody.

33. Power to transfer cases to regular courts. Where, after taking cognizance of any offence, a Special Court is of the opinion that the offence is not triable by it, it shall, notwithstanding that it has no jurisdiction to try such offence, transfer the case for the trial of such offence to any court having jurisdiction under the Code and the Court to which the case is transferred may proceed with the trial of the offence as if it had taken cognizance of the offence.

34. Appeal.

(1) Notwithstanding anything contained in the Code, an appeal shall lie from any judgment, sentence or order, not being an interlocutory order, of a Special Court to the High Court both on facts and on law.

EXPLANATION: For the purposes of this Section, "High Court" means a High Court within whose jurisdiction, a Special Court which passed the judgment, sentence or order, is situated.

(2) Every appeal under sub-section (1) shall be heard by a bench of two Judges of the High Court.

(3) Except as aforesaid, no appeal or revision shall lie to any court from any judgment, sentence or order including an interlocutory order of a Special Court.

(4) Notwithstanding anything contained in sub-section (3) of Section 378 of the Code, an appeal shall lie to the High Court against an order of the Special Court granting or refusing bail.

(5) Every appeal under this Section shall be preferred within a period of thirty days from the date of the judgment, sentence or order appealed from:

PROVIDED that the High Court may entertain an appeal after the expiry of the said period of thirty days if it is satisfied that the appellant had sufficient cause for not preferring the appeal within the period of thirty days.

35. Transitional provisions and transfer of pending proceedings.

(1) The jurisdiction conferred by this Act on a Special Court, shall, until a Special Court is constituted under Section 23, in the case of any offence punishable under this Act, notwithstanding anything contained in the Code, be exercised by the Court of Session of the division in which such offence has been committed and it shall have all the powers and follow the procedure provided under this Chapter.

(2) On and from the date when the Special Court is constituted under Section 23, every trial under the provisions of this Act, which would have been required to be held before the Special Court, shall stand transferred to that Court on the date on which it is constituted.

CHAPTER - V : INTERCEPTION OF COMMUNICATION IN CERTAIN CASES

36. Definitions. In this Chapter, unless the context otherwise requires,—

(a) "electronic communication" means any transmission of signs, signals, writings, images, sounds, data or intelligence of any nature transmitted in whole or in part by a wire, radio, electromagnetic, photo-electronic or photo-optical system that affects inland or foreign commerce but does not include—

(i) the radio portion of a cordless telephone communication that is transmitted between the wireless telephone hand-set and the base unit; or

(ii) any wire or oral communication; or

(iii) any communication made through a tone only paging device; or

(iv) any communication from a tracking device;

(b) "intercept" means the aural or other acquisition of the contents by wire, electronic or oral communication through the use of any electronic, mechanical or other device;

(c) "oral communication" means any oral communication uttered by a person exhibiting an expectation that such communication is not subject to interception under circumstances justifying such expectation but such term does not include any electronic communication;

(d) "wire communication" means any aural transmission made in whole or part through the use of facilities for the transmission of communications by the aid of wire, cable or other like connection between the point of origin and the point of connection, between the point of origin and the point of reception (including the use of such connection in switching station) and such term includes any electronic storage of such communication.

37. Appointment of Competent Authority. The Central Government or the State Government, as the case may be, may appoint an officer not below the rank of Secretary to the Government in the case of State Government and not below the rank of Joint Secretary to the Government in the case of Central Government, to be the Competent Authority for the purposes of this Chapter.

38. Application for authorization of interception of wire, electronic or oral communication.

(1) A police officer not below the rank of Superintendent of Police supervising the investigation of any terrorist act under this Act may submit an application in writing to the Competent Authority for an order authorising or approving the interception of wire, electronic or oral communication by the investigating officer when he believes that such interception may provide, or has provided evidence of any offence involving a terrorist act.

(2) Each application shall include the following information:—

(a) the identity of the investigating officer making the application, and the head of the department authorising the application;

(b) a statement of the facts and circumstances relied upon by the applicant to justify his belief that an order should be issued, including—

(i) details as to the offence of terrorist act that has been, is being, or is about to be committed;

(ii) a particular description of the nature and location of the facilities from which or the place where the communication is to be intercepted;

(iii) a particular description of the type of communications sought to be intercepted; and

(iv) the identity of the person, if known, committing the terrorist act whose communications are to be intercepted;

(c) a statement of the period of time for which the interception is required to be maintained, if the nature of the enquiry is such that the authorisation of interception should not automatically terminate after the described type of communication has been first obtained;

(d) a particular description of facts establishing probable cause to believe that additional communications of the same type will occur thereafter; and

(e) where the application is for the extension of an order, a statement setting forth the results thus far obtained from the interception, or a reasonable explanation of the failure to obtain such results.

(3) The Competent Authority may require the applicant to furnish additional oral or documentary evidence in support of the application.

39. Decision by Competent Authority on application for interception.

(1) Upon such application, the Competent Authority may reject the application, or issue an order, as requested or as modified, authorising or approving

interception of wire, electronic or oral communications, if the Competent Authority determines on the basis of the facts submitted by the applicant that -

(a) there is a probable cause for belief that an individual is committing, has committed, or is about to commit, a particular offence described and made punishable under Sections 3 and 4 of this Act;

(b) there is a probable cause of belief that particular communications concerning that offence may be obtained through such interception;

(c) there is probable cause of belief that the facilities from which, or the place where, the wire, electronic or oral communications are to be intercepted are being used or are about to be used, in connection with the commission of such offence, leased to, or are listed in, the name of or commonly used by such person.

(2) Each order by the Competent Authority authorising or approving the interception of any wire, electronic or oral communication under this Section shall specify—

(a) the identity of the person, if known, whose communications are to be intercepted;

(b) the nature and location of the communication facilities as to which, or the place where, authority to intercept is granted;

(c) a particular description of the type of communication sought to be intercepted, and a statement of the particular offence to which it relates;

(d) the identity of the agency authorised to intercept the communications, and the person authorising the application; and

(e) the period of time during which such interception is authorised, including a statement as to whether or not the interception shall automatically terminate after the described communication has been first obtained.

40. Submission of order of interception to Review Committee.

(1) The Competent Authority shall, immediately after passing the order under sub-section (1) of Section 39, but in any case not later than seven days from the passing of the order, submit a copy of the same to the Review Committee constituted under Section 60 alongwith all the relevant underlying papers, record and his own findings, in respect of the said order, for consideration and approval of the order by the Review Committee.

(2) An order authorising the interception of a wire, electronic or oral communication under this Section shall, upon request of the applicant, direct that a provider of wire or electronic communication service, landlord, custodian or other person shall furnish to the applicant forthwith all information, facilities and technical assistance necessary to accomplish the interception unobtrusively and with a minimum of interference with the services that such service provider, landlord, custodian or person is providing to the person whose communications are to be intercepted.

41. Duration of an order of inception, etc.

(1) No order issued under this Section may authorise or approve the interception of any wire, electronic or oral communication for any period longer than is

necessary to achieve the objective of the authorisation, nor in any event longer than sixty days and such sixty days period shall begin on the day immediately preceding the day on which the investigating officer first begins to conduct an interception under the order or ten days after order is issued whichever is earlier.

(2) The extension of an order may be granted, but only upon an application for an extension made in accordance with sub-section (1) of Section 38 and the Competent Authority making the findings required by sub-section (1) of Section 39, and the period of such extension shall be no longer than the Competent Authority deems necessary to achieve the purposes for which it was granted and in no event for longer than sixty days at a time.

(3) Every order and extension thereof shall contain a provision that the authorisation to intercept shall be executed as soon as practicable and shall be conducted in such manner as to minimise the interception of communications not otherwise subject to interception under this Section and shall terminate upon attainment of the authorised objective, or in any event on the expiry of the period of said order or extension thereof.

42. Authority competent to carry out interception.

(1) An interception under this Chapter may be conducted in whole or in part by a public servant, acting under the supervision of the investigating officer authorised to conduct the interception.

(2) Whenever an order authorising an interception is issued pursuant to this Section, the order may require reports to be made to the Competent Authority who issued the order showing that progress has been made towards achievement of the authorised objective and the need for continued interception and such report shall be made at such intervals as the Competent Authority may require.

43. Interception of communication in emergency.

(1) Notwithstanding anything contained in any other provision of this Chapter, an officer not below the rank of Additional Director-General of Police or a police officer of equivalent rank who reasonably determines that—

(a) an emergency situation exists that involves—

(i) immediate danger of death or serious physical injury to any person; or

(ii) conspiratorial activities threatening the security or interest of the State; or

(iii) conspiratorial activities, characteristic of a terrorist act, that requires a wire, electronic or oral communication to be intercepted before an order from the Competent Authority authorising such interception can, with due diligence, be obtained; and

(b) there are grounds on which an order should be issued under this Section to authorise such interception, may authorise, in writing, the investigating officer to intercept such wire, electronic or oral communication, if an application for an order approving the interception is made in accordance with the provisions of sub-sections (1) and (2) of Section 38 within forty-eight hours after the interception has occurred, or begins to occur.

(2) In the absence of an order approving the interception made under sub-section (1), such interception shall immediately terminate when the communication sought is obtained or when the application for the order is rejected, whichever is earlier; and in the event of an application for permitting interception being rejected under sub-section (1) of Section 39 or an application under sub-section (1) of this Section for approval being rejected, or in any other case where the interception is terminated without an order having been issued, the contents of any wire, electronic or oral communication intercepted shall be treated as having been obtained in violation of this Section.

44. Protection of information collected.

(1) The contents of any wire, electronic or oral communication intercepted by any means authorised by this Chapter shall, as far as possible, be recorded on tape or wire or other comparable device and shall be done in such manner as to protect the recording from editing or other alterations.

(2) Immediately upon the expiration of the period of order, or extension thereof, such recording shall be made available to the Competent Authority issuing such order and shall be sealed under his directions and kept in the custody of such person or authority as the Competent Authority orders, and such recordings shall not be destroyed except upon an order of the Competent Authority and in any event shall be kept for ten years.

(3) Applications made and orders issued under this Chapter shall be sealed by the Competent Authority and custody of the applications and orders shall be kept in such manner as the Competent Authority directs, and shall not be destroyed except on an order of the Competent Authority, and in any event shall be kept for ten years.

45. Admissibility of evidence collected through the interception of communications. Notwithstanding anything in the Code or in any other law for the time being in force, the evidence collected through the interception of wire, electronic or oral communication under this Chapter shall be admissible as evidence against the accused in the Court during the trial of a case:

> *PROVIDED that, the contents of any wire, electronic or oral communication intercepted pursuant to this Chapter or evidence derived therefrom shall not be received in evidence or otherwise disclosed in any trial, hearing or other proceeding in any court unless each accused has been furnished with a copy of the order of the Competent Authority, and accompanying application, under which the interception was authorised or approved not less than ten days before trial, hearing or proceeding:*
>
> *PROVIDED further that, the period of ten days may be waived by the judge trying the matter, if he comes to the conclusion that it was not possible to furnish the accused with the above information*

ten days before the trial, hearing or proceeding and that the accused will not be prejudiced by the delay in receiving such information.

46. Review of authorization order.

(1) The Review Committee constituted by the Central Government or the State Government, as the case may be, shall review every order passed by the Competent Authority under Section 39.

(2) Every order passed by the Competent Authority under Section 39, or disapproved by the officer under Section 43, shall be placed before the Review Committee, which shall be considered by the Review Committee within ten days after its receipt, to decide whether the order was necessary, reasonable and justified.

(3) The Review Committee, after examining the entire record and holding such enquiry, if any, deemed necessary may, by order in writing, either approve the order passed by the Competent Authority or may issue order disapproving the same.

(4) On issue of an order of disapproval by the Review Committee, the interception, if any, already commenced shall be forthwith discontinued and the intercepted communication, if any, in the form of tape, wire or other device shall, thereupon, not be admissible as evidence in any case and shall be directed to be destroyed.

47. Interception and disclosure of wire, electronic or oral communications prohibited.
Except as otherwise specifically provided in Section 39, any police officer who—

(a) intentionally intercepts, endeavours to intercept, or procures any other person to intercept or endeavour to intercept any wire, electronic or oral communication;

(b) intentionally uses, endeavours to use, or procures any other person to use or endeavours to use any electronic, mechanical or other device to intercept any oral communication when—

   (i) such device is affixed to, or otherwise transmits a signal through a wire, cable, or other like connection used in wire communication; or

   (ii) such device transmits communications by radio, or interferes with the transmission of such communication;

(c) intentionally discloses, or endeavours to disclose, to any other person the contents of any wire, electronic or oral communication, knowing or having reason to know that the information was obtained through the interception of a wire, electronic or oral communication in violation of this Chapter;

(d) intentionally uses, or endeavours to use, the contents of any wire, electronic or oral communication, knowing or having reason to know that the information was obtained through the interception of a wire, electronic or oral communication in violation of this Chapter;

(e) intentionally discloses, or endeavours to disclose, to any other unauthorised person the contents of any wire, electronic or oral communication, intercepted by means authorised by Section 39;

(f) intentionally continues the interception of wire, electronic or oral communication after the issue of an order of rejection by the Competent Authority under this Chapter;

(g) intentionally continues the interception of wire, electronic or oral communication after the issue of an order of disapproval by the Review Committee under sub-section (3) of Section 46, shall for such violation be punishable with imprisonment for a term which may extend to one year and with fine up to rupees fifty thousand.

48. Annual report of interceptions.

(1) The Central Government and the State Government, as the case may be, shall cause an annual report to be prepared giving a full account of—

(a) the number of applications for authorisation of interceptions received by the Competent Authority from the Police Department in which prosecutions have been launched;

(b) the number of such applications permitted or rejected;

(c) the number of interceptions carried out in emergency situations and the number of approvals granted or rejected in such matters;

(d) the number of prosecutions launched based on such interceptions and convictions resulting from such interceptions, along with an explanatory memorandum giving general assessment of the utility and importance of the interceptions authorised.

(2) An annual report shall be laid by the State Government before the State Legislature within three months of the completion of every calendar year:

PROVIDED that, if the State Government is of the opinion that the inclusion of any matter in the annual report would be prejudicial to the security of the State or to the prevention or detection of any terrorist act, the State Government may exclude such matter from being included in such annual report.

(3) An annual report shall be laid by the Central Government before each House of Parliament within three months of the completion of every calendar year:

PROVIDED that, if the Central Government is of the opinion that the inclusion of any matter in the Annual Report would be prejudicial to the security of the country or to the prevention or detection of any terrorist act, the Central Government may exclude such matter from being included in such annual report.

CHAPTER - VI : MISCELLANEOUS

49. Modified application of certain provisions of the Code.

(1) Notwithstanding anything contained in the Code or any other law, every offence punishable under this Act shall be deemed to be a cognizable offence within the meaning of clause (c) of Section 2 of the Code, and "cognizable case" as defined in that clause shall be construed accordingly.

(2) Section 167 of the Code shall apply in relation to a case involving an offence punishable under this Act subject to the modification that in sub-section (2),—

(a) the references to "fifteen days", "ninety days" and "sixty days", wherever they occur, shall be construed as references to "thirty days", "ninety days" and "ninety days", respectively; and

(b) after the proviso, the following provisos shall be inserted, namely:—

"PROVIDED FURTHER that if it is not possible to complete the investigation within the said period of ninety days, the Special Court shall extend the said period up to one hundred and eighty days, on the report of the Public Prosecutor indicating the progress of the investigation and the specific reasons for the detention of the accused beyond the said period of ninety days:

PROVIDED ALSO that if the police officer making the investigation under this Act, requests, for the purposes of investigation, for police custody from judicial custody of any person from judicial custody, he shall file an affidavit stating the reasons for doing so and shall also explain the delay, if any, for requesting such police custody.".

(3) Section 268 of the Code shall apply in relation to a case involving an offence punishable under this Act subject to the modification that—

(a) the reference in sub-section (1) thereof—

(i) to "the State Government" shall be construed as a reference to "the Central Government or the State Government",

(ii) to "order of the State Government" shall be construed as a reference to "order of the Central Government or the State Government, as the case may be"; and

(b) the reference in sub-section (2) thereof, to "the State Government" shall be construed as a reference to "the Central Government or the State Government, as the case may be".

(4) Sections 366, 367 and 371 of the Code shall apply in relation to a case involving an offence triable by a Special Court subject to the modification that the reference to "Court of Session", wherever occurring therein, shall be construed as the reference to "Special Court".

(5) Nothing in Section 438 of the Code shall apply in relation to any case involving the arrest of any person accused of having committed an offence punishable under this Act.

(6) Notwithstanding anything contained in the Code, no person accused of an offence punishable under this Act shall, if in custody, be released on bail or on his own bond unless the Court gives the Public Prosecutor an opportunity of being heard.

(7) Where the Public Prosecutor opposes the application of the accused to release on bail, no person accused of an offence punishable under this Act or any rule made thereunder shall be released on bail until the Court is satisfied that there are grounds for believing that he is not guilty of committing such offence:

PROVIDED that after the expiry of a period of one year from the date of detention of the accused for an offence under this Act, the provisions of sub-section (6) of this Section shall apply.

(8) The restrictions on granting of bail specified in sub-sections (6) and (7) are in addition to the restrictions under the Code or any other law for the time being in force on granting of bail.

(9) Notwithstanding anything contained in sub-sections (6), (7) and (8), no bail shall be granted to a person accused of an offence punishable under this Act, if he is not an Indian citizen and has entered the country unauthorisedly or illegally except in very exceptional circumstances and for reasons to be recorded in writing.

50. Cognizance of offences. No court shall take cognizance of any offence under this Act without the previous sanction of the Central Government or, as the case may be, the State Government.

51. Officers competent to investigate offences under this Act. Notwithstanding anything contained in the Code, no police officer,—

(a) in the case of the Delhi Special Police Establishment, below the rank of a Deputy Superintendent of Police or a police officer of equivalent rank;

(b) in the metropolitan areas of Mumbai, Kolkata, Chennai and Ahmedabad and any other metropolitan area notified as such under sub-section (1) of Section 8 of the Code, below the rank of an Assistant Commissioner of Police;

(c) in any other case not relatable to clause (a) or clause (b), below the rank of a Deputy Superintendent of Police or a police officer of an equivalent rank, shall investigate any offence punishable under this Act.

52. Arrest.

(1) Where a police officer arrests a person, he shall prepare a custody memo of the person arrested.

(2) The person arrested shall be informed of his right to consult a legal practitioner as soon as he is brought to the police station.

(3) Whenever any person is arrested, information of his arrest shall be immediately communicated by the police officer to a family member or in his absence to a relative of such person by telegram, telephone or by any other means and this fact shall be recorded by the police officer under the signature of the person arrested.

(4) The person arrested shall be permitted to meet the legal practitioner representing him during the course of interrogation of the accused person:

PROVIDED that nothing in this sub-section shall entitle the legal practitioner to remain present throughout the period of interrogation.

53. Presumption as to offences under Section 3.

(1) In a prosecution for an offence under sub-section (1) of Section 3, if it is proved—

(a) that the arms or explosives or any other substances specified in Section 4 were recovered from the possession of the accused and there is reason to believe that such arms or explosives or other substances of a similar nature, were used in the commission of such offence; or

(b) that the finger-prints of the accused were found at the site of the offence or on anything including arms and vehicles used in connection with the commission of such offence, the Special Court shall draw adverse inference against the accused.

(2) In a prosecution for an offence under sub-section (3) of Section 3, if it is proved that the accused rendered any financial assistance to a person, having knowledge that such person is accused of, or reasonably suspected of, an offence under that Section, the Special Court shall draw adverse inference against the accused.

54. Bar of jurisdiction of courts, etc. No civil court or other authority shall have or, be entitled to, exercise any jurisdiction, powers or authority in relation to the matters referred to in Sections 19 and 40 of the Act.

55. Saving.

(1) Nothing in this Act shall affect the jurisdiction exercisable by, or the procedure applicable to, any court or other authority under any law relating to the naval, military or air forces or other armed forces of the Union.

(2) For the removal of doubts, it is hereby declared that for the purposes of any such law as is referred to in sub-section (1), a Special Court shall be deemed to be a court of ordinary criminal justice.

56. Overriding effect. The provisions of this Act shall have effect notwithstanding anything inconsistent therewith contained in any enactment other than this Act or in any instrument having effect by virtue of any enactment other than this Act.

57. Protection of action taken in good faith. No suit, prosecution or other legal proceeding shall lie against the Central Government or a State Government or any officer or authority of the Central Government or State Government or any other authority on whom powers have been conferred under this Act, for anything which is in good faith done or purported to be done in pursuance of this Act:

PROVIDED that no suit, prosecution or other legal proceedings shall lie against any serving member or retired member of the armed forces or other para-military forces in respect of any action taken or purported to be taken by him in good faith, in the course of any operation directed towards combating terrorism.

58. Punishment and compensation for malicious action.

(1) Any police officer who exercises powers corruptly or maliciously, knowing that there are no reasonable grounds for proceeding under this Act, shall be punishable with imprisonment which may extend to two years, or with fine, or with both.

(2) If the Special Court is of the opinion that any person has been corruptly or maliciously proceeded against under this Act, the Court may award such compensation as it deems fit to the person, so proceeded against and it shall be paid by the officer, person, authority or Government, as may be specified in the order.

59. Impounding passport and arms licence of person chargesheeted under the Act. Notwithstanding anything contained in any other law for the time being in force, the passport and the arms licence of a person, who is charge-sheeted for having committed any offence under this Act, shall be deemed to have been impounded for such period as the Special Court may deem fit.

60. Review Committees.

(1) The Central Government and each State Government shall, whenever necessary, constitute one or more Review Committees for the purposes of this Act.

(2) Every such Committee shall consist of a Chairperson and such other members not exceeding three and possessing such qualifications as may be prescribed.

(3) A Chairperson of the Committee shall be a person who is, or has been, a Judge of a High Court, who shall be appointed by the Central Government, or as the case may be, the State Government, so however, that the concurrence of the Chief Justice of the High Court shall be obtained in the case of a sitting Judge:

PROVIDED that in the case of a Union territory, the appointment of a person who is a Judge of the High Court of a State shall be made as a Chairperson with the concurrence of the Chief Justice of the concerned High Court.

61. Power of High Courts to make rules. The High Court may, by notification in the Official Gazette, make such rules, if any, as they may deem necessary for carrying out the provisions of this Act relating to Special Courts within their territories.

62. Power to make rules.

(1) Without prejudice to the powers of the High Courts to make rules under Section 61, the Central Government may, by notification in the Official Gazette, make rules for carrying out the provisions of this Act.

(2) In particular, and without prejudice to the generality of the foregoing powers, such rules may provide for all or any of the following matters, namely:—

(a) regulating the conduct of persons in respect of areas the control of which is considered necessary or expedient and the removal of such persons from such areas;

(b) the entry into, and search of—

(i) any vehicle, vessel or aircraft; or

(ii) any place, whatsoever,

Reasonably suspected of being used for committing the offences referred to in Section 3 or Section 4 or for manufacturing or storing anything for the commission of any such offence;

(c) conferring powers upon—

(i) the Central Government;

(ii) a State Government;

(iii) an Administrator of a Union territory under article 239 of the Constitution;

(iv) an officer of the Central Government not lower in rank than that of a Joint Secretary; or

(v) an officer of a State Government not lower in rank than that of a District Magistrate, to make general or special orders to prevent or deal with terrorist acts;

(d) the arrest and trial of persons contravening any of the rules or any order made thereunder;

(e) the punishment of any person who contravenes or attempts to contravene or abets or attempts to abet the contravention of any rule or order made thereunder with imprisonment for a term which may extend to one year or fine or both;

(f) providing for the seizure and detention of any property in respect of which such contravention, attempt or abetment as is referred to in clause (e) has been committed and for the adjudication of such seizure and detention, whether by any court or by any other authority;

(g) determination of the price of the forfeited property under sub-section (2) of Section 10;

(h) the procedure of making application under sub-section (3) of Section 19; and

(i) the qualifications of the members of the Review Committee under sub-section (2) of Section 60.

63. Orders and rules to be laid before Houses of Parliament. Every order and every rule made by the Central Government under this Act shall be laid, as soon as may be after it is made, before each House of Parliament, while it is in session, for a total period of thirty days which may be comprised in one session or in two or more successive sessions, and if, before the expiry of the session immediately following the session or the successive sessions aforesaid, both Houses agree in making any modification in the order or rule or both Houses agree that the order or rule should not be made, the order or rule shall thereafter have effect only in such modified form or be of no effect, as the case may be; so, however, that any such modification or annulment shall be without prejudice to the validity of anything previously done under that order or rule.

64. Repeal and saving.

(1) The Prevention of Terrorism (Second) Ordinance, 2001 is hereby repealed.

(2) Notwithstanding the repeal of the said Ordinance, anything done or any action taken under the said Ordinance shall be deemed to have been done or taken under the corresponding provisions of this Act.

THE SCHEDULE

[*See* Section 18]

Terrorist Organisations

1. Babbar Khalsa International.
2. Khalistan Commando Force.
3. Khalistan Zindabad Force.
4. International Sikh Youth Federation.
5. Lashkar-e-Taiba/Pasban-e-Ahle Hadis
6. Jaish-e-Mohammed/Tahrik-e-Furqan
7. Harkat-ul-Mujahideen/Harkat-ul-Ansar/Harkat-ul-Jehad-e-Islami.
8. Hizb-ul-Mujahideen/Hizb-ul-Mujahideen Pir Panjal Regiment.
9. Al-Umar-Mujahideen.
10. Jammu and Kashmir Islamic Front.
11. United Liberation Front of Assam (ULFA).
12. National Democratic Front of Bodoland (NDFB).
13. People's Liberation Army (PLA).
14. United National Liberation Front (UNLF).
15. People's Revolutionary Party of Kangleipak (PREPAK).
16. Kangleipak Communist Party (KCP).
17. Kanglei Yaol Kanba Lup (KYKL).
18. Manipur People's Liberation Front (MPLF).
19. All Tripura Tiger Force.
20. National Liberation Front of Tripura.
21. Liberation Tigers of Tamil Eelam (LTTE).
22. Students Islamic Movement of India.
23. Deendar anjuman.
24. Communist Party of India (Marxist-Leninist)—People's War, all its formations and front organisations.
25. Maoist Communist Centre (MCC), All its formations and front organisations.
26. Al Badr.
27. Jamiat-Ul-Mujahidden.
28. Al-Qaida.
29. Dukhtaran-e-Millat (DEM).
30. Tamil Nadu Liberation Army (TNLA).
31. Tamil National Retrieval Troops (TNRT).
32. Akhil Bharat Nepali Ekta Samaj (ABNES).

EXPLANATION: For the purposes of this Schedule, serial numbers 24 and 25 shall be deemed to have been included with effect from the date of publication of S.O. No. 1194(E), dated the 5th December, 2001.

❑❑❑

38

The Reserve and Auxiliary Air Forces Act, 1952[1]

ACT NO. 62 OF 1952 [22ND AUGUST, 1952]

AN ACT to provide for the constitution and regulation of Certain. Air Force Reserve and also an Auxiliary Air Force and for matters connected therewith.

Be it enacted by Parliament as follows:-

CHAPTER - I : PRELIMINARY

1. Short title, extent and commencement.

(1) This Act may be called the Reserve and Auxiliary Air Forces Act, 1952.

(2) It extends to the whole of India.

(3) This Chapter shall come into force at once, and the remaining provisions shall come into force on such date as the Central Government may, by notification in the Official Gazette, appoint, and different dates may be appointed for different provisions.

2. Definitions. In this Act, unless the context otherwise requires,-

(a) "Air Force Reserve" means any of the Air Force Reserves raised and maintained under this Act;

(b) "competent authority" means an air officer or a committee consisting of two or more air officers appointed under Section 3;

(c) "prescribed" means prescribed by rules made under this Act;

(d) all other words and expressions used herein and defined in the Air Force Act, 1950 (15 of 1950) and not hereinbefore defined shall have the meanings respectively assigned to them by that Act.

3. Appointment of competent authority. The Central Government may, by notification in the Official Gazette, appoint an air officer or a committee consisting of two or more air officers to perform all or any of the functions of the competent authority under this Act for such area as may be specified in the notification.

CHAPTER - II : REGULAR AIR FORCE RESERVE

4. Constitution of Regular Air Force Reserve. The Central Government may raise and maintain in the manner hereafter in this Chapter provided an Air Force Reserve to be designated the Regular Air Force Reserve which shall consist solely of persons transferred or appointed to it under Section 5.

5. Recruitment to the Regular Air Force Reserve.

(1) The competent authority may, by general or special order, transfer to the Regular Air Force Reserve -

(a) any officer or airman of the Air Force who under the terms and conditions of his service is liable to serve in any Air Force Reserve if and when constituted;

(b) any officer or airman of the Air Force whose commission or engagement in the Air Force has been terminated before the commencement of this Act and who under the terms of his commission or engagement was liable to serve in any Air Force Reserve if and when constituted;

(c) any officer or airman who has served in the Air Force and has retired therefrom; and any officer or airman so transferred shall be deemed to be a member of the said Reserve.

(2) The competent authority may, in such circumstances and subject to such conditions as may be prescribed, by special order, appoint to the Regular Air Force Reserve any member of the Air Defence Reserve or the Auxiliary Air Force raised and maintained under this Act, and where any such member is so appointed, he shall cease to be a member of the Air Defence Reserve or the Auxiliary Air Force, as the case may be, and shall as from the date of such appointment be deemed to be a member of the Regular Air Force Reserve.

(3) The competent authority may, for reasons which in its opinion are sufficient, cancel any order made under sub-section (1) or sub-section (2) and on the cancellation of such order the person in respect of whom the order had been made shall cease to be a member of the Regular Air Force Reserve.

6. Classes of person in the Regular Air Force Reserve. Members of the Regular Air Force Reserve shall be divided into the following classes, namely:-

(a) general duties officers;

(b) ground duties officers, and

(c) airmen, and every officer shall be entitled on transfer or appointment to the Reserve to hold the same rank as that which he last held in the Air Force, or the Air Defence Reserve or the Auxiliary Air Force, as the case may be, before such transfer or appointment.

7. Period of service.

(1) Every member of the Regular Air Force Reserve shall be liable to serve in the Reserve -

(a) if he is transferred to the Reserve under sub-section (1) of Section 5, for the period of his Reserve liability; and

(b) if he is appointed to the Reserve under sub-section (2) of Section 5, for the remainder of the period for which he was liable to serve in the Air Defence Reserve or the Auxiliary Air Force, as the case may be: PROVIDED that the competent authority may require any such member to serve in the Reserve for such further period or periods not exceeding in the aggregate five years as it may think fit.

EXPLANATION I. For the purposes of this sub-section, "period of Reserve liability" in relation to any member of the Regular Air Force Reserve means the period for which under the terms and conditions of his service in the Air Force he was liable to serve in any Air Force Reserve if and when constituted.

EXPLANATION II. In computing the period of Reserve liability in relation to any member of the Regular Air Force Reserve whose commission or engagement in the Air Force was terminated before the commencement of this Act, the period which has elapsed between such termination and the date of such commencement shall be included.

(2) Notwithstanding anything contained in sub-section (1), no person shall be liable to serve in the Reserve after attaining the prescribed age.

8. Termination of service in the Reserve. Every member of the Regular Air Force Reserve shall, on completion of the period of his service therein, cease to be a member of the Reserve.

CHAPTER - III : AIR DEFENCE RESERVE

9. Constitution of Air Defence Reserve. The Central Government may raise and maintain in the manner hereafter in this Chapter provided an Air Force Reserve to be designated the Air Defence Reserve which shall consist of persons deemed under the provisions of Section 16 to be enrolled therein.

10. Classes of persons in the Air Defence Reserve. Members of the Air Defence Reserve shall be divided into the following classes, namely:-

(a) general duties officers; (b) ground duties officers; and (c) airmen.

11. Obligation to register.

(1) Every citizen of India who-

(a) holds or has held a public transport pilot' s licence ("B" Licence) issued under the Indian Aircraft Rules, 1937, or

(b) has had not less than two hundred hours' experience of solo flying, including not less than thirty landings, or

(c) holds or has held a first class navigator's licence issued under the Indian Aircraft Rules, 1937, or

(d) has had at least four years' aviation experience during which at least six hundred hours shall have been spent in the air, not less than one hundred hours of such experience being experience of navigation in the air, or

(e) holds or has held a first class radio telegraph operator's licence issued under the Indian Aircraft Rules, 1937, or

(f) holds or has held a radio telephone operator' s licence issued under the Indian Aircraft Rules, 1937, or

(g) holds or has held a licence as ground engineer in any of the categories A, B, C, D or X issued under the Indian Aircraft Rules, 1937, or

(h) is or was at any time employed in connection with any aerodrome or in connection with the control and movement of aircraft, in such capacity as may be prescribed, shall within the prescribed period correctly fill up, or cause to be filled up, to the best of his knowledge and belief the prescribed form, and sign and lodge it with the competent authority nearest to his usual place of residence or business:

PROVIDED that nothing contained in this sub-section shall apply -

(i) to any person belonging to any of the classes specified in clauses (a) to (f), if he has attained the age of thirty-seven years; or

(ii) to any person belonging to any of the classes specified in clauses (g) and (h), if he has attained the age of fifty years.

(2) Without prejudice to the provisions contained in sub-section (1), the competent authority may, if it is satisfied that the provisions of that sub-section apply to any person, by order in writing, require that person to furnish within such time such particulars as may be specified in the order and such person shall within the specified time furnish correctly to the best of his knowledge and belief the said particulars to the said authority in such form and manner as may be prescribed.

12. Liability to be called up for inquiry. Every person to whom the provisions of Section 11 are applicable shall be liable to be called up for inquiry under Section 13,-

(a) if he belongs to any of the classes specified in clauses (a) to (f) of sub-section (1) of Section 11, until he has completed his thirty-seventh year, and

(b) if he belongs to any of the classes specified in clauses (g) and (h) of the said sub-section, until he has completed his fiftieth year.

13. Calling-up for inquiry. The competent authority may cause to be served on any person for the time being liable to be called up for inquiry under Section 12 a written notice stating that he is called up for inquiry regarding his fitness for service in the Air Defence Reserve and requiring him to present himself to such person and at such place and at such time as may be specified in the notice and to submit himself to inquiry by the said person.

14. Medical examination. Every person called up for inquiry under Section 13 shall, if and when required by the competent authority, present himself for examination before such medical officer as may be directed by that authority and, for the purposes of such examination, shall comply with the directions of the medical officer.

15. Registration of persons considered fit for enrolment. If, after such inquiry and medical examination as aforesaid, the competent authority considers a person fit for enrolment in the Air Defence Reserve, it shall inform him accordingly and enter his name and other prescribed particulars in a register maintained in such form and manner as may be prescribed.

16. Calling up for service. The competent authority may cause to be served on any person whose name is entered in the register maintained in pursuance of Section 15 a written notice stating that he is called up for service in the Air Defence Reserve and requiring him to present himself at such place and time and to such authority as may be specified in the notice; and the person upon whom the notice is served shall be deemed to be enrolled in the Reserve as from the day so specified.

17. Period of service.

(1) Every person deemed to be enrolled in the Air Defence Reserve shall be liable for service-

(a) if he belongs to any of the classes specified in clauses (a) to (f) of sub-section (1) of Section 11, until he has completed his forty-second year;

(b) if he belongs to any of the classes specified in clauses (g) and (h) of the said sub-section, until he has completed his fifty-fifth year.

(2) Every such person, on attaining the age specified in sub-section (1), shall cease to be a member of the Air Defence Reserve.

CHAPTER - IV : AUXILIARY AIR FORCE

18. Constitution of Auxiliary Air Force.

(1) The Central Government may raise and maintain in the manner hereafter in this Chapter provided an Air Force to be designated the Auxiliary Air Force.

(2) The Central Government may constitute such number of squadrons and units of the Auxiliary Air Force as it thinks fit and may disband or reconstitute any squadron or unit.

19. Classes of persons in the Auxiliary Air Force. Members of the Auxiliary Air Force shall be divided into the following classes, namely:-

(a) general duties officers;

(b) ground duties officers; and

(c) airmen.

20. Officers of the Auxiliary Air Force. The President may grant to such person as he thinks fit a commission as an officer in the Auxiliary Air Force with designation of rank corresponding to that of any commissioned officer in the Air Force.

21. Persons eligible for enrolment. Any citizen of India may offer himself for enrolment in the Auxiliary Air Force and may, if he satisfies the prescribed conditions, be so enrolled on such terms as may be prescribed.

22. Period of service. Every officer and every enrolled person shall, subject to any rules that may be made in this behalf under this Act, be required to serve in the Auxiliary Air Force for a period of five years from the date of his appointment or enrolment but may, after the completion of his period of service, volunteer to serve therein for further periods each of not more than five years' duration.

23. Termination of service. The service of any officer or enrolled person in the Auxiliary Air Force may, at any time before the completion of his period of service, be terminated by such authority and under such conditions as may be prescribed.

24. Advisory Committees.

(1) The Central Government shall, as soon as may be after the commencement of this Act, constitute-
   (a) for the whole of India, a Central Advisory Committee;
   (b) for each State, a State Advisory Committee; and
   (c) for every unit of the Auxiliary Air Force, a Unit Advisory Committee.

(2) It shall be the duty of the Central Advisory Committee to advise the Central Government on matters connected with the Auxiliary Air Force generally, of the State Advisory Committee to advise the Central Government on matters connected with the formation of squadrons or units in the State and squadrons or units already stationed in the State.

(3) The duties, powers and procedure of Advisory Committees and in particular the matters in respect of which the Advisory Committees may be called upon to give advice shall be such as may be prescribed.

CHAPTER - V : LIABILITY AND DISCIPLINE OF MEMBERS OF RESERVE AND AUXILIARY AIR FORCES

25. Liability to be called up for service. Every member of an Air Force Reserve or the Auxiliary Air Force shall, during the period of his service, be liable to be called up-

(a) for training for such period as may be prescribed and for medical examination,
(b) for service in aid of the civil power,
(c) for Air Force service in India or abroad.

26. Application of Air Force Act, 1950. Every member of an Air Force Reserve or the Auxiliary Air Force shall, when called up for training, medical examination or for service under this Act, be subject to the Air Force Act, 1950 (45 of 1950), and the rules made thereunder in the same manner as a person belonging to the Air Force and holding the same rank is subject to the said Act and rules and shall continue to be so subject until duly released from such training, medical examination or service, as the case may be.

CHAPTER - VI : MISCELLANEOUS

27. Reinstatement in civil employ of persons required to perform service under this Act.

(1) It shall be the duty of every employer by whom a person called up under Section 25 is employed to grant him such leave as may be necessary and to reinstate

him in his employment on the termination of the period during which he has been so called up in an occupation and under conditions not less favourable to him than those which would have been applicable to him had he not been so called up:

PROVIDED that if the employer refuses to reinstate such person or denies his liability to reinstate such person, or if for any reason the reinstatement of such person is represented by the employer to be impracticable, either party may refer the matter to the prescribed authority and that authority shall, after considering all matters which may be put before him and after making such further inquiry into the matter as may be prescribed, pass an order-

(a) exempting the employer from the provisions of this Section, or

(b) requiring him to re-employ such person on such terms as that authority thinks suitable, or

(c) requiring him to pay to such person by way of compensation for failure or inability to re-employ a sum not exceeding an amount equal to six months' remuneration at the rate at which his last remuneration was payable to him by the employer.

(2) If any employer fails to obey the order of any such authority as is referred to in the proviso to sub-section (1), he shall be punishable with fine which may extend to one thousand rupees, and the court by which an employer is convicted under this Section shall order him (if he has not already been so required by the said authority) to pay to the person whom he has failed to re-employ a sum equal to six months' remuneration at the rate at which his last remuneration was payable to him by the employer, and any amount so required to be paid either by the said authority or by the court shall be recoverable as if it were a fine imposed by such court.

(3) In any proceeding under this Section it shall be a defence for an employer to prove that the person formerly employed did not apply to the employer for reinstatement within a period of two months from the termination of the period during which he was called up under Section 25.

(4) The duty imposed by sub-section (1) upon an employer to grant leave to a person such as is described in that sub-section or to reinstate him in his employment shall attach to an employer who, before such person is actually called up under Section 25, terminates his employment in circumstances such as to indicate an intention to evade the duty imposed by that sub-section and such intention shall be presumed until the contrary is proved if the termination takes place after the issue of an order relating to that person under Section 25.

28. Preservation of certain rights persons called up for service. When any person called up under Section 25 has any rights under any provident fund or superannuation fund or other scheme for the benefit of employees maintained in connection with the employment he relinquishes, he shall continue, during the period for which he has been so called up and if he is reinstated, until such reinstatement under the provisions of this Act, to have in respect of such fund or scheme such rights as may be prescribed.

29. Pay and allowances.

(1) Every member of an Air Force Reserve or the Auxiliary Air Force shall, during the period of training or active service, receive such pay and allowances as are admissible to an officer or airman, as the case may be, in the corresponding rank, branch or trade of the Air Force.

(2) Where any such member was in any employment immediately before he is called up for training under Section 25, the employer shall, during the period of the training, be liable to pay to him the difference, if any, between the pay and allowances which he would have received from the employer if he had not been called up for such training and the pay and allowances which he receives as such member while under training.

(3) If any employer refuses or fails to pay to any such member the difference in pay and allowances as provided in sub-section (2), such difference in pay and allowances may, on application by the member to the prescribed authority, be recovered from the employer in such manner as may be prescribed.

30. Penalties.

(1) If any person refuses or without lawful excuse (the burden of proving which shall lie upon such person) neglects to comply fully with the requirements of sub-section (1) of Section 11 or of any order made under sub-section (2) of that Section or with the requirements of Section 14, he shall be punishable with fine which may extend to five hundred rupees.

(2) If any person wilfully fails to comply with any notice issued under Section 13 or Section 16, he shall be punishable with imprisonment which may extend to six months, or with fine which may extend to one thousand rupees, or with both.

31. Service of notice. Any notice or order to be served on any person for the purposes of this Act may be sent by post to that person at his last known address or may be served upon him in such other manner as may be prescribed.

32. Competent authority to be public servant. For the purposes of this Act every competent authority and where the competent authority consists of a committee of two or more air officers, every member of the committee shall be deemed to be a public servant within the meaning of Section 21 of the Indian Penal Code (45 of 1860).

33. Power of Central Government to grant exemptions. The Central Government may, for special reasons and subject to such conditions as may be prescribed, by order exempt any person from any obligation or liability under this Act or any particular provision thereof.

34. Power to make rules.

(1) The Central Government may, by notification in the Official Gazette, make rules 1 for carrying out the purposes of this Act.

(2) In particular, and without prejudice to the generality of the foregoing power, such rules may provide for all or any of the following matters, namely:-

(a) the composition and strength of any Air Force Reserve;

(b) the circumstances in which and the conditions subject to which any officer or airman may be transferred or appointed to the Regular Air Force Reserve under Section 5;

(c) the age beyond which persons shall not be liable to serve in the Regular Air Force Reserve;

(d) the form and manner in which the particulars required by sub-section (2) of Section 11 shall be furnished;

(e) the form and manner in which registers shall be maintained in pursuance of Section 15, the particulars to be entered therein, and the correction or revision of such particulars from time to time;

(f) the pay or allowances payable to persons called up for inquiry or medical examination under this Act;

(g) the terms and conditions subject to which a person may be enrolled as a member of the Auxiliary Air Force;

(h) the authority by which and the conditions subject to which the service of any officer or enrolled person in the Auxiliary Air Force may be terminated;

(i) the constitution and the duties, powers and procedure of Advisory Committees to be constituted under Section 24;

(j) the period and manner of training of members of any Air Force Reserve and the Auxiliary Air Force;

(k) the manner in which and the conditions subject to which the rank of any member of an Air Force Reserve may be determined;

(l) the constitution of the authority for the purpose of Section 27 and the manner in which such authority may conduct any inquiry under this Act;

(m) the authority to which an application under sub-section (3) of Section 29 may be made and the manner in which the difference in the pay and allowances may be recovered under that sub-section;

(n) the manner in which any notice or order issued or made under this Act may be served;

(o) the conditions subject to which any person may be exempted from any obligation or liability under this Act or any particular provision thereof;

(p) any other matter which under this Act is to be, or may be prescribed.

(3) Any rule made under this Section may provide that a contravention thereof shall be punishable with fine which may extend to fifty rupees.

(4) [3][Every rule made under this Section shall be laid, as soon as may be after it is made, before each House of Parliament, while it is in session, for a total period of thirty days which may be comprised in one session or in two or more successive sessions, and if, before the expiry of the session immediately following the session or the successive sessions aforesaid, both Houses agree

in making any modification in the rule or both Houses agree that the rule should not be made, the rule shall thereafter have effect only in such modified form or be of no effect, as the case may be; so, however, that any such modification or annulment shall be without prejudice to the validity of anything previously done under that rule.]

35. [Amendment of Sections 2, 4 and 31, Act 45 of 1950.] *Rep. by the Repealing and Amending Act, 1957 (36 of 1957), s. 2 and Sch. I.*

36. [Repeal of Act 36 of 1939.] *Rep. by s. 2 and Sch. I, ibid. or appointed to it under Section 5.*

5. Recruitment to the Regular Air Force Reserve.

(1) The competent authority may, by general or special order, transfer to the Regular Air Force Reserve-

(a) any officer or airman of the Air Force who under the terms and conditions of his service is liable to serve in any Air Force Reserve if and when constituted;

(b) any officer or airman of the Air Force whose commission or engagement in the Air Force has been terminated before the commencement of this Act and who under the terms of his commission or engagement was liable to serve in any Air Force Reserve if and when constituted;

(c) any officer or airman who has served in the Air Force and has retired therefrom; and any officer or airman so transferred shall be deemed to be a member of the said Reserve.

(2) The competent authority may, in such circumstances and subject to such conditions as may be prescribed, by special order, appoint to the Regular Air Force Reserve any member of the Air Defence Reserve or the Auxiliary Air Force raised and maintained under this Act, and where any such member is so appointed, he shall cease to be a member of the Air Defence Reserve or the Auxiliary Air Force, as the case may be, and shall as from the date of such appointment be deemed to be a member of the Regular Air Force Reserve.

(3) The competent authority may, for reasons which in its opi-nion are sufficient, cancel any order made under sub-section (1) or sub-section (2) and on the cancellation of such order the person in respect of whom the order had been made shall cease to be a member of the Regular Air Force Reserve.

6. Classes of person in the Regular Air Force Reserve. Members of the Regular Air Force Reserve shall be divided into the following classes, namely:-

(a) general duties officers;

(b) ground duties officers; and

(c) airmen, and every officer shall be entitled on transfer or appointment to the Reserve to hold the same rank as that which he last held in the Air Force, or the Air Defence Reserve or the Auxiliary Air Force, as the case may be, before such transfer or appointment.

7. Period of service.

(1) Every member of the Regular Air Force Reserve shall be liable to serve in the Reserve -

(a) if he is transferred to the Reserve under sub-section (1) of Section 5, for the period of his Reserve liability; and

(b) if he is appointed to the Reserve under sub-section (2) of Section 5, for the remainder of the period for which he was liable to serve in the Air Defence Reserve or the Auxiliary Air Force, as the case may be:

PROVIDED that the competent authority may require any such member to serve in the Reserve for such further period or periods not exceeding in the aggregate five years as it may think fit.

EXPLANATION I - For the purposes of this sub-section," period of Reserve liability" in relation to any member of the Regular Air Force Reserve means the period for which under the terms and conditions of his service in the Air Force he was liable to serve in any Air Force Reserve if and when constituted.

EXPLANATION II - In computing the period of Reserve liability in relation to any member of the Regular Air Force Reserve whose commission or engagement in the Air Force was terminated before the commencement of this Act, the period which has elapsed between such termination and the date of such commencement shall be included.

(2) Notwithstanding anything contained in sub-section (1), no person shall be liable to serve in the Reserve after attaining the prescribed age.

8. Termination of service in the Reserve. Every member of the Regular Air Force Reserve shall, on completion of the period of his service therein, cease to be a member of the Reserve.

CHAPTER - III : AIR DEFENCE RESERVE

9. Constitution of Air Defence Reserve. The Central Government may raise and maintain in the manner hereafter in this Chapter provided an Air Force Reserve to be designated the Air Defence Reserve which shall consist of persons deemed under the provisions of Section 16 to be enrolled therein.

10. Classes of persons in the Air Defence Reserve. Members of the Air Defence Reserve shall be divided into the following classes, namely:-

(a) general duties officers;

(b) ground duties officers; and

(c) airmen.

11. Obligation to register.

(1) Every citizen of India who-

(a) holds or has held a public transport pilot's licence ("B" Licence) issued under the Indian Aircraft Rules, 1937, or

(b) has had not less than two hundred hours' experience of solo flying, including not less than thirty landings, or

(c) holds or has held a first class navigator' s licence issued under the Indian Aircraft Rules, 1937, or

(d) has had at least four years' aviation experience during which at least six hundred hours shall have been spent in the air, not less than one hundred hours of such experience being experience of navigation in the air, or

(e) holds or has held a first class radio telegraph operator' s licence issued under the Indian Aircraft Rules, 1937, or

(f) holds or has held a radio telephone operator' s licence issued under the Indian Aircraft Rules, 1937, or

(g) holds or has held a licence as ground engineer in any of the categories A, B, C, D or X issued under the Indian Aircraft Rules, 1937, or

(h) is or was at any time employed in connection with any aerodrome or in connection with the control and movement of aircraft, in such capacity as may be prescribed, shall within the prescribed period correctly fill up, or cause to be filled up, to the best of his knowledge and belief the prescribed form, and sign and lodge it with the competent authority nearest to his usual place of residence or business:

PROVIDED that nothing contained in this sub-section shall apply-

(i) to any person belonging to any of the classes specified in clauses (a) to (f), if he has attained the age of thirty-seven years; or

(ii) to any person belonging to any of the classes specified in clauses (g) and (h), if he has attained the age of fifty years.

(2) Without prejudice to the provisions contained in sub-section (1), the competent authority may, if it is satisfied that the provisions of that sub-section apply to any person, by order in writing, require that person to furnish within such time such particulars as may be specified in the order and such person shall within the specified time furnish correctly to the best of his knowledge and belief the said particulars to the said authority in such form and manner as may be prescribed.

12. Liability to be called up for inquiry. Every person to whom the provisions of Section 11 are applicable shall be liable to be called up for inquiry under Section 13,-

(a) if he belongs to any of the classes specified in clauses (a) to (f) of sub-section (1) of Section 11, until he has completed his thirty-seventh year, and

(b) if he belongs to any of the classes specified in clauses (g) and (h) of the said sub-section, until he has completed his fiftieth year.

13. Calling-up for inquiry. The competent authority may cause to be served on any person for the time being liable to be called up for inquiry under Section 12 a written notice stating that he is called up for inquiry regarding his fitness for service in the Air Defence Reserve and requiring him to present himself to such person and at such place and at such time as may be specified in the notice and to submit himself to inquiry by the said person.

14. Medical examination. Every person called up for inquiry under Section 13 shall, if and when required by the competent authority, present himself for examination before such medical officer as may be directed by that authority and, for the purposes of such examination, shall comply with the directions of the medical officer.

15. Registration of persons considered fit for enrolment. If, after such inquiry and medical examination as aforesaid, the competent authority considers a person fit for enrolment in the Air Defence Reserve, it shall inform him accordingly and enter his name and other prescribed particulars in a register maintained in such form and manner as may be prescribed.

16. Calling up for service. The competent authority may cause to be served on any person whose name is entered in the register maintained in pursuance of Section 15 a written notice stating that he is called up for service in the Air Defence Reserve and requiring him to present himself at such place and time and to such authority as may be specified in the notice; and the person upon whom the notice is served shall be deemed to be enrolled in the Reserve a~ from the day so specified.

17. Period of service.

(1) Every person deemed to be enrolled in the Air Defence Reserve shall be liable for service-

(a) if he belongs to any of the classes specified in clauses (a) to (f) of sub-section (1) of Section 11, until he has completed his forty-second year;

(b) if he belongs to any of the classes specified in clauses (g) and (h) of the said sub-section, until he has completed his fifty-fifth year.

(2) Every such person, on attaining the age specified in sub-section (1), shall cease to be a member of the Air Defence Reserve.

CHAPTER - IV : AUXILIARY AIR FORCE

18. Constitution of Auxiliary Air Force.

(1) The Central Government may raise and maintain in the manner hereafter in this Chapter provided an Air Force to be designated the Auxiliary Air Force.

(2) The Central Government may constitute such number of squadrons and units of the Auxiliary Air Force as it thinks fit and may disband or reconstitute any squadron or unit.

19. Classes of persons in the Auxiliary Air Force. Members of the Auxiliary Air Force shall be divided into the following classes, namely:-

(a) general duties officers;

(b) ground duties officers; and

(c) airmen.

20. Officers of the Auxiliary Air Force. The President may grant to such person as he thinks fit a commission as an officer in the Auxiliary Air Force with designation of rank corresponding to that of any commissioned officer in the Air Force.

21. Persons eligible for enrolment. Any citizen of India may offer himself for enrolment in the Auxiliary Air Force and may, if he satisfies the prescribed conditions, be so enrolled on such terms as may be prescribed.

22. Period of service. Every officer and every enrolled person shall, subject to any rules that may be made in this behalf under this Act, be required to serve in the Auxiliary Air Force for a period of five years from the date of his appointment or enrolment but may, after the completion of his period of service, volunteer to serve therein for further periods each of not more than five years' duration.

23. Termination of service. The service of any officer or enrolled person in the Auxiliary Air Force may, at any time before the completion of his period of service, be terminated by such authority and under such conditions as may be prescribed.

24. Advisory Committees.

(1) The Central Government shall, as soon as may be after the commencement of this Act, constitute-
   (a) for the whole of India, a Central Advisory Committee;
   (b) for each State, a State Advisory Committee; and
   (c) for every unit of the Auxiliary Air Force, a Unit Advisory Committee.

(2) It shall be the duty of the Central Advisory Committee to advise the Central Government on matters connected with the Auxiliary Air Force generally, of the State Advisory Committee to advise the Central Government on matters connected with the formation of squadrons or units in the State and squadrons or units already stationed in the State.

(3) The duties, powers and procedure of Advisory Committees and in particular the matters in respect of which the Advisory Committees may be called upon to give advice shall be such as may be prescribed.

CHAPTER - V : LIABILITY AND DISCIPLINE OF MEMBERS OF RESERVE AND AUXILIARY AIR FORCES

25. Liability to be called up for service. Every member of an Air Force Reserve or the Auxiliary Air Force shall, during the period of his service, be liable to be called up-

(a) for training for such period as may be prescribed and for medical examination,
(b) for service in aid of the civil power,
(c) for Air Force service in India or abroad.

26. Application of Air Force Act, 1950. Every member of an Air Force Reserve or the Auxiliary Air Force shall, when called up for training, medical examination or for service under this Act, be subject to the Air Force Act, 1950 (45 of 1950), and the rules made thereunder in the same manner as a person belonging to the Air Force and holding the same rank is subject to the said Act and rules and shall continue to be so subject until duly released from such training, medical examination or service, as the case may be.

CHAPTER - VI : MISCELLANEOUS

27. Reinstatement in civil employ of persons required to perform service under this Act.

(1) It shall be the duty of every employer by whom a person called up under Section

25 is employed to grant him such leave as may be necessary and to reinstate him in his employment on the termination of the period during which he has been so called up in an occupation and under conditions not less favourable to him than those which would have been applicable to him had he not been so called up:

PROVIDED that if the employer refuses to reinstate such person or denies his liability to reinstate such person, or if for any reason the reinstatement of such person is represented by the employer to be impracticable, either party may refer the matter to the prescribed authority and that authority shall, after considering all matters which may be put before him and after making such further inquiry into the matter as may be prescribed, pass an order-

(a) *exempting the employer from the provisions of this Section, or*

(b) *requiring him to re-employ such person on such terms as that authority thinks suitable, or*

(c) *requiring him to pay to such person by way of compensation for failure or inability to re-employ a sum not exceeding an amount equal to six months' remuneration at the rate at which his last remuneration was payable to him by the employer.*

(2) If any employer fails to obey the order of any such authority as is referred to in the proviso to sub-section (1), he shall be punishable with fine which may extend to one thousand rupees, and the court by which an employer is convicted under this Section shall order him (if he has not already been so required by the said authority) to pay to the person whom he has failed to re-employ a sum equal to six months' remuneration at the rate at which his last remuneration was payable to him by the employer, and any amount so required to be paid either by the said authority or by the court shall be recoverable as if it were a fine imposed by such court.

(3) In any proceeding under this Section it shall be a defence for an employer to prove that the person formerly employed did not apply to the employer for reinstatement within a period of two months from the termination of the period during which he was called up under Section 25.

(4) The duty imposed by sub-section (1) upon an employer to grant leave to a person such as is described in that sub-section or to reinstate him in his employment shall attach to an employer who, before such person is actually called up under Section 25, terminates his employment in circumstances such as to indicate an intention to evade the duty imposed by that sub-section and such intention shall be presumed until the contrary is proved if the termination takes place after the issue of an order relating to that person under Section 25.

28. Preservation of certain rights persons called up for service. When any person called up under Section 25 has any rights under any provident fund or superannuation fund or other scheme for the benefit of employees maintained in connection with the employment he relinquishes, he shall continue, during the period for which he has been so called up and if he is reinstated, until such reinstatement under the provisions of this Act, to have in respect of such fund or scheme such rights as may be prescribed.

29. Pay and allowances.

(1) Every member of an Air Force Reserve or the Auxiliary Air Force shall, during the period of training or active service, receive such pay and allowances as are admissible to an officer or airman, as the case may be, in the corresponding rank, branch or trade of the Air Force.

(2) Where any such member was in any employment immediately before he is called up for training under Section 25, the employer shall, during the period of the training, be liable to pay to him the difference, if any, between the pay and allowances which he would have received from the employer if he had not been called up for such training and the pay and allowances which he receives as such member while under training.

(3) If any employer refuses or fails to pay to any such member the difference in pay and allowances as provided in sub-section (2), such difference in pay and allowances may, on application by the member to the prescribed authority, be recovered from the employer in such manner as may be prescribed.

30. Penalties.

(1) If any person refuses or without lawful excuse (the burden of proving which shall lie upon such person) neglects to comply fully with the requirements of sub-section (1) of Section 11 or of any order made under sub-section (2) of that Section or with the requirements of Section 14, he shall be punishable with fine which may extend to five hundred rupees.

(2) If any person wilfully fails to comply with any notice issued under Section 13 or Section 16, he shall be punishable with imprisonment which may extend to six months, or with fine which may extend to one thousand rupees, or with both.

31. Service of notice. Any notice or order to be served on any person for the purposes of this Act may be sent by post to that person at his last known address or may be served upon him in such other manner as may be prescribed.

32. Competent authority to be public servant. For the purposes of this Act every competent authority and where the competent authority consists of a committee of two or more air officers, every member of the committee shall be deemed to be a public servant within the meaning of Section 21 of the Indian Penal Code (45 of 1860).

33. Power of Central Government to grant exemptions. The Central Government may, for special reasons and subject to such conditions as may be prescribed, by order exempt any person from any obligation or liability under this Act or any particular provision thereof.

34. Power to make rules.

(1) The Central Government may, by notification in the Official Gazette, make Rules 1 for carrying out the purposes of this Act.

(2) In particular, and without prejudice to the generality of the foregoing power, such rules may provide for all or any of the following matters, namely -

(a) the composition and strength of any Air Force Reserve;

(b) the circumstances in which and the conditions subject to which any officer or airman may be transferred or appointed to the Regular Air Force Reserve under Section 5;

(c) the age beyond which persons shall not be liable to serve in the Regular Air Force Reserve;

(d) the form and manner in which the particulars required by sub-section (2) of Section 11 shall be furnished;

(e) the form and manner in which registers shall be maintained in pursuance of Section 15, the particulars to be entered therein, and the correction or revision of such particulars from time to time;

(f) the pay or allowances payable to persons called up for inquiry or medical examination under this Act;

(g) the terms and conditions subject to which a person may be enrolled as a member of the Auxiliary Air Force;

(h) the authority by which and the conditions subject to which the service of any officer or enrolled person in the Auxiliary Air Force may be terminated;

(i) the constitution and the duties, powers and procedure of Advisory Committees to be constituted under Section 24;

(j) the period and manner of training of members of any Air Force Reserve and the Auxiliary Air Force;

(k) the manner in which and the conditions subject to which the rank of any member of an Air Force Reserve may be determined;

(l) the constitution of the authority for the purpose of Section 27 and the manner in which such authority may conduct any inquiry under this Act;

(m) the authority to which an application under sub-section (3) of Section 29 may be made and the manner in which the difference in the pay and allowances may be recovered under that sub-section;

(n) the manner in which any notice or order issued or made under this Act may be served;

(o) the conditions subject to which any person may be exempted from any obligation or liability under this Act or any particular provision thereof;

(p) any other matter which under this Act is to be, or may be prescribed.

(3) Any rule made under this Section may provide that a con-travention thereof shall be punishable with fine which may extend to fifty rupees.

(4) [6][Every rule made under this Section shall be laid, as soon as may be after it is made, before each House of Parliament, while it is in session, for a total period of thirty days which may be comprised in one session or in two or more successive sessions, and if, before the expiry of the session immediately following the session or the successive sessions aforesaid, both Houses agree in making any modification in the rule or both Houses agree that the rule should not be made, the rule shall thereafter have effect only in such modified form or be of no effect, as the case may be; so, however, that any such

modification or annulment shall be without prejudice to the validity of anything previously done under that rule.]

35. [Amendment of Sections 2, 4 and 31, Act 45 of 1950.] *Rep. by the Repealing and Amending Act, 1957 (36 of 1957), s. 2 and Sch. I.*

36. [Repeal of Act 36 of 1939.] *Rep. by s. 2 and Sch. I, ibid.*

❑❑❑

Endnotes

1. The Deputy Chief of Air Staff, vide S. R. O. 321. dated the 20th August, 1955, Gazette of India, Pt. II, Sec. 4, p. 189.
2. See the Reserve and Auxiliary Air Forces Act Rules, 1953, Gazette of India 1953, Pt. II, sec. 4, p. 187.
3. Subs. by Act 4 of 1986, s. 2 and Sch. (w.e.f. 15. 5. 1986).
4. The Deputy Chief of Air Staff, vide S. R. O. 321. dated the 20th August, 1955, Gazette of India, Pt. II, Sec. 4, p. 189.
5. See the Reserve and Auxiliary Air Forces Act Rules, 1953, Gazette of India 1953, Pt. II, sec. 4, p. 187.
6. Subs. by Act 4 of 1986, s. 2 and Sch. (w.e.f. 15. 5. 1986).

39

The State Armed Police Forces (Extension of Laws) Act, 1952

1. Short title and extent.

(1) This Act may be called the State Armed Police Forces (Extension of Laws) Act, 1952.

(2) It extends to the whole of India.

2. Definition. In this Act "armed police-force" means any police-force constituted by any of the enactments specified in the Schedule for the time being in force.

3. Extension of disciplinary laws of any State to members of the armed police forces of that State when serving outside that State. Where any detachment of an armed police force of a State is serving in any part of any other State, whether independently or by being attached to the police-force of that other State, then, notwithstanding anything contained in Section 3 of the Police Act, 1888 (3 of 1888), every member of the said detachment, while discharging the functions of a police-officer in that other State, shall continue to be subject to the same laws in respect of discipline and liabilities as would have been applicable to him, if he had been discharging those functions within the State to which the said force belongs.

4. Power to add to, or omit from, the Schedule. The Central Government may, by notification in the official Gazette, add to, or omit from the Schedule any enactment and on the publication of such a notification, the Schedule shall be deemed to be amended accordingly.

5. (Repeal) [*Rep. by the Repealing and Amending Act, 1957 (36 of 1957). S.2 and Sch. i*]

SCHEDULE
[*See* Sections 2 and 4]

1. The Bengal Military Police Act, 1892 (5 of 1892)*
2. The Eastern Frontier Rifles (Bengal BataHon) Act, 1920 (Bengal Act • No. 2 of 1920).
3. The Bombay State Reserve Police Force Act, 1951 (Bombay Act No. 38 of 1951).
4. The Central Provinces and Berar Special Armed Constabulary Act, 1942 (C.P and Berar Act No. 7 of 1942).
5. The Madhya Bharat Special Armed Force Act, Samvat 2007 (Madhya Bharat Act No. 75 of 1950)
6. The Orissa Military Police Act, 1946 (Orissa Act No 7 of 1946).
7. The Rajasthan Armed Constabulary Act, 1950 (Rajasthan Act No 12 of 1950).
8. The United Provinces Provincial Armed Constabulary Act, 1948 (U. P Act No. 40 of 1948).

❑❑❑

40

The Weapons of Mass Destruction and Their Delivery Systems (Prohibition of Unlawful Activities) Act, 2005

ACT NO. 21 OF 2005 [6TH JUNE, 2005]

AN ACT to prohibit unlawful activities, in relation to weapons of mass destruction and their delivery systems and for matters connected therewith or incidental thereto.

WHEREAS India is determined to safeguard its national security as a Nuclear Weapon State;

AND WHEREAS India is committed not to transfer nuclear weapons or other nuclear explosive devices, or to transfer control over such weapons or explosive devices, and not in any way to assist, encourage, or induce any other country to manufacture nuclear weapons or other nuclear explosive devices;

AND WHEREAS India is committed to prevent a non-State actor and a terrorist from acquiring weapons of mass destruction and their delivery systems;

AND WHEREAS India is committed to the objective of global nuclear disarmament;

AND WHEREAS India is committed to its obligations as a State Party to the Convention on the Prohibition of the Development, Production, Stockpiling and Use of Chemical Weapons and on their Destruction and the Convention on the Prohibition of the Development, Production and Stockpiling of Bacteriological (Biological) and Toxin Weapons and on their Destruction;

AND WHEREAS India is exercising controls over the export of chemicals, organisms, materials, equipment and technologies in relation to weapons of mass destruction and their delivery systems under other relevant Acts;

AND WHEREAS it is considered necessary to provide for integrated legal measures to exercise controls over the export of materials, equipment and technologies and to prohibit unlawful activities in relation to weapons of mass destruction and their means of delivery.

Be it enacted by Parliament in the Fifty-sixth Year of the Republic of India as follows:-

1. Short title and commencement.

(1) This Act may be called the Weapons of Mass Destruction and their Delivery Systems (Prohibition of Unlawful Activities) Act, 2005.

(2) It shall come into force on such date as the Central Government may, by notification in the Official Gazette, appoint.

2. Act in addition to other laws. Save as otherwise expressly provided in this Act, the provisions of this Act shall be in addition to any other relevant Act for the time being in force in relation to any matter covered under this Act.

3. Extent and application.

(1) It extends to the whole of India including its Exclusive Economic Zone.

(2) Every person shall be liable to punishment under this Act for every act or omission contrary to the provisions thereof, of which he is held guilty in India.

(3) Any person who commits an offence beyond India, which is punishable under this Act, shall be dealt with according to the provisions of this Act in the same manner as if such act had been committed in India.

(4) The provisions of this Act shall also apply to—

  (a) citizens of India outside India;

  (b) companies or bodies corporate, registered or incorporated in India or having their associates, branches or subsidiaries, outside India;

  (c) any ship, aircraft or other means of transport registered in India or outside India, wherever it may be;

  (d) foreigners while in India;

  (e) persons in the service of the Government of India, within and beyond India.

(5) Notwithstanding the applicability of the provisions of any other Central Act relating to any activity provided herein, the provisions of this Act shall apply to export, transfer, re-transfer, transit and trans-shipment of material, equipment or technology of any description as are identified, designated, categorised or considered necessary by the Central Government, as pertinent or relevant to India as a Nuclear Weapon State, or to the national security of India, or to the furtherance of its foreign policy or its international obligations under any bilateral, multilateral or international treaty, Covenant, Convention or arrangement relating to weapons of mass destruction or their means of delivery, to which India is a Party.

4. Definitions. In this Act, unless the context otherwise requires,-

(a) "biological weapons" are-

(i) microbial or other biological agents, or toxins whatever their origin or method of production, of types and in quantities that have no justification for prophylactic, protective or other peaceful purposes; and

(ii) weapons, equipment or delivery systems specially designed to use such agents or toxins for hostile purposes or in armed conflict;

(b) "brought in transit" means to bring goods from any country into India by land, air, or amphibious means of transportation, where the goods are to be taken out from India on the same conveyance on which they are brought into India without any landing in India, but does not include a conveyance in innocent passage through Indian territory, Indian territorial waters or Indian airspace of a foreign conveyance carrying goods.

EXPLANATION I: A conveyance is a foreign conveyance if it is not registered in India.

EXPLANATION II: A conveyance is in "innocent passage" if it is not engaged in relevant activity and passes through or above Indian territorial waters or airspace without stopping or anchoring in India;

(c) "chemical weapons" means -

(i) the toxic chemicals and their precursors, except where intended for-

(a) industrial, agricultural, research, medical, pharmaceutical or other peaceful purposes;

(b) protective purposes, namely those purposes directly related to protection against toxic chemicals and to protection against chemical weapons;

(c) military purposes not connected with the use of chemical weapons and not dependent on the use of the toxic properties of chemicals as a method of warfare; or

(d) law enforcement including domestic riot control purposes; as long as the types and quantities are consistent with such purposes;

(ii) the munitions and devices, specifically designed to cause death or other harm through the toxic properties of those toxic chemicals specified in sub-clause (i), which would be released as a result of the employment of such munitions and devices; and

(iii) any equipment specifically designed for use directly in connection with the employment of munitions and devices specified in sub-clause (ii), together or separately;

(d) "export" shall have the meaning assigned to this expression in the Foreign Trade (Development and Regulation) Act, 1992 (22 of 1992);

(e) "fissile material" and "radioactive material" shall have the meanings assigned to these expressions in the Atomic Energy Act, 1962 (33 of 1962);

(f) "item" means materials, equipment, and technology, of any description, notified under this Act or any other Act related to relevant activity;

(g) "non-State actor" is a person or entity not acting under the lawful authority of any country;

(h) "nuclear weapon or other nuclear explosive device" means any nuclear weapon or other nuclear explosive device as may be determined by the Central Government, whose determination in the matter shall be final;

(i) "public domain" means domain that has no restrictions upon dissemination of information within or from it; the existence of any legal rights to intellectual property in that information does not remove such information from being in public domain;

(j) "relevant activity" means -

  (i) the development, production, handling, operation, maintenance, storage or dissemination of a nuclear, chemical or biological weapon; or

  (ii) the development, production, maintenance, storage or dissemination of missiles specially designed for delivering any such weapon;

(k) "re-transfer" means transfer of any item notified under this Act from any country or entity to which it has been exported from India, to yet another country or entity;

(l) "technology" means any information (including information embodied in software) other than information in the public domain, that is capable of being used in-

  (i) the development, production or use of any goods or software;

  (ii) the development of, or the carrying out of, an industrial or commercial activity or the provision of a service of any kind.

  EXPLANATION: When technology is described wholly or partly by reference to the uses to which it (or the goods to which it relates) may be put, it shall include services which are provided or used, or which are capable of being used, in the development, production or use of such technology or goods;

(m) "terrorist" shall have the meaning assigned to this expression in the Unlawful Activities (Prevention) Act, 1967 (37 of 1967);

(n) "trans-shipment" means to remove goods from the conveyance on which they were brought into India and to place the goods on the same or another conveyance for the purpose of taking them out of India, where these acts are carried out on a "through bill of lading", "through airway bill" or "through manifest".

EXPLANATION: "through bill of lading", "through airway bill" and "through manifest" means respectively a bill of lading, airway bill and manifest, for the consignment of goods from a place outside India to a destination which is also outside India without a consignee in India;

(o) "unlawful" means without the authority of the Central Government and the expression "unlawfully" shall be construed accordingly;

(p) "weapons of mass destruction" means any biological, chemical or nuclear weapons.

5. Power to identify, designate, categorise or regulate certain activities.

(1) The Central Government may identify, designate, categorise or regulate, the export, transfer, re-transfer, trans-shipment, or transit of any item related to relevant activity in such manner as may be prescribed.

(2) The Central Government may, by order published in the Official Gazette, designate or notify any item related to relevant activity for the purposes of this Act.

6. Power to appoint Advisory Committees. For the purposes of this Act, the Central Government may appoint such Advisory Committees as it deems fit, and may appoint to them persons to exercise such powers and perform such duties as the Central Government may, by rules, prescribe.

7. Delegation of powers.

(1) Subject to the provisions of this Act and any other law for the time being in force, related to relevant activity, the Central Government shall have the power to direct or assign to any authority, in such manner as it may deem appropriate, such powers as may be necessary to implement the provisions of this Act.

(2) The Central Government may appoint a Licensing Authority and an Appellate Authority and make provisions relating to such authority and for licensing in such manner and in such form, as the Central Government may, by rules, prescribe.

(3) Without prejudice to the generality of the provisions contained in this Act, the authorities and mechanisms provided under other relevant Acts shall continue to deal with matters covered under those Acts:

PROVIDED that in case of any doubt as to whether a matter falls within the scope of such relevant Acts or under this Act, the decision of the Central Government thereon shall be final.

8. Prohibition relating to weapons of mass destruction.

(1) No person shall unlawfully manufacture, acquire, possess, develop or transport a nuclear weapon or other nuclear explosive device and their means of delivery.

(2) No person shall unlawfully transfer, directly or indirectly, to any one a nuclear weapon or other nuclear explosive device, or transfer control over such a weapon, knowing it to be a nuclear weapon or other nuclear explosive device.

(3) No person shall unlawfully manufacture, acquire, possess, develop or transport a biological or chemical weapon or their means of delivery.

(4) No person shall unlawfully transfer, directly or indirectly, to any one biological or chemical weapons.

(5) No person shall unlawfully transfer, directly or indirectly, to any one missiles specially designed for the delivery of weapons of mass destruction.

9. Prohibition relating to non-State actor or terrorist. No person shall, directly or indirectly, transfer to a non-State actor or terrorist, any material, equipment and technology notified under this Act or any other Act related to relevant activity:

Provided that such transfer made to a non-State actor shall not include a transfer made as such to any person acting under lawful authority in India.

10. Prohibition as regards intimidating acts. No person shall transfer, acquire, possess, or transport fissile or radioactive material, which is intended to be used to cause, or in a threat to cause, death or serious injury or damage to property for the purpose of intimidating people or a section of the people in India or in any foreign country, or compelling the Government of India or the Government of a foreign country or an international organisation or any other person to do so or abstain from doing any act.

11. Prohibition on export. No person shall export any material, equipment or technology knowing that such material, equipment or technology is intended to be used in the design or manufacture of a biological weapon, chemical weapon, nuclear weapon or other nuclear explosive device, or in their missile delivery systems.

12. Prohibition on brokering. No person who is a resident in India shall, for a consideration under the terms of an actual or implied contract, knowingly facilitate the execution of any transaction which is prohibited or regulated under this Act:

PROVIDED that a mere carriage, without knowledge, of persons, goods or technology, or provision of services, including by a public or private carrier of goods, courier, telecommunication, postal service provider or financial service provider, shall not be an offence for the purposes of this section.

13. Regulation of export, transfer, retransfer, transit and transshipment.

(1) No item notified under this Act shall be exported, transferred, re-transferred, brought in transit or transhipped except in accordance with the provisions of this Act or any other relevant Act.

(2) Any transfer of technology of an item whose export is prohibited under this Act or any other relevant Act relating to relevant activity shall be prohibited.

(3) When any technology is notified under this Act or any other relevant Act, as being subject to transfer controls, the transfer of such technology shall be restricted to the extent notified thereunder.

EXPLANATION. The transfer of technology may take place through either or both of the following modes of transfer, namely:-

(a) by a person or from a place within India to a person or place outside India;

(b) by a person or from a place outside India to a person, or a place, which is also outside India (but only where the transfer is by, or within the control of, person, who is a citizen of India, or any person who is a resident in India).

(4) The Central Government may notify any item as being subject to the provisions of this Act, whether or not it is covered under any other relevant Act; and when

such item is exhibited, sold, supplied or transferred to any foreign entity or a foreigner who is resident, operating, visiting, studying, or conducting research or business within the territorial limits of India, or in its airspace or Exclusive Economic Zone, it shall constitute an offence.

14. Offences and penalties. Any person who contravenes, or attempts to contravene or abets, the provisions of Section 8 or Section 10 of this Act, shall be punishable with imprisonment for a term which shall not be less than five years but which may extend to imprisonment for life, and shall also be liable to fine.

15. Punishment for aiding non-State actor or terrorist.

(1) Any person who, with intent to aid any non-State actor or terrorist, contravenes the provisions of Section 9 of this Act, shall be punishable with imprisonment for a term which shall not be less than five years but which may extend to imprisonment for life, and shall also be liable to fine.

(2) Any person who, with intent to aid any non-State actor or terrorist, attempts to contravene or abets, or does any act preparatory to contravention of sub-section (1), shall be deemed to have contravened that provision and the provision of sub-section (1) shall apply subject to the modification that the reference to "imprisonment for life" therein shall be construed as a reference to "imprisonment for ten years".

(3) While determining the punishment under this section, the court shall take into consideration whether the accused had the knowledge about the transferee being a non-state actor or not.

16. Punishment for unauthorized export.

(1) Any person who knowingly contravenes, abets or attempts to contravene, the provisions of sub-section (4) of Section 13 of this Act, shall be punishable with fine which shall not be less than three lakh rupees and which may extend to twenty lakh rupees.

(2) If any person is again convicted of the same offence under sub-section (1), then he shall be punishable for the second and every subsequent offence with imprisonment for a term which shall not be less than six months but which may extend to five years and shall also be liable to fine.

17. Punishment for violation of other provisions of the Act.

(1) Where any person contravenes, or abets or attempts to contravene, any provision of this Act other than the provisions under Sections 8, 9, 10 and sub-section (4) of Section 13 of this Act, he shall be punishable with imprisonment for a term which shall not be less than six months but which may extend to five years and shall also be liable to fine.

(2) If any person is again convicted of the same offence under sub-section (1), then he shall be punishable for the second and every subsequent offence with imprisonment for a term which shall not be less than one year but which may extend to seven years and shall also be liable to fine.

18. Penalty for using false or making forged documents, etc. Where any person signs or uses, or causes to be signed or used, any declaration, statement or document submitted to the competent authority knowing or having reason to believe that such declaration, statement or document is forged or tampered with or is false in any material particular, and relates to items notified under this Act or any other relevant Act, including those related to relevant activity, he shall be punishable with fine which shall not be less than five lakh rupees or five times the value of the materials, equipment, technology or services, whichever is more.

19. Punishment for offences with respect to which no provision has been made. Whoever contravenes any other provision of this Act or any rule or order made thereunder for which no specific punishment is provided, shall be punishable with imprisonment for a term which may extend to one year, or with fine, or with both.

20. Offences by companies.

(1) Where an offence under this Act has been committed by a company, every person who at the time the offence was committed was in charge of, and was responsible to, the company for the conduct of the business of the company as well as the company, shall be deemed to be guilty of the offence and shall be liable to be proceeded against and punished accordingly:

PROVIDED that nothing contained in this sub-section shall render any such person liable to any punishment, if he proves that the offence was committed without his knowledge or that he had exercised all due diligence to prevent the commission of such offence.

(2) Notwithstanding anything contained in sub-section (1), where any offence under this Act has been committed by a company and it is proved that the offence has been committed with the consent or connivance of, or is attributable to, any neglect on the part of, any director, manager, secretary or other officer of the company, such director, manager, secretary or other officer shall be deemed to be guilty of that offence and shall be liable to be proceeded against and punished accordingly.

EXPLANATION: For the purposes of this section-

(a) "company" means any body corporate and includes a firm and other association of individuals; and

(b) "director", in relation to a firm, means a partner in the firm.

21. Cognizance of offences. No Court shall take cognizance of any offence under this Act without the previous sanction of the Central Government or any officer authorised by the Central Government in this behalf.

22. Bar of jurisdiction of civil courts. No action or proceedings taken under Section 5 and sub-sections (1) and (2) of Section 7 of this Act by the Central Government or any officer authorised by it in this behalf shall be called in question in any civil court in any suit or application or by way of appeal or revision, and no injunction shall be granted by any civil court or other authority in respect of any action taken or to be taken in pursuance of any power conferred under those provisions.

23. Effect of other laws.

(1) The provisions of this Act shall have effect notwithstanding anything inconsistent therewith contained in any enactment other than this Act or any other instrument having effect by virtue of any enactment other than this Act.

(2) Where any act or omission constitutes an offence punishable under this Act and also under any other relevant Act, then the offender found guilty of such offence shall be liable to be punished under that Act which imposes a greater punishment.

24. Protection of action taken in good faith. No suit, prosecution or other legal proceeding shall lie against the Central Government or any officer or authority of the Central Government or any other authority on whom powers have been conferred pursuant to this Act, for anything which is in good faith done or purported to be done in pursuance of this Act or any rule or order made thereunder.

25. Special provisions as to Central Government. Nothing in this Act shall affect the activities of the Central Government in the discharge of its functions relating to the security or the defence of India.

26. Power to make rules.

(1) The Central Government may, by notification, make rules to carry out the provisions of this Act.

(2) In particular and without prejudice to the generality of the foregoing power, such rules may provide for all or any of the following matters, namely:-

(a) manner of regulating any item related to relevant activity under sub-section (1) of Section 5;

(b) appointment of Advisory Committees, their powers and duties under Section 6;

(c) appointment of Licensing and Appellate Authority and the manner of licensing under sub-section (2) of Section 7; and

(d) any other matter which has to be, or may be, prescribed.

(3) Every rule made under this Act shall be laid, as soon as may be after it is made, before each House of Parliament, while it is in session for a total period of thirty days which may be comprised in one session or in two or more successive sessions, and if, before the expiry of the session immediately following the session or the successive sessions aforesaid, both Houses agree in making any modification in the rule or both Houses agree that the rule should not be made, the rule shall thereafter have effect only in such modified form or be of no effect, as the case may be; so, however, that any such modification or annulment shall be without prejudice to the validity of anything previously done under that rule.

27. Power to remove difficulties.

(1) If any difficulty arises in giving effect to the provisions of this Act, the Central Government may, by order published in the Official Gazette, make such

provisions, not inconsistent with the provisions of this Act, as may appear to be necessary for removing the difficulty:

PROVIDED that no order shall be made under this section after the expiry of the period of two years from the date of commencement of this Act.

(2) Every order made under this section shall be laid, as soon as may be after it is made, before each House of Parliament.

❑❑❑

Bibliography

Armed Forces Communications and Electronics Association. *Intelligence and the New National Security Environment: A White Paper Prepared by the AFCEA Intelligence Committee.* Fairfax: Armed Forces Communications and Electronics Association, 2004. 18pp

Bacevich, Andrew J., ed. *The Long War: A New History of U.S. National Security Policy since World War II.* New York: Columbia University Press, 2007. 586pp. (UA23 .L685 2007)

Baker, Dean. *The Economic Impact of the Iraq War and Higher Military Spending.* Washington, D.C.: Center for Economic and Policy Research, May 2007. 10pp

Baker, Stewart A., and John Kavanagh, eds. *Patriot Debates: Experts Debate the USA PATRIOT Act.* Chicago: American Bar Association, 2005. 208pp. (KF9430 .P38 2005)

Ball, Howard. *The USA Patriot Act of 2001: Balancing Civil Liberties and National Security: A Reference Handbook.* Santa Barbara: ABC-CLIO, 2004. 265pp. (KF4850 .B14 2004)

Barnett, Thomas P.M. *Blueprint for Action: A Future Worth Creating.* New York: G.P. Putnam's Sons, 2005. 440pp. (JZ1480 .B37 2005)

Barnett, Thomas P.M. *The Pentagon's New Map: War and Peace in the Twenty-First Century.* New York: G.P. Putnam's Sons, 2004. 435pp. (UA23 .B337 2004)

Bartholomees, J. Boone, Jr., ed. *U.S. Army War College Guide to National Security Policy and Strategy,* 2d ed. Carlisle Barracks: U.S. Army War College, Department of National Security and Strategy, 2006. 397pp

Bearne, Susanna, et al. "Case Study 6: United States." In *National Security Decision-Making Struc- tures and Security Sector Reform,* 16-20. Santa Monica: RAND, 2005

Benjamin, Daniel, and Steven Simon. *The Next Attack: The Failure of the War on Terror and a Strategy for Getting It Right.* New York: Times Books, 2005. 330pp. (HV6432 .B457 2005)

Benjamin, Daniel, ed. *America and the World in the Age of Terror: A New Landscape in Interna- tional Relations.* Washington, D.C.: CSIS Press, 2005. 206pp. (E902 .A52 2005)

Berkowitz, Peter, ed. *The Future of American Intelligence.* Stanford: Stanford University, Hoover Institution Press, 2005. 184pp. (JK468 .I6F77 2005)

Betts, Richard K. *U.S. National Security Strategy: Lenses and Landmarks.* Princeton: Princeton University, Woodrow Wilson School of Public and International Affairs, 2005. 36pp. Biddle, Stephen D. *American Grand Strategy after 9/11: An Assessment.* Carlisle Barracks: U.S. Army War College, Strategic Studies Institute, 2005. 44pp.

Binnendijk, Hans, and Richard L. Kugler. *Seeing the Elephant: The U.S. Role in Global Security.*

Bolt, Paul J., Damon V. Coletta, and Collins G. Shackelford, Jr., eds. *American Defense Policy,* 8th ed. Baltimore: Johns Hopkins University Press, 2005. 479pp.

Bouchat, Clarence J. *An Introduction to Theater Strategy and Regional Security.* Carlisle Barracks:

Brainard, Lael, ed. *Security by Other Means: Foreign Assistance, Global Poverty, and American Leadership.* Washington, D.C.: Brookings Institution Press, 2007. 364pp. (HC60 .S21 2007)

Brenner, Joel F. *Information Oversight: Practical Lessons from Foreign Intelligence.* Heritage Lec- ture No. 851. Washington, D.C.: Heritage Foundation, 30 September 2004. 12pp.

Bruner, Edward F. *Military Forces: What Is the Appropriate Size for the United States?* Washing- ton, D.C.: Library of Congress, Congressional Research Service, January 2006. 6pp.

Brzezinski, Matthew. *Fortress America: On the Front Lines of Homeland Security: An Inside Look at the Coming Surveillance State.* New York: Bantam Books, 2004. 243pp.

Brzezinski, Zbigniew. *The Choice: Global Domination or Global Leadership.* New York: Basic Books, 2004. 242pp.

Caldwell, Dan, and Robert E. Williams, Jr. *Seeking Security in an Insecure World.* Lanham: Row- man & Littlefield, 2006. 241pp.

Campbell, Kurt M., and Michael E. O'Hanlon. *Hard Power: The New Politics of National Security.* New York: Basic Books, 2006. 319pp.

Campbell, Robin A., Annette N. Foster, and Steven J. Smith. *Harnessing the Military's Voice: An Argument for a Greater Role in Public Diplomacy by the U.S. Military.* National Security Pro- gram Discussion Paper Series. Cambridge: Harvard University, John F. Kennedy School of Government, National Security Program, 2005. 82pp.

Carafano, James Jay, and Paul Rosenzweig. *Winning the Long War: Lessons from the Cold War for Defeating Terrorism and Preserving Freedom.* Washington, D.C.: Heritage Books, 2005. 292pp. (HV6432 .C37 2005)

Carafano, James Jay, Baker Spring, and Mackenzie Eaglen. *Four Percent for Freedom: Maintain- ing Robust National Security Spending.* Executive Memorandum No. 1023. Washington, D.C.: Heritage Foundation, 10 April 2007. 2pp.

Carlisle, Rodney P., ed. *Encyclopedia of Intelligence and Counterintelligence.* Armonk: Sharpe Reference, 2005. 2 vols.

Carothers, Thomas, and Marina Ottaway, eds. *Uncharted Journey: Promoting Democracy in the Middle East*. Washington, D.C.: Carnegie Endowment for International Peace, 2005. 302pp.

Cecchine, Gary, and Melinda Moore. *Infectious Disease and National Security: Strategic Informa- tion Needs*. Santa Monica: RAND, 2006. 105pp.

Center for Counterproliferation Research. *At the Crossroads: Counterproliferation and National Security Strategy*. Washington, D.C.: National Defense University, Center for Counterprolifera- tion Research, April 2004. 74pp.

Chapman, Bert. *Researching National Security and Intelligence Policy*. Washington, D.C.: CQ Press, 2004. 452pp.

Charney, Craig, and Nicole Yakatan. *A New Beginning: Strategies for a More Fruitful Dialogue with the Muslim World*. New York: Council on Foreign Relations, May 2005. 88pp.

Chun, Stephen B.T., comp. *National Military Strategy & National Security Strategy*. Maxwell Air Force Base: Muir S. Fairchild Research Information Center, July 2006. 14pp.

Cimbala, Stephen J. *Nuclear Weapons and Strategy: U.S. Nuclear Policy for the Twenty-First Cen- tury*. New York: Routledge, 2005. 124pp.

Clarke, John L., ed. *Armies in Homeland Security: American and European Perspectives*. Washing- ton, D.C.: National Defense University Press, 2006. 251pp. (UA926 .A65 2006)

Clarke, Ronald V., and Graeme R. Newman. *Outsmarting the Terrorists*. Westport: Praeger Secu- rity International, 2006. 303pp.

CNA Corporation. *National Security and the Threat of Climate Change*. Alexandria: CNA Corpora- tion, 2007. 68pp.

Cohen, Ariel. *The National Security Consequences of Oil Dependency*. Heritage Lecture No. 1021. Washington, D.C.: Heritage Foundation, 14 May 2007. 9pp.

Cohen, David B., and John W. Wells, eds. *American National Security and Civil Liberties in an Era of Terrorism*. New York: Palgrave Macmillan, 2004. 248pp.

Commission on the Intelligence Capabilities of the United States Regarding Weapons of Mass De- struction. *Report to the President of the United States*. Washington, D.C.: Commission on the Intelligence Capabilities of the United States Regarding Weapons of Mass Destruction, 2005. 601pp.

Committee for Economic Development. *Education for Global Leadership: The Importance of In- ternational Studies and Foreign Language Education for U.S. Economic and National Security*. Washington, D.C.: Committee for Economic Development, 2006. 58pp.

Cordesman, Anthony H. *Salvaging American Defense: The Challenge of Strategic Overstretch*. Westport: Praeger Security International, 2007. 470pp.

Cordesman, Anthony H. *The Challenge of Biological Terrorism*. Washington, D.C.: CSIS Press, 2005. 208pp.

Cordesman, Anthony H. *The Five Best Resource Decisions in National Security*. Working Draft. Washington, D.C.: Center for Strategic and International Studies, 2 May 2006. 19pp.

Cordesman, Anthony H. *The War after the War: Strategic Lessons of Iraq and Afghanistan.* Wash- ington, D.C.: CSIS Press, 2004. 73pp.

Cordesman, Anthony H., and Ionut C. Popescu. *The Changing Challenges of U.S. Defense Spend- ing.* Washington, D.C.: Center for Strategic and International Studies, 32 August 2007. 43pp.

Costa, Mark R., comp. *Transformation: A Selected Bibliography.* Carlisle Barracks: U.S. Army War College Library, April 2007. 25pp.

Cothran, Helen, ed. *National Security: Opposing Viewpoints.* San Diego: Greenhaven Press, 2004. 208pp.

Council for a Livable World, et al. *National Security Briefing Book: A Look at Key Issues before Congress in 2007.* Washington, D.C.: Council for a Livable World, January 2007. 70pp.

Council on Foreign Relations. *In the Wake of War: Improving U.S. Post-Conflict Capabilities: Re- port of an Independent Task Force Sponsored by the Council on Foreign Relations.* Samuel R. Berger and Brent Scowcroft, Co-Chairs; William L. Nash, Project Director. New York: Council on Foreign Relations, 2005. 53pp.

Council on Foreign Relations. *National Security Consequences of U.S. Oil Dependency: Report of an Independent Task Force.* John Deutch and James R. Schlesinger, Chairs; David G. Vic- tor, Project Director. New York: Council on Foreign Relations, 2006. 67pp.

Cronin, Audrey Kurth, and James M. Ludes, eds. *Attacking Terrorism: Elements of a Grand Strategy.* Washington, D.C.: Georgetown University Press, 2004. 320pp.

Crosston, Matthew. *Fostering Fundamentalism: Terrorism, Democracy and American Engage- ment in Central Asia.* Burlington: Ashgate, 2006. 186pp.

Crowley, Thomas D., et al. *Transforming the Way DOD Looks at Energy: An Approach to Es- tablishing an Energy Strategy.* McLean: LMI Government Consulting, 2007. 121pp.

D'Arcy, Michael, et al. *Protecting the Homeland, 2006/2007.* Washington, D.C.: Brookings In- stitution Press, 2006. 212pp.

Dalgaard-Nielsen, Anja, and Daniel S. Hamilton, eds. *Transatlantic Homeland Security: Protect- ing Society in the Age of Catastrophic Terrorism.* New York: Routledge, 2006. 206pp.

Darmer, M. Katherine B., Robert M. Baird, and Stuart E. Rosenbaum, eds. *Civil Liberties vs. Na- tional Security: In a Post-9/11 World.* Amherst: Prometheus Books, 2004. 387pp.

Defense Science Board. *2005 Summer Study on Reducing Vulnerabilities to Weapons of Mass Destruction.* Washington, D.C.: U.S. Department of Defense, Office of the Under Secretary of Defense for Acquisition, Technology, and Logistics, May 2007. 66pp.

Dempsey, Thomas. *Counterterrorism in African Failed States: Challenges and Potential Solu- tions.* Carlisle Barracks: U.S. Army War College, Strategic Studies Institute, 2006. 36pp.

Echevarria, Antulio J., II. *Toward an American Way of War.* Carlisle Barracks: U.S. Army War College, Strategic Studies Institute, 2004. 29pp.

Ellis, Jason D., and Geoffrey D. Kiefer. *Combating Proliferation: Strategic Intelligence and Se- curity Policy.* Baltimore: Johns Hopkins University Press, 2004. 287pp.

Ellis, R. Evan. *U.S. National Security Implications of Chinese Involvement in Latin America.* Carlisle Barracks: U.S. Army War College, Strategic Studies Institute, 2005. 44pp.

Feaver, Peter D., and Richard H. Kohn, eds. *Soldiers and Civilians: The Civil-Military Gap and American National Security.* Cambridge: MIT Press, 2001. 545pp.

Fishel, John T., and Max G. Manwaring. *Uncomfortable Wars Revisited.* Norman: University of Oklahoma Press, 2006. 340pp. (U240 .F37 2006)

Flournoy, Michèle A., and Shawn W. Brimley. "Strategic Planning for National Security: A New Project Solarium." *Joint Force Quarterly*, no. 41 (2d Quarter 2006): 80-87.

Flynn, Stephen. *America the Vulnerable: How Our Government Is Failing to Protect Us from Terrorism.* New York: Harper Perennial, 2005. 242pp.

Flynn, Stephen. *The Edge of Disaster: Rebuilding a Resilient Nation.* New York: Random House, 2007. 240pp.

Forest, James J.F., and Matthew V. Sousa. *Oil and Terrorism in the New Gulf: Framing U.S. En- ergy and Security Policies for the Gulf of Guinea.* Lanham: Lexington Books, 2006. 329pp.

Foulon, Mark, and Christopher A. Padilla. "In Pursuit of Security and Prosperity: Technology Con- trols for a New Era." *Washington Quarterly* 30 (Spring 2007): 83-90.

Gaddis, John Lewis. *Surprise, Security, and the American Experience.* Cambridge: Harvard Uni- versity Press, 2004. 150pp.

Gaffney, Frank J., et al. *War Footing: Ten Steps America Must Take to Prevail in the War for the Free World.* Annapolis: Naval Institute Press, 2006. 301pp.

Gardner, Hall. *American Global Strategy and the "War on Terrorism".* Burlington: Ashgate, 2005. 231pp.

Garrett, Laurie. *HIV and National Security: Where Are the Links? A Council on Foreign Relations Report.* New York: Council on Foreign Relations, July 2005. 67pp.

Gartner, Heinz, and Ian M. Cuthbertson, eds. *European Security and Transatlantic Relations af- ter 9/11 and the Iraq War.* New York: Palgrave Macmillan, 2005. 271pp.

Gattuso, Joseph A. "Trading Places: How and Why National Security Roles Are Changing." *Joint Force Quarterly*, no. 45 (2d Quarter 2007): 62-65.

George, Roger Z., and Robert D. Kline, eds. *Intelligence and the National Security Strategist: Enduring Issues and Challenges.* Washington, D.C.: National Defense University Press, 2004. 564pp.

Gerstein, Daniel M. *Leading at the Speed of Light: New Strategies for U.S. Security in the Infor- mation Age.* Washington, D.C.: Potomac Books, 2006. 185pp.

Gibish, Jane E., comp. *U.S. National Security and Strategy: A Selected Bibliography.* Carlisle Bar- racks: U.S. Army War College Library, February 2004. 40pp.

Gordon, Michael R. "Break Point? Iraq and America's Military Forces." *Survival* 48 (December 2006): 67-81.

Gordon, Vikki. "The Law: Unilaterally Shaping U.S. National Security Policy: The Role of Na- tional Security Directives." *Presidential Studies Quarterly* 37 (June 2007): 349-367.

Gorman, Martin J, and Alexander Krongard. "A Goldwater-Nichols Act for the U.S. Government: Institutionalizing the Interagency Process." *Joint Force Quarterly*, no. 39 (4th Quarter 2005): 51-58.

Gormley, Dennis M. "Securing Nuclear Obsolescence." *Survival* 48 (October 2006): 127-148.

Gray, Colin S. "How Has War Changed since the End of the Cold War?" *Parameters* 35 (Spring 2005): 14-26.

Hart, Gary. *The Fourth Power: A Grand Strategy for the United States in the Twenty-First Cen- tury*. Oxford: Oxford University Press, 2004. 187pp.

Hart, Gary. *The Shield and the Cloak: The Security of the Commons*. Oxford: Oxford University Press, 2006. 194pp.

Hentz, James J., ed. *The Obligation of Empire: United States' Grand Strategy for a New Century*. Lexington: University Press of Kentucky, 2004. 226pp.

Heritage Foundation. Mandate for Leadership: Principles to Limit Government, Expand Freedom, and Strengthen America. Washington, D.C.: Heritage Foundation, 2005. 142pp.

Howard, Russell D., and Reid L. Sawyer, eds. *Defeating Terrorism: Shaping the New Security Environment*. Guilford: McGraw-Hill, 2004. 158pp.

Klare, Michael, and Daniel Volman. "The African 'Oil Rush' and US National Security." *Third World Quarterly* 27 (May 2006): 609-628.

Klare, Michael. "The Futile Pursuit of 'Energy Security' by Military Force." *Brown Journal of World Affairs* 13 (Spring-Summer 2007): 139-153.

Kristensen, Hans M. "U.S. Strategic War Planning after 9/11." *Nonproliferation Review* 14 (July 2007): 373-390. http://cns.miis.edu/pubs/npr/vol14/142/142kristensen.pdf

Kupchan, Charles A., and Peter L. Trubowitz. "Grand Strategy for a Divided America." *Foreign Affairs* 86 (July-August 2007): 71-83.

Kydd, Andrew H., and Barbara F. Walter. "The Strategies of Terrorism." *International Security* 31 (Summer 2006): 49-80.

Lantis, Jeffrey S. "America's Nuclear Addiction." *Defense & Security Analysis* 22 (December 2006): 373-385.

Le Gallo, André. "Covert Action: A Vital Option in U.S. National Security Policy." *International Journal of Intelligence and CounterIntelligence* 18 (March 2005): 354-359.

Lebl, Leslie S. "Security Beyond Borders." *Policy Review* 130 (April-May 2005): 23-43.

Mapel, David R. "The Right of National Defense." *International Studies Perspectives* 8 (February 2007): 1-15.

Marlatt, Greta E., comp. *Intelligence and Policy-Making: A Bibliography.* Monterey: U.S. Naval Postgraduate School, Dudley Knox Library, April 2007. 113pp.

McConnell, Mike. "Overhauling Intelligence." *Foreign Affairs* 86 (July-August 2007): 49-58.

Monten, Jonathan. "The Roots of the Bush Doctrine: Power, Nationalism, and Democracy Promo- tion in U.S. Strategy." *International Security* 29 (Spring 2005): 112-156.

Morgan, Matthew J. "An Evolving View of Warfare: War and Peace and the American Military Profession." *Small Wars & Insurgencies* 16 (June 2005): 147-169.

Morris, Justin, and Nicholas J. Wheeler. "The Security Council's Crisis of Legitimacy and the Use of Force." *International Politics* 44 (March-May 2007): 214-231.

Moyer, Jeanette M., comp. *Homeland Security: A Selected Bibliography.* Carlisle Barracks: U.S. Army War College Library, May 2006. 27pp.

Moyer, Jeanette M., comp. *Post Conflict Reconstruction: A Selected Bibliography.* Carlisle Bar- racks: U.S. Army War College Library, January 2007. 24pp.

Peterson, Susan. "Epidemic Disease and National Security." *Security Studies* 12 (December 2006): 43-81.

Phillips, Nicola. "The Limits of 'Securitization': Power, Politics and Process in US Foreign Eco- nomic Policy." *Government and Opposition* 42 (Spring 2007): 158-189. Blackwell-Synergy.

Powell, Colin L. "The Craft of Diplomacy." *Wilson Quarterly* 28 (Summer 2004): 60-68.

Pudas, Terry J. "Disruptive Challenges and Accelerating Force Transformation." *Joint Force Quar- terly*, no. 42 (3d Quarter 2006): 43-50.

Reynolds, Kevin P. "Building the Future Force: Challenges to Getting Military Transformation Right." *Contemporary Security Policy* 27 (December 2006): 435-471.

Rothkopf, David J. "Inside the Committee That Runs the World." *Foreign Policy* 147 (March-April 2005): 30-40.

Russell, James A. "WMD Proliferation, Globalization, and International Security: Whither the Nexus and National Security?" *Strategic Insights* 5 (July 2006): 1-11.

Russell, Kevin. "The Subjectivity of Intelligence Analysis and Implications for the U.S. National Security Strategy." *SAIS Review* 24 (Winter 2004): 147-163. ProQuest

Russell, Richard L. "A Weak Pillar for American National Security: The CIA's Dismal Perform-ance against WMD Threats." *Intelligence & National Security* 20 (September 2005): 466-485.

Sadjadpour, Karim. "The Nuclear Players." *Journal of International Affairs* 60 (Spring 2007): 125-135.

Schmidt, Todd. "U.S. National Security Policy: Framing an Authentic Preemptive Strategy in the 21st Century." *Military Review* 86 (September-October 2006): 75-83.

Schmitt, Michael N. "U.S. Security Strategies: A Legal Assessment." *Harvard Journal of Law & Public Policy* 27 (Summer 2004): 737-763.

Shope, Virginia C., comp. *Jointness: A Selected Bibliography.* Carlisle Barracks: U.S. Army War College Library, 2007. 24pp.

Shultz, George P. "Sustaining Our Resolve." *Policy Review* 138 (August-September 2006): 3-17.

Sicherman, Harvey. "Cheap Hawks, Cheap Doves, and the Pursuit of Strategy." *Orbis* 49 (Fall 2005): 613-629. Wilson OmniFile

Sofaer, Abraham D. "Presidential Power and National Security." *Presidential Studies Quarterly* 37 (March 2007): 101-123.

Stavridis, James G. "Strategic Communication and National Security." *Joint Force Quarterly*, no. 46 (3d Quarter 2007): 4-7.

Steinberg, James. "Preventive Force in US National Security Strategy." *Survival* 47 (December 2005): 55-72.

Stevenson, Jonathan. "Demilitarising the War on Terror." *Survival* 48 (June 2006): 37-54.

Strachan, Hew. "The Lost Meaning of Strategy." *Survival* 47 (October 2005): 33-54.

Taipale, Kim. "Rethinking Foreign Intelligence Surveillance." *World Policy Journal* 23 (Winter 2006-2007): 77-81.

Talmadge, Caitlin. "Deterring a Nuclear 9/11." *Washington Quarterly* 30 (Spring 2007): 21-34.

Ting, Jan C. "Immigration and National Security." *Orbis* 50 (Winter 2006): 41-52.

Trachtenberg, D.J. "Finding the Forest among the Trees: The Bush Administration's National Security Policy Successes." *Comparative Strategy* 23 (January-March 2004): 1-8.

Twining, Daniel. "America's Grand Design in Asia." *Washington Quarterly* 30 (Summer 2007): 79-74.

Ulrich, Marybeth P., and Martin L. Cook. "US Civil Military Relations since 9/11: Issues in Ethics and Policy Development." *Journal of Military Ethics* 5 (November 2006): 161-182.

Vandermolen, Thomas D. "Molecular Nanotechnology and National Security." *Air & Space Power Journal* 20 (Fall 2006): 96-127.

Vego, Milan. "Searching for a Strategy." Sea Power 21. *Armed Forces Journal* 144 (April 2007): 16-19.

Walton, C. Dale. "Not Only Islamism: Great Power Politics and the Future of Terrorism." *Com- parative Strategy* 26 (January 2007): 21-37.

Wester, Eric. "Last Resort and Preemption: Using Armed Force as a Moral and Penultimate Choice." *Parameters* 37 (Summer 2007): 59-70.

Wilson, Isaiah, III. "Rediscovering Containment: The Sources of American-Iranian Conduct." *Journal of International Affairs* 60 (Spring 2007): 95-112.

Yue, Wu. "US Foreign and National Security Policies: An Explanation Based on Theoretical Ap- proaches." *Defense & Security Analysis* 22 (June 2006): 191-196.

Zelnick, Bob. "National Security and Freedom of Speech." *Hoover Digest*, no. 3 (Summer 2006): 51-53.

Index

D

R

S

W